# PHYSICAL ANTHROPOLOGY

# PHYSICAL ANTHROPOLOGY

**SEVENTH EDITION**

**Philip L. Stein**
Los Angeles Pierce College

**Bruce M. Rowe**
Los Angeles Pierce College

Boston   Burr Ridge, IL   Dubuque, IA   Madison, WI   New York
San Francisco   St. Louis   Bangkok   Bogotá   Caracas   Lisbon
London   Madrid   Mexico City   Milan   New Delhi   Seoul
Singapore   Sydney   Taipei   Toronto

*McGraw-Hill Higher Education*  ⚛
*A Division of The **McGraw-Hill** Companies*

## PHYSICAL ANTHROPOLOGY

This book is printed on acid-free paper.

1 2 3 4 5 6 7 8 9 0 DOW/DOW 9 0 9 8 7 6 5 4 3 2 1 0 9

ISBN 0-07-228229-0

Editorial director:   *Phillip A. Butcher*
Senior sponsoring editor:   *Alan McClare*
Editorial assistant:   *Miriam Beyer*
Marketing manager:   *Leslie A. Kraham*
Project manager:   *Kimberly D. Hooker*
Production supervisor:   *Debra R. Benson*
Designer:   *Kiera Cunningham*
Cover design:   *Z Graphics*
Senior photo research coordinator:   *Keri Johnson*
Photo research:   *Charlotte Goldman*
Senior supplement coordinator:   *Cathy L. Tepper*
Compositor:   *York Graphic Services, Inc.*
Typeface:   *10/12 Palatino*
Printer:   *R. R. Donnelley & Sons Company*

**Library of Congress Cataloging-in-Publication Data**

Stein, Philip L.
    Physical anthropology / Phillip L. Stein, Bruce M. Rowe. — 7th
  ed.
        p.        cm.
    Includes bibliographical references and index.
    ISBN 0-07-228229-0
    1. Physical anthropology.   I. Rowe, Bruce M.   II. Title.
  GN60.S72      2000
  599.9—dc21                                                                99-15559
                                                                                CIP

INTERNATIONAL EDITION ISBN 0-07-116991-1
Copyright © 2000. Exclusive rights by The McGraw-Hill Companies, Inc. for manufacture and export.
This book cannot be re-exported from the country to which it is consigned by McGraw-Hill.
The International Edition is not available in North America.
http://www.mhhe.com

*To our families and in memory of*
*Eleanor Frances Blumenthal Rowe Michael*
*Barbara Stein Akerman*
*Arnold L. Freed, M.D.*

# CONTENTS IN BRIEF

# CONTENTS

# PREFACE

In the history of science, each decade and each century can be characterized by landmark developments. In the realm of biology, the nineteenth century was the time during which the first valid explanations of biological evolution were published and debated. The twentieth century can be characterized as a time of meteoric insight into genetic processes.

If we dare to predict, we would characterize the twenty-first century as the era during which humans will gain the ability to manipulate their own genes. Society will be able to design more biological changes for the human species in a few decades than the natural processes of evolution did over tens of thousands of years. Of course, science fiction writers have dealt with this topic for most of the twentieth century. Most of these treatments, such as Aldous Huxley's *Brave New World* (1932), see human interference with our "natural" biological nature as disastrous. Yet others see the control of human genetics as the next step in the long evolution of hominids from small-brained primates to organisms capable, through our changing technology, of influencing their own evolution.

This book traces our present understanding of human biological evolution, the main theme of the field of physical anthropology. Chapter 1 outlines the history and development of ideas in the area of human biological evolution. Chapters 2 through 4 explore our knowledge of genetics and the importance of this knowledge as a basis for the understanding of evolutionary processes. Chapter 5 examines in detail Charles Darwin's main contribution to the understanding of evolution, his concept of natural selection. Chapters 6 through 10 place humans, both physically and behaviorally, in the context of the rest of the animal kingdom. In doing this, we emphasize the relationship of humans to their closest relatives, the living primates. Chapters 11 to 15 outline the evolutionary history of the primate order with emphasis on human evolution. Chapters 16 and 17 describe aspects of the biology of modern human populations, including exploration of the reasons why people vary physically from one another.

This text incorporates a number of pedagogical devices that will aid the reader in understanding and learning the information contained within. Each chapter is divided by headings into manageable segments, and the three levels of headings can assist the student in outlining the material. A summary is found at the end of each major section. All technical terms are in boldface type at their first appearance, and their definitions can be found in the Glossary. There is also a second Glossary that lists and identifies major taxonomic groups among the living and fossil primates. Suggested Readings, Study Questions, and Suggested Web Sites are found at the end of each chapter.

This text is also accompanied by four supplements, one for the student, two for the instructor, and one for both. For the student, Rebecca Stein has written a completely new and exciting *Workbook* with original art by Erik Even. Each chapter includes exercises illustrating or expanding on ideas presented in the text, a directory of over 200 relevant web sites, activities (including Internet-based activities), and exercises. The activities include suggestions for student projects that involve work outside class, such as research paper topics or experiments. Exercises involve working through problem sets related to concepts from the text. Each exercise includes a short introduction that serves to emphasize and review material presented in the text.

The *Workbook* also includes a CD developed by Rebecca Stein, Erik Even, and Robert Frankle. The CD provides chapter summaries with links to appropriate Internet sites and to the searchable Glossary, many activities and exercises, important terms, as well as computer-graded quizzes.

Physical anthropology is a rapidly changing field. For the instructor and student, McGraw-Hill publishes the authors' *Physical Anthropology Update.* Instructors may order complementary copies through their McGraw-Hill representative; everyone can read the updates on the Internet at http://www.mhhe.com/socscience/anthropology/newsletters.mhtml.

For the instructor, the *Instructor's Manual* provides over 1000 exam questions, also available as exam-writing software. For this seventh edition, we welcome Rebecca Stein, who has revised the *Instructor's Manual* and added a great many new exam questions. The manual also includes lists of films, videos, and software, along with suppliers, and sources of supplies and equipment. Transparencies of many illustrations are also available.

McGraw-Hill and the authors would like to thank many reviewers for their helpful comments and suggestions. The names of the reviewers are listed in the acknowledgments.

Finally, special appreciation goes to our families—especially Carol Stein and Christine L. Rowe—for their encouragement and help, and the representative of the second generation, Rebecca Stein, for taking on the task of the *Instructor's Manual* and *Workbook.*

Philip L. Stein
Bruce M. Rowe

# ACKNOWLEDGMENTS

David Abrams, Sacramento City College
Leslie Aiello, University College, London
Clifton Amsbury
James Baker, Okanagan College
Robert L. Blakely, Georgia State University
Rita Castellano, Los Angeles Pierce College
Russell L. Ciochon, University of Iowa
Glenn C. Conroy, Washington University School
    of Medicine
Mildred Dickerman
Daniel Evett, Cornell University
Marc Feldsman, Portland State University
Robin Franck, Southwestern College
Everett L. Frost, Eastern New Mexico University
Janet O. Frost, Eastern New Mexico University
Douglas R. Givens, St. Louis Community College
Glenn A. Gorelick, Citrus College
Philip G. Grant
Joseph Guillotte III, University of New Orleans
Van K. Hainline, Citrus College
Mark E. Harlan
C. C. Hoffman, University of Nevada, Reno
Cheryl Sorenson Jamison, Indiana University
L. Lewis Johnson, Vassar College
Gail Kennedy, University of California, Los
    Angeles
Karen Kovac
Andrew Kramer, University of Tennessee,
    Knoxville
William Leonard, University of Florida

Leonard Lieberman, Central Michigan University

Mary Jean Livingston, Wayne County Community College

Jonathan Marks, University of California, Berkeley

James H. Mielke, University of Kansas

Edward E. Myers

Robert L. Pence, Los Angeles Pierce College

Louanna Pettay, California State University, Sacramento

Gary D. Richards, University of California, Berkeley

Peter S. Rodman, University of California, Davis

Irwin Rovner, North Carolina State University

Jeffrey H. Schwartz, University of Pittsburgh

Paul W. Sciulli, Ohio State University

J. Richard Shenkel, University of New Orleans

Richard J. Sherwood, University of Wisconsin, Madison

Paul E. Simonds, University of Oregon

Sandra L. Snyder

William A. Stini, University of Arizona

Soheir Stolba, American River College

Linda L. Taylor, University of Miama

Mayl L. Walek, North Carolina State University

Tim White, University of California, Berkeley

## CHAPTER 1

# Investigating the Nature of Humankind

*We have now seen that man is variable in body and mind; and that the variations are induced, either directly or indirectly, by the same general causes, and obey the same general laws, as with the lower animals. Man has spread widely over the face of the earth, and must have been exposed, during his incessant migrations, to the most diversified conditions.[1]*
—Charles Darwin

---

[1]C. Darwin, *The Descent of Man,* 2nd rev. ed. (London: J. Murray, 1874), p. 47.

The ideas embodied in the opening quotation, taken from *The Descent of Man*, were revolutionary for their time. Darwin's message was that humans, like all animals, were not specially created and that human characteristics arise from the actions of the same natural forces that affect all life.

Darwin is thought to have been a great discoverer of new facts and ideas, and indeed he was. On the other hand, Darwin's ideas, like all ideas, were formed, nurtured, and brought to maturity in the context of particular intellectual backgrounds. The things we think, the relationships we see, and the very process of creativity are determined, in part, by our cultural environment. The knowledge that a person has at any one time represents the accumulation of information and ideas from his or her whole lifetime. The theory of evolution was not developed by one person. It was part of a chain of intellectual events, each link being necessary to the continuity of that chain.

## THE WORLD OF PHYSICAL ANTHROPOLOGY

The anthropologist is an explorer in pursuit of answers to such questions as: What is it to be human? How did humans evolve? What is the nature of humankind? Anthropology is such a broad discipline, however, that it is divided into several subfields or branches. One of the oldest subfields is that of **physical anthropology,** the study of human biological evolution, which is the process of biological change by which populations of organisms come to differ from their ancestral populations.

### Studies of Physical Anthropology

Physical anthropology is a very diverse field. Some areas of interest lie within the realm of biology and medical science; others are more tuned to cultural anthropology and archaeology.[2]

Anthropologists who specialize in the study of growth and development and anatomy are often found in departments of anatomy, health sciences, and schools of medicine. These investigators frequently conduct research on human populations in

various parts of the world, allowing them to compare different modern populations. For example, physical anthropologists might study the growth patterns of children growing up at high altitude in the Peruvian Andes Mountains. Many anthropologists who specialize in anatomy have a special interest in the skeleton and dentition. Other anthropologists study a wide range of health-related topics such as nutrition, disease, and aging.

A focal area of study in physical anthropology is the study of evolution. Anthropologists join with their colleagues in biology in the study of evolutionary theory. Anthropologists are particularly interested in the reconstruction of human and non-human primate evolution. Key evidence in these studies is the evidence provided through the fossil record (paleontology) and through analysis of cultural remains (archaeology). Paleontology and archaeology join to create the study of paleoanthropology. More recently, the comparative study of protein molecules and DNA, the heredity material, has created the field of molecular evolution, which has brought forth new understandings about the relationships among contemporary organisms.

As we will see later, the critical unit of evolution is the population, a group of closely related organisms. Anthropologists carefully document the characteristics of extant human populations in a number of ways. From these studies, we can learn about how different human populations adapt to their environments. The study of human variation is especially important in our shrinking world as more and more people from diverse parts of the world become economically and politically influenced by one another.

Many physical anthropologists specialize in the study of the fossil record or in skeletal remains found in an archaeological context. For these reasons, anthropologists have become very interested in the biology of the skeleton. As a result, some anthropologists are employed in forensic anthropology, a branch of forensic science. Often found in coroner offices, forensic anthropologists analyze skeletal remains from criminal scenes to determine biological factors about the individual, such as sex and age at death, as well as to determine the probable cause of death.

The members of the animal kingdom most closely related to humans in an evolutionary sense

---

[2]For further information about the diversity of disciplines within physical anthropology, see C. W. Wienker and K. A. Bennett, "Trends and Developments in Physical Anthropology," *American Journal of Physical Anthropology* 87 (1992), pp. 383–393.

**FIGURE 1–1  The Study of Primates**
Primatologist Dian Fossey discusses the fine points of photography with some of her subjects. Her life is recounted in the book and the movie *Gorillas in the Mist.*

are the primates, a group of animals that include the living prosimians, monkeys, apes, and humans in addition to a wide variety of now-extinct forms. Many anthropologists are in the field studying primate behavior and ecology while others are in the lab working on problems in primate anatomy and evolution (Figure 1–1).

A major key in understanding evolutionary processes is an understanding of the mechanisms of heredity—the field called genetics. Many anthropologists are active in studying topics in many subfields of genetics, including human and primate genetics.

### Physical Anthropology in the World of Anthropology

When you tell someone that you are an anthropologist, a usual reply is "Have you dug up any bones lately?" Anthropology is not all old bones. Physical anthropology is one of four main branches of the study of people; the others are cultural anthropology, archaeology, and linguistics (Figure 1–2). Many anthropologists see applied an-

thropology as a distinct fifth field. While traditionally anthropologists are trained in all of the four main fields and see anthropology as a holistic discipline, in recent years, the discipline of anthropology has become more and more diverse and specialized, and many new anthropologists are given minimal training outside their own specializations. This has become very much the case in physical anthropology.

**Cultural anthropology** is the study of human social organization and culture. A central concept in cultural anthropology is that of **culture.** Culture is learned, transmittable behavior that employs the use of symbols, such as words. Cultural behavior, the focus of Chapter 10, is the main way by which humans adjust to their environments.

**Archaeology** is the study of the material remains of human activity, artifacts, and the context in which they are found. Both artifacts and their context are used to reconstruct how different cultures have adjusted to varying situations through time and to explain stability and change. Although some archaeologists study contemporary societies, most archaeologists study the cultural anthropology of the past. **Anthropological linguistics** examines the history, function, structure, and physiology of one of a people's most definitive characteristics—language. **Applied anthropology** is concerned with the application of anthropological ideas to current human problems.

While many physical anthropologists work closely with biologists and other related specialists, physical anthropologists are keenly aware of the special nature of the human species. Herein lie the special emphasis and approach of the physical anthropologist. For example, the biologist who is studying human populations may note that one population has a higher frequency of dark skin than another. The biologist's approach is to describe this variation, perhaps by investigating the genetic mechanisms that led to the differentiation. The anthropologist goes one step further: he or she attempts to discover cultural conventions that may be keeping the dark-skinned populations from interbreeding with the light-skinned ones. For instance, cultural conventions involving concepts of beauty, class distinctions, kinship considerations, economic relationships, and so on all affect breeding patterns. In other words, the biological anthropologist takes

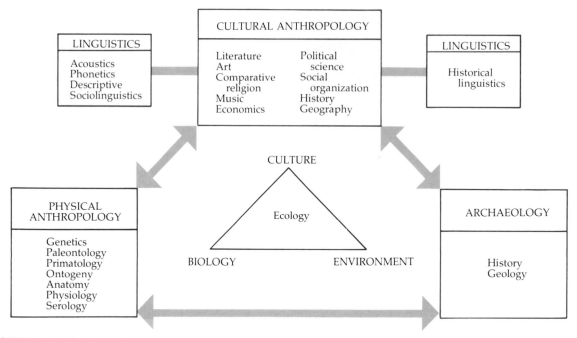

**FIGURE 1–2  The Branches of Anthropology**
The diagram shows the interrelationships of the branches of anthropology with some of their major areas of interest and related fields. Applied anthropology is the practical application of knowledge gained from any of the branches of anthropology. Cultural, biological, and environmental factors interrelate to produce human behavior and human anatomy and physiology. The study of these factors is called *human* or *cultural ecology.*

note of the fact that culture both builds upon and modifies biology.

## Conclusion

Physical anthropology is a vast and dynamic field, and no single textbook can adequately cover all of its aspects. The basic goals of this textbook are twofold. First, we hope to provide a general introduction to physical anthropology as a discipline. Second, the emphasis of the text will be on human evolution.

This text deals with many issues about the nature of humanity, a very complex and difficult topic. There are no simple answers to the many questions that are raised in this book. The purpose of the book is to provide a basic understanding of humans, their development, and their place in nature. We cannot promise that all your questions about people will be answered; in fact, we can promise that they will not. A great deal has been learned about human nature over the centuries, especially in the last 140 years, yet anthropology is

still a dynamic subject. With each publication of a research project, new information is added to our knowledge of humanity. In other words, data that are needed to answer crucial questions about the human species are still being uncovered.

Why study anthropology? Because anthropology provides empirical knowledge about the human condition. On one level, this serves to feed our curiosity about ourselves. However, anthropological studies also provide data useful to the fields of medicine, environmental maintenance, urban planning, education, and so forth. Anthropology also attempts to provide a profile of human potentials and limitations. For instance, it explores the question of whether or not humans are violent by nature. We will attempt to give, in each part of this text, a fuller statement of the relevance of anthropology.

## THE NATURE OF SCIENCE

The physicist investigating the relationship between time and space, the chemist exploring the properties of a new substance, the biologist probing the mysteries of the continuity of life, and the anthropologist searching for human origins share a common trait—curiosity. This is not to say that nonscientists are not curious; most people possess curiosity. The scientist, however, uses scientific reasoning as a specific method to delve into enigmatic problems.

Unfortunately, science often is misunderstood. The multiplication of our knowledge in medicine and technology has led to the idea that science can cure all and explain all and that only enough time, money, and intelligence are needed. In truth, science cannot provide all the answers. In fact, many phenomena are not even subject to scientific explanations.

Science has also been attacked as a cause of most contemporary problems. It is said to be responsible for depersonalizing the individual, for stripping creativity from human behavior, and for creating massive threats to the species through the development of nuclear power, insecticides, and polluting machinery. If we analyze the situation, we can see that the people who developed computers did not intend to debase humankind, nor did those who introduced mass production wish to crush creativity. It is what society, policy makers especially, does with scientific achievements that makes them social or antisocial. There is nothing inherently good or bad about science.

## The Many Aspects of Science

Just what is **science?** Here is where the dictionary fails, for science is not something that can be easily defined. It is an activity, a search, and a method of discovery that results in a body of knowledge.

Science is the activity of seeking out **reliable** explanations for phenomena. *Reliable* here means "predictable." *Predictability* does not mean "assurance"; it may simply indicate the percentage of cases in which, under a given set of conditions, a particular event will occur.

Science is also a search for order. Nature does not categorize; people do. Through classifications, systematic similarities and differences can be found. This display of ordered relationships allows for discoveries that might otherwise never be made.

## Scientific Thinking

The precise mental steps taken in thinking scientifically about a problem may vary depending on the nature of the problem being studied. For instance, because of the different nature of the variables involved, scientific inquiry in the physical sciences differs significantly from that in other sciences.

The first step in scientific studies is to make an observation. Scientific observations are **empirical observations,** observations based upon information received through the senses (seeing, touching, smelling, hearing, tasting). The information can be received directly through the senses or indirectly through an instrument that enhances the senses, such as a microscope or telescope. Some observations are accidental; some are deliberate, such as when a paleontologist goes to a specific geological formation to look for a specific fossil; and some are the results of an experiment.

Next, a question is asked about the observation. For instance, one might observe that the brains of a sequence of related fossils of human ancestors get larger as the fossils get closer to modern times. The question might then be asked: "What advantages might increasing brain size have had in the prehuman and human evolutionary line?

The next step is to identify the variables to be studied. A **variable** is any property that may be displayed in different forms. For example, the volume of the brain case, that part of the skull that houses the brain, is a variable; it may measure 400 cubic centimeters in one animal and 1600 cubic centimeters in another. In order for a variable to be the subject of a scientific study, we must be able to measure it precisely. Different people measuring the same variable should arrive at the same measurement.

The next step in scientific studies is proposing a hypothesis. A **hypothesis** is a tentative answer to a question posed about the relationship of one variable to another. Is one variable independent of the other variable, or does one variable cause another variable to occur? For example, one might hypothesize that among the ancestors of modern humans, as the average size of the brain case increases, so does the ability of the population to manufacture tools. Brain case size is one variable, and the number of tools found in association with the skull is a second variable. The hypothesis proposes a direct relationship between the two variables: as one increases, so does the other. While this particular hypothesis proposes a relationship between two variables, it does not propose that one variable causes the other to occur.

Once proposed, the hypothesis must be tested against reality. In the above example, we could measure brain case size in fossil skulls and count the number of stone tools found in association with each skull. If, upon analysis, we find that as the average size of the brain case increases, so does the number of tools, then we have identified one line of evidence that supports the validity of the hypothesis.

Evidence is not necessarily absolute proof. There could be unknown factors responsible for the observed correlation of the variables. For instance, an increase in the population density at a series of sites might influence the number of stone tools found. Perhaps some habitats are more easily exploited with simpler technologies than are others. In other words, the relationship between the variables in the hypothesis may turn out to be accidental or to be the result of a variable or variables not identified in the original hypothesis.

After a number of studies exploring the relationships of all the variables have been completed, we might develop some generalizations. We might suggest that an increase in the volume of the brain case is correlated with a whole range of behaviors that differentiate earlier humanlike organisms from later ones. Each of these new hypotheses would then have to be tested by some research design. Each test might reveal hidden variables that will either disprove or modify the original and related hypotheses. This hypothesis-test-hypothesis-test cycle is a self-corrective feature of science. Scientists realize that results are never final.

Science is cumulative. It is constantly open to repeated criticism and testing by other scientists. Experiments performed in one lab must yield the same results when duplicated in another lab, and new discoveries must be consistent with previous ones.

**Theory** After many tests have been conducted on a set of similar hypotheses with confirming results, a **theory** may be proposed. One meaning of *theory* is that a theory is a statement based upon highly confirmed hypotheses that generalizes about conditions not yet tested. For example, the testing of thousands of hypotheses on the reasons for change in anatomy and behavior has led to great confidence in the theory of evolution.

Another meaning of the word *theory* is that a theory shows the relationship among scientific facts. It explains how data are related to each other. For instance, facts derived from the study of anatomy, physiology, genetics, and paleontology show that evolution has occurred.

There are more components to scientific thinking than we can discuss in this book. The main point is that scientific thinking is a way to test one's ideas against the real world in a disciplined way. Each step in the process must be made clear so that the procedure can be repeated and yield the same results.

### Science as a Creative Process

Science is a creative process. The scientist must be a keen observer, possess a questioning mind, and ask unique, nonstereotyped questions. The scientist must be clever in suggesting possible answers to his or her own queries. Above all, the scientist must be innovative in designing experiments that will test the validity of the hypothesis. However, it is a mistake to believe that intuition and passion are absent from science. A hunch, along with persistence, has more than once led to a revolutionary discovery. This happened when Mary Leakey and her husband, Louis Leakey, found evidence of early humans in an area that they had been combing for 28 years.

The passion involved in the search for a new truth or simply a new fact can be as intense as that of the artist attempting to create a masterpiece. From Copernicus's calculations to modern methods of charting the entire human genetic system, the scientist displays an ability to see unique solutions to problems that most people do not even recognize as problems.

### Applying Scientific Thinking to Anthropological Problems

In many instances, it is difficult to apply the experimental method to the investigation of humans. For one thing, physical scientists, such as physicists and chemists, can design experiments that can be repeated—in many cases, as many times as desired. The physical anthropologist is often limited in the degree and manner in which the phenomena being studied can be repeated for the sake of experimentation. For instance, how does one repeat the past in an attempt to test hypotheses on early human ancestors?

To explore hypotheses about fossil populations, physical anthropologists might use various methods of comparison. For instance, a series of fossils from older to younger could be compared to determine relationships among anatomical structures. Comparative research can also involve the study of living organisms through comparing embryological development, as well as molecular similarities and differences. These studies are used to determine the degree of relationship between living organisms and propose ideas about the ancestral relationships between these organisms.

Another major problem faced by the anthropologist is that the subjects of anthropological study, humans, are more complex than anything dealt with by the physical scientist. The latter may find a single element that explains the subject under study. This would be a **monocausal explanation.** Water turns to ice at sea level when the temperature is 0°C (32°F), and that's that. Anthropologists are much less likely to find single causes for anything they study; their explanations are usually **multicausal.** All things about humans are due to an interplay of factors at different levels of being. After all, a human is a physical entity and a chemical substance, as well as a biological organism and a social and cultural being. Human behavior, evolution, variation, growth and development, and so on, are subject to explanations on all these levels.

Because of the complexity of the subject matter, anthropology approaches its hypotheses from numerous angles. For example, the general theory of evolution has been validated not only by the study of the fossil record, but also through comparative anatomy, comparative growth and development, molecular biology, and cytogenetics. The confidence in any hypothesis is increased when several lines of evidence all point to the same conclusion. In the case of evolutionary theory, they all do point to the same thing—a dynamic, changeable world.

Anthropology is a newer discipline than physics and chemistry, and its subject matter is more complex. It is thus understandable that the methods and techniques of anthropology are still in a formative stage. Yet, because of its integrative approach and commitment to the scientific exploration of human nature, anthropology perhaps offers us the greatest chance at attaining a general "theory of humanity."

## Science and Religion

The theologian deeply involved in an interpretation of scriptures, the bereaved individual looking to scripture to explain death, and the shaman dancing for rain are putting their trust in traditional doctrines that, for the most part, they do not question. In contrast, the biologist examining cell structure, the anthropologist studying death rituals, and the meteorologist investigating the weather rely on methods and techniques that are aimed at producing new information and validating or correcting old explanations. Thus, they build a body of knowledge from which accurate predictions about natural occurrences can be made. The credibility of scientific conclusions is based on the concepts of accuracy, validity, and reliability; belief in religious doctrines is based on faith.

Scientists can attempt to answer only some questions; others cannot be subjected to scientific inquiry and are therefore not in the domain of empirical or objective research. For example, science cannot deal with the question of the existence of an omnipotent force. In order for an experiment to be carried out, a **control,** a situation that differs from the situation being tested, must be possible. If a phenomenon is present always and everywhere, how can its absence be tested?

Scientists do not claim that their conclusions are final. They realize that their statements are only as good as the data they have and that new information may alter their concepts. A religious belief can change in response to personal interpretation and public opinion, but such interpretations or new information are not necessarily linked to new empirical facts. To a believer, his or her religious belief or faith is taken as being absolutely true, whereas at no time is a scientific statement considered totally and irrefutably correct.

The scientific approach has been consciously and consistently used in Western societies since the 1600s; however, it is not just the industrial societies that practice science. All people make conclusions on the basis of experimenting with observations. The phenomena that they can treat in this way make up their objective knowledge; the more mysterious facets of life are treated religiously or magically. For example, the Trobriand Islanders of the Pacific do two types of fishing: one in the shallow coastal pools and the other far out at sea. The first type is safe and is undertaken by men, women, and children; the second, filled with the unknown, is dangerous and is considered a male activity. Since shallow fishing is undertaken with regularity, time is spent making observations of fish behavior and experiments are performed on how best to catch the prey. Nothing is done religiously or magically to protect the fishing party or to ensure a catch. The story is different with deep-sea fishing. Men occasionally do not return from the expeditions, so elaborate rituals are performed in order to appease or appeal to the gods of the unpredictable seas.

In conclusion, a scientific statement asserts the natural causality of phenomena. One thing happens because of preceding events that led up to it. Things happen and conditions exist because of the physical, chemical, biological, behavioral, and/or cultural characteristics of the thing in question and the context in which it is found. Religious or magical statements assert causality beyond the natural; when natural causality cannot be determined or is not sought, spiritual causality is often assumed.

### Summary

Science is the activity of seeking out reliable explanations for phenomena. Science is also the search for order and a method for discovery. The result of the activity of science is a body of empirical knowledge that can be used to understand the universe better and to predict the processes, structure, form, and function of natural occurrences. Scientific thinking provides a systematic way of investigation and includes the identification of variables, hypothesis formation, and tests of the validity of the hypothesis, and of postulating theories. Scientific thinking also includes the comparative method. All scientific statements are tentative. It is because new evidence is always possible that a scientific statement can never be completely proved.

Science is not a mere mechanical pursuit for knowledge but involves creativity and the passion of discovery and accomplishment. Many breakthroughs, as well as more mundane discoveries, have resulted from a hunch followed by long years of persistent examination.

The scientist and the theologian are both interested in giving answers. However, the scientist proceeds by testing questions about the nature of empirical observation, whereas the theologian consults the philosophy of his or her particular religion and interprets the meaning of that philosophy for a particular situation. Scientific statements are never considered absolute, but at any one time religious doctrine often is. All people have a body of scientific knowledge, but for the things they fear or cannot understand in an empirical way, religion and magic provide a measure of comfort and assurance.

## VIEWS ON THE ESSENCE OF HUMANS, NATURE, AND TIME

Although there were many variations in the early ideas about the universe, they were often the opposite of those embodied in present evolutionary theory. These old ideas had to be challenged before a new concept of reality could arise.

First among the early views was the idea of human superiority, or **anthropocentricity.** This belief was that the earth is the center of the universe and that all the celestial bodies revolve around it. Humans placed themselves on a pedestal, believing that God provided the animals and plants for people's use and fancy. The similarities that people observed between humans and animals and among various animal species were seen as reflecting the design of the Creator. Many people believed that certain shapes and forms are pleasing to God and that God therefore used these as models for all creations.

People of that era, as well as many people today whose beliefs are based upon a literal interpretation of the Bible, thought that life had been formed from nonlife at the will of the Creator. Some believed that this process of creation continued even after the original six days of Genesis; this concept is known as **spontaneous generation.** People also believed that once a type of organism is created, its descendants will remain **immutable,** in the same form as the original, from generation to generation.

The original creation, as described in Genesis, supposedly took place a few thousand years before the Greek and Roman empires. Archbishop James Ussher of Armagh, Ireland (1581–1656) used the generations named in the Bible to calculate that the earth's creation took place at noon on October 23, 4004 B.C. The idea of a spontaneously created and static life, a life brought into being only 6000 years ago, is directly counter to modern evolutionary theory. The development of evolutionary theory depended upon an increasing disbelief in these old ideas.

### Questioning the Old Ideas

What a shock it must have been to European scholars of the sixteenth century when Nicolaus Copernicus (1473–1543) showed conclusively that the earth was not the center of the universe and was not even the center of the solar system! This was but one of a series of revelations that were to bombard the old ideas.

A tired, lost sea captain, who was fearful that he was going to fall off the edge of the earth, might have been both elated and confused at the greeting he received from an exotic people living on a shore that he thought could not possibly exist. The Age of Exploration, which began for Europeans in the late 1400s with the voyages of explorers such as Christopher Columbus, revealed variations of life not dreamed of before. By 1758, 4235 species of animals were cataloged. Today, about 1,032,000 species are known. During the Age of Exploration, strange animals never mentioned in the Bible were seen by Europeans for the first time. Naturalists were overwhelmed by the quantity of new discoveries and the problems of organizing this rapidly growing wealth of data.

**Carolus Linnaeus's Classification**    Although all cultures classify plants and animals into some kind of scheme, it was not until the seventeenth and eighteenth centuries that comprehensive written classifications were made. The Swedish naturalist Carolus Linnaeus (1707–1778) succeeded in classifying every animal and plant known to him into a system of categories (Figure 1–3). This type of classification is absolutely necessary for a scientific understanding of the relationship of one plant or animal to the next. Yet at first it reinforced traditional ideas. Linnaeus saw each category as fixed and immutable, the result of divine creation.

---

**BOX 1-1**

## Science, Religion, and Political Intrigue—The Trial of Galileo

In 1633, the Roman Inquisition found Galileo Galilei (1564–1642), at the age of 69, guilty of supporting the Copernican view that the sun, not the earth, is at the center of the universe. In 1616, the Catholic Church had condemned this sun-centered **(heliocentric)** view of the universe as "false and opposed by the Holy Scripture." In 1600, even before this official condemnation, Giordano Bruno had been burned at the stake for his support of the Copernican view. Galileo was saved from that fate and was instead put under "house arrest" for the last nine years of his life.

Pietro Redondi, an Italian historian of science, has proposed another account of the trial of Galileo. He believes he has uncovered an ancient case of plea bargaining.

Redondi believes that a Jesuit named Orazio Grassi wrote the note, indirectly accusing Galileo of heresy. In 1623, Galileo had professed his belief that all matter consists of small, unchangeable atomic particles. The letter suggested that this view contradicted the idea that the bread and wine of communion could be transformed into the body and blood of Christ. It would have been extreme heresy to suggest such a thing.

Pope Urban VIII, a personal friend of Galileo, had given Galileo permission to publish his ideas on Copernicanism. In 1632, the Copernican idea was not as controversial as it had been in 1600 and 1616, but the Jesuits, who wished to control the Vatican, knew that the atomic theory was a much more profound contradiction of church doctrine. They continued to place pressure on the Pope by attempting to discredit his friend Galileo. In 1624, nothing was done about the Jesuit attack on Galileo; the Jesuits did not have enough influence at that time. However, developments in the European Thirty Years' War had made Pope Urban VIII more politically vulnerable, so, in the 1630s, the Jesuits attempted to reopen their attack. The Pope now, for political reasons, had to pay attention to the Jesuits or be discredited himself.

The Pope defused the situation by allowing Galileo to plead guilty to supporting the Copernican theory. In return, the Inquisition would not charge Galileo for promoting the atomic theory. Galileo agreed to cooperate. In this way, Galileo was saved from burning at the stake, and the Pope showed he still had control. In 1984, Galileo was given a full pardon by the Catholic Church.

*Source:* D. Dickson, "Was Galileo Saved by Plea Bargain?" *Science* 233 (1986), pp. 612–613; and L. S. Lerner and E. A. Gosselin, "Galileo and the Spector of Bruno," *Scientific American* 255 (November 1986), pp. 126–133.

**FIGURE 1–3  Carolus Linnaeus (1707–1778)**
Born with the name Carl von Linné, Linnaeus was a Swedish naturalist and botanist. He established what became the modern method of naming the living world.

Linnaeus's scheme became important to modern biological sciences for many reasons. First, it imposed order upon nature's infinite variation. Linnaeus saw that the analysis of anatomical structures could be used to group plants and animals into categories. The most specific groups included organisms that were very much alike, whereas the more general levels encompassed the specific groups, thereby representing a wider range of variation. Linnaeus wrote that the first order of science is to distinguish one thing from the other; his classification helped do just that.

Second, although Linnaeus considered organisms to be immutable, paradoxically his classification provided a means for "seeing" changes and possible ancestral relationships. Scientists wondered if similar organisms were related by common ancestry. If two or more types had a common origin but were now somewhat different, it followed that evolution must have occurred. Linnaeus, who had been so emphatic about the idea of unchang-

ing species, began in later life to question this concept of fixity. He had observed new types of plants resulting from crossbreeding, and he had decided that perhaps all living things were not immutable.

Third, Linnaeus included people in his classification. Although he did not contend that humans are related to other animals, his placement of humans in this scheme was sure to raise the question.

**Could Nature Be Dynamic?**  Many people of the eighteenth century were intrigued with the rapidly increasing information brought to the fore by exploration. Not only were new varieties of plants and animals being discovered, but so were new people. Who were the Native Americans, the Polynesians, the Africans? Were they human, or were they part human and part ape? Credible answers to these and other questions could not be supplied by traditional explanations.

The effect of exploration in guiding people to new realities was intensified by the great revolutions of the eighteenth and nineteenth centuries. These revolutions included technological changes in the industrial age as well as political upheavals, such as the American and French revolutions. Technological and political developments that brought about major social changes created an atmosphere in which the idea of immutability could be questioned. If people could change their social systems so rapidly, if human life could be so dynamic, then perhaps so was nature. It was in the late eighteenth century that the first modern theories of organic evolution emerged.

### Early Evolutionary Ideas

Georges-Louis Leclerc Comte de Buffon (1707–1788), a contemporary of Linnaeus, proposed many major points that Darwin would later include in *On the Origin of Species*. Buffon recognized the tendency of populations to increase at a faster rate than their food supply, hence the struggle for survival. He noted the variations within species and speculated on methods of inheritance. He questioned spontaneous creation. He also challenged the church's dating of the earth, proposing that the earth is much older than 6000 years. Buffon's importance was diminished by his lack of conciseness, but he might have been vague and apologetic about his thoughts for fear of being considered a heretic.

Although Buffon was one of the first people to scientifically investigate evolution, it was left to Jean-Baptiste de Lamarck (1744–1829) to articulate a systematic theory of evolution as an explanation of organic diversity. Lamarck used the previous nonevolutionary idea that organisms could be ranked in a progressive order, with humans at the top. He envisioned evolution as a constant striving toward perfection and believed deviations were due to local adaptations to specific environments.

Lamarck is remembered by many for his explanation of the cause of these deviations. He again used an idea that had been around for centuries. He proposed that an organism acquired new characteristics in its lifetime by virtue of using or not using different parts of its body and that these newly acquired characteristics could then be inherited by the individual's offspring. For instance, if an animal constantly had to stretch its neck to get at food in the branches of a tree, its neck would get longer. If the trees were to get taller, the animal would then have to stretch more, and its neck would get longer still. This was Lamarck's explanation of the giraffe. He believed that a trait, once acquired, would be passed on to the next generation. This concept is known as the **theory of acquired characteristics.**

Lamarck's importance lies in his proposal that life is dynamic and that there is a mechanism in nature that promotes ongoing change. The method of change he suggested, however, is incorrect. Acquired characteristics are not transmitted to offspring. A person who is very muscular as a result of lifting weights will not be more likely to have a muscle-bound child (Figure 1–4).

Lamarck, like so many famous people of science, was a synthesizer. He combined previously existing notions (such as Linnaean classification and the idea of acquired characteristics) into a new system with new meaning. Although the details of his ideas are incorrect, his emphasis on change gave support to the thoughts of those investigators who would ultimately discover accurate explanations for the changes he proposed.

**Catastrophism**  The work of Lamarck and other early evolutionists, along with increasing evidence that changes had occurred in the living world, prompted thinkers to attempt to reconcile the tra-

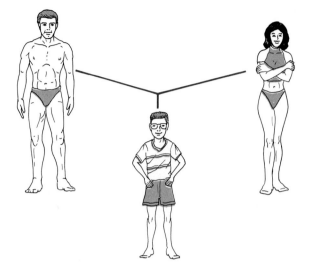

**FIGURE 1–4  Inheritance of Acquired Characteristics**
Today, biologists do not believe that the increase or decrease in the size or strength of parts of the body due to use or disuse is transmitted to offspring. For example, if a couple lift weights and become muscular, their newly acquired physical condition will not be passed on genetically to their offspring.

ditional view of a divinely created changeless world with new evidence and ideas. The French scholar Georges Cuvier (1769–1832) is known for developing the idea called the theory **catastrophism.** Cuvier recognized the fact that as we dig down into the earth, we see different assemblages of plants and animals. In many cases, specific layers of flora and fauna seem to be almost totally replaced by new types overlying them. Cuvier believed that the living organisms represented in each layer were destroyed by a catastrophic event and that the next set of plants and animals represented a new creation event. Although Cuvier did not construct his ideas to bolster a literal interpretation of the Bible, others saw the last catastrophic event as the biblical flood.

According to the proponents of catastrophism, not all plants and animals need be destroyed by a cataclysmic event. For instance, the animals that were collected by Noah survived the flood. Also, Cuvier believed that catastrophes could be localized. Organisms that survived in an area not affected by the cataclysm could then migrate into the areas left vacant by the catastrophe.

Today, evolutionists reject the ideas of divinely created organisms and divinely orchestrated catastrophes. However, just as Linnaeus's classification, originally conceived to explain traditional religious concepts, has become a major tool for modern biologists, some of Cuvier's ideas are still present in the work of some modern evolutionary theorists. As with Linnaeus's ideas, Cuvier's ideas have been expanded upon and reinterpreted in nonreligious terms. For instance, some modern researchers see catastrophic events, such as the effects of meteorites that hit the earth, as the catalysts of major evolutionary events, such as mass extinctions of plants and animals and ensuing rapid evolutionary changes in some of the surviving populations. However, other evolutionists do not view catastrophic events as primary causes of evolutionary change. They see large-scale evolution as the result of the gradual accumulation of small changes over time. This idea of gradual modification of a species is the basic thesis of Darwin's model of evolution. Before we discuss Darwin, however, we turn to a scientist who directly influenced him.

### What Is the Age of the Earth?

By the early nineteenth century, masses of new data had been gathered that threw doubt on traditional interpretations. Charles Lyell (1797–1875) synthesized this new information in a textbook, *Principles of Geology,* the first of three volumes being published in 1830 (Figure 1–5). In it he popularized the principle of **uniformitarianism,** first proposed by James Hutton (1726–1797), which was a main prerequisite to the development of a credible evolutionary theory. The principle of uniformitarianism states that physical forces, such as wind, rain, heat, cold, moving water, volcanism, and earthquakes, that are at work today altering the earth were also in force, working in the same way, in former times. Therefore, "the present is the key to the past."

Lyell also realized that, as they operate today, the processes resulting in physical alteration of the earth would require very long periods of time to form the layers of the earth known as **strata** (Figure 1–6). Therefore, it could be inferred that the large number and often great thickness of strata formed in the past must have taken a long time to develop. This inference also challenged biblical

**FIGURE 1–5  Charles Lyell (1797–1875)**
The main purpose of his book, *Principles of Geology*, was to establish the principle of uniformitarianism, as the book's subtitle indicates: "Being an attempt to explain the former changes of the earth's surface, by reference to causes now in operation."

chronology because it showed that the earth's age was many times greater than previously thought. In popularizing the theory of uniformitarianism, Lyell was also setting the stage for a theory of the evolution of the living world.

William Smith (1769–1839), who was nicknamed "Strata Smith," had found that each stratum was characterized by distinct fossils that could be used to indicate the age of strata. In 1815, he released the first geological maps of English strata.

Charles Lyell also studied fossil plants and animals that were embedded in the various strata. These and other similar investigations suggested that the earth is extremely old and that life had existed in various forms, some now extinct, for hundreds of centuries. Lyell, himself, did not become convinced of the antiquity of living things until later in his life when, in his text *The Antiquity of*

**FIGURE 1–6 Stratigraphy**
The Grand Canyon shows the various strata that have accumulated over millennia.

*Man* (1863), he supported Charles Darwin's theory of natural selection.

## Humans before Adam and Eve?

Fossils of extinct forms of plants and animals had been known long before Lyell's time, and many valid interpretations had been made. However, as often happens, the evidence was more frequently viewed in terms of predispositions and the special interests of the observer; it was not analyzed critically. For instance, early proponents of catastrophism believed that extinct animals were creatures "who did not make the Ark." After Lyell's systematic investigation, some scientists began at last to speculate on the idea of a more dynamic

world. Yet the notion of prehistoric people was still heresy. Were not all people descendants of Adam and Eve?

In the early 1800s, Jacques Boucher de Crèvecoeur de Perthes (1788–1868) made a systematic attempt to demonstrate the existence of a prehistoric period. While digging on the banks of the Somme River in southwestern France, he discovered that many stones were not made of the same material as the walls of the pit in which they were uncovered. In addition, the stones had obviously been shaped into specific forms (Figure 1–7). Other people had also observed these types of rocks. They considered them to be "figured stones" of an unknown origin or "lightning stones," petrified lightning cast to the earth by God during thunderstorms. Boucher de Crèvecoeur de Perthes was convinced that they were made by ancient people. To back up this conviction, he collected what he thought was an immense amount of evidence to

**FIGURE 1–7 Lightning Stone**
This is an example of a hand ax from the Lower Paleolithic of southwestern France.

support his case. He submitted his report in 1838 to various scientific societies, where it was rejected. Not until 20 years later, a year before the publication of Darwin's *On the Origin of Species*, were his conclusions accepted.

By the time of Darwin, the notions of anthropocentrism, immutability, and a date of 4004 B.C. for the earth's origin had been altered or reversed. For most of the scientific community, the final discrediting of spontaneous creation would have to wait until the time of the French chemist Louis Pasteur (1822–1895). Pasteur, who had developed the pasteurization process and vaccinations against anthrax and rabies, also disproved spontaneous creation.

### Darwin's Voyage of Discovery

It was Charles Darwin (1809–1882) who proposed a compelling theory for the mechanism of organic evolution that accurately synthesized the available evidence (Figure 1–8). At the age of 22, Darwin was invited to accompany a scientific investigation on the ship *HMS Beagle*. On December 27, 1831, the *Beagle* sailed from Plymouth, England, on what was to be a five-year voyage of discovery (Figure 1–9). Darwin spent much of the five years confined on the small ship, which measured 90 feet in length and less than 25 feet at the widest point. He was one of 74 aboard.

The purpose of the voyage was to chart the southeastern coast of South America and to calculate an accurate fixing of longitude around the world. It was the role of the voyage in Darwin's life, however, that made it one of the most famous journeys in history. On this voyage, Darwin gained new insights into the origin of coral reefs, described in detail fauna and flora, and studied fossilized animals.

In the Andes, Darwin found seashells in rocks at 3962 meters (13,000 feet), and in Valdivia, Chile, he personally experienced a devastating earthquake that elevated the shore by several feet. These and other experiences showed how dynamic the earth is. He realized that the tops of mountains once had been under the sea and that coastlines could be significantly altered by earthquakes.

Throughout his trip, Darwin witnessed the great diversity in nature. His five-week visit to the Galápagos Islands, a volcanic group of islands some 965

**FIGURE 1–8  Charles Darwin (1809–1882)**
The 1250 copies of the first printing of his book *On the Origin of Species* sold out on the day of its issue in 1859. Darwin's concept of natural selection has been firmly established as a hallmark of modern biological science.

kilometers (600 miles) west of Ecuador, possibly provided a major stimulus for his most famous contribution to science: the concept of natural selection. It was there that he observed giant tortoises, seagoing lizards, ground finches, and other animals that showed variations related to differences in the different island habitats. Ultimately he hypothesized that environmental forces acted to weed out those individuals whose characteristics were not as well-suited to a particular situation.

Darwin was not the only person who was developing a theory of evolution based on species adaptation to the environment. As often happens in science, two people came up with basically the same conclusion simultaneously. In the summer of 1858, Darwin must have got quite a jolt when he received an essay from Alfred Russell Wallace (1823–1913), another naturalist, with whom he had been corresponding (Figure 1–10). Wallace had come up with basically the same ideas that Darwin

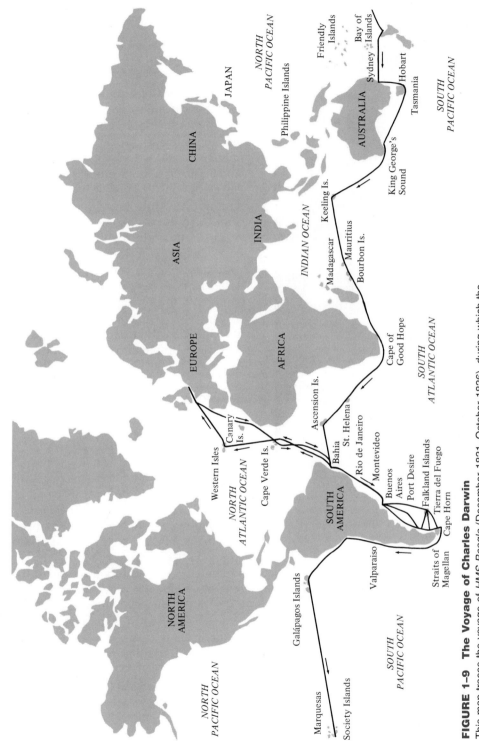

**FIGURE 1-9  The Voyage of Charles Darwin**

This map traces the voyage of *HMS Beagle* (December 1831–October 1836), during which the young Charles Darwin gathered data that he would use to formulate the theory of natural selection.

**FIGURE 1–10  Alfred Russell Wallace (1823–1913)**
Darwin was about halfway through writing *On the Origin of Species* in 1858, when he received an essay from Wallace that outlined Darwin's ideas. Darwin published an extract of his book along with Wallace's essay later in 1858. Neither piece received much attention at the time.

had been working on for two decades. Both men received credit for their work at a meeting of the Linnaean Society in 1858. Because Darwin was the first to publish his work, in his book *On the Origin of Species* in 1859, he has since received most of the credit for modern evolutionary theory. Wallace certainly deserves more credit than he is usually given.

### Darwinian Natural Selection

The concept of **natural selection** emerged from the analysis of the observations made and specimens collected by Charles Darwin on his voyage. Natural selection is the process of favoring or weeding out individuals with different characteristics from a population. Those individuals that are well-suited for their environment will be "favored" in the sense that they will pass on their heritable attributes to the next generation at a higher rate than individuals not as well-suited to the environment.

Darwin noted that within any group of plants or animals there existed much variability. With very few exceptions, each offspring of a pair of sexually reproducing adults is unique. (The exceptions include identical twins and the results of cloning.) While the majority of organisms resemble some type of average or norm, there will always be individuals that are smaller or larger, lighter or darker, or possess some unique features when compared with the average.

Darwin also realized that all living creatures have the capacity to reproduce in very great numbers. For example, if one pair of houseflies bred in April and all eggs hatched and in turn lived to reproduce, by August the total number of houseflies descending from the original pair would be 191,010,000,000,000,000,000. Of course, in real life, not all eggs do hatch, and not all individuals that are born live to reproduce. However, the numbers of individuals born or hatched tend to be vast.

This capacity for organisms to rapidly increase in number was noted by Thomas R. Malthus (1766–1834) in his *Essay on the Principles of Population*. Malthus wrote that the human population is growing at a faster rate than food production, and famine and economic chaos would result as the population grew and food resources dwindled. In general, populations have the potential of dramatically increasing in numbers. However, such growth is limited by such factors as space, food, predators, and disease.

Because of limitations in population growth, Darwin concluded that only a proportion of animals that are born live to reproduce. Since individuals differ from one another, those individuals who possess features that increase the chance of surviving are likely to pass on these features to the next generation. On the other hand, organisms with traits that reduce the chance of successfully reproducing are less likely to pass on these traits. Thus, populations of organisms changed through time as those features that contribute to survival are inherited by future generations.

**Darwin's Finches: A Case of Natural Selection**
Darwin believed that natural selection operated over extremely long periods of time. Therefore, natural selection could not be directly observed, although it could be deduced through the study of the end products or through individuals that have been fossilized. Darwin believed that his logic was sound—natural selection had to be occurring—but at a pace that was impossible to observe within the human life span.

Contemporary field biologists, however, have discovered many situations where natural selection is operating on a time scale that can be observed during the professional lifetime of the investigator. One such case involves the finches found on the Galápagos Islands. These birds, studied by Charles Darwin on his voyage, are today called Darwin's finches.

Finches are songbirds that belong to the same family as sparrows and canaries. Darwin observed several species of finches that had beaks of different sizes and shapes and generally ate different foods. Finches with large, powerful beaks could break open hard seeds that other finches could not. One variety of finch had a short, thick beak; its diet consisted mainly of leaves, buds, blossoms, and fruits. Another finch had a long, straight beak; it subsisted mainly on nectar from the prickly pear cactus.

Darwin believed that competition led to diversity in animal and plant types. For example, the small-beaked birds could not compete for hard seeds with the birds that had more powerful beaks. Unless the birds with smaller beaks possessed characteristics that would allow them to exploit a different segment of the habitat, they might become extinct.

Darwin was impressed by the fact that animals on the Galápagos Islands had "cousins" on the South American mainland. He postulated that since these volcanic islands were younger than the mainland, the animals must have originated on the mainland. He then reasoned that as members of the original population became isolated from each other, they evolved differently, depending on the local environment.

**FIGURE 1–11 Darwin's Finches**
(*a*) The medium ground finch, *Geospiza fortis*, and (*b*) the cactus finch, *Geospiza scandens*.

In 1973, biologists Peter and Rosemary Grant arrived on the very small island of Daphne Major where they began a study that would involve several of their students and would last over two decades. Out of this work would come direct proof that natural selection did indeed occur in a real-life situation.[3]

Daphne Major is a small island of about 100 acres, small enough to be studied intensively. The Grants studied two species of finch that lived on the island, the medium ground finch and the cactus finch (Figure 1–11). Eventually all

[3]P. R. Grant, *Ecology and Evolution of Darwin's Finches* (Princeton, N.J.: Princeton University Press, 1986); J. Weiner, *The Beak of the Finch* (New York: Knopf, 1994).

of the finches on the island were captured and re-leased. They were carefully weighed and measured, and photographed; colored rings placed on their legs ensured that the investigators were able to identify each and every bird in the field. New-born chicks were examined and banded before they left the nest. Their habitats were also carefully studied and available food supplies were quantified.

No rain fell on Daphne Major between mid-1976 and early 1978. Because of the lack of water, fewer seeds were produced and the small, soft seeds that were the preferred food for the ground finches soon disappeared. What was left were the larger, harder seeds that were very difficult to eat. In this situation, birds with larger and more powerful beaks had a distinct advantage. For example, it is very difficult to reach the four to six seeds within the hard fruit of *Tribulus*. On the average, the large ground finch is able to crack the fruit in about 2 seconds and within an additional 7 seconds is able to eat all of the seeds. On the other hand, the smaller ground finch takes about 7 seconds to get into the fruit and another 15 seconds to eat the one or two seeds it can wrestle out of the shell. The smaller bird is using more energy to get less food than the larger bird.

These estimates of time illustrate differences between species. Similar differences are found between birds of different sizes within the same species. Those animals with larger beaks expend less time and energy to more successfully exploit the large tough seeds that are left at the height of the drought.

Not surprisingly, a large number of birds died as a result of the drought. Of the 1200 medium ground finches living on the island at the beginning of 1977, only 180 remained at the end of that year—only 15 percent of the birds survived. The rest had died primarily of starvation. However, when the Grants measured the beaks of the surviving medium ground finches, they discovered that the survivors had an average beak size that was 4 percent greater than the size found before the start of the drought. Since beak size is to a large extent inherited, this increased beak size also characterized the new generation of birds born after the end of the drought. Clearly, natural selection had produced an increase in average beak size.

## Evolution and Creationism

On departing from Plymouth in 1831, the captain of the *Beagle*, Robert Fitzroy, presented Charles Darwin with a gift. That gift, a copy of the newly published *Principles of Geology* by Charles Lyell, influenced the development of Darwin's ideas and was the source of some heated debates between Darwin and Fitzroy, a religious fundamentalist. Had Fitzroy read the book, he may never have given it to Darwin.

After the voyage, Lyell became Darwin's friend. In 1859, Lyell recommended that a partial disclaimer of sorts be added to *On the Origin of Species*, one that would recognize the role of the "Creator" in evolution. The book was first published on November 24, 1859, with no disclaimer; it sold out its first printing that same day. *On the Origin of Species* became the focus of a controversy between those who believed in the divine creation of life (creationists) and those who believed in a natural origin of life (evolutionists).

**"Creation-Science"** Darwin's concept of natural selection has survived the scrutiny of almost 140 years of biological study to become one of the foundations of modern biological science. Yet there are those who, for various reasons that lie outside of science, feel that the concept of evolution must be disproved in favor of a creationist interpretation. In recent times, creationists modified an old strategy. They called the concept of the divine creation of life a scientific view, and the term **creation-science** was born. Even creationists of the nineteenth century had used the argument that the biblical account of creation could be scientifically proved. Creation-science advocates began to sue teachers and school districts to force them to teach creation-science alongside evolutionary theory. They also put pressure on publishers to de-emphasize evolution in biology textbooks.

Under such pressure, several states passed balanced-treatment acts, which required that teachers present "scientific" evidence for creation concurrent with the teaching of evolution. Because it ultimately came before the U.S. Supreme Court, the 1981 Balanced Treatment Act of Louisiana became one of the most important of these acts. On June

19, 1987, the Supreme Court, by a vote of 7 to 2, declared the Louisiana act, and therefore all others like it, unconstitutional on the same grounds that Clarence Darrow had argued 62 years before (Box 1–2). The court agreed that the act

> advanced a religious doctrine by requiring either the banishment of the theory of evolution from public classrooms or the presentation of a religious viewpoint that rejects evolution in its entirety.[4]

The Court ruled that the Louisiana act violated the First Amendment's prohibition of the state's promotion of religious beliefs. Although many biologists believed that creation-science advocates had been dealt a coup de grace to their legal battle over establishing laws that prohibit or cripple the teaching of evolution, creationists developed other strategies.

A school teacher named Ray Webster attempted to teach "creation-science" in an Illinois public school. In the 1990 case, *Webster v. The New Lenox School District,* the Seventh Circuit Court of Appeals found that creation-science was religious advocacy. They further ruled that the school district did not violate Webster's rights to free speech by prohibiting him from teaching religion in his social science classes.

In 1994, John E. Peloza sued the Capistrano School District (California) for requiring him to teach evolution. He contended that the District's actions established a state-supported religion of evolutionism. The Ninth Circuit Court of Appeals dismissed his claim saying that evolution is a scientific theory, not a religion. In 1997, the United States District Court for the Eastern District of Louisiana rejected the Tanipahoa Parish Board of Education's policy of requiring teachers to read aloud a disclaimer whenever they taught evolution.

For some time, creationists have been lobbying school districts to choose textbooks that eliminate or minimize mention of evolution and other subjects that are not in line with fundamental Christian beliefs. This type of censorship may also be in trouble. In 1990, the Board of Education in Texas approved biology textbooks for grades 1 through 12 that "teach the theory of evolution unimpeded by creationist

views."[5] The California Department of Education has enacted similar policies. Perhaps this is the beginning of a new trend to insist that science be in science books and religion be prominent in theology (and history, philosophy, humanity, and art) books.

**Evolutionary Theory after Darwin: The Synthetic Theory**   The basic concepts of Darwin's theory of evolution remain the cornerstone of modern evolutionary theory, yet much has been added to this base. Darwin, Wallace, and other naturalists of their day did not have an accurate picture of inheritance. They therefore were not sure of how characteristics were passed on from generation to generation or how new characteristics might arise. Progress in this area began to be made by Gregor Mendel, who will be discussed in the next chapter. Mendel discovered the basic laws of heredity, which he published in 1868.

Mendel's work began to answer basic questions of inheritance. Since Mendel's time, our knowledge of genetics has grown enormously. In the 1930s, population geneticists began to explain, in mathematical and statistical terms, how evolution could be seen as a change in the genetic composition of populations. From the 1970s through the 1980s, dramatic new discoveries about the genetic material (DNA and RNA) have allowed us to see evolutionary processes that occur at the molecular level. In addition, advances in the study of embryology, paleontology, animal behavior, and other disciplines have all contributed to a modern understanding of evolution. Because this understanding is based on a synthesis of information from diverse fields, it is sometimes called the **synthetic theory of evolution.**

**Summary**

Evolutionary theory has been shown to be a valid and reliable explanation of basic questions about life. Modern evolutionary theory grew out of a European intellectual climate. Before the nineteenth century, most Europeans saw humans as the superior center of a world populated by spontaneously created organisms that did not change once created. Each of these ideas fell in the light of new knowledge

---

[4]C. Norman, "Supreme Court Strikes Down 'Creation-Science' Law as Promotion of Religion," *Science* 236 (1987), p. 1620.

[5]C. Shulman, "Texas Votes for Evolution," *Nature* 348 (1990), p. 271.

**BOX 1-2**

# The Scopes Trial

By the 1920s, many Western theologians, as well as much of the public, had reconciled the concept of natural selection and organic evolution with their religious beliefs. Yet, in some quarters, there was still strong opposition to Darwinism. This opposition had its most dramatic airing in the summer of 1925 in a public spectacle called the "Scopes trial."

John T. Scopes was a high school teacher in Dayton, Tennessee, who decided to challenge that state's new law, the Butler Act, which prohibited the teaching of evolution. After teaching evolution in the classroom, Scopes was arrested. The trial focused national attention on the controversy. Clarence Darrow helped defend Scopes; William Jennings Bryan, the Democratic nominee for president in 1896, 1904, and 1908, worked for the prosecution.

Darrow argued the case on the basis that Scopes's academic freedom had been violated and that Scopes also had the constitutional guarantee of the separation of church and state. Bryan, an old man by 1925, did not argue well and was severely embarrassed by the defense. Yet Scopes *had* broken the state law and was fined $100. The conviction was later overturned on a technicality. It was not the conviction that was important but the fact that the publicity over the trial acted to increase public acceptance of evolution and to discourage many states from enacting so-called monkey laws.

Clarence Darrow (left circle) defends high school science teacher John T. Scopes (right circle) in 1925 for teaching evolution in the state of Tennessee.

gathered by hundreds of scholars, including Copernicus, Linnaeus, Buffon, Lamarck, Lyell, Boucher de Crèvecoeur de Perthes, Darwin, Wallace, and Mendel. Darwin's concept of natural selection has fused with Mendel's concept of genetics; to this mixture new ingredients continue to be added, including concepts about the genetics of populations. Also, ideas of what embryos, fossils, and animal behavior can tell us about the past have become part of what is called the synthetic theory of evolution.

## STUDY QUESTIONS

1. The development of the evolutionary concept was part of the general changes that were occurring in Western society from the fifteenth through nineteenth centuries. How were such historical events as the discovery of North America and the American Revolution related to the development of the theory of evolution?
2. What were some of the concepts about human nature and the relationship between humans and nature that had to change before an evolutionary concept could develop?
3. How does the idea of "catastrophism" differ from Darwin's concept of natural selection?
4. Who were some of the scholars who contributed to the development of evolutionary ideas? What did each contribute to that development?
5. Darwin, Wallace, and other naturalists of the nineteenth century did not have an accurate notion of one aspect of modern evolutionary theory. What element of modern theory was missing from their writings? Who began to provide accurate analyses of this missing element?
6. What is meant by the phrase "the synthetic theory of evolution"?
7. Many antievolutionists believe that since science does not have answers for all questions, scientific conclusions are not necessarily correct. This attitude reflects a failure to understand the nature of science. What is the general nature of scientific thinking? In what way is science "self-correcting"?
8. In what way does a scientific statement differ from a doctrine?

## SUGGESTED READINGS

Darwin, C. *On the Origin of Species by Means of Natural Selection, or the Preservation of Favored Races in the Struggle for Life.* London: J. Murray, 1859. Many editions have been produced of this classic, including a 1967 facsimile of the first edition.

Desmond, A., and J. Moore. *Darwin: The Life of a Tormented Evolutionist.* New York: Warner, 1991. This biography of Darwin makes use of newly available sources and places Darwin and his ideas in the context of Victorian science and society.

Edey, M., and D. C. Johanson. *Blueprints: Solving the Mystery of Evolution.* New York: Penguin, 1989. This volume is a fascinating survey of the "evolution" of the theory of evolution. It gives interesting biographical portraits of the main figures in the development of evolutionary theory.

Futuyma, D. J. *Science on Trial: The Case for Evolution.* Sunderland, Maine: Sinauer Publishing, 1995. This volume is an interesting overview of the conflict between evolutionary teaching and fundamentalist ideas.

Giere, R. N. *Understanding Scientific Reasoning,* 4th ed. Fort Worth: Holt, Rinehart and Winston, 1996. This book explains scientific thinking using examples of scientific discoveries and everyday events.

Gould, S. J. *Time's Arrow Time's Cycle.* Cambridge, Mass.: Harvard University Press, 1987. The author discusses the historical development of the concept of deep time in geology, including a discussion of Charles Lyell's contributions.

Lyell, C. *Principles of Geology,* 3 vols. London: J. Murray, 1830–1833; rpt. New York: Johnson Reprint, 1969. This was the first geology "textbook," and it influenced Darwin's perceptions of nature.

Mayr, E. *The Growth of Biological Thought: Diversity, Evolution, and Inheritance.* Cambridge, Mass.: Harvard University Press, 1985. This is an award-winning book on the history and development of modern biology.

Milner, R. *The Encyclopedia of Evolution.* New York: Facts on File, 1990. This is a very useful encyclopedia with entries on important people and concepts.

Rudwick, M. J. S. *Georges Cuvier, Fossil Bones, and Geological Catastrophes: New Translations and Interpretations of Primary Text.* Chicago: University of Chicago Press, 1997. This volume includes a translation of Cuvier's papers and corrects misconceptions about his ideas and motivations.

*Scientific Genius and Creativity: Readings from Scientific American.* San Francisco: Freeman, 1987. This book includes biographies of 10 great scientists and explores the role of genius and creativity in scientific discoveries.

Simpson, G. G. (ed.). *The Book of Darwin.* New York: Washington Square Press, 1982. The great biologist George Gaylord Simpson presents selections from the writings of Charles Darwin with insightful commentary.

Young, D. *The Discovery of Evolution.* Cambridge, England: Cambridge University Press, 1991. Richly illustrated by many historical photographs and drawings, this volume traces the development of evolutionary theory. It is an excellent introduction to evolution for the new student.

In addition to books, the journals and magazines listed below consistently have materials useful to physical anthropology students.

The following are popular magazines:

*American Scientist*
*Archaeology*
*BioScience*
*Discover*
*National Geographic*
*Natural History*
*Science News*
*Scientific American*
*Smithsonian*

The following are scientific journals:

*American Anthropologist*
*American Journal of Human Biology*
*American Journal of Physical Anthropology*
*American Journal of Primatology*

*Annals of Human Biology and Human Ecology*
*Current Anthropology*
*Evolutionary Anthropology*
*Human Biology*
*Human Evolution*
*Journal of Animal Behavior*
*Journal of Forensic Science*
*Journal of Human Evolution*
*Nature*
*Science*

## SUGGESTED WEB SITES

American Anthropological Association:
   http://www.aaanet.org
Biography of Charles Darwin:
   http://userwww.sfsu.edu/~rsauzier/Darwin.html
History of evolutionary theory from the University of California Museum of Paleontology:
   http://www.ucmp.berkeley.edu/history/evolution.html

Additional Web sites are listed in the *Workbook* that accompanies this text.

# The Study of Heredity

*Charles Darwin, not knowing of Gregor Mendel's work, was making some experiments of his own, which led him within an ace of obtaining results paralleling Mendel's. Whether or not he would have analyzed the results as masterfully as Mendel did is a moot point.[1]*

—Theodozius Dobzhansky (1900–1975)

Charles Darwin's concept of natural selection explains why variants within a population increase or decrease in number over generations. As we saw in the previous chapter, one of the foundations of natural selection is the observation that populations are variable and that part of this variation is the result of heredity. When a particular individual has an increased fertility rate and produces

---

[1]T. Dobzhansky, "Mendelism, Darwinism, and Evolution," *Proceedings of the American Philosophical Society* 109 (1965), p. 205.

a significantly greater number of offspring than other organisms, that individual passes on certain traits to the next generation.

Although Darwin recognized the relationship between the processes of inheritance and natural selection, he was never able to define the rules of heredity. He did not discover how new variants, the raw material of natural selection, arose. Nor did he figure out how characteristics were transmitted from generation to generation. Although some of the basic principles of genetics were worked out during Darwin's time, he was unaware of this new knowledge.

This is the first of two chapters on genetics. In this chapter, we will lay out the basic mechanisms of heredity.

## DISCOVERING THE MECHANISMS OF HEREDITY

Almost everyone would agree with the statement that children resemble their parents and that distinctive physical traits often characterize family lines. Moving from a simple and obvious statement about family likenesses to an actual determination of the genetic mechanisms involved is a long jump.

### Problems in the Study of Heredity

One early attempt at explaining family resemblances was the the idea that hereditary units merged as one might mix two colors of paint. This is known as the **blending theory.** However, if such were the case, traits would be irreversibly changed from generation to generation and would not persist. For example, red paint mixed with white paint yields pink, but both the red and the white colors cease to exist. Neither the red nor the white color can be reconstituted from the pink.

Although Charles Darwin recognized some examples of nonblending, he never came to a correct understanding of genetics. He believed that particles present in the body were influenced by activities of the organism throughout its life. These particles traveled to the reproductive cells through the circulatory system. There they modified the sex cells in such a way that the acquired characteristics of the individual organism could now be passed on to the next generation, a concept called **pangenesis.** Because of poor methodology, inappropriate

materials, and incorrect hypotheses, many of Darwin's contemporaries went equally astray in their quest for an explanation of the transmission and differentiation of life.

Much of the nineteenth-century interest in genetics revolved around the study of human characteristics. However, the study of human heredity is many times more difficult than the study of heredity in other organisms. This is perhaps the main reason so many early biologists failed to discover the underlying principles of genetics.

The experimental method requires control over the object of experimentation, yet no scientist can control human matings. The study of human genetics must accept matings that have already occurred. Many basic genetic principles were developed from the statistical examination of large numbers of progeny; human families tend to be very small. Also, the length of the human generation is much too great to allow one investigator to follow the inheritance of a particular trait for more than a few generations.

Another major problem in the study of genetics is the selection of the trait to be studied, as many traits are difficult to measure and quantify. Until quite recently, when sophisticated instruments came into use, skin color was difficult to measure accurately. Also, many traits are greatly affected by the environment—for example, skin color is affected by sunlight. A further complicating factor is that the inheritance of many traits is complex; it involves more than one genetic factor.

### The Work of Gregor Mendel

It is not surprising that the breakthrough in the understanding of heredity took place outside the arena of human genetics. In 1865, a monk by the name of Gregor Mendel (1822–1884) first wrote about many of the principles of heredity.[2]

Mendel was born in what is now the Czech Republic. As he grew up, he decided to be a teacher. Many teachers were also priests and, in 1843, Mendel joined the monastery of Saint Thomas in what is now Brno, Czech Republic. He became a

---

[2]G. Mendel, "Versuche über Pflanzen-Hybriden," *Verhandlungen des Naturforschenden Vereins Brünn* 4 (1866), pp. 3–37. Translation in C. Stern and E. R. Sherwood (eds.), *The Origins of Genetics* (San Francisco: Freeman, 1966), pp. 1–48.

priest in 1847 and the monastery, which was both a religious and scientific institution, sent Mendel to the University of Vienna in 1851. On his return to Brno, he taught biology and physics at a high school. During his years as a teacher, he performed the breeding experiments to which we now turn.

In his experiments, Gregor Mendel realized that the best traits for the study of heredity were those that are either obviously present or completely absent, rather than those that have intermediate values and must be measured on some type of scale. Mendel chose seven contrasting pairs of characteristics of the common pea plant: flower color (violet or white), stature (tall or dwarf), shape of the ripe seed (smooth or wrinkled), and four others. Using as large a sample as possible to eliminate chance error, he observed each pea plant separately and kept the different generations apart. The results were quantified and expressed as ratios.

In the first series of experiments, Mendel started with **true-breeding** plants. These are plants that have been bred only with plants of the same kind and show the same traits over many generations. Mendel cross-pollinated true-breeding plants that produced only violet flowers with true-breeding plants that produced only white flowers. These plants made up the parental, or $P_1$, generation.

Next, Mendel grew plants from the seeds produced by the parental plants. These were plants of the first filial, or $F_1$, generation. He observed that plants of the $F_1$ generation produced only violet flowers; he observed no white flowers or flowers of intermediate color, such as pink. These $F_1$ plants are termed **hybrids.** The hybrid plant produced violet flowers, as did one of the parental plants, yet it differed from the true-breeding parents in having one parent that produced flowers unlike its own, in this case white.

Mendel then allowed the hybrids to self-pollinate to produce the next generation, called $F_2$. In this generation, he found that some plants produced violet flowers while others produced white flowers. When he counted the number of plants showing each trait, he found that approximately three-fourths of the plants bore violet flowers while one-fourth bore white flowers.

As we saw, the $F_1$ hybrid plants bore violet flowers only, although these plants had parents with white flowers. When the $F_1$ generation was self-pollinated, some of the offspring had white flowers. The trait that is seen in the hybrid is said to be **dominant.** The trait that is not seen and yet can be passed on in a later cross is termed **recessive.** Mendel noted that violet flowers, tallness, and smooth seeds were dominant features, while white flowers, dwarfness, and wrinkled seeds were recessive.

The fact that the $F_1$ generation produced *only* violet flowers and the $F_2$ generation produced violet *and* white flowers showed that the blending theory was erroneous. No plant with pink flowers appeared in the $F_1$ generation, and in the $F_2$ generation white flowers reappeared. This confirmed the fact that the genetic unit for white flower color had not blended but had persisted without having been altered in any way.

**A Model of Genetic Events**   A **model** is a representation of an object or an ideal. It is a simplified representation of a real-world phenomenon. Models help us test hypotheses, make predictions, and see relationships. The model may be a diagrammatic representation of some phenomenon, a statistical description, or a mathematical formula. For instance, the mathematical formula $A = \pi r^2$ allows us to predict exactly how a change in the radius of a circle will affect the area of that circle.

Models act as summaries of the known characteristics of a phenomenon. They provide a means of testing hypotheses about the phenomenon by measuring the effect of one element (variable) of the model on other elements. Gregor Mendel was not aware of the physical or chemical realities of the hereditary mechanism, but he did develop a model to explain what he had observed.

**Principle of Segregation**   Mendel concluded that the hereditary factors maintain their individuality by not blending with one another. He may not have fully understood why this is so. We now know that the hereditary factors exist as discrete pairs. In the formation of the sex cells of plants—pollen and ova—the paired hereditary factors separate, forming sex cells that contain either one or the other factor. For example, they may contain the factor for violet or white flower color, but not both. This is now known as the principle of **segregation.**

Thus, Mendel reasoned that in the parental generation, the violet-flowered plant produces sex cells

# Mendel and the Creative Interpretation of Data

We are shocked when we learn that a medical researcher has made up data to support a hypothesis on how to treat a serious illness. We may be angry that he or she did this to advance in academic rank or to gain fame or fortune. Serious instances of this type of fraud have been reported in recent years.[1]

In 1936, statistician R. A. Fisher published an analysis of Mendel's work. From the standpoint of statistics, Fisher thought that Mendel's results for crosses between hybrid peas were too close to the expected results considering the sample size and other statistical factors.[2] The numerical results of Mendel's crosses of two $F_1$ plants are shown in the accompanying table.

Current evaluation of Fisher's own analysis and more recent reanalysis of Mendel's experiments have shown that it was Fisher who was incorrect. Mendel's ratios come closer to the expected because of situations having to do with

germination in the pea plant, not because of Mendel's conscious "adjusting" of the data. Still, Mendel may have done other things that would not be acceptable today.[3]

Mendel's observations of nature and his knowledge of statistics led him to believe that two genetic units must exist for each characteristic. He concluded that a specific ratio would be shown in matings between plants with specific combinations of dominant or recessive units. He *expected* certain results. When his results were close to the expected but not precisely so, he possibly assumed that it was his ability to discriminate between variations in characteristics, not the purity of the concept, that was at fault. For instance, some peas are smooth (round), while others are wrinkled. Mendel expected to find three smooth peas (they are dominant) for each wrinkled one (recessive) in crosses of hybrid pea plants. Yet some seeds are not

clearly smooth or wrinkled. Mendel counted the results of his experiments, and then he may have placed the intermediate cases in whichever group made the ratios approximate the ideal.

To Mendel, this was not cheating. He knew that there was bias in his observational abilities, but he believed in the validity of his hypothesis. To him, the only logical place for the intermediate forms was in the category that maximized agreement with his expected ratios. There "is subjectivity in the process of inventing categories for comprehending nature and there is subjectivity in assigning objects to these categories."[4] Not only is science a creative process, but the standards for designing experiments, the way in which evidence is interpreted, and the data that are accepted as proof change with time.[5] What cannot be denied is that after decades of experimentation, Mendel's basic principles of segregation and independent assortment stand as the valid foundations of modern genetics.

| Form of seed | 5474 round | 1850 wrinkled | 2.96 to 1 |
|---|---|---|---|
| Color of albumen | 6022 yellow | 2001 green | 3.01 to 1 |
| Color of seed coats | 705 gray* | 224 white* | 3.15 to 1 |
| Form of pod | 882 inflated | 299 constricted | 2.95 to 1 |
| Color of unripe pods | 428 green | 152 yellow | 2.82 to 1 |
| Position of flowers | 651 axial | 207 terminal | 3.14 to 1 |
| Length of stem | 787 long | 277 short | 2.84 to 1 |
| Average | | | 2.98 to 1 |

*Gray seed coats are associated with violet flowers while white seed coats are associated with white flowers.

[1] J. Horgan (ed.), "Science and the Citizen: Doctored Data," *Scientific American* 256 (April 1987), pp. 68–69; D. E. Koshland Jr., "Fraud in Science," *Science* 235 (1987), p. 141.
[2] R. A. Fisher, "Has Mendel's Work Been Rediscovered?" *Annals of Science* 1 (1936), p. 121.
[3] J. A. Miller, "A Matter of Genius or of Guile?" *Science News* 125 (1984), pp. 108–109.
[4] R. S. Root-Bernstein, *History of Science* 21 (1983), p. 275.
[5] D. E. Chubin, "Research Malpractice," *BioScience* 35 (1985), pp. 80–89.

that carry the factor for violet flowers only, while the white-flowered plant produces sex cells that carry the factor for white flowers only. The hybrid develops from the union of two sex cells, one carrying the unit for violet color and one carrying the unit for white color. The hybrid therefore contains a pair of units—one is for violet color and the other is for white. Since the unit for violet color is dominant, the flowers blooming on the hybrid plant are all violet.

When the hybrid produces sex cells, the two units segregate, producing sex cells of two types. Half the sex cells carry the unit for violet flowers, while the other half carry the unit for white flowers. When fertilization takes place, four different combinations may occur in the new plants. Some $F_2$ plants may inherit two units for violet flowers; others may inherit two units for white flowers; and still others may inherit one unit for violet flowers and one unit for white flowers (this last combina-

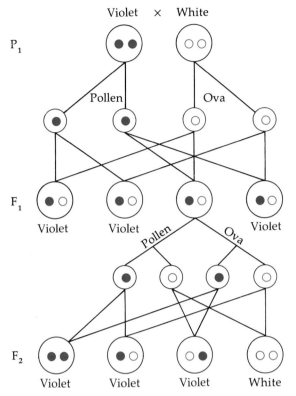

**FIGURE 2–1 Segregation**
In the formation of sex cells, the hereditary factors separate, forming sex cells that contain either one or the other factor. Individual sex cells combine at fertilization, producing new combinations of hereditary units.

tion can occur in two ways: violet-white or white-violet). Since the violet-violet, violet-white, and white-violet combinations all produce violet flowers, three out of every four plants yield violet flowers. Only the white-white combination (one out of every four plants) produces white flowers. This experiment is illustrated in Figure 2–1.

To test his hypothesis, Mendel planned another experiment. He predicted the results before beginning, and he managed to predict them correctly. He crossed an $F_1$ hybrid with a true-breeding, white-flowered plant. This is called a **back cross.** Figure 2–2 shows the result of this experiment.

**Principle of Independent Assortment** Mendel next studied the simultaneous inheritance of more than one trait. For example, he crossed a normal-stature (tall) plant bearing violet flowers with a dwarf plant bearing white flowers. The $F_1$ hybrid

was a tall plant with violet flowers. When the $F_1$ hybrids were crossed, four distinct types of offspring resulted: tall plants with violet flowers, tall plants with white flowers, dwarf plants with violet flowers, and dwarf plants with white flowers, with the frequencies of $9/16$, $3/16$, $3/16$, and $1/16$, respectively. The explanation for these results is seen in Figure 2–3.

From these data, geneticists formulated the principle of **independent assortment,** which states that the inheritance patterns of differing traits are independent of one another. Whether a plant is tall or dwarf is unrelated to whether that plant bears violet or white flowers.

Mendel's experiments were conducted over a period of about 15 years. He was elected abbot of his monastery in 1868, and his duties in this position prevented him from conducting further research. His single important paper on the subject of his research, published in 1865, was generally ignored. The recognition of the importance of Mendel's work did not emerge until the beginning of the twentieth century.

### What Is a Trait?

An organism's observable or measurable characteristics make up its **phenotype.** Whether a pea plant or a human being, the phenotype includes, among other things, physical appearance, internal anatomy, and physiology.

**FIGURE 2–2 Back Cross**
The hybrid violet-flowered plant is crossed with the true-breeding white-flowered parent.

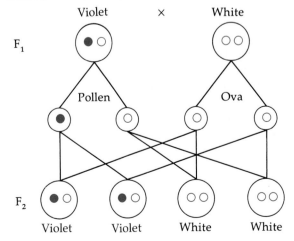

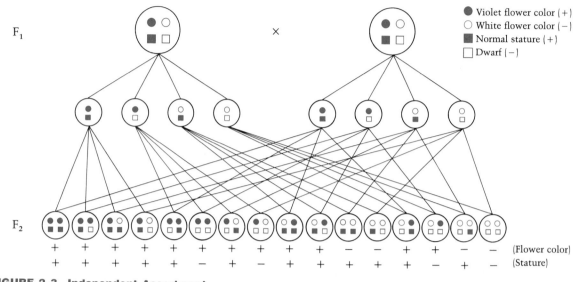

**FIGURE 2–3 Independent Assortment**
The inheritance of flower color is independent of the inheritance of stature.

In describing the phenotype of a person, we can observe certain features such as skin color, eye color, hair color and texture, and general body build. We can also measure such traits as stature, head circumference, nose width, and arm length. Various physiological traits, such as the rate of glucose metabolism, can also be analyzed. Even personality and intelligence can be investigated. The result of these examinations is a profile of the individual's total phenotype. A **trait** is but one aspect of the phenotype—a particular hair texture, an allergy, a blood type.

The phenotype results from the interaction of an individual's **genotype** and the **environment.** The genotype is the individual's specific genetic constitution; the environment includes everything that is external to the individual. A trait can be the result of the interaction of many genetic and environmental factors.

If genetic mechanisms are to be understood, we must know the degree to which traits are determined genetically. One of the most difficult tasks of the geneticist is to discover the role of the environment in the development of a particular trait.

Many traits are determined solely by heredity—blood type, for example. Other traits are determined by the environment—a pierced ear or a dyed head of hair. Most features, however, are influenced by both genetic and environmental factors. It is the task of the investigator to determine the relative influence of genetic and environmental factors in the development of specific traits.

**Twin Studies** One method of estimating the environmental influence on a particular trait in humans is studying twins. Identical, or **monozygotic, twins,** which are derived from a single fertilized ovum, or **zygote,** share identical genotypes. On the other hand, fraternal, or **dizygotic, twins** are derived from separate zygotes; they have genotypes that differ to the same extent as those of brothers and sisters who are not twins. Monozygotic twins are always of the same sex, while dizygotic twins can be of the same sex or different sexes.

Since monozygotic twins share the same heredity, it follows that differences in their phenotypes are due entirely to the effects of the environment. On the other hand, differences between dizygotic-twin partners are due to both genetic and environmental factors. Therefore, we can use twin data to estimate the importance of genetic versus environmental factors with respect to a given trait.

Several methods exist for making such an estimate. One is to locate one twin with a particular trait and see if the other twin also has that trait. In one study, both twins had cardiovascular disease in 19.6 percent of the monozygotic twins and 15.5 percent of same-sex dizygotic twins. One could conclude from these data that the genetic factor in the development of cardiovascular disease is relatively unimportant. With respect to schizophrenia, the percentages were 46 percent for monozygotic twins and 14 percent for dizygotic twins. This leads us to the conclusion that there is a strong genetic factor in the development of schizophrenia; but since both twins had the trait in only 46 percent of the monozygotic twins, and not in 100 percent, we must conclude that there still is a very strong environmental factor.[3]

Twin studies give indications of the relationship between heredity and environment, but these studies present problems. For instance, monozygotic twins are treated more similarly by parents, friends, and teachers than are dizygotic twins. Therefore, a similarity in the behavior of a set of monozygotic twins might be due to their parallel treatment rather than to their genetics. Also, the results of twin studies are only valid for the population from which the twins come since twins that are separated at birth are still usually reared in the same culture. Also, the results of studies of the same characteristics will vary in different populations as a reflection of different cultural patterns.

Similarly, an estimate of the relationship between the genetic and environmental effects of a trait is valid only for the specific environment for which the estimate is made. If the environment changes, this relationship may also change. For example, if monozygotic twins are both raised in the same environment, their stature would be similar. However, if one of a set of such twins is deprived of adequate vitamin D while the other is not, the former's stature could be reduced because of bone deformations that would take place.

### Mendelian Inheritance in Humans

There are a number of human characteristics that are inherited in a simple Mendelian manner. One of these is the form of the human earlobe. Some individuals have earlobes that are characterized by

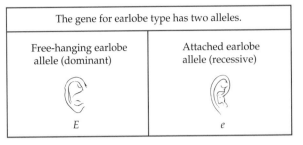

| The gene for earlobe type has two alleles. | |
|---|---|
| Free-hanging earlobe allele (dominant) | Attached earlobe allele (recessive) |
| *E* | *e* |

**FIGURE 2–4  Alleles**
Gregor Mendel determined that each genetically controlled trait is determined minimally by two units of one gene, one unit from each parent. A gene can have different forms, and these different forms of a gene are called alleles. In the illustrated example above, there are two alleles for earlobe type: one for free-hanging earlobes and one for attached earlobes.

the attachment of the lower part directly to the head. Other people have free-hanging earlobes.

The hereditary units that determine earlobe type and other features are called **genes.** Genes occur in alternate forms termed **alleles.** The gene for earlobe type occurs in two forms. We will write the gene using the letter *E* and distinguish the two alleles by using the uppercase *E* for the dominant allele and the lowercase *e* for the recessive allele. *E* represents the allele for free-hanging earlobes, and *e* represents the allele for attached earlobes (Figure 2–4). Remember that in all but the sex cells genes exist as pairs. Thus the gene pair for earlobes can exist as *EE, Ee,* or *ee.*

What are the phenotypes associated with each of these three genotypes? Studies show that a person with a pair of the same alleles for free-hanging earlobes (genotype *EE*) has free-hanging earlobes, while a person with a pair of the same alleles for attached earlobes (genotype *ee*) has attached earlobes. These people are said to be **homozygous.** This means that they have two alleles of the same kind. The former is **homozygous dominant;** the latter is **homozygous recessive.** But what about a person with the genotype *Ee*? An individual with the genotype *Ee* is said to be **heterozygous,** which means that he or she has two different alleles. Since in the heterozygous individual the allele for free-hanging earlobes *(E)* is dominant, it is expressed in the phenotype, whereas the recessive allele *(e)* is not. The heterozygous individual therefore possesses free-hanging earlobes (Figure 2–5).

---

[3]S. E. Nicol and I. I. Gottesman, "Clues to the Genetics and Neurobiology of Schizophrenia," *American Scientist* 71 (1983), pp. 398–404.

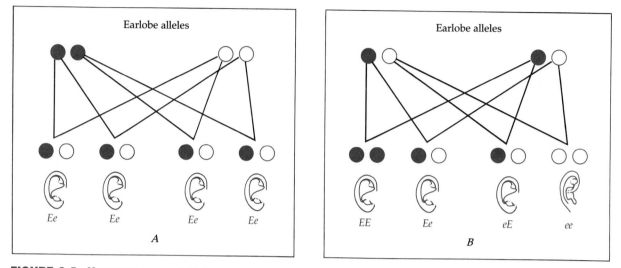

**FIGURE 2–5  Homozygous and Heterozygous**
(*A*) All of the offspring of a homozygous dominant and homozygous recessive parent will be heterozygous. (*B*) The offspring of two heterozygous parents could be (*EE*) homozygous dominant (two dominant alleles), (*Ee* and *eE*) heterozygous (one dominant and one recessive allele), or (*ee*) homozygous recessive (two recessive alleles).

While persons with different earlobe types cannot be mated in the lab, couples of certain phenotypes can be located and their children can be studied. Three basic types of matings are found: free hanging × free hanging, free hanging × attached, and attached × attached. But those with free-hanging earlobes can be either homozygous (*EE*) or heterozygous (*Ee*). The different mating types and their offspring are listed in Table 2–1.

The numbers listed in the table are probability statements. Just as the probability of landing heads when you flip a coin is one out of two, or ½, the probability of two persons heterozygous for earlobe type having a child with attached earlobes is one out of four, or ¼. Similarly, the probability of having a child with free-hanging earlobes is ¾. This does *not* mean that if the couple has four children, three will *necessarily* have free-hanging earlobes, although that is certainly possible. It is also possible that all, or perhaps none, of the children will have free-hanging earlobes, just as it is possible to flip a coin four times and land heads each time.

**An Example of Independent Assortment**   There are several other traits that can be used to demonstrate Mendelian inheritance in humans. An example is the ability to taste the organic chemical **phenylthiocarbamide (PTC).** This ability is tested by having people chew a piece of paper soaked in a concentrated PTC solution. Most people experience a definite bitter taste, but about 30 percent of North American whites and 3 percent of African Americans find the paper has no taste.[4]

What happens when we look at the inheritance of two traits, PTC tasting and the shape of earlobes? We will examine the results of a mating between two

## TABLE 2–1

**POSSIBLE COMBINATIONS AND OFFSPRING FOR A TRAIT WITH TWO ALLELES**

| Mating type | Offspring | | |
| --- | --- | --- | --- |
| | *EE* | *Ee* | *ee* |
| *EE* × *EE* | 1 | 0 | 0 |
| *EE* × *ee* | 0 | 1 | 0 |
| *EE* × *Ee* | ½ | ½ | 0 |
| *Ee* × *EE* | ½ | ½ | 0 |
| *Ee* × *Ee* | ¼ | ½ | ¼ |
| *Ee* × *ee* | 0 | ½ | ½ |
| *ee* × *EE* | 0 | 1 | 0 |
| *ee* × *Ee* | 0 | ½ | ½ |
| *ee* × *ee* | 0 | 0 | 1 |

[4]A. C. Allison and B. S. Blumberg, "Ability to Taste Phenylthiocarbamide among Alaska Eskimos and Other Populations," *Human Biology* 31 (1959), pp. 352–59.

individuals who are heterozygous for both traits. By using the letter *T* to represent the gene for PTC tasting, we can express the mating as *TtEe* × *TtEe*.

In the production of sex cells, the *T* and *t* segregate, as do the *E* and *e*. The segregation of the *T* and the *t* is totally independent of the segregation of the *E* and the *e*. Therefore, four kinds of sex cells will result. Some will carry the *T* and the *E*; others will carry the *T* and the *e*, the *t* and the *E*, or the *t* and the *e*. The sperm and the ova combine at random. A *TE* sperm may fertilize a *TE*, *Te*, *tE*, or *te* ovum, or a *Te* sperm may fertilize a *TE*, *Te*, *tE* or *te* ovum. The same is true for the other two types of sperm. Table 2–2 shows the 16 different combinations that can occur. Four different phenotypes are observed: taster–free hanging, taster–attached, nontaster–free hanging, and nontaster–attached. Since the inheritance of earlobe shape and PTC tasting are independent events, the four different phenotypes will occur in the frequencies of ⁹⁄₁₆, ³⁄₁₆, ³⁄₁₆, and ¹⁄₁₆, respectively.

### Summary

Because of the lack of control over matings, the small size of families, the long generation span, the difficulties in determining what part of a trait is genetic as opposed to environmental, and problems of measurement and quantification, human beings have not been easy subjects for genetic research. The basic principles of heredity were worked out using nonhuman organisms.

Through careful experimentation with the common pea plant, Gregor Mendel was the first scientist to discover the basic principles of heredity. From his data, he formulated two principles based upon a model of genetic events. The principle of segregation states that in the formation of sex cells, the hereditary factors separate, forming sex cells that contain either one or the other of the paired factors. The principle of independent assortment states that the inheritance patterns of differing traits are independent of one another. At the most basic level, these principles are universal among all living organisms, including the human species.

### CYTOGENETICS

The principles of genetics were outlined by Gregor Mendel as an attempt to explain the results of his observations on the production of pea plants. Yet his model was not grounded in the reality of biology since he was unaware of the biological nature of the genetic material. After 1900, biologists began to experiment on the genetics of other organisms, primarily maize and the fruit fly. It rapidly became

---

**TABLE 2-2**

**INDEPENDENT ASSORTMENT: POSSIBLE GENOTYPES AND PHENOTYPES FROM A MATING BETWEEN TWO INDIVIDUALS HETEROZYGOUS FOR TWO TRAITS, PTC TASTING AND EARLOBE TYPE***

| | Offspring | | | | | | | | | | |
|---|---|---|---|---|---|---|---|---|---|---|---|
| | **TE** | | | **Te** | | | **tE** | | | **te** | |
| *TE* | *TTEE* | taster–free-hanging lobe | *TTEe* | taster–free-hanging lobe | *TtEE* | taster–free-hanging lobe | *TtEe* | taster–free-hanging lobe |
| *Te* | *TTEe* | taster–free-hanging lobe | *TTee* | taster–attached lobe | *TtEe* | taster–free-hanging lobe | *Ttee* | taster–attached lobe |
| *tE* | *TtEE* | taster–free-hanging lobe | *TtEe* | taster–free-hanging lobe | *ttEE* | nontaster–free-hanging lobe | *ttEe* | nontaster–free-hanging lobe |
| *te* | *TtEe* | taster–free-hanging lobe | *Ttee* | taster–attached lobe | *ttEe* | nontaster–free-hanging lobe | *ttee* | nontaster–attached lobe |

| Summary of phenotypes | Probability of phenotypes |
|---|---|
| 9 taster–free-hanging lobe | ⁹⁄₁₆ |
| 3 taster–attached lobe | ³⁄₁₆ |
| 3 nontaster–free-hanging lobe | ³⁄₁₆ |
| 1 nontaster–attached lobe | ¹⁄₁₆ |

*The mating can be written in terms of their genotypes, *TtEe* × *TtEe*. Each individual will produce four types of gametes—*TE*, *Te*, *tE*, *te*—in equal frequency.

apparent that the genetic material resided within the nucleus of the cell.

**Cytology** is the branch of science that specializes in the biology of the cell. This term is derived from *cyto,* meaning "cell." The study of the heredity mechanisms within the cell is called **cytogenetics,** the subject of this section.

The **cell** is the basic unit of all life. In fact, cells are the smallest units that perform all the functions that are collectively labeled "life." These include taking in energy and excreting waste; using and storing energy; combining nutrients into substances for growth, repair, and development; adapting to new situations; and, perhaps the most important of all, reproducing new cells.

The great variety of cells all share several structural characteristics (Figure 2–A of the color insert). A cell is bounded by a **plasma membrane** that allows for the entry and exit of certain substances and maintains the cell's integrity. A **nucleus** in the cell is contained within its own **nuclear membrane.** The material between the nuclear membrane and the cell membrane is called the **cytoplasm.**

### The Chromosomes

When a cell begins to divide, long ropelike structures become visible within the nucleus. Because these structures stain very dark purple, they are called **chromosomes**—*chroma* means "color" and *soma* means "body." Viewed under the microscope, a single chromosome is seen to consist of two strands—the **chromatids.** These chromatids are held together by a structure called the **centromere.**

Figure 2–B of the color insert is a photograph of chromosomes prepared from a human blood sample. The chromosomes have been stained by a special process that produces a pattern of bands so that individual chromosomes can be identified.

Much information can be obtained from a photograph of chromosomes. First, the chromosomes can be counted. Different organisms are characterized by specific chromosome numbers per cell. For example, the Indian fern has the highest number, with 1260 chromosomes; the roundworm has only 2. More typical numbers of chromosomes are found in humans (46), boa constrictors (36), and garden peas (14).

Second, not all chromosomes are alike; they differ in relative size and in the position of the centromere. In some, the centromere is centered, so the

"arms" of the chromosomes are of equal length; in others, the centromere is off center, so the arms are of unequal length. Thus, it is possible to classify and identify chromosomes. Each chromosome in a photograph can be cut out and arranged in a standardized representation known as a **karyotype.**

Looking at the karyotypes in Figure 2–6 and Figure 2–C of the color insert, we can see that all the chromosomes, with one exception, exist as pairs. The chromosomes that make up a pair are called **homologous chromosomes.** Homologous chromosomes have the same shape and are of the same size. They also carry the same genes, but they may carry different alleles for specific genes.

The **sex chromosomes** of the male, however, are not homologous. The normal female possesses two homologous sex chromosomes, the **X chromosomes,** but the male has only one X chromosome, which pairs with a different type, the **Y chromosome.** In both sexes, there are 22 pairs of nonsex chromosomes, referred to as **autosomes.** These autosomal pairs are numbered from 1 to 22. The 23rd pair consists of the sex chromosomes. In addition, all chromosomes are classified into seven major groups, A through G, on the basis of relative size and the position of the centromere.

### Cell Division

The physical basis of Mendelian genetics becomes clear when we observe the movement of chromosomes during cell division. There are two basic forms of cell division, mitosis and meiosis. **Mitosis** is the process by which a one-celled organism divides into two new individuals. In a multicellular organism, mitosis results in the growth and replacement of body cells. **Meiosis,** on the other hand, is specialized cell division that results in the production of sex cells, or **gametes.**

**Mitosis**   The events of mitosis follow each other in a continuous fashion. Various studies show that it takes 30 to 90 minutes for one complete mitotic division in humans, depending on the type of cell. Some cells, such as skin cells, are constantly being replaced, so they divide often. On the other hand, nerve cells stop dividing at birth or shortly thereafter. In order to make the events of this process clear, mitosis is divided into several arbitrary phases defined by specific landmark events. The

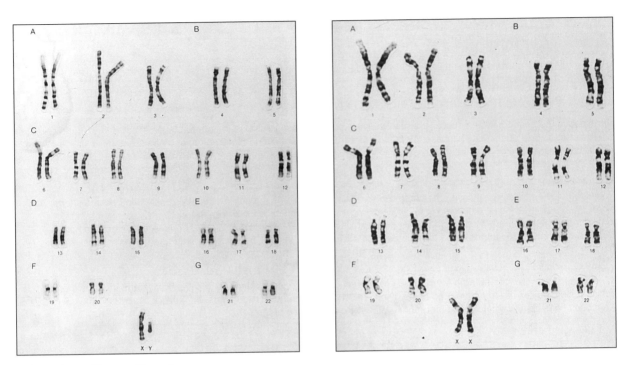

**FIGURE 2–6  Human Karyotypes**

Karyotypes of (*a*) a normal male and (*b*) a normal female. In both sexes, there are 22 pairs of non-sex chromosomes or autosomes and a pair of sex chromosomes. The autosomal pairs are numbered from 1 to 22 and are classified into seven major groups, A through G, on the basis of relative size and the position of the centromere. The X chromosome belongs to group C and the Y chromosome belongs to group G.

phases of mitosis are listed in Table 2–3 and are illustrated in Figure 2–E of the color insert.

**Meiosis**  Meiosis differs from mitosis in many ways. Meiosis takes place only in specialized tissue in the testes of the male and in the ovaries of the female. Meiotic division results in the production of gametes, which are the sperm in the male and the ova in the female.

A significant feature of meiosis is the reduction in chromosome number from 46 to 23. If a sperm and an ovum each contained 46 chromosomes, the cell resulting from the fertilization of an ovum by a sperm would have 92 chromosomes. In the next generation, there would be 184 chromosomes, and so on. Instead, meiosis in humans produces gametes with 23 chromosomes each. When fertilization takes place, the number of chromosomes remains constant at 46. The events of meiosis are described in Table 2–4 and are illustrated in Figure 2–F of the color insert.

**Sperm and Ova Production**  **Spermatogenesis,** or sperm production, begins in the average American male at 12 to 13 years of age and usually continues throughout life. However, the onset of spermatogenesis is variable, not only among individuals but also among the averages for different populations. The male normally produces millions of sperm at any one time.

**Oogenesis,** or ova production, is different. The beginnings of the first division of meiosis occur within the ovaries during fetal development, between the fifth and seventh month after conception. These cells remain in metaphase I until they are stimulated, beginning at puberty, by certain hormones to complete their development.

The first meiotic division is different in the female than in the male. In the female, the spindle does not form across the center of the cell; instead, it forms off to one side. During cell division, one nucleus carries the bulk of cytoplasm. This is also true of the second meiotic division. Thus, a single

---

**TABLE 2-3**

### THE STAGES OF MITOSIS

To make the events of mitosis clear, mitosis can be divided into a number of arbitrary phases. These phases are diagrammed in Figure 2–E of the color insert.

#### Interphase

Interphase is the period between successive mitotic divisions. Interphase is divided into three stages, labeled $G_1$, S, and $G_2$. The cell increases in size during the $G_1$ phase, replication of the DNA occurs during the S stage, and processes associated with the preparation for mitosis occur during the $G_2$ stage. Chromosomes appear as an undifferentiated mass.

#### Prophase

Prophase is the first stage of mitosis. The chromosomes become visible as threadlike structures; they then become shorter and thicker. At this point, each chromosome is made up of two strands, each called a **chromatid,** that are connected by the **centromere.** The two **centrioles,** located within the **centrosomes,** move apart and end up at opposite poles of the nucleus. Protein structures called **kinetochores** form on each side of the centromere. The nuclear membrane begins to break down.

#### Prometaphase

The structure known as the **spindle** forms during prometaphase. The spindle is formed of several units and includes the poles, radiating microtubules called **asters,** and fibers. The kinetochores, each associated with a chromatid, attaches to the spindle. The chromosomes begin to migrate to the **metaphase plate** or central plane of the cell.

#### Metaphase

At metaphase, the chromosomes are lined up at the metaphase plate.

#### Anaphase

In anaphase, the chromatids separate at the centromere, resulting in two separate chromosomes. Each chromosome now consists of a single chromatid. Each chromatid of a pair is pulled by the kinetochore spindle fibers to an opposite pole.

#### Telophase

In telophase, new nuclear membranes appear around the two groups of chromosomes as the spindle disappears. The cell then divides to form two new cells.

---

large ovum and two very small cells, the **polar bodies,** are produced from the one original cell. The large ovum contains enough nutrients to nourish the embryo until the embryo implants itself in the wall of the uterus.

Oogenesis is cyclical. The length of the cycle is highly variable, not only within the female population but also in the same female at different times of her reproductive life. The median length of the cycle among American women between the ages of 20 and 40 ranges from 26.2 to 27.9 days. Ninety percent of the cycle lengths range from a low of 21.8 days to a high of 38.4 days.[5]

At the midpoint of the cycle, the ovum has matured and breaks through the wall of the ovary. This event is known as **ovulation.** In contrast to the great quantity of sperm produced by the male, only one ovum is usually produced during each cycle by the average human female.

Fertilization must take place soon after ovulation. In nonhuman mammals, sexual receptivity is related to the ovarian cycle. The female comes into **estrus,** the period of sexual receptivity, around the time of ovulation. Unlike the case with other mammals, sexual receptivity in the human female is not linked to the periodic occurrence of ovulation.

### Reexamining Mendelian Genetics

The details of cell division can help us understand Mendelian genetics. Mitosis is merely a copying of the genetic material, but in meiosis, the physical re-

---

[5]A. E. Treloar et al., "Variations of the Human Menstrual Cycle through Reproductive Life," *International Journal of Fertility* 12 (1967), pp. 77–126.

## TABLE 2-4

### THE STAGES OF MEIOSIS

To make the events of meiosis clear, meiosis can be divided into a number of arbitrary phases. These events are diagrammed in Figure 2–F of the color insert.

### Prophase I

In prophase I, the chromosomes become visible as they contract and thicken. Homologous chromosomes (members of a pair) come together, and crossing-over may occur.

### Metaphase I

In metaphase I, the paired chromosomes line up at the metaphase plate across the center of the cell.

### Anaphase I

In anaphase I, the paired chromosomes separate and are pulled to opposite poles by spindle fibers.

### Telophase I

In telophase I, a nuclear membrane forms around each set of chromosomes and the cell divides. Each new cell now has one representative of each homologous pair, 23 chromosomes in humans. Each chromosome is still made up of two chromatids.

### Prophase II

In prophase II, the cell prepares to undergo a second division.

### Metaphase II

In metaphase II, the chromosomes line up at the metaphase plate.

### Anaphase II

In anaphase II, the chromatids separate at the centromere, resulting in two separate chromosomes. Each chromosome, now consisting of a single chromatid, is pulled by the kinetochore spindle fibers to opposite poles.

### Telophase II

In telophase II, new nuclear membranes appear around the two groups of chromosomes as the spindle disappears. The cell then divides to form two new cells.

### Spermatogenesis

In spermatogenesis, or sperm production, the products of meiosis are four cells called **spermatids.** Each spermatid becomes a sperm.

### Oogeneis

In oogenesis, or ova production, the cell divides unevenly in meiosis. In the first division of meiosis, the cell divides into one large cell that contains the bulk of the cytoplasm of the original cell and a small cell called a polar body. The large cell then begins the second division of meiosis, again dividing unevenly into a large cell and small polar body. The polar bodies eventually disintegrate.

ality of Mendel's principles of segregation and independent assortment can be observed.

**Segregation and Independent Assortment** Each individual cell contains 23 pairs of chromosomes. One member of each pair is obtained from the mother and one from the father. When the individual then produces gametes, the paired chromosomes will separate during the first meiotic division; this is segregation. Therefore, each gamete will contain only one of each pair and, hence, only the alleles on those particular chromosomes.

When two genes exist on different chromosomes, the inheritance of each gene is independent

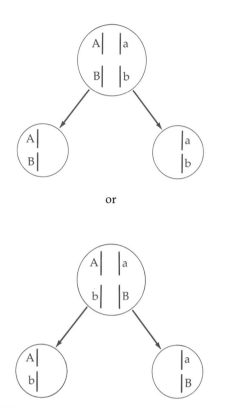

**FIGURE 2–7 Recombination**
The chromosomes can orient themselves in two different
ways, resulting in four distinct combinations of alleles.

of the other. As the chromosomes line up in meiosis, the individual chromosomes can orient in different patterns, as we will see in the next section. This explains Mendel's observations of independent assortment.

As one meiotic division follows another, gamete after gamete is produced, yet each individual gamete is unique, consisting of a particular set of chromosomes. One mechanism of meiosis that is responsible for the uniqueness of each gamete is **recombination.** As the 23 chromosomes line up in meiosis, they can recombine into several configurations.

Let us assume that, in Figure 2–7, the chromosomes with dominant alleles are inherited from the mother *(A, B)* and those with the recessive alleles are inherited from the father *(a, b).* When you are looking at two pairs, they can be oriented in two basic patterns: both paternal chromosomes can lie on one side and the maternal chromosomes on the

other, or one of each can lie on each side. From this, four types of gametes are produced, as shown in Figure 2–7. When all 23 chromosome pairs are considered, there are 8,324,608 possible combinations.

**Linkage** Early studies of inheritance revealed the fact that Mendel's principle of independent assortment does not always work. Traits determined by genes carried on different chromosomes do behave in the way he described, but if different genes are on the same chromosome, they tend to remain together in the formation of gametes. Interestingly, some of the seven traits Mendel studied in the pea plant are located on the same chromosome, but in his experiments demonstrating independent assortment, he by chance chose pairs of traits located on separate chromosomes.

Genes on the same chromosome are said to be linked, and the phenomenon is called **linkage.** Theoretically, if two genes are linked, only two types of gametes are produced instead of the four predicted by the principle of independent assortment. However, during meiosis, genetic material is often exchanged between homologous chromosomes inherited from an individual's father and mother; this event is called **crossing-over.**

As we can see in Figure 2–8, crossing-over provides a mechanism whereby new combinations of alleles can arise among genes that exist on the same chromosome. The farther apart two genes are on a chromosome, the greater the chance that they will cross over. This may be because there are more points between genes at which the chromosome can break and then reunite. As a result, each individual chromosome within each gamete may contain genetic material from both parents. Variation among gametes is the rule. The variations that result among living individuals form the basic raw material for the operation of natural selection.

**Sex Linkage** The X and Y chromosomes are not homologous; each has genes unique to it. Genes on the Y chromosome are said to be **Y-linked,** whereas genes on the X chromosome are said to be **X-linked.** Because of this nonhomogeneity, inheritance of traits carried on the X and Y chromosomes does not follow the simple Mendelian pattern.

The Y chromosome is small and carries few genes. The story is different with the X chromo-

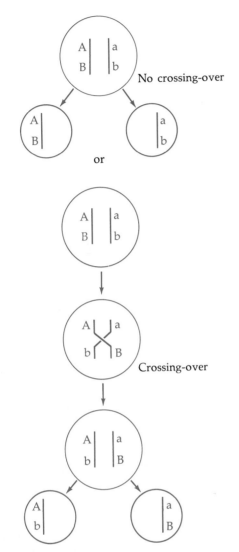

**FIGURE 2–8  Linkage**
Genes located on the same chromosome will be inherited as a unit, except when crossing-over occurs.

some. About 320 genes are known to lie on it, and more is known about the X chromosome than any of the other chromosomes. The inheritance of X-linked genes differs from classical Mendelian inheritance in one important way. Males inherit X-linked genes only from their mothers. Therefore, if the mother is heterozygous, a son will inherit one or the other allele from his mother, but he will not inherit an allele for this gene from his father. A deleterious recessive allele will always be expressed since the carrier state cannot exist in a male. A

daughter, of course, will inherit both an allele from her mother and an allele from her father (Figure 2–9). An example of an X-linked gene will be given in the next chapter.

## Summary

Stimulated by Mendel's work, early geneticists began to search for the physical reality of the gene. Their work led them to the cell and to those small bodies within the nucleus of the cell, the chromosomes.

By means of special techniques, chromosomes can now be routinely observed through the microscope. Each chromosome consists of two strands,

**FIGURE 2–9  X-Linked Inheritance**
The gene identified by the letter *H* is located on the X chromosome, but not on the Y. Genes located on the X chromosome display the X-linked pattern of inheritance.

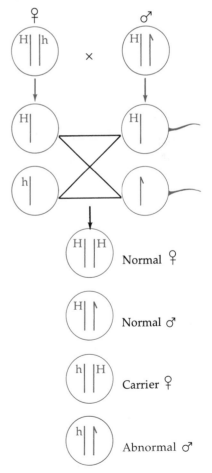

the chromatids, held together by the centromere. For a particular species, there is a characteristic chromosome number, but abnormalities in number and structure occur.

There are two basic forms of cell division. Mitosis is the division of body cells, while meiosis is the production of gametes—sperm and ova—in special body tissues. Detailed studies of the behavior of the chromosomes during cell division have provided a physical explanation for Mendelian genetics.

Deeper probing of the mechanisms of inheritance has shown that Mendel's principles do not always apply. This is not because they are wrong, but simply because the real hereditary mechanisms are very complex. For example, some traits are inherited on the sex chromosomes, so their pattern of inheritance differs from the patterns seen by Mendel.

## THE MOLECULAR BASIS OF HEREDITY

The previous section focused on the behavior of chromosomes as a means of explaining and expanding the observations of Mendel. However, the chromosome is not the gene itself. What is the gene, and how does it operate? To answer this question and others, we must turn to an examination of the chemical nature of the hereditary material.

All substances are composed of **atoms,** the basic building blocks of matter. Of the 92 kinds of atoms that occur in nature, 4 are found in great quantity in living organisms: carbon, hydrogen, oxygen, and nitrogen. Others that play extremely important roles, but are less common, include calcium, phosphorus, sulfur, chlorine, sodium, magnesium, iron, and potassium (Table 2–5).

Atoms can join to form **molecules,** which can vary tremendously in size depending on the number of atoms involved. The molecules found in living organisms are usually of great size because carbon atoms form long chains that can consist of hundreds or thousands of atoms and often include rings of five or six carbon atoms. Other kinds of atoms are attached to the carbon backbone.

### Molecules of Life

Most of the molecules found in living organisms fall into four categories: carbohydrates, lipids, proteins, and nucleic acids. The **carbohydrates** include the sugars and starches. **Lipids** include the fats, oils, and waxes.

Some of the most important molecules of the body are **proteins.** Proteins include muscle fibers, enzymes, and hormones. An understanding of the protein molecule is essential in comprehending the action of the genes. Proteins are long chains of basic units known as **amino acids.** All 20 basic amino acids share a common subunit, which contains carbon, oxygen, hydrogen, and nitrogen. Attached to this subunit are various groups of atoms that define the specific amino acid. These groups range from single hydrogen atoms to very complicated groups containing several carbon atoms. The end of one amino acid can link up with an end of another, forming a **peptide bond.** Short chains of amino acids are called **polypeptides.** A protein forms when several polypeptide chains join together.

Proteins are further complicated by other bonds. These bonds can involve sulfur and hydrogen and can lead to a folding, looping, or coiling of the protein molecule. The three-dimensional structure of proteins is important in determining how they function.

### The Nucleic Acids

Early in the twentieth century, biologists debated whether the gene was in fact a protein or a nucleic acid. It was soon determined that it was the latter.

**Nucleic acids** are the largest molecules found in living organisms. Like the proteins, the nucleic acids are long chains of basic units. In this case, the basic unit is a **nucleotide.** The nucleotide itself is fairly complex, consisting of three lesser units: a five-carbon sugar, either **ribose** or **deoxyribose;** a **phosphate unit;** and a **base.** The bases fall into two categories, **purines** and **pyrimidines,** both con-

### TABLE 2–5

#### COMMON ELEMENTS IN LIVING ORGANISMS

| Element | Approximate composition of human body, by weight (%) |
|---|---|
| Oxygen | 65.0 |
| Carbon | 18.5 |
| Hydrogen | 9.5 |
| Nitrogen | 3.3 |
| Calcium | 1.5 |
| Phosphorus | 1.0 |
| Others | 1.2 |

taining nitrogen. The purine consists of two connected rings of carbon and nitrogen atoms; the pyrimidine consists of a single ring.

The nucleic acid based upon the sugar ribose is called **ribonucleic acid (RNA).** The nucleotides that make up the RNA contain the following bases: the purines **adenine** (A) and **guanine** (G) and the pyrimidines **uracil** (U) and **cytosine** (C). The nucleic acid based upon the sugar deoxyribose is called **deoxyribonucleic acid (DNA).** DNA also contains adenine, guanine, and cytosine, but in place of uracil is found the pyrimidine **thymine** (T) (Figure 2–10).

**The DNA Molecule**  As with the proteins, the three-dimensional structure of the nucleic acids can be critical in understanding how the molecule works. The basic structure of DNA consists of a pair of extremely long chains composed of many nucleotides lying parallel to one another. The units are linked in such a way that a backbone of sugar and phosphate units is formed with the bases sticking out. The chains are connected by attrac-

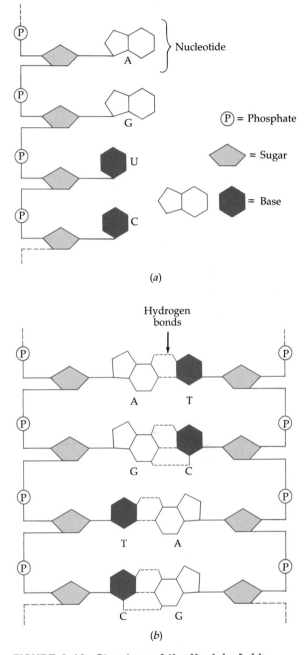

**FIGURE 2–10  Structure of the Nucleic Acids**
(*a*) Short segment of mRNA molecule. Note the presence of the base uracil and the absence of thymine. (*b*) Short segment of DNA showing four varieties of bases. Each base is joined to a deoxyribose molecule, and each deoxyribose molecule is held in the chain by phosphate molecules.

**BOX 2–2**

## Facts about DNA

James Watson and Francis H. C. Crick received a Nobel Prize in 1954 for their work on decoding the structure of DNA.

A human cell contains at least two meters of DNA.

All of this DNA is packaged into a nucleus that is about five microns (5/1000 millimeter) in diameter.

A human gene can contain over a hundred million base pairs; the entire human genetic code is made up of about three billion base pairs.

Because the sequence of base pairs can occur in any order, genetic variability is virtually unlimited.

Between 90 and 97 percent of human DNA is noncoding; it does not code for the production of proteins.

Some noncoding DNA serves as regulatory genes, but the function of most noncoding DNA is still unknown.

The same basic genetic code applies to all life on earth; that is, the same codons code for the same amino acids in all life from bacteria to humans.

The DNA sequences that control for specific proteins are about 99 percent the same for chimpanzees, gorillas, and humans.

tions between the hydrogen atoms of the two bases. Since the distance between the two chains must be constant, one of the two bases must be a pyrimidine and the other a purine. Two pyrimidines would be too narrow and two purines too wide. In addition, because of the nature of the bonding, bonding can take place only between an adenine and a thymine and between a cytosine and a guanine. These are said to be **complementary pairs.**

In 1953, J. D. Watson and F. H. C. Crick proposed a model for the three-dimensional structure of DNA.[6] DNA consists of two long chains wound around each other, forming a double helix, with a complete turn taking 10 nucleotide units (Figure 2–11 and Figure 2–D in the color insert).

**Mitochondrial DNA**   Not all DNA is found within the nucleus of the cell. A small amount is found in the cytoplasm in structures known as **mitochondria.** Mitochondria convert the energy in the chemical bonds of food into **adenosine triphosphate (ATP).** ATP is the main fuel of cells.

**Mitochondrial DNA (mtDNA)** is a double-stranded loop of DNA. There can be one or many mitochondria per cell. Each mitochondrion possesses between 4 and 10 mtDNA loops. Cells with high energy demands, such as muscle cells, have high numbers of mitochondria.

Human mitochondrial DNA contains the codes for only 13 proteins, whereas **nuclear DNA (nDNA)** codes for as many as 100,000 proteins. Viewed another way, nDNA contains about 3 billion base pairs, whereas mtDNA has only 16,569 base pairs.

The inheritance of the genes in mtDNA does not follow Mendelian principles. Mitochondrial DNA is inherited only from one's mother. The mitochondria of the zygote are supplied by the cytoplasm of the ovum; the sperm does not contribute mitochondria.

**Replication of DNA**   At the end of mitosis and meiosis, each chromosome is composed of a single chromatid that will eventually replicate itself to become double-stranded again. A chromatid is basically a single DNA molecule. In molecular terms, the DNA molecule has the ability to replicate itself to become two identical molecules.

In replication, the bonds holding the complementary pairs together are broken and the molecules come apart, with the bases sticking out from the sugar-phosphate backbone. Individual nucleotides of the four types (ultimately obtained from the digestion of food) are found in the nucleus, and the bases of these nucleotides become attracted to the exposed bases on the chain, forming complementary pairs. Thus, a nucleotide with an adenine becomes attracted to a thymine, and so on. When the nucleotides are in place, they bond to one another (Figure 2–12).

**The Genetic Code**   In order for the DNA molecule to function as the hereditary material, there must be a method by which information is stored in the DNA molecule. Remember, there are four bases that can be arranged in several ways. In the following hypothetical example, the DNA backbone of sugar and phosphate units is indicated by a single line, the bases by letters on the line:

C T C G G A C A A A T A

The above sequence codes for amino acids. Each amino acid is determined by specific three-base units called **codons.** This code has been broken and is given in Table 2–6 on page 44.

**Protein Synthesis**

The blueprint for a specific protein is located in the DNA molecule within the nucleus of the cell or the mitochondria. The actual production of proteins by the joining of specific amino acids in a specific sequence takes place within the mitochondria for genes encoded by mtDNA. For genes encoded by nDNA, protein production also occurs in the cytoplasm in extremely small, spherical bodies known as **ribosomes.** How is the information transmitted from the nDNA to the ribosomes?

The carrier of the information is **messenger RNA (mRNA).** This molecule copies the sequence of base pairs from the nDNA molecule. A segment of DNA that contains the code for a particular polypeptide chain unwinds, leaving a series of bases on the DNA chain exposed. Nucleotide units of RNA, which are found in the nucleus, are attracted to the complementary bases on the nDNA chain; the adenine of the RNA is attracted to the thymine on the nDNA, the guanine to the cytosine, the cytosine to the guanine, and the uracil of RNA

[6]J. D. Watson and F. H. C. Crick, "Molecular Structure of Nucleic Acids: A Structure for Deoxyribose Nucleic Acid," *Nature* 171 (1953), pp. 737–738.

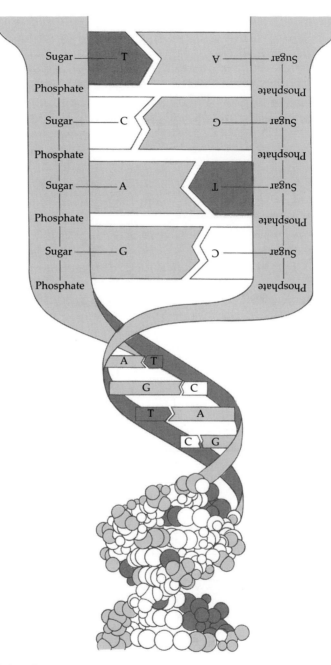

**FIGURE 2–11  The DNA Molecule**

This illustration shows different representations of the DNA molecule. Note that adenine and thymine are always across from each other, as are guanine and cytosine. A sugar molecule (deoxyribose) bonds with each base and each sugar bonds to a phosphate. This sugar–phosphate–sugar–phosphate arrangement forms the "backbone" of the DNA molecule.

Parent DNA

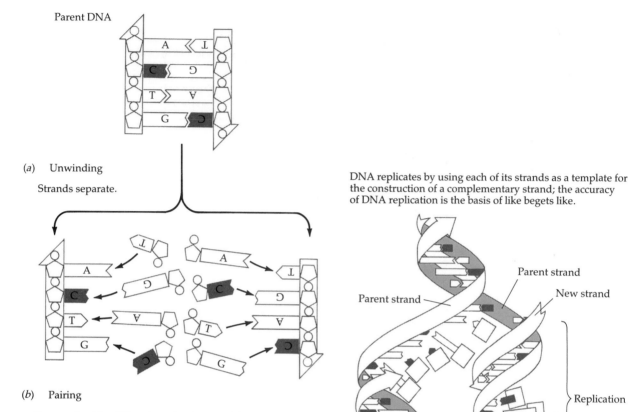

(a) Unwinding

Strands separate.

DNA replicates by using each of its strands as a template for the construction of a complementary strand; the accuracy of DNA replication is the basis of like begets like.

Parent strand

New strand

Parent strand

New strand

*B*

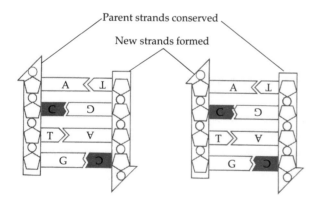

(b) Pairing

Free nucleotides diffuse in and pair up with bases on the separated strands.

Parent strands conserved

New strands formed

Replication

(c) Joining

Each new row of bases is linked into a continuous strand.

*A*

**FIGURE 2–12 Replication of the DNA Molecule**

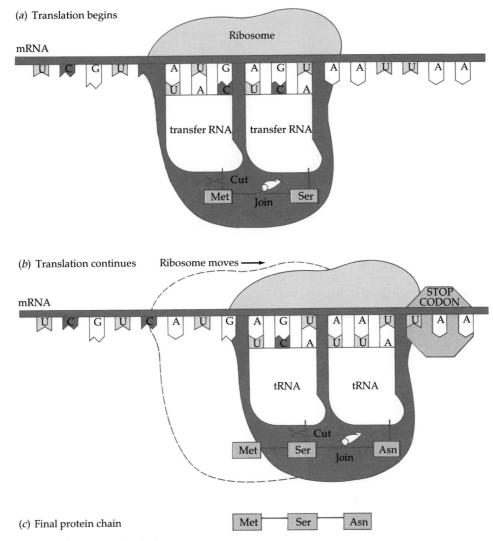

**FIGURE 2–13 Protein Synthesis in the Ribosome**
This is a highly simplified representation of protein synthesis. A start codon on the mRNA (AUG) signals the beginning of the production of a protein as a tRNA molecule brings the amino acid methionine into place. A second tRNA brings the second amino acid (serine, in this example) into place based on the code on the mRNA. The methionine and serine form a polypeptide bond as the first tRNA molecule is ejected. This process continues as more amino acids are linked. A code on the mRNA (stop codon) indicates that the protein is finished. The entire protein is now free of the RNA and is used by the body in the way specific to the type of protein that it is. (Asn stands for the amino acid asparagine.)

(remember, uracil replaces thymine) to the adenine on the nDNA.

After the nucleotide units are in place, they link together and the newly formed messenger RNA leaves the nDNA molecule as a unit. A molecule of mRNA is considerably shorter than a molecule of nDNA, since the mRNA contains the code of a single polypeptide chain.

In the ribosome is another form of RNA, called **transfer RNA (tRNA)** (Figure 2–13). The tRNA is extremely short, consisting in part of a series of three nucleotide units. The three bases form an

## TABLE 2-6

### THE GENETIC CODE

| Amino acid | Codons* |
|---|---|
| Alanine | CGA, CGG, CGT, CGC |
| Arginine | GCA, GCG, GCT, GCC, TCT, TCC |
| Asparagine | TTA, TTG |
| Aspartic acid | CTA, CTG |
| Cysteine | ACA, ACG |
| Glutamic acid | CTT, CTC |
| Glutamine | GTT, GTC |
| Glycine | CCA, CCG, CCT, CCC |
| Histidine | GTA, GTG |
| Isoleucine | TAA, TAG, TAT |
| Leucine | AAT, AAC, GAA, GAG, GAT, GAC |
| Lysine | TTT, TTC |
| Methionine | TAC |
| Phenylalanine | AAA, AAG |
| Proline | GGA, GGG, GGT, GGC |
| Serine | AGA, AGG, AGT, AGC, TCA, TCG |
| Threonine | TGA, TGG, TGT, TGC |
| Tryptophan | ACC |
| Tyrosine | ATA, ATG |
| Valine | CAA, CAG, CAT, CAC |

*The code is given in terms of the nucleotide sequence in the DNA molecule. In addition, there are specific codons signaling the beginning and end of a sequence.

anticode for a particular amino acid; that is, if the code on the mRNA is ACG, then the code on the tRNA consists of the complementary bases, UGC. Attached to the tRNA is the amino acid being coded.

The tRNA moves in and lines up opposite the appropriate codon on the mRNA molecule. For example, GUA is the code for valine on the mRNA, so the tRNA that carries the amino acid valine will have the base sequence CAU. After the amino acids are brought into their proper positions, they link together by means of peptide bonds and the polypeptide chain moves away from the mRNA and tRNA.

### Summary

Processes like inheritance can be understood on many levels. In the years after Mendel proposed his model for inheritance, scientists began investigating the chemical nature of genetic transmission. Their examinations revealed that the genetic material is a nucleic acid, DNA. DNA controls cell activities and hence determines inherited physical characteristics. DNA, which has the ability to replicate itself, is also the mechanism through which one generation passes its characteristics on to the next.

The information contained in the DNA molecule is coded by the arrangement of base pairs. The information on the nuclear DNA molecule is transmitted by messenger RNA to the ribosome, the site of protein manufacture, where transfer RNA functions to bring the appropriate amino acids into position.

On the molecular level, a gene is a segment of the DNA molecule that codes for a particular functioning protein or segment of a protein. When random changes occurs in this code they increase genotypic variation by creating "new" alleles. The various alleles of a particular gene are simply slight variants in the code itself.

### STUDY QUESTIONS

1. Describe the concepts of segregation and independent assortment. In what ways do these concepts differ?
2. Many people take the term *dominant* to mean that an allele is common. However, dominance and recessiveness have nothing to do with frequency. What, precisely, do these two terms signify?
3. Why have the major breakthroughs in the understanding of the mechanisms of heredity been made with bacteria, plants, and nonhuman animals, such as fruit flies and mice, rather than with humans?
4. An individual's phenotype results from the interaction of the genotype and the environment. How does a geneticist proceed to demonstrate the relative importance of these two factors?
5. How does the process of meiosis tend to confirm Mendel's observations of segregation and independent assortment? Is independent assortment an unbroken rule, or are there exceptions?
6. In what ways does oogenesis differ from spermatogenesis? Because of these differences, does the mother's genetic contribution differ from that of the father? In what way?
7. An important feature of meiosis is the reduction in chromosome number. What is the significance of this reduction?
8. In terms of the chemical structure of DNA, what is the gene? Is the concept of the gene a valid one?
9. What is mitochondrial DNA? How does it differ from nuclear DNA?

### SUGGESTED READINGS

Lewin, B. *Genes,* 6th ed. Oxford: Oxford University Press, 1997. This is a popular introductory text on general genetics. It presents an encyclopedic treatment of genetics and as such is an excellent reference book.

Orel, V. *Gregor Mendel: The First Geneticist.* New York: Oxford University Press, 1996. This is an analysis of Mendel's life and work. It discusses the attitudes that his contemporaries had about his experiments.

Watson, J. D., et al. *Molecular Biology of the Gene,* 4th ed. Menlo Park, Calif.: Benjamin/Cummings, 1987. This two-volume set, written by five researchers and teachers, including one of the discoverers of the structure of DNA, gives a detailed discussion of DNA and gene structure.

Weaver, W. F., and P. W. Hedrick. *Genetics,* 3rd ed. Dubuque: Wm C. Brown, 1997. This is a basic introductory text in genetics.

## SUGGESTED WEB SITES

Experimenting with Mendel's Pea:
http://www.biology.uc.edu/vgenetic/Vmendel/index.html
Primer on Molecular Genetics:
http://www.ornl.gov/hgmis/publicat/primer/intro.html
MendelWeb (classic papers, plant science, and data analysis):
http://www.netspace.org/MendelWeb/

Additional web sites are listed in the *Workbook* that accompanies this text.

# GENETICS: FROM CELLS TO DNA

cell    nucleus

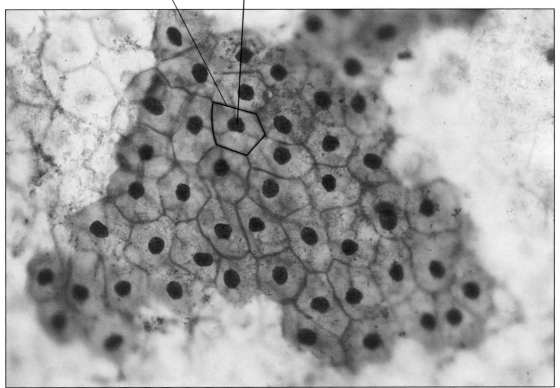

**FIGURE 2–A**   Most living organisms are either single cells or are made up of cells. Here is a picture of human skin cells as they appear under a microscope. The nuclei appear dark because they have been stained with a purple dye. The chromosomes, which contain the genetic material, are found within the nuclei.

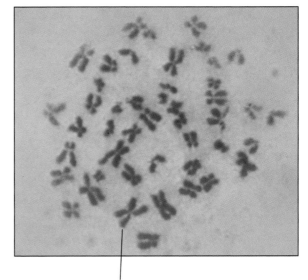

**FIGURE 2–B**   The genetic material is contained within bodies known as chromosomes. Pictured here is a complete set of 46 chromosomes obtained from a white blood cell from a normal human female.

A chromosome

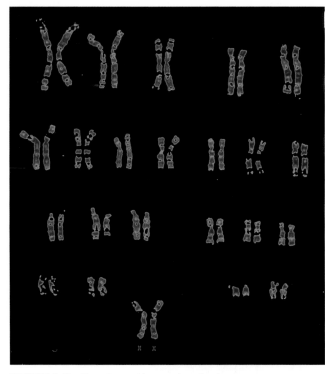

**FIGURE 2–C**  Karyotype of human female chromosomes.

**FIGURE 2–D**  The genetic information is coded in the DNA molecule, located within the chromosome. This molecule, the largest molecule in living organisms, is composed of units that form a double helix. The three-dimensional structure of DNA is seen in this model.

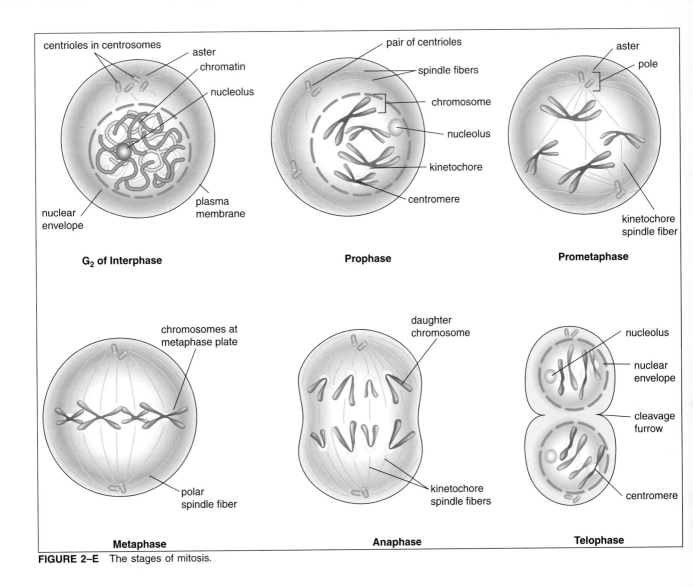

**FIGURE 2–E** The stages of mitosis.

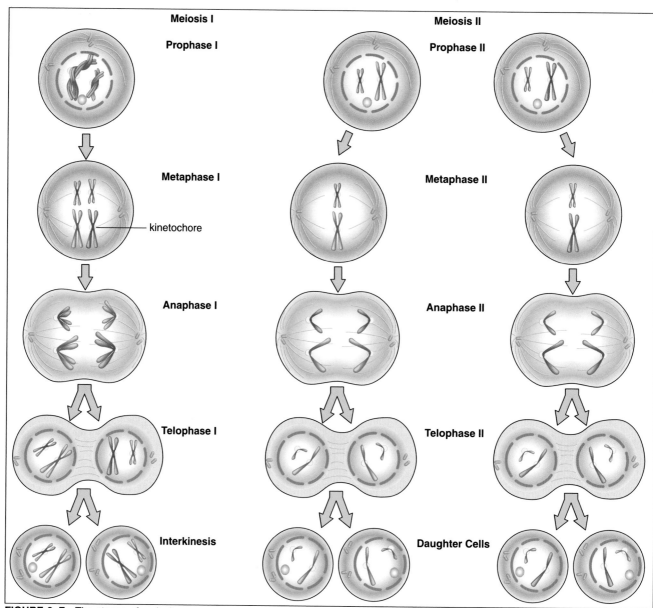

**FIGURE 2–F**  The stages of meiosis.

# The Modern Study of Human Genetics

*...Like other creatures, man evolves, but unlike other creatures, man knows that he evolves. The control of this biological evolution is therefore the change from reproductive success caused by natural selection to reproductive success caused by human choice.[1]*
—M. W. Strickberger

The modern study of genetics began in 1900 when several scholars uncovered the same basic mechanisms of heredity that were first suggested by the experiments of Gregor Mendel. From this beginning emerged a period of experimentation using laboratory plants and animals that could be bred in large numbers. From these experiments, many of the details and complexities of genetics came to light.

It was clear that most new information about how genetics work would come from experimentation.

---

[1]M. W. Strickberger, *Genetics*, 3rd ed. (New York: Macmillan, 1985), p. 782.

Yet there was always a special interest in human heredity. In the nineteenth century, Sir Francis Galton (1822–1911) was encouraged by the writing of his cousin, Charles Darwin. Galton published in 1869 a study entitled *Hereditary Genius,* in which he attempted to show that human intellectual talents were inherited.

In 1902, a physician, Archibald Garrod, wrote a paper in which he demonstrated that the human disease alcaptonuria appeared to be inherited as a simple recessive. This was the first demonstration of Mendelian inheritance in humans. From this beginning, investigators have cataloged today over 10,000 inherited traits in humans.

This chapter will examine various aspects of human genetics. In doing so, we will see how the basic rules of Mendelian genetics apply to humans. We will also see that the principles of genetics are a great deal more complex than those revealed by the work of Mendel.

## MEDICAL GENETICS

The rapid development of the science of genetics in the twentieth century was the result of the application of the scientific method using plants and animals whose breeding could be controlled. Nevertheless, there was always a great interest in the application of genetic principles to humans. The focus of much of this interest was in the arena of medical genetics, the subject of this section.

### Blood-Type Systems

In 1900, the same year Mendel's experiments were being rediscovered, Karl Landsteiner at the University of Vienna discovered that proteins in human blood existed in several different normal forms. The discovery of blood types led to the development of safe blood transfusions and an understanding of the cause of certain medical conditions. Blood types also became an important tool in the study of human variation.

A large number of proteins are found in blood. Since they often occur in several forms, these proteins are said to be **polymorphic,** from *poly,* meaning "many," and *morph,* "structure."

Through blood transfusions and occasional mixing of maternal and fetal blood at birth, proteins can be introduced into the blood of a person whose blood naturally lacks them. The body reacts to these foreign proteins by producing or mobilizing **antibodies,** whose role is to destroy or neutralize foreign substances that have entered the body. A protein that triggers the action of antibodies is known as an **antigen.** Antigen–antibody reactions are of great medical significance and help define differences in blood proteins that exist in humans.

**The ABO Blood-Type System**   The best-known set of blood antigens is the **ABO blood-type system.** This system consists of two basic antigens, which are called simply antigens A and B. Other antigens do exist in the system, and the actual situation is more complex than is presented here.

There are four phenotypes in the ABO system, depending on which antigens are present. Type A indicates the presence of antigen A, while type B shows the presence of antigen B. Type AB indicates the presence of both antigens; type O indicates the absence of both antigens. The antigens themselves are large protein molecules found on the surface of the red blood cells.

In our examples in Chapter 2, we looked at genes that possess two alleles. However, **multiple alleles** frequently occur. The inheritance of ABO blood types involves three alleles, which we will write as $I^A$, $I^B$, and $i$. Two of these alleles are dominant with respect to $i$: $I^A$ results in the production of the A antigen and $I^B$ in the production of the B antigen. In relationship to each other, alleles $I^A$ and $I^B$ are said to be **codominant,** in that an $I^A I^B$ individual produces both antigens. The allele $i$ is recessive and does not result in antigen production. The various genotypes and phenotypes are summarized in Table 3–1.

The ABO system is unusual in that the antibodies are present before exposure to the antigen. Thus, type A individuals have anti-B in their blood. Furthermore, an AB individual has neither antibody, while an O individual has both.

Because of the presence of antibodies in the blood, blood transfusions can be risky if the blood is not accurately typed and administrated. If, for example, type A blood is given to a type O individual, the anti-A present in the recipient's blood will agglutinate all the type A cells entering the recipient's body. **Agglutination** refers to a clumping together of red cells, forming small clots that may block blood vessels.

## TABLE 3-1

**PHENOTYPES AND GENOTYPES OF THE ABO BLOOD-TYPE SYSTEM**

| Type | Antigen | Antibody | Genotype |
|------|---------|----------|----------|
| A | A | Anti-B | $I^A I^A$, $I^A i$ |
| B | B | Anti-A | $I^B I^B$, $I^B i$ |
| O | — | Anti-A, Anti-B | $ii$ |
| AB | A, B | — | $I^A I^B$ |

Table 3–2 shows the consequences of various types of blood transfusions. Blood-type O is often referred to as the universal donor because the entering O cells lack antigens of this system and therefore cannot be agglutinated. However, type O blood does contain anti-A and anti-B, which can cause damage in an A, B, or AB recipient. Although such damage is minimal, since the introduced antibodies become diluted and are rapidly absorbed by the body tissues, the safest transfusions are between people of the same blood type.

**Other Blood Type Systems**   Another major blood-type system, which is a great deal more complex than the ABO system, is the **Rh blood-type system.** This blood-type system is also polymorphic and has multiple alleles resulting in many antigens. The inheritance of Rh blood type and that of ABO blood type are independent of one another, an example of independent assortment.

In the United States and Europe, a problem arises with respect to one of these antigens ($Rh_0$). About 15 percent of the people in this population lack this antigen; these people, who are homozygous recessive, are Rh-negative (Rh−).

Although Rh compatibility can cause problems in transfusion, it is of greater interest as the cause of **erythroblastosis fetalis,** a **hemolytic** (blood-cell-destroying) **disease** affecting 1 out of every 150 to 200 newborns. The problem occurs when an Rh-negative mother carries an Rh-positive fetus. At birth, Rh antigens in the fetal blood can mix with the maternal blood, causing the production of the antibody anti-Rh in the mother's blood. Although the first few pregnancies usually do not present any danger to the fetus, eventually the anti-Rh levels in the mother's blood become fairly high. At this point, if the anti-Rh comes into contact with the fetal bloodstream, it can cause destruction of the fetal blood cells (Figure 3–1).

The Rh problem can be handled by an interesting medical technique. During and shortly after each birth of an Rh-positive child to an Rh-negative mother, the mother is given an injection of synthetic anti-Rh, which suppresses her own production of the antibodies. Soon the injected antibodies disappear, leaving the mother's blood free of any anti-Rh and, therefore, safe for future pregnancies. It is now also possible to transfuse the fetus while it is still in the uterus.

**The Use of Blood Types in Forensic Science**
There are many other blood-type systems that are known for human blood, including the MNSs, Diego, P, Lutheran, Kell, Lewis, Duffy, Kidd, Auberger, Sutter, and Xg. Because each of these systems consists of many diverse antigens, the probability of two persons having an identical combination of antigens is small. If a blood sample is found at a crime scene, it is often possible to determine which of the many blood antigens are present. The particular combinations of blood types in the blood sample, for example, can be compared with the blood types found in blood on the accused person's clothing to see if they are the same.

Of course, it is possible for two people to have the identical combination of blood types. The probability of this occurring can be calculated if the frequency of the occurrence of particular blood types is known in the population. However, a failure to match two blood samples can be used to conclusively prove that they did not come from the same person.

## TABLE 3-2

**RESULTS OF BLOOD TRANSFUSIONS***

| Recipient | Donor | | | |
|-----------|-------|-------|-------|-------|
| | **A** | **B** | **O** | **AB** |
| A | − | + | (+) | + |
| B | + | − | (+) | + |
| O | + | + | − | + |
| AB | (+) | (+) | (+) | − |

*+ indicates heavy agglutination of donor's cells. (+) indicates no agglutination of donor's cells, but antibodies in donor's blood may cause some agglutination of recipient's cells. − indicates no agglutination of donor's cells.

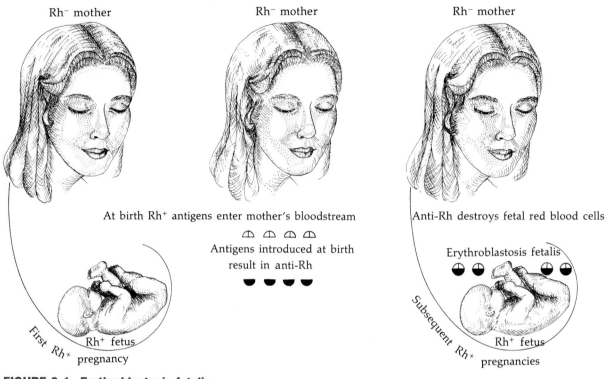

Rh⁻ mother      Rh⁻ mother      Rh⁻ mother

At birth Rh⁺ antigens enter mother's bloodstream

Antigens introduced at birth result in anti-Rh

Anti-Rh destroys fetal red blood cells

Erythroblastosis fetalis

*First* Rh⁺ pregnancy     Rh⁺ fetus

*Subsequent* Rh⁺ pregnancies     Rh⁺ fetus

**FIGURE 3–1 Erythroblastosis fetalis**

The use of blood proteins in criminal identification is enhanced by the fact that the A, B, and other antigens are found in most cells of the body in some individuals and are secreted in body fluids such as saliva, often found at crime scenes. The ability to secrete A and B antigens is determined by the secretor gene. About 22 percent of the American "white" population are homozygous recessive and hence are nonsecretors.

### Human Inherited Abnormalities

In 1966, Victor A. McKusick's first edition of *Mendelian Inheritance in Man* listed 1487 inherited human traits. By 1999, the number of known inherited characteristics had reached 10,503.[2] Due to recent advances in determining the genetic nature of traits, our knowledge of genetics is exploding, with new genetic traits being discovered almost daily. Still, the known number of genetically influenced or controlled traits represents only a small percentage of the number of genes that have been estimated to exist in humans. Since genetic research is costly, most studies of human genes have focused on inherited abnormalities and have been motivated by the hope that cures or treatments can be found. As a result, most of the known inherited traits are abnormalities.

The majority of genetic abnormalities are caused by the interaction of genes and the environment. Although the role of the environment in these situations is difficult to determine, many abnormalities are primarily the result of the action of the genotype. Some of the better-known ones, listed in Table 3–3, are the result of the inheritance of a simple dominant or recessive allele.

Many inherited abnormalities involve errors in metabolism. One of the best known of these is **phenylketonuria (PKU),** an abnormality inherited as a recessive. PKU involves an error in the enzyme

---

[2]Number of entries on May 22, 1999. Online Mendelian Inheritance in Man, OMIM (TM). Center for Medical Genetics, Johns Hopkins University (Baltimore, Md.) and National Center for Biotechnology Information, National Library of Medicine (Bethesda, Md.), 1999. World Wide Web URL: http://www3.ncbi.nlm.nih.gov/Omim/.

## TABLE 3-3

### SOME HUMAN GENETIC ABNORMALITIES

| Abnormality | Symptoms | Inheritance | Incidence* | |
|---|---|---|---|---|
| Cystic fibrosis | Excessive mucus production, digestive and respiratory failure, reduced life expectancy. | Recessive | 1/2500 | (Caucasians, U.S.) |
| Albinism | Little or no pigment in skin, hair, eyes. | Recessive | 1/200 | (Hopi Indians) |
| Tay-Sachs disease | Buildup of fatty deposits in brain, blindness, motor and mental impairment, death in early childhood. | Recessive | 1/3600 | (Ashkenazi Jews) |
| Thalassemia | Anemia due to abnormal red blood cells, bone and spleen enlargement. | Recessive | 1/10 | (some Italian populations) |
| Sickle-cell anemia | Sickling of red blood cells, anemia, jaundice; fatal. | Codominant | 1/625 | (African Americans) |
| Achondroplastic dwarfism | Heterozygotes display long bones that do not grow properly, short stature, other structural abnormalities; homozygotes stillborn or die shortly after birth. | Dominant | 1/9100 | (Danes) |
| Familial hypercholesterolemia | High levels of cholesterol, early heart attacks. | Dominant | 1/500 | (general U.S. population) |
| Huntington's disease | Progressive mental and neurological damage leading to disturbance of speech, dementia, and death. | Dominant | 1/2941 | (Tasmanians) |

*In population with high incidence of the disease.

phenylalanine hydroxylase, which is responsible for the conversion of the amino acid phenylalanine to tyrosine.

A child with PKU is unable to convert phenylalanine into tyrosine. Not only does this result in an inadequate supply of tyrosine, but the levels of phenylalanine build up in the blood. As this buildup progresses, the excess phenylalanine is broken down into toxic by-products. These by-products usually cause, among other things, severe brain damage and mental retardation. This defect occurs in about 1 out of 100,000 live births among northern Europeans and in lower frequencies in most other populations. PKU accounts for about 1 percent of all admissions to mental institutions.

Another type of genetic abnormality is one that leads to an anatomical problem; an example is **achondroplastic dwarfism.** A achondroplastic dwarf is a person whose head and trunk are of normal size but whose limbs are quite short. In contrast with PKU, this abnormality results from the inheritance of a dominant allele. A person who is heterozygous *(Dd)* for this gene would be a dwarf. A homozygous dominant *(DD)* individual is usually stillborn or dies shortly after birth; a normal person is homozygous recessive *(dd)*.

**The Study of Pedigrees** Studies of human genetics are often after-the-fact studies; that is, after a child with PKU has been born, an attempt is made to reconstruct the matings that have already occurred. Such a reconstruction is called a **pedigree.** In the pedigree in Figure 3–2, the males are indicated by squares, the females by circles. Matings are indicated by horizontal lines, while descent is shown by vertical lines. Individuals with the trait in question are solid in color. As you examine the pedigree in Figure 3–2, note that the trait is infrequent. In every case, the parents of PKU children are normal, since a PKU individual generally does

## Spoonerisms and Albinism

You hissed my mystery lecture, you hissed all my mystery lectures! You tasted the whole worm!!

This strange reprimand was uttered by the famous eighteenth-century classicist Reverend Dr. W. A. Spooner. Garbled speech, in which sounds are unintentionally interchanged, has come to be known as spoonerisms. Reverend Spooner meant to admonish an often absent student by saying:

You missed my history lecture, you missed all my history lectures! You wasted the whole term!!

What does this have to do with genetics? It appears that **albinism**—a simple recessive abnormality that leads to little or no production of skin pigment—may be associated with spoonerisms. The allele that causes albinism also affects vision. Albinos often display a neurological problem in which the eyeballs move spasmodically. This condition may have caused Rev. Spooner, an albino, to transpose letters when he read. These experiences may then have affected his speech pattern. Thus, a behavioral characteristic that most people assumed was due to Spooner's level of excitement or anger may have been influenced by inheritance.

*Sources:* A. G. Levinthal, D. J. Vitek, and D. S. Creel, "Abnormal Visual Pathways in Normally Pigmented Cats That Are Heterozygous for Albinism," *Science* 229 (1985), p. 1395; and J. B. Jenkins, *Human Genetics,* 2nd ed. (New York: Harper & Row, 1990), p. 79.

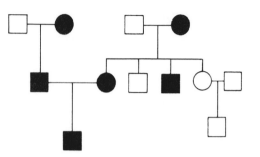

**FIGURE 3–3  Pedigree of Dwarfism**
This type of dwarfism is inherited as a dominant trait. Dwarfs are shown in color.

not reproduce. Therefore, it can be assumed that the parents are heterozygous for the trait while the affected individual is homozygous recessive.

Now let us compare this pedigree of a recessive trait with that of a dominant trait. Figure 3–3 shows a pedigree of achondroplastic dwarfism. Note that all dwarf children have at least one parent who is also a dwarf. Since the abnormality is the result of a dominant allele, it is expressed in the heterozygous individual. A mating between two nondwarfs produces nondwarf children only.

You might think that a good way to identify the mode of inheritance from a pedigree is to look for the characteristic Mendelian proportions, but such proportions are rarely found. The size of families is too small to provide a large enough sample. Although the data from several families can be pooled, this requires specific mathematical procedures.

**Other Patterns of Inheritance**  The basic principles of genetics as worked out by Gregor Mendel are seen in all living organisms. However, the inheritance of many traits does not follow these basic patterns. In fact, because the actual modes of inheritance are usually more complex, traits inherited in the basic Mendelian pattern are the exception rather than the rule. We have already examined the case of multiple alleles and codominance in our discussion of ABO blood types. These and other deviations from Mendel's rules are summarized in Table 3–4.

**Y-Linkage and the Determination of Sex**  Since male progeny inherit the Y chromosome, all males inherit the Y-linked genes. Y linkage, however, is difficult to distinguish from a **sex-limited gene.** These genes behave as if they were on the Y chromosome, but they are actually carried on an autosome and are expressed only in the male. The most significant gene that is found on the Y chromosome is the one that establishes the sex of the individual.

**FIGURE 3–2  Pedigree of PKU**
Phenylketonuria is inherited as a recessive trait. Individuals with PKU are shown in color. Note that neither of his parents has the disease; they are both carriers.

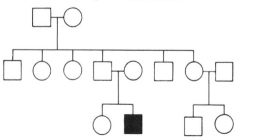

**TABLE 3-4**

**SOME DEVIATIONS FROM MENDELIAN GENETICS**

| Deviation | Definition | Example |
| --- | --- | --- |
| Environmental influences | Nongenetic factors that influence the phenotype. | Dyed hair color. |
| Polygenic inheritance | A specific trait is influenced by more than one gene. | Stature. |
| Codominance | Both alleles are expressed in the heterozygous genotype. | In sickle-cell anemia, the heterozygous genotype produces both hemoglobin A and S. |
| Multiple-allele series | Three or more alleles exist for a specific gene. | In the ABO blood-type system, the four major blood types are determined by three alleles. |
| Modifying gene | One gene alters the expression of another gene. | One gene controls whether a person who has inherited the alleles for cataracts will get cataracts. |
| Regulatory genes | Genes that initiate or block the activities of other genes. | Genes that control aging. |
| Incomplete penetrance | The situation in which an allele that might be expected to be expressed is not. | A person who inherits the alleles for diabetes may not express the symptoms of the disease. |
| Sex-limited trait | A trait expressed in only one sex. | A beard in a male. |
| Pleiotropy | A single allele may affect an entire series of traits. | Sickle-cell anemia may cause blindness, stroke, kidney damage, etc. |

Most people accept the fact that people are born either as female or male. However, we need to distinguish between different kinds of sex. **Phenotypical sex** refers to how an individual's phenotype is viewed and is based upon a person's sex organs and secondary sexual characteristics. Sometimes, an individual's phenotypical sex is ambiguous. **Chromosomal sex** refers to the number of X and Y chromosomes. However, some individuals are born with abnormal numbers of sex chromosomes, as we will see later in this chapter. **Genetic sex** refers to the presence of the gene that determines sex. This gene, called *Sry*, is located on the Y chromosome.

A human embryo develops a set of generalized organs and tubes that will eventually turn into the sex organs. Between the fifth and seventh weeks of development, the *Sry* gene, if present, produces a chemical that influences the undifferentiated **gonad** (sex organ) to become a testis. Once the testis begins to develop, it will produce testosterone that will turn the other structures into the male sex organs. If this does not occur by the 13th week, the gonad begins to develop into an ovary, and under the influence of ovarian hormones, the tubes will develop into female structures.

How can a person with two X chromosomes become a male? If the *Sry* gene breaks off of a Y chromosome in the father's sperm and attaches to an X chromosome, the *Sry* gene will still operate even though it is on the X chromosome.

Can an XY individual be a female? This can happen if the *Sry* gene is not operating or if the receptor sites on the undifferentiated gonads do not respond to the presence of the hormone. In addition to these examples, other problems result in ambiguous phenotypic sex.

One area of human endeavor where this has become a major issue is athletic competition, especially the Olympics. Fearing that a phenotypic female who is a genetic or chromosomal male will have an unfair advantage, all phenotypic female athletes have been forced to undergo testing. Female athletes are put through this demeaning process in spite of the fact that several decades of testing have demonstrated that the few phenotypic females who, for example, carry an X and a Y chromosome do not have any particular athletic advantage.

The Spanish hurdler, Maria Patino, is a phenotypic female, yet carries an X and a Y chromosome in her cells. Because of an androgen insensitivity syndrome, there are no masculinizing effects and she has no advantage over other female athletes in terms of speed and strength. Women with this syndrome have breasts and vaginas and are socialized as females, but lack a uterus and ovaries and have testes located within their bodies. Patino made her case public, and after several years has been certified a female by the International Olympic Committee.

A total of 2406 female athletes competing in the 1992 Barcelona Olympics were tested for the presence of the male-sex producing gene. Five athletes, about 1 in 500, "failed" the test. Four athletes that agreed to a follow-up physical exam exhibited physical abnormalities. The International Olympic Committee has not revealed whether or not these women were allowed to compete. Many geneticists have called for an end to genetic screening for athletes.[3]

**X-Linked Abnormalities**  In the last chapter, we saw that genes that are found on the X and Y chromosomes show a distinctive pattern of inheritance. Here we study an example of an X-linked abnormality. Hemophilia is a recessive X-linked trait that is characterized by excessive bleeding due to a faulty clotting mechanism.

During the nineteenth and twentieth centuries, hemophilia occurred with some frequency in the royal houses of Europe. The disease probably originated with Queen Victoria of England, because all the people involved are descended from her. None of her ancestors had the disease, but of Queen Victoria's nine children, two daughters were carriers, three daughters were possible carriers, and one son (Leopold) had the disease. These people brought the disease into the royal families of England, Spain, Russia, and probably Germany (Figure 3–4).

A famous case of the relationship of hemophilia to history involved Alix, granddaughter of Victoria, who married the future czar of Russia, Nicholas II, and became known in Russia as Alexandra. She had four daughters and one son, Alexis, who was a hemophiliac. Historians have suggested that the preoccupation of Nicholas and Alexandra with their son's disease brought them under the control

of Rasputin and hastened the overthrow of their government.

## Chromosomal Abnormalities

Besides abnormalities in specific genes, problems also occur with chromosomes. The processes of mitosis and meiosis are precise, yet errors do occur. Such errors lead to **chromosomal aberrations,** which consist of two types: abnormal chromosome number and abnormal chromosome structure.

**Abnormal Chromosome Number**  A common error of meiosis is that of **nondisjunction.** When two members of a chromosome pair move together to the same pole instead of to opposite poles, nondisjunction has occurred. This leads to abnormal chromosome numbers in the second-generation cells. Thus, two second-generation cells are formed: one contains 22 chromosomes and the other has 24. The union of a gamete having the normal complement of 23 chromosomes with a gamete having an abnormal number of chromosomes will produce a zygote with either an extra or missing chromosome. For example, if a sperm with 24 chromosomes fertilizes an ovum with 23, the zygote will have 47 chromosomes.

What phenotype is found in an individual developing from a zygote with an abnormal karyotype? Figure 3–5a on page 57 shows a karyotype of an individual with 47 chromosomes, one too many. Since the extra chromosome is a number 21, a fairly small chromosome, a relatively small number of genes are involved. Figure 3–5b shows a child with this karyotype; the condition is called **Down syndrome** or **trisomy 21.** (The term *trisomy* refers to the presence of three chromosomes instead of a pair, in this case three chromosome 21s.)

Down syndrome is characterized by a peculiarity in the eyefolds (which some seem to think resembles the Mongoloid eye, although it is different), short stature with stubby hands and feet, and congenital malformations of the heart and other organs. Perhaps the most significant feature is mental retardation.

Down syndrome is not rare. The risk of giving birth to a Down syndrome child increases with the age of the mother and perhaps the father. Women who are 20 years of age have a 1 in 2000 chance of having a child with trisomy 21, but, for a 30-year-old woman, the risk is 1 in 300 and, for a 42-year-

---

[3]J. Diamond, "Turning a Man," *Discover,* June 1992, pp. 71–77; and D. Grady, "Sex Test of Champions," *Discover,* June 1992, pp. 78–82.

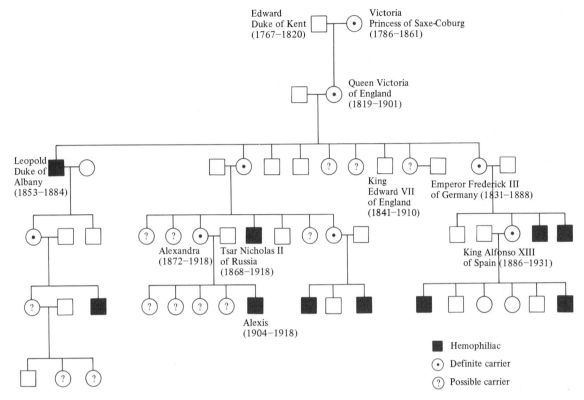

**FIGURE 3–4a Queen Victoria's Pedigree**

old woman, 1 in 20. Although it was once thought that Down syndrome was due exclusively to nondisjunction in the ova, it is now thought that in about 5 percent of all Down syndrome children, the disease is the result of defective sperm.[4]

More common than nondisjunctions of autosomes are extra or missing sex chromosomes. Among these are such abnormal sex chromosome counts as X– **(Turner syndrome)**, XXY **(Klinefelter syndrome)**, XXX, and XYY (Table 3–5). While these individuals have a higher survival rate than do infants with extra or missing autosomes, possessors of abnormal sex chromosome numbers often show abnormal sex organs and abnormal secondary sexual characteristics, sterility, and, sometimes, mental retardation.

**Structural Aberrations of Chromosomes** In addition to abnormal numbers of chromosomes due to nondisjunction, several types of structural abnormalities can occur. Structural abnormalities are the result of breaks in the chromosome.

**Deletion** occurs when a chromosome itself breaks and a segment of it that is not attached to the spindle fails to be included in the second-generation cell. The genetic material on the deleted section is "lost." **Duplication** is the process whereby a section of a chromosome is repeated. **Inversion** occurs when parts of a chromosome break and reunite in a reversed order. No genetic material is lost or gained, but the position of the alleles involved is changed. **Translocation** is the process whereby segments of chromosomes become detached and then reattach to other nonhomologous chromosomes.

Abnormal chromosome numbers and structural aberrations account for a significant number of defects in newborns and a large number of spontaneous abortions (miscarriages). About 50 percent of the miscarriages in the United States are due to chromosomal abnormalities. Approximately 1 in 160 live births is accompanied by a chromosomal

---

[4]C. Ezzell, "New Clues to the Origin of Down's Syndrome," *Science News* 139 (1991), p. 292.

**FIGURE 3–4*b***
This photograph shows Queen Victoria and some of her descendants: Princess Alix (Alexandra) of
Hesse (left), Queen Victoria (center), Princess Irene of Prussia (right).

abnormality.[5] One way of preventing what is very
often a tragedy is to identify the abnormality before birth. Karyotypes can be made from the fetal
cells found in the amniotic fluid; if chromosomal
abnormalities are seen, the early fetus can be
aborted. The procedure is recommended to all
mothers over 35 years of age as a means of identifying fetuses having Down syndrome or other
chromosomal abnormalities.

### Genetic Abnormalities as Mistakes in Proteins

A great number of genetic abnormalities result from
abnormal protein molecules. Since the blueprints

for proteins are located in the DNA molecule, it follows that these abnormal proteins are the result of
an incorrect sequence of nucleotides in the DNA
molecule itself. This can be demonstrated with respect to sickle-cell anemia.

**The Molecular Structure of Hemoglobin** Blood
is a very complex material composed of a liquid
and a solid portion. The solid portion consists of
the **erythrocytes (red blood cells),** the **leukocytes
(white blood cells),** and the **platelets.** The liquid
portion is the **plasma.** Dissolved in the plasma are
a wide variety of materials, including salts, sugars,
fats, amino acids, and hormones, along with the important plasma proteins.

Packed into the erythrocytes are millions of molecules of the red pigment **hemoglobin A (HbA).**
The major constituent of the molecule is a larger

[5]R. H. Tamarin, *Principles of Genetics*, 2nd ed. (Boston: Prindle, Weber, Schmidt, 1986), pp. 246–247.

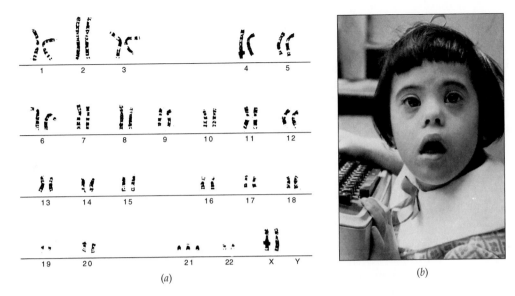

**FIGURE 3-5 Down syndrome**
(*a*) Karyotype of Down syndrome. Note the extra chromosome 21. (*b*) Girl with Down syndrome.
Down syndrome is characterized by a peculiarity in the eyefolds, short stature with stubby hands
and feet, congenital malformations of the heart and other organs, and significant mental retardation.

**TABLE 3-5**

### SOME EXAMPLES OF ABNORMAL CHROMOSOME NUMBERS

| Type | Incidence | Phenotype |
|---|---|---|
| **Autosomal abnormalities** | | |
| Trisomy* 13 (Patau syndrome) | 1/15,000 | Severely malformed. Small head, sloping forehead, cardiac and other defects. |
| Trisomy 18 (Edward syndrome) | 1/7500 | Growth and developmental retardation, death usually before 6 months. |
| Trisomy 21 (Down syndrome) | 1/700 | See text for description. |
| **Sex-chromosome abnormalities** | | |
| 47, XXY (Klinefelter syndrome) | 1/850 males | Phenotypically male. Sterile, small penis, breast enlargement in 40% of cases, average IQ scores. |
| 45, X– (Turner syndrome) | 1/5000 females | Phenotypically female. Variable characteristics. Short stature, relatively normal IQ scores, small chin, webbing of neck in 50% of cases, shield-shaped chest, cardiovascular disease in 35% of cases, affectionate, sterile. |
| 47, XYY (XYY syndrome) | 1/900 males | Phenotypically male, fertile. Tendency for delayed language development, cognitive problems, suggested tendency toward aggressive and generally antisocial behavior. |
| 47, XXX (XXX syndrome) | 1/1250 females | Phenotypically female. Some impairment of intellectual development in about two-thirds of cases, suggested increase in risk for schizophrenia, sometimes menstrual disorders and early menopause. |

*Trisomy refers to three of a given chromosome; an individual with trisomy 13 has 47 chromosomes with 3 chromosome 13s. *Data from:* Clark F. Fraser and James J. Nora, *Genetics of Man,* 2nd ed. (Philadelphia: Lea & Febiger, 1986), pp. 31–68.

globin unit, to which are attached four **heme** groups. The latter are small, iron-containing molecular units. The globin unit consists of four chains, two **alpha** and two **beta** chains. Each alpha chain consists of 141 amino acids, and each beta chain consists of 146.

Several other hemoglobins are known. **Hemoglobin A$_2$** is found in small amounts in adult human blood. **Fetal hemoglobin (HbF)** is found in the fetus but usually disappears within the first year after birth. These hemoglobins differ somewhat in their abilities to carry oxygen.

**Abnormal Hemoglobins** Perhaps the best known of all the hemoglobin abnormalities is **hemoglobin S (HbS),** which is responsible for **sickle-cell anemia.** This disease is characterized by periodic sickling episodes during which the red blood cells become distorted and rigid (Figure 3–6). These abnormal cells clog the minute capillaries by forming small clots. Cells located beyond the clots are deprived of oxygen and die. Depending upon the location of the clots, they may cause heart failure, strokes, blindness, kidney damage, and other serious physical injuries.

The genetics of sickle-cell anemia is quite simple. The individual homozygous for HbA is normal, while the person homozygous for HbS has abnormal hemoglobin and the potential of developing the disease sickle-cell anemia. The heterozygous individual has a mixture of normal and abnormal hemoglobin but very rarely has symptoms related to HbS. Such an individual is said to have the **sickle-cell trait.** This is an example of codominance.

Identification of the individual heterozygous for sickle-cell anemia is relatively simple, and many methods now exist, including the use of **electrophoresis.** In this method, a hemoglobin sample is placed in a solution containing atoms that carry electric charges. These, in turn, cause the proteins to develop electric charges of their own. The sample is then placed in an electric field, and the proteins migrate to one of the poles. The speed of travel depends on the weight of the molecule and the strength of the charge. The proteins are stopped before they reach the poles, and the relative position of the proteins can be used to identify them. Figure 3–7 shows the result of such a procedure.

The precise molecular structure of HbS has been worked out. The hemoglobin molecule consists of

**FIGURE 3–6 Normal and Sickled Erythrocytes**
The electron microscope reveals the distinctive shape of (*a*) the normal erythrocyte and (*b*) the sickled erythrocyte.

(*a*)

(*b*)

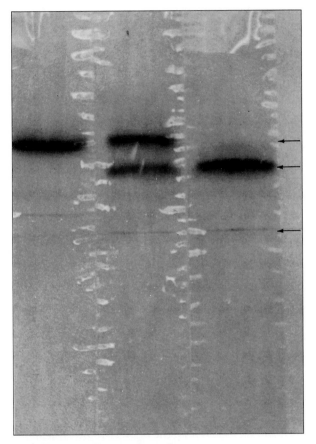

**FIGURE 3–7 Electrophoresis**
Charged hemoglobin molecules, placed initially at the point of origin, migrate differentially in an electric field.

four heme units and a globin. The globin, in turn, consists of a pair of alpha and a pair of beta chains. In HbS the alpha chains are normal; the defect is found in the beta chains. Out of the 146 amino acids in each of the beta chains, the sixth from one end is incorrect: instead of glutamic acid, which is found in HbA, the amino acid valine is present in HbS. The rest of the chain is the same. The codons that code for glutamic acid and valine differ in only one base pair. One code for glutamic acid is CTT, while one code for valine is CAT. There are 146 amino acids in the chain; a mistake in only one, brought about by a single mistake in the code, produces an abnormal hemoglobin with such drastic consequences.

Many other abnormal hemoglobins are known. More than 30 of them are caused by defects on the alpha chain, and more than 50 involve the beta chain. They all result from a substitution of one amino acid for another at some point in the polypeptide chain. The substitution, in turn, results from some alteration of the genetic code, following which the inheritance of the altered code conforms to rules of normal Mendelian inheritance.

### Summary

Blood studies have traditionally been important to anthropology because they provide a relatively easy way to study genetically controlled variability in human populations. They also play an important role in forensic science. A large number of polymorphic blood proteins are found in blood that are inherited in known Mendelian patterns. The best-known system of blood proteins is the ABO system, which consists of three basic blood antigens.

Over 10,000 genes have now been recognized in humans; a majority of these are associated with a genetic abnormality. Phenylketonuria is an example of an abnormality that is inherited as a simple recessive; achondroplastic dwarfism, on the other hand, is inherited as a simple dominant. Not all patterns of inheritance follow these simple Mendelian rules. Many apparent exceptions, in reality complexities, are summarized in Table 3–4.

One distinctive pattern of inheritance occurs when the gene in question is located on the X chromosome. Since males inherit only one X chromosome from their mothers and a Y chromosome from their fathers, genes on the X chromosome are not paired as they are in females. Because of their distinctive inheritance pattern, X-linked traits are relatively easy to identify, such as the example of hemophilia.

A number of abnormalities are not due to single genes but to errors in the number and structure of chromosomes. Such errors, when they involve autosomes, tend to lead to major abnormalities. Individuals with errors in number of sex chromosomes do survive with varying degrees of problems.

Finally, looking at the molecular level, we see that genetic abnormalities can be specific errors in the genetic code. The specific error in the DNA molecule has been worked out for hemoglobin S, which can lead to the disease sickle-cell anemia.

### GENETICS AND HUMAN AFFAIRS

Perhaps no other area of scientific discoveries affects human affairs more profoundly than that of genetics. In the future, the direct manipulation of the genetic material may prevent or cure genetic disease, extend life span, and allow children to be created "to order." Already, advances in genetics have sparked heated debates over the ethics of manipulating the human **genome,** the totality of genes located within a gamete. In the paragraphs below, we will discuss how our knowledge of genetics, and ultimately our ability to manipulate the genetic material, has and might have an impact on human affairs.

### Tay-Sachs Disease: A Case Study

**Tay-Sachs disease** is a metabolic abnormality caused by an abnormal enzyme. In this case, the enzyme is hexaminidase A, which occurs within the brain cells. Absence of the normal enzyme, which occurs in homozygous recessive individuals, permits the buildup of lipid material in the brain cell, leading to cell death. Appearing normal at birth, the child develops symptoms at about six months of age, and death occurs a few years later. Ashkenazi Jews (Jews of central and eastern European origin) show a high carrier rate for Tay-Sachs disease. A **carrier** is a person who possesses a recessive allele in the heterozygous condition.

When a disease occurs at a high frequency in a specific population, an agency may conduct an educational screening program for carriers. Screening is especially effective for Tay-Sachs disease because the test is very accurate and relatively inexpensive. Screening programs have reduced dramatically the incidence of Tay-Sachs disease among Ashkenazi Jews.

How does screening reduce the frequency of a genetic disease? In order for a child to have Tay-Sachs disease, both parents must be carriers. If screening shows that both are carriers, several options are open. The parents may choose to have no children; they may try to adopt children; or if the woman does become pregnant, she may choose to undergo amniocentesis. In the latter case, if it is determined that she carries an affected child, the parents could elect to abort the fetus.

Unfortunately, because most people do not know of Tay-Sachs disease or falsely believe that it is exclusively a Jewish disease, they do not seek testing. As a result, most of the recent cases of Tay-Sachs disease are among non-Jews. The carrier rate for Ashkenazi Jews is about 1 in 30, but it is about 1 in 150 in the general population, which is still an appreciable rate.

**Probabilities of Inheriting a Specific Genetic Disease**   If both members of a couple are carriers of Tay-Sachs disease, what is the probability of their having an affected child? A carrier has one normal allele and one abnormal one, so each parent in our example has the genotype $Tt$. The mating is represented as $Tt \times Tt$. Since the disease is caused by a recessive allele, the affected individual has the genotype $tt$ (homozygous recessive). Because the alleles $T$ and $t$ each have an equal chance of being included in any sex cell, half the father's sperm carries the $t$ allele, as will half the mother's ova.

What is the probability of two carriers producing a Tay-Sachs child? For a child to inherit the disease, he or she must inherit a recessive allele from each parent. The probability of inheriting a $t$ from a specific parent is $\frac{1}{2}$. What about inheriting a $t$ from both parents? The answer to this question is based upon the statistical principle that the probability of the occurrence of two independent, random events is the product of the events' separate probabilities. Inheriting the recessive allele from the father is independent of inheriting the allele from the mother. Thus, the answer to our question is $\frac{1}{2} \times \frac{1}{2}$, or $\frac{1}{4}$.

When we take population data and individual mating probabilities into consideration, we can calculate the overall probability of having a Tay-Sachs child. In the Ashkenazi Jewish population, the incidence of carriers is $\frac{1}{30}$. The chance that two carriers will mate is $\frac{1}{30} \times \frac{1}{30}$, or $\frac{1}{900}$. Since the probability of two carriers' producing a Tay-Sachs child is $\frac{1}{4}$, the probability of a Tay-Sachs child for any people from this population is $\frac{1}{900} \times \frac{1}{4}$, or $\frac{1}{3600}$. Until recently, this was the actual rate of such births; but as mentioned earlier, because of screening programs, the percentage is much lower today.

There are no tests for most genetic abnormalities. However, genetic researchers are making progress in the detection of carriers. As of 1998, 85 to 90 percent of carriers of cystic fibrosis can be detected by testing. One out of every 25 Americans of North European ancestry is a carrier for this recessive genetic disease, the most common fatal genetic disease of young Americans. (The carrier rate for African Americans is $\frac{1}{65}$; Hispanic Americans, $\frac{1}{48}$; and Asian Americans, $\frac{1}{150}$.)

**Genetic Counseling** When a person suspects that he or she or a relative has a genetic disease or abnormality, that person might seek genetic counseling. A **genetic counselor** is someone who advises prospective parents or an affected individual of the probability of having a child with a genetic problem.

Often, a couple has already conceived a child with an abnormality. They go to a genetic counselor to seek information about the probability of their conceiving another child with a genetic defect.

In other cases, members of a specific cultural or ethnic group that is characterized by a high frequency of some inherited disease might wish to know what the chances are that they are carrying the abnormal allele. This is the case for Tay-Sachs disease among Ashkenazi Jews. As further examples, African Americans and certain other people show a high frequency of the blood disorder sickle-cell anemia (Chapter 5); Mediterranean peoples display a high frequency of another blood disorder, beta thalassemia; the general northern European population has a high rate of cystic fibrosis (a respiratory disease); and Inuit ("Eskimos") have a high frequency of kushokwin (a protein disease).

For many diseases, the inheritance pattern is more complex than in Tay-Sachs or cystic fibrosis. In these cases, a genetic counselor must construct a pedigree to determine the probability of a concerned individual's being a carrier or having an allele or alleles for a specific genetic problem. A genetic counselor can work out probabilities only for genetic disorders with a known mode of inheritance, and the validity of a probability calculation is dependent on how much information is known about the client's relatives.

Genetic counseling has grown as a profession along with the enormous growth in the genetic knowledge gained in the last few decades. As more diseases are found to have a genetic basis, and as the inheritance patterns of more genetic diseases are learned, the job of the genetic counselor will become increasingly complex. Society will benefit from the ability to treat or manage more genetic diseases successfully.

**Identifying Problems in a Fetus** Another approach to genetic problems is the identification of abnormalities in the fetus. If the fetus is found to be defective, a therapeutic abortion may be performed if the parents so decide. Abnormalities in the fetus can be detected by ultrasound, amniocentesis, chorionic villus biopsy, and blood test. **Ultrasound** is a diagnostic method that uses sound waves to take a picture, or **sonogram,** of the fetus. With **amniocentesis,** a sample of **amniotic fluid,** the fluid surrounding the fetus, is taken. The cells in the fluid are of fetal origin, and they can be grown in the laboratory and tested for a variety of enzyme deficiencies. The genetic material itself can also be examined for defects. More than 80 metabolic disorders, including Tay-Sachs disease, and several abnormalities of other types, can be detected in this manner.

The method of **chorionic villus biopsy** involves the analysis of the tissue surrounding the developing embryo. It can provide answers faster than is possible with amniocentesis, but this technique is not generally available and its relative safety has not yet been determined. Also, the blood of the mother can be tested for high levels of **alpha-feto protein (AFP),** which enters the mother's blood through the placenta. Excessive amounts of AFP may indicate neural tube defects or other fetal abnormalities.

## The Control of Human Biological Evolution

Techniques for improving the human gene pool are referred to as **eugenic methods.** The simplest eugenic methods involve the control of breeding. **Negative eugenics** is any process whereby some people are prevented from mating. The people involved are usually labeled undesirable by some group or government. The converse is **positive eugenic** methods for encouraging certain people to mate. Adolf Hitler practiced both positive and negative eugenics. He encouraged and sometimes forced people he called "members of the superrace" to mate with each other in breeding camps. He discouraged others from mating in the most extreme way possible—he had them killed. These practices bestowed a sinister connotation upon the word *eugenics.*

Today, new eugenic methods aim first to eliminate deleterious genes and eventually to alter the human genome. Methods now on the horizon go well beyond changing the frequency of alleles in a population by controlling conceptions and matings. The hope of most eugenic researchers is the actual altering of the genetic material to produce a healthier person. The industrial or experimental technology to do this is called **genetic engineering.** A few of the things that may be applied to human genetic engineering in the near future are discussed in this section.

**Regulatory Genes**  First identified in the 1960s, a **regulatory gene** codes for a protein that acts as a switch for a structural gene or another regulatory gene. A structural gene codes for specific polypeptide chains that make up protein molecules such as insulin. A regulatory gene either allows the second gene to express itself or shuts it down. So, for example, the gene that codes for insulin can be turned on or off by its regulatory gene.

Genetic diseases that result from the faulty action of a regulatory gene may be managed by treatment that leads to either turning the gene on or off. As we discover what chemicals affect what genes, regulation may be controlled. For instance, it is believed that aging is controlled by regulatory genes and that the aging process could be arrested if the cytoplasmic products that influence the aging regulatory genes could be controlled.

**Restriction Enzymes**  In 1973, scientists discovered that certain types of enzymes, called **restriction enzymes,** could be used to "cut" the DNA at specific sites. This has enabled scientists to cut out specific genes, which can then be spliced into a different organism. For instance, the human gene for insulin has been spliced into the genetic system of a bacterium. The resulting bacterial progeny produced human insulin, which is marketed under the name "Humulin."

**Artificial Genes**  In 1976, it was announced that a completely **artificial gene,** used to replace a defective gene in a virus, had been synthesized. Will we be able to manufacture genes that will make us have more endurance, be resistant to disease, and be more intelligent? Perhaps these "designer genes" will be the wave of the future.

**Cloning**  "Humulin" was made possible, in part, by cloning. **Cloning** is the process of producing a group of genes, cells, or whole organisms that have the same genetic constitution. Once the human gene for insulin was introduced into bacteria by re-

combinant DNA techniques, repeated mitosis in the bacteria continued to produce the same gene over and over again. The gene originated from a body (somatic) cell, not from a sex cell.

Whole organisms can be cloned. In fact, a type of cloning has been done with plants for years. In July 1996, the first mammal, a lamb named Dolly, was cloned from adult body cells. In 1998, Dolly gave birth to a normal noncloned offspring. Such clones are not necessarily exact duplicates of the donor. They do possess the exact same genotype, but environmental factors both before and after birth are responsible for some variation. Perhaps it is only a matter of time until humans are cloned.

**Gene Therapy**  Gene therapy involves detecting a genetic defect and correcting it by replacing the DNA sequence that causes the defect with the correct DNA sequence. The first successful gene therapy was performed in 1990. White blood cells of a four-year-old girl suffering from ADA deficiency, an immune deficiency disease, were modified with normal DNA and transfused back into her. By 1998, scientists were discussing altering the genome of sex cells of an individual or of the fertilized ovum.

**Consequences of Genetic Engineering**  Any modification of human genetic material is controversial. Some ethical implications of genetic engineering are discussed in Box 3–2. Here, we will mention two possible biological problems with genetic engineering. The first is the reduction of variability within a population.

Imagine a situation where, by using eugenic means, we could eliminate the allele for a recessive genetic disease through detection of heterozygotes. This is a fine goal. However, as we will discuss in detail in Chapter 5, people who are heterozygous for the sickle-cell allele have considerable protection from malaria. Other heterozygous genotypes seem to provide protection from other diseases, even if the homozygous recessive condition causes severe illness or death. The paradox is that by eliminating the disease, you might be eliminating protection from some other factor.

A second possible biological negative consequence is the fact that a gene can have more than one effect on the phenotype. An engineered change of one gene may have effects on the individual far

## Genetics and Insurance: An Ethical Dilemma

There are numerous ethical concerns that are being ushered into our consciousness due to our growing knowledge of human genetics. Some of those concerns revolve around the question of who will be able to take advantage of the medical techniques that result from this knowledge. For instance, there is hope that in the future more and more genetic diseases will be treated or even cured. Yet in twenty-first-century America, millions of people do not have health insurance and cannot afford basic medical care. In the future, will only the wealthy profit from what might be very expensive management of genetic diseases?

Another concern is that of privacy. We are developing the ability to predict for which diseases a person may be at risk in his or her lifetime. If this information is available to insurance companies, health and life insurance might be denied or be very expensive. Knowing that insurance might be denied, people might avoid having tests to determine if they are at risk for genetic diseases or genetically influenced conditions. In turn, those people who do not have these tests done may not be able to take advantage of medical treatments in time to save their lives. In 1998, these issues were discussed by a U.S. Senate Committee. The government continues to struggle with the issue of who has the right to know a person's potential medical risks.

beyond those that are intended, and some of those effects might be negative.

Although our knowledge of genetics has increased geometrically since the beginning of the twentieth century, there is still much that we do not know. One of the things about which we know little is the multiple effects of genes and the effect of genes on each other.

### Summary

Genetics may be one of the most important concerns of people in the twenty-first century. In the previous century, we learned about the mode of inheritance of many recessive and dominant genetic abnormalities as well as ones with more complex patterns of inheritance. The field of genetic counseling has grown as our knowledge of human genetics has expanded.

Already geneticists can, in a limited way, manipulate the human genome. In the future, human cloning, gene therapy, and other forms of genetic engineering may become common practices to cure genetic abnormalities, create children with specific characteristics, and allow couples to have special types of children, such as clones of themselves. Political, ethical, philosophical, and biological concerns about eugenics will no doubt fill the pages of newspapers, magazines, and journals for decades to come.

## ADVANCES IN THE MOLECULAR STUDY OF GENETICS

The advent of high-tech methods of analyzing nucleic acids has allowed for rapid and accurate recording of the genetic code. This has led to a better understanding of what a gene is as well as providing insights into evolutionary relationships between species and relationships among members of the same species.

### What Is a Gene?

We can examine this question in the light of studies of the structure and function of the hereditary material, the DNA molecule. The concept of the gene was originally developed as part of a model to explain the mechanisms of heredity when the actual physical and chemical nature of the hereditary material was unknown.

A gene is a biological unit of inheritance; it is a section of DNA that has a specific function. That function could be the coding of a particular protein, a polypeptide chain; or it could be a regulatory function, that is, controlling of the activity of other genes. In the first situation, the 438 nucleotides that code for the structure of the hemoglobin beta chain can be thought of as a gene.

**Linkage Maps** Because of the distinctive inheritance pattern of X-linked traits, geneticists have identified many genes that reside on the X chromosome. Hemophilia is perhaps the best known of these X-linked traits. Other genes known to be on the X chromosome include red-green color blindness, congenital night blindness, Xg blood type, vitamin D–resistant rickets, glucose-6-phosphate dehydrogenase deficiency, and one form of muscular dystrophy.

In the 1950s, geneticists identified the first human autosomal genes that are associated on the same chromosome. Such sets of genes are called

**linkage groups.** Genes located close together on the same chromosome tend to be inherited together since crossing-over seldom occurs between them. Genes located far apart on large chromosomes, however, behave as if they were on separate chromosomes, since crossing-over occurs frequently between them. Thus they recombine according to the principle of independent assortment.

Crossing-over data can be used to determine the linear order of genes in a linkage group. Since the frequency of crossing-over is proportional to the distance between genes on a chromatid, genes that are farther apart will cross over more frequently.

Let us assume that there are three genes, *A, B,* and *C,* linked on the same chromosome. *A* and *B* cross over in 2 percent of cell divisions, while *B* and *C* cross over 8 percent of the time. Therefore, *B* and *C* are farther apart from each other than are *A* and *B*. We can predict that *A* and *C* will cross over either 6 or 10 percent of the time (8 − 2 or 8 + 2). This method gives the linear order of genes on a chromosome (Figure 3–8). The relative distance between individual genes is measured in **centiMorgans (cM),** named after Thomas Hunt Morgan (1866–1945), a pioneer in the study of genetics who demonstrated that genes are arranged on chromosomes in a fixed linear order. One centiMorgan represents a crossing-over rate of 1 percent.

**FIGURE 3–8  Calculating Gene Distances**
This diagram shows possible arrangements of three genes on a chromosome. In this example, genes *A* and *C* cross over in 2 percent of the cell divisions, and genes *B* and *C* cross over 8 percent of the time. In order to learn whether *A* or *B* is first in this sequence of three genes, the number of cross-overs between *A* and *C* must be determined. If *A* and *C* cross over 10 percent of the time (8% + 2%), the gene sequence would then be *A-B-C* (a). If *A* and *C* cross over 6 percent of the time (8% − 2%), the gene sequence would be *B-A-C* (b).

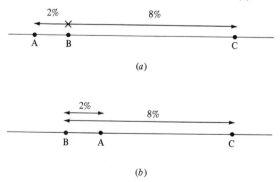

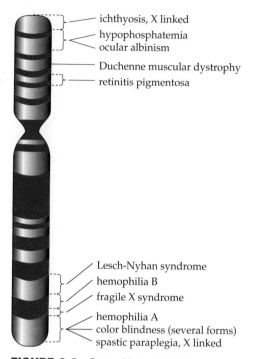

**FIGURE 3–9  Gene Map of X Chromosome**

The next step is to associate linkage groups with specific chromosomes. Small chromosomal aberrations are often associated with unusual inheritance patterns. These can be used to determine the location of specific autosomes on a specific chromosome. Today we know that cystic fibrosis is located on chromosome 7, sickle-cell anemia on chromosome 11, phenylketonuria on chromosome 12, and Tay-Sachs disease on chromosome 15.

**Sequencing DNA and Gene Mapping**  The next stage is the development of a physical map. A physical map includes specific features of the chromosome and the banding patterns that develop when the chromosome is treated with certain dyes. These features are then associated with specific genes and DNA sequences called gene markers. The first physical maps were published in 1992. By 1993, simple physical maps were produced for all human chromosomes. Figure 3–9 is a map of the X chromosome.

**The Human Genome**

We are living in an age of communication. Through computers and other advanced technologies, information moves around the world at the speed of light, complex problems are analyzed in seconds instead of lifetimes, and vital information is readily available to a wide audience. Yet as data moves through wires, optic fibers, or as electromagnetic waves through the atmosphere, we must remember that we are basically dealing with very simple codes, such as the presence or absence of an electric charge.

The genetic material, DNA, communicates through a code. Computer scientists as well as biologists appreciate the elegance of the DNA code. Some futurists envision computer storage devices based on codes at the molecular level. The words in this text, maintained on a hard disk in the authors' office, might some day be actually coded in the computer of the future by artificial DNA or a molecule like it.

Geneticists today are actively studying the genetic code in order to understand how the code works. In 1977, researchers developed the first efficient methodology for determining the sequence of nucleotides or base pairs in a strand of DNA. Almost immediately, biologists began to ponder the possibility of determining the base pair sequence for all human genes. Although in 1977 such a dream appeared technologically light years away, by the second half of the 1980s, molecular biologists were beginning to think that such a project was feasible.

It is estimated that the entire human genome contains about three billion base pairs or nucleotides. In the mid-1980s, biologists estimated that one technician could sequence 100,000 base pairs a year, which meant that it would take 30,000 person-years to sequence the entire human genome. The cost was established at $3 billion. Out of this early interest came the Human Genome Project. In 1988, the National Center for Human Genome Research was established by the National Institutes of Health. The first director, from 1988 through 1992, was James Watson, who, with Francis Crick, had first determined the structure of DNA in 1953. The project formally began in 1990 and was seen as a 15-year project, although new technologies are speeding up the process. Other governments have established similar programs that work cooperatively with the American effort.

The Human Genome Project is not without controversy. Some people ask if we should undertake the task of mapping the human genome. What would be the consequences? A complete human gene map would lead to improved diagnosis of hereditary diseases and the development of new drugs for genetic abnormalities. The mapping of the human genome could also lead to ethical dilemmas and abuses. Whose genome should be taken as prototypically human? Would only the rich be able to take advantage of the health benefits gained

## BOX 3-3

# DNA in the News

In the 1880s, Sir Francis Galton, cousin of Charles Darwin, reported that no two people could have exactly the same fingerprint pattern. Since that time, the use of fingerprint analysis has played a central role in criminal investigation. A century later, another powerful identification tool was developed—DNA fingerprinting. DNA fingerprinting played a major role during the 1995 O. J. Simpson trial.

This method relies on the analysis of the genetic material. Except for identical twins, each person's genetic code is unique. DNA analysis can be done using blood, skin, hair, saliva, or semen

that is left at a crime scene. In this way, an individual can either be identified or excluded as the culprit.

The method involves the use of enzymes to break up the DNA recovered at the crime scene and the DNA obtained from the suspect. The DNA fragments are then separated in an electric field producing a specific pattern. These patterns are the "fingerprints" that can then be compared.

The area of controversy in the courtroom today revolves around the probability that any particular fingerprint is unique. Since forensic scientists do not

analyze the entire genome of an individual, it is theoretically possible for two people to show the same pattern. The probability of this occurring with today's methods varies from 1 in 100,000 to 1 in 100 million. More complex methods being developed will reduce this probability to about zero.

*Sources:* K. C. McElfresh, D. Vining-Forde, and I. Balazs, "DNA-Based Identity Testing in Forensic Science," *BioScience* 43 (1993), pp. 149–157; R. Nowak, "Forensic DNA Goes to Court with O. J.," *Science* 265 (1994), pp. 1352–1354.

BOX 3-4

## Landmarks in Genetics: The DNA Sequence of an Animal Genome Is Decoded

In 1900, the modern age of genetics began with the rediscovery of Mendel's principles of segregation and independent assortment. Ninety-eight years later, essentially the entire genetic code of an animal was decoded for the first time. Although few humans feel akin to that animal, the methods used to determine its genetic code have proven useful to the Human Genome Project. The animal is *Caenorhabditis elegans,* one of a group of small invertebrates known as nematodes or roundworms. Its DNA sequence is made up of about 97 million base pairs representing about 19,000 genes. More than 40 percent of the proteins coded by these genes match known genes in other organisms.

Just as Mendel's discovery of the basic principles of genetics was the jumping off point for the understanding of more complex principles of genetics, the decoding of the DNA sequence in *C. elegans* is providing new strategies useful in other genome projects. It is also providing a method of comparison that will help gauge what genes are common to all or most organisms. This landmark will help usher in a new world of human genetic engineering, many of the applications of which can only be imagined at this time.

*Source:* The *C. elegans* Sequencing Consortium, "Genome Sequence of the Nematode *C. elegans:* A Platform for Investigating Biology," *Science* 282 (1998), pp. 2012–2017.

from the new technology? And who would control the technology? Control of the human genome could lead to the engineering of specific types of humans and it could create an elitist society. Yet work continues on the project with the proponents believing that the benefits of its success will far outweigh any problems it creates.

**The Human Genome Diversity Project**   The first-year medical student is often pictured bent over a human cadaver learning the size, shape, location, and name of all parts of the human body. Today, human anatomy is entering the computer age. One recent project involves taking cadavers of anatomically average individuals, one male and one female, and cutting the cadaver into thin sections. The sections are then scanned into a computer. Using these data, the computer can then present a cross section of the human body at any level, and can electronically put together the data to represent three-dimensional images for study.

If the software developers are taking a single human male and a single human female as the model for the computer images, how is the selection being made? What is the age of the cadavers selected? What is their height and weight? What is their "race"? In other words, what do we mean by "typical" or "average"?

The same issue has arisen in the Human Genome Project. The investigators are working out the genetic code of the human genome. However, since every individual, except for identical twins, is different genetically, whose code will be selected as the standard? Many geneticists are concerned that the genome being analyzed is essentially "Caucasian."

Geneticist Luca Cavalli-Sforza and his colleagues have been instrumental in the development of the Human Genome Diversity Project. They plan to collect samples of blood, hair, and saliva from which DNA can be extracted for study. The samples are to be collected from anonymous donors in different populations throughout the world. Initially, a small series of DNA sequences will be determined for these DNA samples to study the variation that occurs among different human populations. These data will then be used for studies of the relationships among human groups. The data will also be used to test how much individuals from different populations differ from the sequence being uncovered by the Human Genome Project.

The proposed project has not been met with enthusiasm by all. Some people see the taking of blood samples as desecrating the body. Others believe that these genetic studies will support negative eugenic studies. The major concern is that these studies may lead to new definitions of race based on genetic data and that these studies are basically racist. The researchers are quick to point out, however, that the project is a weapon against racism. Since the major work on the human genome is using "Caucasian" genes, the diverse DNA in the database will provide a means of including all peoples in the benefits that the genome project will bring. In addition, anthropologists also note that genetic data will clearly demonstrate the nonexistence of races in the human species, as we will see in Chapter 17.

## Summary

Today, a gene is seen as a section of DNA that has a specific function, such as the coding of a particular protein. Geneticists have been able to identify the location of specific genes on specific chromosomes. Such mapping has been accomplished through linkage studies and identification of specific DNA sequences with specific genes.

One of the most ambitious scientific ventures of the past decade is the Human Genome Project, which is an attempt to map the entire human genome. On one hand, such knowledge is seen as crucial for research on genetic disease. On the other hand, the project has its critics who point to numerous ways that the information obtained could be used in unethical and elitist ways. One of these concerns is that the genome being documented essentially represents populations derived from Europe. The Human Genome Diversity Project is attempting to remedy this by collecting DNA samples from populations throughout the world.

## STUDY QUESTIONS

1. Why are studies of the genetics of blood types of more use to anthropologists than studies of IQ or skin color?
2. What is meant by the term *multiple alleles*?
3. How does Y-linked and X-linked inheritance differ from autosomal inheritance?
4. What is the difference between phenotypic sex, chromosomal sex, and genetic sex?
5. What is a common error of meiosis and to what type of problems does this error lead?
6. In what ways can human genetics be purposefully altered? What might be possible in the future?
7. The book discusses two possible negative effects of eugenics. What are they? Can you think of other possible negatives of eugenics? What are the positive aspects of eugenics?
8. What is the Human Genome Project? What methods do the scientists working on this project use to accomplish their goals?
9. What is the Human Genome Diversity Project? What are the goals of the scientists working on this project? What are the concerns about the project?

## SUGGESTED READINGS

Lewin, B. *Genes,* 6th ed. Oxford: Oxford University Press, 1997. This is a popular introductory text on general genetics. It presents an encyclopedic treatment of genetics and, as such, is an excellent reference book.

Read, A. P., and T. Strachen. *Human Molecular Genetics.* New York: John Wiley, 1997. This text covers molecular genetics up to the recent developments in eugenics and the Human Genome Project.

Silver, L. M. *Remaking Eden: Cloning and Beyond in a Brave New World.* New York: Avon/Weidenfeld and Nicoson, 1998. This book tells of what can currently be done with genetic engineering and what might be possible in the twenty-first century. It also discusses the ethical, political, and practical concerns people have about genetic engineering.

Watson, J. D., et al. *Molecular Biology of the Gene,* 4th ed. Menlo Park, Calif.: Benjamin/Cummings, 1987. This two-volume set, written by five researchers and teachers, including one of the discoverers of the structure of DNA, gives a detailed discussion of DNA and gene structure.

## SUGGESTED WEB SITES

March of Dimes Fact Sheets (information on various birth defects and genetics):
http://www.noah.cuny.edu/pregnancy/pregnancy.html#BIRTH DEFECTS AND GENETICS
Tay-Sachs Information and Links:
http://www.flmed.net/reference_library/diseases/taysachs.htm
Understanding Gene Testing (U.S. Department of Health and Human Services Information on genetic diseases and testing):
http://www.gene.com/ae/AE/AEPC/NIH/index.html

Additional web sites are listed in the Workbook that accompanies this text.

## CHAPTER 4

# Population Genetics

*The object is to combine certain ideas derived from a consideration of . . . a population of organisms, with the concepts of the factorial scheme of inheritance, so as to state the principle of Natural Selection in the form of a rigorous mathematical theorem.*[1]
—R. A. Fisher (1890–1962)

In 1930, R. A. Fisher published a book that evaluated Darwin's theory in terms of mathematics and statistics. In *The Genetical Theory of Natural Selection,* Fisher described equations that showed how genetic diversity within populations allows more possibilities for adapting to environments.

Up to this point, we have been mainly concerned with the mechanisms of heredity in the individual and in family groups. Evolution, however, occurs in reproductive populations. This chapter focuses on the dynamics of populations

---

[1]R. A. Fisher, *The Genetical Theory of Natural Selection* (Oxford: Clarendon Press, 1930).

and various mathematical principles that measure genetic changes in populations.

## A MODEL OF POPULATION GENETICS

The individual is not the unit of evolution, although a person does change over time. An individual gets taller and heavier, and perhaps his or her hair changes color; other changes occur that are variously labeled "growth," "development," and "decline." Yet although an individual today is not the same individual he or she will be tomorrow, that person is not evolving. Likewise, evolution is not a case of people producing offspring different from themselves. For no two individuals, whether contemporaries or living at different times or whether related or unrelated, are exactly alike. Variation is not evolution.

### Populations

The unit of evolution is the **reproductive population.** The reproductive population can be defined as a group of organisms potentially capable of successful reproduction.

Successful reproduction requires sexual behavior culminating in copulation, fertilization, normal development of the fetus, and production of offspring that are normal and healthy and capable of reproducing in turn. A number of conditions, called **reproductive isolating mechanisms,** can prevent closely related populations from exchanging genes by preventing successful reproduction. One way in which this occurs is if the sexual behavior of the male, such as the mating dance of birds, fails to stimulate the female of a closely related population. Several types of reproductive isolating mechanisms are discussed in Chapter 5.

Of course, successful reproduction of a population requires a rate of reproduction sufficient to sustain the population. As we saw in Chapter 1, Thomas R. Malthus pointed out that although a population has the potential for very rapid growth, environmental factors can severely limit the number of individuals that survive. The number of individuals produced each generation must be great enough to compensate for deaths due to accident, predation, disease, and so on. However, the rate of reproduction cannot be so great that the population will increase to the point at which it can no longer

be supported by its food sources or other elements in the environment. In other words, a successful reproductive rate is one that maintains a balance between population size and the potentials and limitations of the environment.

The largest reproductive population is the **species.** The members of a species are potentially capable of successful reproduction among themselves but not with members of other species. Species can be broken down into smaller reproductive populations, which are to some degree and often temporarily isolated from one another.

**Phenotype of a Population**    Just as one can speak of the phenotype of an individual, one can also speak of the phenotype of a population. Since a population is made up of varied individuals, such a description must be handled statistically. For example, one can calculate the average stature for a population and the variation from that average. It is also possible to calculate the percentage of blood-type O, blue eyes, red hair, and so on, and emerge with a statistical profile.

As stated earlier, no two individuals are ever alike; the possible combinations of alleles are staggering. Nevertheless, the frequency of alleles in a population may remain relatively constant over many generations. What we have are individuals being formed out of a pool of genes that can be combined in an almost infinite number of ways. New combinations do not necessarily change the frequencies of any allele in the next generation (Figure 4–1).

**Genotype of a Population**    The sum of all alleles carried by the members of a population is known as the **gene pool.** Since a population is made up of many individuals, each represented by a unique genotype, a gene pool is described in statistical terms. The frequency of alleles in the gene pool can be calculated with formulas that will be discussed in a moment. Since each body cell has the same genetic components, each individual can be thought of as contributing one of those cells to the gene pool. From these cells, the genes can be extracted and tallied.

For example, if the alleles for PTC tasting in a population are tallied, the result may be that 41.3 percent of them are dominant (*T*) and 58.7 percent

Gene pools                    Genotypes

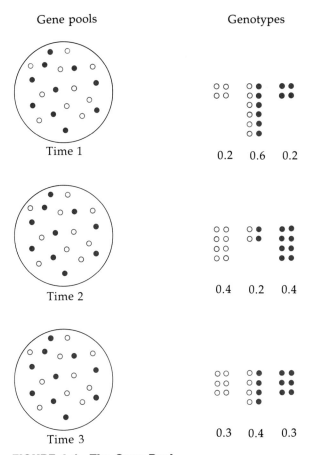

Time 1                    0.2    0.6    0.2

Time 2                    0.4    0.2    0.4

Time 3                    0.3    0.4    0.3

**FIGURE 4–1   The Gene Pool**
Even though the allele frequencies remain constant, the genotype frequencies can differ through time.

are recessive (*t*). Further examination may reveal that 17.1 percent of the genotypes that emerge from the gene pool of PTC alleles are homozygous dominant, whereas 48.4 percent are heterozygous and 34.5 percent are homozygous recessive. A complete statistical description of the genotype of a population would require that we know the frequency of every allele in the gene pool.

## Genetic Equilibrium

Before we discuss the mechanisms of evolution, evolution must first be defined in terms of populations. **Evolution** can be defined as a change in the gene pool of a population. So, for example, if the frequency of the allele *T* changes from 41.3 percent to 42.1 percent, we can say that the population has evolved.

A population is evolving if the frequencies of its alleles are changing. It is not evolving if these frequencies remain constant, a situation termed **genetic equilibrium.** Since several factors can bring about frequency changes, it is best to begin with a consideration of genetic equilibrium and then to follow with a separate consideration of each factor that brings about change.

**A Model of Genetic Equilibrium**   In building a model of genetic equilibrium, we can simplify things by considering a hypothetical gene. We will assume that this gene occurs as two alleles, *A* and *a*, each with a frequency of ½. The symbol *f* will be used to indicate "relative frequency of." Therefore, we can write our example as follows: $f(A) = ½$ and $f(a) = ½$. If these are the only alleles for this gene, the relative frequencies must add up to 1, or unity. This gives us the formula:

$$f(A) + f(a) = ½ + ½ = 1$$

This formula is an example of a model that, when the equation equals 1, reflects a hypothetical situation of no change or genetic equilibrium in a population from one generation to the next. However, the fact that populations *do* change, that is, the equation does not equal 1, is what makes this model important. By being able to specify under what conditions a static situation would exist, we can see, measure, and analyze change.

Certain conditions must be assumed for a population to remain in genetic equilibrium. Mutation must not be taking place. The population must be infinitely large, so change does not occur by chance. Individuals from a neighboring population must not introduce alleles into the population. Mating must take place at random, that is, without any design or propensity of one kind for another. These matings must be equally fertile; that is, they must produce the same number of viable offspring. In other words, natural selection must not be occurring. Deviation from equilibrium shows that one or a combination of these conditions is not being met.

**Doing the Math**   If the relative frequencies of the alleles are each ½, what are the relative frequencies of the different individual genotypes? As we saw in the last chapter, the probability of two independent events both occurring is the product of their separate probabilities. Therefore, if $f(A) = \frac{1}{2}$, it follows that $f(AA) = \frac{1}{2} \times \frac{1}{2} = \frac{1}{4}$. So, one-fourth of the population is homozygous dominant.

Similarly, $f(Aa) = 2 \times \frac{1}{2} \times \frac{1}{2} = \frac{1}{2}$. Why the number 2? Because we are including two separate cases, $Aa$ and $aA$. While the origin of the alleles differs in each, the genotype is the same. We must then add the two cases together. Therefore, one-half the population is heterozygous. Finally, $f(aa) = \frac{1}{2} \times \frac{1}{2} = \frac{1}{4}$; one-fourth of the population is homozygous recessive.

Now suppose the individuals within this population mate at random. The possible matings are $AA \times AA$, $AA \times Aa$, $AA \times aa$, $Aa \times Aa$, $Aa \times aa$, and $aa \times aa$. Three of the six matings can be accomplished in two ways; for example, $AA \times Aa$ could also be $Aa \times AA$. To simplify matters in each of these three cases, the two situations will be combined (added) as one mating.

How frequent is each of the mating types? To find out, one multiplies the frequencies of each genotype. So, for example, the frequency of the first type, $AA \times AA$, is $\frac{1}{4} \times \frac{1}{4} = \frac{1}{16}$. In the case in which mating types can be accomplished in two ways, the separate frequencies must be added together. This is why the number 2 must be included. The relative frequencies of the mating types are shown in Table 4–1; note that the frequencies add up to 1.

Since we are interested in seeing how the relative frequencies of the alleles change between generations, the next step is to calculate the frequency of offspring produced. Table 4–2 presents a series of calculations showing the contribution of each mating type to the next generation. The first case, $AA \times AA$, occurs one-sixteenth of the time and

therefore produces one-sixteenth of all the offspring. Since all these offspring are $AA$, we can say that this mating type contributes $\frac{1}{16}$ $AA$ children to the next generation, as shown in the $AA$ column in Table 4–2.

The second case, $AA \times Aa$, accounts for one-fourth of all matings and therefore this mating type produces one-fourth of all the offspring. Of these offspring, one-half are $AA$ and one-half are $Aa$. Since $\frac{1}{2}$ of $\frac{1}{4}$ is $\frac{1}{8}$, $\frac{1}{8}$ is placed in the $AA$ column and $\frac{1}{8}$ in the $Aa$ column. The same procedure is followed for calculating the contributions of the other mating types.

Next, we add up the numbers in each column. We see that one-fourth of the total offspring are $AA$, one-half $Aa$, and one-fourth $aa$. In other words, the relative frequencies of the varying genotypes have remained unchanged from the previous generation. The population is therefore in genetic equilibrium.

**The Hardy-Weinberg Equilibrium**   In the discussion above, we simplified matters by taking a simple example. However, in the real world, not all pairs of alleles exist in the frequencies of $\frac{1}{2}$ and $\frac{1}{2}$. Now we want to generalize the calculations to fit all possible allele frequencies.

The calculations for genetic equilibrium were first made independently by Godfrey Hardy and Wilhelm Weinberg in 1908 and are known as the **Hardy-Weinberg equilibrium.** This equilibrium

## TABLE 4–1

### FREQUENCIES OF MATING TYPES

| Mating type | Frequency |
|---|---|
| $AA \times AA$ | $\frac{1}{4} \times \frac{1}{4} = \frac{1}{16}$ |
| $AA \times Aa$ | $2 \times \frac{1}{4} \times \frac{1}{2} = \frac{1}{4}$ |
| $AA \times aa$ | $2 \times \frac{1}{4} \times \frac{1}{4} = \frac{1}{8}$ |
| $Aa \times Aa$ | $\frac{1}{2} \times \frac{1}{2} = \frac{1}{4}$ |
| $Aa \times aa$ | $2 \times \frac{1}{2} \times \frac{1}{4} = \frac{1}{4}$ |
| $aa \times aa$ | $\frac{1}{4} \times \frac{1}{4} = \frac{1}{16}$ |
| Total | 1 |

## TABLE 4–2

### CONTRIBUTIONS OF MATING TYPES TO THE NEXT GENERATION

| Mating type | Frequency | Offspring | | |
|---|---|---|---|---|
| | | AA | Aa | aa |
| $AA \times AA$ | $\frac{1}{16}$ | $\frac{1}{16}$ | | |
| $AA \times Aa$ | $\frac{1}{4}$ | $\frac{1}{8}$ | $\frac{1}{8}$ | |
| $AA \times aa$ | $\frac{1}{8}$ | | $\frac{1}{8}$ | |
| $Aa \times Aa$ | $\frac{1}{4}$ | $\frac{1}{16}$ | $\frac{1}{8}$ | $\frac{1}{16}$ |
| $Aa \times aa$ | $\frac{1}{4}$ | | $\frac{1}{8}$ | $\frac{1}{8}$ |
| $aa \times aa$ | $\frac{1}{16}$ | | | $\frac{1}{16}$ |
| Total | | $\frac{1}{4}$ | $\frac{1}{2}$ | $\frac{1}{4}$ |

## TABLE 4-3

### ALGEBRAIC DERIVATION OF HARDY-WEINBERG EQUILIBRIUM

| Allele | Frequency | Genotype | Frequency of genotype in population |
|---|---|---|---|
| $A$ | $p$ | $AA$ | $p^2$ |
| $a$ | $q$ | $Aa$ | $2pq$ |
|  |  | $aa$ | $q^2$ |

#### Offspring resulting from random matings

| Parents | Frequency of mating types | Frequency of offspring | | |
|---|---|---|---|---|
|  |  | $AA$ | $Aa$ | $aa$ |
| $AA \times AA$ | $p^2 \times p^2 = p^4$ | $p^4$ | — | — |
| $AA \times Aa$ | $2 \times p^2 \times 2pq = 4p^3q$ | $2p^3q$ | $2p^3q$ | — |
| $AA \times aa$ | $2 \times p^2 \times q^2 = 2p^2q^2$ | — | $2p^2q^2$ | — |
| $Aa \times Aa$ | $2pq \times 2pq = 4p^2q^2$ | $p^2q^2$ | $2p^2q^2$ | $p^2q^2$ |
| $Aa \times aa$ | $2 \times 2pq \times q^2 = 4pq^3$ | — | $2pq^3$ | $2pq^3$ |
| $aa \times aa$ | $q^2 \times q^2 = q^4$ | — | — | $q^4$ |

$$f(AA) = p^4 + 2p^3q + p^2q^2 = p^2(p^2 + 2pq + q^2) = p^2(1) = p^2$$
$$f(Aa) = 2p^3q + 2p^2q^2 + 2p^2q^2 + 2pq^3 = 2pq(p^2 + pq + pq + q^2) = 2pq(1) = 2pq$$
$$f(aa) = p^2q^2 + 2pq^3 + q^4 = q^2(p^2 + 2pq + q^2) = q^2(1) = q^2$$

can be developed algebraically (Table 4–3). This results in the following general formula for the Hardy-Weinberg equilibrium:

$$p^2 + 2pq + q^2 = 1$$

In this formula, $p = f(A)$ and $q = f(a)$. Therefore, $f(AA) = p^2$, $f(Aa) = 2pq$, and $f(aa) = q^2$.

### Using the Genetic-Equilibrium Model

The assumptions necessary for this formula have already been listed: no mutation, infinite population size, no introduction of genes from neighboring populations, random mating, and equal fertility. Since these conditions can never hold true for any population, the Hardy-Weinberg formula defines a model that can be used to test hypotheses about gene pools and the evolutionary forces that work on them.

While no populations are actually in genetic equilibrium, some do come close. For the sake of illustration, we will first look at a hypothetical population that is large; we will focus on a trait that does not play a role in mate selection and does not influence fertility or survival to any known degree. That trait is PTC tasting, which was discussed in Chapter 2.

**PTC Tasting** In taking a random survey of a hypothetical population, we find that out of 1000 individuals tested, 640 are tasters and 360 are nontasters. What are the relative frequencies of the two alleles, and how many tasters are carriers of the recessive allele?

In our population, 360 out of 1000 individuals, or 36 percent, are nontasters, and hence homozygous recessive or $tt$. We can set up the equation $f(tt) \times q^2 = 0.36$, where $q^2$ is the proportion of homozygous recessive individuals and 0.36 is the decimal equivalent of $^{360}/_{1000}$. If $q^2 = 0.36$, then $q = 0.6$ (0.6 being the square root of 0.36). If $q = 0.6$, then $p$ must equal 0.4 (since $p + q = 1$). Therefore, 40 percent of the alleles in the gene pool are dominant $T$, while 60 percent are the recessive $t$.

The numbers obtained through our calculations may be surprising at first. The majority of individuals are tasters, yet the majority of alleles are for nontasting. This means that most of the recessive alleles are found in the heterozygous individuals and are therefore not expressed in the phenotype.

What proportion of the population consists of heterozygous tasters (carriers)? The answer is $2pq$, or 48 percent ($2 \times 0.4 \times 0.6$). Only 16 percent ($p^2 = 0.4 \times 0.4$) are homozygous dominant tasters, and 36 percent are nontasters.

**Phenylketonuria** In England, approximately 1 out of every 40,000 children is born with the metabolic abnormality PKU.[2] Several questions may be asked: How frequent is the defective allele in the gene pool? What is the probability that an individual in the population will be a carrier? What is the probability that two normal individuals mating at random will have a child with PKU?

This example is not a case of genetic equilibrium, since the assumptions for genetic equilibrium are not being met. For example, until very recently, children with PKU did not grow up and reproduce. However, we can assume genetic equilibrium and use the Hardy-Weinberg formula to estimate the answers to these questions.

If the rate of abnormality is 1 child out of 40,000, the relative frequency of the trait is $\frac{1}{40,000}$, or 0.000025 (0.0025 percent). Therefore, $f(kk) = q^2 = 0.000025$, so $q = 0.005$. This means that 0.5 percent of the gene pool is $k$, while 99.5 percent ($p = 0.995$) is the normal allele $K$.

What is the probability of being a carrier? The answer is $2pq$, which equals 0.00995 ($2 \times 0.995 \times 0.005$), which is rounded off to 0.01. Therefore, approximately 1 percent of the members of the population are carriers, which is 1 out of 100 individuals. This is a large number, especially when we realize that only 1 out of 40,000 actually has the disease.

What is the probability that two persons mating at random will have a PKU child? The probability of being a carrier is 0.01, so the probability of two persons being carriers is $0.01 \times 0.01$, or 0.0001. If both are carriers, one out of every four of their children is expected to have the defect. When 0.0001 (the probability that both will be carriers) is multiplied by $\frac{1}{4}$ (the probability that two carriers will have a PKU child), the answer is 0.000025, or $\frac{1}{40,000}$.

**Genetic Load** It is apparent from the PKU example that populations contain reservoirs of deleterious alleles hidden in the heterozygous condition. In fact, estimates show that every person is carrying an average of three to five recessive alleles that in a homozygous condition would lead to death or

disablement. The term **genetic load** refers to the totality of recessive **lethal** alleles in a population; these are alleles that bring about death before reproductive age. The expression of this genetic load is responsible for the presence of many harmful genetic abnormalities in human populations.

**Demonstrating Genetic Equilibrium** The Hardy-Weinberg formula can also be used to show if a population is in genetic equilibrium with respect to a particular trait. With this information, we can gain some idea of the impact of the forces of evolutionary change upon the population. We can take as an example a hypothetical population with the following genotypic frequencies: $f(AA) = 0.34$, $f(Aa) = 0.46$, and $f(aa) = 0.20$. To find the frequency of $A$, we add the frequency of the $AA$ individuals, who contribute only $A$ alleles to the gene pool, and one-half the frequency of the $Aa$ individuals, since only one-half of their alleles are $A$. Therefore, $f(A) = p = f(AA) + \frac{1}{2}f(Aa) = 0.34 + 0.23 = 0.57$. Since $p = 0.57$, $q = 0.43$.

To determine whether this population is in genetic equilibrium with respect to this gene, we take the calculated allele frequencies and calculate the expected frequencies of the genotypes. Thus, the expected frequencies are

$$f(AA) = p^2 = (0.57)^2 = 0.325$$
$$f(Aa) = 2pq = 2 \times 0.57 \times 0.43 = 0.490$$
$$f(aa) = q^2 = (0.43)^2 = 0.185$$

When these are compared with the observed frequencies, they do not agree. The amount of disagreement between the expected and observed frequencies may or may not be statistically significant. (Methods exist for determining significance, but they will not be discussed here.) Therefore, our population is not in genetic equilibrium with respect to this gene.

**Summary**

The unit of evolution is the reproductive population. Such a population is described, in statistical terms, as having both a phenotype and a genotype. The genotype of a population is referred to as the gene pool. The gene pool is composed of all the alleles carried by the members of a population. As the frequencies of alleles within the gene pool change, the population evolves. Conversely, if the

---

[2]The incidence of PKU in England ranges between 2 and 6 per 100,000; $\frac{1}{40,000}$ falls within this range. See T. A. Munro, "Phenylketonuria: Data of 47 British Families," *Annals of Eugenics* 14 (1947), pp. 60–88.

allele frequencies remain constant, the population does not evolve; it is said to be in a state of genetic equilibrium. Genetic equilibrium, however, can be only a hypothetical state because the evolutionary forces of mutation, finite population size, gene flow, nonrandom mating, and unequal fertility are always present and lead to change.

By using the Hardy-Weinberg formula, we can measure the strength of evolutionary forces by making comparisons between the hypothetical situation of no change and observed situations of change. Also, the formula can be used to calculate the frequencies of specific alleles and specific genotypes, such as carriers, within a population.

## MECHANISMS OF EVOLUTIONARY CHANGE

In the model of a population in genetic equilibrium, the frequencies of the alleles in the gene pool remain constant. Such a population is not evolving. However, in order to have genetic equilibrium, five requirements must be met: (1) no mutation, (2) infinite population size (i.e., no sampling error), (3) absence of alleles being introduced from neighboring populations (i.e., lack of gene flow), (4) random mating, and (5) equal fertility (i.e., natural selection not operating). Since no natural population meets these requirements, it follows that all populations must be evolving.

From the five conditions that must be met for genetic equilibrium to occur, we can list the various mechanisms that bring about evolutionary change. The first is mutation. Next is small population size, which is responsible for three mechanisms of evolutionary change—genetic drift, population bottlenecking, and the founder principle. The movement of alleles into a population from neighboring populations is termed gene flow. Nonrandom mating occurs in several forms, as we will soon see. And finally, and to many, the most important are differential fertility rates, another way of saying natural selection.

### Mutations

A **mutation** is any alteration in the genetic material. A **point mutation** is a change at a particular point on the DNA molecule. Chromosomal aberration are changes in the number or structure of chromosomes.

Mutations are chance events. Organisms do not sense a change or potential change in the environment and then "decide to" mutate; nor are there innate mechanisms that can provide predictions of what future environmental conditions will be like. Mutations arise with no design, no predetermined reason or purpose; in other words, they are random.

Mutations bring about new alleles. When new alleles occur in body cells, the effect may be insignificant unless, of course, it causes a medical problem such as a cancer that can have a direct effect on the viability of the organism. However, when the mutation occurs in the sex cells and brings about new alleles in the ova and sperm, it can change the gene pool in the next generation since the mutation can be passed on to the next generation. Mutation is the ultimate source of all variation within the gene pool. It creates variability rather than directly bringing about evolutionary change.

**Mutations as Random Events** What is the probability that a chance alteration of the genetic code will be advantageous to the organism? Imagine that a Shakespearean sonnet is being transcribed into Morse code. Suppose that in the process a dot is selected at random and replaced with a dash. What is the probability that this change will improve the poem? Most likely, the change will result in a misspelled word; it might even change the word and, hence, the meaning.

Likewise, the probability that a chance alteration in the genetic code will bring about an improvement is very low. Mutations are usually deleterious to individual organisms. Mutations that are advantageous, or at least neutral, are usually very subtle and are seldom noticed in the phenotype.

Whereas mutations are generally deleterious to an individual, they provide genotypic variation for a population. Since environments change over time, mutations within a population represent a potential for meeting new conditions as they arise. Put another way, mutations are often not fit for the environments in which they originate, but they might provide the genotypic variation needed to survive in a new environment. Mutations provide one mechanism to keep the population viable.

**How Do Mutations Occur?** A mutation may occur **spontaneously,** that is, in response to the usual conditions within the body or environment, or it may be **induced** by human-created agents. In both cases, some factor is actively causing the mutation to occur. The exact cause of any specific mutation usually cannot be determined, although, in experimental situations, various agents can be shown to increase the frequency of the occurrence of mutations.

Geneticists believe that many point mutations result from mistakes in the replication of the DNA molecule. For example, consider the replication of a polypeptide that includes the codon ATA, which codes for the amino acid tyrosine. If an incorrect complementary base were incorporated into the DNA molecule, the new codon might read AAA, which codes for phenylalanine. As a result, phenylalanine replaces tyrosine, a substitution that may greatly alter the functioning of the protein.

Once the substitution has occurred, the new codon would be the basis for replication of additional DNA, all with the same error. We would refer to the altered genetic code as a mutation. Not all substitutions produce phenotypic changes. All but two amino acids are coded by more than one codon, so some mutations can be genetically neutral. For example, if the codon ATA mutated to ATG, there would be no change in the amino acid since both codons code for the same amino acid, in this case tyrosine.

The factors that initiate spontaneous mutations are for the most part unknown. It was once thought that background radiation from the general environment accounted for the majority of the observed spontaneous mutations, but most geneticists now believe that this is not true. Naturally occurring chemicals and fluctuations in temperature may account for many spontaneous mutations.

The story is different for induced mutations. In 1927, H. J. Muller demonstrated that mutations could be induced in fruit flies by using x-rays.[3] In fact, the increase in the frequency of mutations was directly proportional to the increase in the dosage of radiation (Figure 4–2). This discovery increased the awareness of the dangers of artificial radiation from medical or occupational exposure and nuclear fallout. The U.S. National Academy of Sciences has concluded that there is no safe level of ionizing radiation, such as x-rays.

Certain chemicals added to foods, compounded in medicines, or poured into the atmosphere or waters are known to cause mutations, cancers, or other adverse effects in human populations. Some of these substances, although they may enter the animal, may be kept from the chromosomes by plasma and nuclear membranes. Since many substances that are commonly used are suspect, it is important that they be fully investigated. In addition, certain viruses are known to cause mutations.

When mutations do occur, they may have no effect on the phenotype of the organism, as is the case, for example, when the mutant allele is a recessive. On the other hand, mutations can produce phenotypic alterations that range from extremely subtle to drastic. If mutations occur in body cells, cell death and abnormal development, including cancer, could result. A single chance mutation taking place in a skin cell, for example, may have virtually no effect on the phenotype, yet the same isolated mutation taking place in a sex cell may have a significant effect on the individual conceived from that sex cell. Such a mutation may result in potentially valuable characteristics, abnormal conditions, or even inviable gametes.

How frequent are mutations? Although mutation rates vary from trait to trait, most estimates for mutations that occur in sex cells are about 1 in every 100,000 gametes per generation per gene (Table 4–4). When the large number of genes per gamete is considered, the probability of a particular gamete carrying at least one new mutation is about ½. Since many of these new mutations are recessive, they probably will not cause any problems in the immediate offspring.

## Genetic Drift, Population Bottlenecking, and the Founders Principle

The model of genetic equilibrium is mathematical and assumes an infinitely large population, but natural populations are not infinitely large. When we deal with small populations, we often see changes in gene frequencies that are due to chance effects.

**Sampling Error**  Political polls that predict the winners of elections can serve as examples of **sampling error.** Imagine it is election time, and you

---

[3]H. J. Muller, "Artificial Transmutation of the Gene," *Science* 66 (1927), pp. 84–87.

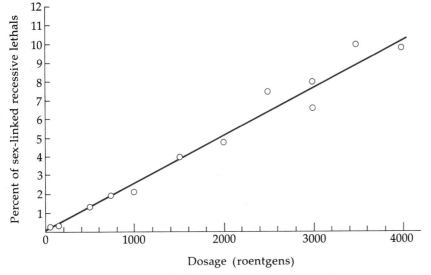

**FIGURE 4–2  Effects of Radiation on the Genetic Material**
X-ray dosage and frequency of sex-linked recessives induced in fruit fly spermatozoa.

have been hired by a candidate to predict the winner. Because of time and money limitations, you cannot possibly reach all 100,000 eligible voters, so you decide to take a sample.

The first question is: How large must the sample be to represent the population adequately? If

you ask only 10 people, they might all be voting for the same person by pure chance. Maybe they are relatives and the only ones voting for this candidate! If you take a sample of 100 individuals, the predictive value of the poll might be increased. Here, too, you must protect against bias by not

TABLE 4–4

### SOME ESTIMATED SPONTANEOUS MUTATION RATES IN HUMAN POPULATIONS

| Abnormality | Inheritance* | Estimated mutation rate (per million gametes per generation) | Population | Source† |
|---|---|---|---|---|
| Retinoblastoma | AD, v | 6–7 | German | 1 |
| Tay-Sachs disease | AR | 11 | Japanese | 2 |
| | | 4 | European | 2 |
| Congenital total color blindness | AR | 28 | Japanese | 2 |
| | | 15 | European | 2 |
| Albinism | AR | 28 | Japanese | 2 |
| | | 15 | European | 2 |
| | | 33–70 | Northern Irish | 3 |
| Hemophilia A | XR | 13 | North American | 4 |
| Hemophilia B | XR | 0.5 | North American | 4 |

*AD = autosomal dominant; AR = autosomal recessive; XR = X-linked recessive, v = incomplete penetrance and/or variable expressivity.
†1 = F. Vogel, "Neue Untersuchen zür Genetik des Retinoblastoms," *Zeitschrift für menschliche Vererbungs und Konstitutionslehre* 34 (1957), pp. 230, 234; 2 = J. V. Neel et al., "The Incidence of Consanguineous Matings in Japan with Remarks on the Estimation of Comparative Gene Frequencies and the Expected Rate of Appearance of Induced Recessive Mutations," *American Journal of Human Genetics* 1 (1949), pp. 175–176; 3 = P. Froggart, "Albinism in Northern Ireland," *Annals of Human Genetics* 24 (1960), pp. 226–227, 231; 4 = I. Barrai et al. "The Effects of Parental Age on Rates of Mutation for Hemophilia and Evidence of Differing Mutation Rates for Hemophilia A and B," *American Journal of Human Genetics* 20 (1968), p. 195.

polling people who might be inclined toward one candidate because of their ethnic background, financial situation, party affiliation, and so forth. One way of achieving an unbiased sample is by randomly polling an adequate-sized sample. The actual size of a representative sample depends on the variation within the population. Statistical formulas can be used to determine what sample size is needed to ensure that predictions will be within a desired level of accuracy.

Consider another example: suppose you wish to take a representative sample of the colors of marking pens in a "population" of such pens. If the entire population is red, a sample of one will be sufficient. However, if there are 10 colors in various frequencies, the sample must be large enough to include all the colors *and* reflect their relative numbers. Any deviation from this would be a sampling error.

One more, slightly different example can be used: flipping coins. Since the odds of landing heads are ½, we would expect that one-half of the flips will always be heads. So, if you flip a coin 10 times, you would expect 5 heads; 100 times, 50 heads; and 1000 times, 500 heads. Yet if the coin is flipped the suggested number of times, the results might deviate from the predicted situation. If, for example, you flip the coin 10 times, you *might* end up with 5 heads; but any number from 0 to 10 is possible. Furthermore, if you flip the coin 10 times repeatedly, the number of heads will fluctuate from series to series (Table 4–5). If a large number of flips, say, 1000, are performed, not only will you come closer to the ideal probability of ½ heads, but the fluctuations from one series to another will not be as dramatic (Table 4–6).

**Genetic Drift**   As the genes in a gene pool are being passed from one generation, we are, in effect, taking a sample. Just as with a sample of voters, colored pens, or coins, all the possibilities may not be represented. If the gene pool is large, and hence the number of matings great, the odds are high that the new gene pool will be fairly representative of the old one. If the gene pool is small, however, the new pool may deviate appreciably from the old. Such chance deviation in the frequency of alleles in a population is known as **genetic drift.**

Figure 4–3 plots the change of allele frequency through time as the result of genetic drift. Note that

### TABLE 4–5

**SAMPLING ERROR IN A SET OF ACTUAL TRIALS**

| Possible combinations for 10 throws | | Times combination thrown | |
|---|---|---|---|
| Heads | Tails | Number | Percent |
| 10 | 0 | 0 | 0 |
| 9 | 1 | 0 | 0 |
| 8 | 2 | 3 | 3 |
| 7 | 3 | 7 | 8 |
| 6 | 4 | 23 | 26 |
| 5 | 5 | 23 | 26 |
| 4 | 6 | 13 | 15 |
| 3 | 7 | 12 | 14 |
| 2 | 8 | 5 | 7 |
| 1 | 9 | 1 | 1 |
| 0 | 10 | 0 | 0 |
| | | 87 | 100 |

the fluctuations appear to be random. However, when the allele frequency is high, there is a strong possibility that it will reach 100 percent, with the alternate allele disappearing from the population.

**Population Bottlenecking**   Another form of genetic drift occurs as the result of **population bottlenecking.** This happens when a population is reduced to a small size for some reason, such as a natural disaster. The initial reduction in the size of the population causes a reduction in variation because of the probability that some variants will be lost by chance as individuals are lost from the population. As the reduced population reproduces, the variability of ensuing populations is less than the variation that existed before the bottlenecking took place.

Naoyuki Takahata and several other population geneticists have proposed that a population bottle-

### TABLE 4–6

**POPULATION SIZE IN A SET OF ACTUAL TRIALS**

| Number of throws | Number of heads expected | Number of heads observed | Deviation from expected (%) |
|---|---|---|---|
| 250 | 125 | 118 | 5.6 |
| 500 | 250 | 258 | 3.2 |
| 1000 | 500 | 497 | 0.6 |

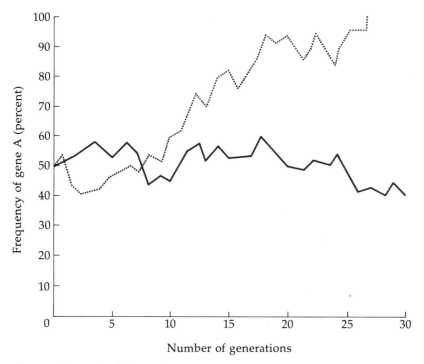

**FIGURE 4–3  Genetic Drift**
This diagram traces genetic drift in two hypothetical populations, beginning with an allele frequency of 50 percent. After 30 generations, one allele has reached a frequency of 100 percent and the other has dropped to 40 percent.

neck occurred sometime around 400,000 years ago.[4] This would explain why there is less genetic variation among humans worldwide than the genetic variation found among geographically close individuals of other species such as gorillas living in the same forest. The proposed bottleneck might have reduced the number of reproducing humans from about 100,000 to 10,000 individuals. Much of the diversity of the original population could have been lost by chance. The new population of 10,000 individuals would then have given rise to new generations of descendants with reduced variation. Not everyone agrees with this explanation for the relative lack of genetic diversity in modern human populations. For example, some statisticians believe that a population of 10,000 is still too large to be an effective bottleneck.

**Founder Principle**  Another form of sampling error in populations is the **founder principle,** which may occur when a segment of a population migrates to another area. The migrating group represents a sample of the original, larger population, but this sample is probably not a random representation of the original group. For instance, it may be made up of members from certain family groups whose gene frequencies vary considerably from the average of the original population. If the migrant population settles down in an uninhabited area or restricts mating to itself, it may become the founder population for the larger population that will develop from it (Figure 4–4). The migrant population may also ultimately merge with other populations, or it may become extinct.

The Xavante of the Amazon Basin provide an example of the founder principle. The Xavante live in villages with average populations of several hundred individuals. When a village becomes too large, it divides into two villages, each with 100 to 200

---

[4]A. Gibbons, "The Mystery of Humanity's Missing Mutations," *Science* 267 (1995), pp. 35–36.

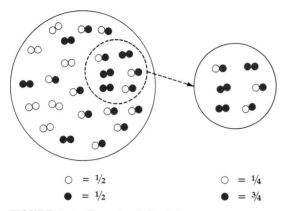

○ = ½          ○ = ¼

● = ½          ● = ¾

**FIGURE 4–4  Founder Principle**
The founders of the new population represent a nonrandom
sample of the original population.

people. Consequently, the breeding size of each
new village is smaller than that of the original village. The split into two villages is largely along
family lines. Since family members stay together,
and many do not mate because of the incest taboo,
the effective breeding size of the population is even
smaller; that is, the number of potential mates is reduced even further from what we may assume
from the size of the population alone. Therefore,
the fission of the original village leads to the establishment of new populations that may by chance
statistically differ from each other in terms of gene
frequencies.

### Gene Flow

Movement of people into areas that are already occupied may serve to introduce new alleles into the
population; this is termed **gene flow**. For example,
travelers may bring a previously absent allele to a
population.

An introduced allele is analogous in effect to a
mutation. If the new allele gives its possessor some
advantage, then this allele will tend to spread
through the population in subsequent generations.
Gene flow may alter the effects of genetic drift, since
alleles lost or reduced in frequency by chance may
be reintroduced into a population by newcomers.
Also, gene flow usually has a homogenizing effect.
The process generally makes two or more populations more similar to each other than would be the
case if gene flow did not occur between them.

Note that the terms *gene flow* and *migration* are
not synonymous. Gene flow refers to the transfer
of alleles into different gene pools, whereas migration connotes a permanent or long-term move to
another area. Thus, one person could migrate but
contribute no alleles to his or her new population,
but a male could go on even a short trip and disperse his genes through his sperm. Soldiers, traveling businesspersons, and others have produced
gene flow without actually migrating.

### Nonrandom Mating

The statistical model of genetic equilibrium calls for
random mating. If matings were truly random, the
probability of mating with any one individual of
the opposite sex would be the same as the probability of mating with any other individual. In reality, mating is not truly random. When you choose
a mate, very definite biases contribute to the choice
—factors such as physical appearance, education,
socioeconomic status, religion, and geographical
location.

There are two basic types of nonrandom matings
that will be discussed here. The first is **consanguineous mating**, which refers to mating between
relatives; the second is **assortative mating**, which
involves preference for or avoidance of certain people for physical and/or social reasons.

**Consanguineous Mating**  For most of American
society, mating between relatives is now rare. Yet
in some other societies, consanguineous mating is
not only common but preferred.

Many societies have cultural patterns of preferential marriage with a particular relative. **Cross-
cousin preferential marriage** is one common type.
In this system, an example of your preferred marriage partner is your mother's brother's child or
your father's sister's child, who in each case is your
first cousin. Yet marriage may be prohibited between you and your mother's sister's child or father's brother's child. Cousin marriage is quite
common in many parts of the world. Table 4–7
shows the incidence of first-cousin marriage in several societies.

Marriages also occur between second and third
cousins, as well as between other types of relatives,
such as uncle and niece. In fact, a preferential marriage that is considered repulsive to most Western

## TABLE 4-7

**FREQUENCIES OF COUSIN MARRIAGES**

| Population | Period | Number of marriages in sample | First-cousin marriages (%) |
|---|---|---|---|
| United States, urban | 1935–1950 | 8,000 | 0.05 |
| Brazil, urban | 1946–1956 | 1,172 | 0.42 |
| Spain | | | |
| Urban | 1920–1957 | 12,570 | 0.59 |
| Rural | 1951–1958 | 814 | 4.67 |
| Japan | | | |
| Urban | 1953 | 16,681 | 5.03 |
| Rural | 1950 | 414 | 16.40 |
| India, rural | 1957–1958 | 6,945 | 33.30 |

*Source:* From *Principles of Human Genetics*, Third Edition, by Curt Stern. Copyright © 1973 by Curt Stern. Reprinted by permission of W. H. Freeman and Company.

societies, brother–sister marriage, was common for the royalty of several societies, including Hawaiians and ancient Egyptians. Some scholars believe that Cleopatra was the offspring of a brother–sister marriage and was at one time married to her brother.

What are the effects of consanguineous matings on a gene pool? Such matings have little effect on common alleles, but their effect on rare alleles is a different story. Geneticist L. C. Dunn gives the following example.[5]

Research in Sweden has determined that the frequency of the recessive allele for juvenile amaurotic idiocy is 0.005. This means that about 1 percent of the total population are heterozygous for the gene. Therefore, the probability of two people mating at random turning out both to be carriers is 0.01 × 0.01, or 0.0001. Since one-fourth of their offspring would have the trait, the probably of two people in the population mating at random having a child with juvenile amaurotic idiocy is 0.000025 or $\frac{1}{40,000}$ (0.01 × 0.01 × ¼), which is the observed frequency of the trait.

Now instead of considering two persons who mate at random, suppose two first cousins mate whose common grandfather is a carrier. If the heterozygous grandfather married a person who is ho-

mozygous dominant (normal), the probability of their offspring being a carrier is ½. The probability of getting carriers in the third generation, assuming that all people marrying into the family are homozygous dominant, is ½ × ½, or ¼. This is because matings between *AA* and *Aa* individuals would have a probability of ½ for the production of *Aa* offspring and, since we know that the probability of the second-generation parents' being *Aa* is ½, we must multiply ½ by ½, the individual probabilities of the two separate events. In the third generation, each cousin has a ¼ probability of being a carrier. The probability of the cousins' mating and both being carriers is ¼ × ¼, or $\frac{1}{16}$. The probability of these cousins having a child with juvenile amaurotic idiocy is $\frac{1}{16}$ (the probability of the cousins both being carriers) × ¼ (the probability of two carriers producing a homozygous recessive child), which equals $\frac{1}{64}$ (see Figure 4–5).

In the above problem, the cousins' grandfather was a carrier. Of course, it is seldom known whether a particular ancestor was a carrier or not, but the probability of a common ancestor can be calculated from gene-frequency data on the population in question. In this case, the probability of two first cousins having a defective child is $\frac{1}{3200}$, compared with $\frac{1}{40,000}$ if the mating were random.

Consanguineous matings increase the probability of homozygous recessive genotypes. In the example above, the probability of producing a homozygous recessive individual is 12½ times greater

[5]L. C. Dunn, *Heredity and Evolution in Human Populations*, rev. ed. (New York: Atheneum, 1965), pp. 125–126.

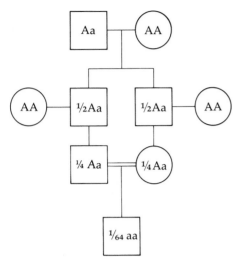

**FIGURE 4–5   Cousin Mating**
See explanation in text.

if first cousins mate than it is if random mating occurs. In fact, some recessive alleles are so rare that the probability of a carrier mating with another carrier at random is just about zero. Some recessive abnormalities are known only from inbred family groups.

The result of consanguineous matings in a population is a reduction in the number of heterozygous individuals and an increase in the number of homozygous individuals. If the homozygous recessive genotype is deleterious, the frequency of the abnormality will increase. Since natural selection can then act upon the abnormal homozygous recessive individuals, there could result a net decrease in the frequency of the allele in the population.

Not all inbreeding is the result of preferential marriage. In a small society, it may be impossible to find a mate who is not a relative. Because of this, the effects of consanguineous marriages and genetic drift are often operating together in the same population, as will be seen in Box 4–1.

**Assortative Mating**   In the United States, consanguineous matings are not common. Nevertheless, mating is far from random. Deviation from random mating stems from the fact that Americans choose spouses by certain cultural conventions that they learn from parents, friends, and the mass media. *Assortative* mating means that people with certain phenotypes tend to mate more or less often than would be expected if matings were random.

Stature provides an interesting example of assortative mating. In American society, a husband is almost always taller than the wife. The reverse is uncommon and is often the source of jokes when it occurs. What effect does this have on the gene pool?

Take two men, one 173 centimeters (5 feet 8 inches) and the other 188 centimeters (6 feet 2 inches). If stature is a convention in mate selection, then the first man would be considering women 173 centimeters (5 feet 8 inches) or less, while the second man would be considering women 188 centimeters (6 feet 2 inches) or less. The second man has a greater population of women from which to choose and might find it easier to find a wife than the first man. Similarly, a woman 183 centimeters (6 feet) tall may have some difficulty finding a mate, since she is "restricted" to men more than 183 centimeters (6 feet) tall. As a result, she may mate later and therefore have a shorter reproductive life and potentially fewer children.

Other important factors that determine mate selection include education and geography. Education is easy to document, and it appears that college-educated people generally prefer to marry other college-educated people. Geography is also important. Before you can marry someone, you must meet that person. People tend to meet and marry in the community in which they live. Ethnicity and religion also play a significant role in mate selection.

Besides showing preferences in choice of a mate, individuals also show avoidances. For example, mentally deficient people would not be selected as mates as frequently as mentally normal individuals.

Assortative mating influences gene combination in the $F_1$ generation. The failure of particular individuals to mate because they are not selected as mating partners would prevent certain alleles (such as those causing mental retardation) from being passed on to the next generation's gene pool. Preferences for particular phenotypes might increase the probability that certain gene combinations will be represented in the gene pool of the next generation. For instance, if a tall individual selected as a mate another tall individual, extremely tall offspring might then appear in the

## BOX 4-1

# The Amish

The Amish are a series of small populations that have remained socially isolated for religious and cultural reasons. There are Amish settlements in 23 states and Ontario, Canada, but the most studied group consists of the 20,000 or so Amish

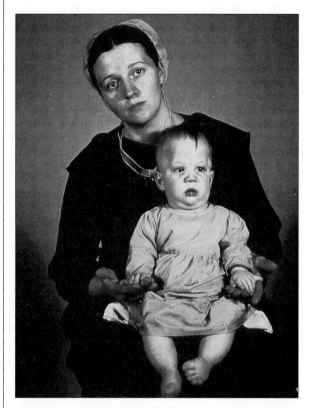

Amish mother holding child with Ellis–van Creveld syndrome.

of Lancaster County, Pennsylvania. The Amish are one of several religious isolates that are ideal for population studies. They are a strictly defined, closed group with good genealogical records, high nutritional and health standards, and good medical care. Almost all the Amish are at the same socioeconomic level, and they tend to have large families.

Most of the Amish of Lancaster County are the descendants of a founder population of about 200 pre–Revolutionary War ancestors who migrated to Pennsylvania from Europe between 1720 and 1770. Because of the small population size, most available mates are related to some degree, although first-cousin marriages are prohibited.

The Amish represent the results of the founder effect, genetic drift, and consanguineous mating. They have a fairly high frequency of some rather rare alleles, such as the one responsible for Ellis–van Creveld syndrome.

The **Ellis–van Creveld syndrome** is characterized by dwarfism, extra fingers on the hand, and, often, congenital malformations of the heart. The syndrome is quite rare, with fewer than 50 cases being known outside the Amish. Yet among the small Amish population alone, over 80 definite cases are known. A great number of these individuals can trace their descent back to three common ancestors, one of whom was probably a carrier.

Many such isolates, like the Amish, have been studied by students of human evolution. Besides showing a higher incidence of several rare recessive traits, these populations also show allele frequencies for such traits as blood type that differ from the frequencies of the surrounding population. For example, among the Dunkers, a group of 3500 individuals in Pennsylvania descended from German ancestors who migrated to America beginning in 1719, more than 44 percent are of blood-type M. This compares with a frequency of 29 percent for blood-type M found in the present-day populations of the United States and West Germany. Since there is no evidence that these blood-type frequencies are due to natural selection, they are most likely due to the founder principle and/or genetic drift.

---

next generation, thus bringing about new variation in the population.

## Natural Selection

The model of genetic equilibrium assumes that all matings are equally fertile, but this is obviously not the case. Some couples have three children, others one, and still others no children at all. This means that the contribution to the gene pool of the succeeding generation varies from couple to couple.

V. A. McKusick presents some interesting figures.[6] He estimates that more than half of all zygotes never reproduce: 15 percent are lost before birth, 3 percent are stillborn, 2 percent are lost in the neonatal period, 3 percent die before maturity, 20 percent never marry, and 10 percent marry but remain childless.

[6]V. A. McKusick, *Human Genetics,* 2nd ed. (Englewood Cliffs, N.J.: Prentice Hall, 1969), p. 167.

Except for identical twins, each zygote is a unique genotype, representing a unique assortment of alleles, a particular combination that will never occur again. Why do more than half of these fail to reproduce at all? Because of some inherited abnormality, many are lost either before or after birth. Others never mate because they are institutionalized. Some die in wars or accidents. Many mate but never have children because of medical problems. And some do not mate or marry, or they marry but choose to have no children.

Of the 47 percent of the original combinations that do reproduce, reproductive rates vary. Some have only one child, others a dozen. What factors determine the differences in fertility? Some are medical, such as blood-type incompatibility, but many are cultural. For instance, many couples today restrict their families to one or two children because of ecological or economic concerns; others believe, on religious grounds, that salvation lies in high fertility. The point is that the next generation is the result of the reproductive activities of the parental generation.

What we have been talking about is natural selection, the heart of the theory of evolution. Natural selection is the fact that certain individuals tend to have more offspring than do other individuals and therefore make a greater contribution to the gene pool of the next generation. Factors that result in greater fertility, *if genetically determined*, will be passed on to the next generation with greater frequency. Factors that result in lowered fertility or higher mortality, such as genetic abnormality, will tend to be eliminated.

## Summary

Natural populations are not in genetic equilibrium because five mechanisms bring about changes in allele frequency. Mutations, the ultimate source of genetic variability, provide one way in which the predicted frequencies deviate from observed frequencies. Since mutations are usually deleterious to the individual, they rarely "catch on." Their importance lies in providing a potential for adapting to new situations.

Random genetic drift is another factor in evolutionary change. With genetic drift, by chance alone, not all alleles in a population will be represented proportionally in the next generation. The smaller the population, the more pronounced this effect. According to the founder principle, a new population based on a small sample of the original population may show distinctive gene frequencies. Again, the smaller the sample, the greater the potential deviation from the original group. Sampling error is in part responsible for much of the physical variation in different human populations.

Gene flow can bring new alleles into a population, where they may be adaptive and increase in frequency. Gene flow also acts to make populations genetically more similar to each other.

The genetic-equilibrium model assumes random mating, but individuals consciously choose mates for myriad reasons. For example, they may prefer to marry a relative in order to keep power and wealth within the family, or they may want to mate with someone with green eyes for personal aesthetic reasons. Nonrandom mating leads to changes in gene frequencies from generation to generation.

Differential fertility, or natural selection, is a powerful force of evolutionary change. This topic will be a major focus of the next chapter.

As a final note, it should be emphasized that the mechanisms of evolution—mutation, drift, gene flow, nonrandom mating, and natural selection—work *together* to create net change. For instance, natural selection would have nothing to "select" for or against if the variability provided by mutation were not present.

## STUDY QUESTIONS

1. Why do we define evolutionary change in terms of changes in relative gene frequencies rather than in terms of changes in phenotype?
2. Genetic equilibrium is a state that never actually exists. Why can it not exist in a real population?
3. What is meant by the term *sampling error?* What types of sampling errors can occur in the reproduction of populations?
4. Cousin marriage is illegal in some states. Does mating between cousins produce more abnormal children than mating between nonrelatives? What genetic factors are involved?
5. What role does mutation play in evolutionary change? Could evolution occur without mutation?
6. Insecticide is sprayed on an insect population. A small percent of the insects survive because of a mutation

that allows them to "neutralize" the toxin. Did the mutation arise because the insect population needed it to? Explain.

7. In what way does natural selection affect a gene pool? How does natural selection interact with other forces of evolution to create changes in the gene pool?

8. Do you believe that the course of human evolution can be predicted? If so, why and how? If not, why not?

## SUGGESTED READINGS

Bowler, P. J. *Evolution: The History of an Idea,* rev. ed. Berkeley: University of California Press, 1989. This book outlines the history of evolutionary theories. Its final chapter looks at modern debates about evolutionary theory, including the ideas of creationists.

Futuyma, D. J. *Evolutionary Biology,* 3rd ed. Sunderland, Mass.: Sinauer Associates, 1998. This book provides one of the best discussions of population genetics available.

Griffiths, A., et al. *An Introduction to Genetic Analysis,* 6th ed. New York: Freeman, 1996. This is a general introduction to genetics with excellent chapters on population genetics. There are numerous solved exercises.

Hartl, D. L., and A. Clark. *Principles of Population Genetics,* 3rd ed. Sunderland, Mass.: Sinauer Associates, 1998. This is a popular introduction to population genetics.

Volpe, E. P., and P. Andrew. *Understanding Evolution,* 7th ed. New York: McGraw-Hill, 1999. This is a short introduction to evolutionary theory with a good overview of population genetics.

## SUGGESTED WEB SITES

Overview of Hardy-Weinberg from Palomar College:
http://daphne.palomar.edu/synthetic/synth_2.htm
Hardy-Weinberg Simulation:
http://cyclone.cs.clemson.edu/~tmiller/java/genetics/genetics.html
Simulation of Genetic Drift:
http://darwin.bio.geneseo.edu/~haynie/java/drift/parse1.html

Additional web sites are listed in the *Workbook* that accompanies this text.

## CHAPTER 5

# Natural Selection and the Origin of Species

*I have called this principle, by which each slight variation, if useful, is preserved, by the term Natural Selection.*
—Charles Darwin (1809–1882)

Evolution is change. Scientists theorize that life began to form more than four billion years ago. Eventually, unicellular organisms evolved, followed by multicellular organisms. From this early life, millions of species evolved, some becoming extinct without leaving descendants, others evolving into species that populate the world today.

The biological evolution that leads to the propagation and diversity of life occurs on at least two levels. What is sometimes called "small-scale" biological evolution, or **microevolution,** is any change in the frequency of alleles within the gene pool of a population, which we examined in the last chapter. These microevolutionary changes occur through several mechanisms that include mutation, gene flow, genetic drift, and, the subject of the first part of this chapter, natural selection.

The second level of biological evolution is often referred to as "large-scale" evolution or **macroevolution.** This is the subject of the second part of this chapter. Macroevolution leads to the evolution of new species and larger categories of life.

## NATURAL SELECTION

We will now revisit the concept of natural selection, which we have already encountered in Chapters 1 and 4. Natural selection remains one of the central concepts in modern evolutionary theory. Charles Darwin first wrote about natural selection in 1842, but most people did not learn of it until 1859 when Darwin presented the concept in his book *On the Origin of Species.* Darwin had collected an enormous amount of facts in the areas of geology, biogeography, biology, animal husbandry, paleontology, and other fields. He presented his data in a way that ultimately convinced the scientific world of the validity of the concept of natural selection.

Natural selection is one of the processes that act to change the frequency of alleles in a population. Darwin and others observed that individuals within a population produce far more individuals than is necessary to replace themselves. He also observed that these populations are variable. Environmental factors such as predators, disease, lack of food, competition over mates, and lack of space will tend to eliminate or reduce the genetic contribution (the number of offspring) of those individuals who cannot cope with these pressures.

Darwin contrasted natural selection with **artificial selection.** Artificial selection or **selective breeding** is the deliberate breeding of domesticated plants and animals. It is similar to natural selection except that it is controlled by humans. People have probably been selectively breeding animals for at least 13,000 years. Darwin believed that if people could selectively breed for thicker wool in sheep, speed in horses, or docile temperaments in dogs, then the pressures imposed on natural populations could similarly, although not deliberately, bring about changes as well.

### The Variability of Populations

All populations, including humans, display variability. Some of this variability is clearly observable: color, size, and shape, for example. Other differences are observable only through dissection or microscopic and biochemical analysis.

Humans are polymorphic. **Polymorphism** refers to the presence of several distinct forms with frequencies greater than 1 percent within a population. An example of this would be the presence of individuals with A, B, AB, and O blood types within a population (Chapter 3).

We can easily observe variation of phenotypes among human populations in different parts of the world; this is the subject of Chapter 17. Even among siblings from a single family, there are differences in physical features, blood types, and psychological patterns. Some of these differences vary with sex and age; others are influenced by the cultural or natural environment; and many, such as blood type, are totally inherited.

How many genetically different individuals are possible? There are theoretically about $10^{963}$ possible combinations of alleles in humans. This number is a 1 followed by 963 zeros—a number trillions of times larger than the total number of people who have ever inhabited the earth. To this genetic variability we can add the effects of differing environments, which further increase variability. (Because of exposure to differences in the environment, even identical twins, which do have identical genotypes, differ from each other.)

**Mechanisms of Variation**   As noted in Chapter 4, mutation is the ultimate source of all genetic variability. Mutations, which provide the raw material for increasing genetic variation, have the potential to enter into new combinations with existing alleles.

Variation also develops in another way. Because of independent assortment and crossing-over, a new combination of alleles is produced every time a gamete is formed. Sperm and ovum then combine to produce a unique genotype, a genotype that has never existed before and will never exist again. Natural selection acts upon new mutations and recombinations of existing alleles.

## Environment, Habitat, and Niche

We have referred to the role of the **environment** in natural selection. The environment, in its most general sense, is anything and everything external to a particular entity. The environment of a specific red blood cell includes other red blood cells, white blood cells, and the plasma. A person's environment would include such things as clothing, furniture, air temperature, trees, and flowers, as well as other people.

This concept of environment is very broad. Therefore, it is often useful to think in terms of the physical environment, biological environment, and cultural environment. The **physical environment** refers to the inanimate elements of the surroundings, such as sunlight, the atmosphere, and mountains. The living elements around us—the trees, grass, birds, and insects, for example—are more specifically referred to as the **biological environment.** The **cultural environment** contains the products of human endeavor, such as tools, shelters, clothing, toxic wastes, and even social institutions.

Sometimes we want to talk about the environmental factors immediately surrounding an organism. This is the **microenvironment.** For example, a particular organism may live in only a certain species of tree and may occupy space on only the end branches of those trees.

A term related to environment is **habitat;** habitat is defined as the place in which an organism lives. Examples of habitats are tropical rain forests, deserts, freshwater marshes, and tundra. Some authors also employ the concept of **microhabitat,** which is a more specific "address" for an organism, such as the upper story of the tropical rain forest.

In the study of natural selection, we are concerned with the specific environmental factors surrounding a specific organism. Yet environment is not enough, for different organisms have evolved different strategies for survival in each specific microhabitat. A useful concept in evolutionary studies is that of **ecological niche.**

A niche, or ecological niche, refers first to the specific microhabitat in which a particular species lives. Sometimes the microhabitat is extremely narrow and includes a very specific set of environmental factors. Other times the niche is very broad in that the organism can function under a wide range of environmental factors.

The term ecological niche also includes the anatomical, physiological, and behavioral methods by which the organism exploits physical space and its relationship to other organisms. Two animals may occupy the same physical area, but one consuming leaves and the other fruits or one being active at night and the other active during the day are occupying different niches (Figure 5–1).

## The Mechanisms of Natural Selection

As we saw in the last chapter, individuals in a population differ from one another in terms of their fertility rates, that is, the number of offspring they produce. Possessors of some phenotypes live to reproduce and do so to varying degrees; possessors of other phenotypes either die before reproductive age or live but do not reproduce. Numerous factors, both environmental and genetic, account for these differences in fertility rate.

Sometimes it is possible to identify a specific factor that brings about differences in fertility rates. For example, in Chapter 1 we looked at Darwin's finches on the island of Daphne Major. The medium ground finches show much variability in the size of their beaks. Differences in beak size, often a matter of only a few millimeters, are related to the ability of the bird to process seeds of particular size and hardness.

Changes in the climate profoundly affect the numbers and types of seeds that are available for finches to eat. During the 1976–1978 drought, Peter and Rosemary Grant documented the fact that small soft seeds rapidly disappeared, leaving only relatively large hard seeds to eat. Since only the birds with the larger beaks were able to effectively handle the larger seeds, these birds survived; birds with smaller beaks died. It has been estimated that about 80 percent of beak size is due to heredity. Therefore, when the rains came again, the surviving birds, which were those with the larger beaks, began to breed. The new generation of birds had beaks that were about 4 percent larger than the average beak size that existed before the drought.

**Selective Agents** Any factor that brings about a difference in fertility among members of a population

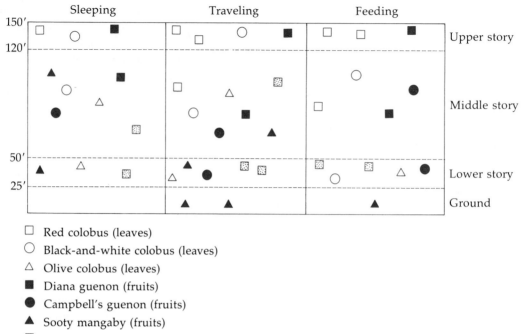

**FIGURE 5–1  Ecological Niche**
This chart shows the spatial distribution of seven species of African arboreal monkeys in relationship to diet and three different activities.

is termed a **selective agent.** A selective agent places **selective pressure** on certain individuals in the population, resulting in a change in the frequency of alleles in the next generation. In the case of Darwin's finches, differences in the size and hardness of seeds were selective agents. (Of course, plants are also subject to natural selection. The lack of rainfall was a selective agent bringing about differences in fertility and mortality among seed-producing plants.)

An example of a selective agent in a human population is the smallpox virus. If a population is exposed to the virus, some individuals will acquire the disease and die, others will develop mild cases, and still others will not contract the disease at all. Environmental factors such as exposure, hygiene, age, diet, and stress play major roles in determining who gets the disease and the severity of the disease. Research suggests that certain biochemical factors, such as ABO blood types, also play a role in determining who acquires smallpox. Thus, possessors of certain phenotypes will have a higher

death rate than others; a high mortality rate is directly related to a low fertility rate. Only those who survive will be available to transmit their genes to the next generation.

Selective agents act upon the phenotype of the members of the population. Only those individuals who survive the smallpox epidemic will be able to reproduce. If the factor that has enabled the organism to survive is determined genetically, then these genes, passed on to the next generation, will aid in the survival from smallpox in the next generation. On the other hand, if the characteristic that led to survival is determined solely by an environmental factor, then natural selection will not occur. Of course, the majority of phenotypic traits have both genetic and environmental components. Therefore, smallpox as a selective agent ultimately operates to produce a subsequent gene pool that is more resistant (better adapted) to the disease environment (Figure 5–2).

Finally, an environmental factor that may cause death but does not "select" one phenotype over an-

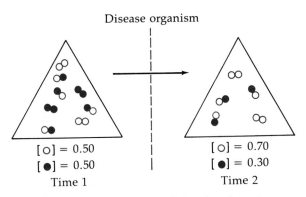

Disease organism

[○] = 0.50
[●] = 0.50
Time 1

[○] = 0.70
[●] = 0.30
Time 2

**FIGURE 5–2  Disease as a Selective Agent**
Disease can bring about different survival rates among the possessors of different genotypes, hence changing the allele frequencies in the gene pool.

other is not a selective agent. If a nuclear bomb were dropped without warning on an area and everyone died, or if only a random sample of people who happened to be in a shelter at the time survived, natural selection would not be taking place. On the other hand, if some people on the periphery of the bomb were biologically more resistant to the radiation than others and hence survived at a greater frequency, this would be an instance of natural selection.

**Fitness**  Individuals (or populations) that have higher fertility rates than other individuals (or populations) in a particular ecological niche are said to display a greater fitness to that niche. **Fitness** is a measure of how well-adapted a particular individual or group is to the requirements imposed by the niche. Survival to reproductive age, successful mating, and fertility are not always related to such factors as size and strength. Fitness also does not necessarily correspond to characteristics that a society values. A highly educated, wealthy, good citizen who has no children has an individual fertility rate of zero.

Fitness varies with the situation. Since environmental factors change and populations may shift into new niches, selective pressures are not always constant. For this reason, a trait that has a high fitness value in one niche may lose this fitness in another. On the other hand, a trait with a low fitness value may gain greater fitness in a new niche.

In general, natural selection affects the frequency of alleles by eliminating alleles and allele combinations that are deleterious to the majority of those who carry them. Natural selection also tends to retain and increase the frequencies of alleles and allele combinations that are adaptive, that is, more fit.

**Types of Natural Selection**  The results of natural selection differ in various situations. We can examine the range of variation within a population. The different types of selection occur because different parts of the range of variation have different reproductive rates. Biologists generally recognize three types of natural selection (Figure 5–3). In all three cases, we start by looking at the distribution of variability—beak size in finches, for example—and observe where on the distribution curve selection is operating. In other words, where on the variation curve do we find significant differences in fertility rate?

Returning to Darwin's ground finch on Daphne Major, we observe that one end of the variability curve is being negatively impacted during the drought. That is, finches with small beaks are dying from hunger because they are unable to process the large, hard seeds that were the only seeds remaining. (The investigators actually measured the beaks of dead birds found on the island.) As a result, the mean of the curve showing variation in the next generation shifted toward larger beaks. This is called **directional selection** because the mean of the variation is moving each generation in a particular direction.[1]

Another situation is where natural selection selects against organisms at both ends of the curve; those individuals near the mean have the higher fertility rate. This is often found in populations that exist in stable habitats. An example is birth weight in humans. Human infants that are lighter or heavier than average do not survive as well as those of average weight. This is termed **stabilizing selection.**

---

[1]One would expect that over time, the beaks of finches on Daphne Major would be getting larger and larger. However, directional selection actually favors smaller beaks during times of heavy rains. The end result is an oscillation of the mean back and forth over time.

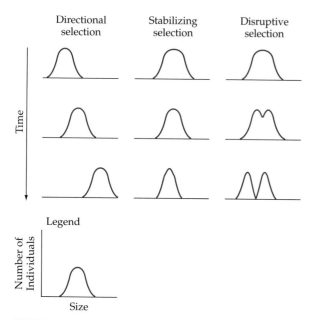

| Directional selection | Stabilizing selection | Disruptive selection |

**FIGURE 5–3  The Types of Natural Selection**
Three recognized types of natural selection exist because
different parts of the range of variation have different
reproductive rates.

The third type of natural selection is **disruptive
selection.** Here, natural selection favors both ex-
tremes; individuals near the mean have the lower
fertility rate. Diversity increases and sometimes the
population actually fragments into two new populations.

## Natural Selection in Humans

Charles Darwin believed that natural selection progressed so slowly that it would be impossible to
see. Yet today, biologists have documented over 100
cases of natural selection occurring in nature within
a time frame that can be studied by human investigators. Natural selection is also occurring in human populations. Because of the long time between
generations, however, examples of selection in human populations are not as easy to document as
they are in birds, for example. Yet several studies
based on indirect evidence have dealt with what
might be real, but subtle, examples.

**Selection against Certain Simple Dominant and
Recessive Alleles**   The least complicated cases of
natural selection in humans are those involving total selection against a simple dominant abnormality that affects all persons that inherit the alleles
and is always fatal. An example is **retinoblastoma,**
a cancer of the retina of the eye in children. This
abnormality is fatal unless the entire eye is removed. Since the trait affects all individuals with
the allele equally and results in death before reproductive age, selection will eliminate the allele
in the next generation. Because none of the individuals with the abnormality can reproduce (assuming surgery is not performed), the appearance
of the trait in any generation will be due to new
mutations.

Such an allele has a **selective coefficient** ($s$) of
1.00—selection is complete. The **relative fitness
(RF)** of an individual with the allele is given by the
formula $RF = 1 - s$. The relative fitness in this case
is 0; no offspring are produced by a person with a
dominant lethal allele.

If selection is not complete, an abnormal dominant allele still will tend to be eliminated, but more
slowly. For example, if the selective coefficient is
0.50, then persons with the trait would leave behind, on the average, only one-half the number of
offspring that those without the trait would leave,
all other factors being equal. Thus, the number of
persons with the trait, barring new mutations,
would be cut by one-half in each generation.

Natural selection acts much more slowly against
a recessive trait. Only homozygous recessive individuals are affected by selection. Heterozygous individuals will carry the allele to the next generation. For example, persons with Tay-Sachs disease
always die as children, but carriers survive to adulthood and have normal reproductive rates. Thus,
the allele will tend to be eliminated, but much more
slowly than a dominant trait with the same fitness
(Figure 5–4).

**Natural Selection and the ABO Blood Types**   Differences in blood-type frequencies exist in different
populations. For example, in a population in India,
35.38 percent of the members were of blood-type
B; 33.21 percent were type O; 24.55 percent were
type A; and 6.86 percent were type AB. This contrasts strongly with a Kwakiutl Indian population
from British Columbia, Canada, in which 67.74
percent of the members were of type O and 32.27

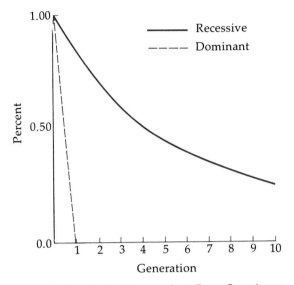

**FIGURE 5–4  Selection against Rare Genotypes**
This graph shows the rate at which frequencies of rare genotypes are reduced by natural selection. One line shows a dominant abnormality and the other a recessive one. In both cases, the frequencies begin at 1 percent, and selection is complete. Assume no new mutations.

percent type A. Types B and AB were totally absent.[2]

Why should these differences exist within and between populations? Likely explanations are random genetic drift and natural selection.

Until relatively recent times, all people lived in small groups. Group differences developed from group to group because of genetic drift. Likewise, when a small group migrated from one group to establish a new population, differences developed because of the founder principle. However, evidence suggests that natural selection also played a role in the evolution of the ABO blood-type system.

In Chapter 3, we discussed hemolytic disease involving the Rh blood-type system. It now appears that, in some respects, ABO incompatibilities may have a greater selective effect than Rh incompatibilities. Several investigators have noted that in situations in which the mother is blood-type O and the fetus is type A or B, hemolytic disease may develop in the newborn infant.

Surveys show that when the mother is type O and the father type A, fewer type A children are produced than when the mother is type A and the father type O. The type O mother carries anti-A and anti-B in her blood. These antibodies often, but not always, cross over into the fetal blood system, where, if the fetus is of type A, damage may occur. In one study, 12 percent of all newborns of type O mothers were of type A and B. Of these newborns, 0.5 percent showed clinical symptoms of blood destruction.[3]

It is important to realize that fertility rates differ for different types of matings. We have seen, for example, that a mating between an O mother and an A father will produce fewer offspring than a mating between an A mother and an O father. Fewer of the former's children will be of blood-type A. These differences in fertility can bring about subtle, but real, changes in allele frequencies over many generations.

Several diseases also appear to act as selective agents against certain blood types. For example, persons with blood-type A have an elevated incidence of cancer of the stomach, cancer of the pancreas, and pernicious anemia. Blood-type O has been linked to duodenal and stomach ulcers. In populations of European descent, the risk of developing a duodenal ulcer is 35 percent higher among persons of type O than among persons of the other three ABO blood types (Figure 5–5).[4]

### Natural Selection and Sickle-Cell Anemia

You have already been introduced to sickle-cell anemia. The genotype $Hb^A Hb^A$ results in the manufacture of hemoglobin A. The genotype $Hb^S Hb^S$ produces hemoglobin S and the disease sickle-cell anemia. The heterozygote $Hb^A Hb^S$ produces both hemoglobins.

---

[2]A. E. Mourant et al., *The Distribution of the Human Blood Groups and Other Polymorphisms*, 2nd ed. (London: Oxford University Press, 1976).

[3]H. Levene and R. E. Rosefield, "ABO Incompatibility," in A. G. Steinberg (ed.), *Progress in Medical Genetics*, vol. 1 (New York: Grune & Stratton, 1961), pp. 120–157.

[4]J. Buettner-Janusch, "The Study of Natural Selection and the ABO(H) Blood Group System in Man," in G. E. Dole and R. L. Carniero (eds.), *Essays in the Science of Culture* (New York: Crowell, 1969), pp. 79–110.

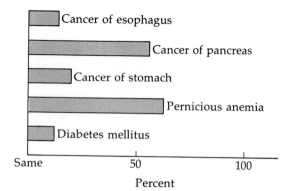

**FIGURE 5–5  Natural Selection and the ABO Blood Types**
This graph shows the relatively greater risk, in percent, of type A individuals developing the diseases listed, compared with that of type O individuals. Other blood types also show relatively greater risks for specific diseases.

The fitness of the individual with sickle-cell anemia is effectively zero. Therefore, as we would expect, natural selection is operating to eliminate the allele $Hb^S$ in many areas, such as the United States. Nevertheless, populations in many parts of Africa, southern Europe, and the Middle East have very high $Hb^S$ allele frequencies, as high as approximately 0.20. This means that as many as 36 percent of the individuals in these populations have the sickle-cell trait or sickle-cell anemia. The high frequency for $Hb^S$ is startling, especially when we remember that the frequency of the allele for PKU, also a deleterious recessive, is only 0.01 or less in all populations for which data are available. What factors are responsible for the high frequency of $Hb^S$?

The British geneticist Anthony Allison was one of the first to realize that the high frequencies of $Hb^S$ are found in areas characterized by high incidences of falciparum malaria.[5] The distribution of hemoglobin S (seen in Figure 5–6) correlates highly with that of malaria. This suggests that the heterozygote, with both hemoglobin A and hemoglobin S, is relatively resistant to malaria and has a higher fitness than either homozygous type. This increased resistance has been confirmed.

Malaria involves parasites that, at one stage of their complex reproductive cycle, reproduce in the red blood cell. The malaria parasite cannot infect cells that contain hemoglobin S. The fitness of the anemic individual is low because of the effects of sickle-cell anemia. The fitness of the individual homozygous for hemoglobin A in malarial areas is depressed because malaria has such a high mortality rate and because malaria often leaves the victim sterile.

The fitness of the heterozygote, however, is relatively high because of lower mortality from malaria. Thus, the heterozygote has the greatest probability of surviving, reproducing, and contributing the most genetic material to the next generation. Yet because the heterozygote produces a certain proportion of children with the disease, the death rate from sickle-cell anemia may be high in areas where the allele is plentiful.

Disease organisms are important environmental factors. Some anthropologists believe that malaria as it is known today did not exist in Africa before the development of agriculture some 10,000 years ago. This cultural change caused an opening of the forest and the creation of stagnant pools of water in which mosquitoes, which are the carriers of the malarial parasites, reproduced. As the rate of malaria increased, so did mortality. A population in a malarial environment has several possible fates. It may die off when the mortality rate is so great that the population is no longer large enough to maintain itself; on the other hand, a chance mechanism for survival might save the population.

Most likely, sickle-cell anemia already existed, but before the rise of malaria, the frequency of the allele $Hb^S$ would have been low because of the low fitness of the anemic individual. With the increase and spread of malaria, the fitness of the heterozygote became greater than the fitness of the homozygous $Hb^A Hb^A$ individual, and the frequency of the allele $Hb^S$ increased. Today, population fitness in malarial areas is balanced between mortality due to malaria and mortality due to sickle-cell anemia. The combined death rate is lower than the rate would be for mortality due to malaria alone if the sickle-cell allele did not exist. This situation, in which the heterozygous individual is best fit, is one form of **balanced polymorphism** (Figure 5–7).

A balanced polymorphism is a condition for which two or more alleles are maintained in a pop-

[5]A. C. Allison, "Protection Afforded by Sickle-Cell Trait against Subtertian Malarial Infection," *British Medical Journal* 1 (1954), pp. 290–294.

ulation by natural selection. Selection produces an equilibrium so that allele frequencies remain the same from generation to generation. Heterozygote advantage, as seen in the case of sickle-cell anemia, is the simplest type of balanced polymorphism. In such a case, if the frequency of the sickle-cell allele decreases, more people who are homozygous for $Hb^A$ are born, and there is increased selection against the $Hb^A$ allele. If the frequency of the $Hb^S$ allele increases, more individuals homozygous for that allele are born, and there is increased selection against the $Hb^S$ allele. If the heterozygote is more fit than either homozygous condition, this produces a balance–counterbalance system that keeps the frequencies of alleles stable.

**Other Diseases and Malaria**  Several other genetic conditions are associated with the distribution of malaria. Some of them have been shown to reduce the impact of malaria upon human populations, and others are suspected of performing this function. The picture is complicated by the fact that more than one type of malaria exists and differing genetic traits may protect the individual against different forms of the malarial parasite.

In northwestern sections of Africa, an abnormal hemoglobin, **hemoglobin C,** overlaps the distribution of hemoglobin S. Perhaps these two hemoglobins protect against different types of malaria.

A series of abnormalities referred to as **thalassemias** differ from the abnormal hemoglobins in that the polypeptide chains are normal. However, some chains, such as the alpha or beta chain, may not be produced, while other hemoglobin types, such as fetal hemoglobin, are produced into adulthood. Thalassemia major, which occurs in the homozygous individual, can be severe and is often fatal. Thalassemia minor, which occurs in the heterozygous individual, is not severe and is believed to be associated with malarial resistance. **Glucose-6-phosphate dehydrogenase (G6PD) deficiency** has also been linked to malaria resistance. Figure 5–6 shows the distribution of some of these traits and malaria.

### Sexual Selection

Natural selection is, in part, about access to resources. Animals who are more successful at finding and processing food, for example, are more likely to survive and produce the greater numbers of offspring. Seen in terms of genes, successful animals will pass on a greater number of their genes to the next generation than others. Earlier, we saw that on the island of Daphne Major, those medium ground finches with larger beaks survived the drought in larger numbers than birds with smaller beaks; the larger-beaked birds later produced offspring, while those with smaller beaks died. Since beak size is, to a large extent, inheritable, the offspring had relatively large beaks.

In natural selection, both males and females are competing for access to resources such as food and space. However, the situation for females and males differs significantly when it comes to reproduction. Among mammals in general, an individual female makes a major investment in each of her offspring in terms of pregnancy, nursing, and protecting the newborn infant. This is often accomplished without any assistance from the male, although, in many species, males do play important roles in the rearing of offspring. The reproductive success of a female, that is, the number of offspring the female produces, is limited by her access to resources such as food and a good hiding place for her young. In contrast with males, all females do generally mate. Thus, differential access to males as mates is not a factor in female reproductive success.

The situation is different for males. A particular male can produce offspring with a number of females. The reproductive success of a male, that is, the number of offspring a male can sire and, ultimately, the number of genes he can pass on to the next generation, is determined by the number of females with which he mates. Therefore, the male's reproductive success is limited by his access to females, resulting in competition among males for females. Characteristics that increase the success of a male in competing for females will increase in frequency over time; this is called **sexual selection.**

**Intersexual Selection**  Evolutionary biologists recognize two forms of sexual selection. The first is **intersexual selection,** selection for traits that make males more attractive to females. This occurs when females consistently select as mates males with particular features that are unique to males. Of course, as in natural selection, sexual selection will only occur if the trait selected is inherited.

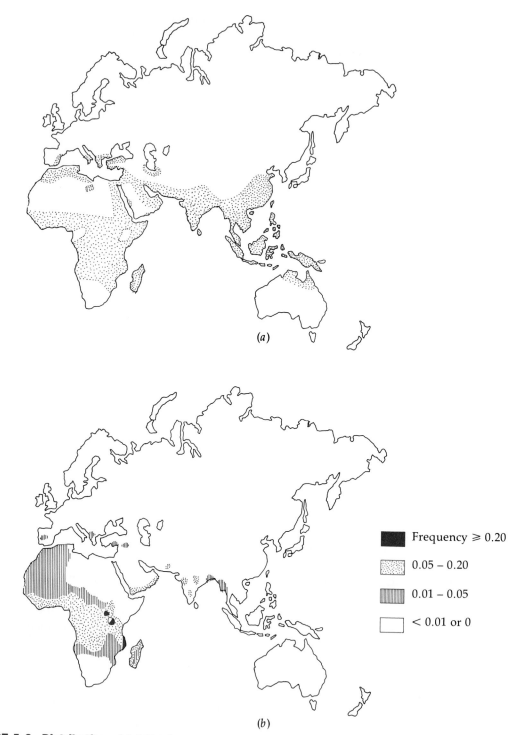

*(a)*

*(b)*

**FIGURE 5–6** Distribution of (*a*) Falciparum malaria, (*b*) Hemoglobin S, (*c*) Hemoglobin C and E, and (*d*) Thalassemia in the Old World

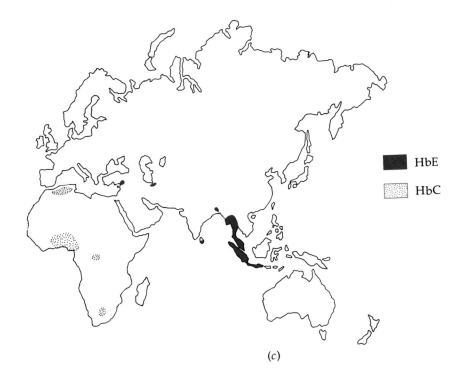

(c)

(d)

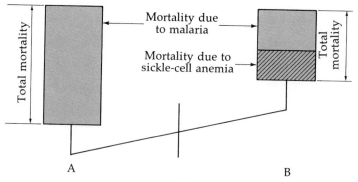

**FIGURE 5–7  Balanced Polymorphism**
The total death rate from malaria in a population lacking the sickle-cell allele (*A*) is greater than the total death rate from malaria and sickle-cell anemia in a population with the sickle-cell allele (*B*).

There are many kinds of intersexual selection. Females often prefer as mates males with traits that confer direct benefit on the female. These traits include those that enable the male to more successfully protect offspring, provide food, or defend the territory where the offspring are kept.

For example, in many species, males will first establish territories as a prelude to competing for females. Females will be attracted to males with large safe territories; the presence of such territories will increase the probability of her offspring surviving.

Another kind of trait that appears to be favored by sexual selection is that which enables the female to distinguish male genetic quality. Many male mammals and birds are characterized by conspicuously colored body parts; the peacock's tail, for example. Often there is a direct correlation between the brightness of a patch of fur or feathers and the health of the animal. For example, parasites often result in a dulling of an animal's coat. Parasite infestation is also affected, to a degree, by the animal's genotype. By favoring a brightly colored male, females are selecting as mates the more healthy animals.

Intersexual competition sometimes leads to an exaggeration of male traits. The classic example is the large and colorful tail of the peacock (Figure 5–8). Female preference for large, brightly colored tails, related to the health status of the male, has led, through time, to extremely large, colorful tails. Yet such tails have a downside. A bird endowed with such a large bright, phenotype will be easily seen by predators. Perhaps the fact that such males are able

to survive means that they possess the right genes for survival. This example also shows that sexual selection is often stronger than natural selection.

**Intrasexual Selection**  The second form of sexual selection is **intrasexual selection.** In this case, males directly compete with one another, with the win-

**FIGURE 5–8  Intersexual Selection**
The male peacock is an example of intersexual selection. Intersexual selection is the selection for traits that make males more attractive to females.

ner enjoying sexual access to the females. Males will engage in fights and displays directed toward one another. Ultimately, one male will drive the other males away and will take possession of the female or females.

In this case, males are competing with one another and the winner has access to the females. The females do not have any choice in the matter. Therefore, sexual selection favors those traits that increase the probability of a male winning the battle with other males.

Success in fights often depends on greater general size and the evolution and enlargement of special anatomical features for fighting such as large canine teeth and large horns, tusks, and antlers. Thus, sexual selection favors large size in males. In many mammalian species, males are significantly larger than are females, and males often exhibit distinct physical features. This phenomenon is referred to as **sexual dimorphism** (Figure 5–9). For example, male orangutans are considerably larger than females, and they also possess a flange of flesh

**FIGURE 5–9  Intrasexual Selection**
Among the orangutans, the adult male, seen here on the right, is much larger than the adult female, seen on the left. This is an example of sexual dimorphism.

around the face. Sexual dimorphism is thought to result from sexual selection.

**Sexual Selection in Humans**   The demonstration of sexual selection in humans is difficult. The heart of the problem is the issue of what aspects of human behavior are genetically determined and what aspects are the results of culture. With the exception of a very small number of genetic abnormalities that include very specific behavioral symptoms, scholars have yet to identify any normal behavior pattern that is clearly inherited. On the other hand there is evidence that some behavioral patterns do have genetic components.

Many scholars are interested in the issue of biological influence on human behavior and the role of natural selection in human behavior. This is in large part the discipline of **Darwinian psychology.** Our example of sexual selection in humans comes from the field of Darwinian psychology. It should be pointed out that this research is very controversial and has more than its share of critics. We do not have room in these pages for a rigorous critique of these ideas, but they should be taken simply as suggestions and an area for future research.

David M. Buss led a major cross-cultural study on the subject of mate choice.[6] In this study, Buss and his colleagues interviewed 9474 individuals from 33 countries on six continents and five islands. In the interviews, each individual was questioned about characteristics desired in a mate.

Some traits on the list showed great variation from culture to culture. These are probably the result of cultural tradition, that is, learned behavior. An example is the importance of chastity in a mate. In some societies, including China, India, Indonesia, and Iran, great importance was placed on chastity. In contrast, many Western European societies, including Sweden, Finland, and West Germany, responded that chastity was irrelevant or unimportant.

A number of traits showed great differences between male and female subjects. In general, males in all societies appear to value appearance in a potential mate more than do females. Females appear to value to a greater degree than males educational background, emotional stability, favorable social status, and intelligence. Such sex differences are fairly consistent among the various cultures.

Buss believes that the differences between what males and what females are looking for in potential mates are examples of sexual selection. Males tend to prefer females who will reproduce successfully. Fertility in women is highest in their early 20s and steadily declines until menopause. A male seeking to maximize his reproductive success would be expected to favor women in their early 20s along with physical features that are associated with youth, features that men consider to be associated with beauty. Although men express their preference in terms of beauty, in effect, men are exhibiting preferences for women with the highest probability of reproductive success.

On the other hand, Buss tells us that women prefer mates who are able to provide resources for her and her children, since resources (such as food, shelter, access to health care, and so forth) will maximize her reproductive success. Beauty is not as critical an issue in selecting her mate. More important are factors associated with financial success, social status, and education. Older males can be quite fertile, and most older males are clearly established in their careers and social status.

**How Sexual Selection in Humans Differs from That of Other Mammals**   In our discussion of sexual selection in mammals, we saw that generally all females mate and the vast majority produce offspring. On the other hand, not all males mate because not all males are selected by females or because only certain males are winners in direct male-to-male competition for females.

Is it ever the other way around? It is occasionally. The classic example is the seahorse where the female deposits her eggs in the male's brood pouch and leaves the male to carry the eggs and care for the young.

The situation in humans is not as clear-cut as it is in most other mammals. In the majority of mammals, the male leaves after the mating and the female raises the offspring; but the offspring grow rapidly and soon reach independence.

---

[6]D. M. Buss et al., "International Preferences in Selecting Mates," *Journal of Cross-Cultural Psychology* 21 (1990), pp. 5–47; D. M. Buss and D. P. Schmitt, "Sexual Strategies Theory: An Evolutionary Perspective on Human Mating," *Psychological Review* 100 (1993), pp. 204–232.

The human infant, however, is very helpless for a relatively long period of time. During the period of infancy, the human female must spend a great deal of time protecting and caring for her offspring as well as obtaining food. This drain on the mother's energy and resources could create a very dangerous situation for the offspring that would lead to a high mortality rate. Parental investment dramatically increases the chances of the offspring surviving. Survival of offspring ensures that the father's genes will be preserved in the next generation.

Because of the long-term investment of the male in the rearing of the offspring, it follows that the male will be more selective in choosing the female. Studies of features that males desire in females are generally those that are associated with high fertility—youth and good health. On the other hand, human females tend to select males that appear to have the resources to care for her and her child over a significant period of time.

## Kin Selection

Both natural selection and sexual selection can be seen in terms of reproductive success for the individual. The finch with the larger beak who can process food during a drought, or a colorful peacock who is more successful than his fellows at attracting a female, will have relatively high reproductive rates. In the first case, the finch succeeds through survival; in the second case, the peacock succeeds by successfully attracting a female. Fitness has been defined in terms of the number of offspring produced by the animal. The large-beaked finch and the colorful peacock have a high degree of fitness since they produce a large number of offspring.

Darwin noted that some behaviors cannot be explained in terms of increased fitness; sometimes we observe behaviors that appear to decrease the reproductive success of the animal. One category of such behavior is **altruism.** Altruism refers to behaviors that decrease the reproductive success of an individual while, at the same time, benefit the reproductive success of another member of the population.

Altruism may actually lead to the death of an individual. For example, a predator creeps close to the hiding place of a group of young animals. The mother attempts to distract the predator and, in the process, is killed, but her offspring survive. More subtle examples are seen in social situations where an individual expends resources and energy for the benefit of others. In a group of monkeys, for example, one animal spies a tree loaded with ripe fruit and calls out, letting other animals know. This results in competition for the fruit in which the original animal may not have as much to eat than if he consumed the fruit alone. Yet animals often behave in ways that contribute to the survival of other members of the community, sometimes placing themselves at a disadvantage.

From these examples, we see that individuals can pass on their genes to the next generation in two distinct ways. In the first and most obvious situation, parents pass their genes directly to an offspring. This is part of the process of natural selection. The second way is more indirect. Relatives share many of the same genes. If an individual assists a relative to reproduce and pass its genes on to its offspring, the individual is also assisting on passing on its own genes, that is, genes shared with the relative, to the next generation. This is referred to as **kin selection** (Figure 5–10).

Fitness is a measure of the reproductive success of an individual, that is, the number of offspring produced. The term **inclusive fitness** refers to the number of offspring produced plus the offspring produced by relatives who share some of the same genes. Therefore, altruistic behavior may increase the inclusive fitness of an individual. The degree of inclusive fitness will depend in large part on the

**FIGURE 5–10 Kin Selection**
Kin selection is the process whereby an individual's genes are selected for by virtue of that individual's increasing the chances that his or her kin's genes will be propagated into the next generation. This diagram shows that more of Altruist A's genes would be contributed to the next generation if his death meant that three (or more) of his siblings would survive to reproduce rather than if he survived but all of his siblings died.

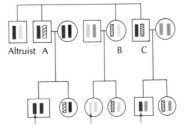

## Social Darwinism

What famous person who lived in the nineteenth century coined the phrase "survival of the fittest"? When asked, many students assertively answer: Charles Darwin. Actually, the phrase was coined by the English philosopher Herbert Spencer (1820–1903), who was greatly influenced by Darwin's ideas. In many of his works, including *First Principles* (1862) and *Principles of Ethics* (1879–1893), Spencer attempted to apply his own and Darwin's notions of biological evolution to psychology, sociology, and other social sciences. The application of the principles of biological evolution to explain topics such as social inequalities became known as social Darwinism.

Spencer and other proponents of social Darwinism viewed social life as a competitive struggle for power, wealth, and general well-being among individuals and nations. Using this concept, Europeans of the nineteenth century could argue that their dominant position in the world was the result of natural superiority that resulted from natural selection.

The Asian, African, Polynesian, and other peoples that Europeans ruled or subdued at the time were seen as belonging to earlier and more primitive stages of evolution. Likewise, the social inequalities among individuals within European society were thought to be variations on which natural selection acted. The prosperous were seen as being "fit," while the poor and powerless were seen as "unfit" individuals against which natural selection would select.

Spencer and other social Darwinists, including the American sociologist William Graham Sumner (1840–1910), believed that government should do nothing to aid the poor or sick. Modern social Darwinists assert that programs such as food stamps, aid to families with dependent children, and free public health clinics would interfere with the natural weeding out of unfit people and thereby weaken society. Or, said in reverse, a laissez-faire approach to social inequalities would lead to a natural cleansing of a population and hence would lead to a society and a world

better adapted to environmental pressures. In the United States and Europe, social Darwinism has been used to justify discriminatory actions against women, nonwhites, and various ethnic groups. It must be noted, however, that Charles Darwin was not a social Darwinist; at least, he avoided any discussion of the social implications of his ideas.

Scientific studies on human populations have not supported the tenets of social Darwinism. It appears that it is discrimination and the ideas of superiority, as well as differential access to natural resources, that produce most inequalities. The fact that some societies are more powerful than others and that some individuals within a society do not have equal access to necessities and luxuries is due to social history. When populations or classes of people within societies are freed from discriminatory practices, they can reach the same levels of wealth, power, and education as those groups who traditionally define themselves as superior.

closeness of the relationship; the closer the degree of kinship, the greater the number of genes that are shared in common. The degree of genetic relationship between two individuals is measured by the coefficient of relatedness, which measures the probability that two individuals share the same allele. The coefficient of relatedness between a parent and offspring is ½. Another way of looking at this is that a parent and offspring share ½ of their alleles. The same is true of full siblings. On the other hand, the number of shared alleles decreases as the relationship becomes more remote. The coefficient of relatedness between an aunt and her nephew is ¼, between first cousins is ⅛. Since more of the same alleles are involved, one would expect to see a greater degree of altruistic behavior between close relatives as opposed to more distant relatives.

Kin selection provides an explanation for many behaviors that we observe when looking at ani-

mals. In Chapter 9, we will closely examine the behavior of several species of living primates. Many of the behavioral patterns that we will examine can be understood in terms of kin selection.

### Summary

Variability is inherent in all populations. The human species is polymorphic and natural selection operates upon this variability. Natural selection can be seen as differences in reproductive rates among the variants within the population. Possessors of some genotypes reproduce to varying degrees, while others leave behind no offspring. Since the possessors of different genotypes produce differing numbers of offspring, their contribution to the next generation differs, and this brings about changes in the gene pool. Individuals or populations with higher survival or fertility rates are said to be better fitted to the environment in which they live.

Still, a genotype that is fit in one environment may lose some or all of its fitness in a new one; the converse is also true.

There are three types of natural selection: directional selection, stabilizing selection, and disruptive selection. All of these are seen as eliminating those individuals from the population who are not fit or less fit than others in the population. In contrast is kin selection, whereby an individual contributes to his or her reproductive success by acting in a manner that allows his or her kin to be reproductively successful.

Still another type of selection is sexual selection. Intersexual selection selects for traits that make males more attractive to females. Intrasexual selection involves males competing with one another with the successful individuals contributing genes to the next generation.

## THE ORIGIN OF SPECIES

Microevolution is the process of establishing and eliminating alleles from a population through such processes as natural selection and genetic drift. It is small-scale evolution that can be seen occurring in living populations, as in the case of Darwin's finches. Thus far we have been discussing microevolution.

Macroevolution, the subject of this section, addresses the evolution of new species and higher taxa such as genera and families. It is evolution, that in part is the cumulative effect of microevolu-

tionary change, that takes place over many generations and can be inferred from fossil and other types of evidence.

### The Evolution of Subspecies

All natural populations of plants and animals vary. For instance, within your community, your classroom, and your family, there are obvious differences in physical appearance in addition to less easily observed differences in such traits as blood type and resistance to disease.

Likewise, small natural populations vary. These local populations or **demes** are groups of organisms of the same species that live together, exploit the same habitat, and mate most frequently with one another. As a result, individuals within the deme tend to resemble one another more closely than they do individuals living in adjacent demes.

Demes, however, do not exist in isolation. Members of one deme, sometimes all of the adult members of one sex, will leave the deme of their birth, often at puberty, and join a neighboring deme. When the newcomer mates with members of the new deme, new alleles are effectively transferred from one deme to another. This is gene flow (Figure 5–11).

As a result of gene flow, nearby demes resemble one another more closely than demes further away. This can be illustrated on a map showing the distribution of demes of a particular kind of animal. When we plot a particular feature, its frequency appears to change as a function of distance. This

**FIGURE 5–11   Gene Flow**

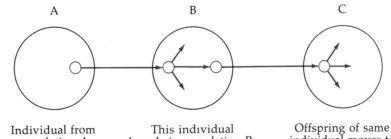

Individual from population A moves to population B.

This individual breeds in population B, and his or her genes become a part of the gene pool of population B.

Offspring of same individual moves to population C and breeds. Thus alleles from population A are ultimately introduced into population C.

systematic change in the frequency of a trait as one moves in a given direction is referred to as a **clinal distribution.**

Because phenotypes may vary with distance, groups of demes at opposite ends of a range may appear to be quite distinct in physical appearance. Such distinct groups are referred to as **subspecies.** Yet in spite of the differences that exist between subspecies, by definition, all members of all subspecies that make up the species are capable of successful reproduction.

While we may define as a separate subspecies groups of demes at opposite ends of a range, we must remember that variation may be continuous from one end of the range to the other. Thus, it is impossible to draw a dividing line where one subspecies ends and another begins. However, distinct boundaries may exist when there are physical barriers that impede gene flow between subspecies.

The development of subspecies often occurs when something is present that prevents or hinders gene flow between groups of demes. The simplest example is **geographical isolation** (Figure 5–12). If a particular animal is not capable of crossing bodies of water, for example, the change in the course of a river that now cuts across an area occupied by the species will create two groups of demes, one on either side of the river. Inability to swim prevents gene flow from occurring, leaving each group to evolve its own unique characteristics and to evolve into two distinct subspecies.

### The Evolution of Species

Once gene flow has ceased, two subspecies will continue to evolve independently as the various mechanisms, such as genetic drift, operate differently in the two populations. Also, subtle differences in microenvironments may exist in the two regions and new alleles may arise through mutation. These factors may lead to changes in the frequencies of alleles in the two subspecies.

If the genetic differences between the two subspecies become great enough, members of the two subspecies will no longer be capable of successful reproduction with each other even if the barrier is later removed. Consequently, the two groups may begin as two distinct subspecies and eventually evolve into two distinct species.

**Geographical Isolation**   Geographical isolation is a primary initiator of the evolution of new species in animals. It is the process in which members of a population become separated by barriers that prevent the interchange of genes. Such barriers include large bodies of water, mountain ranges, and deserts. **Speciation,** the evolution of new species, occurs when the separated populations have evolved characteristics that successfully prevent reproduction between them even if the geographical barriers are later lifted. Species that occupy mutually exclusive geographical areas are called **allopatric species** (Figure 5–13a).

Speciation may result from spatial isolation more subtle than major geographical barriers. Organisms may adapt to narrowly defined ecological niches. Within a tropical forest, for example, the tops of trees present microhabitats that may be quite different from those on the tree trunks or near the ground. In such cases, speciation may take place because of spatial isolation within a relatively small area.

**Reproductive Isolating Mechanisms**   Spatial isolation initiates speciation, but once speciation has

**FIGURE 5–12   First Step in Speciation**
Geographical isolation of two groups of demes prevents gene flow between them. Small circles represent demes, and connecting lines between them represent gene flow.

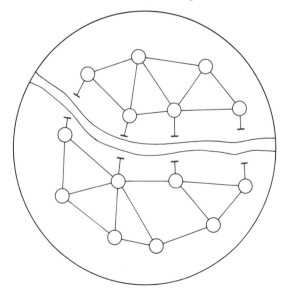

(a)    (b)

**FIGURE 5–13  Allopatric and Sympatric Species**
(*a*) Allopatric species occupy mutually exclusive geographical areas. (*b*) Sympatric species live in
the same area, but they are prevented from successful reproduction by a reproductive isolating
mechanism.

taken place, the species may come to reside within the same region. Such species are called **sympatric species** (Figure 5–13*b*). Eight reproductive isolating mechanisms serve to separate closely related species living side by side.

**Ecological isolation** is the circumstance in which two closely related populations are separated by what is often a slight difference in the niches they occupy. Some species are adapted to such extremely narrow niches that minor differences, such as variations in soil conditions, can effectively separate them, even when they are living next to each other.

**Seasonal isolation** occurs when the breeding seasons of two closely related populations do not correspond. For example, a male from one species whose breeding season is in April will not mate with a female from another species whose breeding season is in June.

**Sexual isolation** is the condition in which an incompatibility in behavior prevents mating between individuals of closely related populations. For instance, one or both sexes of a species may initiate

mating by a pattern of behavior that acts as a stimulus to the other sex of its own species but does not act as a stimulus to the opposite sex in a closely related species. The stimuli might take the form of specific visual signals, such as the mating rituals of certain birds or the light signals sent out by male fireflies. The member of the opposite sex responds only to the signal characteristic of its group. Incompatibility in auditory stimuli, such as calls, and chemical stimuli, such as the release of odoriferous substances, can also act as behavioral isolating mechanisms.

**Mechanical isolation** occurs because of an incompatibility in the structure of the male and female sex organs. In some cases, copulation is attempted, but no sperm is transferred.

Ecological, seasonal, sexual, and mechanical reproductive isolating mechanisms are **premating mechanisms** that prevent species from exchanging gametes. In **postmating mechanisms,** gametes are exchanged but either no offspring result or the offspring that do result are inviable, are sterile, or have reduced fertility. Premating mechanisms are less wasteful than postmating mechanisms, since in the former gametes are not used, but in the latter they are.

**Gametic mortality** is the process by which sperm are immobilized and destroyed before fertilization can take place. This occurs if antibodies in the genital tract of the female kill the sperm or if sperm cannot penetrate the membrane of the egg. The term **zygotic mortality** describes the situation in which fertilization occurs but development ceases soon after.

**Hybrid inviability** occurs when a mating between two species gives rise to a fertile hybrid that does not leave any offspring. This process is not well understood, but the lack of success of the hybrid may depend on its inability to compete effectively with nonhybrid individuals. In other words, the hybrid may not be as well adapted as the nonhybrid parents, or it may not display appropriate mating behavior. These adaptive and behavioral limitations may prevent the production of progeny.

**Hybrid sterility** occurs when the hybrid of two species is sterile. The classic example is the hybrid of the horse and the donkey, the mule, which, with few exceptions, is incapable of reproduction.

### Speciation in Genetic Terms

Why is isolation necessary for speciation to occur? Isolation allows descended populations to develop in an undisturbed manner, without the infusion of genes from another closely related population. In this way, the genetic material in the isolated population can be reconstituted, resulting in the development of one of the reproductive isolating mechanisms previously discussed. As long as there is significant gene flow between populations, these mechanisms cannot develop.

Mutation, drift, nonrandom mating, and selection operate to bring about speciation in isolated populations. The probability that the *same* mutation will occur, or that mutations will occur in the same sequence, in two different isolated populations is effectively zero. Different mutations create different potential genotypes.

Also, alleles can recombine in an almost infinite number of ways, which is important since a particular allele can have differing selective advantages in the context of variable genotypes. Since each isolated population contains unique gene combinations, new combinations may arise by chance, providing some selective advantage to the population.

In addition, no two habitats are identical. Therefore, separate populations are subject to different selective pressures. The genetic systems of separated populations tend to adapt to the changing environments. In fact, they must, or else they will become extinct. The new populations also represent different sectors of the parental population because of the founder principle, so they are somewhat different from each other from the very beginning.

### Ecology and Speciation

Animal populations are able to expand into new geographical regions and occupy some of the ecological niches that exist in those regions. However, the ability to adapt to new niches varies from an extremely limited potential in some populations to an almost unlimited, expansive ability in others. The major factors influencing this capability include the nature of the geographical barriers, the amount of change a group of organisms can tolerate, and the mode or modes of dispersal, that is, the ability of the organism to "get around."

When a population enters a new region, it will occupy niches similar to those it occupied in the original area. The niches will not be identical either, because minor environmental differences may exist or because other niches may already be occupied by another species.

Of course, an important factor that influences movement of a population into a new niche is whether another population of a different species is already present. When two populations occupy the same or parts of the same niche, they are said to be competing with one another. **Competition** does not necessarily mean that individuals belonging to the two species physically fight one another. It simply means that they eat the same food, seek out the same sleeping places, or are active at the same time of day.

When two populations are competing in the same niche, differences in anatomy, physiology, or behavior may give one population the edge. For example, a population that is able to gain access to food at the expense of the other population will be able to maintain itself in the niche. The other population will either die out, move, or—an important factor in speciation—adapt to another or a more restricted niche. Thus, if one population's diet includes fruits, leaves, and occasionally insects and another population's diet consists of fruits and leaves only, the first might increase its intake of insects. This population may ultimately become primarily insectivorous in its habits.

## Preadaptation

Populations entering new geographical regions often occupy niches not found in their original area. These populations will not be totally adapted to the new niches, since the selective pressures characteristic of these new niches would not have been operating on them. Nevertheless, many populations, or individuals within a population, may already have developed characteristics that prove to be adaptive in the new situation. The term **preadaptation** refers to the potential to adapt to a new niche. Organisms do not adapt because they need to but because by chance they have the potential to adapt.

A classic example of preadaptation is the evolution of flight in birds. Ever since the discovery in Germany of an ancient bird in 1861, named *Archaeopteryx,* most paleontologists have seen a connection between modern birds and the dinosaurs (Figure 11–2*b*). Perhaps one of the most specialized traits in modern birds is feathers, structures that are found on no other contemporary animal. Flight is a complicated method of locomotion and the anatomy for flight could not have simply arisen in place. The evolution of feathers was not likely to be in response to any anticipated need for flight.

Recently, two well-preserved dinosaur fossils were discovered in Liaoning Province, in northeastern China, dated between 135 and 120 million years old.[7] These dinosaurs possessed feathers! The two new dinosaur species are *Protarchaeopteryx,* named after *Archaeopteryx,* and *Caudipteryx,* meaning "tail-feather." The feathers are identical to those

of modern birds in structure, and include both down-like and vaned, barbed feathers located on the arms and legs, body, and tail. Nevertheless, these two animals were definitely not birds and, from an analysis of their anatomy, they were clearly not capable of flight. For what purpose did feathers originally evolve? Some possibilities include camouflage, display, or perhaps insulation. The presence of feathers, however, made the later evolution of avian flight possible.

## Specialized and Generalized Species

A species is **specialized** when it exhibits little variation. Thus, it can tolerate little change in its particular niche. A specialized species may not be able to move into new niches, even when the environmental conditions are similar, and may not be able to compete successfully with other populations.

An example of an extremely specialized animal in terms of diet is the Australian koala, which eats almost exclusively the leaves of eucalyptus trees. The distribution and proliferation of these trees therefore determine the distribution of the animal. Any change in tree population, due to a change in climate or in human use, will affect the koala population.

Because a specialized species can tolerate little change in its ecological niche, its ability to disperse is limited. However, as long as the habitat remains stable, a specialized species will be highly competitive toward less specialized species in its habitat. It will experience a high degree of reproductive success.

If a small population does become geographically isolated from the parental population and develops a specialized relationship with the new environment, this ecological specialization will act as an isolating mechanism, preventing gene flow. Hence, speciation will occur.

A **generalized species** exhibits a greater variability than a specialized species and can survive in a variety of ecological niches. Humans are perhaps the most generalized of all species. Humans' variability is also expressed in terms of cultural patterns. Through their cultural ingenuity, human populations can adjust to environments such as the extreme cold of the Arctic and the heat and humidity of the tropics by making tools and building appropriate shelters. Now, with the development

---

[7] J. Qiang et al., "Two Feathered Dinosaurs from Northeastern China," *Nature* 393 (June 25, 1998), pp. 753–761; K. Padian and L. M. Chiappe, "The Origin of Birds and Their Flight," *Scientific American,* February 1998, pp. 38–47; and J. Ackerman, "Dinosaurs Take Wing," *National Geographic* 194 (July 1998), pp. 74–99.

**BOX 5-2**

# Eugenics and the Reduction of Variability

Humans are one of the most ecologically generalized species, primarily because of human culture, which allows for flexible responses to diversity and environmental change. Humans also show considerable biological diversity, which allows for the exploitation of numerous environments.

Eugenics is the study of various methods that can improve the inherited qualities of a species. Nevertheless, in some instances, eugenic programs could have a very negative effect on the human population by reducing genetic variability.

A major question is: What traits should be eliminated? Genetic abnormalities that lead to an early death, extremely low intelligence, and severe skeletal abnormalities will probably never have any advantages in future generations. However, what about certain mild metabolic defects or blood disorders that could conceivably have beneficial effects if the environment should change? Also, alleles that are deleterious in the homozygous state may confer adaptive advantage in the heterozygote.

A classic example of this situation is the relationship between sickle-cell anemia and malaria. Sickle-cell anemia is often a lethal trait, bringing about disability and early death, yet the presence of this deleterious allele in the heterozygous individual brings about a resistance to malaria, a resistance also found in the homozygous individual. Many other examples exist of alleles that, although dis-

advantageous in the homozygous recessive state, bring about a greater adaptation in the heterozygous than in the homozygous normal individual. In 1987, the carrier rate for cystic fibrosis, a fatal lung disease, was found to be higher than expected; one explanatory proposal is that the heterozygous individual has some selective advantage that has as yet been unidentified.

Imagine a situation whereby, by using eugenic means, we could eliminate the allele for sickle-cell anemia through detection of heterozygotes. This is a fine goal. What would happen, though, if the techniques for controlling malaria become ineffective? Because of the disappearance of the sickle-cell allele, the population would lack the protection from malaria conferred by this allele. This

is not farfetched, since the major means of controlling malaria is to destroy the disease-carrying mosquito with insecticides such as DDT. Already, large populations of mosquitoes have evolved resistance to DDT. If malaria became a threat again and the sickle-cell allele no longer existed, the population would be less fit in the new malarial environment than it was in the old one (see figure).

As the situation changes, what was at one time advantageous (the sickle-cell trait) might become disadvantageous, but conceivably it could become advantageous again. Also, new diseases can evolve; if certain types of people are deleted from the population through eugenics, it later might turn out that they were the people who carried the immunity to the new disease.

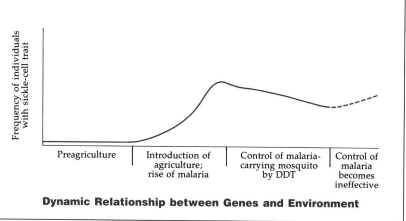

**Dynamic Relationship between Genes and Environment**

of life-support systems, people can live for extended periods of time under the sea and in outer space. This ability to move into a variety of habitats has been responsible for the great dispersal of humans over the earth. Perhaps in the future it will be responsible for their dispersal throughout the solar system.

Because of people's lack of precise environmental requirements, and because of their ability to culturally adjust, geographical barriers have had little chance to isolate human populations effectively.

Since gene flow has been continuous, speciation has not occurred among humans. People are, of course, not the only generalized animals. In fact, *generalized* and *specialized* are relative terms. At one end is the extremely specialized koala and at the other the very generalized *Homo sapiens*. Within these limits are varying degrees of generalization and specialization.

**Specialized and Generalized Traits** We have been using the concepts of generalization and specialization to refer to the relationship between a population and its niche, but we can also use these terms to label specific characteristics displayed by the members of populations. For instance, the human hand is generalized in that it can be used for many purposes, such as carrying objects and manufacturing tools. The foot, on the other hand, is specialized in that it is used for basically one thing, locomotion. What is important here is that the relative specialization or generalization of a specific trait may make that trait more or less important for survival than another trait. Generally, the more specialized anatomical, physiological, or behavioral features an animal has, the more specialized the total phenotype will be.

Specialization can lead not only to speciation but also to evolutionary dead ends. The more specialized an animal becomes, the less likely it will be to move into new niches; hence the animal has less chance of encountering the isolation necessary for further speciation to occur. When a species becomes so specialized in a particular niche that it cannot tolerate change, it is in greater danger of extinction than a more generalized species. If eucalyptus trees die out, so will koalas. On the other hand, if one of the environments that a particular group of humans occupies becomes unlivable, other environments will support this group.

### Rates of Speciation

The rates at which speciation occurs are difficult to determine, and the fossil record is of little help. First, it is difficult or impossible to know when reproductive isolating mechanisms came into being. How is one to know from bones if differences in mating behavior existed between two morphologically similar populations?

Second, even if isolating mechanisms could be observed in the fossil record, they develop in too short a time for the points at which differentiation takes place to be noticed. Reproductive isolating mechanisms might develop quickly, but a fossil sequence most likely consists of forms that lived thousands of years apart.

Although rates of speciation cannot be measured effectively, we can infer that they are dependent on internal and external factors. Internal factors include such things as point mutations, chromosome changes, and other genetic factors that may lead to

the development of reproductive isolating mechanisms. External factors include the types of barriers to gene flow, the types of new ecological niches available, and so forth.

We may assume that related populations that have low mutation rates, that live in homogeneous environments without physical barriers, and that are not under great selective pressure may remain basically stable and not develop sufficient differences for speciation. It follows that high mutation rates, strong selective pressures, differing ecological niches, and separation by geographical barriers may provide the necessary conditions for rapid speciation.

**The Tempo of Evolutionary Change**   There are two general views on the tempo of evolutionary change. Charles Darwin called the first "descent with modification." Known today as **phyletic gradualism,** it sees evolution as a slow process characterized by gradual transformation of one population into others. In 1972, paleontologists Niles Eldridge and Stephen Jay Gould proposed a different scheme, called **punctuated equilibrium.**[8]

The phyletic gradualism model of evolution assumes that the rate of evolutionary change is relatively slow and constant through time. The fossil record, however, reveals what appear to be shifts in the pace of evolutionary change within specific lineages. An evolutionary line that has been very "conservative" for millions of years may seem to suddenly undergo a rapid burst of evolutionary change. Evolution may proceed quickly when a population enters a new habitat, but as the population adapts to its new niche, the rate of evolution will slow. These shifts in the tempo of evolution are seen as an illusion by phyletic gradualists. Such shifts in tempo are explained as reflections of imperfections in the fossil record, caused by such things as changing conditions for fossilization.

The punctuated equilibrium model is consistent with the data from the fossil record. Eldredge and Gould propose that a large population may become fragmented into several new populations by geographical isolation or migration. New populations,

---

[8]N. Eldredge and S. J. Gould. "Punctuated Equilibria: An Alternative to Phyletic Gradualism," in T. J. M. Schopf (ed.), *Models in Paleobiology* (San Francisco: Freeman, Cooper, 1972), pp. 82–115.

now peripheral to the main population, would initially differ from the main population because of the founder effect. In addition, these peripheral populations would be small and therefore subject to the effects of genetic drift. Some researchers believe that in small peripheral populations, genetic drift is a much stronger evolutionary force than has previously been proposed in most microevolutionary models. Thus, natural selection and genetic drift may differ in their importance in microevolu-

tion and macroevolution in different populations (Figure 5–14).

**Regulatory Genes** Other genetic events could be responsible for relatively rapid evolutionary shifts. Among these would be chromosomal mutations such as translocations and inversions. Another possibility involves regulatory genes. Mutations in regulatory genes may play an important role in speciation. Such mutations would not affect the coding

**FIGURE 5–14 Phyletic Gradualism and Punctuated Equilibrium**
(*a*) Phyletic gradualism sees okapi and giraffe evolution as two evolutionary lines slowly diverging from a common ancestor. (*b*) Punctuated equilibrium sees a small population coming off of the pre-okapi group leading to modern okapis, while several more giraffelike species evolved and became extinct through time.

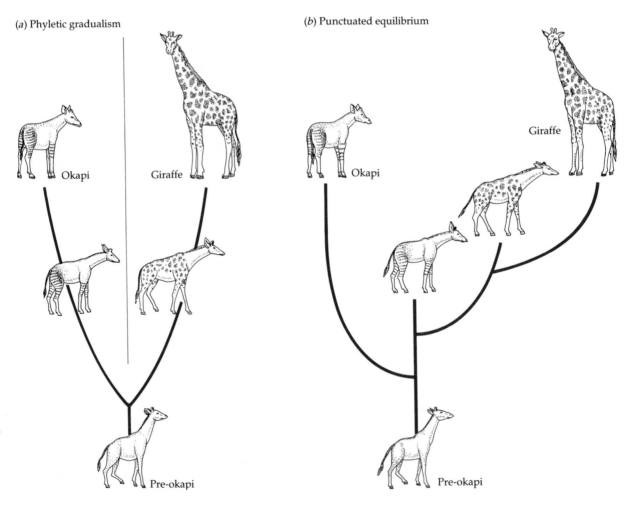

(*a*) Phyletic gradualism

(*b*) Punctuated equilibrium

for a polypeptide chain, but they might change the timing of the production of that structural unit or block its production altogether.

Differences between closely related species may be due more to mutations in the regulation of structural genes than to changes in the structural genes themselves. For example, researchers have found that, on the average, 44 human and chimpanzee proteins are 99 percent identical, yet these organisms are anatomically quite dissimilar. Mary-Claire King and Allan C. Wilson believe that the differences are due mainly to changes in regulatory, not structural, genes.[9] Since one regulatory gene may affect many morphological and behavioral traits, a mutation to a single or a few regulatory genes may lead to rapid evolution. This idea will be discussed further in Chapter 8.

### Adaptive Radiation

Movement into new ecological niches depends on many factors. First, there has to be physical access to the new niche; physical barriers may limit an organism's chance for dispersal. Second, the habitats in which the individuals live must provide a variety of niches. A lowland animal living in a valley surrounded by high mountains has immediate access to a diversity of adjacent altitudinal niches. In contrast, a flatland animal population, while perhaps finding it easier to move more extensively, may encounter only a limited number of flatland niches. Third, the individuals entering the new niche must be preadapted to some degree. Fourth, either the new niche must be unoccupied or the entering individuals must be able to compete successfully with other populations already existing in the niche.

A generalized species is usually able to survive in a variety of habitats. Its members may spread into new ecological niches to which they are preadapted and form new populations. Over time, these populations will take on distinctive characteristics as they become more closely adapted to their new niches. Subspecies will form, and in many cases, new species will emerge. The evolution of new species is most likely to occur in certain situations: when a species enters an uninhabited environment or one in which competition does not exist (as in the example below), or when a species develops new anatomical or physiological adaptations that allow it to compete successfully in a variety of niches. Such a proliferation of new species is called an **adaptive radiation.**

A classic example of adaptive radiation is the case of the finches of the Galápagos Islands, where a single mainland species evolved into 13 new species upon reaching the islands (Chapter 1) (Figure 5-15). Another important example is the case of primates on the island of Madagascar where, isolated from monkeys and apes, earlier primates evolved into a number of forms found nowhere else—lemurs, indris, and aye-ayes. We will look at these primate forms in Chapter 7.

### Extinction

While evolution is constantly bringing about the development of new species, other species are disappearing. When pressures develop in an environment, natural selection does not always bring about new adaptations. In many cases, the organisms involved simply do not have the potential to adapt. Because they are too specialized and are not preadapted to the new situation, they become **extinct.**

Extinction can occur in another way. As a species evolves, there is a point at which a species can be considered to be significantly different from its ancestral species. At this point, paleontologists may give it a new species name. The ancestral species becomes extinct not by dying off, but by evolving into something else.

Extinction is not an unusual event. Extinctions of the past far outnumber the total number of species that are living today. Humans, through their technology, have increased the rate of extinction. Humans use guns to kill animals and bulldozers to destroy their habitats. Although there is usually competition between organisms over particular niches, wherein some of the competitors are displaced, no large animals can compete successfully with *Homo sapiens* for any environment. (Interestingly, those organisms that do compete successfully with humans are small forms, such as

[9]M.-C. King and A. C. Wilson, "Evolution at Two Levels in Humans and Chimpanzees," *Science* 188 (1975), pp. 107–116.

Large seed-eating ground finch

Cactus ground finch

Insectivorous tree finch

Small seed-eating ground finch

Vegetarian tree finch

Woodpecker finch

**FIGURE 5–15 Darwin's Finches**
The diverse bill forms represent adaptations to different niches, an example of an adaptive radiation.

mice, flies, and disease organisms.) Therefore, the give-and-take, the periods of change and reestablishment of new balances, and the derivation of new types do not generally occur when people take over an environment.

## Summary

Macroevolution includes those processes responsible for the evolution of species and higher taxa. The local reproductive population is the deme, and the forces of evolution operate to bring about changes in gene frequencies within the gene pools of demes. Since different demes of the same species occupy slightly different habitats, selective pressures may differ from deme to deme.

When demes or groups of demes become reproductively isolated, subspecies may develop. The elimination of gene flow between demes, which is usually the result of some type of geographical barrier, allows for the accumulation of different mutations within each deme. These accumulations and gene-frequency changes, generated within and restricted to each deme, ultimately make successful reproduction between the demes impossible. Over time, these populations may become distinct species, called allopatric species.

Sympatric species are closely related species that have come to reside in the same general geographical area. Yet gene flow is effectively prevented by one of several reproductive isolating mechanisms: ecological isolation, seasonal isolation, sexual isolation, mechanical isolation, gametic mortality, zygotic mortality, hybrid inviability, and hybrid sterility.

Populations within a species will tend to disperse into new regions where they occupy similar ecological niches, but these new niches can never be identical to the original ones. Certain individuals within the population may possess preadapted variations that increase their adaptation in the new niche. When a population enters an area in which it has no competition, or when a population evolves new anatomical or physiological adaptations, speciation may be quite rapid. This rapid proliferation of species is an adaptive radiation. However, if populations unable to compete in their original niche do not adapt to new or changing niches, extinction may result.

## STUDY QUESTIONS

1. What is meant by the statement that evolution is based on variation within the population and within the niche?
2. What is the difference between microevolution and macroevolution?

3. Often the fitness of a particular trait and the nature of the selective pressures within a population are not obvious. What selective pressures are operating on hemoglobin S in a malarial environment?
4. What are the different types of selection discussed in the chapter? How does kin selection differ from other forms of selection?
5. What is meant by the term *sexual selection?* Does sexual selection operate in human populations?
6. Speciation follows geographical isolation. What occurs genetically after a population becomes geographically isolated? What factors other than geography serve to isolate populations?
7. Why is necessity not the "mother of invention" in evolutionary terms?
8. Contrast the phyletic gradualism model of evolution with the punctuated equilibrium model.
9. What differentiates a generalized from a specialized species?
10. There are two types of extinction. What are they?

## SUGGESTED READINGS

Bowler, P. J. *Evolution: The History of an Idea,* rev. ed. Berkeley: University of California Press, 1989. This book outlines the history of evolutionary theories. Its final chapter looks at modern debates about evolutionary theory, including the ideas of creationists.

Buss, D. M. *The Evolution of Desire: Strategies of Human Mating.* New York: Basic Books, 1994. This is a report of David Buss's study of mate selection in 37 societies.

Edelstein, S. J. *The Sickled Cell: From Myths to Molecules.* Cambridge, Mass.: Harvard University Press, 1986. This book details the history and nature of sickle-cell anemia.

Jones, D. *Physical Attractiveness and the Theory of Sexual Selection.* Ann Arbor: Michigan Museum of Anthropology Publications, 1996. This is a study of human sexual selection. The book includes a discussion of research in five human societies.

Maitland, A. E., and D. C. Johanson. *Blueprints: Solving the Mystery of Evolution.* New York: Penguin, 1989. Written by a journalist and a well-known paleoanthropologist, this book is an extremely readable introduction to evolutionary theory. It tells the story of how evolutionary and genetic ideas developed through time.

Mayr, E. *Toward a New Philosophy of Biology: Observations of an Evolutionist.* Cambridge, Mass.: Harvard University Press, 1989. One of the best-known modern evolutionary theorists discusses his ideas about evolution and the origin of species.

Volpe, E. P., and P. Andrews. *Understanding Evolution,* 7th ed. New York: McGraw-Hill, 1999. This is a short introduction to the theory of evolution and population genetics.

Wright, R. *The Moral Animal.* New York: Vintage Books, 1994. A very readable introduction to evolutionary psychology.

## SUGGESTED WEB SITES

Center for Evolutionary Psychology at UC Santa Barbara: http://www.psych.ucsb.edu/research/cep/
Interview with Richard Dawkins: http://www.rtd.com/~lippard/skeptic/03.4miele-dawkins-iv.html
Speciation in Progress (the example of *Ensatina escholtz,* a lungless salamander): http://www.santarosa.edu/lifesciences/ensatina.htm

Additional web sites are listed in the *Workbook* that accompanies this text.

## CHAPTER 6

# People's Place in Nature

*It was to reveal the divine design that a young Swedish naturalist called Carl von Linné (generally known by his pen-name of Linnaeus) began the first great catalogue of animals and plants which culminated in the publication in 1752 of* Philosophia Botanica, *written in Latin, in which he classified all plants according to class, genus, and species. . . . In his view the universe was static and atemporal, unchanged since it had first been created by God. He was interested only in the number, figure, proportion and situation of the organisms he classified, because these data were essential if the full complexity of God's design were to be revealed. Linnaeus conceived of a perfectly balanced nature, advocating zoos with cages each containing one pair of each type of animal, separated from other types, without interaction between them. According to him such a zoo would reproduce conditions as they had been on earth immediately after Creation.[1]*
—James Burke

## Chapter Outline

**Taxonomy**
Linnaeus's Classification
The Basis of Modern Taxonomy
Determining Evolutionary Relationships
Cladistics
Summary

**People and the Animal World**
The Animal Kingdom
The Phylum Chordata
The Vertebrates
The Mammals
Summary

---

[1]From James Burke, *The Day the Universe Changed* (Boston: Little, Brown, 1985). Copyright ©1985 by London Writers Limited. By permission of Little, Brown and Company and BBC Enterprises Ltd.

Humans are animals. They are part of a great diversity of living things, all of which share certain basic traits. Within the depths of the cell, biochemical mechanisms are remarkably similar wherever they are found. Yet, upon this base, life has evolved into an amazing variety of forms.

Early naturalists, including Carolus Linnaeus, viewed the complexity of life as a manifestation of the divine design that revealed itself at the creation. Although Linnaeus's view was a far cry from the vision of evolutionary change published by Charles Darwin over 100 years later, the classification of the living world was an important step in the development of such a theory. Classification provided biologists with a system for discussing, comparing, and contrasting living forms. This chapter discusses biological classification and looks at how humankind is related to the rest of the animal kingdom.

## TAXONOMY

All human societies attempt to put order into their world. To understand the nature of living things and their diversity, people sort this diversity into a manageable number of categories. These categories can then be related to one another.

Ordering is one of the first steps in science, and the scientist is involved in the development of classification schemes. If we are to consider variability scientifically, we must precisely define the units of study and how they are related to one another. A system of organizing data is a **classification.** The science of classifying organisms into different categories is known as **taxonomy.**

### Linnaeus's Classification

The most significant early attempt to order the living world was that of the Swedish naturalist Carolus Linnaeus (1707–1778). Although fundamental differences exist in theory, the system developed by Linnaeus is the basis of the system of classification used in modern biology.

The basic unit of classification in Linnaeus's scheme is the species, which Linnaeus considered to be a unit of creation, unchanging and distinct through time. His task was to define all the species known to him and to classify them. In his 10th edition of *Systema Naturae,* published in 1758, he listed

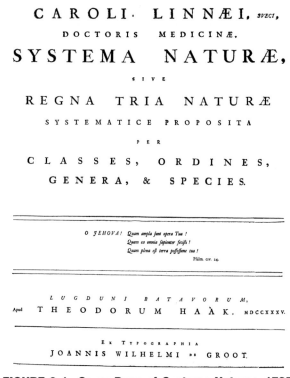

**FIGURE 6–1  Cover Page of *Systema Naturae,* 1735** Carolus Linnaeus's *Systema Naturae* set forth the form of the classification of the living world still in use today.

4235 animal species (Figure 6–1). Today, according to biologist Edward O. Wilson, there are approximately 1,032,000 animal species that have been described in scientific journals.[2]

**Binomial Nomenclature**  Linnaeus realized that a given animal is often known by different names in different parts of the world. Indeed, the same kind of animal often has several names in the same language. For these reasons, he decided to give species new Latin names. He chose Latin not only because it was the language of science but also because it was unchanging and politically neutral.

The system developed by Linnaeus is called a **binomial nomenclature** because each species is known by a **binomen,** or a two-part name. For

---

[2]E. O. Wilson, *The Diversity of Life* (Cambridge, Mass.: Belknap Press, 1992).

**BOX 6-1**

# The Diversity of Life

The typical urban American student is probably aware of only a very small number of animal species. The first that come to mind are those we keep as pets, including the familiar dogs and cats and the less familiar tropical fish, turtles, and parrots. Perhaps more significant are those urban species about which we would rather not think: rats, spiders, flies, and cockroaches. William Jordan describes several animal species that have made notable adaptations to an urban lifestyle in the suburbs of Los Angeles: the opossum, coyote, skunk, crow, parrot, alligator lizard, argentine ant, cellar spider, and feral cat.[1] Yet the totality of urban fauna is rather limited.

Moving to a larger venue, we may ask: How many animals worldwide have been identified and named by biologists? Not surprisingly, this list is a great deal longer. Yet most of the animals on this list are known only from a few specimens in a dusty museum drawer or a drawing in a technical scientific journal. This state of affairs makes it extremely difficult to arrive at an accurate estimate of the number of animal species that do exist on earth. Estimates vary tremendously, and many biologists agree that the number of animal species described and named may be only a fraction of the species that actually exist.

Biologist Edward O. Wilson ponders this question.[2] As a result of his search, he estimates that 1,032,000 animals are presently described and named. If we examine the number of animals in each of the animal phyla as seen in the figure, we observe that the vast number of known animal species are the arthropods, the phylum that includes the beetles, spiders, ants, and butterflies. And of the animal species yet to be discovered, the vast majority will probably turn out to be the arthropods living in the world's tropical rain forests. Biologists are very concerned about the rapid destruction of the rain forest that is destroying tens of thousands, if not millions, of unknown animal species, some of which could have a major impact on human survival and the quality of human life.

And what of the mammals, the group of animals to which we belong? Only about 4000 mammals are known and, except for a few small rodents and similar types, most mammals have been named and described.

George Ward

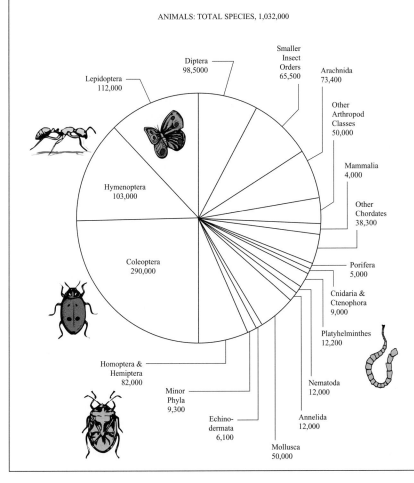

Number of Living Animal Species Currently Known
(According to Major Group)

ANIMALS: TOTAL SPECIES, 1,032,000

Diptera 98,5000
Lepidoptera 112,000
Smaller Insect Orders 65,500
Arachnida 73,400
Other Arthropod Classes 50,000
Mammalia 4,000
Other Chordates 38,300
Hymenoptera 103,000
Porifera 5,000
Cnidaria & Ctenophora 9,000
Platyhelminthes 12,200
Coleoptera 290,000
Nematoda 12,000
Homoptera & Hemiptera 82,000
Minor Phyla 9,300
Annelida 12,000
Echinodermata 6,100
Mollusca 50,000

[1]W. Jordan, "New Eden, City of Beasts," in *Divorce Among the Gulls* (San Francisco: North Point Press, 1991), pp. 70–100.
[2]E. O. Wilson, *The Diversity of Life* (Cambridge, Mass.: Belknap Press, 1992).

example, Linnaeus gave the human species the name *Homo sapiens. Homo* is the generic name, or the name of the **genus** to which humans belong. A genus is a group of similar species. This name is always capitalized, and no two genera (plural of *genus*) in the animal kingdom can have the same name. The second name is the specific name. The specific name is never capitalized, and it must always appear in association with the generic name. The generic and specific names are always in italics or underlined. Thus, humans belong to the genus *Homo* and the species *Homo sapiens.*

**Classification of Species**   According to Linnaeus, the characteristics of each animal species were the result of creation and a reflection of the divine plan. Variations within a species did exist, but these variations were considered irrelevant. The basic unit of study was actually the divine blueprint, or **archetype,** of a particular species.

Linnaeus noted that some species are more alike than others; monkeys resemble humans quite closely and humans resemble dogs more than they do fish. Scientists of the eighteenth century believed that these similarities in structure were due to similarities in archetype. To study the similarities between animal forms, and to classify them on this basis, was to reveal the divine plan.

Archetypes were found on different levels. Each species had an archetype. Because humans, monkeys, and apes shared a great many features, Linnaeus placed them in a common group on the basis of these similarities. The archetype for the group Primates was simply a less specific blueprint than the archetype for the individual species. Going one step further, Linnaeus placed humans, monkeys, dogs, horses, and others into an even larger group, Mammalia. Here again, an archetype existed, but with even more generalized specifications.

### The Basis of Modern Taxonomy

Biologists no longer think of species as fixed units of creation. A species is a population whose members are able to reproduce successfully among themselves but are unable to reproduce with members of other species. The species is a dynamic unit, constantly changing through time and space; a species living at one point in time may be quite different from its descendants living tens of thousands of years later. Segments of a species may develop into subspecies and, finally, may form a separate species. Species are not defined by physical similarities per se but rather on the criterion of their successful reproduction. Species are classified into higher taxonomic levels on the basis of their evolutionary relationships.

**The Taxonomic Hierarchy**   The species is the basic unit of the modern system of classification. Closely related species are placed in a common genus. A genus represents a group of species with a fairly recent common ancestry; these species are populations that in the recent past were merely subspecies of some larger population. A genus is an example of a **taxon** (plural, *taxa*), which is a group of organisms at any level of the taxonomic hierarchy.

Taxa above the level of genus are often referred to as the **higher taxa.** The existing system of classification contains five main higher taxa: **family, order, class, phylum,** and **kingdom.** A family is a group of closely related genera; an order is a group of closely related families; and so forth. As we go higher in the hierarchy, each succeeding level is defined by more generalized characteristics. Because the higher taxa encompass so much variation, the included species have fewer characteristics in common.

Humans belong to the species *Homo sapiens* and the genus *Homo.* Although the genus *Homo* contains only one living species, it includes several extinct species such as *Homo erectus.* The genus *Homo* is part of the family Hominidae, which also includes the extinct genera *Ardipithecus, Australopithecus,* and *Paranthropus.* The family Hominidae belongs to the order Primates, as do the monkeys, apes, tarsiers, and prosimians. The order Primates, in turn, is part of the next higher taxon, the class Mammalia. Other examples of mammals are dogs, cattle, whales, elephants, and bats. The class Mammalia is included in the phylum Chordata, which also encompasses birds, reptiles, amphibians, and fish. Finally, the chordates belong to the kingdom Animalia, which includes all animal forms.

The seven taxonomic levels, however, are not enough for a complete and satisfactory classification. The prefixes *super-, sub-,* and *infra-* are used to create additional levels. Thus, there can be a superfamily, a suborder, an infraclass, and so on.

## TABLE 6-1

### THE CLASSIFICATION OF *HOMO SAPIENS*

KINGDOM: Animalia
  PHYLUM: Chordata
    SUBPHYLUM: Vertebrata
      CLASS: Mammalia
        SUBCLASS: Theria
          INFRACLASS: Eutheria
            ORDER: Primates
              SUBORDER: Anthropoidea
                SUPERFAMILY: Hominoidea
                  FAMILY: Hominidae
                    GENUS: *Homo*
                      SPECIES: *Homo sapiens*

Table 6–1 presents a detailed classification of the species *Homo sapiens.*

### Determining Evolutionary Relationships

**Phylogeny** refers to the evolutionary history of species. Since the development of classifications depends on the knowledge of evolutionary relationships among taxa, this section will discuss some of the problems in determining these evolutionary relationships.

**Homologous Features**  A comparison of two different animals may reveal many anatomical correspondences. In the reconstruction of a phylogeny, the taxonomist looks for structural correspondences that are the result of inheritance from a common ancestor. These are known as **homologies** or homologous features.

To convey the significance of homologous structures, we must point out that evolution is irrevocable. If we examine a series of changes in the genetic code, the probability that it will evolve back into the exact code from which it came is effectively zero. Specific anatomical traits may appear to evolve into an ancestral condition, but these similar appearances are superficial. Such apparent similarities affect only a few traits in a complex animal. An anatomical trait, however, can disappear or evolve further into something else. Furthermore, new structures do not simply appear from nowhere; they evolve from preexisting structures.

Figure 6–2 shows the forelimbs of a series of vertebrates. Externally, these forelimbs are quite different and serve different functions: manipulating objects, running, flying, and swimming. Yet all are derived from the same basic structure found in a common ancestral form. While the whale flipper reminds one of a fish fin, upon dissection the derivation of the flipper becomes obvious. It is an elaboration of the basic structure of the forelimb of a four-footed land vertebrate.

**FIGURE 6–2  Vertebrate Forelimbs**
Homologous bones in the forelimbs of four vertebrates are (H) humerus, (U) ulna, (R) radius, and (C) carpals. Homologies are similarities resulting from inheritance from a common ancestor.

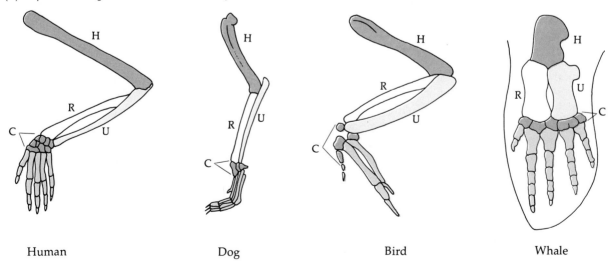

Human          Dog          Bird          Whale

## BOX 6-2

# The Feet of Whales

Transitional forms are very rarely recovered from the fossil record. A very small percentage of the living creatures that once lived are found as fossils. It is rather improbable that we will ever recover a representative of a rapidly evolving transitional form. This makes it difficult for some people to accept evolutionary history as fact.

From comparative anatomical and molecular studies of living forms, investigators hypothesize that modern cetaceans, the order that includes modern whales and porpoises, evolved from the mesonychids, a group of prehistoric even-toed hoofed animals related to modern deer, camels, and pigs. Yet until recently, fossils of early whales had

not been recovered. In December 1989, the husband-and-wife paleontology team of Philip Gingerich and Holly Smith discovered a whale with hind limbs in the Zeuglodon Valley in what is now the Egyptian desert.

The 40-million-year-old Egyptian fossils represent several bones of the pelvis and hindlimbs of *Basilosaurus*. The 20-inch-long leg articulates with a 10-inch-long pelvis, which in turn articulates with the spine of an animal some 50 feet long when adult. Although the hindlimbs are extremely tiny when compared with the body, they are fully functional. Philip Gingerich suggests that they may have been used to align the animal during copulation.

In 1994, fossil evidence of the earliest fully marine ancestor of the whale, *Rodhocetus*, was published. This form dates from about 46 to 47 million years ago and was found in Pakistan. An even older species is *Ambulacetus,* also from Pakistan. Unlike the younger *Rodhocetus, Ambulacetus,* having functioning legs, could move on land as well as in the water. Weighing about 300 kilograms (660 pounds), this early cetacean lived in shallow seas. Its skeleton shows a large, elongated hand, toes ending in hooves, and a long tail. It moved around on land very much like a modern sea lion and swam by means of undulations of the spine and paddling with its hindlimbs (see the figure). Other fossil cetaceans are known, the oldest dating from 52 million years ago, and also found in Pakistan.

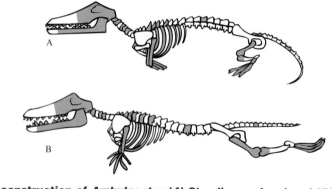

**Reconstruction of *Ambulacetus* (A) Standing on Land and (B) at the End of the Power Stroke during Swimming.**

*Sources:* P. D. Gingerich, "The Whales of Tethys," *Natural History,* April 1994, pp. 86–88; P. D. Gingerich et al., "New Whale from the Eocene of Pakistan and the Origin of Cetacean Swimming," *Nature* 368 (1994), pp. 844–847; P. D. Gingerich, B. H. Smith, and E. L. Simons, "Hind Limbs of Eocene *Basilosaurus:* Evidence of Feet in Whales," *Science* 249 (1990), pp. 154–157; and J. G. M. Thewissen et al., "Fossil Evidence for the Origin of Aquatic Locomotion in Archaeocete Whales," *Science* 263 (1994), pp. 210–212.

**Homoplastic Features**   It is, of course, possible for structures in two different species to be similar without being homologous. Such similarities are said to be **homoplastic.** Homoplasy can come about in four different ways: parallelism, convergence, analogy, and chance.

Homoplastic features may be found in related species that independently evolved similarities that did not exist in the common ancestor. However, the common ancestry did provide initial commonalities that gave direction to a parallel evolution in the two lines. This is called **parallelism.** For example,

while the common ancestor of the monkeys of the New World (Central and South America) and the monkeys of the Old World (Africa, Europe, and Asia) evolved in Africa, the evolution of monkeys in the New World and Old World occurred independently of one another. Many similarities between these two major groups of monkeys arose independently in the two hemispheres but from a common premonkey ancestor (Figure 6–3).

**Convergence** refers to similar developments in less closely related evolutionary lines. Figure 6–4 shows a North American wolf, a Tasmanian wolf,

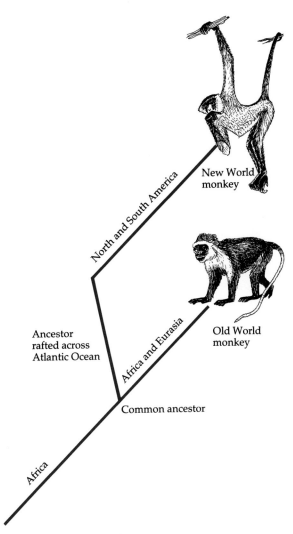

**FIGURE 6–3   Parallelism**
Old World and New World monkeys had a common origin in Africa. After rafting to South America, the New World monkeys evolved along lines similar to those of Old World monkeys because of the common origin and similarities in ecological niches.

and a whale. If a biologist had to classify these animals based on their evolutionary relationships, what criteria would be used?

A comparison of North American and Tasmanian wolves shows similarity in body size and shape, type of dentition, and diet—but it also shows great differences as well. The North American wolf and the whale are both placental mammals. In these species, the fetus is nourished through a placenta

until birth. The placenta is an example of an ancestral structure found in many descendant species. In contrast, the Tasmanian wolf, which is thought to be extinct today, is a marsupial, or pouched mammal, like the kangaroo. The absence of the placenta in the marsupials is evidence of a more distant relationship since the marsupials diverged from the mammalian line before evolution of the placenta.

The complex method of fetal nourishment characterized by the placenta is more indicative of a close evolutionary relationship than are size and shape. Yet the similarities seen in the North American wolf and the Tasmanian wolf are striking. They are due to the fact that similar selective pressures can bring about similar adaptations in divergent evolutionary lines; this is convergence. (For another example of convergence, see Figure 6–12.)

Another type of homoplasy occurs when two structures are superficially similar in very distantly related forms. For example, the wing of a bat and that of an insect are superficially similar and serve the same function—flying; however, there is no common relationship. Such similarities are called **analogies** (Figure 6–5). Of course, similarities can also arise by chance.

**Cladistics**

An important approach to the theory of classification is **cladistics.** This term comes from the word **clade,** which refers to a set of species descended from a particular ancestral species. The practitioner of cladistics looks for homologous features. A major concern in this search is how far back in time the homologies first appeared.

In cladistics, homologies that appeared recently and are therefore shared by a relatively small group of closely related taxa are called **shared derived (synapomorphic) features.** Homologies that first appeared a longer time ago and are shared by a larger group of species are called **shared ancestral (symplesiomorphic) features.** The task of the taxonomist is to identify which features are shared derived and which are shared ancestral, and to separate both these types from features that are **uniquely derived (autapomorphic)** in a particular species or group of species.

Conducting a cladistic analysis is relatively straightforward. Let us say that we wish to

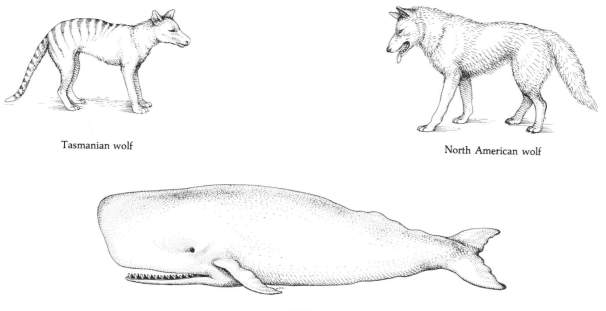

**FIGURE 6–4  Convergence**
The similarities between the Tasmanian wolf and the North American wolf result from convergent evolution. Actually, the North American wolf is more closely related to the whale.

**FIGURE 6–5  Analogy**
The wings of the butterfly, the bird, and the bat are analogous structures. They serve the same function, flying, but were independently evolved in different evolutionary lines.

determine evolutionary relationships among three species (or three genera, families, and so forth). These are species A, B, and C in Figure 6–6. We include in our analysis several other species that are closely related to the three in question; these additional species are called an **outgroup.** Features that appear in all or most of the species including the outgroup (A through F in Figure 6–6) are assumed to be shared ancestral features. (It is possible for a particular shared ancestral feature to be absent from a particular species because the feature has disappeared in that species.) Features that are found in the original set of species (A, B, and C) but not in the outgroup are assumed to be shared derived features.

From a cladistic analysis, a **cladogram** can be drawn that graphically presents the evolutionary relationships among the species (or other taxa) being studied (Figure 6–7). While such a diagram appears to convey an evolutionary history, the time element is not present. Thus, the cladogram, while depicting relationships among taxa, does not depict temporal relationships.

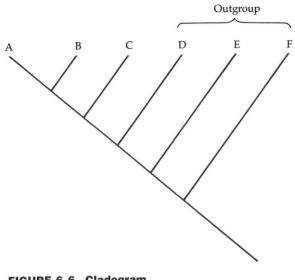

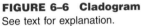

**FIGURE 6–6 Cladogram**
See text for explanation.

## Summary

Central to the scientific study of the diversity of life is a system of ordering data, which is known as classification; the science of classifying organisms into different categories is known as taxonomy. In 1758, Linnaeus published the 10th edition of his classification of the living world; the form of this classification is still used today. Linnaeus gave all living species a binomial name, or binomen, and placed species in genera, genera in families, and so forth up the taxonomic hierarchy. Species were seen as unchanging, divinely created units, each of which had an archetype, or divine blueprint. Similar-looking animals were placed in categories based on increasingly generalized archetypes.

Modern taxonomists think of the species as a dynamic unit defined in terms of reproductive success. Evolutionary relationships between species can be deduced on the basis of structural similarities that are the result of inheritance from a common ancestor; such similarities are known as homologies. On the other hand, structures in two different animals can be similar without being homologous; such similarities are said to be homoplastic. Homoplasy can come about in several different ways. Independent evolution of similarities in related species is referred to as parallelism. Convergence refers to developments that arise in divergent evolutionary lines when similar selective pressures cause similar adaptations. Two structures can be superficially similar in two or more species unrelated to common ancestry; such similarities are called analogies. Similarities can also come about by chance. In cladistics, a distinction is made between homologies that have appeared recently and are shared by a relatively small group of species or taxa (shared derived features) and homologies that first appeared a much longer time ago and are shared by a relatively large group of species or taxa (shared ancestral features).

## PEOPLE AND THE ANIMAL WORLD

### The Animal Kingdom

The first step in the classification of organisms is to divide them into large, basic units known as *kingdoms*. It was once thought that all organisms could be placed in either the plant kingdom or the animal kingdom. Today, however, taxonomists realize that many forms, such as unicellular organisms, bacteria, and fungi, do not fit neatly into either of these two groups; they are placed in other kingdoms, bringing the total number of kingdoms to five (Table 6–2).

Members of the animal kingdom differ from plants in a number of ways. Animals are incapable of synthesizing food from inorganic materials; they must obtain their nutrients by consuming other organisms. Most animals are highly mobile and have contracting fibers such as muscles. In addition, animals are composed of specialized kinds of cells. Most animals can respond quickly to changes in their environment because they have nerves, muscles, and special sensing organs.

The animal kingdom is divided into several units known as *phyla*, with each phylum representing a basic body plan. The number of recognized phyla varies from author to author, but the total number is usually more than 18. Most familiar animals belong to the following nine phyla (examples of animals in each are given in parentheses): Porifera (sponges), Coelenterata (jellyfish, sea anemones), Platyhelminthes (planaria, tapeworms), Aschelminthes (nematode worms), Mollusca (snails, scallops, octopuses), Annelida (earthworms), Echinodermata (starfish), Arthropoda

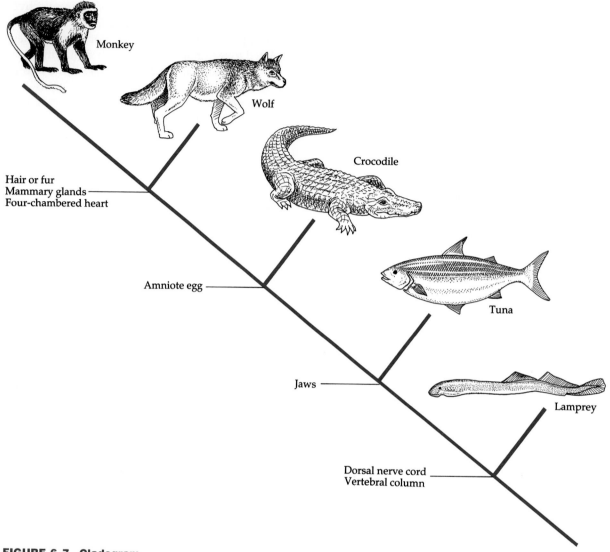

Monkey

Wolf

Crocodile

Hair or fur
Mammary glands
Four-chambered heart

Tuna

Amniote egg

Jaws

Lamprey

Dorsal nerve cord
Vertebral column

**FIGURE 6–7 Cladogram**
This cladogram shows the relationships among representatives of five vertebrates. Each branch
point is defined by one or more newly evolved shared derived features.

(spiders, butterflies, crayfish), and Chordata (fish,
reptiles, birds, mammals).

### The Phylum Chordata

Humans belong to the phylum Chordata. **Chordates** include such forms as the tunicates, fish, amphibians, reptiles, birds, and mammals.

It is instructive to compare the phylum Chordata with another, such as the phylum Arthropoda.

| TABLE 6–2 |
|---|
| **THE FIVE KINGDOMS OF LIFE** |
| KINGDOM: Animalia (sponges, earthworms, grasshoppers, shellfish, starfish, reptiles, mammals) |
| KINGDOM: Planti (pine trees, flowering plants) |
| KINGDOM: Fungi (mushrooms) |
| KINGDOM: Protista (unicellular organisms) |
| KINGDOM: Monera (bacteria, blue-green algae) |

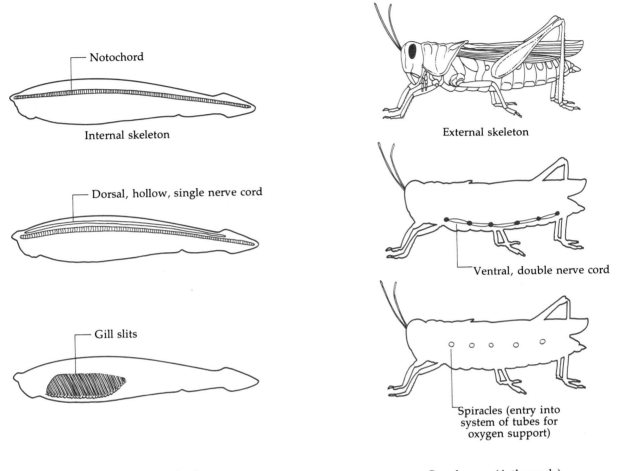

Amphioxus (Chordata)                    Grasshopper (Arthropoda)

**FIGURE 6–8  The Phyla Chordata and Arthropoda**
The major characteristics of the phylum Chordata are contrasted with those of the phylum Arthropoda.

Figure 6–8 compares a grasshopper, an arthropod, with an *Amphioxus*, a small, ocean-dwelling chordate. Some points of similarity can be noted. Each is **bilaterally symmetrical;** that is, each can be cut down the middle to form two halves that are generally mirror images of each other. Each animal has a head and a tail and a digestive system with openings at both ends.

A distinctive feature of the chordates is the presence of an internal skeleton. Part of this skeleton is a cartilaginous rod, called the **notochord,** that runs along the back of the animal. In all chordates, the notochord is present in the embryonic stage, but in most chordates, it is replaced by the spine in the adult. In the grasshopper (arthropod), the skeleton is external; the animal has no notochord.

In chordates, a single hollow nerve cord lies on top of the notochord (**dorsal** to the notochord). In the arthropods, the nerve cord is double and solid, and it is located on the **ventral,** or bottom, side of the animal.

In addition, all chordates have **gill slits** at some time in their life history. Although gills do not actually develop in humans, structures that appear in the human embryo are thought by embryologists to be **gill pouches.** Arthropods such as grasshoppers supply air to their tissues through a series of tubes that open to the outside through their outer covering. Others such as crayfish have feathery gills but no gill slits.

## The Vertebrates

The phylum Chordata includes the subphylum Vertebrata, which includes most of the animals within the phylum. There are seven living classes of vertebrates: the jawless vertebrates, the sharks and rays, the bony fish, the amphibians, the reptiles, the birds, and the mammals (Table 6–3).

The early **vertebrates** were similar in many ways to *Amphioxus,* but in place of a notochord, a true vertebral column, or spine, developed. Like the early chordates, the early vertebrates were filter feeders. Because they lacked jaws, they swam with open mouths; by forcing water into their mouths and out through their gills, they filtered out food particles. Vertebrates ultimately developed bone in place of cartilage, and many early forms were covered by bony plates. Today, the jawless vertebrates are represented by the highly specialized lamprey and hagfish.

A major event in vertebrate evolution was the evolution of jaws. New structures do not simply arise from nothing; they develop as modifications of preexisting structures. The jawless vertebrates have skeletal elements, **gill bars,** that support the gill slits. In the early fish, the first gill bars enlarged to become a primitive jaw (Figure 6–9).

While filter feeding restricted the jawless vertebrates to very small food particles, the evolution of jaws enabled them to prey on one another and to proliferate. Today, these jawed vertebrates are rep-

resented by the cartilagenous fish, the sharks and rays, and the bony fish. Land vertebrates eventually evolved from a population of freshwater bony fish.

**The Origin of Land Vertebrates**  The ancestors of the land vertebrates were freshwater bony fish capable of coping with drought conditions, which were common at the time. Periodically, lakes and streams dried up or became small ponds of stagnant water. These vertebrates had lungs for supplementing their oxygen supply in oxygen-deficient water.

The origin of land vertebrates also depended on the evolution of legs. Unlike the fish of today, these early fish had bony elements in their fins. The constant drying up of lakes and streams gave a local selective advantage to these fish, which could move overland from one pond to the next.

Land vertebrates did not arise because there was opportunity on land. Organisms do not evolve structures to meet the requirements of new potential habitats. No fish ever lifted its head out of the water, surveyed the land, and decided that since the land was devoid of competition and food was plentiful, it would then evolve lungs and limbs. The structures that make life on land possible evolved as adaptations to aid the fish in *water* under drought conditions. In retrospect, it appears as if the population evolved new adaptations in order to enter new niches on land. In reality, the evolution of new adaptations for life in water merely allowed the animal to adapt to new terrestrial habitats, an example of preadaptation.

**Amphibians and Reptiles**  The earliest land vertebrates were the amphibians. Amphibians, however, were tied to the water. Most needed to keep their skin moist, especially to aid in breathing through the skin, and all had to lay their eggs in water. This prevented an extensive exploitation of terrestrial habitats.

A life spent totally on land was made possible by changes in the breathing apparatus, which increased the efficiency of the lungs; a waterproof skin; and the **amniote egg.** The amniote egg may have evolved as a method of protecting eggs in water; but once it had developed, reproduction on land became possible.

---

**TABLE 6–3**

### THE CLASSIFICATION OF THE CHORDATES

PHYLUM:  Chordata
  SUBPHYLUM:  Tunicata (tunicates)
  SUBPHYLUM:  Cephalochordata (*Amphioxus*)
  SUBPHYLUM:  Vertebrata
    CLASS:  Agnatha (lampreys, hagfish)
    CLASS:  Chondrichthyes (sharks, rays)
    CLASS:  Osteichthyes (perch, herring, salmon)
    CLASS:  Amphibia (frogs, salamanders)
    CLASS:  Reptilia (turtles, lizards, snakes)
    CLASS:  Aves (robins, vultures, ostriches, penguins)
    CLASS:  Mammalia (dogs, elephants, whales, gorillas)

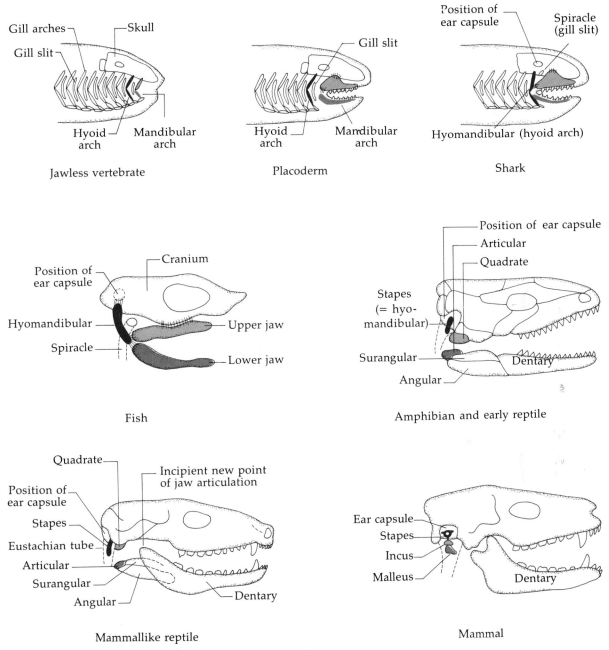

**FIGURE 6-9 Evolution of the Jaws and Middle Ear Bones**
Note the many examples of homologies. For instance, the malleus (a bone of the middle ear) of the mammal is homologous to the articular bone of the lower jaw in the amphibian and early reptile.

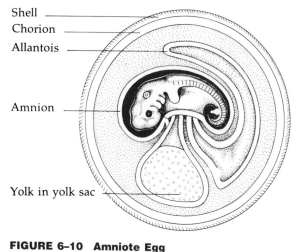

Shell
Chorion
Allantois

Amnion

Yolk in yolk sac

**FIGURE 6–10   Amniote Egg**
This type of egg could be laid on land.

The embryo in an amniote egg develops within a shell (Figure 6–10). Fertilization must take place inside the body of the female before the shell is formed. Within the shell, several membranes develop from embryonic tissue. The embryo is contained inside a fluid-filled **amnion,** which forms from the embryo's side. A second membrane, the **chorion,** is derived from the amnion; the chorion lies just beneath the shell and acts as a surface for oxygen absorption. Growing out of the embryo's digestive tract is the **yolk sac,** which is filled with yolk in reptiles and birds, and the **allantois,** where waste material is deposited.

With the development of the amniote egg, vertebrates were no longer tied to the water. The earliest true land vertebrates were the reptiles, which began to cover the land 300 million years ago. From this radiation evolved the dinosaurs and modern reptiles, as well as the birds and mammals.

## The Mammals

The reptilian group from which the mammals ultimately emerged appeared very early in the reptilian radiation. These early mammallike reptiles did not resemble modern reptiles; from the beginning, they showed marked mammalian features and soon evolved into true mammals. The mammals coexisted with a variety of animals, including the dinosaurs, throughout most of their history. With the demise of the dinosaurs, mammals became the dominant form of large terrestrial animal.

**The Regulation of Body Temperature**   A lizard sleeps through the cold desert night in an underground shelter. When it senses the warmth of the sun, it emerges into the daylight and suns itself. At last it is ready to perform the activities of the day. Yet when the desert sun is high, the lizard must seek shelter, for it cannot function in the desert's fierce heat.

A cold wind is blowing down the mountainside, yet the mouse wakes up before dawn. In the dark, safe from most of its enemies, it forages for food. Unlike the lizard, the mouse can function in the cold of night or in the fierce heat of day.

Contemporary reptiles are said to be "cold-blooded," while mammals are described as "warm-blooded," but these terms are far from descriptive since the body temperature of a lizard may be as high as that of a mammal. The primary distinction between the body temperatures of reptiles and mammals lies in the source of the body heat. Reptiles are **ectotherms;** that is, they derive most of their body heat from outside their bodies. Reptiles can and do maintain a high and constant body temperature, but they accomplish this primarily through behavior. During the cold of the night, the lizard seeks a relatively warm underground burrow; in the early morning, the animal suns itself on a rock; and during the heat of the day, it finds the shade of a plant or rock. This method of maintaining relatively constant temperature is termed **behavioral thermoregulation.** To maintain a constant temperature, the reptile must vary its activity with changes in the environment.

Like the lizard, the mouse also maintains a relatively high, constant body temperature. Unlike the lizard, however, mammals are **homeothermic;** that is, mammals can control their body temperature through physiological means and can maintain a high body temperature largely independent of the environmental temperature. This is accomplished by the ability to generate body heat internally (**endothermy**) and by special physiological and anatomical mechanisms for regulating the body temperature. This means that mammals can maintain a relatively constant, high level of activity with a fair degree of independence from the constraints of environmental temperature.

Homeothermy requires a complex of interrelated features such as the evolution of regulating

**BOX 6-3**

# Were Dinosaurs "Warm-Blooded"?

Characteristically, humans try to understand extinct forms by analogy, thinking of them in terms of modern species. Since the dinosaurs are placed in the class Reptilia, modern reptiles have been used as models for reconstructing how dinosaurs actually lived. Yet prehistoric species may have been quite different from similar-appearing modern ones.

Throughout the museums of the world, dinosaurs were once shown essentially as large lizards, and often as large, lumbering, quadrupedal beasts. Nevertheless, because of the discoveries and new interpretations of the past few decades, our picture of the daily life of the dinosaurs is rapidly changing. One major conclusion of some paleontologists, although it is far from universally accepted, is that some dinosaurs were "warm-blooded." John Ostrom describes the small, predatory dinosaur *Deinonychus*: "It must have been a fleet-footed, highly predacious, extremely agile and very active animal, sensitive to many stimuli and quick in its responses. These in turn indicate an unusual level of activity for a reptile and suggest an unusually high metabolic rate."[1]

Some evidence is highly suggestive of endothermy, although the picture is far from clear and controversy reigns. For example, skeletons and preserved footprints show that most dinosaurs were erect bipeds, a posture and gait that occur today only in the endotherms, mammals and birds. The relatively large vertical distance between the heart and the brain requires that there be sufficient blood pressure to get the blood to the brain, which suggests a fully developed four-chambered heart. Analysis of skeletons leads to the conclusion that these animals were capable of high activity levels and high running speeds.

Other bits of evidence include specialized dentition among the plant-eating dinosaurs that is associated with the processing of large amounts of tough vegetable food that would be required for endothermy. In some species, the anatomical structure of the mouth functionally separates the nasal from the mouth cavity, permitting simultaneous eating and breathing. Microscopic examination of the structure of the bone of some species shows similarities to that of endothermic mammals and birds and differences from that of modern reptiles. Finally, analysis of the skeletons of young dinosaurs shows a rapid rate of growth that is characteristic of modern mammals and birds but quite different from the slow growth rate of modern reptiles.

The largest amount of evidence comes from an analysis of a mixture of the isotopes of oxygen in the bone of a well-preserved fossil of *Tyrannosaurus rex*. In modern reptiles, there is a significant temperature difference between the internal body core and the extremities; such a marked difference is not found in endothermic mammals. Body temperature is reflected in the ratio of isotopes of oxygen. Analysis of such data reveals a mammalian, hence a "warm-blooded," pattern. This conclusion is far from being universally accepted, but this latest evidence adds another piece to this fascinating puzzle.

---

[1]John Ostrom, quoted in J. N. Wilford, *The Riddle of the Dinosaurs* (New York: Knopf, 1985), p. 172.
*Sources:* R. T. Bakker, *The Dinosaur Heresies* (New York: William Morrow, 1986); R. E. Barrick and W. J. Showers, "Thermophysiology of *Tyrannosaurus rex*: Evidence from Oxygen Isotopes," *Science* (1994), pp. 222–224; J. N. Wilford, *The Riddle of the Dinosaurs;* J. H. Ostrom, "The Evidence for Endothermy in Dinosaurs," in R. D. K. Thomas and E. C. Olsen (eds.), *A Cold Look at the Warm-Blooded Dinosaurs* (Washington, D.C.: American Association for the Advancement of Science, 1980).

**Deinonychus, a Predatory Dinosaur from Montana.**

mechanisms in the brain, the growth of fur or hair to provide a layer of insulation, and the development of sweat glands to allow cooling of the body if necessary. In addition, it requires a reliable and fairly large intake of food. A snake may eat once every other week. It simply swallows an entire animal, which then dissolves slowly in the digestive juices in its stomach; the bones and fur are excreted. Mammals do not swallow animals whole. Instead, meat-eating mammals tear their prey into small pieces, and plant eaters bite off small amounts that they then chew into small pieces.

**Some Characteristics of the Mammals** Mammals are characterized by **heterodont** dentition, the regional differentiation of teeth (Figure 6–11). Unlike reptiles, whose teeth are all simple, pointed structures **(homodont),** mammals evolved different types of teeth—incisor, canine, premolar, and molar—that serve the different functions of tearing, piercing, and chewing. Mammals have two sets of teeth **(diphyodonty),** the deciduous teeth and the permanent teeth; reptilian teeth are continuously replaced **(polyphyodonty).**

The growth and development of teeth parallel the pattern of growth and development of the skeleton. Reptiles continue to grow throughout their lives. Their teeth are continuously being replaced, and their long bones are capped with cartilage where bone growth likewise continues to take place. On the other hand, mammalian deciduous teeth are replaced in childhood by permanent teeth that serve the mammal throughout adult life. Growth occurs in plates that are located at a distance from the ends of long bones, which means that in the joint of a growing child, bone is articulating with bone.

The lower teeth of the mammals are embedded in one bone on either side of the lower jaw, or mandible, which is a solid structure able to take the stresses of chewing. The reptilian lower jaw is composed of six bones, while the mammalian lower jaw or **mandible** is composed of two bones that are often fused into a single structure. Two of the reptilian jawbones have been transformed into middle-ear bones, giving mammals three bones in the middle ear in contrast to the single bone in reptiles. While the eardrum, or **tympanic membrane,** is found near the surface of the body in reptiles, the

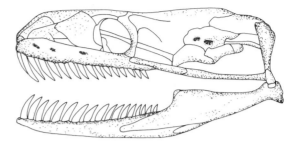

Snake

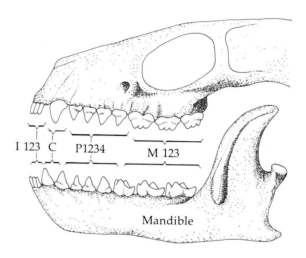

Mammal

**FIGURE 6–11 Mammalian Jaws and Teeth**
The jaws and teeth of a mammal are compared with those of a reptile (a snake). The mammal pictured is a hypothetical generalized placental mammal. The teeth are (I) incisors, (C) canines, (P) premolars, and (M) molars.

mammalian tympanic membrane and middle ear are encased in bone.

Many other anatomical features in mammals aid in dealing with terrestrial habitats. These include the **diaphragm,** which is a muscle lying beneath the lungs that functions in breathing; the **hard palate,** which separates the nasal from the oral cavity and permits the animal to breathe and chew at the same time; and the **four-chambered heart,** which allows for more complete separation of oxygenated and deoxygenated blood than in reptiles. These and other characteristics of the mammals are listed in Table 6–4.

**TABLE 6-4**

## SOME CHARACTERISTICS OF THE MAMMALS

Homeothermy (constant body temperature through physiological mechanisms of thermoregulation)

Fur or hair provides a layer of insulation

Sweat glands permit cooling of the body

Heterodont dentition (regional differentiation of teeth)

Diphyodonty (two sets of teeth: deciduous and permanent)

Bone growth occurs in growth plates between the diaphysis and epiphyses of the bone

Saliva includes the digestive enzyme ptyalin, which initiates the digestive process in the mouth

Lower teeth embedded in one bone on either side of the lower jaw

Three bones in the middle ear

Eardrum, or tympanic membrane, and middle ear are encased in bone

Diaphragm functions in breathing

Hard palate separates the nasal from the oral cavity

Four-chambered heart allows efficient separation of oxygenated and deoxygenated blood

Offspring usually develop inside the mother

Newborns nourished from their mothers' mammary glands

Care is given to the young by the mother and often by the father and other adults

Much of mammalian behavior is learned

Improvements in the nervous system and elaboration of the brain

**Mammalian Reproduction and Behavior** The amniote egg, which is laid on land, evolved with the reptiles. In order to maintain their populations, most reptiles lay eggs in great numbers; however, the eggs of most reptiles are given minimal care.

One of the most important aspects of mammalian reproduction is that the offspring develop inside the mother. The embryo and fetus are not exposed to the outside environment. This ensures a higher chance of survival for the fetus, which means that fewer young are required to maintain the population.

Behavioral changes are as important as anatomical and physiological changes. Newborn mammals cannot obtain their own food; they are nourished by taking milk from their mothers' **mammary glands.** The ability of the mother to produce a high-quality, dependable food also increases the mammalian infant's chances of survival. The care given the young by the mother and often by the father is equally important. Among some mammals, adults other than the parents care for infants. Unlike many reptilian young, who often never see their parents, mammalian young develop close bonds with their mothers and sometimes their fathers and siblings.

Bonding and protection of offspring not only function to protect the offspring but also make the transmission of learned behavioral patterns possible. To a large extent, mammals also adjust to their niches through behavior. In contrast to insect behavior, which is basically innate, much of mammalian behavior is learned. Behavioral adjustments can thereby change rapidly, even within a single generation, in response to changing environmental pressures. Anatomical adaptations, such as improvements in the nervous system, including the elaboration of the brain, are important in creating the potential for behavioral adjustments.

**Classification of the Mammals** The mammals belong to the class Mammalia, which is divided into two subclasses containing three groups that correspond to the three major kinds of mammals. The subclass Prototheria consists of the egg-laying mammals; the pouched mammals and the placental mammals belong to the subclass Theria.

**Prototherian** mammals, also known as the **monotremes,** include only two living forms, the platypus and the echidna (Figure 6–12). These animals lay eggs but also produce milk. In most ways, they possess both reptilian and mammalian characteristics, and for this reason some taxonomists consider them to be mammallike reptiles. Modern mammals did not evolve from prototherianlike ancestors. They represent a branch of the mammalian class that evolved a number of distinctive traits after the monotremes had branched off the main mammalian evolutionary line.

The **therian** mammals, which produce live young, can be divided into two infraclasses. The infraclass Metatheria contains the **marsupials,** or pouched mammals (Figure 6–13). Most of them live in Australia, although the opossums are a well-known North American group. They differ from other mammals in many ways but most importantly in method of reproduction. Metatherian offspring are born while they are still fetuses. The fetus then crawls into the mother's pouch or fold, where it continues to develop and mature.

The remainder of the mammals, and by far the largest number of species, belong to the infraclass

**FIGURE 6–12   The Echidna *(Tachyglossus aculeatus)***
This is an example of a prototherian mammal. The spines on the body resemble those of the porcupine, a placental mammal, yet they have a different internal structure. This is an example of convergent evolution.

Eutheria. These are the **placental mammals.** Their young remain inside the mother, nourished by the **placenta,** until they reach an advanced state of development. The placenta is an organ that develops from fetal membranes. It penetrates the lining of the uterus where the placental blood vessels come into close contact with the mother's blood. Oxygen, nutrients, and other substances pass from the mother's bloodstream into that of the fetus. Waste material passes in the opposite direction.

**The Relationship of Primates to Other Mammals**
Today there are 18 (some count more) living orders of placental mammals, which are listed in the classification in Table 6–5. Since the major subject of physical anthropology is humans, we are most interested in the order Primates, which is the subject of the next several chapters.

The traditional classification of taxa is based on the analysis of anatomy and paleontology. More recently, molecular and chromosome data have been considered, which has led to many discussions about the relationships among various groups of animals, such as the orders of placental mammals. Although there is no consensus on this issue, Figure 6–14 shows one attempt, based on molecular data, to picture the relationship among the mammalian orders.[3]

As can be seen in Figure 6–14, some biologists place the order Primates in a superorder named Archonta. The Archonta includes the primates along with the Scandentia (tree shrews), the Dermoptera (flying lemurs), and the Chiroptera (bats).

**Summary**

People belong to the animal kingdom. This large group of organisms is divided into several phyla

---

[3]M. J. Novacek, "Mammalian Phylogeny: Shaking the Tree," *Nature* 356 (1992), pp. 121–125.

**FIGURE 6–13  Matchie's Tree Kangaroo** *(Dendrolagus matchiei)*
This is an example of a metatherian mammal, or marsupial.

that represent basic body plans. The phylum Chordata is characterized by a notochord, dorsal hollow nerve cord, and gill slits. In the largest subphylum of chordates, the vertebrates, the notochord is replaced by a vertebral column in the embryo. One group of early vertebrates gave rise, through the refinement of lungs and limbs, to the first land vertebrates, the amphibians. With the evolution of the amniote egg, reproduction was no longer tied to water. This evolutionary development resulted in the great reptilian radiation, which included a line of reptiles that were mammallike. Through a long evolutionary history, these reptiles ultimately gave rise to the mammals.

The mammals are a class of vertebrates. They are characterized by homeothermy and endothermy, heterodont dentition, mammary glands, and complex patterns of learned behavior. The mammals have radiated into 20 living orders. Included in one of these orders, the order Primates, are people.

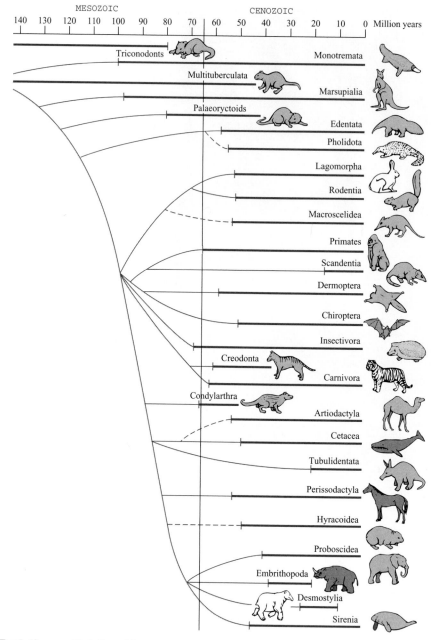

**FIGURE 6–14 Evolutionary Relationships among the Mammals**
See text for explanation.

## TABLE 6-5

### THE CLASSIFICATION OF THE MAMMALS

CLASS: Mammalia
  SUBCLASS: Prototheria
    ORDER: Monotremata (platypuses, echidnas)
  SUBCLASS: Theria
    INFRACLASS: Metatheria
      ORDER: Marsupialia (kangaroos, koalas, opossums)
    INFRACLASS: Eutheria
      ORDER: Insectivora (shrews, hedgehogs, moles)
      ORDER: Macroscelida (elephant shrews)
      ORDER: Scandentia (tree shrews)
      ORDER: Chiroptera (bats)
      ORDER: Dermoptera (flying "lemurs")
      ORDER: Edentata (armadillos, anteaters, tree sloths)
      ORDER: Pholidota (pangolins)
      ORDER: Primates (lemurs, tarsiers, monkeys, apes, humans)
      ORDER: Rodentia (squirrels, beavers, mice, porcupines)
      ORDER: Lagomorpha (rabbits, hares)
      ORDER: Cetacea (whales, porpoises, dolphins)
      ORDER: Carnivora (dogs, bears, cats, hyenas, seals)
      ORDER: Tubulidentata (aardvarks)
      ORDER: Perissodactyla (horses, rhinoceroses, tapirs)
      ORDER: Artiodactyla (pigs, camels, deer, cattle, hippopotamuses)
      ORDER: Proboscidea (elephants)
      ORDER: Sirenia (sea cows, dugongs)
      ORDER: Hyracoidea (hyraxes, conies)

This classification is based upon that of E. H. Colbert and M. Morales, *Evolution of the Vertebrates*, 4th ed. (New York: Wiley-Liss, 1991), pp. 434–437. The classification of other authors may differ. For example, many zoologists place the seals and walruses into their own order, the Pinnipedia. The Cetacea and Chiroptera each is often divided into two orders instead of one.

## STUDY QUESTIONS

1. Although the form of Linnaeus's system of biological classification is still in use, the concept of classification has changed considerably. In what ways does the theory of taxonomy of the eighteenth century differ from that of the twentieth century?

2. One line of evidence for evolutionary relationships is homologous structures. How does the taxonomist distinguish between two similar structures that are truly homologous and those that are the result of convergent evolution?

3. What is the theoretical basis of the cladistic approach?

4. Each animal phylum represents a basic body plan. What features characterize the phylum Chordata? Can these features be identified in humans?

5. What selective pressures operating on the water-dwelling bony fish resulted in a preadaptation for life on land?

6. What major adaptations have been largely responsible for the success of the mammals at the expense of the reptiles?

7. Think about what humans are like today. Why is it unlikely that a humanlike creature would evolve in the class Reptilia?

## SUGGESTED READINGS

Anderson, S., and J. K. Jones, Jr. (eds.). *Orders and Families of Recent Mammals of the World.* New York: Wiley, 1984. This book contains several very detailed discussions of modern mammals, including their characteristics and classification.

Colbert, E. H., and M. Morales. *Evolution of the Vertebrates*, 4th ed. New York: Wiley-Liss, 1991. This book presents the history of the vertebrates, including the fossil record and a survey of living forms.

Mayr, E. *The Science of the Living World.* Cambridge, Mass.: Harvard University Press, 1997. One of the twentieth century's preeminent biologists discusses the nature of science, biology, and evolution.

Nielsen, C. *Animal Evolution: Interrelationships of the Living Phyla.* New York: Oxford University Press, 1995. This book provides a detailed cladistic analysis of animal species, including the primates.

Radinsky, L. B. *The Evolution of Vertebrate Design.* Chicago: University of Chicago Press, 1987. A well-written and easily understood book on the evolution of vertebrate anatomy.

## SUGGESTED WEB SITES

Mammalia:
  http://www.oit.itd.umich.edu/bio108/Chordata/Mammalia.html
The Phylogeny of Life (an exploration of life):
  http://www.ucmp.berkeley.edu/alllife/threedomains.html
Tree of Life (information on phylogenetics and biodiversity):
  http://phylogeny.arizona.edu/tree/phylogeny.html

Additional web sites are listed in the *Workbook* that accompanies this text.

## CHAPTER 7

# The Living Primates

*Humans have a special interest in the group of animals known as primates since, in addition to prosimians, monkeys, and apes, it includes ourselves. This interest is traceable into remote antiquity, long before it was realized that we humans are a part of nature and that primates are our closest relatives. Inquisitiveness is a legacy of those primate origins. Who among us has not wondered about those familiar faces peering at us from the monkey island at the local zoo.[1]*

—Daris R. Swindler

In 1758, Linnaeus classified humans together with the monkeys and apes into the same category, Primates. Since then, many people have attempted, as Richard Passingham says, to "put animals back in their proper place."[2] Different rationales have been posited to put distance between humans and the other primates—for that matter, all animals—but today biologists no longer debate the issue.

---

[1]D. R. Swindler, *Introduction to the Primates* (Seattle: University of Washington Press, 1998), p. 3.
[2]R. Passingham, *The Human Primate* (Oxford: Freeman, 1982), p. 1.

**137**

Humans *are* primates; they share with other primates many basic primate characteristics. This perhaps explains the tremendous fascination that people have for monkeys and apes in zoos. Anthropologists, too, are fascinated by primates. Studies of their natural history, behavior, and anatomy provide important clues for the reconstruction and understanding of human evolutionary history.

This is the first of several chapters that examine the relationship of humans to their nonhuman primate relatives. This chapter defines what a primate is and then surveys the animals that make up this order.

## THE PRIMATE ORDER

The order Primates is one of the 18 orders of placental mammals recognized by biologists today. We can define most of these mammalian orders on the basis of some distinctive specialization. Members of the order Chiroptera, the bats, have wings; members of the order Carnivora, which includes the bears, lions, and dogs, have sharp teeth for slicing and tearing meat; and so on.

Unlike animals in other mammalian orders, members of the order Primates are not characterized by one or more conspicuous traits, such as the wings of bats or the specialized teeth of carnivores. This fact has led to considerable difficulties concerning the definition of the order. In this section, we will examine the features that are usually associated with the living primates.

### The Nature of the Primate Order

The problem of defining the primates was noted by the British anatomist Wilfred LeGros Clark, who pointed out that primates are best defined in terms of their adaptability. This adaptability may be thought of as a response to the **arboreal** habitat. Almost all primates live in trees. Even the more terrestrial forms, such as the baboons, readily take to the trees; humans also have the potential to climb. In fact, children from many cultures enjoy playing in trees, and many athletes and performers achieve great proficiency in arboreal maneuvers.

The arboreal habitat differs significantly from the terrestrial one. An arboreal animal must constantly be aware of the three-dimensional nature of its habitat. In moving through the trees, the animal is moving not only forward and backward, left and right, but also up and down. The arboreal habitat is not a solid one, and any miscalculation can send an animal falling to the ground from great heights. Sometimes branches sway in the wind or shift as an animal leaps from one branch to the next. This habitat is also unpredictable, as can be seen when a primate leaps to a branch that then breaks. The difficulties of living under such circumstances should be kept in mind as we review the characteristics of the order.

Another basic theme in primate evolution is related to the ecological niche thought to have been filled by the earliest primates—arboreal insect predation. Although only some living primates eat insects, many features of today's primates can be seen as having evolved for moving along the thin branches of low-lying bushes and trees hunting for insects.

**The *Scala Naturae*** A major difficulty in discussing primate characteristics is the variability of the group. Early biologists saw humans as the "ideal" primate and placed the primates in a rank order according to how closely they conform to the ideal. Their rank-order sequence might list, in ascending order, the tree shrew (no longer considered a primate), lemur, tarsier, monkey, chimpanzee, and, at the top, human. This model, known as the *Scala naturae*, suggests an evolutionary sequence consisting of living forms, one of which is our direct ancestor.

Of course, a species cannot be a descendant of a contemporary species. Some modern species may have specific characteristics that were present in populations ancestral to ourselves, and so these forms may share a common ancestry with humans. Still, we must remember that modern nonhuman primates are products of long evolutionary sequences, just as humans are; thus, they cannot be our ancestors.

### Characteristics of the Order Primates

Today we realize that we must take great care when isolating the specific characteristics that form the basis of the definition of a taxon. While members of a taxon, such as an order, share many homologous features, as we discussed in Chapter 6, we must be careful to distinguish between different kinds of homologies.

Some similarities found among the primates are shared ancestral traits that are found in many mammalian orders, having been inherited from the same ancestral placental mammal. For example, all primates are characterized by the presence of the clavicle, a pair of bones commonly called the "collarbone." Yet the clavicle is present in other mammalian orders and in fossil placental mammals. This is an example of a trait retained in the primates although it has been lost in some other orders. Of course, we must remember that a trait that is present in the primates and other mammalian orders may have arisen through parallelism or convergence.

Other traits that are found among the primates are shared derived features that are unique to the order and therefore may be used to distinguish the primates from other groups of mammals. Examples include the replacement of the claw by nails (although some primates have retained claws on some digits) and the details of the structure of the skull that houses the middle ear.

**Movement in the Trees**   As has been mentioned, primates are generally arboreal animals, and many shared derived features of their anatomy are related to movement in arboreal habitats. Primates have evolved a degree of prehension of the hand and foot whereby they are able to grasp; a monkey walking along a branch grasps that branch.

The evolution of a grasping big toe is perhaps one of the most important diagnostic features of the primates. Except for humans, all primates can grasp objects with the big toe. The grasping big toe plays an important role in arboreal insect predation by allowing the animal to anchor itself on a branch by its feet as it leaps up and catches an insect with its hands. The adaptation for this niche served to differentiate the early primates from other early mammalian stocks.

Many, but not all, primates have a grasping thumb. In many cases, the thumb has become truly **opposable;** that is, the thumb can rotate so that the terminal pad of the thumb comes into contact with

the terminal pad of one or more of the other digits. This grasping ability is another important factor in the primates' ability to manipulate objects in their habitats.

A squirrel scampers up a tree by digging its claws into the bark. As a primate moves up a tree, it grasps the trunk. In most primates, claws have evolved into nails. The fingers of primates end in **tactile pads;** these pads not only act as friction pads in grasping but also confer a refined sense of touch that helps convey information about the environment.

Besides having these shared derived features, the primates have also retained many shared ancestral features. The forelimb structure of the primate corresponds well to the generalized limb structure of early placental ancestors. For example, all primates have retained the clavicle (collarbone), the two separate bones in the lower arm (the ulna and radius), and five fingers **(pentadactylism).** (See the appendix for a discussion and diagrams of the bones of the skeleton.) This arrangement permits a great degree of flexibility in the shoulder, forearm, and hand, which facilitates movement through the trees.

In many modern placental mammals, one or more of these features have disappeared. We can look at the horse as an example. The horse is suited to high-speed running over hard ground. This means of locomotion results in a great amount of jarring, but it does not require any real degree of flexibility in the forelimb. Such flexibility has been lost in the horse, and, as a result, many elements of the skeleton have been lost. The clavicle has disappeared, the shoulder has lost its flexibility, the two bones of the lower arm have fused, and the five fingers have been reduced to one, the hoof.

The flexibility of the primate skeleton is associated with the wide range of locomotor patterns both within and among the various species. The anatomical structures that play major roles in movement and locomotion will be described in more detail in Chapter 8.

**The Sense of Smell**   Among terrestrial mammals, the **olfactory** sense, or sense of smell, plays a crucial role. Hunters realize that when they approach an animal like a gazelle, the animal is not apt to see them, especially if they freeze when it is looking up; but they had better stalk the animal from downwind to avoid being detected by their smell.

Smells are relatively unimportant in the trees. Most odors hug the ground, and the wind, as it blows through the trees, eliminates their usefulness. Also, the sense of smell does not give an arboreal animal the type of information it needs, such as the exact direction and distance of one branch from another. Thus, in the primates, the sense of smell has diminished; over time, it has proved to have little selective advantage.

In the primates, the nasal structures of the skull are reduced in size, and the muzzle or snout is relatively small (Figure 7–1). While some primates have retained a **rhinarium,** the moist, naked area surrounding the nostrils, most primates lack this feature. The olfactory regions of the brain are reduced.

**Vision** Most mammals see only a two-dimensional black-and-white field; they depend more on the olfactory sense. Most primates see both in three

dimensions and in color, although the degree of development of color vision does vary among different groups of primates. Color vision helps them distinguish detail, since similar colors, such as various shades of green in a tropical forest, may blend if seen only in black and white. In addition, stationary objects stand out in a three-dimensional field.

Primate vision developed in response to the selective pressures of the arboreal environment, where precise information on direction and distance is crucial. Once developed, vision provided the primates with more detailed information about their habitats than was available to any other mammalian form. Also, excellence in vision combined with fine motor coordination and manipulative ability allowed the development of superb hand–eye coordination.

The primate eye is large, and its **retina** contains two types of cells, **rods** and **cones,** that are sensitive to light. Rods respond to very low intensities of light and are responsible for black-and-white vision. Cones, while not as sensitive to low light intensities, sense color and have high acuity. In the central area of the retina is the **macula,** an area

**FIGURE 7–1 The Primate Face**
The facial skeleton of a monkey is compared with that of a tree shrew. Note the reduction of the olfactory apparatus and the relatively flat facial skeleton of the monkey.

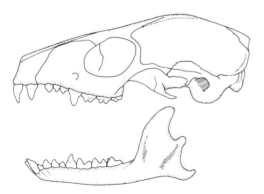

Tree shrew

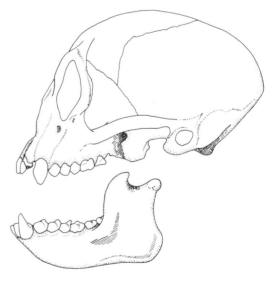

Monkey (*Cebus*)

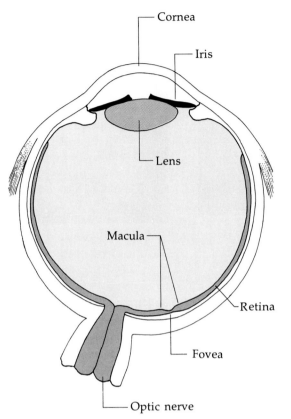

**FIGURE 7–2  The Primate Eye**
A diagrammatic cross section of the human eye.

consisting of only cones. Within the macula of most primates is a depression, called the **fovea,** that contains a single layer of cones with no overlapping blood vessels. This is the area of greatest visual acuity; it permits the fine visual discrimination characteristic of the primate eye (Figure 7–2).

The primate eyes have come to lie on the front of the face. As a result, the visual fields seen by each eye overlap extensively, producing a broad **binocular field.** Thus, the brain receives images of the same objects simultaneously from both eyes. This fact is a prerequisite for three-dimensional or **stereoscopic vision.** The evolution of stereoscopic vision is not only dependent on binocular vision but also on significant changes in the optic nerves and the brain.

Stereoscopic vision enables the arboreal primate to determine distance with a high degree of precision, which aids the animal in moving rapidly through the trees. The origins of stereoscopic vision, however, like those of the grasping big toe, may lie in arboreal insect predation in the early primates. Three-dimensional vision improves the accuracy of the final strike when the primate is pursuing fast-moving insect prey.

In the primates, the eye is supported on the side by a **postorbital bar** (Figure 7–3). This skeletal feature is found in all living primates and in some other mammalian groups. However, the morphological details of the postorbital bar differ among the different mammalian taxa, and the evolution of the postorbital bar in different orders most likely represents a case of convergent evolution.

In some primates, and in other mammal orders, the orbit, the space that contains the eye, is not separated from the muscles behind it. In most primates, a bony **postorbital septum** is found behind the eye that isolates it from these muscles and forms a bony socket in which the eye lies.

Primates are highly social animals, and vision plays a key role in primate communication. Unlike dogs, who smell one another on meeting, primates communicate largely through visual stimuli, although vocalizations also play important roles. Primates frequently use body postures and facial expressions as means of communication. Facial expression is made possible in many primates by differentiation of the muscles of the face. The facial musculature in other mammals is relatively undifferentiated. Also, unlike other mammals, many primates have an upper lip that is not attached to the upper gum. This allows a wide range of gestures, including the kiss.

### The Growth and Development of Primates

The life of an individual can be divided into several phases or periods: **prenatal,** from conception to birth; **infantile,** from birth to the eruption of the first permanent teeth; and **juvenile,** which encompasses the time from the eruption of the first permanent teeth to the eruption of the last permanent teeth. This is followed by the **adult** period. Figure 7–4 shows the relative length of these subdivisions of growth and development in several primate forms.

**The Prenatal Period**  The primate placenta differs from that of other placental mammals. In most

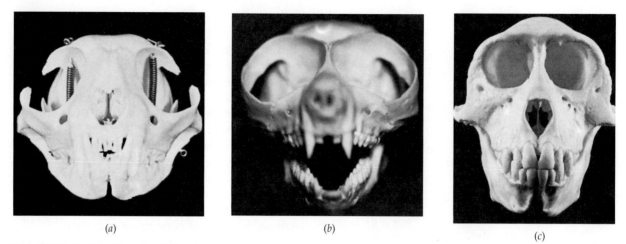

*(a)*        *(b)*        *(c)*

**FIGURE 7–3  The Eye Socket**
(*a*) An eye socket is absent in the cat. (*b*) While an eye socket is absent in the slender loris, the eye is surrounded by a complete bony ring. (*c*) The monkey skull displays a complete eye socket.

mammals, the blood vessels of the fetus and those of the mother come into close contact, and nutrients and other substances pass through two vessel walls from the maternal to the fetal bloodstream. In the **hemochorial placenta,** which is found in many primates, the fetal blood vessels penetrate the lining of the uterus (Figure 7–5). The uterus undergoes cellular changes, and the fine blood vessels of the mother break down to form a spongy, blood-filled mass. The result is that maternal blood surrounds the fetal blood vessels, and so materials pass through only a single vessel wall in moving from one blood system to the other.

The period of time between conception and birth is known as **gestation.** The primates are characterized by a prolonged gestation. To illustrate this point, we can compare three mammals of similar size: the chimpanzee (a primate), the impala (a hoofed mammal), and the coyote (a carnivore). Gestation is 224 days in the chimpanzee, 191 days in the impala, and 63 days in the coyote. Human gestation is 266 days. The length of gestation in several primates is listed in Table 7–1.

Besides the lengthened prenatal period, a rapid rate of growth characterizes the human fetus. For example, the orangutan fetus grows at an average rate of 5.7 grams (0.2 ounces) per day, while the rate for the human fetus is about 12.5 grams (0.44 ounces) per day. Because the placenta develops earlier in humans, rapid growth begins soon after conception and remains rapid throughout the gestation process.

**Life after Birth**  Along with a lengthened childhood period is a lengthened life span in general. Primates are relatively long-lived animals. Among mammals, longevity is related to body size, with the larger mammals, in general, living longer than the smaller ones. Yet when other mammals of similar size are compared with primates, the latter tend to exhibit a longer life span. Other life-cycle events also take longer in primates. The age at which the female gives birth to her first offspring is 14 years in the chimpanzee, 2 years in the impala, and 3 years in the coyote. Finally, the life span is approximately 41 years in the chimpanzee, 12½ years in the impala, and 16 years in the coyote.

## Other Features of the Primates

Dentition is discussed in detail in Chapter 8, but it should be mentioned here that primate dentition is characterized by fewer teeth than the number found in the ancestral placental mammal. This ancestral form had 44 teeth, whereas many primates, including humans, have only 32. Primate teeth are relatively simple in structure, especially when they are compared with those of grazing animals or carnivores. Features of the skeleton are discussed in Chapter 8.

Primates are known for their great intelligence. The primate brain is large in relation to the size of the body, and the areas that control complex behavioral patterns are well-developed. This permits a great degree of behavioral flexibility. The

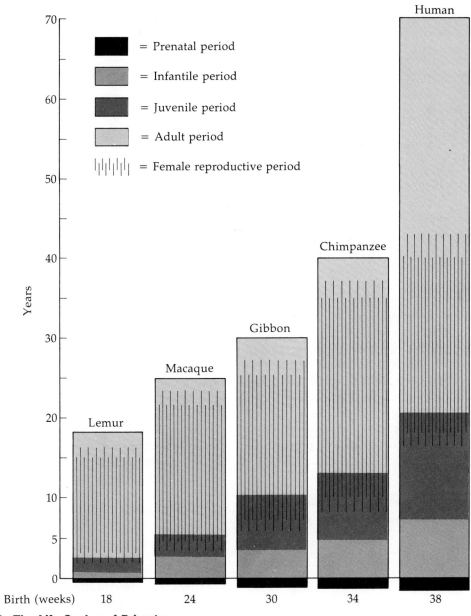

**FIGURE 7–4  The Life Cycles of Primates**

anatomy of the primate brain is discussed in Chapter 8.

Much primate adaptability is the result of learned behavioral adaptations. Most primates live in large social units, usually produce single births, and have a long childhood period; these factors facilitate learning. The social behavior of primates is the topic of Chapter 9.

**Summary**

Unlike animals in other mammalian orders, primates are not characterized by one or more conspicuous traits. Instead, primates are best defined in terms of their adaptability, which may be thought of as a response to the arboreal habitat and arboreal insect predation.

Among the most significant diagnostic features

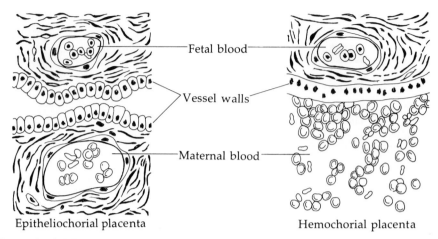

**FIGURE 7–5  Hemochorial Placenta**
The hemochorial placenta (right), found in humans, is compared with the epitheliochorial placenta
(left), found in lemurs.

of the order are a grasping big toe, a grasping thumb that is opposable in many groups, digits ending in nails and tactile pads, pentadactylism, and retention of the clavicle. Among primates, the olfactory sense has been reduced along with the skeletal apparatus for smell and the olfactory areas of the brain. The sense of vision has become predominant; primates see in color and possess stereoscopic vision. The eye is supported by a postorbital bar, and in most primates a postorbital septum forms a bony socket that lies on the front of the face.

During the prenatal period, the primate fetus is nourished through a hemochorial placenta in which the fetal blood vessels are bathed in the maternal blood. The primates are characterized by the prolongation of gestation, during which the fetus grows rapidly, as well as by a long childhood period and a prolonged life span. Other characteristics of the order include the retention of a relatively unspecialized dentition, increased brain size, adjustment through learned patterns of behavior, and life in social groups.

## THE LIVING PRIMATES

Approximately 190 species of primates have been described. The classification of primates, however, like taxonomy in general, is open to some debate. The purpose here is not to enter into these controversies but simply to recognize their existence.

This section will follow the classification shown in Table 7–2. When looking at the classification of the living primates, we see that the order Primates is divided into 3 suborders and 12 families. In this section, we will discuss representative species in each family in terms of their classification and natural history. More detailed information on behavior, anatomy, and other subjects will be presented in subsequent chapters.

### TABLE 7–1

**LENGTH OF GESTATION IN PRIMATES**

| Primate | Gestation period (days) |
| --- | --- |
| Lemur | 120–135 |
| Slender loris | 160–174 |
| Marmoset | 142–150 |
| Spider monkey | 139 |
| Squirrel monkey | 165–170 |
| Guenon | 150–210 |
| Macaque | 162–186 |
| Langur | 196 |
| Baboon | 164–186 |
| Orangutan | 240–270 |
| Gorilla | 270 |
| Chimpanzee | 216–260 |
| Human | 266 |

*Source:* A. G. Hendrick and M. L. Houstion, "Gestation," in E. S. E. Hafez (ed.), *Comparative Reproduction of Nonhuman Primates* (Springfield, Ill.: Charles C. Thomas, 1971). Used with permission of Charles C. Thomas, Publisher.

## TABLE 7-2

### CLASSIFICATION OF THE LIVING PRIMATES

ORDER: Primates
 SUBORDER: Prosimii
  INFRAORDER: Lemuriformes
   SUPERFAMILY: Lemuroidea
    FAMILY: Lemuridae (lemurs)
    FAMILY: Indriidae (indris, avahis, sifakas)
   SUPERFAMILY: Daubentonioidea
    FAMILY: Daubentoniidae (aye-ayes)
  INFRAORDER: Lorisiformes
   SUPERFAMILY: Lorisoidea
    FAMILY: Lorisidae (lorises, galagos)
 SUBORDER: Tarsioidea
   FAMILY: Tarsiidae (tarsiers)
 SUBORDER: Anthropoidea
  INFRAORDER: Platyrrhini
   SUPERFAMILY: Ceboidea
    FAMILY: Callitrichidae (marmosets, tamarins)
    FAMILY: Cebidae (squirrel, spider, howler, and
       capuchin monkeys)
  INFRAORDER: Catarrhini
   SUPERFAMILY: Cercopithecoidea
    FAMILY: Cercopithecidae (guenons, mangabeys,
       baboons, macaques, langurs)
   SUPERFAMILY: Hominoidea
    FAMILY: Hylobatidae (gibbons, siamangs)
    FAMILY: Pongidae (orangutans)
    FAMILY: Panidae (chimpanzees, gorillas)
    FAMILY: Hominidae (humans)

*Source:* J. R. Napier and P. H. Napier, *The Natural History of the Primates* (Cambridge, Mass.: M.I.T., 1985), p. 14. The classification of the Hominoidea has been modified.

## The Prosimians

The first suborder within the Primates is the Prosimii. These animals often lack some of the features described as characteristic of the order. Most, but not all, prosimians are **nocturnal** (active at night), with eyes adapted for nocturnal vision. Their sense of smell is well-developed, facilitated by a long snout ending in a rhinarium. Many also have specialized scent glands, and olfaction plays an important role in their social behavior. Unlike their other fingers and toes, which end in nails, all prosimians possess second toes that end in claws. These **grooming claws** are used by the animal in scratching and cleaning its fur. Finally, in most prosimians, the lower front teeth, the incisors and canines, are thin and narrow and they project forward horizontally to form a **dental comb** (Figure 7–6).

Because the prosimians lack many of the features of the monkeys, apes, and humans, it is easy to think of them as primitive ancestral forms. Although they retain many ancestral features, they are modern, highly specialized animals. Figure 7–7 shows the distribution of the prosimian families.

**The Prosimians of Madagascar** Three closely related families of prosimians—the Lemuridae, Indriidae, and Daubentoniidae—live on the island of Madagascar (Malagasy Republic), which is located about 400 kilometers (250 miles) off the southeast coast of Africa. Primatologists believe that the early ancestors of these animals found their way to the island by rafting across the channel, which was once narrower than it is today, on masses of vegetation. Once on the island, they were isolated from the mainland, and thus they were protected from the later-evolving monkeys and apes. In isolation and lacking competition from other mammals, the Madagascar prosimians were able to move into many diverse niches; this is reflected in their numbers and diversity. However, today their natural habitats are being rapidly destroyed, and many species observed by early explorers are known only from their skeletal remains and preserved museum specimens.

The family Lemuridae includes the lemurs (Figures 7–A and 7–B in color inserts; Box 9–1). In general, the small lemurs are nocturnal, solitary, and **omnivorous** and eat a variety of foods. The larger lemurs, including the well-known ringtailed lemur (Figure 7–8), are more **diurnal** (active during the day), live in large social units, and include plant food as a major part of their diet. The smallest are the mouse lemurs and dwarf lemurs; one species averages only 60 grams (2 ounces) in weight. The largest lemurs weigh only around 4 kilograms (9 pounds).

Stereoscopic vision is not as well-developed in the lemurs as it is in the monkeys and apes. On the other hand, the ringtailed lemur's sense of smell is well-developed. When it is disturbed, it often rubs its anal region against a tree, a behavior termed **scent marking.** The male ringtailed lemur has a specialized gland on his forearm that is also used in scent marking. Like many prosimians, the lemurs possess a dental comb and a grooming claw on the second toe.

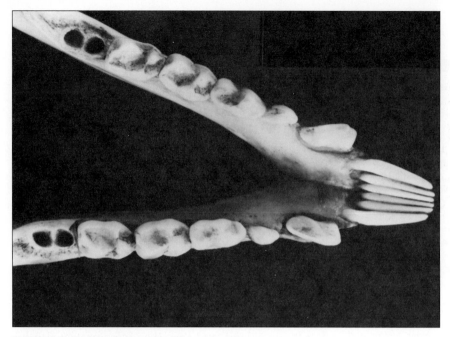

**FIGURE 7-6  The Dental Comb**

The lower jaw of a lemur. The dental comb is made up of the lower two canines and four incisors.

**FIGURE 7-7  Distribution of Prosimian and Tarsier Families**

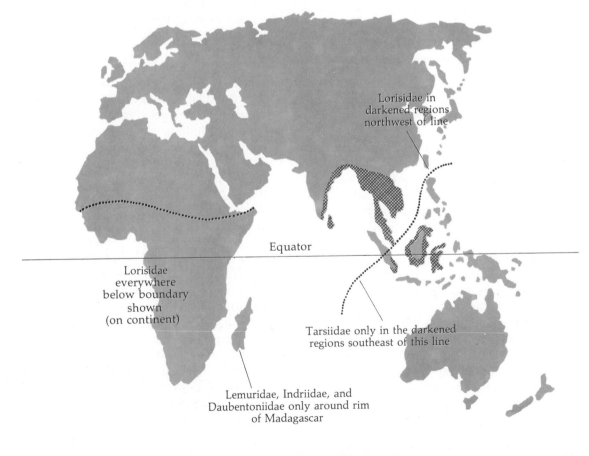

Lorisidae in darkened regions northwest of line

Lorisidae everywhere below boundary shown (on continent)

Equator

Tarsiidae only in the darkened regions southeast of this line

Lemuridae, Indriidae, and Daubentoniidae only around rim of Madagascar

digits except the big toes end in claws. During the night, the aye-aye uses its front teeth to tear open the outer layers of bamboo or the bark of trees to get at the insects inside; the insect is then extracted with the elongated finger.

The aye-aye provides us with an interesting example of convergence of function or analogy. Three animals that feed on insects directly beneath the bark are the aye-aye, the woodpecker (a bird), and *Dactylopsila*, an Australian marsupial. Like the aye-aye, *Dactylopsila* has a thin, elongated finger on each hand and large incisors.

**The Family Lorisidae**   The lorises probably have survived competition with the monkeys and apes in Asia and Africa because of their nocturnal habits. The family is divided into two subfamilies. The subfamily Lorisinae contains species that walk

**FIGURE 7–8   Prosimian**
Representative of the family Lemuridae: Ring-tailed lemur, *Lemur catta.*

Also living on the island of Madagascar, the family Indriidae consists of the indri, avahi, and sifaka (Figure 7–9). The indri, which is totally diurnal, is the largest of the Madagascar prosimians, weighing about 6.3 kilograms (14 pounds). Their diet consists primarily of plant material, especially leaves. When they are resting, they cling upright on a vertical branch; when moving, they use their very long legs to leap from branch to branch, maintaining an upright posture. The indri is the only Madagascar prosimian that lacks a tail.

The family Daubentoniidae contains only one species, the aye-aye, now on the verge of extinction (Figure 7–C in color insert). The aye-aye was once thought to be a rodent since it has large, continuously growing front teeth that are separated from the rest of the teeth by a large gap. The hand is characterized by a long, thin, middle finger, and all the

**FIGURE 7–9   Prosimian**
Representative of the family Indridae: Sifaka, *Propithecus verraeux.*

**FIGURE 7-10   Prosimian**
Representative of the family Lorisidae: Slow loris, *Nycticebus coucang.*

**FIGURE 7-11   Prosimian**
Representative of the family Lorisidae: Galago, *Galago senegalensis.*

along branches very slowly and deliberately, hand over hand (Figure 7–10). These animals have very powerful grips, enhanced by the reduction of their index fingers to mere bumps. Like the lemurs, they have dental combs as well as grooming claws on their second toes. The lorises live alone or in pairs. Their diet is varied, consisting of fruits, leaves, seeds, birds and birds' eggs, lizards, and insects. The Asiatic members of the subfamily are the slender loris and slow loris; the African members are the potto and angwantibo.

The African subfamily Galaginae includes the galagos, also known as bush babies (Figure 7–11). These are small animals weighing between 65 grams (2.3 ounces) and 1.3 kilograms (3 pounds). Although they show a variety of locomotor patterns, these nocturnal primates are noted for their leaping ability, which is made possible by their elongated legs. In one study, the small *Galago senegalensis,* with a center of gravity perhaps 3.75 centimeters (1.5 inches) off the ground, leaped verti-

cally in the air 2.25 meters (7 feet 4.75 inches).[3] This leaping ability enables the animal to move quickly through the branches searching for and catching insects.

## The Tarsiers

The suborder Tarsioidea includes only one family, the Tarsiidae. The five species of tarsier are found on islands in southeast Asia, including Borneo, Sumatra, and the Philippines (Figure 7–12).

The tarsiers are very small primates, weighing between 60 and 200 grams (2 and 7 ounces). Their name is derived from their elongated tarsal (ankle) bones, which enable them to leap long distances. The tarsiers leap among the thin, vertical saplings near the ground, keeping their bodies in a vertical

---

[3]E. C. B. Hall-Craggs, "An Analysis of the Jump of the Lesser Galago *(Galago senegalensis),*" *Journal of Zoology* 147 (1965), pp. 20–29.

**FIGURE 7–12 Tarsier**
Representative of the family Tarsiidae: Mindanao tarsier, *Tarsius syrichta carbonarious.*

position. At rest, they press the lower part of their long tails against the tree trunk for support (Figure 8–2).

Tarsiers are strictly nocturnal. Their eyes have become so large that they cannot be moved by the eye muscles, which have become degenerate. Instead, the animal is capable of turning its head almost 180 degrees to look behind itself. Tarsiers feed on insects and lizards; they do not eat plant food.

The tarsiers share several characteristics with the prosimians, such as the grooming claw on the second toe. (The tarsiers actually have additional grooming claws on the third toes as well.) In contrast to the prosimians, they lack a dental comb. Their eye socket is partially closed; in this they resemble more closely the monkeys and apes than the prosimians. They also show a number of specialized features that are unique among primates, such as the fusion of the tibia and fibula (the two bones of the lower leg). This feature is also found in the rabbits and hares.

At one time, early tarsiers were thought to be ancestral to the monkeys and apes. Today, some paleontologists believe that tarsiers represent an ancient, specialized primate group, perhaps best placed in its own suborder, the Tarsioidea.

### The Monkeys

The third major division of the order Primates is the suborder Anthropoidea. This suborder includes the primates that are familiar to most people: the New World monkeys, Old World monkeys, lesser and great apes, and humans.

The term *monkey* embraces a large number of species found throughout the tropics of the Old World (Africa, Asia, and Europe) and the New World (South, Central, and North America). Although most people see the monkeys as a single group, in reality the monkeys of the Old World and those of the New World are fairly distinct. Many anthropologists theorize that the ancestral monkeys first evolved in Africa. Later, some populations rafted across the Atlantic Ocean to populate the New World. Isolated in their own hemisphere for over 30 million years, each group evolved many unique features. Yet the Old World and New World monkeys, building on the same basic anatomy, retained and evolved many similarities as well. This is an example of parallelism.

These two groups of monkeys are usually divided into two superfamilies: the Cercopithecoidea of the Old World and the Ceboidea of the New World. Figure 7–13 shows the distribution of the two monkey superfamilies.

**The New World Monkeys** The monkeys of the New World belong to the superfamily Ceboidea. These monkeys are easily identified by the **platyrrhine nose,** in which the nostrils are usually separated by a broad nasal partition, or septum, and open facing forward or to the side. This nose form contrasts with the nose of the Old World monkeys, apes, and humans. Consequently, the New World monkeys are often referred to as the platyrrhine monkeys and are sometimes placed in the infraorder Platyrrhini.

The New World monkeys share several features that contrast with those of the Old World monkeys. The New World monkeys tend to be smaller than those of the Old World, and they are strictly

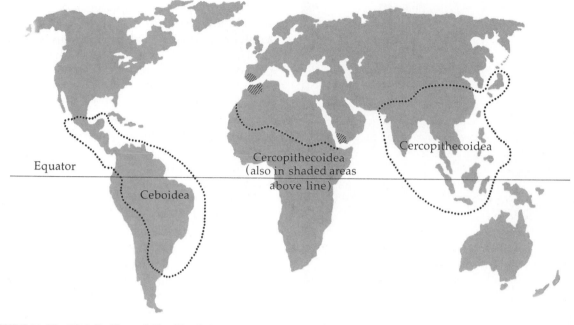

**FIGURE 7–13 Distribution of the Monkeys**

BOX 7–1

## New Discoveries

A modern tragedy is the destruction of the tropical rain forest and the loss of its lush vegetation and the extinction of its diverse animal life. In contrast to the daily stories of destruction and extinction comes the periodic discovery of new species.

In 1984, a new species of guenon was found in an undisturbed primary forest in central Gabon, in west Africa. The primate was named the sun-tailed guenon (*Cercopithecus solatus*). The guenons are the most common African arboreal monkey with over 20 described species.

In 1985 and 1986, a new species of lemur was seen in the southeastern rain forest of Madagascar. This animal was named *Hapalemur aureus,* the golden bamboo lemur, and is the third species within the genus *Hapalemur,* the bamboo lemurs.

In 1989, another lemur was "rediscovered." Although a few individuals had

been seen earlier and five specimens exist in museum collections, the hairy-eared dwarf lemur, *Allocebus trichotis,* has never been studied. This species of dwarf lemur is very small, weighing only 80 grams (2.8 ounces), and was rediscovered in the rain forest on the northeastern coast of Madagascar.

In 1988, a population of tarsiers was observed on the Indonesian island of Sulawesi that appeared to differ from the four known tarsier species in their anatomy, behavior, and chromosomes. The species was named *Tarsius dianae,* in honor of the late primatologist Dian Fossey, known for her work among the mountain gorillas.

In another part of the world, Brazil, coastal rain forests are being rapidly destroyed. In 1990, on a small island south of São Paulo, primatologists discovered a new species of New World monkey, the

black-faced lion tamarin, *Leontopithecus caissara.* All five of these newly found primates, the sun-tailed guenon, the golden bamboo lemur (Figure 7–B in color insert), the hairy-eared dwarf lemur (Figure 7–A in color insert), the Sulawesi tarsier, and the black-faced lion tamarin, are rare and highly endangered.

*Sources:* M. J. S. Harrison, "A New Species of Geunon (Genus *Cercopithecus*) from Gabon," *Journal of Zoology, London* 215 (1988), pp. 561–575; B. Meier et al., "A New Species of *Hapalemur* (Primates) from South East Madagascar," *Folia Primatologica* 48 (1987), pp. 211–215; B. Meier and R. Albignac, "Rediscovery of *Allocebus trichotis* Günther 1985 (Primates) in Northeast Madagascar," *Folia Primatologica* 56 (1991), pp. 57–63; C. Niemitz et al., "*Tarsius dianae:* A New Primate Species from Central Sulawesi (Indonesia)," *Folia Primatologica* 56 (1991), pp. 105–116; W. Stolzenburg, "Tamarin Tale: Tracking Down a New Species," *Science News* 137 (June 30, 1990), p. 406.

arboreal. The New World monkeys have three premolars in each quarter of the mouth; some, but not all, have **prehensile tails** that can be used to hang onto branches and even to pick up objects; the thumb is nonopposable, and in some forms it has disappeared.

The New World monkeys are divided into two families. The first family, the Callitrichidae, includes the marmosets and tamarins (Figure 7–H in color insert). These are small animals weighing between 70 and 550 grams (2.5 and 19.5 ounces). The 34 species of marmosets and tamarins are found throughout the forests of Central and South America. The marmosets and tamarins live in small family units, and the females usually produce twins at birth. The father carries the infants and transfers them to the mother for feeding (Figure 9–1).

Unlike most primates, the marmosets and tamarins possess modified claws on all their digits except their big toes, which have true nails. Like all ceboid monkeys, they have three premolars in each quadrant of the mouth, but this family is distinguished from other New World monkeys in having only two molars per quadrant; all other monkeys have three. They are generally omnivorous and include insects in their diet. Unlike the tamarins, the marmosets rely heavily on sap and gums. This dietary specialization is reflected in their dentition. In contrast to the teeth of the tamarins, the lower incisors of the marmosets are relatively long and the lower canines project only a little above the level of the incisors. The animals use their specialized lower teeth to make holes in the bark of trees to tap the sap and gum.

Most of the New World monkeys belong to the second family, the Cebidae. In contrast to the Callitrichidae, the cebids are larger, weighing between 750 grams and 15 kilograms (1.5 and 33 pounds). They have nails on all digits, have three premolars and three molars per quadrant of the mouth, and are characterized by single births. The larger cebids habitually move and feed while suspended under branches, and many have evolved a prehensile tail as an aid in suspension.

The cebids are divided into five subfamilies. The subfamily Cebinae includes the small squirrel monkeys (Figure 7–14) and the well-known capuchins, the common organ-grinder monkeys. Capuchins

**FIGURE 7–14 New World Monkey**
Representative of the family Cebidae: Squirrel monkeys, *Saimiri sciureus.*

have a moderately developed prehensile tail. The subfamily Aotinae includes the titi monkey and the owl monkey, or douroucolis (Figure 7–15); the owl monkey is the only completely nocturnal mon-

**FIGURE 7–15  New World Monkey**
Representative of the family Cebidae: owl monkey, *Aotus trivirgatus*.

key. The subfamily Pithecinae includes the sakis (Figure 7–16) and uakaris. Uakaris are bald-headed primates with very short tails whose naked faces are often bright pink (Figure 7–I in color insert).

The next two subfamilies are characterized by the presence of a prehensile tail. The subfamily Alouatinae contains the howler monkeys (Figure 7–17). This genus possesses a highly specialized larynx and a modified hyoid bone that forms a chamber that acts as an amplifier and is responsible for the monkey's loud and distinctive call. The spider monkeys, the woolly monkeys, and the rare muriquis are in the subfamily Atelinae. Spider monkeys are noted for their dexterous prehensile tail, which serves as a third "hand." The underside of the lower part of the tail lacks hair and appears to be sensitive to touch. This monkey's hand lacks a thumb, and the remaining four fingers form a hook that the animal uses as it suspends itself underneath a branch (Figure 8–1).

**The Old World Monkeys**  Old World monkeys, apes, and humans make up the infraorder Catarrhini. Members of this infraorder are characterized by the **catarrhine nose,** where the nostrils are separated by a narrow nasal septum and open downward. They possess two premolars per quadrant of the mouth, and the thumb is well-developed in most forms and is opposable. This infraorder can be divided into two superfamilies. The superfamily Cercopithecoidea are the Old World monkeys, which consists of the single family Cercopithecidae;

**FIGURE 7–16  New World Monkey**
Representative of the family Cebidae: hairy saki, *Pithecia monachus*.

**FIGURE 7–17  New World Monkey**
Representative of the family Cebidae: red howler monkey, *Alouatta seniculus*.

the superfamily Hominoidea includes the apes and humans.

Old World monkeys, superfamily Cercopithecoidea, comprise a large number of species that are spread over Africa and Asia, and they include one small population in Europe. In contrast to the New World monkeys, some Old World monkeys tend to be fairly large. Although many are arboreal, some genera are semiterrestrial. None has a prehensile tail.

The Cercopithecidae are divided into two subfamilies. Except for the macaques, members of the subfamily Cercopithecinae live in sub-Saharan Africa. Macaques are found in north Africa, on the Rock of Gibraltar in Europe, and in southern and southeast Asia and southern Japan (Figure 7–18 and Box 9–1). Members of this subfamily weigh between 1.2 and 15 kilograms (2.7 and 33 pounds), and many species exhibit a marked **sexual dimorphism,** that is, a major difference in size and nonsexual features between sexes. A distinguishing feature of these monkeys is the presence of **ischial callosities** in the anal region of the animal; these callouses are in contact with the branch or ground when the animal sits. The female usually has a **sexual skin** that often turns bright pink or red and sometimes swells when the female is in **estrus,** the period of sexual receptivity (Figure 7–19). The Cercopithecinae are omnivorous, and they have **cheek pouches** that open into the mouth and are used for temporary food storage.

Many arboreal and all of the semiterrestrial monkeys of Africa belong to the Cercopithecinae. The many species of guenons and mangabeys are spread throughout the African rain forest, woodland, and savanna habitats (Figure 7–20). The ground-dwelling monkeys of the savanna are the baboons (Figures 7–19, 9–7, and 9–8). One species,

**FIGURE 7–18 Old World Monkey**
Representative of the subfamily Cercopithecinae: Barbary "ape" macaque, *Macaca sylanus.*

the hamadryas baboon, lives in the semidesert regions of southern Ethiopia where the baboons sleep at night on cliffs rather than in trees. Baboons are often referred to as the "dog-faced monkeys" because of their well-pronounced muzzles. Associated with the muzzle are large, formidable canine teeth, especially in the adult males. Other African cercopithecoids include the patas monkey, vervet monkey, drill, mandrill (Figure 7–D in color insert), and gelada (Figures 7–21, 9–4, and 9–5).

The Asiatic representatives of the Cercopithecinae are the macaques. The dozen macaque species live in a great diversity of habitats, including tropical rain forests and semideserts; in contrast, the Japanese macaque endures winter snow. The only European monkey is a macaque living on the Rock of Gibraltar. The diet of the macaques is quite varied, including fruits, roots, and other vegetable material, as well as insects and shellfish.

The other subfamily, the Colobinae, or leaf-eating monkeys, also inhabits both Africa and Asia. The members of this subfamily lack cheek pouches. They are able to digest mature leaves because of the presence of a complex sacculated stomach in

which bacterial action is able to break down the cellulose found in leaves.

A major group of leaf-eating monkeys is the langurs of south and southeast Asia (Figure 7–22). One population lives in the Himalayas at elevations up to 3650 meters (12,000 feet). Others are found in very dry habitats, where they can survive because of their ability to digest dry, mature leaves and bark. Other Asiatic forms include the snub-nosed langurs (Figure 7–F in color insert) and the proboscis monkey. The African representatives of this subfamily are the colobus monkeys, or guerezas (Figure 7–23).

### The Apes

The last four primate families belong to the superfamily Hominoidea. Figure 7-24 shows their distribution. The first three families are referred to as the apes; these are the Hylobatidae, Pongidae, and Panidae. Note that the primates that are considered to be apes are classified in different families than those considered to be monkeys. Although apes are frequently called monkeys, they actually are very distinct kinds of animals.

**The Family Hylobatidae** The family Hylobatidae includes the smallest of the apes, the gibbons and siamangs, which are sometimes called the **lesser apes.** Gibbons range over a larger area than any of the other apes. They are found in much of southeast Asia, including Indonesia, Malaysia, Thailand, Burma, and the east Indian state of Assam. The gibbons are the smaller of the lesser apes, weighing about 6 kilograms (13 pounds) and standing about 90 centimeters (3 feet) tall (Figures 7–25, 9–2, and 9–3). They exhibit virtually no sexual dimorphism. They have short, compact bodies with exceedingly long arms—a body build suited for **brachiation,** which is hand-over-hand locomotion under a branch (Figure 8–3). The gibbons are the classic brachiators in the primate order.

While gibbons are primarily arboreal, they do walk bipedally when on the ground. Their diet consists of fruits, leaves, and buds, supplemented with birds' eggs, young birds, and insects. Gibbons live in small family groups consisting of a mature pair with several young. Each group occupies a distinct territory that is defended by loud vocal displays by the male.

**FIGURE 7–19  Old World Monkey**
Representative of the subfamily Cercopithecinae: Chacma baboon, *Papio ursinus.* A female chacma
baboon shows a swelling of the sexual skin. Underneath the swelling on the left can be seen part
of the ischial callosity.

The siamangs are found in Sumatra and on the
Malay Peninsula (Figure 7–26). They are similar to
the gibbons, but they are larger (10.7 kilograms or
23.5 pounds) and have longer arms in proportion
to their bodies. A distinctive feature is an air sac
under the chin that inflates when the animal vo-
calizes, producing a very loud call.

**The Family Pongidae**  Until comparatively recent
times, the family Pongidae was considered synonymous with the **great apes,** which included the

two African great apes, the chimpanzee and gorilla,
and the Asiatic great ape, the orangutan. However,
studies of molecular biology and cytogenetics have
demonstrated the very close evolutionary relationship of the African great apes to humans. Therefore, many anthropologists today have moved the
chimpanzee and gorilla out of the Pongidae, leaving the orangutan as the sole member of this
family.

The orangutan is found today only on the islands
of Sumatra and Borneo (Figure 7–G in color insert;

**FIGURE 7–20 Old World Monkey**
Representative of the subfamily Cercopithecinae: Hamlyn's guenon, *Cercopithecus hamlyni.*

Figure 5–9). Orangutans are quiet, slow-moving, arboreal vegetarians. Young orangutans stay close to their mothers; adult orangutans, however, are solitary. They sleep in nests that can be as high as 24 meters (80 feet) above the ground. Their locomotor behavior can be described as **quadrumanous;** that is, they use their upper arms to hold onto branches above their heads, but they do not actually suspend themselves from these branches. They exhibit great sexual dimorphism; the males are large, weighing more than 70 kilograms (154 pounds) at maturity, while the females average about 37 kilograms (81.5 pounds). Males average 1.37 meters (4½ feet) in height, and females average about 1.15 meters (3 feet 10 inches) in height. Some males develop large pouches under the chin and flanges of flesh on the cheeks. These physical features are not found in the females.

**The Family Panidae** The increase in the number of comparative studies of the African great apes, in addition to new theoretical approaches to the study of taxonomy, has led many anthropologists to reconsider traditional classifications. This has led to

several new schemes that attempt to show more accurately the relationship between the apes and humans. Table 7-3 shows some examples of proposed classifications. In this text we will adopt the classification that places the African great apes in the family Panidae and humans in the family Hominidae.

The family Panidae includes the gorilla, chimpanzee, and the bonobo. The largest living primates are the gorillas of Africa; an adult male gorilla weighs about 150 kilograms (331 pounds) and is about 1.83 meters (6 feet) tall. Females weigh about 92 kilograms (203 pounds). Gorillas are divided into three subspecies: the lowland gorilla of west Africa, the lowland gorilla of east Africa, and the highland gorilla of east Africa (Figure 7–E in color insert; Figure 7–27). Lowland gorillas are the ones that are usually seen in zoos. The highland gorillas have been the subject of several studies in the wild.

Gorillas are basically terrestrial vegetarians. They walk on all four limbs, but instead of placing the palms of their hands flat on the ground, they walk on their knuckles. Although their size prevents them from moving easily through the trees, gorillas sometimes choose to build their sleeping nests there.

Perhaps the best known ape is the chimpanzee (Figures 7–28 and 8–4). This genus includes three subspecies of chimpanzees, found north of the Zaire River. However, analysis of the DNA found in hair samples shed in the wild suggests that the western subspecies may actually be a separate species.[4] The other known species is the rare bonobo found south of the river (Figure 7–29). Bonobo males average about 45 kilograms (100 pounds) in weight, with females averaging about 37 kilograms (82 pounds). Chimpanzees range in height from 1 to 1.7 meters (3¼ to 5½ feet). On the average, females are only 6 percent smaller than males. The bonobo is only slightly smaller than the chimpanzee and more slender in body build.

Sociable and curious, chimpanzees are much more active than gorillas. They live in flexible social groups, which is not generally true of other

---

[4]See P. A. Morin et al., "Kin Selection, Social Structure, Gene Flow, and the Evolution of Chimpanzees," *Science* 265 (1994), pp. 1193–1201.

**FIGURE 7–21 Old World Monkey**
Representative of the subfamily Cercopithecinae: gelada, *Theropithecus gelada.*

nonhuman primates. Like the gorillas, chimpanzees build nests in trees and are also knuckle walkers.

### The Hominids

The family Hominidae contains only one living species—*Homo sapiens.* Humans display moderate sexual dimorphism, with the average height of women generally between 5 and 10 percent less than the average height for men. The average height in different populations, however, can differ significantly. The world's shortest people are the Efe of Zaire, Africa. Efe males average about 1.42 meters (4 feet 8 inches) in height. On the other hand, the Dinka of the Sudan, also in Africa, display the greatest average height, with males averaging 1.85 meters (6 feet 1 inch) in height.

Unlike the other primates, humans have lost much of their locomotor flexibility. While they are still capable of climbing trees, and some individuals do become skillful aerialists, humans are essentially habitually erect, terrestrial bipeds. This pattern of posture and locomotion is not unique to *H. sapiens,* but only this species among all primates has become anatomically specialized for it. While

**FIGURE 7–22 Old World Monkey**
Representative of the subfamily Colobinae: common langur, *Presbytis entellus*.

**FIGURE 7–23 Old World Monkey**
Representative of the subfamily Colobinae: Kikuyu colobus, *Colobus guereza*.

**FIGURE 7–24 Distribution of the Apes**

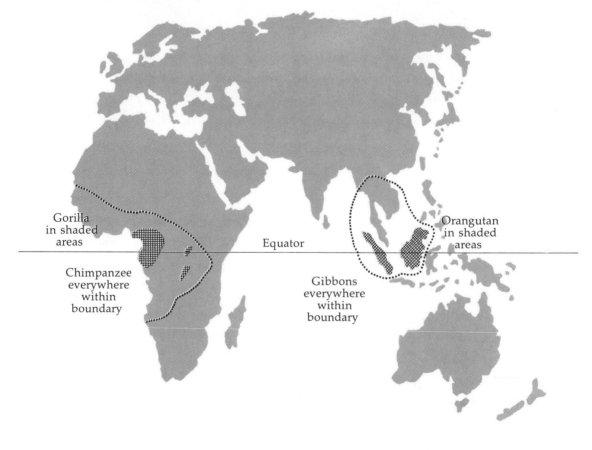

**FIGURE 7–25  Lesser Ape**
Representative of the family Hylobatidae: white-handed gibbon, *Hylobates lar lar.*

**FIGURE 7–26  Lesser Ape**
Representative of the family Hylobatidae: island siamang, *Symphalangus syndactylus.*

| **TABLE 7-3** | | |
|---|---|---|

**THREE DIFFERENT CLASSIFICATIONS OF HUMANS AND APES**

| Simpson (1945)[*] | Andrews and Cronin (1982)[†] | Andrews (1990)[‡] |
|---|---|---|
| Superfamily: Hominoidea | Superfamily: Hominoidea | Superfamily: Hominoidea |
|   Family: Pongidae |   Family: Hylobatidae |   Family: Hylobatidae |
|     Subfamily: Hylobatinae |     Genus: *Hylobates* |     Genus: *Hylobates* |
|       Genus: *Hylobates* |     Genus: *Symphalangus* |     Genus: *Symphalangus* |
|       Genus: *Symphalangus* |   Family: Pongidae |   Family: Hominidae |
|     Subfamily: Ponginae |     Genus: *Pongo* |     Subfamily: Ponginae |
|       Genus: *Pongo* |   Family: Hominidae |       Genus: *Pongo* |
|       Genus: *Pan* |     Subfamily: Gorillinae |     Subfamily: Homininae |
|       Genus: *Gorilla* |       Genus: *Pan* |       Tribe: Gorillini |
|   Family: Hominidae |       Genus: *Gorilla* |         Genus: *Pan* |
|     Genus: *Homo* |     Subfamily: Homininae |         Genus: *Gorilla* |
| |       Genus: *Homo* |       Tribe: Hominini |
| | |         Genus: *Homo* |

[*]G. G. Simpson, "The Principles of Classification and a Classification of Mammals," *Bulletin of the American Museum of Natural History* 85 (1945), pp. 1–350.
[†]P. Andrews, and J. E. Cronin, "The Relationships of *Sivapithecus* and *Ramapithecus* and the Evolution of the Orang Utan," *Nature* 297 (1982), pp. 541–546.
[‡]P. Andrews, cited in L. Aiello and C. Dean, *Human Evolutionary Anatomy* (London: Academic Press, 1990), p. 9.

**FIGURE 7–27  Great Ape**
Representative of the family Panidae: lowland gorilla, *Gorilla gorilla gorilla*.

## The Discovery of the Gorilla

The nineteenth century was an age of exploration as Europeans learned of new lands, plants, animals, and peoples. These discoveries provided fresh data for the scientists of the time who were developing new ideas to explain the natural world, a world suddenly made more complex. One of these ideas was that of evolution. Throughout the nineteenth century, reports reached Europe of new species of monkeys and apes that provided important clues to the mystery of human origins.

The gorilla was the last of the apes to be discovered by Europeans. Although the largest of the great apes may have been seen by early explorers, "as object of scientific study this ape simply did not exist at the beginning of the nineteenth century, and it was not until the middle of the century that it was definitely described and generally accepted as a new genus of anthropoid ape."[1]

The first scientific account of the gorilla was an article by Thomas Savage in 1847. The creature was named after the "hairy people" or "gorillae" described in

the fifth century B.C. by the Carthaginian, Hanno, who had sailed along the western coast of Africa. (In all probability, however, Hanno's "gorillae" were monkeys.) Additional studies of the animal followed as bones and preserved specimens were sent to Europe. The first living gorilla seen in Europe was exhibited in England in 1855.

The early accounts of gorilla behavior were based on rumors and stories that were more fanciful than factual. Little was known about the behavior of gorillas in the wild, and this ignorance enabled storytellers to create images of gorillas as large terrifying beasts, exemplified in the movie *King Kong*. As Robert Yerkes wrote in 1929:

Creature of mystery, the gorilla long played hide and seek in the reports of hunters and naturalists. Even now the name holds peculiar fascination because imaginative descriptions abound. Relatively rare, inaccessible, powerful, reputedly dangerous, difficult to capture, and untamable, it has

yielded slowly to human curiosity. For centuries rumors of the existence of such a huge anthropoid, native superstitions, and alarming tales stirred popular and scientific interest.[2]

Today, we have a very different understanding of the natural history and behavior of the gorilla through the studies of several primatologists, including George Schaller and Dian Fossey. In contrast to the image of King Kong, George Schaller writes: "The gorilla is by nature reserved and shy and, whenever it can possibly do so, it avoids contact with its human neighbors."[3] Dian Fossey's book *Gorillas in the Mist* and the movie of the same name show gorillas as gentle vegetarians characterized by only rare acts of aggression.

---

[1] R. M. Yerkes, *The Great Apes* (New Haven: Yale University Press, 1929), p. 31.
[2] Ibid., p. 381.
[3] G. B. Schaller, *The Year of the Gorilla* (Chicago: University of Chicago Press, 1964), pp. 101–102.

the human skeleton is similar to the ape skeleton in the upper torso, from the pelvis down, the human skeleton has become highly specialized for bipedal walking and running.

Humans are omnivorous, with meat eating playing a significant role in almost all human societies. The only other primates known to kill and eat other mammals are baboons and chimpanzees. While chimpanzees have been observed to manufacture a limited number of tools, the manufacture of large numbers of complex tools by humans has led to the development of elaborate and complex technologies.

Humans have one of the longest gestation periods of any primate, although they produce the most helpless infants. The period of infant dependency is very long, with adult status often not reached un-

til the second decade of life. This long childhood provides an opportunity for the development of complex patterns of learned behavior. Indeed, this is *H. sapiens's* most significant distinction: the dependence on culture for adjusting to the environment.

### Summary

This section has introduced the various primate groups in anticipation of the chapters to follow. The order Primates is divided into three suborders. The first, Prosimii, includes the lemurs, sifaka, aye-aye, lorises, and galagos. The second, Tarsioidea, contains the tarsiers. The final suborder, Anthropoidea, includes the New World and Old World monkeys, apes, and humans.

**FIGURE 7–28 Great Ape**
Representative of the family Panidae: chimpanzee, *Pan troglodytes*.

**FIGURE 7–29 Great Ape**
Representative of the family Panidae: bonobo, *Pan paniscus*.

**BOX 7-3**

# Vanishing Primates

Today, over half of the living primate species are in some danger of becoming extinct. Leading the list of endangered species are the muriqui and lion tamarin of the Atlantic forests of eastern Brazil, the mountain gorilla of Africa, the 28 species of primates on the island of Madagascar, and the lion-tailed macaque and the snub-nosed monkeys from Asia. The color insert presents photographs of several endangered primates.

The major threat to primates in the wild is destruction of their habitats, which is occurring primarily in the tropical forests where the vast majority of modern primates live. Because the rapidly increasing human populations in these parts of the world cannot be supported on the traditional agricultural land or in the large cities, vast areas of tropical forest are being converted into farmland and ranchland. Other factors responsible for much of the destruction of the tropical forest are the need for firewood, poor management of industrial logging, and the construction of hydroelectric projects.

In many parts of the world, primates are hunted for food or to procure skins and other body parts. The skins of the black-and-white colobus monkey have been used for rugs, coats, and native headdresses.

Finally, primates are used extensively for scientific research. Although today the importation of primates from the wild has markedly decreased, only a few decades ago, thousands of animals were imported for research and the pet trade.

Today, major efforts to preserve the primate fauna have been initiated in many countries. Yet while laws have been passed to promote the conservation of primates, they are often impossible to enforce. The major problem is the exploding population characteristic of many tropical countries. The need to feed and house this expanding population has made it difficult to preserve endangered primate species.

*Source:* R. A. Mittermeier and D. L. Cheney, "Conservation of Primates and Their Habitats," in B. B. Smuts et al. (eds.), *Primate Societies* (Chicago: University of Chicago Press, 1986), pp. 477–490.

## STUDY QUESTIONS

1. What is meant by the idea that adaptability is the primate's way of coping with its habitat? How is this related to the arboreal environment?

2. In what ways can the primate be said to possess a generalized anatomy? In what ways is a generalized anatomy more advantageous than a more specialized one?

3. An animal's awareness of its environment depends on data received through the sense organs. What senses have been refined in the primates? How do the refinements of these senses provide adaptations to arboreal habitats?

4. What are some of the characteristics of the primates that can be considered shared derived (synapomorphic)? What characteristics can be considered shared ancestral (symplesiomorphic)?

5. How does the suborder Prosimii as a group contrast with the suborder Anthropoidea?

6. In what ways have the evolution of New World monkeys and Old World monkeys paralleled each other? What features can be used to distinguish between the two groups?

## SUGGESTED READINGS

Ciochon, R. L., and R. A. Nisbett (eds.). *The Primate Anthology: Essays on Primate Behavior, Ecology, and Conservation from Natural History.* Upper Saddle River, N.J.: Prentice Hall, 1998. This volume contains a series of articles that appeared originally in *Natural History.*

Fleagle, J. G. *Primate Adaptation and Evolution,* 2nd ed. San Diego: Academic, 1999. The first half of this book is a discussion of the primate order and the various primate taxa.

Martin, R. D. *Primate Origins and Evolution.* Princeton, N.J.: Princeton University Press, 1990. This large volume presents a wealth of detailed information about many aspects of the primate order.

Napier, J. R., and P. H. Napier. T*he Natural History of the Primates.* Cambridge, Mass.: M.I.T., 1985. The first five chapters of this book deal with characteristics of the primates, primate origins, anatomy, and behavior. This is followed by profiles of each primate genus, illustrated with black-and-white and color photographs.

Richard, A. F. *Primates in Nature.* New York: Freeman, 1985. This book focuses on primate ecology, with excellent discussions of distribution, diet, demography, and social organization.

Sleeper, B., and A. Wolfe. *Primates: The Amazing World of Lemurs, Monkeys and Apes.* San Francisco: Chronicle Books, 1997. This is primarily a book of photographs of primates with brief descriptive material, and excellent photographs.

Swindler, D. R. *Introduction to the Primates.* Seattle: University of Washington Press, 1998. This is a comprehensive introduction to the primate order.

Tylinek, E., and G. Berger. *Monkeys and Apes.* New York: Arco, 1985. After a general introduction, this book proceeds to present a paragraph or so on each primate species. The book is abundantly illustrated with line drawings as well as black-and-white and color photographs.

Wolfheim, J. H. *Primates of the World: Distribution, Abundance, and Conservation.* Seattle: University of Washington Press, 1983. This listing of all living primate species includes a distribution map with data on abundance and diversity, habitat, factors affecting populations, and conservation activities. An extensive bibliography is provided for each species.

## SUGGESTED WEB SITES

African Primates at Home (information, photographs, vocalizations):
http://www.indiana.edu/~primate/primates.html

Primate Gallery Archive (pictures, links to information):
http://www.selu.com/~bio/PrimateGallery/main.html

Primate Info Net (from the Wisconsin Regional Primate Research Center; lists of primate organizations, information resources:
http://www.primate.wisc.edu/pin/

Additional web sites are listed in the *Workbook* that accompanies this text.

# A PORTFOLIO OF ENDANGERED PRIMATES

The tropical forests of the world are home to the greatest diversity of plant and animal species on the planet, yet many of these unique life forms are rapidly disappearing, primarily because of deforestation brought about by human activity. On these pages are just a few primate species that are classified as endangered or vulnerable by the International Union for Conservation of Nature and Natural Resources. Species classified as *endangered* are those that are in great danger of extinction, especially if conditions do not change. Some endangered species may already be extinct. Species classified as *vulnerable* are those that are very likely to be reclassified as endangered in the near future.

## MADAGASCAR

**FIGURE 7–A**   Hairy-eared dwarf lemur, *Allocebus trichotis,* a representative of the family Lemuridae from Madagascar, was thought to be extinct but was rediscovered in the middle 1990s. It is considered critically endangered.

**FIGURE 7–B**   Golden bamboo lemur, *Hapalemur aureus,* a representative of the family Lemuridae from Madagascar, is recently discovered and is classified as critically endangered.

**FIGURE 7–C**   Aye-aye, *Daubentonia madagascariensis,* representative of the family Daubentoniidae, from Madagascar, is classified as endangered.

**FIGURE 7–D** Mandrill, *Mandrillus spinx,* a representative of the family Cercopithecidae from Cameroon, Congo, Equatorial Guinea, and Gabon, is classified as near threatened.

**FIGURE 7–E** Mountain gorilla, *Gorilla gorilla beringei,* a representative of the family Panidae from Rwanda, Uganda, and Zaire, is critically endangered.

**FIGURE 7–F**  Golden snub-noted monkey, *Rhinopithecus roxellanae*, a representative of the subfamily Colobinae from China, is considered to be vulnerable and is likely to be classified as endangered in the near future.

**FIGURE 7–G**  Orangutan, *Pongo pygmaeus,* the sole member of the family Pongidae, lives on the islands of Sumatra and Borneo, and is classified as vulnerable.

**FIGURE 7–H** Golden lion tamarin, *Leontopithecus rosalia,* a representative of the family Callitrichidae from Brazil, is critically endangered. This primate has been successfully bred in several zoos in the United States and is currently being introduced back into its natural habitat in Brazil.

**Figure 7–I** Red uakari, *Cacajao calvus,* a representative of the family Cebidae from Brazil, Colombia, and Peru, is considered to be vulnerable and is likely to be classified as endangered in the near future.

# Comparative Studies: Anatomy and Genetics

*In order to interpret the fossils, to determine what hominid fossils were like in life, it is necessary to compare the structure of their fossil bones and teeth to those of humans, apes and other primates. This can help us to determine not only that they were on the human line, but also details about their function, how they moved and what they ate. Only by such analogy with modern humans and non-human primates can we have confidence in our conclusions about the nature of our evolutionary ancestors.[1]*
—Leslie Aiello and Christopher Dean

---

[1]L. Aiello and C. Dean, *An Introduction to Human Evolutionary Anatomy* (London: Academic, 1990), p. 1.

The fossil record provides, in a sense, the "hard evidence" of evolutionary history. Yet, as we will see in later chapters, the fossil record is difficult to read because of its fragmentary and incomplete nature. Evolutionary history can also be reconstructed from the study of living primates. New features, anatomical and genetic, do not suddenly arise from nowhere. Instead, they develop gradually as modifications of preexisting structures. By comparing anatomical features, as well as chromosomes, proteins, and DNA, of living primates, anthropologists are able to gain an understanding of the evolutionary relationships among living forms. Such comparisons also allow anthropologists to make educated guesses about the nature of the hypothetical common ancestors of contemporary primates. This chapter will examine these comparative studies.

## COMPARATIVE ANATOMY OF LOCOMOTION AND MANIPULATION

Humans are erect bipeds, but they are not the only erect bipeds in the animal kingdom, nor are they the only primates capable of this method of locomotion. Unlike other primates, however, hominids habitually depend on this mode of locomotion. They have evolved many anatomical features that have made efficient and habitual erect bipedalism possible. As we will see in later chapters, these anatomical features evolved over the last 4½ million years or more.

Likewise, primates in general share a refined manual dexterity. For example, most Old World monkeys and the apes share with humans an opposable thumb. Humans, however, have evolved a high degree of manual dexterity that permits the creation of a complex technology. This section will explore the anatomy of locomotion and manual dexterity.

### Locomotor Patterns among Primates

Locomotor specializations characterize most mammalian orders; some obvious examples are the bats, the whales, and the hoofed mammals. On the other hand, primates retain a rather large repertoire of locomotor behaviors. This is consistent with the theme of primate adaptability. The primates, as a group, display a variety of locomotor patterns, and

| **TABLE 8–1** | |
| --- | --- |
| **PRIMATE LOCOMOTOR PATTERNS** | |
| Type of locomotion | Representative primates |
| QUADRUPEDALISM | |
| Slow climbing | Loris |
| | Potto |
| Branch running and walking | Lemur |
| | Tamarin |
| | Capuchin monkey |
| | Guenon |
| Ground running and walking | Macaque |
| | Gelada |
| | Baboon |
| | Mandrill |
| New World semibrachiation | Spider monkey |
| | Howler monkey |
| Old World semibrachiation | Colobus monkey |
| | Langur |
| VERTICAL CLINGING AND LEAPING | |
| Vertical clinging and leaping | Tarsier |
| | Galago |
| | Sifaka |
| APE LOCOMOTION | |
| True brachiation | Gibbon |
| | Siamang |
| Quadrumanous | Orangutan |
| Knuckle walking | Chimpanzee |
| | Gorilla |
| ERECT BIPEDALISM | |
| Erect bipedalism (heel-toe stride) | Human |

a wide range of locomotor patterns may characterize a single species. Table 8–1 lists several general types of locomotor behavior.

**Locomotor Patterns of Prosimians, Tarsiers, and Monkeys** The basic locomotor pattern of terrestrial vertebrates is **quadrupedalism.** The quadruped moves on all four limbs with its body held parallel to the ground, a position known as **pronograde** posture.

We can recognize several categories of quadrupedalism. In **branch running and walking,** the primates walk, climb, jump, and leap on and among the branches. The branches may be quite small and uneven, and they are frequently unstable as they move in the wind or in response to the

**FIGURE 8–1  New World Semibrachiation**
A spider monkey (*Ateles geoffroyi*) is seen suspending itself by an
arm and prehensile tail.

motion of another animal. Arboreal quadrupeds
use their hands and feet to grasp a branch as they
move along the top of the branch. Their arms and
legs are of roughly equal length, although all their
limbs tend to be shorter than those of other primates; shorter limbs bring the body closer to the
branch, thus aiding stability. Branch runners and
walkers also have long tails that aid in balancing
on top of the branches. Their fingers and toes are
relatively long to facilitate grasping the branches,
but they are not as long as those of primates that
suspend themselves under branches.

Some arboreal quadrupeds suspend themselves
and move beneath branches. In **New World semi-**
**brachiation,** the animal, such as the spider monkey
or the howler monkey, uses its prehensile tail and
arms to suspend its body (Figure 8–1). In **Old World**
**semibrachiation,** where a prehensile tail is not involved, leaping is common, with the arms extended
to grasp a branch. The colobus monkeys and langurs frequently use this form of locomotion. Both
types of semibrachiation are forms of **suspensory**
**behavior.** Suspensory behavior is not only a method
of locomotion but also a major means of feeding.

Some monkeys are more terrestrial in their
habits. In **ground running and walking,** the animal spends much of its time on the ground feeding. Movement on the ground does not involve

grasping with their hands. Also, these animals do not leap or climb as they move along a relatively flat, continuous surface. Compared with arboreal quadrupeds, terrestrial quadrupeds have shorter fingers and toes, longer arms and legs of nearly equal length, and often a short or externally absent tail. Terrestrial quadrupeds include such monkeys as the baboons and gelada.

**Vertical clinging and leaping** is the dominant locomotor pattern of the tarsiers and many prosimians such as the galagos and sifakas (Figure 8–2). As the term suggests, the animal rests on a tree trunk in a clinging position; it keeps its body in a vertical, or **orthograde,** posture. In moving from one tree to another, it leaps, landing vertically with its hindlimbs on the new trunk. On the ground, the animal either hops or moves bipedally. These animals have long, powerful hindlimbs.

**Hominoid Locomotion** A highly specialized form of suspensory behavior is **true brachiation,** which is found in the lesser apes, the gibbons and siamang (Figure 8–3). In true brachiation, the body, suspended from above, is propelled by arm swinging. The animal rapidly moves hand over hand along a branch, maintaining an orthograde posture.

When feeding, a gibbon can suspend itself under a branch by one arm for up to 20 minutes at a time. In this position, the gibbon, because of its very long arms, can collect various fruits, berries, buds, and flowers growing on branches beneath it with its free hand. A quadruped would be unable to reach many of these items since they often grow on the ends of branches that would not support the animal's weight. The true brachiators are bipedal on the tops of large branches and on the ground, where they also maintain an orthograde posture.

Orangutans are much larger and more cautious animals than lesser apes. While they often suspend themselves under branches, their movements are slow and they use their forelimbs and hindlimbs to a great extent, a locomotor pattern described as **quadrumanous.** Quadrupedal on the ground, the orangutan usually does not walk on the palm of the hand as monkeys do, but often walks on the side of the hand or fist.

The locomotor behavior of the African great apes is best described as **knuckle walking** (Figure 8–4). Unlike orangutans, which frequently move from tree to tree without descending to the ground, the chim-

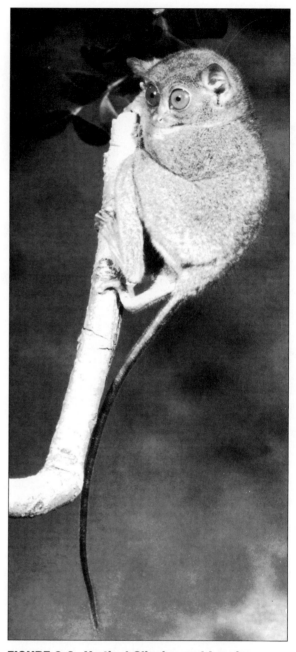

**FIGURE 8–2  Vertical Clinging and Leaping**
A tarsier (*Tarsius syrichta*) is shown clinging to a vertical branch.

panzees, bonobos, and gorillas usually move on the ground. Having arms that are longer than their legs, they are essentially semierect quadrupeds. They support the upper part of their bodies on the knuckles of their hands, unlike the monkeys, which use

**FIGURE 8–3  Brachiation**
A siamang (*Symphalangus syndactylus*) is caught in the act of brachiating.

their palms. In knuckle walking, the fingers are flexed and the animal places its weight on special knuckle pads that lie on the backs of the fingers.

Many primates exhibit **erect bipedalism** over short distances, but only in humans is erect bipedalism the habitual means of locomotion. Humans maintain an orthograde posture while standing and walking. As a human walks, the heel of the foot strikes the ground first; the cycle ends when the individual pushes off with the big toe. This is called the **heel-toe stride.**

### Comparative Anatomy of Primate Locomotion

A major topic in early hominid evolution is the origin of erect bipedalism. If hominid and ape locomotor patterns share a common ancestry, evidence should be found by comparing those parts of the anatomy that relate to locomotion. From such an analysis, a hypothetical common ancestor can be reconstructed. In comparing modern forms and the

reconstructed ancestor, the evolutionary history of habitual erect bipedalism reveals itself.

This section is not intended as a complete survey of comparative anatomy. Rather, it discusses the method of comparative anatomy and some of the major conclusions of this method. This section focuses on the parts of the skeleton that function in locomotor activities. An introduction to the skeleton, including the identification of the various bones, is presented in the appendix.

### Variations of the Basic Mammalian Skeleton

The basic mammalian skeleton is greatly modified in many mammalian orders. For example, the horse skeleton is adapted for high-speed running (Figure 8–5). This type of locomotion involves constant jarring of the body and transmits great forces through the limbs to the body. As the horse skeleton has no clavicle, the scapula attaches directly to the rib cage by muscles that absorb the forces generated by running. Of course, flexibility in the shoulder has been

**FIGURE 8–4   Knuckle Walking**
A chimpanzee (*Pan troglodytes*) is seen in a knuckle-walking stance.

lost, but a grass-eating animal running across the plains has little need to lift its forelimb above its head. The radius and ulna in the horse skeleton have fused; four of the five digits on each limb have been lost, and the remaining digit has evolved into a hoof.

In contrast to the horse and most other mammals, the primates have retained a basically generalized skeleton. All primates have retained the clavicle, and most are able to rotate their forearms. With a few exceptions, primates have five fully developed fingers and toes at the end of each limb.

**The Hominoid Skeleton**

In contrast with the hominoids (apes and humans), monkeys carry their bodies parallel to the ground. The spine forms an arch supported by the limbs; the trunk is relatively long and narrow. The hominoid trunk is relatively short and broad; for example, the spine of the gorilla contains three to four lumbar vertebrae compared with seven in the rhesus monkey. Unlike the monkey's back, the homi-

noid back does not play any important role in locomotion. The ape body is semivertical to the ground, whereas the human body is completely erect. The back muscles of the hominoids are fairly small, and the spine is relatively inflexible.

Figure 8–6 shows the relative positions of the bones of the shoulder girdle. In a monkey, the

**FIGURE 8–5   Limb Skeletons of a Horse and a Human**
While the forelimb of the horse has been highly specialized for running on hard ground, the primate forelimb has remained relatively generalized. Note the fusion of the radius and ulna and the loss of four of the five digits in the horse.

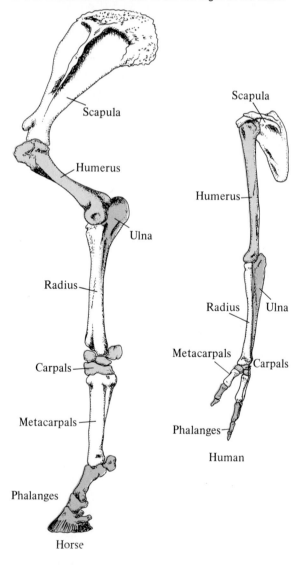

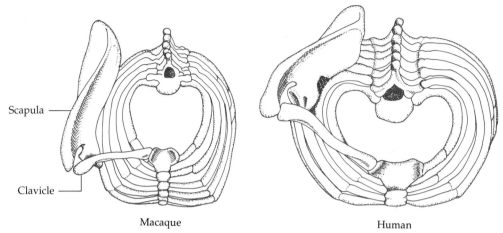

Scapula

Clavicle

Macaque

Human

**FIGURE 8–6  Cross Section of Trunk**
Note the differences in the shape of the rib cage and the relative positions of the clavicle and scapula.

scapula lies on the side of the trunk, with the head of the humerus pointing backward. In a hominoid, the long clavicles place the arms well to the side of the body. The clavicles extend backward so that the scapula lies on the back and the head of the humerus points inward.

The socket of the scapula is relatively shallow in humans and apes, permitting a greater degree of rotation of the humerus than occurs in monkeys. Thus, a hominoid can easily hold its arms directly overhead, as when an ape suspends itself from an overhead branch. In addition, hominoids can rotate their forearms to a much greater extent than can monkeys. Humans can rotate their forearms about 160 degrees, allowing them to do pull-ups with palms either toward the body or away from it.

These are some of the many characteristics common to apes and humans in the shoulder and arm. These features are adaptations to suspensory behavior and suggest that hominids evolved from an ancestor adapted to arboreal locomotion. This does not mean that the ancestor was a specialized brachiator like the modern gibbon, with elongated forearms and fingers; the ancestor may have simply been an animal that engaged in some degree of suspensory behavior and emphasized the arms in locomotion.

The length of the leg in quadrupedal monkeys is nearly the same or somewhat longer than the arm. The ratio of arms to legs is seen by comparing the **intermembral index.** This index compares the length of two bones in the arm (the humerus and the radius) with the length of two bones in the leg (the femur and the tibia). The equation for calculating the intermembral index is

$$\frac{\text{Length of humerus} + \text{length of radius}}{\text{Length of femur} + \text{length of tibia}} \times 100$$

The number that results from this formula provides an indication of the relative proportion of the forelimb and the hindlimb. An index of 100 means that the arms and legs (excluding the hand and foot) are of equal length. An index over 100 indicates longer arms than legs, while an index under 100 means that the legs are longer. Note that this index in the quadrupedal monkeys is nearly or somewhat below 100. On the other hand, apes, with their characteristically elongated arms, typically have intermembral indices above 100. Table 8–2 lists this index for several primates.

**Adaptations for Erect Bipedalism**

In general, the skeleton of the human trunk, shoulders, and upper limbs shows adaptations to suspensory behavior similar to those found in apes. However, other parts of the human anatomy, particularly the pelvis, leg, and foot, show specializations for erect bipedalism.

A chimpanzee occasionally assumes an upright stance. For the bipedal ape, the major problem is

## TABLE 8-2

PRIMATE INTERMEMBRAL INDICES

| Type of locomotion | Representative primates | Intermembral index* |
|---|---|---|
| QUADRUPEDALISM | | |
| Slow climbing | Loris | 92 |
| | Potto | 88 |
| Branch running and walking | Lemur | 70 |
| | Tamarin | 82 |
| | Capuchin monkey | 81 |
| | Guenon | 84 |
| Ground running and walking | Macaque | 89 |
| | Gelada | 94 |
| | Baboon | 95 |
| | Mandrill | 94 |
| New World semibrachiation | Spider monkey | 105 |
| | Howler monkey | 98 |
| Old World semibrachiation | Colobus monkey | 79 |
| | Langur | 78 |
| VERTICAL CLINGING AND LEAPING | | |
| Vertical clinging and leaping | Tarsier | 55 |
| | Galago | 62 |
| | Sifaka | 64 |
| APE LOCOMOTION | | |
| True brachiation | Gibbon | 129 |
| | Siamang | 148 |
| Quadrumanous | Orangutan | 144 |
| Knuckle walking | Chimpanzee | 107 |
| | Gorilla | 117 |
| ERECT BIPEDALISM | | |
| Erect bipedalism (heel-toe stride) | Human | 70 |

*Average for sample.
*Source:* Data taken from J. R. Napier and P. H. Napier, *A Handbook of Living Primates* (London: Academic, 1967), pp. 393–395. Used with permission of Academic Press and J. R. Napier. Human index taken from A. H. Schultz, "Proportions of Long Bones in Man and Apes," *Human Biology* 9 (1937), pp. 281–328.

maintaining a balance of the trunk since in an upright position the center of gravity shifts to the front of the pelvis and legs. The chimpanzee must therefore bend the leg at the knee, resulting in an awkward and inefficient form of bipedalism. In humans, habitual erect bipedalism is facilitated by the fact that the knee joint is locked and stabilized when fully extended. The human ankle is also more stable than is that of the ape.

In humans, the position of the skull on top of the spine and the development of curvatures of the spine, especially the **lumbar curve,** have resulted in a trunk balanced over the pelvis. The ilium of

the pelvis has become short and broad, which provides the surfaces necessary for the attachment of muscles involved in erect bipedalism. With changes in the shape and position of the ilium, the human sacrum has come to lie in a new position, closer to the point of articulation between the femur and the pelvis than it is in the ape. Consequently, the weight of the trunk is transmitted more directly to the legs (Figure 8–7).

Three muscles having an important role in hominoid stance and movement are the **gluteus maximus, gluteus medius,** and **gluteus minimus.** In the ape, all three act as **extensors,** extending the

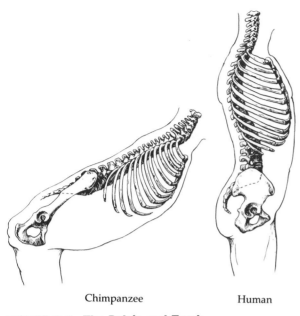

Chimpanzee          Human

**FIGURE 8–7  The Pelvis and Trunk**
A comparison of the pelvis and trunk in the chimpanzee and human.

leg at the hip. In the chimpanzee, the gluteus medius is the largest of the three (Figure 8–8).

The modification of the pelvis in human evolution has brought about reorganization of the muscles involved in movements of the leg. In hominids, changes in the structure and orientation of the ilium have resulted in repositioning of the gluteus medius and gluteus minimus. These muscles now act as **abductors,** moving the thigh away from the midline of the body and rotating it laterally as well. Both muscles are responsible for keeping the trunk in a stable, upright position during walking. The gluteus maximus has become a very large muscle and acts as a major extensor of the leg in running and climbing.

The leg and foot have also been modified for erect bipedalism. The leg is long and powerful (see Table 8–2 for the human intermembral index). Instead of extending straight down from the pelvis, the thigh extends down at an angle, bringing the knees close together for better balance (Figure 13–26).

The foot shows great evolutionary changes and is among the most specialized of human features. In other primates, the big toe is well-developed and is capable of movements to the side of the foot; this capability allows these primates to grasp with their feet. In walking, their body weight is borne between the first and second toes. In contrast, the human foot is fairly inflexible, and an arch has developed. The toes are short, including the big toe, and they are incapable of extensive sideways movement. Thus, humans have only a limited grasping ability; they are not capable of manipulating objects with their feet to the degree found in other primates (Figure 8–9). In walking, the heel hits the ground first and the push of the step-off is on the big toe itself.

## Comparative Anatomy of the Hand

A major feature of the hominids is their ability to manufacture tools. Evidence for toolmaking comes from two sources. The first is the discovery of stone tools; the earliest archaeological material dates to about 2½ million years ago. It is also very likely that tools made of perishable materials such as wood and vines date back much earlier in time. The second line of evidence is the anatomy of the hand, whose structure permits the fine coordination required for tool manufacture.

The hand serves a number of functions. It is an organ of locomotion, manipulation, and sensation. In most primate species, the locomotor function dominates the manipulative function. In humans, who normally use only their lower limbs in getting from one place to another, the hands are freed for exclusive manipulative activity. This activity is enhanced by a refined sense of touch.

As we have already seen, the primates are characterized by pentadactylism; they have retained the five fingers characteristic of the early placental mammals (Figure 8–10). (In a few species—the spider monkey and the colobus monkey, both semibrachiators—the thumb has been lost.) The palm and fingertips of the primate hand are devoid of hair and are covered with fine **epidermal ridges** that are richly endowed with nerve endings and are responsible for the highly developed sense of touch. The claws characteristic of many mammals have been replaced with nails.

Most prosimians, tarsiers, and New World monkeys can draw their fingers back against the palm of the hand, facilitating the grasping of branches and other objects. In these primates, movement of the thumb is restricted to the joint between the metacarpal and first phalanges, and to the joint between phalanges.

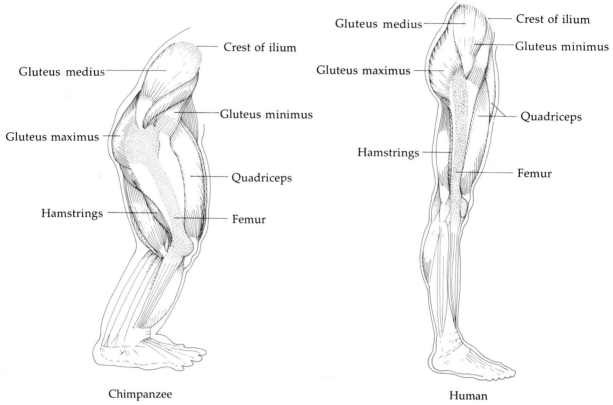

Chimpanzee

Human

**FIGURE 8–8  Gluteal Musculature in a Chimpanzee and a Human**

**FIGURE 8–9  Foot Skeletons of a Gorilla and a Human**

**FIGURE 8–10  Hands of a Chimpanzee and a Human**

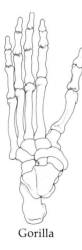 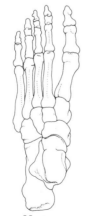 

Gorilla

Human

Human

Chimpanzee

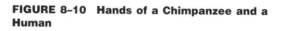

In the Old World monkeys, apes, and humans, the development of a saddle configuration in the joint between the carpal and metacarpal allows the thumb to be directly opposed to the other fingers (Figure 8–11). Humans differ primarily in the degree of movement possible at this joint. The human thumb is able to oppose the other fingers, and so the fleshy tip of the thumb comes into direct contact with the fleshy tips of all the fingers. In the apes, the fingers are elongated, and the metacarpals and phalanges are curved; in humans these bones are straight.

The hand is capable of several types of prehensile functions. In the **power grip,** the animal grabs an object between the palm and the fingers; in this position, much force can be applied (Figure 8–12). All primates are capable of the power grip. More important for fine manipulation of objects is the **precision grip,** where the animal holds an object between the thumb and the fingers. This is made possible by the presence of an opposable thumb. Humans have developed precision handling to a degree not found in other primates.

## Summary

Primates display a variety of locomotor patterns, not only among the various species within the order but also within a given species itself. Many fundamental locomotor patterns can be identified within the primate order. These include branch running and walking, ground running and walking, New World semibrachiation, Old World semibrachiation, vertical clinging and leaping, true brachiation, quadrumanous locomotion, knuckle walking, and erect bipedalism.

While the skeleton of most mammals, such as the horse, is highly specialized for locomotion, the primate skeleton is relatively generalized. It has retained many traits of the generalized mammal, such as five fingers on all limbs and the clavicle, but some degree of skeletal specialization does exist.

The skeletons of living apes and humans are adapted to suspensory behavior. Some of the skeletal features needed for suspension include a short, broad trunk; fewer lumbar vertebrae in the spine; clavicles that extend backward; a scapula that lies on the back of the trunk, with the head of the humerus pointed inward; a shallow socket on the scapula; and the ability to rotate the lower arm 160

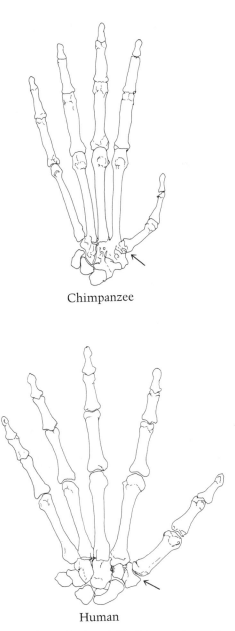

Chimpanzee

Human

**FIGURE 8–11 Hand Skeletons of a Chimpanzee and a Human**
Arrows point to the joint between the carpal and metacarpal of the thumb. In humans, this joint has a saddle configuration that permits the thumb to be directly opposed to the other fingers.

degrees. From studies of the anatomy of the hominoids, many anthropologists have concluded that the common ancestor of humans and apes was an arboreal primate adapted to some degree of suspensory behavior.

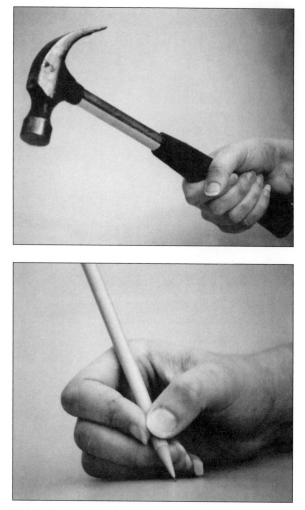

**FIGURE 8–12 Human Hand Showing (a) Power Grip and (b) Precision Grip**

Unlike the skeletons of most primates, the human skeleton has become specialized for erect bipedalism. Some modifications that made this possible include the development of the lumbar curve, changes in the shape and orientation of the pelvis, changes in the function of the gluteal musculature, elongation of the leg relative to the arm, and the evolution of a short, stout big toe and an arch of the foot.

One of the most significant characteristics of the hominids is the development of the hand as a fine instrument of manipulation. The primate hand possesses five fingers and fingernails and is covered with fine epidermal ridges. The thumbs of the Old

World monkeys, apes, and humans are opposable and thus capable of fine precision handling.

## COMPARATIVE ANATOMY OF THE SKULL AND THE BRAIN

The skull is a very complex part of the skeleton, composed in humans of 28 separate bones plus 32 teeth in the adult. A description of the skull and an identification of the individual bones are included in the appendix.

The skull contains the brain and the sense organs for seeing, hearing, tasting, and smelling, as well as the jaws and teeth, the organs of mastication. The structure of the skull reflects its position on the spine and the nature of the animal's diet. This section discusses these points, as well as the structure of the brain itself.

### Some Features of the Skull

The skull articulates with the spine by the **occipital condyles,** two rounded projections on the cranial base. The occipital condyles are located on the sides of a large hole, the **foramen magnum,** in the cranial base; the spinal cord passes through the foramen magnum to merge with the brain.

Figure 8–13D shows a bottom view of the skulls of a cat and several primates. The occipital condyles on the cat skull are located far to the rear of the skull. This animal is pronograde; the skull attaches directly to the front of the spine, where the powerful **nuchal muscles** keep the head up. These muscles in animals such as the cat are relatively large. In the cat, a flange, known as the **nuchal crest,** has formed on the back section of the brain case where it provides additional surface area for attachment of the nuchal musculature.

Apes are characterized by a degree of orthograde posturing. Consequently, the occipital condyles are in a more forward position on the cranial base to articulate better with the top of the spine in a vertical position. In the gorilla, the massive facial skeleton weights the head so that powerful nuchal muscles are needed, hence the presence of a prominent nuchal crest. In humans, the condyles and the foramen magnum lie in a position almost directly in the center of the underside of the skull. With the reduction of the facial skeleton and the enlargement of the brain case, the skull has achieved a good balance on top of the spine. Note the absence of a prominent nuchal crest.

**The Sense Organs**   Seeing, smelling, and hearing are characterized by special sense organs: the eye, nose, and ear. These organs are, in part, housed within the skull. Therefore, the structure of the skull reflects the nature of these organs.

The eyes of most primates are located on the front of the head instead of on the sides of the head as in most other animals. This allows for binocular vision. The lower part of the eye in most mammals is supported on the side by the **zygomatic arch,** or cheekbone; the eye itself is separated from the musculature behind it by a membrane. In living primates, the eye is further supported by the **postorbital bar** created by the fusion of a process coming down from the top of the orbit and a process com-

ing up from the zygomatic arch. In the anthropoids, and to a large degree in the tarsiers, a bony **postorbital septum** is found behind the eye. It connects the postorbital bar to the brain case, creating a complete eye socket in the anthropoid skull. While a postorbital bar is found in some other mammals, the postorbital septum is a primate specialization (Figure 7–3).

In primates, because of the general reduction in the sense of smell, the nasal region of the skull is relatively small. This results in a general flattening of the face. Associated with the reduction in olfaction is a reduction in the surface area of the nasal membranes and the bony plates that support these membranes.

The organ of hearing, the ear, consists of the external ear, a tube leading to the eardrum, the eardrum itself, the three middle-ear bones, a coiled

**FIGURE 8–13  Comparative Anatomy of the Skull**
(A) Front view, (B) side view, (C) back view, and (D) bottom view of the skulls of a (*a*) cat, (*b*) rhesus monkey, (*c*) chimpanzee, (*d*) human. (Note: Not to scale.)

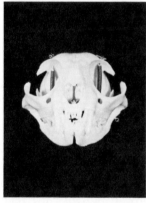
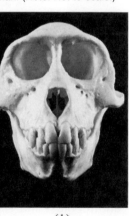
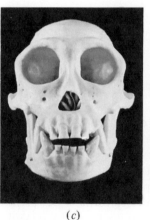

(*a*)          (*b*)          (*c*)          (*d*)

A

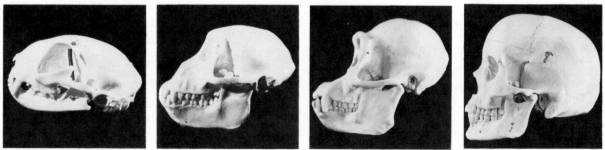

(*a*)          (*b*)          (*c*)          (*d*)

B

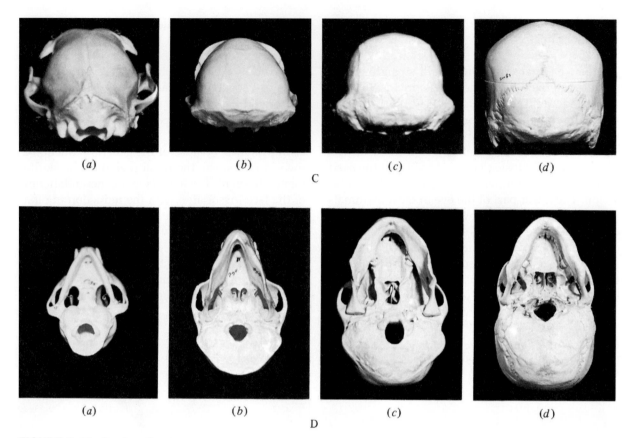

(a)          (b)          (c)          (d)

C

(a)          (b)          (c)          (d)

D

**FIGURE 8–13** (continued)

tube containing the nerve endings that sense the vibrations created by sound, and fluid-filled chambers associated with movement and orientation. Most of the ear is housed within the skull.

The middle ear, containing the three middle-ear bones, lies within the **auditory bulla,** a flat or inflated structure that forms in the floor of the skull. The tympanic membrane, or eardrum, is supported by a bony element called the **ectotympanic.** The relationship of the ectotympanic to the auditory bulla differs among living primates. In the lemurs, the ectotympanic is a simple ring, while in the lorises and New World monkeys, the ectotympanic is fused to the rim of the auditory bulla. In the tarsiers, Old World monkeys, apes, and humans, the ectotympanic is fused to the outer margin of the auditory bulla and extends into a tube.

The architecture of the skull is a reflection of the organization of the brain, teeth, and sense organs.

In the primates, the facial skeleton has become relatively small primarily because of the reduction of the sense of smell. This contrasts with the enlargement of the cranium. In prosimians, the facial skeleton is located to the front of the brain case, but in anthropoids, and especially in humans, the relatively small facial skeleton has moved below the large brain case. Although the nasal apparatus is reduced in size, the massiveness of the teeth and jaw in some species, such as the baboon and gorilla, results in a **prognathism,** which is a jutting forward of the jaw.

## The Evolution of the Primate Brain

The human brain, which allows for the complexity of behavior and culture, is a remarkable organ and is one of the most distinctive features of *Homo sapiens.* The anatomy of the brain is discussed in the appendix.

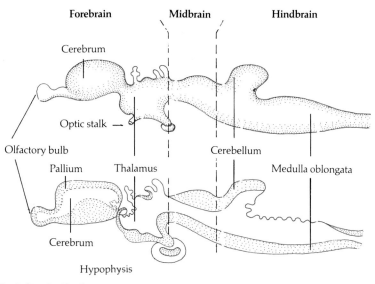

**FIGURE 8–14  The Vertebrate Brain**
A generalized and schematized representation of the vertebrate brain. The lower figure is a longitudinal section showing differences in the thickness of the brain wall.

The major element of the nervous system in the primitive vertebrate is the single, hollow nerve cord. At the front end of the cord, the primitive brain developed. Here are the sense organs; information gathered by these structures is fed into the brain, which then produces some type of response. The primitive vertebrate brain consists of three swellings in the hollow nerve cord associated with a thickening of walls: the **forebrain, midbrain,** and **hindbrain.** These swellings established the basic structure of all vertebrate brains, including those of the primates (Figure 8–14).

In early vertebrates, differentiation of each of the three divisions of the brain already had taken place. Three sections make up the forebrain: the thalamus, the cerebral hemispheres, and the olfactory bulbs. The midbrain also developed special structures, including the optic lobes. The cerebellum developed as a large swelling on the hindbrain, with the thick lower portion becoming the medulla oblongata. These are only the major features of the early vertebrate brain, for many other structures were also developing. In the early vertebrates, the paired cerebral hemispheres of the forebrain were smooth swellings; they were associated primarily with the sense of smell.

In the early reptiles, the cerebrum enlarged. Although it is still associated with smell, a new area appeared, the **neocortex,** a gray covering on the cerebrum. This cortex is involved with the association and coordination of various impulses coming from the sense organs and other areas of the brain.

In early mammals, the area of the cerebrum associated with smell was important, but the neocortex shows some expansion. The neocortex is separated from the rest of the cortex by a groove. This new area is the major part of the covering, or cortex, of the brain. This part of the mammalian brain expanded in size, and convolutions are seen on the surface in many species. In this expanded cortex, many of the functions that were controlled in the early mammals by other sections of the brain are associated with the cerebral cortex. For example, in mammals visual stimuli are received by the cerebral cortex rather than by the optic lobes of the midbrain. Several vertebrate brains are compared in Figure 8–15.

**The Primate Brain**  The evolution of the primate brain is characterized by a general increase in brain size relative to body size. As the size of the body increases, so does the size of various parts of the

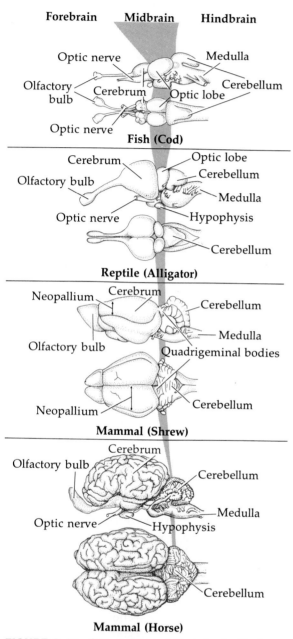

Forebrain    Midbrain    Hindbrain

Optic nerve — Medulla
Olfactory bulb — Cerebrum — Optic lobe — Cerebellum
Optic nerve
**Fish (Cod)**

Cerebrum — Optic lobe — Cerebellum
Olfactory bulb — Medulla
Optic nerve — Hypophysis — Cerebellum
**Reptile (Alligator)**

Neopallium — Cerebrum — Cerebellum
Olfactory bulb — Medulla — Quadrigeminal bodies
Neopallium — Cerebellum
**Mammal (Shrew)**

Cerebrum
Olfactory bulb — Cerebellum
Optic nerve — Medulla — Hypophysis
Cerebellum
**Mammal (Horse)**

**FIGURE 8–15  Comparison of Vertebrate Brains**
Side and top views of four vertebrate brains. Note expansion of the forebrain in the mammals.

body. Not all body parts increase at the same rate; some parts of the body, such as the brain, increase at a faster rate. This is the concept of **allometric growth.** In many large animals, the brain is rela-

tively larger than it is in closely related smaller species.

Since humans are large primates, we expect to see a large brain due to allometric growth. The increase in the size of the hominid brain through time, however, is greater than can be explained by allometric growth alone. The increase in brain size over and beyond that which can be explained by an increase in body size is termed the **encephalization quotient (EQ).** Table 8–3 gives several examples of this measure. Note the tremendous difference between humans and other primates.

**The Cerebral Cortex**  The neocortex covers the entire cerebrum in the Anthropoidea. Many convolutions greatly increase its surface area, and the cerebral cortex in humans completely covers the olfactory lobes and the midbrain. In the course of primate evolution, the different areas that are associated with specific functions have become more clearly defined (Figure 8–16). Areas of the brain concerned with the sense of smell have undergone reduction, while areas associated with vision and the sense of touch have become elaborated.

The evolution of toolmaking abilities, language, and other human characteristics has affected the evolution of the brain. The cortical areas associated with hand coordination are about three times as extensive in the human brain as they are in the ape brain, and the expansion of the areas concerned with language is even greater.

| TABLE 8–3 | |
|---|---|
| **ENCEPHALIZATION QUOTIENT IN SOME PRIMATES** | |
| **Primate** | **EQ** |
| Tarsier | 1.29 |
| Spider monkey | 2.33 |
| Rhesus monkey | 2.09 |
| Hamadryas baboon | 2.35 |
| Gibbon | 2.74 |
| Orangutan (male) | 1.63 |
| Gorilla (male) | 1.53 |
| Chimpanzee (male) | 2.48 |
| Human (male) | 7.79 |

*Source:* H. J. Jerison, *Evolution of the Brain and Intelligence* (New York: Academic, 1973).

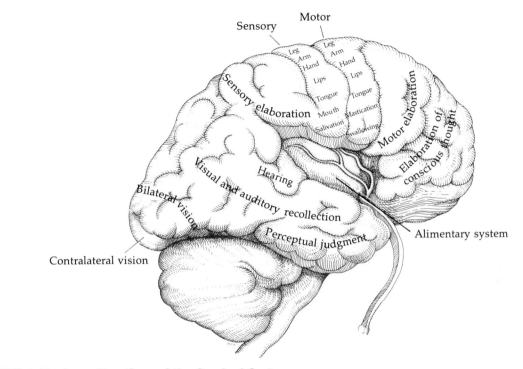

**FIGURE 8–16  Some Functions of the Cerebral Cortex**

The cerebral cortex makes possible a level of complex behavior that we call intelligence, which is most highly developed in humans. The cortex also allows for **social intelligence,** through which the knowledge and images that originate in an individual's brain can be transferred by speech (and, in the last 5000 years, writing) to the brains of others. The knowledge of an entire society, which is always greater than the knowledge of any one individual, can be drawn on to meet crises. This is one major factor that differentiates humans from other species.

### Erect Bipedalism and the Human Brain

In the evolution of the human pelvis, discussed earlier, a repositioning of the sacrum in hominids has created a complete bony ring through which the birth canal passes. In the chimpanzee, the articulations of the sacrum to the innominate bones and the pelvis to the femur are farther apart than in humans, which means that the birth canal has a bony roof at one point and a bony floor at another. In humans, the bony roof has moved over the bony floor, creating a complete bony ring through which the head of the child must pass at birth (Figure 8–17). The flexibility of the human infant's skull, however, allows for a certain degree of compression as the child passes through the birth canal, and for a great deal of growth after birth.

Other animals' brains are almost completely developed at birth. For instance, the rhesus monkey at birth has a brain that is approximately 75 percent of its adult size, and the brain of a chimpanzee newborn is 45 to 50 percent of its adult size. In contrast, the human newborn has a brain less than 30 percent of its adult size, attaining over 90 percent of its adult size by the fifth year of life. Consequently, the child is dependent upon others for a long time, and it is during this extended period that learning occurs and mental abilities develop.

### The Brain Case

As the brain enlarges, so does the neurocranium in which the brain is housed. In most mammals, as in

**BOX 8-1**

# Hemispheric Asymmetry—One Brain or Two?

In general, the brain is bilaterally symmetrical, as are many other anatomical features of all chordates. Yet the human brain does show one-sidedness, or **asymmetry of function (lateralization),** within this general context of bilateral symmetry. The left cerebral hemisphere in most people contributes more than the right hemisphere to language abilities. The right hemisphere, on the other hand, plays a larger role in nonverbal communication.

Clinical experiments have indicated that the left hemisphere analyzes the outside world in a more precise, more analytic, and more literal way than the right side does. In contrast, the right side appears to perceive the world in a more general, more geometric, and more holistic way than the left cerebral hemisphere does.

Asymmetry of function should be viewed in terms of the contributions each side makes; no function is the exclusive domain of one side. The role of the corpus callosum, which connects the two hemispheres, makes intimate teamwork possible between the two sides of the brain.

Clear-cut hemispheric asymmetry has been demonstrated only for humans and song birds. The evolutionary significance of lateralization of function in these two quite different groups of animals appears related to vocalization.

In humans, the fact that the left hemisphere is usually dominant for language may be related to an advantage gained from motor asymmetry for the control of speech. The organs used in speech include the lips, tongue, nose, throat, and vocal cords. These structures are midline organs; they lie in the center of the body. These midline organs are innervated, that is, connected to the brain, by nerves on both sides of the body. Since midline organs are equally innervated from the right and left sides, the problem arises of which side of the brain would control the midline function—speech in humans and songs in birds. One hypothesis is that natural selection favored those individuals for whom hemispheric conflict was least likely to occur. These individuals would be those with hemispheric asymmetry, since such asymmetry would prevent potential confusion in the control of organs located on the midline. Asymmetry in the control of speech production may have led to asymmetry for speech comprehension, which is also basically a left-side function in most people. This language asymmetry may then have allowed the right hemisphere to do other things.

The idea of brain asymmetry has lead to a provocative question: Are male and female brains lateralized differently? Some researchers have hypothesized that the brains of females show less differentiation of function between the right and left side than do the brains of males. This has been used to explain a number of differences such as the fact that on the math section of the Scholastic Aptitude Test (SAT) 13 boys score above 700 for every 1 girl.[1] Math is seen as a specialized left-hemisphere function. Some evidence suggests that females are not as specialized as males for this function, but the relationship between greater lateralization and superior ability is not clear. As with math, women are less lateralized for verbal skills than men, yet as a group they do better than men in tests of language skills.

Although the validity of the research designs that have led to these types of conclusions about male–female brain differences has been questioned, the verdict on the precise nature of such differences is not in yet. It is perhaps consistent with evolutionary theory to hypothesize that some differences would exist between male and female brains. For more than 99 percent of *H. sapiens'* tenure on earth, hunting and gathering, or scavenging, was the only pattern of subsistence. Since men predominantly hunt or scavenge and women predominantly gather, different selective forces working on males and females could possibly have led to brain differences along with the well-documented differences in overall size and shape, fat and muscle composition, and other sexual dimorphisms that will be discussed in Chapter 16.

Now let us return to the question posed in the title of this box: Does a human have one brain or two? The resounding answer is one. Jerre Levy puts it this way: ". . . normal people have not half a brain nor two brains but one gloriously differentiated brain, with each hemisphere contributing its specialized abilities."[2]

[1]Bruce Bower, "The 'Math Gap' Puzzling Sex Differences," *Science News* 130 (December 6, 1986), p. 357.
[2]Jerre Levy, "Right Brain, Left Brain: Fact or Fiction," *Psychology Today* 16 (May 1985), p. 44.

the cat, the facial skeleton is relatively large in relation to the brain case, and it is located in front of the brain case. In primates, the brain case is larger than the facial skeleton, and the facial skeleton is located underneath the brain case rather than in front of it.

The volume of the interior of the brain case is the **cranial capacity.** Note that cranial capacity is the volume of the brain case, *not* the size of the brain (Table 8–4). Although the two are close, the brain itself is covered by tissue, nerves, and blood vessels, and so its volume is always less than that of the cranium.

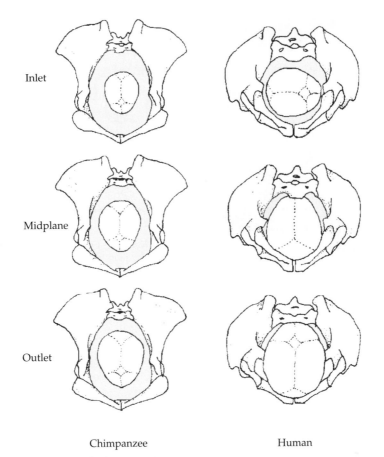

Inlet

Midplane

Outlet

Chimpanzee                    Human

**FIGURE 8-17  Pelvis and Fetal Head**
This diagram shows a female pelvis of a chimpanzee and a human from below. Note the size of the
head of the fetus in childbirth at the level of the pelvic inlet, midplane, and pelvic outlet.

| TABLE 8-4 | |
|---|---|
| **CRANIAL CAPACITIES OF THE LIVING HOMINOIDEA** | |
| **Primate** | **Average cranial capacity (cubic centimeters)** |
| Gibbon | 102 |
| Chimpanzee | 399 |
| Orangutan | 434 |
| Gorilla | 535 |
| Human | 1350 |

*Source:* P. V. Tobias, "The Distribution of Cranial Capacity Values among Living Hominoids," *Proceedings of the Third International Congress of Primatology, Zurich, 1970,* vol. 1 (Basel: Karger, 1971), pp. 18–35.

Wide variation of cranial capacity is usually seen within a given species. While we note that the average cranial capacity of modern humans is 1350 cubic centimeters, the nonpathological range runs from about 900 to more than 2000 cubic centimeters. Within this range, there appears to be no correlation between brain size and intelligence. Even between species, the structure and physiology of the brain are more important than its size.

Since the inside of the brain case does conform roughly to the outside surface of the brain, it can convey some information about the brain itself. Often, a cast is made of the inside of a cranium of a

**FIGURE 8–18  An Endocranial Cast**
An endocranial cast of *Homo erectus*, a fossil hominid from China.

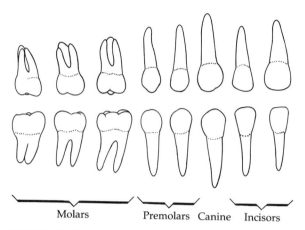

Molars  Premolars Canine  Incisors

**FIGURE 8–19  Four Types of Primate Teeth**
Human dentition from half of the upper jaw and half of the lower jaw.

fossil find; the result is an **endocranial cast** like the one in Figure 8–18. From such a cast the relative proportion of the lobes of the brain and other information can be inferred. Remember, however, that this is not a fossil brain but simply a cast of the inside of the brain case.

### Primate Dentition

The ingestion of food is a major prerequisite for life in animals and involves several parts of the anatomy. In vertebrates, the teeth, jaw, and muscles used for chewing are employed in preparing food for intake into the digestive system of the body. We have already seen that mammals are characterized by heterodonty, the regional differentiation of teeth into different kinds of teeth that serve different functions, and diphyodonty, the development of two sets of teeth, the deciduous dentition (milk teeth) followed by the adult dentition. In general, the primates have retained a fairly unspecialized tooth structure; the reduction in the number of teeth has not progressed to the degree that it has in many other mammalian orders.

**Primate Teeth**  Among mammals, we recognize four different kinds of permanent teeth: incisors, canines, premolars, and molars (Figure 8–19). Among primates in general, the incisor tends to be a broad, cutting type of tooth with a rather simple

structure; it is often described as "spatulate." The incisors are used to grasp food. Primates that eat fruit use their incisors to tear off small pieces that can then be properly masticated (chewed) by the premolars and molars. Smaller food objects, such as seeds and grasses, are usually passed directly back to the chewing teeth. Primates that specialize in this type of diet often have smaller incisors than do the fruit eaters.

As we saw in Chapter 7, prosimians are characterized by the development of a dental comb, which is formed by lower incisors and canines that project forward horizontally. The lower canine often takes on the appearance of an incisor and is included in the comb (Figure 7–6). In this situation, the functions of the canine are taken over by the first premolar, which then becomes caninelike in appearance. The upper incisors are frequently reduced in size. The animal uses the comb for grooming the fur and for scraping gum and resins off the bark of trees.

The canine is a simple, pointed, curved tooth, usually larger than the other teeth. This tooth serves many functions, such as grasping, stabbing, ripping, and tearing food, and plays a role in defense and displays of dominance. Canines of the Anthropoidea tend to be much larger in males than in females, another example of sexual dimorphism. Canines, highly developed in the terrestrial male baboon, act as a weapon in troop defense.

The premolars and molars are often called the **cheek teeth;** these are the teeth used in chewing. The premolars, or bicuspids in dental terminology, are simple teeth that usually have two **cusps,** or points. In many mammals, including some primates, the premolar either has developed additional cusps to become more molarlike or possesses only a single cusp; for this reason, anthropologists do not call the premolars bicuspids.

The molars are the most complex teeth in structure due to the formation of several cusps and minor cusps, ridges, and valleys. The molars chew and prepare the food for passage to the stomach for digestion. The smaller the food particles, the greater the surface area per unit of volume upon which the digestive enzymes can act.

Some types of foods are more difficult to process than others, and primates tend to specialize in different kinds of diets. Most living primates show three basic dietary adaptations; they may be classified as **insectivores** (insect eaters), **frugivores** (fruit eaters), and **folivores** (leaf eaters). Many primates, such as humans, show a combination of these patterns and are called **omnivores,** which in a few primates includes eating meat. Since the teeth play major roles in the procurement and processing of food, we would expect to find special dental adaptations that are related to the special requirements of various types of diets (Figure 8–20). Once we understand these adaptations in living primates, we can look for similar adaptations in fossil primates, and we can attempt to gain some understanding of their dietary habits.

The ingestion both of leaves and of insects requires that the leaves and the insect skeletons be broken up and chopped into small pieces. The molars of folivores and insectivores are characterized by the development of shearing crests on the molars that function to cut the food into small pieces. Insectivores' molars are further characterized by high, pointed cusps that are capable of puncturing the outside skeleton of insects.

---

**BOX 8-2**

## The Ultrastructure of Tooth Enamel

The development of the scanning electron microscope has made possible the development of comparative studies on a microscopic level. This technology has been used to study tooth enamel, the hard outer layer of the tooth. These studies are exciting because enamel changes very little during the process of fossilization and teeth are very common in the fossil record. In fact, many extinct species are known by their teeth alone.

Tooth enamel is 96 percent mineral—crystals of apatitic calcium phosphate. These crystals form into rods or prisms that are then assembled into even larger units. Electron microscope studies have shown that the structure of tooth enamel is very regular, yet variations exist among species.

There are three major patterns in the arrangement of prisms. Distinct differences in pattern exist between living hominids and living and fossil anthropoids. Pattern 1 prisms are found in insectivores and many bats. Pattern 2 prisms are found in most hoofed mammals, rodents, and marsupials. Prisms with pattern 3, often called the "keyhole" pattern, are commonly found in humans. Many subtypes also exist. All three enamel types can be found in the primate order. While pattern 3 is found in human enamel, pattern 2 is frequently found in the enamel of the rhesus monkey, and pattern 1 in the lemurs.

Differences are also found among the various species of hominoids. In general, pattern 3 enamel characterizes the great apes and humans. However, the relative abundance of some of the subtypes differs. A specialist in the microstructure of tooth enamel can distinguish human enamel from chimpanzee and gorilla enamel when viewed with a scanning electron microscope.

Because of variation in structure, pattern differences become a valuable diagnostic tool. Remember that teeth are the most common parts of the skeleton to be preserved in the fossil record. Since teeth are largely composed of minerals, few changes are found in teeth that have been buried in the ground. Analysis of the microstructure of tooth enamel can therefore provide valuable clues as to the evolutionary relationship of a particular fossil tooth and living primate forms.

---

*Sources:* A. Boyde and L. Martin, "The Microstructure of Dental Enamel," in D. J. Chivers, B. A. Wood, and A. Bilsborough (eds.), *Food Acquisition and Processing in Primates* (New York: Plenum, 1984), pp. 341–367; T. G. Bromage and M. C. Dean, "Reevaluation of the Age at Death of Immature Fossil Hominids," *Nature* 317 (1985), pp. 525–527; and D. B. Gantt, "Enamel Thickness and Ultrastructure in Hominoids: With Reference to Form, Function, and Phylogeny," in D. R. Swindler and J. Erwin (eds.), *Systematics, Evolution, and Anatomy* (New York: Liss, 1986), pp. 453–475.

| Diet | Dentition | Example | Drawing |
|------|-----------|---------|---------|
| Frugivorous (fruit-eating) | Low cusps for crushing soft fruits | Spider monkey |  |
| Folivorous (leaf-eating) | Well-developed shearing crests for cutting tough leafy material into small pieces | Langur | 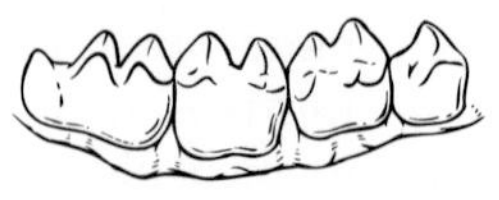 |
| Insectivorous (insect-eating) | Sharp crests for puncturing the outer skeleton of insects | Goeldi's monkey | 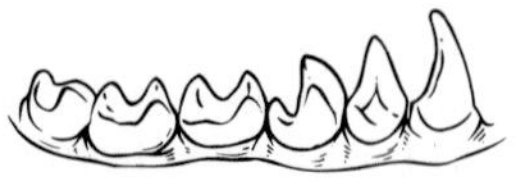 |

**FIGURE 8–20  Molar Morphology and Diet**

Frugivores, on the other hand, have molar teeth with low, rounded cusps; their molars have few crests and are characterized by broad, flat basins for crushing and mashing the food. Low, rounded cusps are also seen on molars of primates that consume hard nuts or seeds, but these molars are also characterized by very thick enamel.

**Dental Formulas**   The types and numbers of teeth are designated in **dental formulas,** some of which are listed in Table 8–5. Since dentition is bilaterally symmetrical, we need only note the numbers and kinds of teeth on one side of the jaw. The teeth of the upper jaw are shown above the line, and those of the lower jaw, below the line. While the notations for the upper and lower jaws are generally the same, there are exceptions. In the formula, the four numbers, separated by dots, are the number of incisors, canines, premolars, and molars, respectively, per quadrant. Paleontologists have reconstructed the dental formula of the common ancestor of living placental mammals as

$$\frac{3.1.4.3}{3.1.4.3}$$

Primate evolution is characterized by a loss of teeth in the dental formula, although the total reduction in tooth number in primates is not as great as that found in some other mammalian orders.

The different prosimian groups have different numbers of teeth. All the Ceboidea are characterized by three premolars per quadrant; among the ceboids, the cebids have retained three molars while the marmosets and tamarins have two. All the Old World anthropoids have 32 teeth and the dental formula

$$\frac{2.1.2.3}{2.1.2.3}$$

In apes and humans, a further reduction in the dental formula is possible since one or more of the third molars (wisdom teeth) do not develop at all in some individuals. Also, when the third molars erupt, the human jaw is often too small to accommodate them, and the resulting impacted molars require surgical removal.

**Ape Dentition**   Because of a common ancestry, the dentition of the apes and that of the hominids have many traits in common. Even so, each evolutionary line has evolved several distinctive features (Figure 8–21). The incisors of the great apes are quite broad and spatula-like, and the upper incisors of these animals are implanted in the jaw at an angle.

## TABLE 8-5

### ADULT DENTAL FORMULAS OF LIVING PRIMATES

| Primate | Dental formula | Total number of teeth |
|---|---|---|
| Lemurs | $\dfrac{2.1.3.3}{2.1.3.3}$ | 36 |
| Indris | $\dfrac{2.1.2.3}{1.1.2.3}$ | 30 |
| Aye-ayes | $\dfrac{1.0.1.3}{1.0.0.3}$ | 18 |
| Marmosets | $\dfrac{2.1.3.2}{2.1.3.2}$ | 32 |
| New World monkeys | $\dfrac{2.1.3.3}{2.1.3.3}$ | 36 |
| Old World monkeys, apes, and humans | $\dfrac{2.1.2.3}{2.1.2.3}$ | 32 |

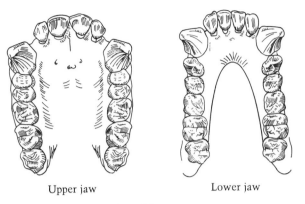

Upper jaw        Lower jaw

**FIGURE 8–21  Ape Dentition**
Note that the premolar and molar teeth of the chimpanzee on each side of the mouth are approximately parallel to each other; there are two diastemata in the dental arcade of both the upper and lower jaw; and the canine teeth are longer than the other teeth. See the text for other features of ape dentition.

The ape canine is large and projecting. When the animal closes its mouth, the canines interlock, each fitting into a space, or **diastema,** in the opposite jaw. In the upper jaw, the diastema is in front of the canine, while in the lower jaw, it is behind the canine. Thus, in chewing, the chimpanzee cannot use the more rotary motion characteristic of hominids. The canines of all great apes show marked sexual dimorphism.

When the mandible of a prosimian is looked at from above, the row of teeth, or **dental arcade,** presents the outline of the letter V. With the evolution of large, projecting canines in the ape, the front of the mandible has broadened so that the ape dental arcade is in the shape of the letter U.

The first lower premolar in the ape is also specialized because the canine in the upper jaw shears directly in front of it. This premolar is larger than the other and has an enlarged cusp. This tooth, known as a **sectorial premolar,** presents a sharpening edge for the canine. The cheek teeth, the premolars and molars, are arranged in two straight rows that parallel each other, although they often converge toward the back of the jaw.

The basic structure of the molars in humans is the same as that in chimpanzees. The upper mo-

lar contains four cusps, and the lower molar has five. The arrangement of the five cusps and the grooves between them suggests a letter Y and therefore is called the **Y-5 pattern** (Figure 8–22). This contrasts with the **bilophodont** molar structure in the monkey, whose lower molar consists of four cusps with a small constriction separating them into two pairs.

**Modern Hominid Dentition**   In the evolution of hominid dentition, the size of the teeth has decreased and the length of that portion of the jaw that holds the cheek teeth has decreased relative to the length of the skull. When viewed from the side, all the teeth are at the same level; the canine is not projecting, and the first lower premolar is not sectorial. As shown in Figure 8–23, the teeth are arranged in a curved, or parabolic, dental arcade with no diastema.

The human incisors, in contrast to those of the ape, are narrower and are implanted vertically in the jaw. Human canines are small, with a spatulate cutting edge; they do not project or interlock, nor do they show much sexual dimorphism. This contrasts markedly with the ape canines, which are pointed, projecting, and interlocking and show

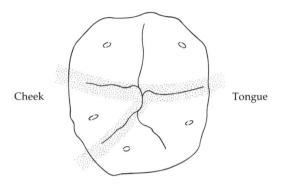

**FIGURE 8–22  The Y-5 Molar Pattern**
Note the arrangement of the valleys and five cusps in the lower hominoid molar.

Cheek

Tongue

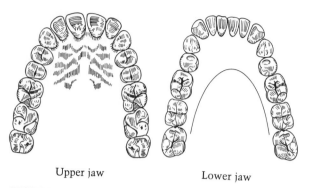

Upper jaw

Lower jaw

**FIGURE 8–23  Human Dentition**
Human dentition contrasts in a number of ways from ape dentition. Note that the premolars and molars of the human are not parallel to each other; there are no diastemata; and the canine teeth are not any longer than the other teeth. See the text for other features of human dentition.

great sexual dimorphism. Diastemata associated with the ape canines are absent in humans.

Like the ape molars, the human upper molars have four cusps (although the upper third molar tends to have only three), while the lower molars exhibit the Y-5 pattern. In contrast to ape molars, human molars show more rounded and compacted cusps. These features are due to the fact that hominid teeth have relatively thick enamel (the outer covering of the teeth). Thick enamel, characteristic of both living and fossil hominids, is suited to the increased crushing and grinding required in the processing of hard, tough food materials. Most of the apes possess relatively thin enamel; the thickness of enamel in the orangutan is intermediate between that of humans and that of the other apes.

The permanent teeth normally erupt in a predictable pattern (Chapter 16). Monkeys and apes are similar in that the canine tends to be the tooth that erupts last or next to last. This may be related to the fact that the large, projecting canine can be an effective and dangerous weapon. The monkey and ape canine erupts after the animal has attained full adult size and social status. The human canine erupts before the second and third molars and, in some individuals, may even erupt before one or more of the premolars.

Besides differences in the order of eruption, the time over which the teeth erupt is extended in humans as a consequence of the extended childhood

period. Thus, by the time the second molar erupts, the first molar has had the opportunity to be partially ground down by abrasion from some types of food particles. When the third molar erupts, it shows a high relief with its patterns of cusps and valleys, compared with the second molar, which is somewhat ground down, and the first molar, which is ground down even further. This steplike wear pattern in a fossil jaw may be indicative of an extended childhood period.

The reduction in the size of the teeth may be related to the development of tool use and a more meat-oriented diet. The apes, for example, use their large front teeth to break open hard fruits; humans might use a chopping tool held in the hand in the same situation. Another suggestion is that a major function of the large, projecting canine is its role in aggressive displays. With the development of cooperative hunting in human societies, such displays probably no longer occurred. Also, humans use weapons instead of canines for defense.

Remember, however, that use and disuse of a structure during a lifetime does not directly affect the evolution of that structure. The reduction of the canine represents a shift in frequencies from the alleles that produce larger canines to those that produce smaller ones; that is, mutations were originally responsible for creating a range of variation in canine size. When the large canines lost their selective advantage, the smaller canines may have gained some selective advantage; through time, the frequency of large canines gradually decreased.

## The Jaw

The modern human jaw is smaller and shorter relative to the skull than is the ape jaw. Since human food is usually cut up or in some way processed into smaller pieces so that it is easier to chew, humans do not need to exert as much pressure when chewing as the apes do. In time, of course, fire was used to cook meat, thus tenderizing it.

In the anthropoids, the mandible, or lower jaw, consists of two fused symmetrical halves. In the ape, the forces generated by the jaw in eating are great and the curved front section of the mandible, where the two halves of the mandible have fused, is reinforced internally by a buttress, the **simian shelf.** This shelf rarely occurs in the hominids. In modern humans, the evolution of a small jaw has resulted in a **chin,** a product of changes in the growth and development pattern of the jaw (Figure 8–24).

The muscles that operate the jaw have also changed in the course of human evolution, becoming smaller. The **temporalis** muscle arises on the side of the skull and inserts on the jaw (Figure 8–25). In the gorilla, this muscle is very large while the brain case is relatively small, and so a large flange, the **sagittal crest,** develops across the top of the skull, providing the surface area necessary for muscle attachment. The **masseter,** another muscle that functions in chewing, arises on the zygomatic arch of the skull and inserts on the mandible. An animal with large teeth and jaw and, consequently, a large masseter has a robust zygomatic. Since the temporalis passes through the opening formed by the zygomatic and the side of the skull, a large temporalis is associated with a flaring zygomatic arch. In modern humans, the zygomatic arch is slender and not flaring.

## Summary

The human skull, composed of 28 separate bones plus 32 teeth in the adult, is a very complex part of the skeleton. The skull articulates with the spine by means of the occipital condyles on the base of the skull. In most mammals, the condyles are located toward the rear of the skull, while in primates they are located underneath the skull. In humans, they are positioned almost directly in the center of the skull; this achieves a good balance of the skull atop the spine. In general, the primate facial skeleton is reduced in relationship to the rest of the skull. The nasal apparatus is reduced in size, and the eyes are

**FIGURE 8–24  Simian Shelf and Chin**
Note (*a*) the simian shelf in the ape mandible and (*b*) the chin or mental protuberance on the human mandible.

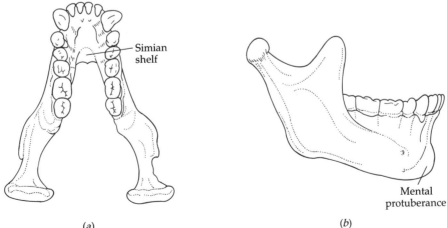

(*a*)                (*b*)

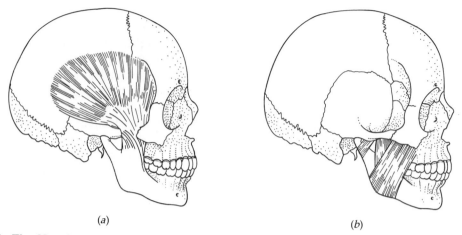

**FIGURE 8–25 The Muscles of the Jaws**
The temporalis muscle (*a*) and masseter muscle (*b*) as seen on on a human skull.

encased in bony eye sockets located on the front of the skull.

Within the primate order, we see the progressive enlargement of brain volume and development of the cerebral cortex. The human neocortex makes possible higher mental activities. In association with other features, such as bipedalism and manual dexterity, the cerebral cortex allows for social as well as individual intelligence. It is this social intelligence that enables humans as a species to significantly alter the environment. These alterations can be advantageous, as seen in the general increase in comfort and living standards that technology can bring, or devastating, as evidenced by pollution, the effects of war, and depletion of resources.

The increase in the size of the human brain is reflected in the increased volume of the cranium, or brain case. While the average cranial capacity is 1350 cubic centimeters, the range of variation is large. Within normal limits, no correlation between brain size and intelligence exists.

The primates have retained a fairly unspecialized tooth structure. The New World monkeys have three premolars per quadrant of the mouth, and most have a total of 36 teeth. All the Old World anthropoids have only two premolars, for a total of 32 permanent teeth. General characteristics of modern hominid dentition are a reduction in tooth size, lack of a sectorial premolar, a parabolic dental arcade, lack of a diastema and projecting canine, vertical implantation of the incisors, early eruption of the canine, a differential wear pattern of the molars, and thick tooth enamel.

The human jaw is smaller and shorter, relative to the skull, than is the ape jaw, and a chin is present. The muscles that operate the jaw are smaller. The temporalis muscle in the ape is very large, while the brain case is relatively small. A large flange, the sagittal crest, often develops across the top of the ape skull, providing the surface area necessary for muscle attachment. The large masseter muscle is associated with a robust, flaring zygomatic arch. The modern human skull always lacks a sagittal crest and is characterized by small or absent brow ridges and a slender, nonflaring zygomatic arch.

## MOLECULAR BIOLOGY AND CYTOGENETICS

Evolution has been defined on the genetic level as changes in the gene pool of a population. Ultimately, this refers to changes in the genes themselves. This section examines **comparative cytogenetics,** the comparative study of chromosomes, and **molecular biology**, the comparative study of the molecules of living organisms.

### Comparative Cytogenetics

The genetic material within the cell is found in small bodies called chromosomes (Chapter 2).

Comparative cytogenetics is the comparative study of chromosomes from the cells of different species of plants and animals. Such studies shed light on the evolutionary relationships and histories of these species.

**Chromosome Number** A species is associated with a characteristic number of chromosomes. In *Homo sapiens*, nondividing body cells contain 46 chromosomes. Table 8–6 lists the chromosome numbers of a variety of primate species, varying from 34 in the spider monkey to 62 in the woolly monkey.

Chromosome number is not necessarily consistent within any given taxonomic group such as a family; closely related species may have differing chromosome numbers. For example, the white-handed gibbon has 44 chromosomes, while the crested gibbon has 52, yet both species belong to the same genus. On the other hand, widely differing species may share the same number of chromosomes. The Old World patas monkey and the New World owl monkey both have the same chromosome number, 54. It therefore follows that chro-

### TABLE 8–6

**SOME CHROMOSOME NUMBERS OF PRIMATES**

| Primate | Family | Chromosome number |
| --- | --- | --- |
| Owl monkey | Cebidae | 54 |
| Spider monkey | Cebidae | 34 |
| Capuchin monkey | Cebidae | 54 |
| Woolly monkey | Cebidae | 62 |
| Squirrel monkey | Cebidae | 44 |
| Common marmoset | Callitrichidae | 46 |
| Red-crowned mangabey | Cercopithecidae | 42 |
| Vervet monkey | Cercopithecidae | 60 |
| Patas monkey | Cercopithecidae | 54 |
| Rhesus monkey | Cercopithecidae | 42 |
| Baboon | Cercopithecidae | 42 |
| Indian langur | Cercopithecidae | 44 |
| White-handed gibbon | Hylobatidae | 44 |
| Crested gibbon | Hylobatidae | 52 |
| Siamang | Hylobatidae | 50 |
| Orangutan | Pongidae | 48 |
| Gorilla | Panidae | 48 |
| Chimpanzee | Panidae | 48 |
| Human | Hominidae | 46 |

*Source:* T. C. Hsu and K. Benirschke, *Atlas of Mammalian Chromosomes,* vol. 10 (Berlin: Springer, 1977), pt. 4.

mosome number is not evidence of evolutionary relationships. All the great apes, however, share the same chromosome number of 48.

### The Nature of Chromosome Evolution

As we saw in Chapter 2, chromosomes differ in size and position of the centromere. On the basis of these characteristics, chromosomes may be classified and arranged in a standard way; this standardized arrangement of chromosomes is a **karyotype.** Human karyotypes are shown in Figure 2–6.

Figure 8–26 shows a composite karyotype comparing chimpanzee and human chromosomes. Although the chromosome numbers differ, the chromosomes exhibit a high degree of similarity in their appearance. Hypothetically, their similarity is the result of a common inheritance; in other words, these chromosomes are homologous. Through gene mapping, homologous genes are being found in the same position on human and chimpanzee chromosomes.

The chromosomes seen in Figure 8–26 are giemsa-banded. Detailed analysis of the banding patterns leads to the conclusion that "essentially every band and subband observed in man has a direct counterpart in the chimpanzee chromosome complements."[2] Since the banding pattern is largely a reflection of the genetic content of the chromosomes, this supports the theory of close genetic similarity between chimpanzees and humans.

**Human and Chimpanzee Chromosomes Compared** Although human and chimpanzee chromosomes are very similar, comparisons of human and chimpanzee banded chromosomes reveal many interesting differences. Figure 8–27*b* illustrates a **pericentric inversion** in which two breaks occur, one on either side of the centromere. The centerpiece turns around and rejoins the two outside pieces. Thus, human chromosome 4 and its chimpanzee counterpart both contain the same bands, but their relative positions are different. Nine

---

[2]J. J. Yunis, J. R. Sawyer, and K. Dunham, "The Striking Resemblance of High-Resolution G-Banded Chromosomes of Man and Chimpanzee," *Science* 208 (1980), p. 1145.

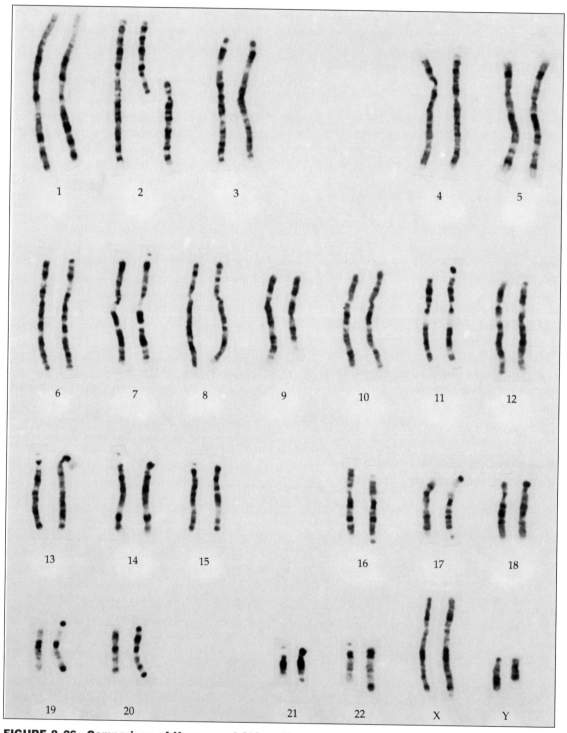

**FIGURE 8–26  Comparison of Human and Chimp Chromosomes**
The great similarity of human and chimpanzee chromosomes is shown in this composite karyotype.
For each pair, the human chromosome is shown on the left and the chimpanzee chromosome on
the right.

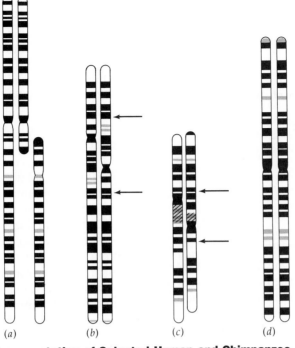

**FIGURE 8–27   Schematic Representation of Selected Human and Chimpanzee Chromosomes**
Human chromosomes are on left. (*a*) Human chromosome 2 shows similarities with two chimpanzee chromosomes. (*b*) Chromosome 4 shows an inversion; breaks (shown by arrows) occur on either side of centromere, and centerpiece becomes turned around. (*c*) Chromosome 9 shows an inversion plus chromosomal material, indicated by hatched lines, that is not thought to contain any actual genes. (*d*) Chromosome 3 shows virtually no variation between human and chimpanzee.

human chromosomes differ from their chimpanzee counterparts in such a manner.

Ten other chromosomes, including the X chromosome, differ from their chimpanzee counterparts because they contain extra chromosome material called **constitutive heterochromatin.** Geneticists believe that this material does not contain any actual genes (Figure 8–27*c*).

We have already noted that the human karyotype contains one less chromosome pair than the chimpanzee karyotype does. When we carefully pair up each human chromosome with a chimpanzee chromosome that appears to be similar, we find that human chromosome 2 does not have a homologous chromosome from the chimpanzee set. Also, two small chimpanzee chromosomes, both possessing centromeres near one end, are left unmatched.

One hypothesis proposes that human chromosome 2 evolved from a fusion of two ancestral chromosomes. Such an event is illustrated in Figure 8–28. The two short arms of the two chromosomes break off. If these small, short arms carry no important genes, their loss would not adversely affect the organism. Then the two centromeres fuse, forming a new, larger chromosome. Once this becomes fixed in the population, the number of chromosomes is reduced from 48 to 46.

We can conclude that the common ancestor of humans and chimpanzees possessed 48 chromosomes, which is the chromosome number of the other great apes as well. Figure 8–27*a* compares human chromosome 2 with two chimpanzee chromosomes. The matching bands support the hypothesis that this human chromosome arose through a fusion of the two smaller ancestral chromosomes.

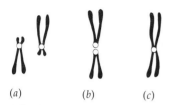

(a)          (b)          (c)

**FIGURE 8–28   The Evolution of Human Chromosome 2**
It is hypothesized that human chromosome 2 evolved from a fusion of two small ancestral chromosomes: (a) ancestral chromosomes; (b) short arms broken off; (c) centromeres fused together.

## The Study of Protein Structure

In the previous sections, we saw how evolutionary relationships can be established upon analysis of the genetic material on the cellular level. In the following sections, we will examine similarities on the molecular level, looking first at protein molecules and then at the DNA molecule itself.

In sickle-cell anemia, the abnormal hemoglobin S differs from the normal hemoglobin A by a single amino acid substitution. This substitution is a reflection of a single base change in the DNA molecule controlling beta-chain synthesis (Chapter 3). However, not all substitutions produce abnormalities. In the course of evolution, occasional substitutions occur that either produce no undesirable changes or, less commonly, produce an improvement. Thus, in the divergence of two evolutionary lines that begins with common protein structures, successive substitutions will occur. In time, the two divergent populations will possess proteins with similar yet differing structures. The amino acid sequences of the same types of protein or, more accurately, homologous proteins, may be compared. Those with the more recent common ancestor should show the greatest similarities in the amino acid sequence; that is, they should show the least number of amino acid substitutions.

**Immunological Studies**   The determination of the exact sequence of amino acids in a protein can be time-consuming. Other methods of comparing proteins can be used, such as **immunological comparison.** As an example, we will summarize the

studies of the serum albumins conducted by Vincent Sarich.[3]

The serum albumins are single chains of about 570 amino acids found in all land vertebrates. Sarich took samples of purified serum albumin from human and nonhuman primate blood and injected them into rabbits. The rabbits responded by manufacturing antibodies against the injected proteins. These antibodies were used as the test reagent since they reflect the structure of the injected protein.

The antisera that developed from the injection of human serum albumin reacted strongly to human serum albumin. The reaction of antihuman serum albumin to chimpanzee serum albumin, however, was less strong, and to rhesus monkey serum albumin it was even weaker. The strong reaction between the antisera and the sera from which the antisera were derived is said to indicate an **immunological distance (ID)** of zero; therefore, the ID between one human and another is zero. The weakest measurable ID is about 200. Antisera were developed to serum albumin samples from humans, chimpanzees, rhesus monkeys, and spider monkeys and were then tested against the serum albumins from these four species. The results are listed in Table 8–7. The smaller the ID, the closer the evolutionary relationship.

**Studies of Amino Acid Sequences**   Since each amino acid is specified by one or a few codes in the DNA molecule itself, the determination of amino acid sequences provides us with a reconstruction of the genetic code. Since some amino acids are determined by more than one code, some changes in the code itself will not result in an amino acid substitution. Therefore, the amino acid sequence provides us with the minimum number of changes or substitutions in the nucleotide sequence of the DNA molecule.

As an example, we can look again at the hemoglobin molecule. The alpha chain of a hemoglobin molecule consists of 141 amino acids. In a group of primates studied, all but 17 of these 141 were iden-

[3]V. Sarich, "A Molecular Approach to the Question of Human Origins," in P. Dolhinow and V. Sarich (eds.), *Background for Man* (Boston: Little, Brown, 1971), pp. 60–81.

## TABLE 8-7

### IMMUNOLOGICAL DISTANCE SEPARATING PRIMATE PAIRS

| Pair | ID |
|------|-----|
| Human–chimpanzee | 7 |
| Human–rhesus monkey | 32 |
| Human–spider monkey | 58 |
| Chimpanzee–rhesus monkey | 30 |
| Chimpanzee–spider monkey | 56 |
| Rhesus monkey–spider monkey | 56 |

*Source:* Adapted from Vincent Sarich, "A Molecular Approach to the Question of Human Origins," in P. Dolhinow and V. Sarich (eds.), *Background for Man* (Boston: Little, Brown, 1971), p. 66.

tical. Table 8–8 lists the variable positions in the polypeptide chain and identifies the variant amino acid in each position for several representative primates. Molecular biologists have determined amino acid sequences for several proteins in over 100 primate species.

### Phylogenetic Trees

The quantitative data derived from the comparisons of homologous proteins or DNA may be used to develop phylogenetic trees. These are graphic representations of the evolutionary relationships among animal species.

A phylogenetic tree appears as a series of points connected by lines to form a branching pattern. The single most ancestral point is the root of the tree, and each ancestral point produces two, and only two, descendants. Earlier we noted that changes in amino

acids can be accounted for by more than one pattern of change in the genetic code; therefore, alternate branching patterns can be constructed. An important principle in the construction of phylogenetic trees is the **maximum parsimony principle.** Simply stated, the most probable phylogenetic tree is the one based on the fewest changes in the genetic code.

Figure 8–29 is an example of a phylogenetic tree. It is based on the combined amino acid sequence of six proteins: alpha- and beta-hemoglobin, myoglobin, fibrinopeptides A and B, cytochrome *c,* and alpha lens crystallin. Let us read this tree from the top down.

All the primates listed in Figure 8–29 exhibit a common ancestry distinct from the other eutherian orders shown. The order Primates appears to be most closely related to the orders Lagomorpha and Insectivora. The first group of primates to branch off the line leading to humans is the prosimians; shown in the diagram are the slender loris, the slow loris, and the Lemuroidea (lemurs). The next primates to branch off are the tarsiers, followed by the New World monkeys, represented by *Saimiri* (the squirrel monkey), *Cebus* (the capuchin), Atelinae (spider monkeys), and the marmosets.

Following the New World monkeys, the Old World monkeys branched off, forming a distinct group consisting of the langur, vervet monkeys, the patas monkey, the rhesus and Japanese macaques, mangabeys, and baboons. Finally, the phylogenetic tree shows the close relationships among the members of the Hominoidea and the especially close relationship of humans to chimpanzees.

## TABLE 8-8

### VARIABLE AMINO ACIDS IN PRIMATE ALPHA-GLOBIN CHAINS

| | Amino acid number | | | | | | | | | | | | | | | | | |
|---|---|---|---|---|---|---|---|---|---|---|---|---|---|---|---|---|---|---|
| | 8 | 12 | 15 | 19 | 21 | 23 | 53 | 57 | 67 | 68 | 71 | 73 | 78 | 111 | 113 | 118 | 129 |
| Primate ancestor | Thr | Ala | Gly | Gly | Ala | Asp | Ala | Ala | Thr | Asn | Ala | Val | Ser | Ser | His | Asp | Leu |
| Anthropoid ancestor | — | — | — | — | — | — | — | Gly | — | — | — | — | Asn | Ala | — | — | — |
| Tarsier | — | — | Asp | — | — | — | Ser | Gly | — | Thr | Gly | Ile | Asn | Cys | — | — | Val |
| Capuchin monkey | — | Thr | — | — | — | — | — | Gly | Ser | — | — | — | Asn | Ala | — | — | — |
| Rhesus macaque | Ser | — | — | — | — | Glu | — | Leu | Gly | Leu | Gly | — | Asn | Ala | Leu | Glu | — |
| Human | — | — | — | Ala | — | Glu | — | Gly | — | — | — | — | Asn | Ala | Leu | Glu | — |

*Source:* Adapted from J. M. Beard and M. Goodman, "The Hemoglobins of *Tarsius bancanus,*" in M. Goodman, R. E. Tashian, and J. H. Tashian (eds.), *Molecular Anthropology* (New York: Plenum, 1976), p. 243.

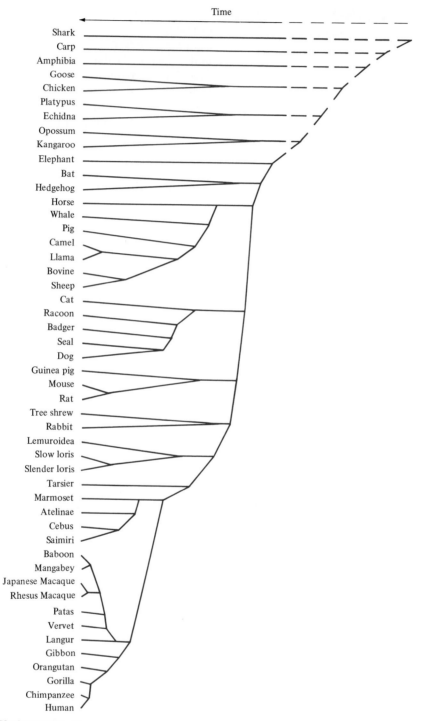

Time

Shark
Carp
Amphibia
Goose
Chicken
Platypus
Echidna
Opossum
Kangaroo
Elephant
Bat
Hedgehog
Horse
Whale
Pig
Camel
Llama
Bovine
Sheep
Cat
Racoon
Badger
Seal
Dog
Guinea pig
Mouse
Rat
Tree shrew
Rabbit
Lemuroidea
Slow loris
Slender loris
Tarsier
Marmoset
Atelinae
Cebus
Saimiri
Baboon
Mangabey
Japanese Macaque
Rhesus Macaque
Patas
Vervet
Langur
Gibbon
Orangutan
Gorilla
Chimpanzee
Human

**FIGURE 8–29  Phylogenetic Tree**
See text for explanation.

## TABLE 8-9

### AMINO ACID DISTANCES BETWEEN HUMANS AND SELECTED PRIMATES

| Primate | Amino acid distances between human and nonhuman primates* |
|---|---|
| Chimpanzee | 0.27 |
| Gorilla | 0.65 |
| Orangutan | 2.78 |
| Gibbon | 2.38 |
| Macaque[†] | 3.89 |
| *Cercopithecus*[†] | 3.65 |
| Squirrel monkey[‡] | 8.78 |
| Spider monkey[‡] | 6.31 |
| Capuchin monkey[‡] | 7.56 |
| Slow loris[§] | 11.36 |

*Percent of differing amino acids.
[†]Old World monkey.
[‡]New World monkey.
[§]Prosimian.
*Source:* Adapted from M. Goodman, "Protein Sequence and Immuno-logical Specificity," in W. P. Luckett and F. S. Szalay (eds.), *Phylogeny of the Primates* (New York: Plenum, 1975), p. 224.

## TABLE 8-10

### DIFFERENCES IN THE AMINO ACID SEQUENCES OF HUMAN AND CHIMPANZEE PROTEINS

| Protein | Number of amino acid differences | Number of amino acids in protein |
|---|---|---|
| Fibrinopeptides A and B | 0 | 30 |
| Cytochrome *c* | 0 | 104 |
| Lysozome | 0* | 130 |
| Hemoglobin $\alpha$ | 0 | 141 |
| Hemoglobin $\beta$ | 0 | 146 |
| Hemoglobin $^A\gamma$ | 0 | 146 |
| Hemoglobin $^G\gamma$ | 0 | 146 |
| Hemoglobin $\delta$ | 1 | 146 |
| Myoglobin | 1 | 153 |
| Carbonic anhydrase | 3* | 264 |
| Serum albumin | 6* | 580 |
| Transferrin | 8* | 647 |
| Total | 19 | 2633 |

*Approximation based on methods other than analysis of known amino acid sequences.
*Source:* Reprinted from M.-C. King and A. C. Wilson, "Evolution at Two Levels in Humans and Chimpanzees," *Science* 188 (1975), p. 108. Copyright 1975 American Association for the Advancement of Science.

**Human–Ape Relationships**  The construction of hominoid phylogenetic trees has ultimately led to a restructuring of hominoid taxonomy. Traditionally, the superfamily Hominoidea was divided into three families: Hylobatidae (gibbons and siamang), Pongidae (orangutan, gorilla, and chimpanzees), and Hominidae (humans). Molecular data, however, have clearly shown the closeness of the human–chimpanzee evolutionary tie and, to a slightly lesser degree, the human–gorilla tie. Orangutans appear to be more distantly related to humans than are the African great apes, which has led many primate taxonomists to keep *Pongo*, the orangutan, in the family Pongidae and to move the chimpanzees and gorillas into the family Panidae. We have followed this practice in this text.

Table 8–9 illustrates the differences between humans and several primate species by measuring the percentage of differing amino acids in a series of proteins. The close relationship between *Homo sapiens* and the African great apes is apparent. Table 8–10 summarizes the differences in the amino acid sequences of 12 proteins in humans and chimpanzees. From these data, we see that 99.3 percent of the human and chimpanzee polypeptides studied are identical.

We may conclude, then, that the differences in structural genes between *Homo sapiens* and the living chimpanzees are very small. They are of the same order of magnitude as differences existing between similar-appearing, very closely related species such as the horse and the zebra or the grizzly and the polar bear. On the other hand, the anatomical differences between humans and chimpanzees are substantial. It has been suggested that most of the changes that have taken place in hominid evolution are based on changes in regulatory or modifier genes and on the relative positions of the genes on the chromosomes, rather than on mutations of structural genes.

**The Molecular Clock**  The construction of phylogenetic trees enables anthropologists and biologists to establish the relative evolutionary distances and relationships between different taxonomic groups. Early investigators of the structure of hemoglobin and cytochrome *c* went one step further and proposed the existence of a "molecular clock." They felt that by using this clock, the molecular distance between groups could be translated into a known period of time.

The existence of a molecular clock is based on the assumption that the rate of amino acid replacement for any given protein is relatively constant. If this assumption is correct, then the clock can be calibrated by correlating a particular evolutionary distance between two groups with the actual time of divergence as known through the dating of the fossil record. Thus, the molecular clock is only as good as the calibration date. (The problems of dating the fossil record will be discussed in Chapter 11.) Once this calibration has been accomplished, investigators can use the clock to establish the divergence time for pairs of taxa for which fossil records do not exist.

If the concept of a molecular clock is to be valid, several assumptions must be shown to be true. First, the rate of amino acid substitutions in protein molecules, or nucleotide substitutions in DNA, must be constant over time. This may not be the case, however; research suggests that different proteins exhibit different substitution rates. Also, substitution rates may differ in different evolutionary lines. In comparisons with other mammalian groups, the molecular clock may actually run slower in the Hominoidea and slower still in the Hominidae. The critical factor in this difference in clock rate may be the length of the generation. Second, for the concept of the molecular clock to be valid, the majority of mutations or substitutions must be neutral so that these substitutions can accumulate without being acted upon by natural selection. Anthropologists do not agree on the validity of these assumptions.

### Summary

Since the genes are located within the chromosomes, comparative analysis of human and nonhuman chromosomes has provided information for determining evolutionary relationships. When we examine human and chimpanzee karyotypes, we can easily pair up each human chromosome with a chimpanzee counterpart. The only exception is human chromosome 2, which appears to have evolved from the fusion of two smaller chromosomes.

In recent years, detailed biochemical studies of protein molecules have added a valuable perspective to evolutionary studies. By a comparison of protein and DNA molecules from various living species, the evolutionary closeness of these species can be estimated. From these data, phylogenetic trees can be drawn to illustrate the most probable evolutionary relationships among species.

### STUDY QUESTIONS

1. How does the anthropologist use data from comparative anatomy to determine evolutionary relationships?
2. In what ways can the primate skeleton be said to be generalized?
3. What is meant by the term *suspensory behavior*? Discuss the evidence for the hypothesis that hominids evolved from a generalized suspensory ancestry.
4. Some hominid fossils show the presence of crests, ridges, and pronounced brow ridges on the skull. How can these features be interpreted?
5. Compare the dentition of modern humans with that of modern apes.
6. What are the major features of the evolution of the primate brain?
7. Describe the evolution of the human karyotype from an ancestral ape karyotype.
8. As animals evolve, so do protein molecules. Discuss the use of comparative biochemical studies in the determination of evolutionary relationships.

### SUGGESTED READINGS

Aiello, L., and C. Dean. *An Introduction to Human Evolutionary Anatomy.* London: Academic, 1990. A detailed description of human anatomy, this book emphasizes the anatomical evidence for human evolution.

Ankel-Simons, F. *A Survey of Living Primates and Their Anatomy.* New York: Macmillan, 1983. This is a rather complete introduction to the primate order, emphasizing various aspects of their anatomy, including the skeleton.

Martin, R. D. *Primate Origins and Evolution: A Phylogenetic Reconstruction.* Princeton: Princeton University Press, 1990. This book contains several detailed chapters summarizing comparative primate anatomy.

Napier, J., revised by R. H. Tuttle. *Hands.* Princeton, N.J.: Princeton University Press, 1993. This book includes discussions of the anatomy, evolution, and social and cultural aspects of the hand.

Swindler, D., and C. D. Wood. *An Atlas of Primate Gross Anatomy.* Melbourne, Fla.: Krieger, 1982. This book contains a series of detailed line drawings illustrating the comparative anatomy of the baboon, chimpanzee, and human.

Zihlman, A. L. *The Human Evolution Coloring Book.* New York: Barnes & Noble, 1982. This "coloring book" is not a children's book but a very complete workbook written by a noted physical anthropologist. It includes an important "lesson" on human evolution including anatomy and molecular genetics.

## SUGGESTED WEB SITES

Atlas of the Human Body (exploration of human anatomy from the American Medical Association): http://www.ama-assn.org/insight/gen_hlth/atlas/atlas.htm

Comparative Anatomy of Teeth: http://www.uic.edu/classes/osci/osci590/2.3TheComparativeAnatomyofTeeth.htm

Additional web sites are listed in the *Workbook* that accompanies this text.

## CHAPTER 9

# Primate Behavior

*Studies of nonhuman primates form an important part of a scientific enterprise that is giving us increased understanding of the world about us, of the evolutionary processes that gave rise to it, and of our place within it. Beyond that, however, nonhuman species, and especially nonhuman primates, provide an important source of data for understanding many aspects of human behavior and physiology in terms of causation, developmental processes, function, and evolution.[1]*

—Robert A. Hinde

From casual observers at a zoo to scientists engaged in research, people are fascinated with animal behavior. The physical anthropologist is most interested in the nonhuman primates since all primates, including humans, are united by a common ancestry.

Millions of years have passed since all primates had a common ancestor, or even since humans and apes did. Yet studies of nonhuman primate behavior throw light on current human behaviors—such as the need for physical contact. By studying

---

[1] R. A. Hinde, "Can Nonhuman Primates Help Us Understand Human Behavior?" in B. B. Smuts et al. (eds.), *Primate Societies* (Chicago: University of Chicago Press, 1987), p. 413. ©1986 by the University of Chicago. All rights reserved.

contemporary nonhuman primate behavior, we can develop ideas on what some of the selective pressures operating on early hominid populations might have been.

Although there are many similarities between human and nonhuman primate behavior, humans have taken a different evolutionary path from any other primate. This chapter considers the behavior of the nonhuman primates, while the next chapter discusses human behavior from the perspective of the behavior of nonhuman primates.

## PRIMATE BEHAVIOR

A majority of mammals do not live in large social units; many are solitary or live as mated adults with offspring. Of course, even solitary mammals have to engage in some social activity for mating, and the mother usually spends time feeding and protecting her infants. However, primates, including humans, do tend to form social groups.

### Why Primates Form Groups

Why do primates form groups? No single variable explains why this occurs. Many ideas, however, have been proposed.

One hypothesis is the **resource-defense model.** This model is based on the idea that a group of individuals can defend access to resources such as food and keep other animals and other groups away from these resources better than an individual can. The importance of defending resources depends on the nature of the resource. For example, leaves tend to be plentiful and they are spread fairly evenly through the forest. On the other hand, fruit is not as plentiful. In a tropical forest, only a few trees will produce fruit at any one time, yet at that time a tree may be loaded with enough fruit to satisfy the needs of all members of a group. Primates that emphasize fruit in their diets tend to live in larger social groups than primates that emphasize leaves or insects in their diet.

Another model is the **predation model.** This hypothesis emphasizes the risk that primates face from predators. The presence of a large group and defense behavior often associated with such groups help protect individuals from the dangers of carnivores. Semiterrestrial primates are perhaps the

most vulnerable to predation; such primates tend to form large groups.

Neither model explains all of the variation and complexity of primate social organization. Both may be operating together and other, as-yet-unknown factors may be present. There is a great deal of research yet to be done before these and other models can be fully evaluated.

### Kinds of Primate Social Organization

In studying primate social groups, we see great variation not only among the various primate species, but also within a particular species. **Primatologists** have conducted studies about what factors determine the form that a primate group takes. From these studies, we can make some generalizations.

Several factors appear to determine to some degree the size of a particular primate social group. As predicted by the predation model, more terrestrial primates tend to live in larger groups than more arboreal ones. **Nocturnal** primates, those who are active at night, often develop strategies where single animals or small groups are able to successfully prevent being seen by predators. **Diurnal** primates, those that are active during the day, are more easily seen. Here there is an advantage of living in a larger group since predators have a much more difficult time approaching such a group without being seen by at least one animal.

Diet also appears to be related to group size. Folivores (leaf-eaters) tend to live in smaller groups, probably because leaves are plentiful and can be exploited by several small groups spread out through the forest. As we saw in the discussion of the resource-defense model, frugivores (fruit-eaters) tend to live in larger groups.

Primate groups also vary greatly in terms of group membership. One way of making sense of group organization is to think of different primate groups in terms of relationships among females. Since females carry the developing fetus, nurse the infant, and generally carry and care for the young offspring, we would expect that their success in producing offspring will be closely related to the state of their health and nutrition. The latter is closely related to their access to food. Essentially, all females do mate, but the differences in reproductive success among females are related to the female's ability to bring a fetus to term and to raise the newborn. This contrasts with the reproductive success of males, which is related to their access to females for purposes of mating.

One way of looking at variation among primate social groups is to examine the relationship of adult females to food resources. Since the reproductive success of a female is related to her access to food, we would assume that females generally compete for food. Many females forage for food on their own, establishing individual control over resources. However, there are some situations in which a female may enhance her ability to procure food by forming alliances with other females, especially female kin. Groups that are based on associations among related females are termed **female-bonded kin groups.**

**Types of Groups** A relatively simple form of social grouping is found in many small nocturnal prosimians, such as the galagos, mouse lemurs, and dwarf lemurs, as well as in the orangutan (Table 9–1). The basic social unit is the female and her immature offspring. Each female–offspring unit occupies a specific space termed a **home range.** The ranges of females may overlap extensively, and, among prosimians, females with their young often share the same nest. Males occupy larger ranges that overlap several ranges occupied by females. Males and females do not interact with each other on a regular basis; for example, they do not feed together.

They do have periodic contact, and when the female is sexually receptive, mating occurs. The social unit of the mouse lemur is described in Box 9–1.

The **monogamous pair** is a relatively simple unit that consists of an adult female–male pair, usually mated for life, and their offspring. The young normally leave the group when they reach puberty. This type of social unit is characteristic of some prosimians, some New World monkeys, and the lesser apes.

Among the marmosets and tamarins, small New World monkeys, males play major roles in the rearing of offspring. Twins are usually born, and the father carries the infants, transferring the young to the female only for feeding (Figure 9–1). The group often contains three sets of twins of successive ages. This social unit, however, is not as simple as it might first appear. Young animals may transfer from one family group to another, and in some groups a second adult male may be present. Among humans, the term *polyandry* is used to refer to a marriage system where a female is married to two or more males. Therefore, this type of primate social organization is sometimes referred to as a **polyandrous group.**

A more common form of group organization consists of several females associated with a single male. This type of group may exist as a small, independent **one-male group,** or it may be a subunit, sometimes called a **harem,** of a larger unit. The social organization of the hamadryas baboon

### TABLE 9–1

**PRIMATE SOCIAL GROUPS**

| Group | Description | Examples |
|---|---|---|
| Female—offspring unit | Range overlaps ranges of other female–offspring groups and the larger ranges of the males | Mouse lemurs, galagos, orangutans |
| Monogamous pair | Male–female pair and preadult offspring | Owl monkey, gibbons |
| Polyandrous group | Female with one or more males and offspring | Marmosets, tamarins |
| One-male–several-female group | Male with several females; called a harem when the group is a subunit of a larger unit | Hamadryas baboons, geladas, langurs |
| Multimale group | Several males with several females and offspring | Savanna baboons, rhesus macaques |
| Fission-fusion society | Several groups varying in size and composition | Chimpanzees |

**BOX 9-1**

# The Behavior of the Mouse Lemur

While primates are usually thought of as highly social animals, some of the small nocturnal prosimians lead a relatively solitary existence. Among the smallest of the primates are the mouse lemurs of Madagascar. The head and body of the lesser mouse lemur are only 13.3 centimeters (5 inches) long; the tail adds another 14 centimeters (5.5 inches). Mouse lemurs spend the daylight hours

in leaf nests built in the dense foliage or in holes in trees. During the night hours, they forage for a variety of plant and animal food including fruits, insects, spiders, and frogs. A very important part of their diet is gums and insect secretions that they scrape off the bark and leaves with their dental comb. Here we will look briefly at the social behavior of the slightly larger Coquerel's mouse lemur, *Microcebus coquereli.*

Adult mouse lemurs occupy relatively small core areas that average 1.5 hectares (3.7 acres) for males and 2.5 to 3 hectares (6.2 to 7.4 acres) for females. The core area is surrounded by a larger peripheral area of over 4 hectares (10 acres). There is some overlapping of the home range, especially in the case of a female and her young or a male and a female. Peripheral areas overlap more extensively, allowing adults of the same sex to come into social contact. However, although the core area makes up only 30 percent of the home range, 80 percent of their activity occurs here. Like most lemurs, the mouse lemur marks its core area with urine, feces, and secretions from specialized glands.

While occupying the core area, the mouse lemur engages in solitary activities such as self-grooming, feeding, and resting; these activities typically occur during the earlier part of the night. After midnight, the animal may move out into the peripheral area, where it may contact another mouse lemur. These include encounters between the sexes and territorial activities between males.

*Source:* E. Pages, "Ethoecology of *Microcebus conquereli* during the Dry Season," in P. Charles-Dominique et al., *Nocturnal Malagasy Primates* (New York: Academic Press, 1980), pp. 97–116.

**FIGURE 9–1  Golden Lion Tamarin**
Marmosets and tamarins usually produce twins, which are carried by the father and transferred to the mother for nursing.

consists of harems and all-male groups bound together in a hierarchy of larger social groupings. This basic type of organization is also found among howler monkeys, langurs, and geladas.

When circumstances lead to the development of larger social units called the **multimale group,** we find that group membership includes many adult males and adult females. The large number of females requires the presence of several males. Females in such groups tend to form close bonds while males usually migrate at puberty to neighboring groups. However, the distinction between one-male and multimale groups is not always clear. The social organizations of baboons, macaques, and other Old World monkeys, some colobus monkeys, and some New World monkeys are examples of multimale group societies.

Finally, there are many primates that exhibit a variety of social groupings. The size and organization of the various types of groups often depend on the activity of the group and the season of the year. This is typical of chimpanzees, whose social organization may be referred to as a **fission-fusion society** because large groups break into smaller units and smaller groups coalesce into larger ones.

### Methods in the Study of Primate Behavior

Early studies of primate behavior were conducted primarily with zoo populations, and data from these studies led to many erroneous conclusions. Today we realize that these data reflect the unnatural and overcrowded conditions in the cage. When a zoo population is given adequate space and a good food supply and is maintained in a natural social grouping, its behavior is very similar to that of wild populations.

Perhaps the most valid type of primate behavior study is the **field study.** The field observer spends enough time with a natural population to recognize individuals. Since animals become familiar with the observer as well, close observation becomes possible. The disadvantages of such studies are that it takes long periods of time to make contact with the animals and the yield of data is relatively low.

Many of these problems are solved to a great extent through studies of **provisioned colonies,** which are natural populations in which feeding stations are established. Because the primate group travels to the feeding stations daily, the researcher can observe individuals closely and can collect census data, such as information on births and deaths. Studies conducted away from the feeding stations are made easier by the primate group's increased tolerance of the observer. The yield of data is greater than that achieved with the standard field study of a nonprovisioned group, and new observers can be introduced into the research situation quite readily. Well-known provisioned colonies include those of the Japanese macaque at Takasakiyama, Japan, and the rhesus macaque colony on Cayo Santiago, Puerto Rico (Box 9–2).

While natural and provisioned populations are the most frequently studied, many universities and research stations maintain artificial colonies. In addition, laboratory studies, conducted primarily by psychologists, involve manipulation of the animals in a laboratory situation.

### Summary

Most primates live in groups, that is, primates are social animals. Primates that subsist on sparse resources are most likely to live in groups because they can defend resources from other populations better than could a solitary animal. Primates that are vulnerable to predators, like those that spend time on the ground, might form groups as protection from those predators. In both cases, there is power in numbers.

Primates form many different types of groups. The type formed by a particular species varies based on the lifestyle of the group—semiterrestrial or arboreal, diet, how the young are cared for, and other factors. Table 9–1 summarizes the major types of primate groups.

Perhaps the most ideal way to study any animal is in the field where the natural behavior of the animal can be observed in the animal's own habitat. However, it is often not possible or practical to conduct a field study. In these cases, provisioned colonies become an alternative to field studies. Primates are also studied in the zoo and in the laboratory.

## CASE STUDIES OF PRIMATE BEHAVIOR

This section deals with the social organization and social behavior of the monkeys and apes. We will examine a small series of anthropoids—the gibbon, gelada, baboon, and chimpanzee—by outlining their basic social organizations and discussing selected aspects of their social behaviors. This is not an exhaustive study, but it is one that will provide some understanding of the basic patterns and general nature of primate behavior. A fifth case study, that of humans, will be presented in Chapter 10.

### Social Behavior of the Gibbon

The monkeys and apes are generally characterized by relatively large, complex social units, although small social groups do exist. Since many basic concepts are easier to understand in the context of small groups, we will begin our discussion with a description of the monogamous group.

The monogamous group is a relatively small social unit consisting of a single mated pair and their young offspring. It is found among the lesser apes (Hylobatidae)—the gibbons and the siamang (Figure 9–2). In this section, we will examine some aspects of the social behavior of the white-handed gibbon, *Hylobates lar,* which was studied by J. O. Ellefson in the lowland rain forests of the Malay Peninsula.[2]

**The Gibbon Social Group**  In the monogamous group, the adult male and female mate for life. The close relationship between the adult pair is seen in both grooming and sexual activity.

**Grooming** is a behavioral pattern common to most primates. In grooming, the animal uses its hands to search and comb through the fur, although

---

[2]J. O. Ellefson, "A Natural History of White-Handed Gibbons in the Malayan Peninsula," in D. M. Rumbaugh (ed.), *Gibbon and Siamang,* vol. 3 (Basel: Karger, 1974), pp. 1–136.

**BOX 9-2**

# The Rhesus Monkeys of Cayo Santiago

Cayo Santiago is a 15.2-hectare (37.6-acre) island located 1 kilometer (0.6 mile) from the southeast coast of Puerto Rico. In 1938, a population of rhesus monkeys *(Macaca mulatta)* from India was established on this uninhabited island. The colony has been continuously maintained since 1938.

The idea of developing a colony of free-ranging monkeys in the New World was developed by Clarence Ray Carpenter. In 1938, there was much interest in the project because of the possibility that the political situation in Europe might result in the cutting off of the importation of monkeys from Asia, especially the rhesus macaque, commonly used in laboratory studies. Carpenter traveled to India to trap 500 rhesus

macaques, including 100 females with infants. All were tested for tuberculosis, a major cause of illness and death among monkeys, and those showing a positive reaction were not shipped. It took 47 days to transport the animals from India to New York. The animals arrived on the Santiago Island on November 14, 1938, and, beginning in December, 409 rhesus monkeys were set free.

Before the arrival of the monkeys, Santiago Island was covered primarily with grass and was used as pasture for goats. A variety of trees and shrubs were planted in anticipation of the monkeys. Little was known about the naturalistic behavior of rhesus monkeys. For example, some people thought that rhesus monkeys were cave dwellers and they

constructed many small artificial caves; none were ever used.

By 1941, the colony was firmly established, and many primatologists were using the animals in their research. However, the financial support of the colony was becoming precarious and large numbers of monkeys were removed from the island and transported to laboratories in the United States. In 1956, the Laboratory of Perinatal Physiology of the National Institute of Neurological Disease and Blindness (NINDB) and the University of Puerto Rico took over administration of the island colony.

Under new management, improvements in the care of the animals were made and major research was initiated on the island. It was at this time that animals were marked so that individuals could be identified. Annual censuses were conducted and longitudinal studies of specific animals following their development from birth to death were begun. These long-term studies are extremely difficult in natural populations. Although many animals were removed for laboratory studies, the population increased in size annually. In the 1960s, Santiago Island macaques were used to found new monkey colonies on other islands in the area. In 1970, the island became part of what is now the Caribbean Primate Research Center of the University of Puerto Rico School of Medicine.

A rhesus mother and her infant rest in the branches of a tree on Cayo Santiago.

*Source:* R. G. Rawlins and Matt J. Kessler, "The History of Cayo Santiago Colony," in R. G. Rawlins and M. J. Kessler (eds.), *The Cayo Santiago Macaques: History, Behavior and Biology* (Albany, N.Y.: State Univ. of New York Press, 1986), pp. 13–45.

prosimians use the dental comb instead. Grooming involves the search for dirt, dry pieces of skin, and parasites in the fur. The removal of this material keeps the fur relatively clean and groomed. An animal may spend time grooming itself as a part of this cleaning process; this is called **autogrooming.**

The animals also spend a great deal of time grooming one another; this is referred to as **allogrooming.**

Allogrooming in primates is an important form of social behavior, as it aids in the development and maintenance of close social bonds. It is especially common between closely related individuals and is

**FIGURE 9–2 The Monogamous Social Unit of the Gibbon**
Adult male (black) and female (blond) with offspring

characteristic of close social ties such as those be-tween mother and child. Among gibbons, groom-ing is important in the maintenance of the adult male–female bond. The adult gibbon pair groom one another several times a day, primarily in the afternoon. This grooming is reciprocal; the male grooms the female for about as long as the female grooms the male.

Sexual behavior is another important aspect of social behavior. An analysis of the spacing of births suggests that sexual behavior in the white-handed gibbon takes place during short periods every two years or so.

**The Gibbon Life Cycle**   The infant stage of gib-bon development lasts from birth to approximately 2 to 2½ years of age. Within a few months after birth, the infant begins to eat solid food. At the end of this stage, it is weaned and also stops sleeping with its mother. Even the very young infant can cling tightly to its mother's fur as she rapidly moves through the high branches of the trees. The mother and other members of the group do not pay a great deal of attention to the infant. As the infant grows older, it moves farther away from its mother for longer periods of time and interacts with older siblings if it has any.

The juvenile period begins between 2 and 2½ years and ends between 4 and 4½ years. Important during this stage of gibbon development is **play** be-havior. Play is difficult to define, yet play behavior appears to be important among primates and it oc-cupies a great deal of the waking hours of juveniles. Play often involves intense, repetitive physical ac-tivity that results in the development and refine-ment of physical skills. Ellefson describes the play of the white-handed gibbon as including "chasing, grappling, hitting, kicking, jerking, holding, biting, stretching, pushing and dropping."[3] It is through play that young primates learn rules of objects, that is, the relationship between the body and objects—for example, what objects the juvenile can move and how trees respond to jumping on a branch. Play also provides a setting for the development of social skills and the formation of social bonds be-tween specific individuals.

There is a major difference, however, between the play activities of gibbons and those of many other primates. In larger primate groups, several **play groups** may form, each including many ani-mals of similar age. In the small gibbon family, the

[3]Ibid., p. 84.

sole playmate of an older juvenile is its younger sibling. Thus, the older juvenile is always larger and stronger than the younger, and the physical activity of the older must be controlled to avoid injuring the younger. Also, gibbons spend less time playing than do most other primates.

During the juvenile period, the adults become less and less tolerant of the juvenile's feeding close by. When the juvenile is about four years of age, the adults actively threaten it away from many food sources. Their **threat gestures** include staring, shaking a branch, and lunging toward the young animal.

The adolescent gibbon is between four and six years of age. At about 6 years of age, the animal attains full adult size and full sexual maturity. This is the period of **peripheralization.** At this time, the adults (more often the adult male) become aggressive toward the adolescent and actively keep it away from the area in which they are eating. Also, the adolescent gibbon begins to move away from the group to forage and feed on its own.

The subadult phase of gibbon development lasts from the age of six until the animal mates, but the age of first mating is variable. As the animal becomes more and more separated from its group of birth, possibilities arise for the formation of a new social unit. Although the exact mechanisms are not known, peripheral subadult males do attract subadult females, and new male–female pairs are established.

**Territoriality**  All animals occupy space. The area in which a group feeds, drinks, grooms, sleeps, plays, and so forth, is its home range. The home ranges of gibbon groups measure about 40 hectares (100 acres) in size. We must always keep in mind, however, that primates utilize three-dimensional space and that the actual space occupied in a tropical forest, with its tall trees, is considerably larger than that suggested by the ground measurement. The area that a group defends against other members of its own species is its **territory.** The territory, which is usually smaller than the home range, represents the boundaries at which the animal actively begins to defend an area against another group.

Gibbons are highly territorial animals, and most of the home range is defended territory. Among the white-handed gibbons studied by Ellefson, territo-

ries overlap about 20 percent, and so the neighboring group may be found within the overlapping area. Actual conflict between neighboring males takes place, on the average, about every other day. Conflicts always occur in the area of overlapping territories, which is usually about 23 to 69 meters (25 to 75 yards) wide.

Territorial conflict is expressed primarily in terms of vocalization and display (Figure 9–3). Early in the morning, the southeast Asian forest rings with the sound of the great call of the gibbon. These morning calls broadcast the location of the various gibbon groups. Upon hearing the morning call of a nearby group, a male may lead his group over to the vicinity of that neighboring group. A typical conflict period lasts about an hour, the first

**FIGURE 9–3  Gibbon Vocalization**

half of which is spent in vocalizations and displays by adult males. These are usually followed by chases, but the chases rarely penetrate deep into any group's territory. Actual contact between adult males is rare.

Territorial behavior serves several functions. It spreads individual members of a population over a large area, thereby preventing a concentration of animals and overutilization of resources in a relatively small area. A map of gibbon territories shows a mosaic of small territories throughout a relatively large area. Territoriality also serves to control population size, since an animal cannot begin to produce offspring until it has found a mate and established its own territory. The number of territories available is stable.

### Social Behavior of the Gelada

Geladas, *Theropithecus gelada,* are large, primarily terrestrial monkeys. They once ranged over large areas of east Africa, and they are even represented in the fossil record. Today, the geladas are found only in a dry, desolate, mountainous region of Ethiopia. Although the geladas are not true baboons (baboons belong to the genus *Papio*), they are similar to baboons in many ways.

The social organization found in this hot, dry habitat may be an adaptation to the environment. Primates that spend a great deal of time on the ground searching for food tend to form large groups for protection against predators. Primates that are more arboreal are relatively secure in the trees, and so they tend to form smaller and more loosely organized groups. Although trees are few and far between in the barren wastes where the geladas live, large social units are not always able to locate adequate food supplies in the hot, dry habitat. Thus, when food is scarce, the larger gelada group breaks up into its constituent groups. These smaller units are a better size for foraging for food under the harsh conditions. The following description of gelada social organization is based on the field studies of Robin and Patsy Dunbar.[4]

---

[4]R. Dunbar and P. Dunbar, *Social Dynamics of Gelada Baboons* (Basel: Karger, 1975).

**Age-Sex Categories**   Different animals behave in different ways within a social group. The most important differences in social behavior are determined by the sex and age of the individual. Therefore, we need to divide the members of the gelada groups into a series of age-sex categories, as we previously did with the white-handed gibbon.

The infant phase lasts from birth to 18 months of age. The young infant is black or dark brown in color, a marked contrast to the reddish coat color of the adult. This distinctive difference in color between infant and adult, which is characteristic of many primate species, makes the infant easily recognizable. The black gelada infant is a focal point of the group, and all members will protect the infant if it is in danger. During infancy, the young gelada stays very close to its mother. Toward the end of this phase, when the coat color begins to change to the adult color, the adults relax their vigilance and the infant is freer to move around and explore its environment.

The 6- to 18-month-old infant is adult in color, yet it still spends considerable time near its mother. At about 1 to 1½ years of age, the infant is weaned. Then the animal is classified as a juvenile, a phase lasting from 1½ to 3½ years of age. During this period, the juvenile becomes increasingly independent of its mother, and most of its social interactions take place in play groups.

The subadult female, aged 3½ to 4½ years, is sexually mature but has not quite reached adult size. As the female completes growth, she associates primarily with other adult females and their offspring and is soon bearing offspring of her own.

The male is considered a subadult for a much longer time than the female—from 3½ to 6 years of age. In part, this is because the male continues to grow for a longer period of time than the female. While the canine teeth erupt early in the subadult period, full growth of the large canines characteristic of males does not take place until the end of the subadult period. Only at this time do the males take their place in adult life. Because of this longer growth period, the adult male is larger than the female. This larger size, plus other distinctive features such as the cape of fur around the shoulders, makes it easy to distinguish the adult male from the adult female (Figure 9–4). Such a difference in the phys-

**FIGURE 9–4  The Gelada**
A female gelada sits behind and grooms an older male.

ical appearance between the male and female is an example of sexual dimorphism (Figure 7-21).

Sexual dimorphism is common among the more terrestrial monkeys. Monkeys spending considerable time on the ground are vulnerable to predation and hence tend to live in larger social units. This means that a greater number of females are in the troop, which leads to an increase in intrasexual selection. As we saw in Chapter 5, increased intrasexual selection is correlated with an increase in sexual dimorphism. In addition, the larger size of the males provides the group with a mechanism for defense against predators.

Instant recognition of individuals is relatively easy in small units such as the gibbon family, but recognition becomes a problem in larger social groups. In case of danger, a gelada female needs to identify an adult male, and the distinctive physical appearance of the male makes this easy.

**Social Organization of the Harem Units**   The basic social unit of the gelada is the one-male–several-females unit, or harem. Besides harems, small all-male groups also exist.

A typical harem consists of about 11 members: one adult male, five adult females, and five juveniles and infants. The most cohesive bonds in the unit appear to exist between females, who express their closeness in terms of grooming. In many ways, the male is peripheral to the group. The females form a stable unit that maintains itself with little herding by the male. If a female from a neighboring harem comes too close, the females will chase her off. Similarly, males threaten females from other groups who come too close.

One form of behavior that is often seen in social interactions within the harem or between harems is **agonistic behavior.** This is behavior involving "fighting, threats, fleeing and other related displays."[5] Much agonistic behavior takes the form of display and gesture instead of actual fighting. Agonistic gestures and facial expressions include staring, raising the eyebrows, and lunging in space (Figure 9–5).

**Social Development**   The juvenile male spends most of his time in play groups with other young animals within his harem, although juveniles from adjacent harems play with one another. As he grows older, he pays less attention to the members of the harem of his birth and begins to associate with an all-male group consisting of older juveniles, young subadults and adult males without females. The older subadult male begins to show interest in the harem groups, and he attaches himself to one as a follower. These follower males are peripheral to the unit; they interact primarily with the juveniles and a few females of the group and generally avoid the adult males.

The juvenile female also participates in play groups until the time of puberty. She then begins to show interest in the adult males, mothers, and young infants and spends her time following the infants around and attempting to play with them.

---

[5]N. Chalmers, *Social Behavior in Primates* (Baltimore: University Park Press, 1980), p. 63.

**FIGURE 9–5   The Gelada**
Two males are fighting on the right. Note threat gesture at left.

As she reaches sexual maturity, she becomes interested in the group leader. Since the adult male usually has little interest in the young female, the possibility arises that the female will become attached to a young male.

New harem units may arise in a variety of ways. Typically a follower male forms an attachment with a young female. Once this bond becomes established, the young male and female slowly move away from the larger unit to form a new unit. A less frequent possibility is that a young male will attack an older harem male and take over the harem.

**Larger Gelada Units**   While the basic social units of the gelada are the harem and the all-male group, these groups do not wander independently of one another. Instead, they gather into **bands** consisting of harems and male groups that share a home range. During certain seasons, the band comes together in areas where food is plentiful. During times when food is less plentiful, the band breaks up and forages as individual harems and all-male groups.

Under very good grazing conditions, many bands come together to form a **herd.** Herds form in areas where band ranges overlap. In the Dunbars' study at Sankaber, Ethiopia, the herd contained 762 animals divided into 6 bands; in all there were 68 harems and 9 all-male groups.

### Social Behavior of the Savanna Baboon

Perhaps one of the best-studied primates other than humans is the savanna baboon. In large part, this is because savanna baboons live on the open grassland where humans can easily observe them. This contrasts with the very difficult observing conditions in forest areas. Also, many anthropologists have been intrigued by the fact that both baboons and early hominids are primates that left the forest and became adapted to life on the savanna.

Baboons range throughout large areas of Africa where they are the most commonly seen monkeys; in some places, they are considered agricultural pests. The savanna baboons are divided into four kinds: olive (or anubis), yellow, chacma, and Guinea baboons. Many primatologists believe that the four groups represent four subspecies of the species *Papio cynocephalus.*

Many populations of savanna baboon have been studied in many parts of Africa. Baboon social organization is quite flexible and varies from one group to another. For example, the baboon troops at Amboseli, Kenya, exhibit intergroup aggression when in close proximity, yet baboons studied in Uganda show frequent movement of individuals from one group to another. In contrast, the baboons of Nairobi Park, Kenya, show much stability.

The conclusion we must draw from the wealth of field observations of baboons and other primates is that primate societies are variable in their adjustments to the environment. Differences in physical habitat, for example, are reflected in differences in the size of the home range, the troop size, and the general nature of intergroup interactions. This variability is a reflection of the fact that, in general, primate social behavior is not biologically determined. Through the formation of learned behavioral patterns, each primate population has developed its particular guide for survival.

The following discussion is based on studies of two populations of savanna baboons living in Kenya, the baboons of Nairobi Park, studied by Irvin DeVore and his colleagues, and the baboons of Amboseli, studied by Stuart and Jane Altmann and their associates.[6]

**The Baboon Troop**  Baboons live in a social unit called a **troop.** In both Nairobi Park and Amboseli, troops average about 40 animals. The baboon troop remains within a home range with distinct boundaries, a fact illustrated by the inability of an ob-

server to drive a troop across these boundaries. Boundaries are never defended; hence, territories do not exist. The home ranges of neighboring troops usually overlap extensively (Figure 9–6). In contrast to the territorial behavior of the gibbon, when more than one baboon troop occupies sections of an overlapping area, the troops tend to ignore one another and to avoid contact. When contact between baboon troops is unavoidable, such as around a water hole during the dry season, several troops often drink side by side. They ignore one another, or the smaller troop simply gives way to the larger.

The baboons of Kenya occupy ranges of about 23 to 24 square kilometers (8.9 to 9.3 square miles). The size appears to depend on the size of the troop and the concentration of food. Within the home range are certain **core areas,** which may contain a concentration of food, a water hole, a good resting area, or sleeping trees. The core areas are used exclusively by a single troop, which spends more than 90 percent of its time within the two or three core areas that are found in its home range.

Baboons inhabit the savanna, which is essentially a dry grassland with scattered groups of trees. The primary food of the baboon is grass, which makes up about 90 percent of its diet during the dry season. This is supplemented by other vegetable matter such as seeds, flowers, and fruits. The baboon also consumes insects and some small reptiles and occasionally eats mammalian flesh.

Although food is easily found, the baboon must obtain much of this food on the ground, where danger from predators poses a real threat. The location of sleeping trees is extremely important for safety during sleeping hours, and the troop must reach the safety of these trees by nightfall. During the day, the troop depends on the collective protection of the large males, and it relies to an extent on the alarm calls of other animals to warn it of the proximity of predators.

**Structure of the Baboon Troop**  Within the baboon troop, several distinct classes of individuals can be identified. The age-sex categories, similar to those of the gelada, include infants, juveniles, subadult males, adult females, and adult males.

The adult males play an especially important role in baboon social life, for the troop is dependent upon

[6]I. DeVore and K. R. L. Hall, "Baboon Ecology," and K. R. L. Hall and I. DeVore, "Baboon Social Behavior," in I. DeVore (ed.), *Primate Behavior: Field Studies of Monkeys and Apes* (New York: Holt, 1965), pp. 20–52, 53–110; S. A. Altmann and J. A. Altmann, *Baboon Ecology: African Field Research* (Chicago: University of Chicago Press, 1970); J. Altmann, *Baboon Mothers and Infants* (Cambridge, Mass.: Harvard University Press, 1980).

Boundary of Nairobi Park

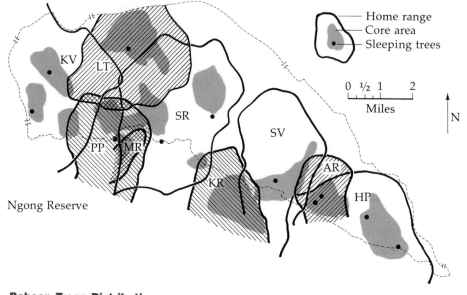

**FIGURE 9–6   Baboon Troop Distribution**
Home ranges and core areas of nine baboon troops in Nairobi Park, Kenya. The troops vary in size
from 12 to 87.

them for protection when foraging in the open. The baboons show a greater degree of sexual dimorphism than do most other monkey species. The very long canine teeth of the male are deadly weapons even against the most powerful carnivores.

The adult males are arranged in a **dominance hierarchy.** While this hierarchy is usually thought of as strictly linear, the relative ranks of the lower-ranking males are not always sharply defined. Also, a pair of males may form an alliance that permits the pair to occupy a position in the system at a higher level than either could occupy alone. The existence of a hierarchy makes it possible for several aggressive adult males to coexist within the same troop.

The most dominant males are usually in good physical condition. They appear to be confident and aggressive, and they are able to attract the support of other males. The most dominant males also seem to be the offspring of the highest-ranking females. The presence of a high-ranking mother enables a male offspring to intimidate other animals higher in rank than himself but lower in rank than the mother, who is quick to back up her young

in a conflict situation. Also, the offspring of high-ranking mothers associate more closely with the dominant males than do other offspring.

Once formed, the hierarchy is stable, although changes do occur, especially as members grow old and die. Young males entering the system cannot simply challenge the most dominant male for his position, for the dominant male is likely to be supported by other dominant males. Some high-ranking males are able to maintain their high rank even after they have become old and weak, with their canine teeth worn down to the gums.

Physical aggression is rare, and most aggression is expressed by gesturing rather than by actual fighting. Such agonistic behavior includes staring, raising the eyebrow to expose the distinctively colored eyelid, slapping the ground, or jerking the head back and forth. When you next visit the zoo and observe a baboon male "yawning," do not feel that he is bored or tired. He is probably displaying his canine teeth as a threat gesture directed toward you, the observer (Figure 9–7).

The dominance system operates in a variety of situations. A dominant male receives his preference

**FIGURE 9-7 Baboon Threat Gesture**
The canine display.

of choice food and can monopolize sexually receptive females. A subordinate gives up his sitting place to a more dominant male, a behavior that is termed **displacement.** A subordinate male approaching a more dominant male will **present** his anal region to him and often will be **mounted** by him. The observer uses data on such behaviors as displacement, presenting, and mounting to gain a picture of the dominance system within the troop.

Adult females also form dominance hierarchies, although dominance interactions are not observed as often among females as they are among males. The rank of a female is determined largely by the rank of her mother, and she usually ranks just below her mother. The relative rank of a female baboon with respect to her mother, sisters, and daughters is more significant among females than among males since a female spends most of her time in the company of family members.

In contrast to females, subadult males leave the troop of their birth and migrate to other troops. These migrations often cover long distances and expose the young males to much danger. This is a ma-

jor reason why males have a higher death rate than females. As a result, adult males in a given troop have all migrated in from other troops and do not form close kinship bonds as do females.

The relative position of a female varies somewhat depending on whether she is sexually receptive to the male or is associated with a young infant. These changes are related, in part, to the interest of the adult male in receptive females and the concern of the male about the safety of the young. Females in either situation find themselves close to the dominant males, thus elevating their social rank in the troop. In addition, other females show great interest in infants, and they present to or groom the mother in an attempt to come into close association with the infant.

**Sexual Relationships** The reproductive cycle in the baboon female is about 35 days long. At approximately the midpoint of the cycle, a mature ovum moves from the ovary to the fallopian tube; this event is called **ovulation.** If sperm are present in the female reproductive tract around the time of ovulation, conception may occur.

Sexual activity in most primates occurs only around the time of ovulation. This period of sexual receptivity is termed **estrus.** Since sexual behavior functions to ensure the presence of sperm in the female reproductive tract at the time when an ovum is available for fertilization, sexual activity is normally restricted to the estrus period.

During most of her life, the female baboon is not sexually receptive to the male. She is receptive only during estrus, but estrus does not occur during pregnancy or **lactation** (nursing). In addition, sexual activity among many monkey species is restricted to a definite mating season, in which case no sexual activity may take place within a troop for many months of the year. It is therefore apparent that sexual activity is limited among baboons and may be absent for long periods of time.

Estrus in the savanna baboon is marked by certain physical and behavioral changes, and prominent among them is the swelling of the sexual skin. As the swelling enlarges, the female becomes receptive to the advances of the males. The swelling, in turn, serves as a signal to the males that the female is indeed in estrus. In most mammals, olfactory cues signal sexual receptivity. While this is true to a degree in primates, the prominence of a visual cue underscores the importance of vision to primates.

Early in a female's ovulation period, the more subordinate males make sexual advances; they are short in duration. As the female approaches the time of ovulation, she actively solicits sexual interest from the dominant males. The dominant male and female form a **consort pair,** and they will remain together for several hours to several days. Since the dominant males are copulating around the time of ovulation, they probably will father most of the young.

**Group Cohesion** Unlike many mammalian societies, most monkey troops are not held together by herding on the part of the males. The members of the troop appear to prefer to remain with the group of their birth, among familiar individuals with whom they have formed social bonds. Consequently, it is difficult to force a member to leave a troop or to introduce a new member into a troop.

Group cohesion appears to be based on the attraction of troop members to three categories of individuals: dominant males, infants, and old females. At rest, the dominant males are surrounded by females and young, who are attracted to their presence. This is especially true of very young animals and mothers of newborns. Infants also become focal points of troop interest. When a newborn appears in a troop, the female members attempt to look at it and handle it and they pay a great deal of attention to the mother.

Lengthy studies of some monkey species have demonstrated a bond that exists between mothers and their adult daughters. A basic subunit of the troop is an old female with her grown daughters and their respective offspring. When the troop is at rest, the females settle down in **grooming clusters** that are composed of several closely related females. As we have seen in other species, grooming symbolizes a closeness between individual primates.

Other close relationships exist among baboons. Barbara Smuts has recognized friendships that occur between adult males and females among the olive baboons in Kenya.[7] Female baboons are wary

around the larger adult males, yet females form friendships with specific males in which the relationship is quite different. An adult female is relaxed around her male friend and often grooms him (Figure 9–8). A male friend appears to protect both the female and her offspring from aggression from other animals. The male may carry the infant as a way of inhibiting aggression against himself on the part of other males. When in estrus, the female is more likely to form a consort pair with her friend, which means that the infant being protected is very likely to be his offspring.

### Social Behavior of the Chimpanzee

Perhaps one of the most extensive studies of a primate population in its natural habitat is that of the chimpanzee, *Pan troglodytes,* in the Gombe Stream National Park in Uganda. Begun in 1960 by Jane Goodall, this study continues today.[8] Although chimpanzees normally inhabit dense forests, the more open forest of the park has made observation easier.

The chimpanzee is primarily arboreal. Its food is found principally in trees, and about 50 to 70 percent of the day is spent feeding and resting in trees. The animals sleep in trees, building new nests each evening. Yet most traveling between trees is done on the ground. Chimpanzees travel many miles each day, with the availability of food determining the length and direction of travel.

The diet of the chimpanzee is primarily vegetarian, including fruits, leaves, seeds, and bark. In addition, the animal occasionally eats insects, such as ants and termites, and sometimes hunts and eats meat. Six to seven hours each day are spent actively feeding.

**Chimpanzee Social Organization** Like that of the gibbon, gelada, and baboon, the life cycle of the chimpanzee can be divided into stages. The most notable difference between the life-cycle stages of chimpanzees and those of monkeys is that chimpanzees have a longer life span and mature more

---

[7]B. B. Smuts, *Sex and Friendship in Baboons* (New York: Aldine, 1985).

[8]J. van Lawick-Goodall, *In the Shadow of Man* (Boston: Houghton Mifflin, 1971); J. Goodall, *The Chimpanzees of Gombe: Patterns of Behavior* (Cambridge, Mass.: Belknap Press, 1986); g. Goodall, "Gombe: Highlights and Current Research," in P. G. Heltne and L. A. Marquardt (eds.), *Understanding Chimpanzees* (Cambridge, Mass: Harvard University Press, 1989), pp. 2–21.

**FIGURE 9–8  Baboon Friends**
Pegasus, an adult male, grooms his best friend, Cicily, who is nursing her first infant. These
baboons are members of the Eburru Cliffs troop who live near the town of Gilgil, Kenya.

slowly. The stages in the life of chimpanzees are
summarized in Table 9–2. Chimpanzees probably
live into their 50s.

The chimpanzee social unit is an ever-changing
association of individuals that is perhaps best described as a fission-fusion type of society. In contrast to the savanna baboon troop, with its relative
day-to-day stability and constancy, the chimpanzee
**community** consists of a series of small units whose
membership is constantly changing. A community
consists of individuals who occupy a particular
range and who, in the course of a year, have some
contact with one another. The size of the community varies depending on births, deaths, and migrations. In 1980, the Gombe Stream community
consisted of 42 individuals.

An individual chimpanzee may display a great
deal of independence as he or she establishes new
associations, sometimes on a day-by-day basis; or,
on occasion, he or she may travel alone. The typical chimpanzee group usually contains five or
fewer adults and adolescents in addition to juveniles and infants, but a number of different kinds
of groups can form (Figure 9–9). The eight different kinds of groups are summarized in Table 9–3.

Many variables are responsible for the changes in
group composition, including the availability of
food, the presence of infants, the number of estrus
females, and the invasion of a home territory by
neighbors.

**Social Relationships among the Chimpanzees**
As with monkeys, social interactions between
chimpanzee males can be described by the terms
*dominance* and *submission*. Many instances of dominance interactions between two males have been
described. For example, if two males go after the

**TABLE 9–2**

**STAGES IN THE LIFE OF CHIMPANZEES**

| Stage | Male | Female |
|---|---|---|
| Infancy | 0–5 years | 0–5 years |
| Childhood | 5–7 years | 5–7 years |
| Adolescence | 8–15 years | 8–14 years |
| Maturity | 16–33 years | 14–33 years |
| Old age | 33 years–death | 33 years–death |

**FIGURE 9–9 Chimpanzee Social Unit**
Fifi (left), a chimpanzee in Africa's Gombe Stream National Park, nuzzles her brother, Flint, while their mother, Flo, holds the baby.

| TABLE 9–3 | |
|---|---|
| **COMPOSITION OF CHIMPANZEE SOCIAL GROUPS** | |
| **Types of social groupings** | **Description** |
| All-male party | Two or more adults and/or subadult males |
| Family unit | A mother and her offspring |
| Nursery unit | Two or more family units; may include unrelated childless females |
| Mixed party | One or more adult or adolescent males with one or more adult or adolescent females, with or without offspring |
| Sexual party | A mixed party in which one or more females are in estrus |
| Consortship | One adult male with one adult female with or without offspring |
| Gathering | A group including at least half of the members of the community and at least half of the adult males |
| Lone individual | A single animal |

same fruit, the subordinate male holds back. Likewise, if a dominant male shows signs of aggression, the subordinate male responds with gestures of submission, such as reaching out to touch the dominant animal and crouching. Although clear-cut dominance interactions do take place, a rigid dominance hierarchy, such as that found among baboons, does not exist.

Much of chimpanzee aggression takes the form of gesture and display, and one animal can achieve dominance over the others by the fierceness of his display activity. One such male, Mike, rose from the bottom of the ladder to the top by incorporating into his display some of Goodall's kerosene cans. He would hurl the cans in front of him as he charged the other males, and they would quickly get out of his way and respond with a submissive gesture. Goodall sees Mike's behavior as evidence of his superior intelligence relative to that of the other chimpanzees in his community.

Goodall and other researchers have discovered that adult male chimpanzees are usually more sociable (interactive) than adult females. In contrast to the baboons, it is the female chimpanzee that usually migrates from one community to another. Thus, closely related males, often brothers, form a close bond within the community in contrast to the females, who often spend time alone with their offspring. Closely related males are more likely to travel and cooperate with one another.

Most male interactions are with other males. Goodall found that males groom each other about twice as long as males and females groom each other. Males also display their affinity for each other by holding and embracing one another much more than they hold and embrace females. Unlike human groups and some nonhuman primate groups, "male chimpanzees do not have long-lasting close relationships with particular females; their closest relationships are with other adult males."[9]

---

[9]R. C. Baily and R. Avunger, "Humans as Primates: The Social Relationships of Efe Pygmy Men in Comparative Perspective," *International Journal of Primatology* 11 (1990), p. 141.

**BOX 9-3**

# The Sexual Behavior of the Bonobo

The bonobo *(Pan paniscus)* lives in a small, dense tropical forest in Zaire south of the Congo River. As early as 1929, the bonobo population had been reduced by the hunting practices of local peoples. Today, few natural groups exist and even fewer captive populations are available for study. Beginning in the 1970s, considerable research has been carried out on the remaining wild populations.

The social behavior of this ape differs in many ways from that of the chimpanzee and bears some interesting resemblances to human behavior. Bonobos live in communities of about 50 animals, but they spend most of their time in smaller groups of 2 to 10 individuals.

Compared with chimpanzees, the bonobos are more social and more peaceful and spend more of their time in groups.

Bonobo sexual behavior shows some features that are not found in other apes. Bonobos mate face to face (ventroventral) about a quarter of the time. This copulatory position is not found among chimpanzees and is rare among mammals in general; it is found primarily among whales, porpoises, and humans. Female bonobos exhibit a prolonged period of sexual receptivity, with copulations occurring during early phases of the estrus cycle.

Among chimpanzees, males usually initiate sexual behavior; among the bonobos, males and females initiate sex-

ual behavior in an egalitarian manner. Finally, investigators have observed behavior, primarily among females, that has been labeled "homosexual" behavior. The behavior observed is described as genitogenital rubbing and is usually seen during feeding sessions or before or after heterosexual mating by one or both of the females.

_____

*Sources:* B. G. Blout, "Issues in Bonobo *(Pan paniscus)* Sexual Behavior," *American Anthropologist* 92 (1990), pp. 702–714; T. Kano, "The Bonobo's Peaceable Kingdom," *Natural History,* November 1990, pp. 62–70; and R. L. Susman (ed.), *The Pygmy Chimpanzee* (New York: Plenum, 1984).

Two adult female bonobos in a typical genitogenital rubbing position. The older female carries the younger one.

The female reproductive cycle is evidenced in the chimpanzee by the periodic swelling of the sexual skin. The female may initiate sexual contact, but generally sexual behavior is a consequence of male courtship displays. The male leaps into a tree and for about a minute swings from branch to branch with the hair of his head, shoulders, and arms erect. As the male approaches the female, she crouches down in front of him. Consort pairs do not always form and a female will often mate with several males.

The mother–infant bond is extremely close. At first, the infant is totally dependent upon its mother and is constantly held and carried by her. Later, the infant sits upright on her back and begins to move away from her. Mothers frequently play with their babies, and the babies' playmates also include other young and adult animals. After the young stops riding on its mother's back, the juvenile chimpanzee associates more frequently with a play group. Play becomes less important when puberty is reached and the animal begins to enter adult life.

**The Termite Stick** The chimpanzee's practice of feeding on termites is of special interest to students of human evolution, for the chimpanzee manufactures and uses a tool for this purpose. At one time, anthropologists defined humans as *the* toolmaking animal. This definition has now been revised since chimpanzees and other animals have been observed deliberately manufacturing tools.

Termite feeding becomes an important activity at the beginning of the rainy season. For as many as nine weeks, chimpanzees spend one or two hours each day feeding on termites. This is the time when sexually mature termites grow wings in order to leave the termite mound to found new colonies. Passages within the mound are extended to its surface, but the openings to the outside are sealed over while the termites await ideal flying conditions.

The chimpanzee, upon locating a mound in this condition, scrapes away the thin seal over one of the passages. It then takes a **termite stick** and pokes it down the hole. After a moment, the tool is withdrawn with the termites hanging on it, ready to be licked off by the chimpanzee (Figure 9–10).

In manufacturing a termite stick, the chimpanzee pays attention to the choice of material and the nature of the tool. The termite stick is fashioned from a grass stalk, twig, or vine, and it is usually less than 30.5 centimeters (12 inches) long. If a twig is too long to use, the chimpanzee breaks it to the right length. If a twig or vine is leafy, the animal strips it of its leaves before using it.

Young chimpanzees do not appear to have an interest in collecting termites. Goodall reports that while a mother chimpanzee spends hours termiting, the young become impatient and attempt to get her to leave. The art of termiting and termite-

**FIGURE 9–10 The Termite Stick**
A five-year-old chimpanzee uses a tool she made herself, by stripping down a blade of grass, to fish for insects in a termite mound.

stick making is learned. When young chimpanzees begin to show an interest, their first termite sticks are poorly made. They have difficulty inserting the stick into the hole and withdrawing it without losing the termites hanging on to it. Through watching their mothers, the young chimpanzees learn, although some are better students than others and are able to make better tools.

Goodall and others describe other examples of tool manufacture. For example, a chimpanzee will make a sponge by chewing a leaf and then use it to sponge up water. One chimpanzee was observed making a series of different tools to extract honey from a dead stump.

Many natural objects are used as tools: sticks as clubs, rocks as missiles, and leaves as towels. Nevertheless, although chimpanzees do make tools in the wild, their inventory of tools does not even begin to approach the complexity of human technology or the degree of human dependence upon tools for survival.

**FIGURE 9–11 Chimpanzee Eating Meat**
Adult male chimpanzee (hair wet from rainstorm) dismantles and eats a juvenile baboon carcass.

**Chimpanzees as Hunters** Unlike most primates, chimpanzees eat meat. Chimpanzees have been observed killing and eating a variety of animals, including bushbucks, bushpigs, rodents, and young and adult monkeys, such as the baboon and the red colobus monkey (Figure 9–11). Cannibalism and the attacking of human infants have also been reported. While chimpanzees may simply surprise an animal in the undergrowth and then kill and eat it, they also appear to hunt animals deliberately for food.

The decision to hunt is often triggered by the distress call of a young baboon, and a spontaneous kill frequently leads to more purposeful activity. Hunting is most often a male activity in which several males cooperate in trapping the animal. The prey is killed by slamming it against a tree or the ground, by crushing its skull between their teeth, or simply by tearing it apart.

After the kill, other chimpanzees arrive to share the meat. They form temporary groupings called **sharing clusters,** and most members of a cluster eat some of the prey. Observations show that the time spent in eating the meat varies from 1 hour and 40 minutes to more than 9 hours.

Some individuals, especially subadults and adult females, simply pick up pieces of meat that have been dropped by other individuals. Other animals tear off a section of a larger piece being consumed by another animal, usually a female. Often, a particular animal requests meat by the characteristic gesture of holding a hand, open and palm up, under the possessor's chin while making characteristic vocalizations. Any chimpanzee may make such a request, but it is more often ignored than rewarded.

The head seems to be the choicest part of the kill by chimpanzee standards. The animals enlarge the foramen magnum (the large hole in the base of the skull) with their teeth and fingers to get at the brain. They eat the soft tissue together with leaves.

**Summary**

We have just examined some aspects of the social behavior of four primate species: the gibbon, the gelada, the savanna baboon, and the chimpanzee. None of these species is typical, for each represents its own set of adaptations and adjustments to the environments in which it lives. Yet certain themes of behavior emerge from our studies. For example, agonistic behavior appears to be characteristic of each of our groups. In multimale groups, male dominance hierarchies tend to form, yet most dominance behavior is expressed by gesturing rather than actual fighting. Grooming behavior occurs frequently among primates as an expression of close social ties. The protection and care of the infant by the mother and other adults of the social unit also appear to be a universal theme of primate social behavior.

**STUDY QUESTIONS**

1. Describe some of the different kinds of social groups found among primates.
2. What is grooming behavior? How does grooming affect the social relationships of the members of a primate group?
3. Gelada society is organized into a hierarchy of groups. Describe this organization and explain how it relates to changes in the environment.
4. Compare the use of space by the savanna baboon troop with that by the gibbon group. What differences in their habitats would help explain differences in their use of space?
5. Baboon troops are relatively stable and peaceful. In-group fighting is rare. How does the existence of the dominance hierarchy promote the stability of the group?
6. Periods of sexual activity in primates are usually limited. Describe the sexual cycle of a female monkey and

discuss how the period of receptivity in the female affects the social unit.
7. What is meant by a fission-fusion type of social organization? Describe the various types of social groups found among chimpanzees.
8. In the context of hunting, chimpanzees exhibit several behavioral traits that are usually not encountered in other social activities. What are some of these traits?

**SUGGESTED READINGS**

Goodall, J. *The Chimpanzees of Gombe: Patterns of Behavior.* Cambridge, Mass.: Belknap Press, 1986. This book brings together the data gathered from over two decades of research on the chimpanzees of the Gombe.

Heltne, P. G., and L. A. Marquardt (eds.). *Understanding Chimpanzees.* Cambridge, Mass.: Harvard University Press, 1989. This volume includes 33 papers on chimpanzees.

Jolly, A. *The Evolution of Primate Behavior,* 2nd ed. New York: Macmillan, 1985. This is an excellent introduction to the general topic of primate behavior.

Peterson, D., and J. Goodall. *Visions of Caliban.* Boston: Houghton Mifflin, 1993. Written for a general audience, this volume discusses chimpanzee behavior and the relationship between humans and chimpanzees.

Richard, A. F. *Primates in Nature.* New York: Freeman, 1985. This is an excellent introduction to the general topic of primate behavior. The author also discusses primate distribution, diet, and communication.

Smuts, B. B., D. L. Cheney, R. M. Seyfarth, R. W. Wrangham, and T. T. Struhsaker. *Primate Societies.* Chicago: University of Chicago Press, 1987. This is a collection of papers covering a variety of topics including primate socioecology, communication, and intelligence.

van Lawick-Goodall, J. *In the Shadow of Man.* Boston: Houghton Mifflin, 1971. This is a nontechnical discussion of the behavior of chimpanzees and the early experiences of Jane Goodall in the field.

**SUGGESTED WEB SITES**

East African Primate Research Sites:
http://www.indiana.edu/~primate/sites.html
Primate Info Net (Wisconsin Regional Primate Research Center):
http://www.primate.wisc.edu/pin/

Additional web sites are listed in the *Workbook* that accompanies this text.

# Human Behavior in Perspective

*The human condition has led to an open adaptive system based on culture. Culture may have its own set of biological restraints. Mental patterns may be partially shaped by genes, but these can only set the outer limit on the range of possible human behavior. Actual behavior, in specific conditions, can never be understood without an understanding of the cultural and historical process that shapes it. The nature of human nature is essentially cultural.[1]*
—Alexander Alland Jr.

**M**any anthropologists have studied the structure of nonhuman primate society for clues to the origins of human society. They have assumed that human societies were derived from social systems similar to those of the living monkeys and apes. Yet the social systems of modern nonhuman primates also have been developing through the millennia,

---

[1] A. Alland Jr., *To Be Human* (New York: Wiley, 1980), pp. 621–622.

so they do not necessarily represent ancestral patterns. However, comparative studies of all behavioral systems can provide us with new insights as to the limits and possibilities of human behavior.

## SOCIAL BEHAVIOR OF HUMAN FORAGERS

In the previous chapter, we examined the social behavior of four primates: the gibbon, the gelada, the baboon, and the chimpanzee. This chapter focuses on another primate, the study of which is at the center of anthropology—the species *Homo sapiens*.

Most humans today live in farming and industrial societies. Yet farming is a recent human development, probably no older than 13,000 years, and industrialism is a product of the eighteenth century. When anthropologists compare humans with other animal societies, they turn to contemporary societies that practice a foraging (hunting-gathering) strategy.

All contemporary foraging societies have been affected by technologically more advanced peoples. In recent centuries, foragers have lived essentially in marginal areas where farming is not practical. Today these societies are rapidly changing as they increasingly come under the influence of neighboring agricultural or industrial peoples. For this reason, most of the data for our comparisons come from the many anthropological studies of hunter-gatherers conducted during the first half of the twentieth century.

### The Structure of the Human Band

The basic social unit of foraging peoples is the **band,** which typically contains about 35 to 50 members. Bands, however, can be much larger, and band membership is often quite variable. Small bands may join into larger, multiband units when food is plentiful.

Like the monkey troop and the chimpanzee community, the human band consists of many males and females—adults, subadults, juveniles, and infants. In contrast to the nonhuman primate societies we have surveyed, the adult members of the human band, for the most part, are involved in exclusive male–female relationships. The gibbon social unit consists of a single male and female with their immature offspring, but a third adult normally is not tolerated; within the human band, several male–female partnerships coexist (Figure 10–1).

Among the many factors related to permanent male–female bonding may be the fact that human females do not exhibit any conspicuous physical indication of estrus, and hence of ovulation, such as the swelling of the sexual skin in baboons and chimpanzees. The lack of estrus in the human female is a feature that clearly defines the human condition, yet anthropologists are not sure why this should be the case. Many hypotheses have been proposed as explanations.

One of the earlier ideas is that the lack of a clearly defined estrus in humans may be related to the development of bonds of cooperation among the males of the band and the lessening of male–male competition over estrus females. Since all females are potentially receptive throughout the year, males do not need to compete for the few females in the band who are near the time of ovulation.

More recent hypotheses center on the role of the female in human society. Some scholars see the result of a lack of estrus as creating a situation where a male must copulate frequently with his mate in order to ensure fertilization. A male's close bonding with a female is also necessary to prevent the female from mating with other males. This increases the probability that a male bonded to a female is the father of her offspring.

On the other hand, other scholars see the hiding of ovulation as a strategy for permitting the female to copulate with a number of males, thus confusing the paternity issue. Therefore, several males would have a vested interest in the female's offspring, which would enhance the protection of the helpless infant. Students of primate behavior have observed that males will often kill infants that are not their own; confused paternity would prevent such behavior.

Monkey troops and chimpanzee communities are, to a large degree, closed units. Relationships with adjacent groups are often hostile. Animals of one particular sex remain with the troop into which they were born for their entire lives and form close bonds with siblings of the same sex. Adolescent animals of the other sex, male baboons and female chimpanzees, for example, leave the group of their birth and migrate to other groups. Once the animal has left the unit of its birth, it no longer has any social relationships with its parents or siblings.

Human bands are similar to baboon troops and chimpanzee communities in that members of one sex, usually females in foraging societies, leave the

**FIGURE 10–1  San Family**

group of their birth and join—in the case of humans, marry into—a neighboring group. What is different with humans is that they continue to maintain close ties throughout their lives with relatives in other bands. Thus, a woman lives in a band with her husband and children, yet she maintains close relationships with the bands of her parents and brothers, the band of her sister and her sister's husband, the band of her daughter and her daughter's husband, and so on. She visits these other bands, and may even live with another band for a period of time. As a result, important social and economic relationships are formed among these bands. Kinship is the basic means of social organization in which the relationships of the family extend throughout the society (Figure 10–2).

The extent of territoriality among hunter-gatherers varies. In many parts of the world, these people do not look upon an area of land as something owned by a particular group, even though some locations, such as particular water holes and sacred areas, are often traditionally regarded as be-

ing within the realm of a particular group. In the case of a water hole, other groups show their courtesy by asking permission to use it; this permission is seldom refused. Warfare as we know it in agricultural and industrial societies does not occur among hunter-gatherers, but formalized skirmishes or feuds do occur.

Dominance is a recurrent feature of male–male and female–female social relationships among nonhuman primates. In the human band, the typical nature of male–male and female–female relationships is essentially egalitarian. Although individuals, usually males, may be considered leaders because of their skills and leadership abilities, hunting and gathering societies are characterized by cooperation, equal access to resources, and the absence of strict hierarchical systems. Cooperation is essential for successful hunting-gathering.

## Summary

For a significant part of human evolution, people lived as foragers. The present human condition was

**FIGURE 10–2 San Mother and Children**

shaped, in part, by evolutionary forces acting on hunting-gathering groups. The basic social unit of foragers is the band, which consists of adult males and females, subadults, juveniles, and infants. Bands are characterized by exclusive long-term male–female relationships. In human bands, women often leave the band of their birth and marry into a neighboring group. Continuing social relationships function to maintain social and economic relationships between bands. The degree of territoriality and intragroup fighting varies in different hunting-gathering societies. However, the concept of private ownership of land or warfare over territory is foreign to foragers.

## THE ORIGIN AND NATURE OF HUMAN SOCIETY

Much of the research into hominid origins centers around the anatomy of the early hominids as seen in the fossil record; yet a proper understanding of our origins must include investigations into the be-

haviors of the early hominids. In the study of anatomy, clear relationships often can be determined through the identification of homologous structures, and, through such studies, an ancestral anatomy reconstructed. Primate behavior, however, is to a very large extent learned. Even among the apes, specific populations display unique behaviors that are the products of learned traditions. Thus, the behaviors of present-day primate societies cannot be used as models of prehistoric social behavior. They can only be used to provide us with ideas of possibilities.

Prehistoric behavior does not fossilize in the same way as do bones. Archaeologists have recovered stone tools that are the products of behavior, but the earliest stone tools appeared about 2½ million years ago. However, we do not have a record of tools made of perishable materials that most likely were manufactured and used by even earlier hominids.

Thus, most of the evidence of early hominid behavior is circumstantial. Using such evidence, anthropologists have developed a number of hypotheses. We will examine some of these hypotheses here.

### Humans as Hunters

Humans are primarily omnivores. Although different societies emphasize different foods, humans eat a variety of animal and vegetable material. What a society considers edible or inedible is defined by its culture. The significance of meat eating varies from society to society, but all foraging societies appear to emphasize meat as an important source of sustenance. Hunting is considered an important social activity (Figure 10–3 and color inserts).

During the 1960s, many anthropologists viewed "man the hunter" as the key to understanding human evolution. The hunting activities of contemporary foragers were projected back to prehistoric times. Hunting became the main explanation for the evolution of manual dexterity, erect bipedalism, the human brain, and culture.

Predatory activity is rare in primates. Many primates consume insects, birds, small reptiles, and small mammals, but only three primates—baboons, chimpanzees, and humans—have been observed eating the flesh of medium to large mammals that

**FIGURE 10–3  San Hunters and Gatherers**
Two San men carry home palm hearts.

they have killed. Although baboons and chimpanzees deliberately hunt, hunting is a minor activity in terms of the total diet and social behavior. For example, a group of chimpanzees living in Tanzania consumed 3 kilograms (6.6 pounds) of meat per offspring, 8 kilograms (17.6 pounds) of meat per female, and 25 kilograms (55 pounds) of meat per male in an average year.[2]

In 1969, George Schaller and Gordon Lowther proposed that social systems are determined to a large extent by ecological conditions.[3] Schaller and Lowther noted that, in some respects, human society bears a closer resemblance to that of the social carnivores, such as lions, tigers, and wild dogs, than to that of the apes. Among the many characteristics that are shared, to a degree, by both human and carnivore societies are large ranges, cooperative hunting, food transport, food sharing, an egalitarian social system, cooperation, and the establishment of home bases (Figure 10–4).

This interpretation of human origins was based, in part, on early interpretations of the archaeological remains from South Africa (Chapter 13). Much of the fossil and archaeological evidence has been interpreted as supporting the idea that these early

[2]R. W. Wrangham and E. van Z. B. Riss, "Rates of Predation on Mammals by Gombe Chimpanzees, 1972–1975," *Primates* 31 (1990), p. 167. Dividing these figures by 365 days gives an approximation of 22 grams of meat for females and 68½ grams of meat for males per day for chimpanzees. Richard Lee reports for the !Kung San, a foraging people from southern Africa, an average of 230 grams of meat per day. See R. Lee, "What Hunters Do for a Living, or, How to Make Out on Scarce Resources," in R. B. Lee and I. DeVore (eds.), *Man the Hunter* (Chicago: Aldine, 1968), pp. 30–48.

[3]G. B. Schaller and G. R. Lowther, "The Relevance of Carnivore Behavior to the Study of Early Hominids," *Southwestern Journal of Anthropology* 25 (1969), pp. 307–341.

**FIGURE 10–4  Wild Dogs, Tanzania**
Female (not the mother) regurgitates meat to pups. These adult dogs transport food and share the meat with other animals.

hominids were actually killer apes. Anthropologist Matt Cartmill writes:

> During the 1960s, the central propositions of the hunting hypothesis—that hunting and its selection pressures had made men and women out of our apelike ancestors, instilled a taste for violence in them, estranged them from the animal kingdom, and excluded them from the order of nature—became familiar themes of the national culture, and the picture of *Homo sapiens* as a mentally unbalanced predator threatening an otherwise harmonious natural realm became disseminated not only through popular-science books but also through novels, cartoons, films, and television.[4]

### Woman the Gatherer

Not all anthropologists agree that hunting was the primary factor in the development of hominid society. They note that in modern foraging societies, when the sources of the diet are accurately noted and weighed, women often provide the bulk of the calories (Figure 10–5). For example, Richard Lee notes that among the !Kung San of South Africa, women, in one study over a 28-day period, provided 57 percent of the calories and men provided another 13 percent *through gathering;* only 30 percent of the calories came from the hunt.[5]

Unlike gathering, hunting is not predictable. Anthropologist Dean Falk comments:

---

[4]M. Cartmill, *A View to a Death in the Morning: Hunting and Nature through History* (Cambridge, Mass.: Harvard University Press, 1993), p. 14.

[5]R. B. Lee, *The !Kung San* (Cambridge, Mass.: Harvard University Press, 1979), p. 262.

**FIGURE 10–5  San Hunters and Gatherers**
San women gathering.

In modern hunting and gathering societies that live in habitats similar to those of early hominids, the men may go hunting, but, on a day-to-day basis, it is the women who end up providing most of the nourishment for the entire group. While *he is* out trying his luck at hunting, *she* (often accompanied by children) collects the more widely available plant food, insects, and small animals. She ensures that neither her children nor her hunter will go hungry tonight![6]

It is much more likely that small social groups of men and woman began to exploit a wide variety of food resources. The greater the resource base,

the more likely it is that the San will be able to obtain an adequate supply of food.

Another issue revolves around the archaeological evidence of hunting. Very early stone tools, which first appear in the archaeological record from about 2.6 million years ago in east Africa, were more likely to have been butchering implements than hunting weapons. Careful examination of fossilized butchered bones under the scanning electron microscope shows that the marks of stone butchering implements often overlie the tooth marks of carnivores. This suggests that the animals were killed by one of the many carnivores present and that later a group of hominids came along and used stone tools to cut away the remaining scraps of meat or to break open the long bones to obtain the marrow. In other words, early hominid society may have developed as a scavenger-gathering society.

### Reproductive Strategies and the Origins of Human Society

Anthropologist Owen Lovejoy believes that the key to understanding the evolution of early hominid society lies in an understanding of reproductive strategies.[7] Among nonvertebrate animals, a female produces an enormous quantity of ova, but she gives the ova little or no care. From millions of ova, only a few offspring are produced who survive to adulthood.

In mammals, and especially in primates, far fewer offspring are produced, and the intervals between successive births are longer. Instead of spending reproductive energy to produce numerous progeny, primates often have single rather than multiple births. Children are helpless at birth, and a fairly long childhood is required to learn the behaviors required for survival in adulthood. This increase of parental care helps ensure their survival.

This reproductive strategy can lead to a situation in which the population declines in size and becomes in danger of extinction because of an inadequate birthrate. For example, there has been a steady decline in the ape populations over the centuries. The average female chimpanzee produces

---

[6]From *Braindance* by Dean Falk. Copyright ©1992 by Dean Falk. Reprinted by permission of Henry Holt and Co., Inc.

[7]C. O. Lovejoy, "The Origin of Man," *Science* 211 (1981), pp. 341–350; C. O. Lovejoy, "Modeling Human Origins: Are We Sexy Because We're Smart, or Smart Because We're Sexy?" in D. T. Rasmussen (ed.), *The Origin and Evolution of Humans and Humanness* (Boston: Jones and Bartlett, 1993), pp. 1–28.

one offspring every 5.6 years. She does not reach sexual maturity until 10 years of age. This means that she must live until 21 years of age if she is to produce two offspring to replace her and her mate. However, there are many biological and environmental factors that may prevent this from happening.

A chimpanzee mother must forage for food in the trees. Movement in trees creates dangerous situations during which an infant may fall; this is a major cause of infant mortality. The child must be carried, and the mother is not able to carry two young offspring at the same time. A long interval between successive births allows one offspring to be independent of the mother before another offspring is born.

Lovejoy postulates that a solution to these problems developed among the earliest hominids through a partial separation of the feeding ranges of the males and females. The males were able to exploit a much larger range because they were unrestricted by the presence of a young infant. Since there was less competition from the males, the females could confine their foraging to a much smaller area. Less mobility resulted in a lowered accident rate, and this permitted an increase in parenting behavior.

Male access to a female is necessary for reproductive purposes. A system by which the male was associated exclusively with a single female provided a condition whereby the male was guaranteed access to a female. This decreased the competition with other males, while at the same time the male did not compete with the female and offspring for food supplies.

According to Lovejoy's hypothesis, the next step was the collection of distant food by the male, who transported the food to the female and her offspring. The mother spent more time caring for her offspring, and she could take care of more than one immature offspring at a time. This reduced the time between successive births. The total birth and survival rates increased. All of this benefited the male, who increased the probability of his genes being represented in the next generation. Habitual erect bipedalism allowed the male to carry food more efficiently with his hands. Lovejoy believes that the earliest tools made were devices for carrying food.

Once this stage had been reached, other features that characterize human social organization emerged. For example, the loss of the outward signs of estrus and the development of continual sexual receptivity on the part of the female increased the intensity of the male–female bond. Increased participation of the male in parenting led to the development of the nuclear family.

This model, however, has not found universal acceptance. Direct evidence of early hominid behavior is practically nonexistent. While anthropologists may develop hypotheses using data from a variety of sources, our knowledge of what really occurred is strictly limited.

### Summary

Our knowledge of the origin and nature of early hominid social and cultural behavior is largely circumstantial. Behavior does not fossilize; and it is likely that the behavior of modern humans and other primates has evolved substantially since the evolution of the first hominids over $4\frac{1}{2}$ million years ago. Although some things about behavior can be deduced from the anatomy of fossils—locomotor patterns, for example—anatomy cannot tell us much about social interactions and the concepts that formed in the minds of early hominids.

Some anthropologists see human societies as having evolved along parallel lines with carnivore societies; some see great significance in the gathering activities of women, while others see human reproductive biology and behavior as the prime factor. Owen Lovejoy sees human society as having evolved in relation to the separation of male and female feeding ranges; this allowed females to stay close to their home base and to care for young more effectively than if they had to compete with males for food.

### ARE HUMANS UNIQUE?

Throughout history, many philosophers have attempted to distance humans from other living organisms. Social scientists have searched for characteristics that mark humanity as unique. On the other hand, modern evolutionary biologists and sociobiologists see continuity in the living world. They see differences, especially differences in closely related species, as quantitative rather than qualitative. In this section, we will explore the question of the uniqueness of the human species.

## Culture

The lives of nonhuman animals are controlled primarily by genes. Nevertheless, many animals have been extremely successful in their adaptations to a variety of habitats. Humans, on the other hand, are primarily dependent on learned behavior. In fact, the emergence of the human species and its continuance are dependent on what is called **culture.**

*Culture* is one of those words that everyone uses but almost everyone uses differently. A person may say, "Those people belong to the Art Society; they certainly are cultured." To the anthropologist, there is one thing culture is not, and that is a level of sophistication or formal education. Culture is not something that one person has and another does not.

Anthropologists have defined culture in hundreds of ways. Fortunately, most definitions have points in common, and these points are included in our definition: Culture is learned, nonrandom, systematic behavior and knowledge that is transmitted from person to person and from generation to generation.

**Culture Is Learned and Patterned**   Culture is learned; it is not biologically determined or coded by the hereditary material. When termites emerge from their pupae, workers, soldiers, and queens crawl away to their respective predetermined tasks. They are innately equipped to brave the hazards of their environment. Humans do not function in this manner. A baby abandoned at birth has *no* chance of surviving by itself. In fact, most six- or seven-year-olds would probably perish if left to their own resources. Survival strategies, as well as other behaviors and thoughts, are learned from people such as parents, other relatives, teachers, peers, and friends.

Culture is patterned in two ways. First, it is nonrandom behavior and knowledge; that is, specific actions or thoughts are usually the same in similar situations. For example, in Western societies, when two people meet, they usually shake hands. Second, it is patterned in the sense that it is systematic; that is, one aspect of behavior or thought is related to all others. Taken together, they form a system.

A **system** is a collection of parts that are interrelated so that a change in any one part brings about specifiable changes in the others. For example, in eastern Europe, the change from a communist government to a more democratic one has had repercussions on the educational, economic, moral, and social elements of society. In addition, a group's cultural traditions and the way in which its members relate to one another reflect certain underlying principles about the basic characteristics of people and nature.

**Culture Is Transmittable**   Culture is transmittable; it spreads. Information is learned, stored in the cortex of the brain, interpreted, and then transmitted to other people. Knowledge builds on information from past generations. In societies with writing, each generation can continue to influence future generations indefinitely. Therefore, a particular culture is the result of its history as well as its present state. Although there is now evidence that certain nonhuman animals also possess some ability to pass on acquired behavior, in no other animal has this ability evolved to the same degree as in humans.

**Coping with Change**   Over time, nonhuman animals usually adapt to changing environments through changes in their physical form. Humans usually adjust to a change in environment with changes in behavior or knowledge (including beliefs, values, and customs).

Of course, physical changes have been important in human evolution, and they account for why we no longer look like our distant ancestors. The size and proportions of the human body and the size and structure of the brain have changed over time. These changes have led to upright posture, which freed the hands from locomotor function; they have also led to the evolution of a brain that is capable of mental functions at a higher level than other animals'.

Such changes allow for today's cultural potential. Humans can sometimes substitute cultural innovation for biological alteration. If you were to transplant a group of temperate-zone nonhuman animals to an arctic environment, they might all die. On the other hand, those that were somewhat different from the average, possibly by having more fur, might survive. If you put humans into the same environment, they might make systematic changes in their culture that would lead to appropriate technological and social innovations; they might build an igloo, start a fire, or even kill a polar bear to make a coat.

Humans adapt biologically to changing environments as well as adjusting to environments through the human biological potential for culture. This is one reason why the human species is so widely dispersed. Physical features do not need to change in order for humans to move into a new environment. Instead, human biological potentials allow for behavioral flexibility, which results in an enormous range of adjustments.

### Protoculture among Nonhuman Primates

Humans have been described as cultural animals who cope with the conditions of their niches largely by means of cultural adjustments. Primatologists are becoming increasingly aware of the fact that not only can nonhuman primates adjust to new situations by means of learned behavior, but also that many behavioral patterns are passed down from generation to generation as a type of social tradition. Those who feel that the transmission of learned behavior is common among these forms believe that primates do have a **protoculture;** that is, they are characterized by the simplest, most basic aspects of culture.

**Protoculture in Monkeys** Many behavioral patterns in monkeys are certainly genetically determined. Laboratory studies, in which animals have been reared away from the social unit or reared by a human substitute mother, have shown that certain vocalizations and dominance gestures occur in the isolated monkey. Since the animal had no contact with its natural mother or troop, such similarities between isolated and troop-reared behavior must be interpreted as being genetically determined.

On the other hand, many behavioral patterns are apparently learned. One infant raised with its natural mother never learned to use its cheek pouches for food; its mother never used hers. Later the animal was placed in a cage with another monkey. The second monkey would rush to the food and place much of it in his cheek pouches, leaving lit-

tle for the first. Very quickly, however, the original animal learned the proper use of the pouches.

Some of the best data on the degree to which learned behavior is developed in nonhuman primates come from studies of the Japanese macaque. Primatologists have attempted to introduce new foods in provisioned populations. The Japanese macaque does not eat everything available in its natural habitat and does not always accept the introduction of new foods. Candy was accepted readily by the infants, who generally show a greater amount of exploratory activity than do adults, but even after several years, candy was not accepted by the entire troop. On the other hand, the dominant males accepted the introduction of wheat immediately, and this behavior spread throughout the troop in only four hours.

Examples of behavioral changes occurred on Koshima Island, Japan, where primatologists introduced sweet potatoes as a food. Normally, macaques rub dirt off food with their hands, but one day a young female took her sweet potato to a stream and washed it (Figure 10–6). Apparently providing greater efficiency in dirt removal, the pattern of sweet-potato washing soon spread to the other members of her play group and then to the mothers of these young monkeys. Four years later,

**FIGURE 10–6 The Japanese Macaque**
Sweet-potato washing.

**FIGURE 10–7  The Japanese Macaque**
Bipedal transport of sweet potato to the ocean for washing.

80 to 90 percent of the monkeys in the troop were washing sweet potatoes. Later, some monkeys began to wash their sweet potatoes in salt water, the salt probably improving the flavor. Often they carried the sweet potatoes a short distance to the shore, and in carrying sweet potatoes, the animals moved bipedally (Figure 10–7).

This later development is of interest to students of human evolution. Erect bipedalism evolved in the earliest hominids as a dominant form of locomotion. The shift to erect bipedalism was not necessarily sudden; rather, a slow increase in the frequency of this mode of locomotion could have occurred in response to some environmental factor. Anthropologists are not quite sure what this environmental change was, although the replacement of tropical forest by grassland has been suggested.

On Koshima Island, the investigators saw the increased use of this locomotor pattern in response to a new learned behavioral pattern, washing sweet potatoes in salt water. Conceivably, if a behavioral pattern like this had some selective advantage, animals biologically more capable of bipedalism might contribute more genes to the gene pool of the next generation. At any rate, the behavioral changes in the Japanese macaque at least suggest

how changes in the frequency of an anatomical trait might result from a change in a behavioral pattern.

**Protoculture in Chimpanzees**  Protocultural behavior is also present in the chimpanzee. Some of this learned behavior was discussed in Chapter 9 in relation to the use of termite sticks by young chimpanzees and the use of human-made objects to obtain status. In addition, young chimpanzees learn a great deal about chimpanzee society in their play groups. For instance, they learn who the dominant adult females are by the actions taken against them if they get into a fight with another youngster. Chimpanzee females also appear to learn how to be effective mothers from watching their own mothers and taking care of their siblings. Jane Goodall reports that a young female who took care of her orphaned brother seemed to be a more experienced mother when she had her first offspring than other first-time mothers.

The point of this discussion is that the beginning of cultural behavior can be seen in monkey and ape societies. Continuing investigations into these phenomena can aid the physical anthropologist in understanding the possible ways in which culture developed in humans.

### Human Universals

Many anthropologists, probably most of them, are skeptical of statements that generalize about what all peoples do. But are there not generalizations of that sort that really do hold for the wide array of human populations? There are—and not enough has been said about them. This skepticism and neglect of human universals is the entrenched legacy of an era of particularism in which the observation that something *doesn't* occur among the Bongo Bongo counted as a major contribution of anthropology. The truth of the matter is, however, that anthropologists probably always take for granted an indefinite collection of traits that add up to a very complex view of human nature.[8]

Just as all baboons share many behavioral characteristics, all humans share certain behavioral potentials. For instance, except for individuals profoundly affected by disease or injury, all humans

---

[8]D. E. Brown, *Human Universals* (New York: McGraw-Hill, 1991), p. 1.

can learn a language—baboons cannot. The potential for learning language, and other characteristics of human nature, evolved as a result of evolutionary and cultural forces acting on these behaviors. Just as there is a "prewired" genetic potential for learning language, it is equally true that a specific language, such as English, Chinese, or Navaho, is learned by exposure to an environment in which that language is spoken (or signed). There is no biological propensity to learn one specific language over another. These facts are relatively noncontroversial.

**The Sexual Division of Labor** The general relationship between nature (biological destiny) and nurture (learning) concerning language abilities may be relatively clear. However, what about other behaviors, say, the division of labor between males and females? Is this behavior a result of nature or nurture or some combination of both factors?

One way that this issue has been approached is by asking questions such as this: Are women as a category universally subordinate to men as a category? However, this question is perhaps too loaded with emotion to deal with objectively. Also, a scientific explanation depends on precisely defined concepts, but it is hard to define *subordinate*.

> So who is right? Are women subordinate to men in all societies or not? Certainly, ethnographers have been biased—but does this bias explain their consistent reports of female subordination? Certainly, the Iroquois and other peoples demonstrate that women in some societies have achieved considerable control over their own lives and even over public decision making—but do such cases represent full equality of males and females? Indeed, would we know "full general equality" if we saw it in a society? What would it look like? Would men and women have to carry out the same kinds of economic tasks before we could say they are equal? Is monogamy necessary, or can a society be polygynous and still qualify? Shall we require that women occupy 50 percent of all leadership roles before we say they have equal rights? How should domestic life be organized before we can say that husbands in general do not dominate their wives?[9]

So perhaps the question about the relationship between the sexes should be phrased something like this: Are there biological differences between the sexes that universally affect behavior in a consistent manner? Besides the most apparent primary sexual differences between men and women, other biologically controlled differences exist. The average man is stronger (more muscular) than the average woman. Many women seem to experience a decrease in fertility if they engage in very heavy exercise; men are not affected in this way. Women not only give birth, but in all societies they care for infants and young children more than men do.

The character of each culture determines the precise way that the above biological facts are interpreted. For instance, in modern industrial societies, in which machines often substitute for human muscle power and in which the birth rate is low, biological differences between men and women have fewer social consequences than in nonindustrial societies. Yet these biological factors are at least partially responsible for the male–female division-of-labor specializations found in societies throughout the world. Hunting, trapping, mining, lumbering, butchering, building boats, and working with stone, bone, shell, and metal seem to be overwhelmingly male activities in all societies studied. Gathering wild plant foods, shellfish, and mollusks; collecting resources for use as fuel; fetching water; making clothing; weaving; and taking care of small animals are predominantly female tasks.

**Other Human Universals** We have been discussing sexual differences in task specialization as an example of a human universal. Donald E. Brown lists hundreds of other possible human universals.[10] There are different degrees of consensus on the universality of the items he lists, but various anthropologists, psychologists, sociologists, sociobiologists, and others have suggested each item as a candidate for universal status.

Some researchers believe that all human societies change through time, have some concept of privacy, have some form of art, practice body ornamentation, distinguish between good and bad behavior (have a moral system), make jokes, have

---

[9]Reprinted by permission from *Humanity: An Introduction to Cultural Anthropology* by Peoples and Bailey. ©1994 by West Publishing Company. All rights reserved.

---

[10]Brown, *Human Universals*, pp. 157–201.

languages that conform to a universal set of grammatical rules, display universal stages of language acquisition, distinguish between general and particular, display ethnocentrism, solve some problems by trial and error, use tools, have kinship terms, have rules about sexual behavior, are aware of the individual self as distinct from others, have a social structure influenced by accumulated information, show collective decision making, have leadership, have some form of play and games, have a world view, and have children that show a fear of strangers. Some people also believe that individuals within all societies have the potential for aggression, hope, anxiety, lying, and feeling loss and grief in respect to the death of close kin; have a sense of duty; and feel boredom.

Humans share some of the above characteristics with other animals. Chimpanzees make a limited number of tools, and some researchers suggest that they might feel grief when certain other chimpanzees, such as a mother, die. Yet the list of human universals taken as a whole describes only one animal—*Homo sapiens.*

## Communication

In his book *Language, Thought and Reality,* the linguist Benjamin Lee Whorf claims, "Speech is the best show man puts on."[11] Indeed, anthropologists consider language to be such an important aspect of our nature that an entire branch of anthropology—**anthropological linguistics**—is devoted to its description and analysis. The understanding of linguistic behavior is important to the anthropologist's understanding of human adjustments, adaptations, and adaptability.

Language is but one means of communication. **Communication** is a very general term that, in its broadest application, simply means that some stimulus or message is transmitted and received. On more specific levels, communication means different things to the physicist, mathematician, engineer, and behavioral scientist. We are concerned with its usage in relation to animals; in this context, communication means that one animal transmits information to another animal. This information

[11]B. L. Whorf, in J. B. Carroll (ed.), *Language, Thought and Reality: Selected Writings of Benjamin Lee Whorf* (Cambridge, Mass., and New York: Technology Press and Wiley, 1956), p. 249.

can simply convey the presence of the animal, or it can indicate such things as dominance, fear, hunger, or sexual receptiveness. Communication does not necessarily imply thought, but as neurological complexity evolves, so do the methods, mechanisms, and potential of communication.

**Methods of Primate Communication** Social animals are constantly communicating with one another; even the spatial positions they assume in relation to one another can be forms of communication. Primates communicate through olfactory, tactile, visual, and auditory signals.

Compared with other mammals, the primates, in general, have a reduced olfactory sense. The sense of smell is much more important to prosimians and New World monkeys than to Old World monkeys and apes. Some prosimians, such as the ring-tailed lemur, have specialized skin glands that excrete odoriferous substances. The animal uses this material, along with urine and feces, to mark off territory. Many of the New World monkeys use the olfactory sense also and, like prosimians, have permanent scent glands.

Although the sense of smell is less important in Old World monkeys and apes, it still serves as a means of communication. Male rhesus monkeys, for example, recognize an estrus female by specific odors originating in the vagina. The great emphasis on deodorants and perfumes indicates the role played by olfactory signals in human communication.

The tactile sense is likewise important in primates, and they spend long periods of time touching one another. Grooming, for example, functions not only to remove dirt and parasites from the fur but to communicate affection. Grooming is found among all categories of individuals: between adult males, between a male and an estrus female, and between a female and her infant. The close physical contact between a mother and her infant appears to be essential for the normal development of the individual.

Visual communication is of great importance to primates. The positioning of animals in relationship to one another conveys information about dominance, feeding, sexual behavior, and attitude, and general body posture can signal tension or relaxation. Motivational researchers have concluded that a political candidate, newscaster, or other person talking to a large group should stand slightly sideways rather than face directly ahead. The latter position, supposedly taken as a dominance display, is said to make an audience nervous.

In addition to the positioning of the body, facial gestures are used extensively among primates to convey information. Various examples of gestures were given in the discussion of the social behavior of the baboon in Chapter 9.

**Vocal Communication**   One thing is certain: primates, including people, do not have to open their mouths to communicate a wide range of information. Many primate sounds are nonvocal. For instance, the gorilla beats its chest, shakes branches, or strikes the ground to communicate frustration. Likewise, a bit of silence is often as meaningful as noise itself and often indicates danger. Anyone who has been to a zoo, however, and heard the vocalizations of the siamangs, or, for that matter, anyone who has visited a schoolyard knows that primates not only vocalize but do so with a great deal of noise. Some arboreal monkeys and apes are among the loudest and most vocal of mammals.

Nonhuman primates produce a number of vocalized sounds. In prosimians and some monkeys, these sounds tend to be **discrete.** A discrete signal is one that does not blend with other signals; it is individually distinct. Anthropoids also produce some discrete calls, but other calls grade into one another, forming a **call system.** This blending makes it difficult to estimate the number of calls, or specific messages, produced, but the number of calls for most species seems to average between 10 and 20.

Although the meaning of different sounds varies a great deal from one species to another, some generalizations can be made. Barking sounds serve as alarm signals among gorillas, chimpanzees, baboons, rhesus monkeys, and langurs. Screeching and screaming sounds often signal distress; growling indicates annoyance. Animals produce different types of grunts while moving around, seemingly to maintain contact between the animals in a group.

One animal can produce sounds that direct the attention of another toward specific objects. Other sounds convey quantitative information, specify a particular type of behavior that should be used, or initiate a whole sequence of related behaviors. Primates also have a great ability to inform one another about their moods at particular moments through subtle changes in their vocalizations.

### Language

Nonhuman animals, especially other primates, share many of the features of human language. Nevertheless, several characteristics of language are, as far as we know, unique. Other features are developed to a higher degree in human language than in any other communication system.

Human language is both **open** and discrete. Openness refers to the expansionary nature of language, which enables people to coin new labels for new concepts and objects. The hunter-gatherer who sees an airplane for the first time can attach a designation to it; in the same manner, a biologist who discovers a new species can give it a name.

Most nonhuman primate signals are not discrete. The gibbon who is content one moment and frightened the next simply grades one call into the next. Recently, research has shown that a limited number of nonhuman anthropoid signals do seem to be discrete, such as the two very acoustically different alarm calls of vervet monkeys, one that signals the initial approach of a neighboring group and another that signals a more aggressive approach. However, all the messages of language are discrete. Through language, the human can say, "I am content" or "I am frightened," delivering a distinct message that never blends with any other message.

The discrete units of language are **arbitrary.** A word, for example, has no real connection to the thing to which it refers. There is nothing about a pen that is suggested by the sound "pen." If we all agreed, a pen could be called a "table." Even though the potential for sound formation is innate, the meanings of the arbitrary elements of a language must be learned.

One of the most important and useful things about human language is **displacement,** which is the ability to communicate about events at times and places distant from those of their occurrence. Displacement enables a person to talk and think about things not directly in front of him or her. This is the characteristic of language that makes learning from the past, as well as planning for the future, possible. Displacement is to a large degree responsible for creativity, imagination, and illusion.

For a communication system to be called language, it must have a lexicon and a grammar. A **lexicon** is a vocabulary, a set of meaningful units such as words (or hand positions in sign language). A **grammar** is a set of rules used to make up these words and then to combine them into larger utterances such as phrases and sentences. Most rules of a grammar are unconsciously known. If a system has a lexicon and a grammar, it need not be oral to be considered language. Thus, a system such as American Sign Language (ASL) is considered a language, since specific rules govern the combination of the nonvocal signs used.

**Symbolic Behavior in Apes**   As research on primates continues, the uniqueness of humankind diminishes. Research involving several apes—including the chimpanzee Washoe, the bonobo Kanzi, and the gorilla Koko—has cast doubt on

the claim that language is exclusively a human characteristic.

For almost half a century, researchers have been attempting to teach chimpanzees language. In the 1940s, a chimpanzee named Vicki, after years of training, was with difficulty and lack of clarity able to say three words: *mama, papa,* and *cup.*

The chimpanzee's larynx (voice box) is higher in the throat than is the human larynx. This and other anatomical features of the chimpanzee prevent the animal from producing sounds with the qualities of human speech sounds. Also, chimpanzees do not show development of **Broca's area** of the brain, the area that in humans controls the production of speech (Figure 14–28). However, recent research suggests that chimpanzees may have limited abilities to understand language. For this reason, systems of nonvocal communication, which have a lexicon and a grammar as well as the design features of language not related to speech, have been tried in experimental situations. Washoe and Koko

BOX 10-1

## The Question of the Innateness and Uniqueness of Language

Anyone concerned with the study of human nature and human capacities must somehow come to grips with the fact that all normal humans acquire language, whereas acquisition of even its barest rudiments is quite beyond the capacities of an otherwise intelligent ape.[1]

Noam Chomsky, one of the best known linguists of the twentieth century, expressed the above sentiment in 1972. It mirrored the traditional view about people: humans are distinct from all other animals in possessing language. In an attempt to explain this uniqueness, Chomsky and others proposed that there is a yet-to-be-found language acquisition area of the brain that allows children to unconsciously, and without being directly taught, learn language. If this language acquisition area exists, it would be an innate feature of humans that is prewired for what Chomsky calls

a Universal Grammar. The Universal Grammar is a set of proposed rules that underlies the specific grammars of all languages. All that is needed for a child to learn any language is a sample of utterances provided by the linguistic environment.

There is no doubt that a human brain evolved specially equipped for language acquisition. Although linguists debate the existence of a Universal Grammar, it is an established fact that all human children go through the same stages of language development at about the same age, regardless of the language of their culture.

Also, there is no doubt that the ability to acquire language is much more developed in humans than in any other species. However, Chomsky's contention that "acquisition of even its barest rudiments is quite beyond the capacities of an otherwise intelligent ape" may not be correct.

Research on bonobos, such as Kanzi, indicates that they can "use symbol combinations as a means of specifying more than a single symbol can express."[2] Some of Kanzi's two-element combinations are *bite-chase, slap-grab, tickle-hide, chase-ball, grab-head, grab-Matata,* and *food-orange.* The use of these two-element combinations may reflect the bonobo's ability to reach, very rudimentarily, what is called the two-word stage of language development. So, as with many other characteristics once thought to be the exclusive province of humankind, very simple and partial language-type abilities may be found in nonhuman primates.

[1]N. Chomsky, *Language and Mind* (New York: Harcourt Brace Jovanovich, 1972).
[2]E. S. Savage-Rumbaugh, "Language Acquisition in a Nonhuman Species: Implications for the Innateness Debate," *Developmental Psychobiology* 23 (1990), p. 615.

**FIGURE 10–8  Washoe**
Washoe uses the ASL sign for "hat."

have been taught to use systems of signs based on the American Sign Language for the deaf, and Kanzi has been taught to use a computer that employs arbitrary symbols to represent words or concepts.

By 1991, Washoe had a signing vocabulary of 240 signs (Figure 10–8). In 1992, she was moved to a new research facility at Central Washington University. Here she joined other signing chimpanzees and is participating in many projects, including the study of chimp-to-chimp signing.

In the late 1980s, reports of a young bonobo named Kanzi began to appear. Although raised around chimpanzees who were being taught to use a computer, Kanzi had no training in this skill (Figure 10–9). The computer had 250 symbols on a keyboard. Each symbol, called a **lexigram,** represented a word. Investigators at the Yerkes Regional Primate Center in Georgia were amazed when Kanzi spontaneously began to use the computer and "asked" to be chased. Kanzi also seems to understand spoken language and responds correctly to certain oral commands.

Some of those who work with Kanzi maintain that he has a simple understanding of grammar. For instance, if a chimpanzee named Matata initiated an action, Kanzi would describe the incident by putting the verbal aspect second—"Matata bite." However, if Matata was acted upon, the verb would go first, as in "grabbed Matata," meaning someone grabbed Matata. By 1991, Kanzi's custodians said the six-year-old bonobo knew 90 lexigrams and understood 200 spoken words and 650 sentences.

Gorillas were once thought to be less intelligent than chimpanzees, but this is being challenged by the work with the gorilla Koko (Figure 10–10). By the age of seven years, Koko had an active vocabulary of 375 ASL signs, many more than Washoe or other chimpanzees had acquired at any age. According to her handlers, Koko identifies herself in the mirror and in photographs, and invents words and phrases. In 1998, Koko went online in what her handlers called the first interspecies chat over the Internet. Through her tutor Francine Patterson, Koko answered questions posed by humans online. These and other behaviors indicate an intelligence far beyond what was expected before studies of the language ability of apes began.

**Skepticism about Ape-Language Studies**  The above information has been presented from the point of view of the researchers involved in the studies. With few exceptions, the general scientific community of the 1960s and 1970s accepted these reports at face value, but in 1979 and the early 1980s, the first extensive criticisms began to appear.

One of the most vocal critics of the ape-language studies is H. S. Terrace.[12] Terrace is not convinced that the apes display an understanding or use of grammar. He points out that in word sequences, the ape might simply be using two or more behaviors that individually get the same reward. For example, Terrace believes that Washoe's use of the sequence "more drink" does not display the animal's knowledge of *more* as a modifier of *drink.* Instead, he believes that the ape has learned through conditioning that either the word *more* or the word *drink* will be rewarded with food, a hug, a pat, or other positive reinforcement; the combination of signs maximizes the chance of reward and need not imply any knowledge of grammar.

The contention that Kanzi understands word order may also be premature. Not enough data have

---

[12]H. S. Terrace, "How Nim Chimpsky Changed My Mind," *Psychology Today* 13 (November 1979), pp. 65–77.

**FIGURE 10-9  Kanzi**
Kanzi is a bonobo who, in some ways, seems more adept at learning language than chimpanzees.
Kanzi communicates by pointing to symbols on keyboards.

been presented to make a strong argument for his understanding of grammar. If the apes have no real understanding of grammar, then this might mean that ASL or a computer readout does not have the same meaning for the ape as it does for the human. If this is so, then the ape's lack of a true lexicon and grammar indicates a lack of language abilities, at least as reflected in the ape-language studies done so far.

Terrace also offers another type of criticism. He believes that ape researchers of the 1960s and 1970s were giving their subjects subtle subconscious clues as to the correct response. He noted this in his own research with Neam Chimpsky ("Nim" for short), the chimpanzee named for the famous linguist Noam Chomsky. When Terrace studied videotapes of his own assistants communicating with Nim, he discovered subtle nonverbal prompting. He saw the same type of prompting in films of other subjects.

Terrace also found that Nim's utterances did not increase in length over time and that Nim's re-

sponses were not usually spontaneous but followed the researcher's utterances 88 percent of the time. In addition, many of Nim's responses were imitations of the human utterances; the ape rarely added information to a "conversation" and had no concept of turn taking. In other words, to Terrace, what Nim and other apes were doing did not look like human language.

There is much debate over Terrace's observations. Researchers A. Allen Gardner and Beatrice Gardner, who worked with Washoe, have labeled Terrace's Nim project "poor" and a "gross oversimplification."[13] Others have said that Terrace is making distinctions between human language and ways in which apes produce utterances that have no basis in fact.

If Terrace is correct, then language may indeed be a uniquely human potential. On the other hand,

---

[13]J. Greenberg, "Ape Talk: More Than 'Pigeon' English?" *Science News* 117 (1980), p. 298.

**FIGURE 10–10  Koko**
Koko was the first gorilla to be taught a form of American Sign Language. Here she is shown making the sign "smoke" for her cat Smoky.

if Washoe, Kanzi, and Koko are really using language, then language can no longer be qualitatively considered the exclusive domain of our species. In the long run, both schools of thought may be missing the point. Duane Rumbaugh points out that language may not be simply an all-or-none phenomenon.[14] If apes are evolutionarily as close to humans as all areas of study indicate, then perhaps ape and human linguistic abilities evolved from a common ability of an ancient ancestor. The two abilities may have simply evolved differently, maintaining some similarities because of a common source. Whatever the answers are, the ape-

language studies in the twenty-first century are guaranteed to be exciting and controversial.

### Intelligence in Nonhuman Primates

The concept of intelligence is an elusive one. Social scientists cannot even form a consensus on the nature of intelligence in humans. Most psychologists see intelligence generally as a capacity to deal effectively with the environment by acting rationally and purposefully. The concept is more problematic when related to nonhumans. For instance, apes have learned to use American Sign Language to some degree. The fact that they can use arbitrary and discrete symbols in an open way to convey displaced information suggests a continuity with human thought processes. Recent research on monkeys also displays this continuity. Does this mean that they

---

[14]Ibid., pp. 298–300.

are acting rationally or purposefully? Some researchers say yes; others say that their actions are simply conditioned by their human handlers.

**What Do Monkeys Know?** Dorothy L. Cheney and Robert M. Seyfarth provide insight into the question of monkey intelligence.[15] They designed experiments to see whether African vervet monkeys understand the concept of rank within their dominance hierarchy.

To form powerful alliances, individual vervet monkeys attempt to groom other monkeys that are higher in rank. If a monkey approaches a grooming pair, the invader will displace the monkey it outranks. If the intruder outranks both grooming monkeys, which one will the intruder displace? In 29 out of 30 cases, the more dominant intruder displaced the lower-ranking monkey of the pair (Figure 10–11). Cheney and Seyfarth conclude that the monkey who stays put knows its own rank relative to the invading monkey and knows its rank relative to the monkey who is displaced. The monkey who stays also knows the other two monkeys' relationship to each other. "In other words, she [the monkey who stays] must recognize a rank hierarchy."[16]

Cheney and Seyfarth also explore the extent to which vervets understand their own calls. Vervet monkeys are territorial; when a monkey from one group first sights a neighboring group approaching, they produce a *wrr wrr* warning. If the neighboring group approaches aggressively, the members of the invaded group produce a chuttering sound (Figure 10–12).

The researchers conducted an experiment in which they played a recording of one vervet's *wrr*s to its group when no neighboring group was in sight. The other animals soon learned to ignore the false alarm and also ignored the chutters of the recorded monkey. However, the animals reacted normally to all other calls of the monkey who had "cried wolf." Cheney and Seyfarth conclude that

since the *wrr*s and chutters are acoustically dissimilar, the vervets can perceive that *wrr*s and chutters carry similar meaning. Since the recorded monkey was unreliable with one alarm call *(wrr)*, the vervets also ignored its other alarm call (chutter).

Cheney and Seyfarth's work, and the work of several other primatologists, suggests that monkeys generalize about relationships between individuals and represent meaning in their calls. Unlike the case with humans, the monkeys' potential in these areas is very limited. Even if every primate call had meaning, a primate species usually has fewer than 20 calls; the English language contains about 500,000 words. This represents an enormous quantitative difference. Cheney and Seyfarth point out that there are also qualitative differences between monkeys and humans. For instance, monkeys do not know what they know; that is, they do not seem to be aware that they know things. Also, monkeys seem unable to "attribute mental states to others or to recognize that others' behavior is . . . caused by motives, beliefs, and desires."[17]

**What Distinguishes Primates?** The work with vervet monkeys suggests that intelligence is not an all-or-none characteristic. The developing body of evidence from monkey and ape research projects has led Susan Essock-Vitale and Robert M. Seyfarth to summarize some of the things that set primates apart, at least quantitatively, from most other animals. These behaviors include the facts that primates

> recognize each other as individuals, distinguish kin from nonkin, and behave differently toward those of different dominance ranks. Experiments suggest that these social skills are learned and that they develop with experience. Moreover, primates can remember past interactions, seem able to predict the behavior of others based on prior observations, and discriminate among their own and other individuals' close associations. . . . Finally, although primates are not qualitatively different from other animals in this respect, they do seem outstanding in their ability to maintain simultaneously many different kinds of relationships,

---

[15]D. L. Cheney and R. M. Seyfarth, *How Monkeys See the World* (Chicago: University of Chicago Press, 1990).
[16]Ibid., p. 82.

[17]Ibid., p. 312.

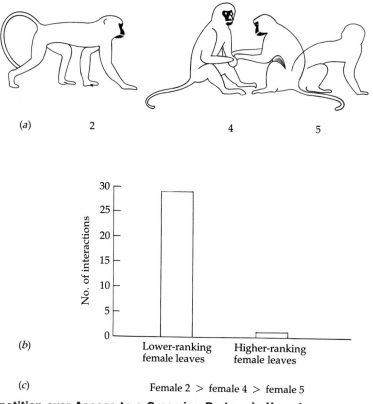

(a)      2           4          5

(b)

(c)                    Female 2 > female 4 > female 5

**FIGURE 10–11   Competition over Access to a Grooming Partner in Vervet Monkeys**
(a) A high-ranking female (2) approaches two lower-ranking females (4 and 5). (b) The lower-ranking female (5) is almost always supplanted. (c) This suggests that the monkeys recognize a rank hierarchy.

each finely tuned to the individual characteristics of the participants.[18]

These qualities point to the nonhuman primates' great mental abilities as compared with those of other animals. Yet we can only speculate as to the evolutionary meaning of this complex behavior. As with humans, behavior based on learning allows for more behavioral flexibility than that determined strictly by heredity. This behavioral flexibility allows the animal to choose a variety of strategies, which is especially important when unusual events occur and biologically stereotyped behavior may

prove disastrous. In the complexity of the nonhuman primates' social behavior, and in their ability to manufacture tools, we see reflections of what may have been the roots of human culture.

**The Evolution of Intelligence**   Studies of intelligence in nonhuman primates have focused on their ability to solve complex problems. Certainly, problem solving is one aspect of what we call intelligence. Several hypotheses have been proposed for the evolution of intelligence and an increase in brain size among primates. These ideals generally fall into two areas. One hypothesis centers around the fact that most primates live in large social units. Successful living in such societies provides situations of conflict, competition, and cooperation. Animals that have the capabilities to form close ties

[18]S. Essock-Vitale and R. M. Seyfarth, "Intelligence and Social Cognition," in B. B. Smuts et al. (eds.), *Primate Societies* (Chicago: University of Chicago Press, 1987), p. 452. ©1986 by the University of Chicago. All rights reserved.

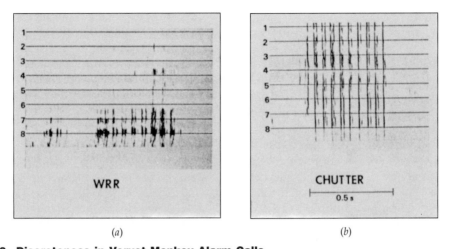

**FIGURE 10–12 Discreteness in Vervet Monkey Alarm Calls**
The *wrr* and chutter are both calls that are given in the presence of another group. (*a*) The *wrr* is given when a neighboring group has first been spotted. (*b*) The acoustically different chutter is produced under more aggressive conditions of contact. Pictured are spectrograms, which are visualizations of sound.

and minimize conflict, for example, are those who are most likely to successfully reproduce.

The other hypothesis centers on the shift to frugavory, the emphasis on fruit in the diet as opposed to leaves and insects. Trees that are producing fruit at a given point in time are widely scattered in the tropical forest and primates must move from one area to another through the forest in order to find food. However, particular trees will bear fruit in a predictable pattern over time. Unlike grazing for leaves, the successful primate forager must develop a mental map of fruit resources that includes the location of fruiting trees as well as the path to those trees. This map is further complicated by the periodic production of fruit at certain times of the year. Some anthropologists believe that the evolution of the capability of learning such mental maps and timetables is the basis of primate intelligence.

In reality, intelligence is a complex characteristic and the forces of natural selection that favored its evolution were most likely also complex. Factors that may have led to the evolution of intelligence may have included living in large social units, concentration on the eating of fruits, behaviors to defeat or avoid predators, and behaviors that would allow for increased size of range. In other words, there was most likely a complex interplay of many factors that led to the evolution of greater intelligence.

## Summary

Research into primate behavior reveals that many nonhuman primates, especially monkeys and apes, show protocultural behavior. The study of the ways in which behavior is learned and transmitted in nonhuman primates, we hope, will aid in the understanding of the development and nature of human culture.

The terms *communication* and *language* are not synonymous. All organisms communicate in that they transmit and receive messages. These messages need not be symbolic or involve any form of thought; they simply give information. Language has been regarded as a uniquely human form of communication that involves symbolic representations that are arbitrary and discrete. These characteristics, along with openness and displacement, as well as other features not discussed in this text, when taken as a whole differentiate language from the call systems of nonhuman primates and the communication systems of all other organisms.

Nevertheless, experimental work on apes has raised questions regarding the linguistic abilities of nonhuman primates. Can apes be taught human language and then transmit this knowledge to their offspring or other untrained apes? Some investigators believe that the research done with Washoe, Kanzi, Koko, and other apes shows that they have at least rudimentary linguistic ability. Other researchers see the supposed linguistic behavior of apes as nothing more than stimulus-response learning. Still others take a position somewhere between these two conclusions. As new research methods are developed, the early twenty-first century may be a time when more concrete answers are provided to the question of the ape's linguistic abilities.

Perhaps most anthropologists would agree that members of our species are the only living organisms with the capability of asking the questions: What am I? and Why am I? In the search for the answers to these questions, anthropologists are carefully studying the behavior of closely related species. Some nonhuman primates display mental characteristics that were once thought to be distinctly human. These include the ability to categorize experiences and convey distinct and discrete meaning in their calls.

## STUDY QUESTIONS

1. What is the nature of the human band? What are some points of comparison between the human band and other primate social arrangements?
2. What characterizes male–female relationships in human societies? In what ways do these relationships differ from those of other primates?
3. Are the words *language* and *communication* synonymous? Explain.
4. In what ways is language different from other animal communication systems?
5. Why is there controversy over the contention made by some researchers that apes can learn human language?
6. Research on vervet monkeys has shown these animals to be capable of behaviors once thought to be unique to humans. What are these behaviors, and in what ways did investigators discover that monkeys were capable of them?
7. What is meant by the term *protoculture*? How do monkeys show protocultural behavior?

## SUGGESTED READINGS

Cheney, D., and R. Seyfarth. *How Monkeys See the World.* Chicago: University of Chicago Press, 1990. This book explores such questions as: What do monkeys know about the world? Are they aware of what they know?

It presents the results of research into these and other questions dealing with the issues of primate intelligence and cognition.

Fouts, R., and S. T. Mills. *Next of Kin: What Chimpanzees Have Taught Me about Who We Are.* New York: Morrow, 1998. This is the fascinating story of Roger Fouts' 32-year relationship with Washoe, the signing chimpanzee.

Goodall, J. *The Chimpanzees of Gombe: Patterns of Behavior.* Cambridge, Mass.: Belknap Press, 1986. This book brings together the data gathered from over two decades of research on the chimpanzees of the Gombe.

Heltne, P. G., and L. A. Marquardt (eds.). *Understanding Chimpanzees.* Cambridge, Mass.: Harvard University Press, 1989. This volume includes 33 papers on chimpanzees, 7 of which deal with ape-language studies and chimpanzee intelligence.

Michel, A. *The Story of Nim: The Chimp Who Learned Language.* New York: Knopf, 1980. This is a short book with marvelous photographs explaining how H. S. Terrace attempted to teach language to a chimpanzee.

Parker, S. T., R. W. Mitchell, and M. L. Boccia. *Self-Awareness in Animals and Humans: Developmental Perspectives.* New York: Cambridge University Press, 1994. This collection of original articles explores the meaning of self-awareness, how to measure self-awareness, and which species are capable of it and why.

Sebeok, T. A., and J. Umiker-Sebeok. *Speaking of Apes: A Critical Anthology of Two-Way Communication with Man.* New York: Plenum, 1980. This book looks at ape language from a skeptical point of view.

Terrace, H. S. *Nim.* New York: Knopf, 1979. This book presents the first systematic and extensive negative criticism of the ape-language studies of the 1960s and 1970s.

## SUGGESTED WEB SITES

Central Washington University: Chimp and Human Communication Institute:
http://www.cwu.edu/~cwuchci/

Evolution of Primate Intelligence:
http://hcs.harvard.edu/~husn/BRAIN/vol2/Primate.html

!Kung foragers:
http://www.lawrence.edu/dept/anthropology/kungsan/kungsan.html

Additional web sites are listed in the *Workbook* that accompanies this text.

# THE EFE: FORAGERS OF THE CONGO BASIN

Between 150,000 and 200,000 short-statured people, known to outsiders as Pygmies, live in the tropical rain forest in seven African countries. Anthropologist Robert C. Bailey has studied a group called the Efe. The semi-nomadic Efe are foragers who provide the Lese, a larger-statured group of farmers, with forest products and field labor in return for the garden food that provides the Efe with two-thirds of their calories.

Major Pygmy populations

**FIGURE 10–A**  An Efe man carries an 18-kilogram (40-pound) duiker, a type of antelope, which he killed with a metal-tipped arrow.

GHANA
NIGERIA
BENIN
TOGO
CAMEROON
CENTRAL AFRICAN REPUBLIC
SUDAN
EQUATORIAL GUINEA
Zaire (Congo)
Author's study area
UGANDA
GABON
CONGO
Lake Victoria
RWANDA
BURUNDI
CABINDA (ANGOLA)
ZAIRE
TANZANIA
Lake Tanganyika
ANGOLA
MALAWI
ZAMBIA
ZIMBABWE
MOZAMBIQUE
BOTSWANA
SWAZILAND
SOUTH AFRICA
LESOTHO

**Figure 10–B**   A group of men divide up a kill. The largest portion of meat always goes to the hunter who first wounds the animal. Because the men do many things besides hunt as a group, they spend a lot of time together. However, the one individual a married man spends the most time with is his wife.

**Figure 10–C**   An Efe man repairs arrows while his wife sits at the entrance of the hut preparing food. The man's daughter-in-law (far left) is also involved in the food preparation. Efe women do much of the heavy work, as well. They gather and carry large pieces of fire wood to the camp and carry most of the family's belongings when the camp is moved. When Bailey asked an Efe man why the women carry more than the men, the man dismissed the question by replying: "Women are stronger than men. ...I could never carry all that weight. Besides, men have to be free to use their weapons. What if an elephant charges?"

*R.C. Bailey, "The Efe: Archers of the African Rain Forest," *National Geographic,* 176 (November 1989), 686.

## CHAPTER 11

# The Record of the Past

*Most fossil animals no longer possess soft tissues like muscles, flesh, and brain; their bones are no longer articulated, and some of their bones are broken or destroyed. Their bones and teeth have been mineralized. Fossil animals do not live in social groups; they have no home range or preferred habitat; and they do not move, feed, play, learn, reproduce, fight, or engage in any other behaviors. Their bones are not associated with those of the animals they interacted with in life. In short, through death most evidence of the interesting information about animals—what they look like, what they eat, how they move, where they live, and so on—is lost. Only through indirect evidence and painstaking study can any information about their habits and lifestyle be reconstructed.*[1]

—Pat Shipman

## Chapter Outline

**C**onfucius wrote, "Study the past, if you would divine the future." Through the ages, people have pondered their history. The anthropologist is interested in the past for what it will reveal about the nature and development of humans as biological, social, and cultural beings. The anthropologist

---

[1]P. Shipman, *Life History of a Fossil: An Introduction to Taphonomy and Paleoecology* (Cambridge, Mass.: Harvard University Press, 1981), p. 3. Reprinted by permission of Harvard University Press.

believes, as Confucius did, that a knowledge of the events leading to the present human condition is an important tool for coping with the problems that confront us.

The past reflects a type of biological immortality. Life begets life, and through the processes of reproduction, the present becomes a slightly modified reconstruction of the immediate past. There is, however, still another type of immortality—that of the fossilized remains of an organism. It is through the preservation of body parts that the anthropologist can see into the past and attempt to reconstruct the history of life.

## FOSSILS AND THEIR INTERPRETATION

A **fossil** is the remains or traces of an ancient organism. Fossils have interested people for thousands of years; in fact, prehistoric societies may have attached magical or religious significance to fossils. The Greeks and Romans not only knew of fossils but also made some assumptions about their meaning. About 500 B.C., some believed that fossil fish represented the ancestors of all life. During the Middle Ages, knowledge and theories about fossils changed. Fossils were considered remnants of attempts at special creation, objects that had fallen from the heavens, and even devices of the devil.

In the fifteenth century, Leonardo da Vinci wrote: "The mountains where there are shells were formerly shores beaten by waves, and since then they have been elevated to the heights we see today." From that time on, debate has raged over the true meaning of geological formations and the fossils found in them. Only in the past few hundred years have scholars agreed that fossils are the remains of ancient organisms and that they can tell us much about the history of life.

### The Nature of Fossils

The "immortality" of the body is limited; most organisms have left no traces of their existence upon our planet. Their dead bodies were consumed by other organisms and eventually, through the process of decay, were absorbed into the soil.

**Taphonomy** is the study of the processes that affect an organism after death, leading in some cases to fossilization. Fossilization is actually a rare event, since several conditions must be met in order for an organism to be preserved.

First, the remains of the organism must be suitable for fossilization. Different parts of the body decay at different rates. It is therefore not surprising that the vast majority of fossils uncovered are those with hard tissues such as teeth, bones, and shell. These decay more slowly than soft tissues such as skin, brain, and muscles. Vast numbers of ancient organisms that lacked hard material probably will never be known.

Second, a deceased organism must be buried very quickly after death, before it is consumed by scavengers or destroyed by natural elements. The probability of fossilization is greatly increased when the body settles in stagnant water. The lack of oxygen discourages bacterial decay, and the lack of currents in the water minimizes movements of the body. More unusual are volcanic eruptions or violent storms that quickly cover the body with layers of volcanic ash or mud.

Finally, the material in which the remains are buried must be favorable for fossilization. Some soils, such as the acidic soils of the tropics, actually destroy bone. Also, minerals must be present that will infiltrate the bone, teeth, or shell and replace the organic matter. This is the process of fossilization.

Only on rare occasions are entire organisms found that include soft tissue. In 1991, a partially freeze-dried body of a man was found at an elevation of 3200 meters (10,500 feet) in the Italian Alps near the Austrian border. The corpse was not the victim of a recent skiing accident; it was the victim of a misfortune that took place about 5300 years ago. Even the man's internal organs, clothing, and tools had been preserved (Figure 11–1).

Although less ancient, the remains of gold-laden, ritually sacrificed Inca children were found in the Andes in the late 1990s. Even better preserved than the body from the Italian Alps, studies of these 600- to 500-year-old children will tell us about diseases and cultural practices in pre-Columbian America. In 1995, a frozen mummified body of a 12- to 14-year-old Inca girl was discovered at the 6300-meter (20,700-foot) level of Mount Ampato in the Peruvian Andes, where she had been sacrificed about 500 years ago.

Mummified remains are also known from the

**FIGURE 11–1 The "Ice Man"**
The partially freeze-dried body of a man who died about 5300 years ago.

hot, dry regions of Egypt, the American Southwest, and the western coastal deserts of South America. Other preserved bodies have been discovered in the peat bogs of northern Europe. These rare finds are extremely valuable because they provide direct evidence of skin, hair, stomach contents (for diet analysis), and much more. Although not of direct interest to anthropologists, insects and spiders are found embedded in amber, which is fossilized tree resin.

The vast majority of fossils exist in the form of mineralized bone (Figure 11–2a). As the bone lies buried in the ground, minerals replace the organic matter in the bone. Traces of ancient life forms also may be found as molds and casts. A **mold** is a cavity left in firm sediments by the decayed body of an organism; nothing of the organism itself is left. This mold, if filled with some substance, becomes a **cast** that reflects the shape of the fossil (Figure 11–2b). Tracks and burrows of animals have been preserved this way (Figure 11–2c). Materials that were ingested and excreted by animals also can be preserved; they tell us much about the diet of the animals. These forms of preservation, however, are

rarely found in the primate fossil record; ancient primates are best known by their fossilized bones and teeth.

**Biases in the Fossil Record**

The fossil record is not a complete record of the history of living organisms upon the face of the earth. It is but a sample of the plants and animals that once lived. Charles Darwin wrote:

> I look at the natural geological record, as a history of the world imperfectly kept, and written in a changing dialect; of this history we possess the last volume alone, relating only to two or three countries. Of this volume, only here and there a short chapter has been preserved; and of each page, only here and there a few lines.[2]

**Sampling Error in the Fossil Record** Because the probability of preservation varies from region to region, some organisms are better represented in the

[2]C. Darwin, *On the Origin of Species by Means of Natural Selection* (London: J. Murray, 1859), pp. 310–311.

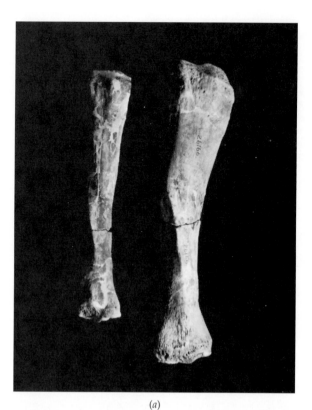

(a)

(b)

**FIGURE 11–2 Fossils**
The remains of prehistoric life may take the form of (a) fossilized bone (limb bones of *Baluchterium*), (b) cast (*Archeopteryx*), and (c) tracks (dinosaur).

(c)

fossil record than others, while still others are totally unknown. Species living under conditions in which the odds of fossilization are good, such as freshwater lakes and ponds, will be common as fossils. Terrestrial animals, especially those living in tropical areas, are fossilized much less often.

Because of differential preservation, the frequency of fossil specimens does not necessarily reflect the size of the living populations represented by the fossils. Birds, for example, are not preserved as frequently as mammals, and so the fossil record shows a scarcity of bird species. In reality, birds may have been a predominant life form in a particular area at a particular time.

Another factor in sampling is the accessibility of sites. In some areas, important fossil beds may have formed, but they are not exposed at the surface. Some areas, such as southwestern France and

Kenya, have been extensively explored, while other areas, such as southeast Asia, remain virtually untouched. A major reason for this geographical sampling error is politics. Some governments have been hostile to anthropological research, and military activity has made visits to other areas impossible. On the other hand, many governments and governmental institutions, such as the National Museums of Kenya, have been extremely active in this type of research. The result has been an uneven sampling of sites in various regions of the world.

An important factor determining the locations excavated is the individual interests of paleoanthropologists. Most excavations occur in deposits representing geographical areas and geological periods that are considered important at the time the research is planned. As time goes on and our knowledge of human paleontology grows, new areas and new periods are considered critical.

Another factor that affects geographical sampling is money. Fieldwork can be very expensive, and the research interests of a scientist must be mirrored by the agencies financing the project. Several factors affect the cost of paleoanthropological research. A low-paid graduate student working in his or her own country may be able to conduct a short-term project for relatively little money. On the other hand, a full-scale overseas multidisciplinary operation may cost several hundred thousand dollars.

**Gaps in Fossil Sequences**  It is sometimes possible to follow the evolution of successive populations for millions of years, only to encounter a period characterized by an absence of fossils. This, in turn, may be followed by the reemergence of the population or by the appearance of a descendant of that population. Such gaps are common, and we will see many examples in subsequent chapters.

Several factors can cause gaps to appear in the fossil record. For one thing, organisms do not necessarily stay in the same habitat or niche. If a species moves into a new habitat, the probability of fossilization may change. Although the population seems to have disappeared, in reality it simply may not have been preserved during the time it resided in that habitat.

Another factor bringing about gaps in the fossil record is a change in **sedimentation,** which is the deposition of materials carried in water, wind, or glaciers. Most fossils are found in sedimentary deposits. If sedimentation ceases in a particular area, preservation may also cease and a gap in the fossil record will result. In addition, erosion may destroy sedimentary beds that have already been laid down.

**Sampling of Populations**  Within a given species, the collection of actual specimens recovered represents a sample of the individual organisms that once lived. Anna K. Behrensmeyer estimates that only 0.004 percent of the hominids once living at Omo, Ethiopia, are represented in the fossil record.[3]

Fossilization is a chance phenomenon; it represents a sample of individuals of a given population. This forces us to question if a specific individual is an average member of the population, especially if a species is known only from fragmentary remains or from a single individual. Since the probabilities for fossilization are so low, it is very difficult to know the range of variation of a species and we must often define a species on the basis of a single specimen.

In situations in which a species is defined on the basis of a reasonable sample of individuals, some unrepresentative fossils are known. For example, the first relatively complete Neandertal skeleton to be discovered is the one from La Chapelle-aux-Saints, France. This skeleton became the prototype of the Neandertals. The Neandertals were pictured as creatures with unusual posture, hunched over and bowlegged, with massive brow ridges and bestial features.

The specimen from La Chapelle-aux-Saints is not an average Neandertal, however, but the skeleton of an old man suffering from an advanced case of arthritis of the spine. If a number of Neandertals are compared, this particular individual is one of the least modern in appearance. Today we know that the term *Neandertal* is a general designation for a group of hominids that show a great deal of intraspecific variation.

[3]A. K. Behrensmeyer, "Taphonomy and Paleoecology in the Hominid Fossil Record," *Yearbook of Physical Anthropology 1975* (Washington, D.C.: American Association of Physical Anthropologists, 1976), pp. 36–50.

## Differential Preservation

As we have seen, whether a particular organism or parts of an organism are preserved or not depends on a number of factors. The probability of a bone's being preserved after death is known as that bone's **preservation potential.** By observing the fate of dead bodies in the field and by conducting many laboratory experiments, taphonomists have gathered data showing that the preservation potential of a particular bone depends on its size, shape, and composition and its behavior in water.

Bone size can be thought of in terms of volume. Very large bones, such as skulls and mandibles, are preserved more frequently than small bones. Bone composition is also a factor. Because carnivores prefer spongy bone, compact bones are more frequently left to be incorporated into the fossil record. Also important is the shape of the bone. Relatively thin, flat bones, such as the innominate and scapula, tend to break easily. These bones are infrequently found as fossils and, when recovered, are often broken and fragmented.

The **hydraulic behavior** of a bone refers to its transport and dispersal in water. Most fossils are derived from bodies that have been deposited in water environments; the fossils are found in sedimentary beds that are formed in water. A bone's composition, its size, and its shape are all important factors in determining what will happen to the bone in water. Ribs and vertebrae are easily transported by water, and so they are frequently moved by water considerable distances from the rest of the skeleton. As they move, they are often abraded by the gravel beds of the stream or river. On the other hand, skulls and mandibles are transported only by rapidly moving streams. Table 11–1 and Figure 11–3 summarize the forces that act to destroy bones after the death of an organism.

## What Can Fossils Tell Us?

The fossil record is like a puzzle with many pieces missing and still others distorted. Yet a picture, although incomplete, does emerge. Often the image is only an outline of the past; sometimes it is a well-documented history.

With a few exceptions, the fossil record consists solely of skeletal remains, but much can be inferred

### TABLE 11–1

**DESTRUCTIVE FORCES ACTING ON BONE**

| Destructive force | Effects |
| --- | --- |
| Predators and scavengers (including hominids) | Consumption, gnawing, breakage |
| Use of bones as tools | Breakage, wear |
| Hydraulic transport | Winnowing of assemblage, abrasion |
| Subaerial transport (rolling, sliding along streambed) | Abrasion, breakage |
| Aeolian (wind) transport | Pitting, winnowing of assemblage |
| Weathering | Cracking, crumbling, exfoliation |
| Decay by chemicals, roots, insects, soil, water | Disintegration, breakdown of structure |

*Source:* Adapted from P. Shipman, *Life History of a Fossil: An Introduction to Taphonomy and Paleoecology* (Cambridge, Mass.: Harvard University Press, 1981), p. 41. Reprinted by permission of the Harvard University Press.

about the body from the skeleton. For example, areas of muscle attachment can be seen on the surface of bone, often as ridges or roughened areas. From this information, the shape, size, and function of various muscles can be reconstructed. This is important in the reconstruction of locomotor patterns.

Once the musculature has been reconstructed, we can get some idea of what the organism might have looked like by placing a skin over the musculature (Figure 11–4). The fossil record, however, gives no indication of the color of the skin or of the amount of hair on the body.

The relative size of the eye socket, nasal cavities, and hearing apparatus can tell us a great deal about which senses were most important when the animal was alive. The evolution of vision in the primates can be seen in the formation of the eye socket and the frontal position of the eyes on the skull.

Brains are never fossilized, although brain matter has been found from fairly recent times in bodies preserved in wet sites such as bogs. However, some inferences about brain size can be made from the brain case. An examination of the inside sur-

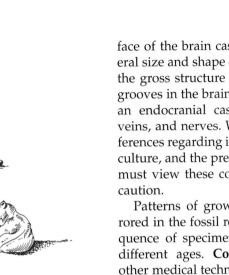

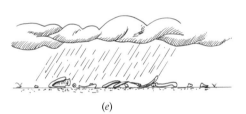

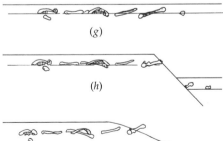

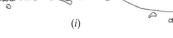

face of the brain case, which conforms to the general size and shape of the brain, gives some idea of the gross structure of the brain itself. In addition, grooves in the brain case, which are clearly seen in an endocranial cast, are indications of arteries, veins, and nerves. While such data have led to inferences regarding intelligence, the development of culture, and the presence or absence of speech, one must view these conclusions with a great deal of caution.

Patterns of growth and development are mirrored in the fossil record when one discovers a sequence of specimens representing individuals of different ages. **Computerized tomography** and other medical technologies are being used by paleoanthropologists to discover features such as nonerupted teeth that are embedded within the fossil jaw. These findings provide evidence for reconstructing age at death and patterns of dental development and maturation, as well as for reconstructing life expectancies and population structure. **Paleopathology** deals with investigations of injuries and disease in prehistoric populations, such as arthritis and dental caries (cavities in teeth) in Neandertal skeletons.

In addition to information about the individual and the species, the presence of fossil remains of animals in association with human remains, the remains of human activity, and the geological context all tell us much about the living patterns and ecological relations of the early hominids. Figure 11–5 shows the interrelationships of various types of data and interpretations that can be used to build a picture of the early hominids.

Hominid fossils and **artifacts,** the material remains of human behavior, are the primary data used in the reconstruction of technology, subsistence activities and diet, land-use patterns, and

**FIGURE 11–3  The Process of Fossilization**
(*a*) A living animal. (*b*) The carcass of the recently dead animal. (*c*) Predators feed on the carcass, destroying and disarticulating many bones. (*d*) Trampling by other animals further breaks up the bones. (*e*) Weathering by rain, sun, and other elements cracks and splits many of the bones. (*f*) The roots of plants invade many bones. (*g*) The bones are fossilized. (*h*) Faulting displaces and further breaks bones. (*i*) Fossils are exposed on surface by erosion.

**FIGURE 11–4  Flesh Reconstruction**
A flesh reconstruction of *Homo erectus* from China.

even, to a limited extent, group social structure. **Paleoanthropology,** the interdisciplinary study of prehistoric hominids and related forms, combines data from many disciplines, such as geology, **paleontology** (the study of fossils), **palynology** (the study of fossil pollen), **paleoecology,** and taphonomy, to reconstruct the environment in which the hominids functioned. Of course, the most important information anthropologists derive from the fossil record is evidence of evolutionary processes. For it is in the fossil record that the actual remains of early forms are found.

### Taxonomy and the Fossil Record

In 1963, George Gaylord Simpson wrote:

> Men and all recent and fossil organisms pertinent to their affinities are animals, and the appropriate language for discussing their classification and relationships is that of animal taxonomy. . . . It is notorious

that hominid nomenclature, particularly, has become chaotic.[4]

Prerequisite to any discussion of the fossil record is an understanding of the problems of taxonomy and fossils.

**The Species Concept in the Fossil Record**   Fossil taxonomy is one of the most provocative areas in paleoanthropology. With each new find, a new debate begins over the fossil's placement in the evolutionary scheme, and a major problem is the definition of species when applied to fossils. Since the definition of species for living populations is based on the criterion of reproductive success, the difficulties of applying this concept to the fossil record are obvious.

There are two schools of thought concerning the definition of species in the fossil record, and they are diametrically opposed to each other in philosophical outlook. The **typological** viewpoint embodies the ancient philosophy developed by Plato, which holds that basic variation of a type is illusory and that only fixed ideal types are real. According to this concept of the archetype, which was introduced in the discussion of taxonomy in Chapter 6, two fossils that differ from each other in certain respects represent two types and, hence, are two different species.

The typological viewpoint has dominated human paleontology for what are probably psychological reasons more than anything else. The discovery of a new fossil is a highly emotional experience, and a new find becomes more significant if it can be said to represent a new species rather than simply being another specimen of an already known species.

The **populationist** viewpoint, on the other hand, maintains that only individuals have reality and that the type is illusory. More precisely, the populationists argue that since no two individuals are exactly alike, variation underlies all existence.

---

[4]G. G. Simpson, "The Meaning of Taxonomic Statements," in S. C. Washburn (ed.), *Classification and Human Evolution*, Viking Fund Publications in Anthropology, No. 37 (New York: Wenner-Gren Foundation for Anthropological Research, 1963), pp. 4–5.

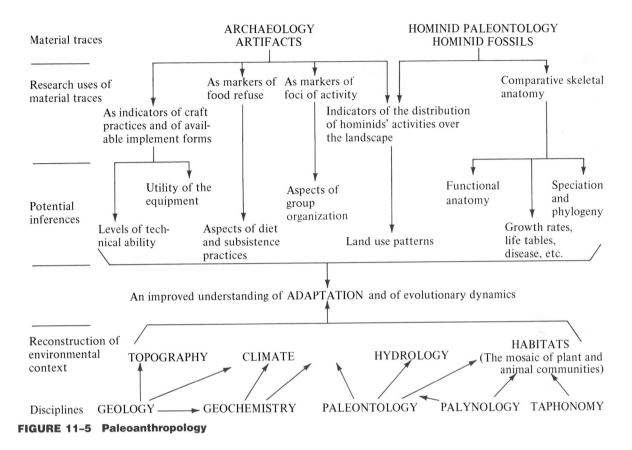

**FIGURE 11–5  Paleoanthropology**

Let us consider an example of the populationist viewpoint. The heights of four individuals are 155 centimeters (5 feet 1 inch), 160 centimeters (5 feet 3 inches), 170 centimeters (5 feet 7 inches), and 178 centimeters (5 feet 10 inches). Their average height is 166 centimeters (5 feet 5 inches). First, note that the individuals in the sample vary by 23 centimeters (9 inches), and second, note that no one individual in the sample is average. According to this reasoning, variation in fossil finds can be explained as divergence from a statistical average. If this variation is no greater than that which might be found within a related living species, the populationist sees no reason to separate the finds into different taxonomic categories.

To illustrate this point, Figure 11–6 shows a series of skulls that display a fair degree of variation in appearance. How many species are represented here? In this case, they are all modern gorillas, members of the species *Gorilla gorilla*. Yet a series of hominoid fossils that show this degree of varia-

tion would be broken up by many paleoanthropologists into a number of distinct species.

**The Paleospecies**  Among living organisms, the species is defined in the objective terms of reproductive isolation, yet neither reproductive isolating mechanisms nor gene frequencies can be seen in the fossil record. At best, geographical isolation can be inferred in some situations. In dealing with the fossil record, the taxonomist is restricted to an analysis of morphological variation, and, as has already been noted, variation within a species can be great.

Many anthropologists have concluded that since reproductive criteria cannot be applied to the fossil record, the species concept cannot be legitimately applied to fossil forms. Instead, we must speak of the **paleospecies,** which resembles the species but is defined in terms of morphological variation rather than in terms of genetic isolation and reproductive success. (Some paleoanthropologists speak of **chronospecies,** which are arbitrarily

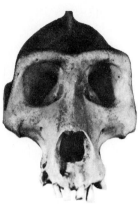

*(a)*      *(b)*

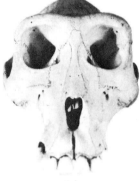
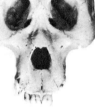

*(c)*      *(d)*

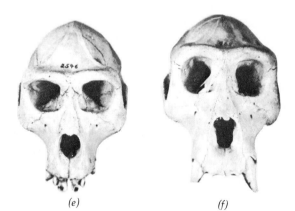

*(e)*      *(f)*

**FIGURE 11–6  Intraspecific Variation**
A series of six skulls, all members of the same species, *Gorilla gorilla*. Note the degree of variation: (*b*) and (*f*) are males, (*a*) and (*c*) are probably males, and (*d*) and (*e*) are probably females.

defined divisions of an evolutionary line.) A paleospecies is a group of similar fossils whose range of morphological variation does not exceed the range of variation within a closely related living species. Determination of a paleospecies requires detailed statistical analysis of both the fossil series and the living species being used for comparison.

Yet some paleontologists suggest that the range of variation may have been greater in some earlier populations than among related contemporary species. For example, over 1000 apelike fossils have been recovered from Lufeng, China. Some paleoanthropologists see clear evidence of two distinct species, *Ramapithecus lufengensis* and *Sivapithecus yunnanensis*. Charles E. Oxnard writes: "The marked differences between *Ramapithecus* which is always smaller and *Sivapithecus* is clear. These differences are far greater than those generally found between the sexes of extant forms, even between the sexes of such markedly dimorphic species as gorillas and orang-utans."[5] On the other hand, an analysis by Jay Kelley and Xu Qinghua leads them to the conclusion that these specimens represent a single species that exhibits a degree of sexual dimorphism in dimensions of the teeth that exceeds the degree of sexual dimorphism found among living orangutans and gorillas.[6]

It may be difficult to resolve this difference of opinion. The evidence consists primarily of teeth, although other parts of the skeletal anatomy are known; determination of sex on the basis of dental evidence is difficult. It is also very possible that a group of fossils includes the remains of individuals that originally lived at different times.

**Reasons for Variability in the Fossil Record**
Many differences among fossil specimens represent the emergence of new species and higher taxonomic groups. Nevertheless, much of the variation that often is interpreted as interspecific actually is intraspecific.

One form of intraspecific variation is that of age. Figure 11–7 shows the skulls of an infant and an

---

[5]C. E. Oxnard, *Fossils, Teeth and Sex* (Seattle: University of Washington Press, 1987), p. 93.
[6]J. Kelley and X. Qinghua, "Extreme Sexual Dimorphism in Miocene Hominoids," *Nature* 352 (1991), pp. 151–153.

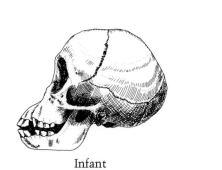

Infant

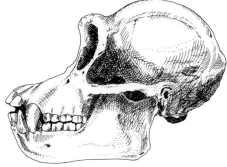

Adult

**FIGURE 11-7   Age Differences in Chimpanzee Skulls**
The skulls of an infant and an adult chimpanzee.

adult chimpanzee; note the absence of a prominent brow ridge and the generally more "human" appearance of the infant's skull. One must be extremely careful when using anything other than adult material in interpreting the fossil record.

Sexual dimorphism was discussed in Chapter 7. We saw that the male adult baboon is larger than the female, has longer canines, and has a mantle of fur over his shoulder. Thus, the sex of an adult baboon is easy to determine even from a skull alone. On the other hand, the gibbon shows little sexual dimorphism; unless the female is nursing a child, male and female gibbons cannot be distinguished at a distance. Evidence suggests that the early hominids showed a greater degree of sexual dimorphism than *Homo sapiens* does today.

Finally, variation within a species can be due to the simple fact that, as we saw in the discussion of genetics, no two individuals are phenotypically identical. One cannot expect any two fossil specimens to be exactly alike. Consider, for example, the tremendous variation within the species *Homo sapiens* with respect to stature, body build, and cranial capacity.

## Summary

The remains and traces of ancient organisms make up the fossil record, yet this record is far from being a complete history of life on earth. The process of fossilization is the subject matter of taphonomy. Fossilization is a rare event, because it depends on an organism's having hard parts, such as bones, teeth, or shells, and being buried immediately af-

ter death. The work of predators and scavengers, and the weathering effects of rain, heat, cold, and wind, often serve to destroy most or all of an organism before final burial takes place.

Because of the nature of fossilization, the fossil record is a biased sample of the totality of life that once existed. Fossilization is more apt to occur in some areas, such as at the bottom of lakes, than others, such as in tropical rain forests. Aquatic animals are preserved more frequently than those living in terrestrial habitats. Some parts of the world and some geological time spans have been more thoroughly explored for fossils than have others. A major problem of sampling is the realization that a fossil is a single individual. Is that individual typical of the species, or does it represent a deviation from the norm?

Fossils provide a great deal of information if they are studied carefully. From skeletal remains, the musculature can be reconstructed; from the musculature, one can get a good picture of the physical appearance of the animal when it was alive. The brain case provides some information about the brain itself. In addition, fossils provide data on growth and development patterns and injury and disease. The associated remains of animals, artifacts, and the geological context tell us much about ecological relationships and even, to some extent, the behavior of prehistoric populations.

A major problem in paleoanthropology is the application of taxonomic principles to the fossil record. The species concept as defined in terms of reproductive success cannot be applied to the fossil record. Instead, we must speak of pale-ospecies, which are defined in terms of morphological similarities and differences.

## GEOLOGICAL TIME

It is somewhat paradoxical that in order to learn more about the earth, scientists have investigated the nature of the moon. Yet both bodies, along with the sun and the other planets, are thought to have been formed at about the same time. Because the crust of the moon has not undergone as much alteration as that of the earth, the examination of moon rocks may give a better estimate of the age of the earth than an examination of the earth itself. This estimate now stands at about 4.6 billion years.

When people believed that the earth was only about 6000 years old, it was impossible to conceive of evolutionary theory in both the biological and the geological senses. While microevolution can be observed within a human life span, as we saw in the case of Darwin's finches, macroevolution requires an extremely long time span. Because the concept of deep time is so central to paleoanthropology, we must attempt to gain a feeling for long periods of time. This section looks at methods for

determining the age of fossils and the way in which geologists and paleontologists organize geological time.

## Stratigraphy

If a glass of river water sits for a period of time, a thin layer of material soon appears on the bottom of the glass; this layer consists of dirt and other debris that were suspended in the moving water of the river. The atmosphere, through wind and corrosive activities, and bodies of water, through their movements, erode away the land. When the water stops moving, the eroded material, called **sediment,** settles to the bottom under the influence of gravity, and a thin layer forms. In lakes, this process occurs on a much greater scale. Dead animals wash into lakes, where many settle into the bottom mud and become a part of the sedimentary deposit.

Over time, many layers develop, one on top of another. These layers, called **sedimentary beds,** or **strata,** are said to be stratified. Eventually, a lake will dry up, leaving a series of strata that, at some later point in time, may give up their fossils to the paleontologist. The investigation of the composition of the layers of the earth and their relationship to one another is the study of **stratigraphy.**

---

**BOX 11-1**

# What Is a Billion?

Paleontologists today hypothesize that the first life arose on earth about 4.4 to 3.8 billion years ago. The Cenozoic era, or the Age of Mammals, began about 65 million years ago. In the chapters to come, there are many dates more than 1 million years before the present.

Part of the student's task is learning these dates, as they are approximations of when the major events of primate evolution took place. It is one thing to memorize a date; it is quite another to comprehend that date, which is so many times greater than the human life span.

Yet failure to comprehend this vastness of time is failure to understand a major aspect of evolutionary history. Evolutionary changes are slow changes

that take place over vast durations of time. Even relatively fast changes, such as those postulated by the concept of punctuated equilibrium, occur over enormous stretches of time.

A million is 1000 thousand; a billion is 1000 million. Thus, saying that life began 3800 million years ago is the same as saying it began 3.8 billion years ago. A trillion is 1000 billion. These are huge numbers. The late astronomer Carl Sagan tells us how long it would take to count to these numbers if we were to count one number per second, night and day, starting with 1: it would take 17 minutes to count to a thousand, 12 days to count to a million, and 32 years to count to a billion![1]

To get a better feel for the depth of time, we can equate time with distance. Let us say that the history of the earth is represented by a highway stretching from New York to Los Angeles and that New York represents 4½ billion years ago, the age of the earth, and Los Angeles represents today. As we travel along this highway from east to west, the first forms of life appear in Indianapolis, the first animal life in Phoenix, and the first primates around Disneyland. The hominids are evolving on the shores of the Pacific Ocean.

---

[1] C. Sagan, "Billions and Billions," *Parade Magazine,* May 31, 1987, p. 9.

The basis of stratigraphic studies is the principle of **superposition.** Simply stated, this principle says that under stable conditions, the strata on the bottom of a deposit are older than the ones on top. The reasoning behind the principle of superposition is relatively straightforward: the materials from a given point in time are deposited on top of materials deposited earlier. Since the compositions of these materials differ at different times, the various layers can often be visually identified. Areas such as the Grand Canyon in Arizona graphically illustrate stratigraphic succession (Figure 1–6).

In excavating a paleontological or archaeological site, one encounters progressively older remains at increasingly deeper levels. In general, an object that is found deeper in the ground is older than one located closer to the surface. Fossil and cultural remains can be relatively dated based on their position in a deposit (Figure 11–8).

In practice, stratigraphic sequences are not easy to interpret. Neat layers are not always present, and intrusions, such as burials, can place more recent fossils at the same level as much older material (Figure 11–9). Careful analysis of the soil can often reveal such intrusions. Earthquakes, volcanic eruptions, and other cataclysmic events can also alter stratigraphic sequences.

In addition, if long periods of time elapsed during which deposits did not form or deposited sediments were eroded away, long gaps in time will occur between a particular stratum and the layer just above and/or below it. The surfaces of layers that represent such breaks in the geological record are called **unconformities.** For a particular stratigraphic sequence, unconformities may represent more unrecorded time than the time represented by the strata that are present.

**Index Fossils** In the late eighteenth century, an English geologist, William Smith (1769–1839), noted that particular combinations of fossil animals and plants occurred together in certain sedimentary formations. He realized that if these combinations of fossil species were found in areas other than the original, the periods in which the sedimentary layers were laid down in the two areas must be approximately the same. Therefore, strata from one area could be correlated with strata from another.

In this way, certain fossils or combinations of fossils become markers for particular periods of time;

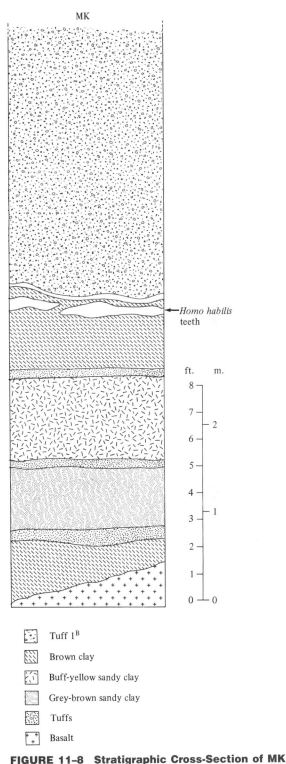

Tuff 1^B
Brown clay
Buff-yellow sandy clay
Grey-brown sandy clay
Tuffs
Basalt

**FIGURE 11–8 Stratigraphic Cross-Section of MK Site, Olduvai Gorge, Tanzania**
Note the location of teeth belonging to the extinct hominid species *Homo habilis,* to be discussed in Chapter 14.

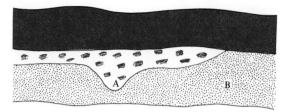

**FIGURE 11–9 Stratigraphic cross-section**
In this hypothetical cross-section of an archaeological site, a hole has been dug into a lower layer. An object lying at the bottom of the hole (A) is therefore found at the same level as much older material (B).

certain key fossils are known as **index fossils.** An index fossil is a species that had a very wide geographical distribution but existed for a short period of time. The appearance of an index fossil in a particular stratum immediately provides the investigator with a relative date for that stratum. If a date is established for an index fossil, any other fossil found in association with it is given the same date.

**Fluorine Dating** Paleontologists have developed several ways to test whether or not objects in a site are contemporary. As bones and teeth lie in the ground, they absorb fluorine and other minerals dissolved in the groundwater. On the other hand, the nitrogen content of the bones decreases as the material ages. The amount of minerals absorbed and the amount of nitrogen lost can be used to calculate the relative chronology of the material in a site. Since the rates of absorption and loss depend on the specific nature of the groundwater, however, these methods can be used only for fossils found in the same area.

The most frequent application of these methods is in determining whether bones found in association are indeed of equal age. If one could show that a human skull and a mammoth rib lying next to it contained the same amount of fluorine, then it follows that both creatures were alive at the same time. On the other hand, if the mineral contents of the two bones differ, with the skull containing less fluorine, one could conclude that the human skull was placed at the lower level through burial. Box 11–2 describes a famous hoax that was resolved through the use of fluorine dating.

## Chronometric Dating Techniques

**Chronometric dates** refer to specific points in time and are noted on specific calendrical systems. **Calendrical systems** are based on natural recurring units of time, such as the revolutions of the earth around the sun or the appearance of the new moon; they note the number of such units that have preceded or elapsed with reference to a specific point in time. For instance, *On the Origin of Species,* by Charles Darwin, was first published in 1859. This date is based on the Gregorian calendar, and it refers to 1859 revolutions of the earth around the sun since the traditional date of the birth of Christ. The same book was published in 5620 according to the Hebrew calendar and in the year 1276 according to the Muslim calendar. The former date is based on the biblical origin of the world, the latter, on the flight of Mohammed.

A chronometric date is often given as 10,115 years ago or 10,115 B.P., in which B.P. stands for "before the present." The problem with this type of designation is that one must know the year in which the date was determined. For example, if a date was determined to be 780 B.P. in 1950, it would have to be changed to 830 B.P. in the year 2000. Many anthropologists use 1950 as the reference point for all B.P. dates.

Chronometric dates in paleontology are often given in the following form: 500 B.P. ± 50 years. The "plus or minus 50 years" does *not* represent an error factor. It is a probability statement that is necessary when certain types of determinations are made. This probability is expressed as a **standard deviation.** For example, a standard deviation of 50 years means that the probability of the real date's falling between 550 and 450 B.P. is 67 percent. The probability of the real date's falling between two standard deviations, in our example between 600 and 400 B.P., is 95 percent.

Chronometric dates are sometimes called *absolute dates,* yet some paleontologists and archaeologists believe that this term is misleading. The paleontologist Chris Paul writes:

> There is a natural human tendency to believe that mathematical calculations are somehow more reliable than logic expressed in words. Thus chronometric dates given in years are often thought to be more accurate than relative ages. In fact we *know* with

**BOX 11-2**

# The Piltdown Skull

In 1912, Charles Dawson found a skull in a site on Piltdown Common, England, which became known as *Piltdown Man*. The find consisted of a brain case, which was very much like that of a relatively modern human, and a lower jaw, which was similar to that of an ape (see figure). Some additional material was discovered later at a nearby site (Site II).

In the years that followed, paleontologists discovered other transitional forms that differed considerably from Piltdown. Piltdown showed a large, developed brain case associated with a modified apelike jaw. More recently discovered forms showed a relatively small brain case associated with essentially modern teeth and jaws.

In 1953, the Piltdown skull was declared a hoax. When paleontologists subjected the fossils to fluorine analysis, they found that many of the different fossils contained different percentages of fluorine. The "hominid" material contained less fluorine than did the bones of other extinct animals found with it, indicating that the Piltdown brain case was more recent than the estimates made on the basis of soil analysis.

Fluorine analysis also revealed that the jaw did not belong to the rest of the skull. Although the brain case appeared to be a real fossil of fairly recent date, the jaw was a modified orangutan mandible.

The culprit who had masterminded the hoax had filed down the canine teeth and stained the bones to make them appear to be of the same age as known prehistoric animals. These diverse fragments were then secretly placed in the sites.

Not until 1996 was it finally announced that the perpetrator had been unmasked. The hoax had been created by Martin A. C. Hinton, a curator of zoology at the Natural History Museum in London, who specialized in the study of fossil rodents. A canvas traveling trunk belonging to Mr. Hinton was discovered in the southwest tower of the museum. Inside were several bones and teeth, all carved and stained in the same manner as the bones placed in the Piltdown site. It is believed that Mr. Hinton, a well-known practical joker, created the hoax to embarrass Arthur Smith Woodward, Keeper of Geology at the museum, as revenge over a pay issue.

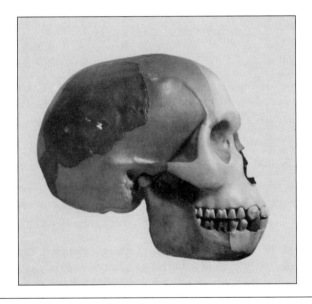

*Sources:* C. Blinderman, *The Piltdown Inquest* (Buffalo, N.Y.: Prometheus, 1986); F. Spencer, *Piltdown: A Scientific Forgery* (London: Oxford University Press, 1990); J. S. Weiner, *The Piltdown Forgery* (London: Oxford University Press, 1955); and H. Gee, "Box of Bones 'Clinches' Identity of Piltdown Palaeontology Hoaxer," *Nature* 381 (May 23, 1996), pp. 261–262.

---

absolute certainty that the Jurassic preceded the Cretaceous, but the current best estimate of fifty-five to sixty million years for the duration of the Jurassic is very much open to question.[7]

Often the paleontologist must use both chronometric and relative dates together. For example, if one fossil is dated at 30,000 ± 250 B.P. and another at 30,150 ± 250 B.P., it is not possible to tell which of the two fossils is older since the ranges of most-probable date overlap (29,750 to 30,250 B.P. and 29,900 to 30,400 B.P.). Deciding which fossil is older would be impossible with only the chronometric dates, but a relative dating technique might solve the problem.

---

[7]C. Paul, *The Natural History of Fossils* (New York: Holmes & Meier, 1980), p. 182. Reprinted by permission of Holmes & Meier.

## Radiometric Dating Techniques

A number of dating methods exist that produce chronometric dates. Examples are **tree-ring dating,** or **dendrochronology,** in which the age of a wood sample is determined by counting the number of annual growth rings, and amino acid racemization, which we will discuss later. Nevertheless, the development of **radiometric dating methods,** based on the decay of radioactive materials, has brought about a major revision of the age of the earth and the fossils it contains.

As we saw in Chapter 2, all matter is composed of one or more elements. The elements carbon, oxygen, nitrogen, and hydrogen are important constituents of all plants and animals, while the elements potassium, silicon, and oxygen are important elements in rocks and minerals.

Although most elements are stable, that is, one element does not change into another, many are unstable, or **radioactive.** Also, an element often occurs in more than one form; the different forms of an element are called **isotopes.** Some isotopes of a particular element may be radioactive, while other isotopes may not.

Radioactivity means that the atom is unstable and will decay into another type of atom. Predicting when a particular atom will decay is impossible, but we can express the rate of decay as a probability statement. If we have a given number of atoms, we can say that one-half of those atoms will have decayed in a specified number of years. This number is known as the **half-life.**

Radioactive decay is uniform throughout time and is unaffected by external conditions such as temperature, pressure, or the presence of other elements. Figure 11–10 plots the rate of decay of radioactive carbon; the number of half-lives is shown on the horizontal axis. In one half-life, exactly one-half of the original atoms have decayed and one-half are left. In two half-lives, three-quarters (one-half plus one-half of one-half) of the original atoms have decayed and one-quarter remain. Notice that this is a geometric curve.

Some radioactive elements have been around from the time the earth was formed. Because their half-lives are so long, they still exist in measurable quantities within the crust of the earth. About 20 such elements have been found, and four exist in enough quantity to be useful for dating: potassium

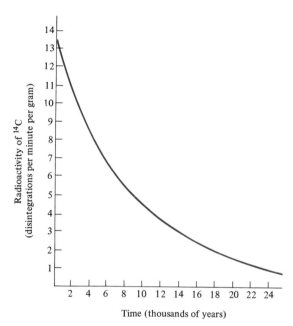

**FIGURE 11–10  Decay Curve of $^{14}$C**
At time 0, the $^{14}$C in the animal tissue is in equilibrium with $^{14}$C in the atmosphere, with the radioactivity of $^{14}$C in the tissue sample measured at 13.56±0.07 disintegrations per minute per gram (dpm/g). When the animal dies, no new $^{14}$C is incorporated into the tissue, and the radioactivity decreases over time.

40, rubidium 87, uranium 235, and uranium 238. Although all four, and some others, have been used as a basis for radiometric dating, potassium 40 has proved to be the most useful.

**Potassium-Argon Dating**  Potassium-argon dating is based on the radioactive decay of potassium 40, which has a half-life of 1250 million years. One out of 10,000 potassium atoms found in rocks is the radioactive isotope potassium 40 ($^{40}$K). Over time, $^{40}$K decays into calcium 40 ($^{40}$Ca) and argon 40 ($^{40}$Ar); the latter is a gas that accumulates within certain minerals.

In order to make use of this technique, the mineral must meet two criteria. First, although potassium is a common constituent of minerals, the method can be used only on material with a sufficiently high potassium content. Second, the material must arise in association with volcanic activity. Under the very high temperatures that accompany volcanic activity, the argon gas is expelled. When the material cools and solidifies, it contains a certain amount of potassium 40 but no argon 40. As time goes on, the amount of $^{40}$K decreases while the amount of $^{40}$Ar increases. These two variables are used in the determination of the chronometric date.

Another form of the potassium-argon technique is **argon 40/argon 39** ($^{40}$Ar/$^{39}$Ar) dating. The material is radiated so that the nonradioactive $^{39}$K is transformed into $^{39}$Ar. The argon gas is extracted and the amounts of $^{40}$Ar and $^{39}$Ar are measured. A variation of this technique involves the use of a laser to melt individual crystals to release the argon. This is termed **single-crystal fusion.** This method reduces the effects of contamination and reduces the size of the sample needed. Recently, this dating method was used to date the most ancient hominid find.

The potassium-argon technique is limited, with few exceptions, to volcanic ash falls and lava flows. The technique is seldom used to date an actual object, but it is used to date fossilized bones with respect to their placement in relationship to volcanic layers in the surrounding material (Figure 11–11).

Similar techniques can be used with other radioactive isotopes. Table 11–2 lists the radioactive isotopes used in radiometric dating. In practice, several different isotopes are used; if similar dates result from the application of two or more techniques, the determined date is considered reliable.

**Radiocarbon Dating**  **Radiocarbon dating,** developed by Willard F. Libby in the late 1940s, was the first radiometric dating technique. One isotope of

**FIGURE 11–11  Potassium-Argon Dating**
(a) Hypothetical live animal. (b) After death, the body of the animal becomes incorporated into a sedimentary bed (lake deposit). Periodic volcanic eruptions have created volcanic lenses in this bed, and the volcanic material can be dated by the potassium-argon technique. The age of the fossil is inferred from its context in relationship to the dated volcanic lenses.

(a)

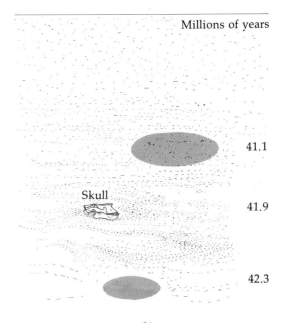

Millions of years

41.1

Skull

41.9

42.3

(b)

**ISOTOPES USED IN RADIOMETRIC DATING**

| Isotopes | | Half-life (years) | Useful time range (years) |
|---|---|---|---|
| Parent | Daughter | | |
| $^{238}U$ | $^{206}Pb$ | $4.50 \times 10^9$ | $10^7$ to origin of earth* |
| $^{235}U$ | $^{207}Pb$ | $0.71 \times 10^9$ | $10^7$ to origin of earth |
| $^{87}Rb$ | $^{87}Sr$ | $4.7 \times 10^{10}$ | $10^7$ to origin of earth |
| $^{40}K$ | $^{40}Ar$ | $1.3 \times 10^9$ | $10^5$ to origin of earth |
| $^{14}C$ | | $5730 \pm 40$ | 0–50,000 |

*Currently estimated at $4.55 \times 10^9$ years.
*Source:* C. Paul, *The Natural History of Fossils* (New York: Holmes & Meier Publishers, Inc., 1980), p. 184. Reprinted by permission of Holmes and Meier.

carbon, carbon 14 ($^{14}C$), is radioactive and will eventually decay into nitrogen 14 ($^{14}N$). The half-life of $^{14}C$ is 5730 years.

Carbon 14 forms in the upper atmosphere by the bombardment of nitrogen by cosmic radiation. The amount of $^{14}C$ formed in the atmosphere is relatively constant over time; although variations in the amount of solar radiation produce fluctuations in the amount of $^{14}C$, it is often possible to correct for these fluctuations.

The $^{14}C$ in the atmosphere combines with oxygen to form carbon dioxide. Carbon dioxide, in turn, is incorporated into plants by photosynthesis and into animals by consumption of plants or other animals (Figure 11–12). As long as the organism is alive, the proportion of $^{14}C$ to nonradioactive $^{12}C$ in the body remains constant since the amount of new $^{14}C$ being incorporated into the body balances the amount being lost through decay. When the organism dies, no new $^{14}C$ atoms are incorporated into the body, and the atoms present at death continue to decay. The age of the organism at death is calculated by comparing the proportion of $^{14}C$ to $^{12}C$ in the prehistoric sample with that in a modern sample. Since nitrogen 14 is a gas, it moves from the body into the atmosphere, where it is indistinguishable from the atmospheric nitrogen, and hence it cannot be measured.

In the conventional method of radiocarbon dating, the $^{14}C$ is measured by means of a special counter that measures the emissions given off by carbon-14 atoms when they decay. Another method of radiocarbon dating uses accelerator mass spectrometry to measure the ratio of $^{14}C$ to $^{12}C$ directly.

Radiocarbon dating can be used to date any organic material, including, but not limited to, wood and charcoal, cloth, seeds and grasses, bones, ivory, and shell. Unlike the case with potassium-argon dating, carbon 14 dates the actual material. The material that is being dated is consumed in the process. The maximum age that can be determined by the conventional method at the present time is 40,000 to 50,000 years. The direct method has a theoretical maximum of 100,000 years, but under present conditions, the maximum is between 40,000 and 60,000 years. The direct method uses much smaller quantities of the sample being dated.

None of the radiometric dating methods is infallible. The accuracy of the equipment used and the skill of the technician can influence the validity of the date determination. Also, a sample may have been contaminated with radioactive materials in the soil or by substances that contacted the sample after excavation, such as oils from a sweaty hand or smoke from a cigarette. Therefore, samples should be picked up with forceps and placed in a special container, but an inexperienced excavator may forget to do this or may not know that it should be done.

**Fission-Track Dating** Another type of radiometric dating technique is **fission-track dating.** Like potassium-argon dating, fission-track dating dates the minerals in a deposit. Minerals are crystalline in nature, which means that their atoms form an orderly three-dimensional structure based on the repetition of modular units. As the nucleus of a heavy isotope such as uranium 238 breaks apart, its decay particles rip holes in the orderly crystal structure of the mineral. In so doing, the particles leave tracks in these crystals.

The tracks can be used to determine a chronometric date. After being chemically treated to make them larger, such tracks can be seen under magnification and counted. The number of atomic disintegrations is directly related to the number of tracks produced. If the concentration of the isotope under study is known, then a count of the tracks left will indicate the age of the mineral being dated. This method can give us dates as far back as the beginning of the solar system.

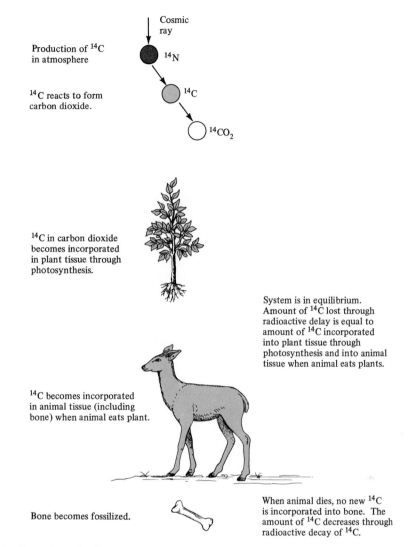

Production of $^{14}C$
in atmosphere

Cosmic
ray

$^{14}N$

$^{14}C$ reacts to form
carbon dioxide.

$^{14}C$

$^{14}CO_2$

$^{14}C$ in carbon dioxide
becomes incorporated
in plant tissue through
photosynthesis.

System is in equilibrium.
Amount of $^{14}C$ lost through
radioactive delay is equal to
amount of $^{14}C$ incorporated
into plant tissue through
photosynthesis and into animal
tissue when animal eats plants.

$^{14}C$ becomes incorporated
in animal tissue (including
bone) when animal eats plant.

Bone becomes fossilized.

When animal dies, no new $^{14}C$
is incorporated into bone. The
amount of $^{14}C$ decreases through
radioactive decay of $^{14}C$.

**FIGURE 11–12  Radiocarbon Dating**

**Thermoluminescence Dating**   When some materials, such as crystals, are heated, they give off a flash of light, a phenomenon known as **thermoluminescence.** Minerals in the ground are constantly exposed to radiation from naturally occurring radioactive elements, primarily uranium, thorium, and potassium 40. The radioactivity causes some electrons to separate from the atoms; these electrons then fall into defects in the structure of the crystal where they remain, accumulating through time. When the material is exposed to heat, the trapped electrons are liberated and, in the process,

give off characteristic wavelengths of light at particular temperatures.

If the mineral has been exposed to constant radiation through time, then the amount of light will be proportional to the age of the material. In addition, immediately after heating, no more light is seen until the mineral has been exposed to new radiation. Thus, the zero point for determining a date is the last heating of the material or the point at which the mineral was crystallized.

Thermoluminescence can be used to date archaeological finds, such as ceramics, burnt stones (such as those that make up a fire pit), and burnt flint tools, as well as geological material, such as volcanic material. This technique can be used to date fairly young objects, as well as objects from as far back as 300,000 years ago, depending on the nature of the material being dated.

**Electron Spin Resonance Dating** In our discussion of thermoluminescence, we saw that naturally occurring radioactivity causes some electrons to separate from the atoms and then fall into defects in the structure of the crystal. Most of the time, these electrons are trapped as pairs, but when an odd number of electrons become trapped, they behave like small magnets. In **electron spin resonance (ESR) dating,** an analysis of this property is used to establish a chronometric date.

Electron spin resonance dating can be used for dates back to the Paleozoic, depending on the material being dated and other conditions. The method can be used to date many materials, including limestone, coral, shell, and teeth. In Chapter 15, we will see how ESR dating has provided dates that have helped paleontologists understand the evolution of our species.

**Amino Acid Racemization** An example of chronometric dating is **amino acid racemization.** Many organic molecules, such as the amino acids, occur in two forms that are identical in structure but are mirror images of each other. The amino acids found in proteins in living organisms, by convention, are called left-handed or L-amino acids; the L refers to *levo-*, or "left." Mirroring them are the right-handed or D-amino acids; the D refers to *dextro-*, or "right." When an organism dies, the L-amino acids slowly turn into D-amino acids, a process known as racemization.

Amino acid racemization is used to date fossil material that contains amino acids; such material includes bone, teeth, **coprolites** (fossilized fecal material), corals, and sea shells. The process can be used to determine the age of material up to 200,000 years old. Its reliability decreases with age, however, and some types of material can be dated more accurately than others.

Amino acids are found in fossils since only 40 to 70 percent of the amino acids in datable material decompose. Each amino acid is associated with a characteristic speed of racemization at a given temperature. This is expressed as the racemization rate, which is the time it takes for half of the molecules to change to the D form. For example, the racemization rate of aspartic acid is 15,000 years at 20°C (68°F).

Problems occur with the use of this method, however, since many variables can affect the speed of racemization. The most significant variables are temperature and acidity of the soil. Because of this, calibrated ratios can be used only in a specific geographical area, and the consistency of temperatures over long periods of time needs to be demonstrated.

### The Geomagnetic Time Scale

The invention of the compass made possible long distance ocean voyages of exploration. The needle of a compass points toward the north magnetic pole. Today, geologists believe that the earth's magnetism arises from motions within the outer liquid core of the earth caused by the rotation of the earth. The positions of the magnetic north and south poles are not stable, however. They move their position, reverse their polarity, and change in intensity over time.

No one has ever observed the occurrence of reversals in the polarity of the earth. Geologists, however, have found crystals in rock that act as small magnets. In molten rock, these crystals orient themselves to the poles before the rock solidifies. Once "frozen," they leave a record of the polarity of the earth at that point in time. The study of the polarity of these materials, both on land and on the sea floor, enables geologists to create a chart showing the sequence of magnetic reversals. When specific reversals are dated by radiometric techniques, a **geomagnetic reversal time scale (GRTS)** can be drawn. If a pattern of normal and reversed polarity is found in a rock formation, the pattern can be matched with the GRTS and dates can be assigned to the formation. Fossils are given approximate dates with respect to their context within the formation.

Figure 11–13 shows a portion of the GRTS. In the figure, intervals of normal polarity, that is, polarity that corresponds to what we find today, are pictured as solid black, while intervals of reversed polarity are seen as white. This scale is constantly be-

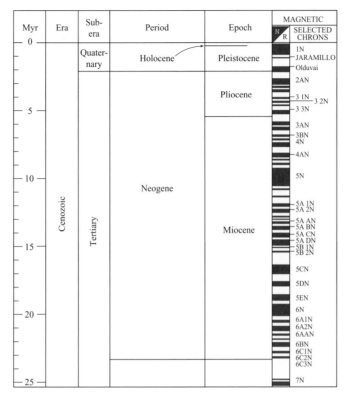

**FIGURE 11–13  The Geomagnetic Reversal Time Scale**

ing improved as new dates or more detailed profiles are determined. Large divisions of the scale that show primarily a single polarity are called **chrons,** while small subdivisions within a chron are known as **subchrons.** Geomagnetic patterns are known back as far as the Middle Jurassic, but some sections are better known and better dated than others. This method is most useful for 10,000 to 10,000,000 years ago. A major advantage of this technique is that it can be applied to sedimentary deposits where radiometric techniques cannot be used.

### The Geological Time Scale

Large sections of stratigraphic sequences are exposed in many parts of the world. The layers, of various colors and textures, are composed of different types of materials that represent the diverse environmental conditions existing at the time the layers were laid down. In addition, the fossil contents also differ. The study of the stratigraphic sequence of geological features and fossils provides the basis for the geological time scale.

Geologists have divided the history of the earth, as revealed in the stratigraphic record, into a hierarchy of units: the **era, period,** and **epoch.** Each division of geological time is characterized by a distinct fossil flora and fauna and major geological events such as extensive mountain building. In general, the farther back in time we go, the more difficult it is to determine the events that occurred since more recent events often obliterate signs of earlier events. The geological time scale is outlined in Figure 11–14.

### Plate Tectonics

The surface of the earth can loosely be compared to a cracked eggshell. Like the fractured shell, the earth's surface is made up of several areas separated by distinct boundaries. These areas, called **tectonic plates,** are segments of the **lithosphere,** the hard outer layer of the earth. Unlike the segments

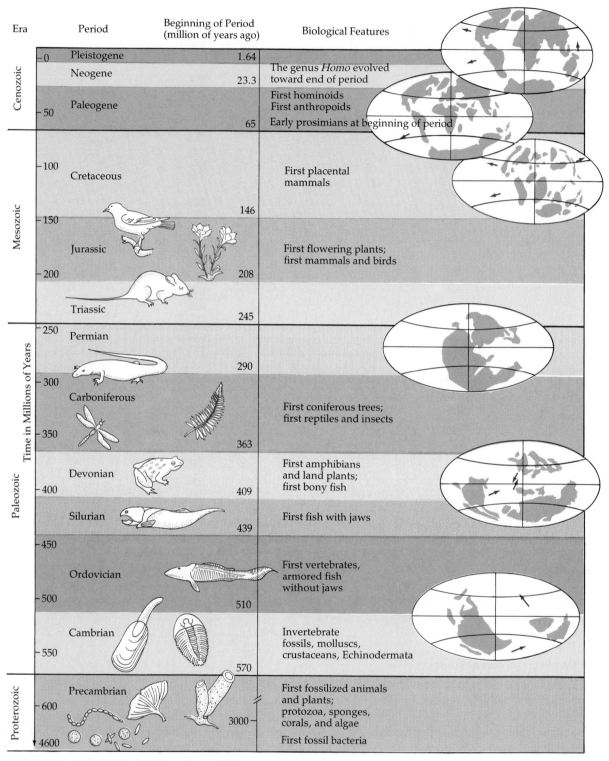

| Era | Period | Beginning of Period (million of years ago) | Biological Features |
|---|---|---|---|
| **Cenozoic** | Pleistogene | 0 / 1.64 | |
| | Neogene | 23.3 | The genus *Homo* evolved toward end of period |
| | Paleogene | 50 / 65 | First hominoids First anthropoids Early prosimians at beginning of period |
| **Mesozoic** | Cretaceous | 100 / 146 | First placental mammals |
| | Jurassic | 150 / 200 / 208 | First flowering plants; first mammals and birds |
| | Triassic | 245 | |
| **Paleozoic** | Permian | 250 / 290 | |
| | Carboniferous | 300 / 350 / 363 | First coniferous trees; first reptiles and insects |
| | Devonian | 400 / 409 | First amphibians and land plants; first bony fish |
| | Silurian | 439 | First fish with jaws |
| | Ordovician | 450 / 500 / 510 | First vertebrates, armored fish without jaws |
| | Cambrian | 550 / 570 | Invertebrate fossils, molluscs, crustaceans, Echinodermata |
| **Proterozoic** | Precambrian | 600 / 3000 / ▼4600 | First fossilized animals and plants; protozoa, sponges, corals, and algae First fossil bacteria |

Time in Millions of Years

**FIGURE 11–14  The Geological Time Scale**

of the eggshell, lithospheric plates move relative to one another as they float at about the rate of 2.5 centimeters (1 inch) a year atop a softer, more fluid layer of the earth. This process of constant plate movement, called **plate tectonics,** is in large part responsible for the formation of mountains and valleys, for earthquakes and volcanoes, for the rise of islands out of the sea, and for many other geological occurrences.

Some plates are completely covered by the sea, while others contain landmasses such as the continents and islands. Since the plates move, it follows that continents move, or "drift." Continents may move into each other; "slide" past each other; or break up, with the parts moving away from each other. Except for earthquakes, this movement occurs so slowly in relationship to a human lifetime that it can be detected only with very sensitive equipment.

Yet continents have been mobile for hundreds of millions of years. Approximately 225 million years ago, plates carrying all the major landmasses that existed at the time came together, forming one large continent called Pangaea (which is Greek for "all the earth"). By about 200 million years ago, this single landmass was breaking up.

Figure 11–14 illustrates the relationship of the continents to each other at various points in time. An important point about continental drift is that it constantly, but slowly, has established and destroyed migration routes. Therefore, understanding the patterns of continental drift is extremely important in explaining why animals and plants are where they are today, that is, their distribution. The fact that different boundaries existed at different times for a population means that the population was at various times subject to different availability of food, different patterns of predation, different climates, and other changes in environmental pressures.

## A Brief History of the Cenozoic

Geological time is divided into three large eras: the Paleozoic, the Mesozoic, and the Cenozoic; the time before the beginning of the Paleozoic is called the Proterozoic. The Cenozoic is called the Age of Mammals because it represents the time of the adaptive radiation of mammals into the numerous and various ecological niches that they occupy to-

day. The Cenozoic began about 65 million years ago. The dividing line between the Mesozoic and the Cenozoic is marked by the relatively rapid extinction of a very large number of organisms, including the dinosaurs, which had dominated the earth for so long.

The Cenozoic can be divided into two **suberas,** the Tertiary and the Quaternary, concepts first defined in the eighteenth century. Today, many geologists and paleontologists divide the Cenozoic into three periods: the first two, the Paleogene and the Neogene, are divisions of the Tertiary; the Pleistogene is the only period within the Quaternary subera. As can be seen in Table 11–3, these periods are further divided into epochs: the Paleocene, Eocene, Oligocene, Miocene, Pliocene, Pleistocene, and Holocene (or Recent). In paleoanthropology, the Cenozoic era and its periods and epochs are of major concern since, during this time, the primates, including *Homo sapiens,* evolved.

**The Paleogene** The most ancient period of the Cenozoic, the Paleogene, contains three epochs: Paleocene, Eocene, and Oligocene. The first mammals evolved in the Mesozoic era, but it was not until the beginning of the Cenozoic, the Paleocene, that they began their major adaptive radiation. At the beginning of this epoch, the mammals found new opportunities for diversification into the ecological niches left vacant by the dinosaurs, which were by that time extinct. Although no modern mammalian

---

| TABLE 11–3 | | | |
|---|---|---|---|

**THE GEOLOGICAL TIME SCALE:
THE CENOZOIC ERA**

| Subera | Period | Epoch | Beginning date (millions of years) |
|---|---|---|---|
| Quaternary | Pleistogene | Holocene | 0.01 |
| | | Pleistocene | 1.64 |
| Tertiary | Neogene | Pliocene | 5.2 |
| | | Miocene | 23.3 |
| | Paleogene | Oligocene | 35.4 |
| | | Eocene | 56.5 |
| | | Paleocene | 65.0 |

*Source:* W. B. Harland et al., *A Geologic Time Scale 1989* (Cambridge: Cambridge University Press, 1990).

BOX 11-3

# Where Have All the Dinosaurs Gone?

At 5 A.M. on July 10, 1990, an asteroid (a small rocky interplanetary object) traveling about 35,406 kilometers per hour (22,000 miles per hour) sped across the earth's orbit at a distance of about 4.8 million kilometers (3 million miles) from the earth. Although 4.8 million kilometers may seem very distant, in astronomical terms, it represents a near miss. Since 1973, observers at Palomar Observatory in California have spotted 39 asteroids that have passed close to earth. None of these objects hit the earth, but scientists have now identified about 150 "impact structures" left from previous strikes, and about three to five new ones are identified each year. We may assume that many craters have yet to be found, while others have been obliterated by geological processes such as volcanism, erosion, and sedimentation.

One of the best known impact structures is Meteor Crater in Arizona (see figure). It was formed when an asteroid hit the earth about 30,000 years ago. The result was a crater that is 1200 meters (4000 feet) in diameter and 200 meters (700 feet) deep. The July 10, 1990, asteroid could have been three times as large as the one that formed Meteor Crater.

Although a dramatic sight, Meteor Crater represents a minor impact compared to that made by an asteroid or comet that may have crashed into the earth 65 million years ago. Some scientists believe that at that time, an extraterrestrial object 10 kilometers (6 miles) or more across struck the planet. The object would have hit the earth with a force 10,000 times more powerful than that of all the world's nuclear weapons. A candidate for the crater that resulted from the impact is located on the Yucatan Peninsula of Mexico. Although some scientists believe that other forces such as massive volcanic eruptions caused or contributed to the Cretaceous/Tertiary extinctions, the impact may have been responsible for the extinction of about 75 percent of all animal species living directly before the impact. This mass extinction is one of at least 12 such episodes that have occurred over the last 800 million years.

The discovery that led to the impact-extinction hypothesis dates back to 1978. At that time, a thin layer of iridium-rich clay was discovered in Gubbio, Italy. Since 1978, iridium, a rare element on earth but frequently found in meteorites (the earthly remains of asteroids), has been discovered in 65-million-year-old layers of the earth worldwide. The 65-million-B.P. date corresponds to the boundary between the Cretaceous and Tertiary periods and to the mass extinction.

If an interplanetary object was responsible for the extinctions, the impact may have created an enormous dust cloud of global proportions; as a consequence, sunlight was blocked and plants could not photosynthesize. As plants died out, the animals that were dependent on them for food also perished. Predators became extinct as their herbivorous prey succumbed. Because solar energy reaching the earth's surface was partially blocked, the planet also cooled. After the initial cooling period, a study of plant life suggests that a heating period occurred (the greenhouse effect). Many organisms that initially survived may have been wiped out by these climatic changes.

Another idea is that hot ejecta (objects thrown upward) were thrown into the atmosphere on the impact of the asteroid. On returning to earth, these objects could have caused global wildfires that precipitated a variety of cataclysmic effects, including acid rain that killed off sea, lake, and river life, creating a rippling food chain die-off.

It is probable that a large asteroid or comet will again hit the earth. This possibility has been exploited in such popular movies as the 1998 film *Armageddon*. Some scientists are now discussing the possibility of using the Star Wars Defense System, originally designed to destroy incoming enemy missiles, to divert the course of potentially dangerous interplanetary objects.

We are currently experiencing the 13th mass extinction. This time the cause is earth-bound. People, through their destruction of the world's environments and overhunting, are the direct and indirect cause of most of the approximately 100 extinctions of plants and animals that are now occurring every day.

For further information see the following:
L. W. Alvarez, "Experimental Evidence That an Asteroid Impact Led to the Extinction of Many Species 65 Million Years Ago," *Proceedings of the National Academy of Sciences* 80 (1983), pp. 627–642; H. J. Melosh et al., "Ignition of Global Wildfires at the Cretaceous/Tertiary Boundary," *Nature* 343 (1990), pp. 251–254; V. E. Courtillot, "A Volcanic Eruption," *Scientific American* 263 (October 1990), pp. 82–92; G. S. Paul, "Giant Meteor Impacts and Great Eruptions: Dinosaur Killers?" *BioScience* 39 (1989), pp. 162–172; and J. A. Wolfe, "Palaeobotanical Evidence of a Marked Temperature Increase Following the Cretaceous/Tertiary Boundary," *Nature* 343 (1990), pp. 153–156.

families came into being during this epoch, the ancestors of modern families were present.

During the Paleocene, North America and Europe were connected as a single continent. The western and eastern parts of North America were separated by a large sea, and northwestern North America was connected by land to northeastern Asia. Other waterways covered parts of what is now South America, Africa, and Eurasia.

During the Paleocene, climates were warm and wet and mountains rose to new heights. Deciduous broad-leaved forests extended northward to approximately the latitude of today's Oslo, Norway, and Seward, Alaska, and conifer forests extended farther northward. Much of the present-day western United States was covered with subtropical forests and savanna. The early primates evolved within this setting.

During the Eocene, the land bridge between North America and Europe began to separate; the connection was gone by the end of this epoch. Large seas in Eurasia effectively isolated western Europe from the rest of the Old World. South America, Africa, and Australia were all surrounded by water. In the latter part of the Eocene, temperatures began to cool, seasons became more pronounced, glaciers began to form in Antarctica, and climates became drier and more diverse. Nearly all the modern orders of mammals were present by the Eocene. Primates were widespread, and the earliest anthropoids were present by the end of this epoch.

During the Oligocene, climates continued to be characterized by increased cooling, drying, and alternating seasons. Africa and South America were closer than they are today and many islands existed in the southern Atlantic Ocean. Many paleoanthropologists believe that African anthropoids could have rafted across the Atlantic Ocean to South America. Some Oligocene primates are known from South American sites. All Old World primate fossils, which include early anthropoids, come from Africa, which was separated from Europe and Asia.

**The Neogene**   The Neogene period consists of the Miocene and Pliocene epochs. In the early Miocene, we find the earliest Old World monkeys and apes in east Africa; the first hominids may have appeared during this epoch as well. By the middle

Miocene, African primates had begun to migrate over a newly formed land bridge into Asia and Europe. In general, climates in the Miocene were somewhat warmer than those in the Oligocene; by the late Miocene, climates were becoming cooler and drier. The continents were pretty much in their present position, but sea levels were higher than they are today and seas still covered large areas of land.

During the Pliocene, climates became cooler and more varied, as the Antarctic ice cap continued to expand. Mountain building continued, and the mammals reached their high point in variety and size. During this epoch, the direct ancestors of *Homo sapiens* evolved.

**The Pleistogene**   The epoch comprising all but the last 10,000 years of the Pleistogene period is the Pleistocene, an epoch marked by major fluctuations in the earth's geology and climate. The Pleistocene was the time of many giant mammals, such as the giant ground sloths, mammoths and mastodons, and the saber-toothed cat; it was also the time of their extinction. During the Pleistocene, hominids became efficient hunters, and they were probably responsible for the extinction of many of these mammals.

The Pleistocene is noteworthy because during this time, large, long-lasting masses of ice, glaciers, were extensive. Great ice ages had already occurred several times in the history of earth, but the Pleistocene Ice Age is the most recent, and it is certainly the best known. When one speaks of an ice age, the image of a world dominated by freezing temperatures and covered with ice comes to mind; but ice never covered the entire earth. The extent of the continental glaciers is shown in Figure 11–15.

The Pleistocene was not a time of continuous glaciation; rather, it was marked by both **glacial** and **interglacial** periods. During glacials, the glacial ice expanded, but during interglacials, the climates were as warm as or even warmer than those prevailing today. Actually, each of the major glacials and interglacials was a complex event, comprising cooler and warmer episodes.

During the last glacial, sea levels dropped at least 100 meters (330 feet) below their present level, primarily because large amounts of water were "locked up" in glacial ice. Land connections came

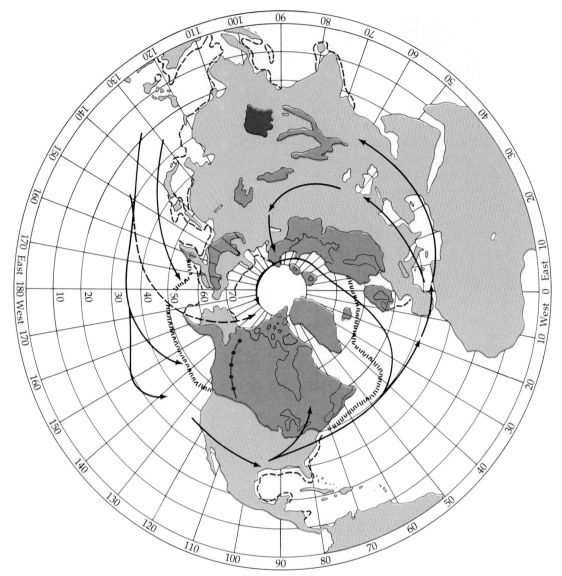

Key:

Principal areas covered by glacier ice. *(Very small areas not shown. In central and northeastern Asia, includes areas of more extensive earlier glaciation.)*

Area not completely glaciated but in which glaciation was extensive.

ᴧᴧᴧᴧᴧᴧᴧᴧ Inferred outer limit of pack ice at annual maximum.

⟶ Inferred major storm tracks *(annual mean)*.

--▸ Inferred occasional and seasonally important storm tracks *(annual mean)*.

•–•–•–•– Zones of contact between coalescent major glaciers.

– – – – – 100-meter isobath.

**FIGURE 11–15 Pleistocene Glaciations**
Glacial ice did not cover the entire earth during the Pleistocene but was confined to areas of Europe, North America, and Siberia.

into existence wherever shallow water had separated two or more landmasses. For example, during the periods of glaciation, Asia was connected by land to North America; thus animals, including humans, were able to cross between the two at the point of connection. The Pleistocene Ice Age also caused changes in vegetation patterns: as glaciers advanced and retreated, forests turned into grasslands. Great herds of mammals flourished, fed by the grasslands at the foot of glacial ice; but as forests again replaced the grasslands, the herds declined.

Figure 11–16 presents a general timeline of the glacials and interglacials during the Pleistocene. The sequence and duration of glacial episodes differed from area to area, however, and the later glacials destroyed much of the detailed evidence of earlier glacials. Therefore, the chart in Figure 11–16 must be viewed in very general terms.

## Summary

The interpretation of the fossil record demands accurate dating of fossils. Relative dating provides information on the sequence of fossils in terms of which are older and which are younger. Stratigraphy is based on the principle of superposition, which states that the lower strata in a deposit are older than those above. One major difficulty with stratigraphy is the possibility that newer material has intruded into older material via burial or cataclysms. Methods like fluorine analysis can help establish whether two bones are contemporary.

Chronometric dating provides an actual calendrical date. The most important chronometric dating methods are based on the decay of radioactive elements. Carbon-14 dating was the first radiometric technique developed, but it is theoretically limited to the last 100,000 years. Potassium-argon dating is based on the radioactive decay of potassium 40, which has an extremely long half-life; consequently, this method can be used to date the age of the earth. Other dating techniques are fission-track dating, amino acid racemization, thermoluminescence, electron spin resonance, and geomagnetism.

The history of the earth is divided, in terms of geological and paleontological events, into four eras. Each era is divided into periods, which, in turn, are divided into epochs. Thus, the Cenozoic era, which is the Age of Mammals, can be discussed in terms of its many subdivisions.

The evolution of life has been greatly affected by earth dynamics. Landmasses move in relationship to each other, thus creating new migratory routes and destroying others. In addition, plate tectonics is responsible for many climatic alternations, and it may have been a prime cause of the cooling that led to the Pleistocene Ice Age. This was a time of fluctuating temperatures and environments, and as such, it presented a series of changing selective pressures that helped to shape human evolution.

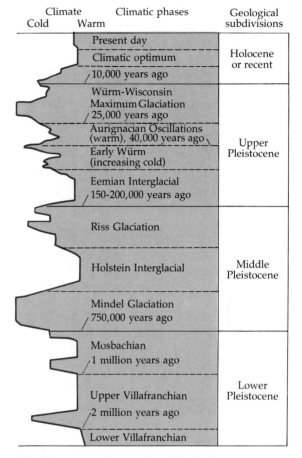

**FIGURE 11–16 Chronology of Glacials and Interglacials**
This chart presents one of several ways of dividing up the Pleistocene. Also, different names are applied to glacial and interglacial episodes in different parts of the world. Note the fluctuations in temperature within the glacials and interglacials.

## STUDY QUESTIONS

1. What does the field of taphonomy tell us about the development of the fossil record? Why is fossilization a relatively rare event?
2. Why are some animals better represented in the fossil record than others? What are the various "sampling errors" found in the fossil record?
3. Although the fossil record is fragmentary, paleontologists are able to reconstruct a great deal about once-living animals. Describe some of the types of information that can be deduced from fossil evidence.
4. Species are defined in terms of reproductive isolation. Since evidence for this cannot be inferred from the fossil record, how does the paleontologist handle the concept of prehistoric species?
5. Individual fossils that were considered representatives of different species have sometimes turned out to belong to a single species. What factors are responsible for variation within species as represented in the fossil record?
6. Distinguish between relative and chronometric dating. What are some examples of each type of dating method?
7. Geological events often have a profound influence on the evolution of living organisms. Briefly describe the impact of continental drift on the evolution of plants and animals.

## SUGGESTED READINGS

Binford, L. R. *Bones: Ancient Men and Modern Myths.* Orlando, Fla.: Academic, 1987. This is a provocative book on the science of taphonomy.

Gould, S. J. *Time's Arrow and Time's Cycle: Myth and Metaphor in the Discovery of Geological Time.* Cambridge, Mass.: Harvard University Press, 1987. In this book, Stephen Jay Gould discusses the history of the discovery of deep time, particularly the writings of Thomas Burnet, James Hutton, and Charles Lyell.

McCown, T. D., and A. R. K. Kennedy (eds.). *Climbing Man's Family Tree: A Collection of Major Writings on Human Phylogeny, 1699–1971.* Englewood Cliffs, N.J.: Prentice Hall, 1972. This collection of essays shows how methods of collecting fossils and interpreting these data have changed over the past three centuries.

Paul, C. *The Natural History of Fossils.* New York: Holmes & Meier, 1980. This is a basic introduction to paleontology with information on the nature of fossils, why fossils form, dating, and more.

Roth, E., and M. Ménager (eds.). *Nuclear Methods of Dating.* Dordrecht, Netherlands: Kluwer Academics, 1989. This book contains a series of articles that discuss, in technical detail, many of the radiometric dating techniques.

Shipman, P. *Life History of a Fossil: An Introduction to Taphonomy and Paleoecology.* Cambridge, Mass.: Harvard University Press, 1981. This book can serve as an introductory text to taphonomy.

Spindler, K. *The Man in the Ice.* New York: Harmony Books, 1994. The lead archaeologist studying the "Ice Man" describes the 5300-year-old frozen fossil and the artifacts found with him.

Taylor, R. E. *Radiocarbon Dating: An Archaeological Approach.* Orlando, Fla.: Academic, 1987. This volume discusses the history, methodology, and problems of carbon-14 dating.

## SUGGESTED WEB SITES

UC Berkeley Museum of Paleontology:
http://www.ucmp.berkeley.edu
Dating Techniques (Minnesota State University):
http://emuseum.mankato.msus.edu/dating/
United States Geologic Survey Geologic Time Online Edition:
http://pubs.usgs./gov/gip/geotime

Additional web sites are listed in the *Workbook* that accompanies this text.

# EXCAVATIONS AT DIK DIK HILL, OLDUVAI GORGE

Paleontological excavation is a difficult and exacting activity. In these photographs, we observe some of the phases in the excavation of a *Homo habilis* skeleton. (The species *H. habilis* is discussed in Chapter 14.)

**FIGURE 11–A**   A group of paleoanthropologists are working at the base of Dik Dik Hill, named for the dik dik, a small east African antelope. This is one of several sites within Olduvai Gorge. The formation known as the Castle is in the foreground.

**Figure 11-B** The first fragment of hominid bone, a piece of right ulna, is found at the site.

**Figure 11-C** The research team sets up to begin excavation.

**Figure 11-D** Paleoanthropologists (right to left) Prosper Endeessokia, Tim White, and Mrisho Ramadhani excavate Dik Dik Hill.

**Figure 11–E** In this aerial view of the completed excavation, white cards indicate where important fragments of the skeleton were found.

**Figure 11–F** Soil is passed through a screen to recover small fragments.

**Figure 11–G** The elbow region is represented by the partial remains of a humerus, an ulna, and a radius.

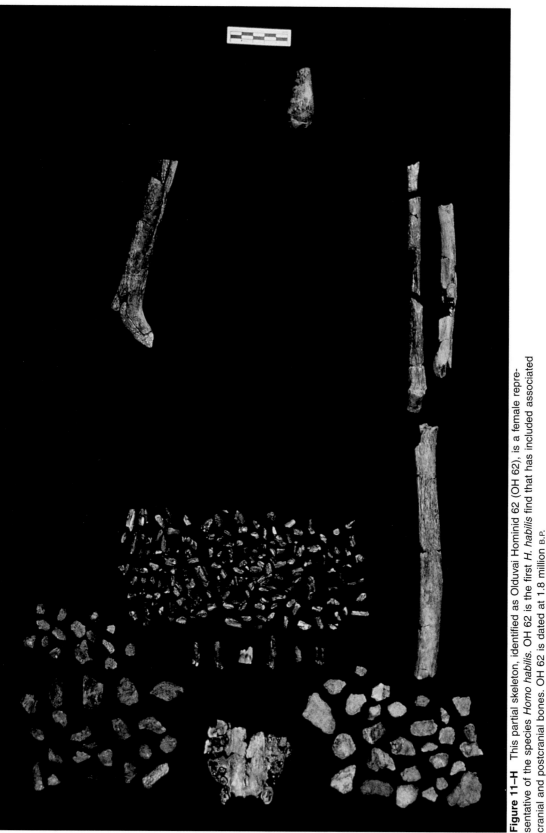

**Figure 11–H**  This partial skeleton, identified as Olduvai Hominid 62 (OH 62), is a female representative of the species *Homo habilis*. OH 62 is the first *H. habilis* find that has included associated cranial and postcranial bones. OH 62 is dated at 1.8 million B.P.

*Sources:* D. Johanson et al., "New Partial Skeleton of *Homo habilis* from Olduvai Gorge, Tanzania," *Nature,* 327 (1987), 205–209; D. Johanson and J. Shreeve, *Lucy's Child: The Discovery of a Human Ancestor* (New York: William Morrow, 1989).

# The Early Primate Fossil Record

*If we are to place our origins in proper perspective, we must . . . be concerned not only with identifying our immediate and processional ancestors, but also with developing an appreciation of the true extent of primate diversity in the past, for it is from amidst this diversity that we emerged.[1]*
—Russell L. Ciochon and Dennis A. Etler

**A** dominant theme in evolutionary studies is that of origins—the origins of humans, of primates, of animals, and, indeed, of life itself. Yet evidence of origins is difficult to identify since the earliest members of a taxonomic group often lack many of

---

[1]R. L. Ciochon and D. A. Etler, "Reinterpreting Past Primate Diversity," in R. S. Corruccini and R. L. Ciochon (eds.), *Integrative Paths to the Past: Paleoanthropological Advances in Honor of F. Clark Howell* (Englewood Cliffs, N.J.: Prentice Hall, 1994), p. 37.

the characteristics of the later and better-known members of that group. Perhaps they resemble more closely the members of the group from which they evolved. Certainly in our search for the earliest primates, we would hardly expect to find a monkeylike or an apelike creature with a fully evolved set of features like those that characterize contemporary animals.

## EVOLUTION OF THE EARLY PRIMATES

Overshadowed by the dinosaurs, the earliest mammals evolved during the Mesozoic era. By Paleocene times at the beginning of the Cenozoic era, all of the dinosaurs, as well as many other forms of life, were extinct and mammals began their adaptive radiation into numerous orders. By the start of

---

**BOX 12-1**

## Discovering the Earliest Primate

Until recently, a major candidate for the honor of being labeled the earliest primate has been a group of fossils known from the Late Cretaceous through the Early Eocene that make up the suborder Plesiadapiformes. The earliest specimen, known exclusively from a single right lower molar, is *Purgatorius,* from the Purgatory Hills of Montana. Yet it is risky to draw any major conclusions from such an isolated piece of evidence.

The plesiadapiforms were first discovered over 100 years ago, and they are known primarily from teeth and jaw fragments; some postcranial materials, including quite recently discovered finds, are known. These fossils are divided into four to six families and they have been found in both North America and Europe.

The plesiadapiforms lack most of the features we associate with the order Primates, and they display a relationship with the primates only through similarities of molar morphology; to many paleoanthropologists, these similarities are far from convincing. These animals lacked a grasping foot; all digits ended in large claws that suggest a locomotor pattern quite different from those we associate with living primates. The relatively small orbits, the lack of a forward rotation of the orbits, and the lack of a postorbital bar all suggest that the vision was not highly developed. The brain was

relatively small. Many of the plesiadapiforms possessed rodent-like teeth with large incisors, no canine, and a large diastema separating the incisors from the premolars. These differences that separate the plesiadapiforms from the more familiar primates led many primatologists to label the plesiadapiforms "archaic primates," as compared with the "primates of modern aspect" or euprimates ("true" primates).

The interpretation of the plesiadapiforms as early primates has changed because of discoveries in the late 1980s of postcranial material. Rather than showing features suggesting distinctive primate locomotor patterns, the bones strongly suggest that these animals possessed a gliding membrane anatomically similar to that of the flying lemurs, or colugo, of the Philippines. (The modern flying lemurs, however, do not fly, nor are they lemurs; indeed they are not even primates, but form their own order, Dermoptera.) For example, while the phalanges, or finger bones, closest to the palm are the longest in most mammals, the middle bone is the longest in the plesiadapiform *Phenacolemur* and in the modern flying lemur; this is an adaptation for support of a gliding membrane.

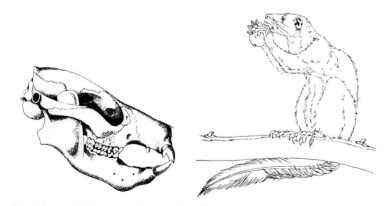

*Plesiadapis,* a Paleocene plesiadapiform. (From "The Early Relatives of Man" by E. L. Simons. Copyright ©1964 by Scientific American, Inc. All rights reserved.)

*Sources:* K. C. Beard, "Gliding Behaviour and Palaeoecology of the Alleged Primate Family Paromomyidae (Mammalia, Dermoptera)," *Nature,* 345 (1990), 340–341; R. F. Kay, R. W. Thorington, Jr., and P. Houde, "Eocene Plesiadapiform Shows Affinities with Flying Lemurs, Not Primates," *Nature,* 345 (1990), 342–344.

the Eocene most of the modern orders of mammals had appeared, including the order Primates.

At the end of the Mesozoic, great forests evolved with flowering trees that provided protection and food for early primates. Some of the early primates, who were quite unlike the primates of today, became extinct without leaving ancestors; others eventually evolved into modern species. This chapter describes what we know about the complex evolutionary history of the early primates.

## The Earliest Primates

In 1990, 10 tiny teeth were recovered from the Late Paleocene of Morocco; dated at 60 million B.P., they were named *Altiatlasius* after the High Atlas Mountains. These fossils suggest that the primates may have originated earlier, perhaps during the Early Paleocene, or possibly as far back as the Late Cretaceous.

Whether or not *Altiatlasius* is the earliest primate, the existing fossil record, in addition to studies of comparative anatomy, gives us a picture of what the early primates were probably like. Robert Martin sees the earliest primates as small, arboreal, nocturnal mammals living in tropical and subtropical forests.[2] They occupied niches characterized by small, thin branches and saplings. Weighing no more than 500 grams (1.1 pounds), they showed anatomical specializations, such as a grasping foot, for effective life in trees. The skin of the palm and fingers was covered with epidermal ridges that are associated with a refined sense of touch. The diet of these earliest primates consisted of plant material, such as fruits, and small animals, primarily insects.

The evolution of precise stereoscopic vision in the early primates aided in the hunting of small animal prey. A typical hunting pattern consisted of carefully stalking the prey; then, anchoring its body with its grasping feet, the animal reached forward and grabbed the prey with its hands. The primate then brought the prey to its mouth, where it was killed by biting.

[2]R. D. Martin, *Primate Origins and Evolution* (Princeton: Princeton University Press, 1990), pp. 656–660.

## The Eocene Primates

The Eocene began about 56½ million years ago, and it lasted about 21 million years. At the start of the Eocene, North America and Europe were still joined, but they had separated by the end of the epoch. This separation isolated animals that had evolved on what had previously been a single landmass.

The Early and Middle Eocene were very warm and wet with less seasonality than found at other times. This changed in the Late Eocene when climates became more diverse with marked seasons. Whales, rodents, bats, horses, and numerous other types of mammals were present by the end of the Eocene.

Two distinct groups of primates appeared at the beginning of the Eocene in both Europe and North America. They both possess a group of distinctive features, such as a postorbital bar and nails, that suggest that all primates are descended from a single ancestor. These two groups make up the families Adapidae and Omomyidae.

**The Adapids** Members of the Adapidae resemble in many ways the modern lemurs and lorises, yet they do not possess the dental comb that is so characteristic of modern prosimians. They are generally larger than the omomyids; many are as large as the larger lemurs living today. Nails are present on fingers and toes. The several relatively complete skeletons exhibit long torsos, legs, and tails, along with grasping feet with divergent big toes; these were adaptations for leaping and grasping behavior (Figure 12–1).

The adapid skull exhibits an elongated snout. The size of the brain case relative to the size of the facial skeleton is larger than in most mammals, and studies of the brain case show an enlargement of the frontal portion of the brain. A complete bony ring encircles the eye, and the forward position of the eyes results in overlapping fields of vision; the relatively small orbits suggest that the animal was diurnal.

The adapid incisors are short and spatulate and are vertically implanted in the jaw. The upper and lower canines interlock and show a marked sexual dimorphism; the anterior lower premolar is sectorial. Most adapids retained four premolars in each

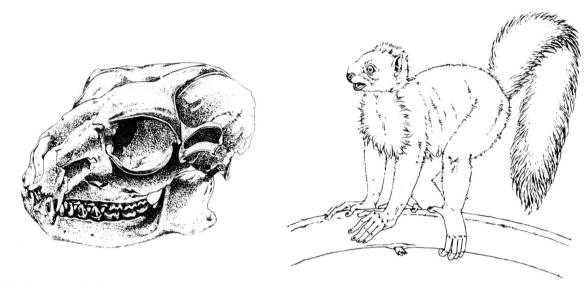

**FIGURE 12–1** *Smilodectes*
An Eocene adapid. (From "The Early Relatives of Man" by E. L. Simons. Copyright ©1964 by Scientific American, Inc. All rights reserved.)

quadrant of the jaw. Various adapid dentitions show differing dietary adaptations, including specializations for eating insects, fruits, and leaves.

The features of the adapids are summarized in Table 12–1.

**The Omomyids**   The family Omomyidae consists of a variety of small, nocturnal primates that contrast with the adapids in many ways (Table 12–1). The tarsal bones are elongated, which gives the omomyids a tarsier- and galago-like appearance.

The skull exhibits a short snout with a V-shaped jaw. The orbit is encircled by a complete bony ring, and some species possess the beginning of a postorbital closure. The large size of the orbits relative to the length of the skull suggests that the omomyids were nocturnal (Figures 12–2 and 12–3).

The lower incisors protrude and are moderately or sharply pointed. The canine teeth are relatively small; they are not interlocking, nor do they show marked sexual dimorphism. The anterior lower premolars are not sectorial. Most omomyids show a reduction in the number of teeth, and most show a dental formula with fewer than four premolars in each quadrant of the mouth. Details of their dentition suggests an insectivorous diet. The omomyids were generally smaller than the adapids.

**Plesiopithecidae**   While most of the early primate fossils belong to the Omomyidae or Adapidae, the fossil record is full of surprises. In 1994, a new fossil was described from Locality 41 at a site in Egypt known as the Fayum. This site is an important source of early primate fossils and will be discussed in detail shortly.

The new fossil, *Plesiopithecus*, is unlike any other known fossil. In fact, it belongs in its own new family, Plesiopithecidae, within the suborder Prosimii.[3] Investigators have recovered an almost complete, but badly crushed, skull of *Plesiopithecus*. As in other prosimians, the skull possesses a postorbital bar, but it lacks a complete eye socket. Elongated lower front teeth resemble a dental comb. The upper canines are sharp and dagger-like. The fossil is

---

[3]E. Simons and D. T. Rasmussen, "A Remarkable Cranium of *Plesiopithecus teras* (Primates, Prosimii) from the Eocene of Egypt," *Proceedings of the National Academy of Science* 91 (1994), pp. 9946–9950.

**TABLE 12-1**

**CHARACTERISTICS OF THE ADAPIDAE AND OMOMYIDAE**

| Characteristic | Adapidae | Omomyidae |
|---|---|---|
| Average body size | Above 500 grams | Below 500 grams |
| Snout | Elongated | Short |
| Mandibular symphysis | Usually fused | Unfused and mobile |
| Tooth row | Almost parallel | V-shaped |
| Incisors | Spatulate and more vertically implanted | Pointed and protruding |
| Size of central incisor relative to lateral incisor | Smaller | Equal or larger |
| Canines | Large, with marked sexual dimorphism | Small, with no sexual dimorphism |
| Lower anterior premolar | Sectorial | Not sectorial |
| Size of orbit | Small | Large |
| Number of premolars | Usually four | Usually fewer than four |
| Activity | Diurnal | Nocturnal |
| Postorbital closure | Absent | Absent or beginning |
| Nails | Present | Present |
| Tibia and fibula | Unfused | Fused |
| Tarsal bones | Not elongated | Elongated |
| Probable diet | Insects, fruit, leaves | Insects |

dated by geomagnetic dating and faunal correlations to about 36 million years B.P.

## The Evolution of Modern Prosimians and Tarsiers

A single upper molar from Egypt suggests that a loris was present in Africa in the Early Oligocene; other lorises are known from the Early Miocene of Africa and the Late Miocene of Asia. The galagos first appeared in the Early Miocene of Africa.

Although fossil lemurs have not been found in Africa, there are many similarities between the fossil lorises from the African continent and the lemurs of Madagascar. Anthropologists believe that the ancestral lemurs reached the island from the African mainland by rafting across the Mozambique Channel; even today, natural rafts of tangled vegetation form in the large rivers that flow into the Indian Ocean. Although the island is 400 kilometers (250 miles) from the mainland, in Early Eocene times the distance was only about 80 kilometers (50 miles).

Many paleoanthropologists consider the omomyids to be closely related to the tarsiers, but the relationship is far from clear. Over the past 10 years, a number of fossil tarsiers of great antiquity have been recovered. These fossils suggest that the tarsiers are a part of the initial radiation of the primates. While they may be related to the omomyids, the latter are most likely not their direct ancestors.

Since 1992, paleontologists have been excavating important beds located near the village of Shanghuang in the southern Jiangsu Province of China. Many primate fossils have been recovered that date about 45 million years ago, or from the Middle Eocene. Both adapid and omomyid fossils have been found. An important discovery is that of teeth

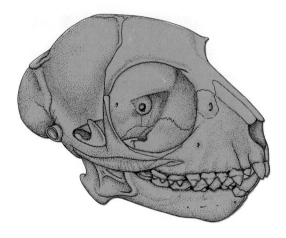

**FIGURE 12-3** *Necrolemur*
*Necrolemur*'s possible appearance is seen in this drawing by E. L. Simons.

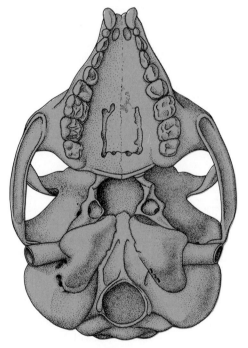

**FIGURE 12-2** *Necrolemur*
The skull of the omomyid *Necrolemur*.

about 50.5 million years ago. Its orbits are large relative to skull length, and it possesses a postorbital bar; however, a postorbital plate is not present.

**Summary**

In 1990, teeth were recovered from the Late Paleocene of Morocco; dated at 60 million years, they were named *Altiatlasius*. These are the earliest known primates in the fossil record. The primates probably originated during the Early Paleocene or the Late Cretaceous. The early primates were very small animals characterized by a grasping foot, epidermal ridges on palm and fingers, and stereoscopic vision. Their diet probably consisted of fruits and insects.

Among the Eocene primates, two distinct morphological patterns are found in North America and Europe; one characterizes the family Adapidae and the other the family Omomyidae. In some ways, the adapids resemble modern lemurs and lorises, although they lacked many features of these modern animals, including the dental comb. On the other hand, the omomyids resemble the tarsiers, although many of the tarsierlike features may be superficial. Their important characteristics are summarized in Table 12-1.

The early tarsiers are known from the Early Eocene of Wyoming, the Middle Miocene of China, the Late Eocene of Egypt, and the Early Miocene deposits in southeast Asia. A loris was present in Africa in the Early Oligocene, and the galagos first appeared in the Early Miocene of Africa.

belonging to a new species that has been placed into the genus *Tarsius,* the same genus that includes the modern tarsier.

Another fossil that appears to be a member of the tarsier family is *Shoshonius* (Figure 12–4). This fossil genus was first recovered during the mid-1980s in Wyoming; it dates to the Early Eocene,

**FIGURE 12–4** *Shoshonius*
Reconstruction of the omomyid *Shoshonius cooperi*.

## EVOLUTION OF THE ANTHROPOIDEA

The suborder Anthropoidea is the division of the order Primates that includes the living monkeys, apes, and humans. The earliest anthropoids in the fossil record date from the Middle Eocene and are known from sites in Africa and Asia. Elwyn Simons and Tab Rasmussen list the major specialized features that the Late Eocene and Oligocene anthropoids share with living anthropoids that distinguish the early anthropoids from the prosimians and tarsiers.

> These include (1) complete bony "eye sockets" or post-orbital closure; (2) a fused metopic suture (i.e., there is a single frontal bone rather than a right and a left); (3) an annular ectotympanic bone attached to the lateral bullar margin (the ear drum is supported by a bone hoop tightly anchored to the bony wall of the ear); (4) lower molars that have reduced trigonids and are bunodont in structure (having rounded puffy cusps for crushing and grinding); and (5) deep mandibles with broadly curved angular regions, steep ascending rami, and fused midline symphyses (indicating a chewing system capable of generating great forces).[4]

In 1927, G. E. Pilgrim described a jaw fragment from the Late Eocene of Burma that he named *Amphipithecus*; another jaw fragment was found in 1938 representing a second species, *Pondaungia*. In 1978, two additional jaw fragments were found in the same geological beds in central Burma (Figure 12–5). Again, each specimen represented one of the two species discovered earlier.

A site near Shanghuang, China, contains several fossils that may be early anthropoids. At least four primate species have been described; the best known belong to the genus *Eosimias*. The early fossil anthropoids are also known from a number of sites from North Africa and the Arabian Peninsula in the countries of Angola, Morocco, Algeria, Tunisia, Egypt, and Oman.

The evidence suggests that since the anthropoids were widely distributed by the Middle Eocene, their origins must lie in a much earlier time. The Late Eocene witnessed an important adaptive radiation of early anthropoids. Many of the early anthropoids closely resemble their prosimian contemporaries. In fact, it is often difficult to distinguish early anthropoids from prosimians, especially from dental evidence alone. An additional problem is that the anthropoid suite of features did not apparently appear all at once; specific traits appear to have evolved at different times.

### The Anthropoids of the Fayum

The richest fossil site from the Late Eocene and Early Oligocene is the Fayum in Egypt. During the Eocene and Oligocene, the Fayum was a tropical forest bordering on a large inland sea. The dense forests, swamps, and rivers were the homes of rodents; insectivores; bats; crocodiles; rhinoceros-size herbivores; miniature ancestors of the elephants; water birds such as herons, storks, and cranes; and many species of primates. Today, the once-lush tropical forest is a desert with little plant or animal life.

The rich deposits of fossil primates are a part of a series of sedimentary beds that make up the Jebel Qatrani Formation. This formation, some 350 meters (1150 feet) thick, spans the period from 36 to 33 million B.P., which includes the Late Eocene and Early Oligocene. Figure 12–6 shows a cross-section of the Jebel Qatrani Formation and the location of the discoveries of several genera.

**The Parapithecidae** The fossils discovered before 1988 were found in the upper levels of the Jebel Qatrani Formation, and they are referred to as the *upper-sequence primates*. They are classified into two families, the Parapithecidae and the Propliopithecidae. These primates are listed in Table 12–2.

The parapithecids are very small and similar in size to the living marmosets and tamarins. One species, weighing about 300 grams (0.7 pound), is the smallest known living or extinct Old World anthropoid. The few postcranial bones recovered suggest that they were probably branch runners and walkers and leapers; the structure of the teeth suggests that their diet most likely consisted of fruits rather than insects. One genus of this group, *Apidium*, is known from hundreds of individual fossils, and it is one of the most common mammals in the Fayum beds (Figure 12–7).

[4]E. L. Simons and T. Rasmussen, "A Whole New World of Ancestors: Eocene Anthropoidean from Africa," *Evolutionary Anthropology* 3 (1994), pp. 128–139.

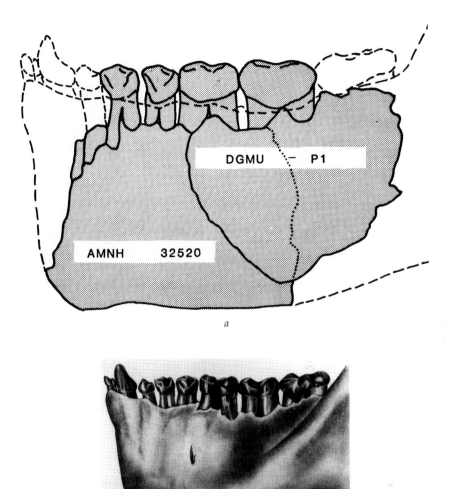

*a*

*b*

**FIGURE 12–5  Eocene Anthropoids**
Reconstruction of the lower jaw of *Amphipithecus mogaungensis* from the Late Eocene of Burma.

The parapithecids display several anthropoid features, yet they resemble the tarsiers in some details of dentition and other features. The mandible is V-shaped, and the canines show a marked sexual dimorphism. The molars show low, rounded cusps characteristic of living fruit eaters, and the thick enamel of the molars suggests the inclusion of hard nuts in the diet as well. Their dental formula is 2.1.3.3/2.1.3.3. This is the dental formula found today among New World monkeys, and it may represent the primitive dental formula of all anthropoids.

The Parapithecidae are most likely a branch that split off as part of the early anthropoid radiation.

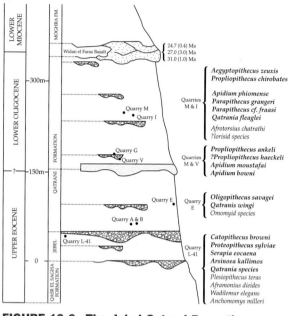

**FIGURE 12–6   The Jebel Qatrani Formation, Fayum**

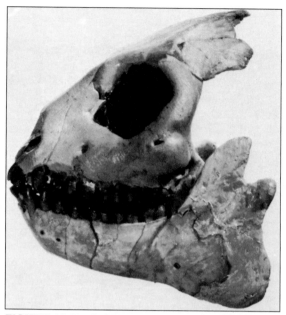

**FIGURE 12–7   *Apidium***

A reconstruction of *Apidium,* a member of the family Parapithecidae from the Fayum.

---

**TABLE 12-2**

**SOME FOSSILS FROM THE FAYUM, EGYPT**

| Quarry* | Epoch | Age (myr) | Species | Family |
|---------|-------|-----------|---------|--------|
| Quarries I, M | Early Oligocene | 33.1–33.4 | *Aegyptopithecus zeuxis* | Propliopithecidae |
| | | | *Propliopithecus chirobates* | Propliopithecidae |
| | | | *Apidium phiomense* | Parapithecidae |
| | | | *Parapithecus grangeri* | Parapithecidae |
| | | | *Qatrania fleaglei* | Parapithecidae |
| | | | *Afrotarsius chatrathi* | Tarsiidae |
| Quarries V, G | Early Oligocene | 33.8–34.0 | *Propliopithecus haecheli* | Propliopithecidae |
| | | | *Propliopithecus ankeli* | Propliopithecidae |
| | | | *Apidium moustafai* | Parapithecidae |
| Quarry E | Late Eocene | 34.0–35.1 | *Oligopithecus savagei* | Propliopithecidae |
| | | | *Qatrania wingi* | Parapithecidae |
| Quarry L-41 | Late Eocene | 35.6–35.9 | *Catopithecus browni* | Propliopithecidae |
| | | | *Proteopithecus sylviae* | Propliopithecidae |
| | | | *Serapia eocaena* | Parapithecidae |

*Quarries refer to specific deposits where fossils have been excavated.
Dates from E. L. Simons and T. Rasmussen, "A Whole New World of Ancestors: Eocene Anthropoidean from Africa," *Evolutionary Anthropology* 3 (1994), pp. 128–139.

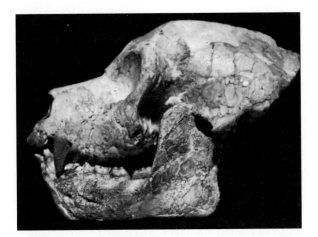

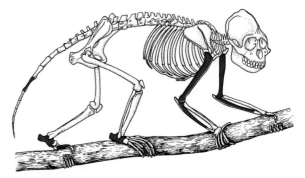

**FIGURE 12–9** *Aegyptopithecus*
The reconstructed postcranial skeleton of *Aegyptopithecus zeuxis*. Bones shown in color have been recovered.

**FIGURE 12–8** *Aegyptopithecus*
The reconstructed skull of *Aegyptopithecus zeuxis* from the Oligocene of the Fayum.

Although they possessed many features found in living anthropoids, the lineage probably became extinct.

**The Propliopithecidae** The best known propliopithecid is *Aegyptopithecus.* Although the first sparse fossil remains of *Aegyptopithecus* were discovered in 1906, today we are able to study many skulls and some postcranial material (Figure 12–8). The *Aegyptopithecus* male probably weighed about 6 kilograms (13 pounds) and is the largest of the Fayum primates.

*Aegyptopithecus* is a good example of a transitional form. Its long snout and relatively small brain case remind us of the adapids. The dentition points to an affinity with the hominoid line. Details of the teeth and jaw are similar to those of the Miocene and Pliocene hominoids.

The size of the eye sockets suggests that *Aegyptopithecus* was diurnal. The relative expansion of the visual areas of the brain and the relative decrease in the olfactory areas, as seen in the endocranial cast, provide evidence for the importance of vision over smell.

The locomotor behavior of *Aegyptopithecus* is known from the analysis of several postcranial bones (Figure 12–9). It was probably an arboreal quadruped capable of some degree of leaping and suspensory behavior.

The large number of *Aegyptopithecus* specimens makes it possible to analyze the material for variation within the species. Differences in tooth size suggest a marked sexual dimorphism. Living primates that live in large social units containing several adults of both sexes (such as the baboons) exhibit a high degree of sexual dimorphism. In contrast, primates that live in small social units (for example, the gibbons) show very little difference in size and proportions between the male and female. The fact that *Aegyptopithecus* shows a marked sexual dimorphism suggests that these primates lived in complex social groups.

The many similarities between *Aegyptopithecus* and modern apes have led some paleoanthropologists to view it as an early member of the Hominoidea. Yet recent studies have emphasized the many features that are more similar to those of the New World and Old World monkeys. It is very likely that the propliopithecids represent a group of primates ancestral to both the cercopithecoids and the hominoids.

An area of the Fayum known as Locality 41 is located in the lower strata of the Jebel Qatrani Formation. Several nearly complete skulls of *Catopithecus,* an early member of the family Propliopithecidae, were recovered in 1992 and 1993.[5] These

[5]E. L. Simons, "Skulls and Anterior Teeth of *Catopithecus* (Primates: Anthropoidea) from the Eocene and Anthropoid Origins," *Science* 268 (1995), pp. 1885–1888.

were small animals about the size of a modern marmoset. The dentition suggests a diet of insects and fruits. The diameter of the eye socket falls within the smaller numbers characteristic of living diurnal primates. Analysis of the few known postcranial bones suggests that *Catopithecus* was a branch runner and walker and leaper, moving through its habitat in a way that resembles the smaller living New World monkeys today.

## The Evolution of the New World Monkeys

The New World monkeys most likely evolved from the early African anthropoids. Throughout most of the Cenozoic, South America was separated from North America. Although there was never a land connection between South America and Africa during that era, a major lowering of sea levels occurred in the Middle Oligocene. This event would have exposed much of the African continental shelf, and many islands would have surfaced above the South Atlantic waters. Aided by these islands, the ancestral ceboid monkeys could have crossed the Atlantic Ocean on naturally formed rafts.

Although the New World monkeys and Old World monkeys evolved independently, the fact that they are descended from a common ancestor and that they occupy similar ecological niches have led to many similarities in their appearances. This is an example of parallelism. The earliest New World monkeys appear in the Late Oligocene.

The oldest fossil member of the superfamily Ceboidea is *Branisella*. It lived in Bolivia about 27 million years ago, during the Late Oligocene. This and another Late Oligocene fossil, *Dolichocebus*, which was found in Patagonia in southern Argentina, show little similarity with any contemporary primate population.

It appears that the differentiation of New World monkeys into their present subfamilies had occurred by Middle Miocene times. Known fossils include possible ancestors of the subfamily Cebinae (the modern squirrel and capuchin monkeys), the subfamily Alouattinae (the modern howler monkeys), and the subfamily Pithecinae (the modern sakis and uakaris). The similarity between the fossil and the modern owl monkey (subfamily Aotinae) is so close that they have been placed in the same genus, *Aotus* (Figure 12–10). Finally, an early

representative of the marmosets, family Callitrichidae, may also be present.

## The Evolution of the Old World Monkeys

The earliest fossils of the Old World monkeys belong to the genera *Prohylobates* and *Victoriapithecus*; they make up the family Victoriapithecidae. Specimens have been found in fossil beds from the Early and Middle Miocene in north Africa, Kenya, and Uganda. Both genera are known primarily from dental remains that are more primitive than the teeth of the later monkeys. Recent discoveries of dental, cranial, and postcranial material on Maboko Island in Kenya suggest that *Victoriapithecus* was a small primate weighing about 3.5 to 4 kilograms (7.7 to 8.8 pounds). It moved quadrupedally in the trees and on the ground.

The origin of the Cercopithecoidea is uncertain. Some paleoanthropologists view the Old World monkeys as a very specialized primate group that evolved as part of an earlier and more generalized anthropoid radiation. Certainly, the anthropoids had undergone a major adaptive radiation, and by

**FIGURE 12–10** *Aotus*
The mandible of *Aotus dindensis* from the Middle Miocene (below) and of the modern *Aotus trivigatus* (above).

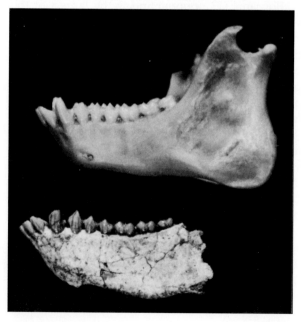

Early Miocene times they had become very diverse and numerous. Yet at this time, the cercopithecoids, represented by the victoriapithecids, were fairly uncommon. Hominoids occupied many of the ecological niches that would later be occupied by the monkeys. Only later, when the diversity and number of hominoids diminished, did the cercopithecoids assume a dominant role in the mammalian fauna.

There is a gap of 10 million years between the last record of the Victoriapithecidae and the next-oldest known fossil evidence of the Old World monkeys. The monkeys became more frequent in the Late Miocene fossil record. By this time, the Old World monkeys had divided into the two subfamilies seen today: the Cercopithecinae and the Colobinae.

The fossil cercopithecines closely resemble living populations to which they were undoubtedly ancestral or closely related. The earliest macaques lived in the Late Miocene or Early Pliocene of northern Africa. *Parapapio*, from the Lower Miocene of eastern and southern Africa, is probably close to the origin of the baboons and the mangabeys. The geladas, found today in a small range in the Ethiopian desert, were once widespread throughout Africa and extended eastward to India. One species belonging to the genus that includes the living gelada, *Theropithecus oswaldi*, is the largest known monkey (100 kilograms, or 220 pounds) (Figure 12–11). The guenons, today one of the most common monkeys in Africa, are represented by

**FIGURE 12–11** *Theropithecus*
A reconstruction of the skeleton of *Theropithecus oswaldi*, an extinct species of gelada from the Pleistocene at Olduvai Gorge.

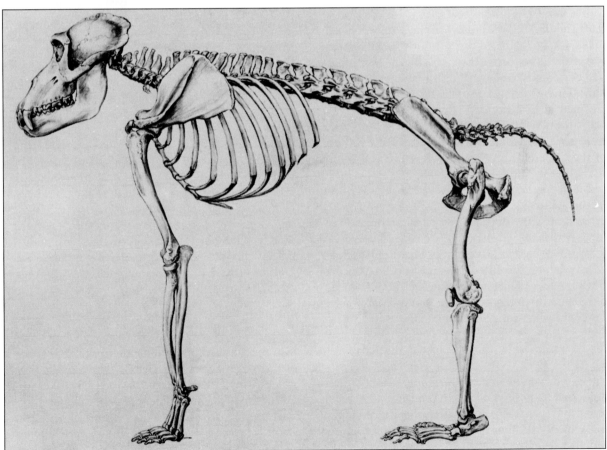

fragmentary dental remains that are found in Pliocene and Pleistocene beds in east Africa.

While the prehistoric cercopithecines are very similar to extant populations, this is not true for the colobines. Fossil members of the subfamily Colobinae are quite different from modern forms, and they are also found throughout a greater range. They were present in Late Miocene and Pliocene Europe. While they were also present in Asia, the fossils have been fragmentary.

## Summary

The suborder Anthropoidea includes the living monkeys, apes, and humans. They are characterized by complete bony eye sockets, a fused metopic suture, lower molars that have rounded puffy cusps, deep mandibles with fused midline symphyses, and other features.

The Jebel Qatrani Formation, of the Fayum of Egypt, dates from the Late Eocene and Early Oligocene. The primates of the upper levels belong to the families Parapithecidae and Propliopithecidae. The Parapithecidae, which includes *Aegyptopithecus*, may represent a group of primates ancestral to both the cercopithecoids and the hominoids.

The ceboids, or New World monkeys, are probably derived from early African anthropoids that traveled across the then-narrower Atlantic Ocean on natural rafts. The earliest-known ceboid dates from the Late Oligocene of Bolivia. The evolution of the ceboids into their present subfamilies took place by the Middle Miocene.

The cercopithecoids, or Old World monkeys, were relatively scarce in the Miocene; yet by the Pliocene and Pleistocene, they became common animals, especially in Africa. The earliest-known fossil primates belong to the family Victoriapithecidae, which dates from the Early and Middle Miocene. Beginning in the Late Miocene, the monkeys underwent a divergence into the two subfamilies, the Cercopithecinae and the Colobinae.

## EVOLUTION OF THE HOMINOIDEA

The living members of the superfamily Hominoidea include the living apes and humans. Fossil hominoids are well-known from the Miocene, during which time they underwent a major adaptive radiation.

Paleoanthropologists have known of the Miocene hominoids for well over a century; the first was described in 1856, three years before Charles Darwin published *On the Origin of Species*. Today they are well-represented in the Miocene fossil record. A few thousand individual hominoid fossils have been found, the majority of which are teeth and jaws. They have been given many different scientific names, and the result has often been a confusing and inaccurate taxonomy. Some paleoanthropologists refer to these paleospecies as "dental apes" because their dentition resembles the dentition of modern apes in many ways, while their postcranial skeleton is monkey-like, or perhaps simply primitive. We will not refer to them as apes here even though some of these forms are certainly related to the later apes; indeed, some may be related to the later hominids.

The earliest hominoids to appear in the fossil record date between 22 and 18 million B.P. from Early Miocene fossil beds of east Africa and Saudi Arabia. They most likely evolved from Oligocene primates, perhaps the propliopithecids. Most of the Miocene hominoids disappeared from the fossil record by around 8 million years ago during the Late Miocene. However, one genus, *Gigantopithecus*, survived into the Pleistocene of China and southeast Asia, where it was a contemporary with members of our genus, *Homo*.

## Hominoids of the Early Miocene

The fossil hominoids of the Early Miocene radiation belong to a number of genera including *Afropithecus*, *Heliopithecus*, *Limnopithecus*, *Nyanzapithecus*, *Proconsul*, *Rangwapithecus*, and *Turkanapithecus*. They range in size from that of small monkeys to that of chimpanzees, and they show a marked degree of sexual dimorphism. Their dentition suggests that fruit and leaves were both a part of their diet.

**Proconsul** Perhaps the best-known of the Early Miocene African hominoids are the several species of *Proconsul*. The cranial remains show many primitive features that characterize the early Old World anthropoids such as a slender mandible and a robust zygomatic arch. Dental features include incisors and canines that are more vertically implanted than they are in modern apes, slender

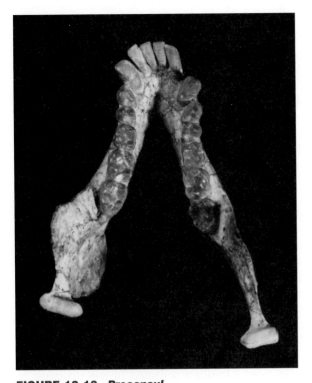

**FIGURE 12–12** *Proconsul*
The lower jaw of *Proconsul africanus* from Rusinga Island, Kenya.

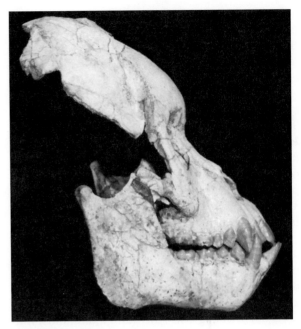

**FIGURE 12–13** *Proconsul*
The skull of *Proconsul africanus* from Kenya.

**FIGURE 12–14** *Proconsul*
A reconstruction of the skeleton of *Proconsul africanus*. Bones shown in color have been recovered.

canines, semisectorial lower anterior premolars, and thin enamel on the molars. The relative width of the jaw between the canines is less than that in modern apes; this results in a more V-shaped dental arcade (Figure 12–12). The V-shape contrasts with the U-shaped dental arcade of the modern chimpanzee and gorilla. The skull of *Proconsul africanus* is shown in Figure 12–13; note the prognathous face and the lack of brow ridges. The skull appears more delicate in build than the skulls of contemporary apes.

Some *Proconsul* postcranial material is known, but the fossils are primarily unassociated fragments rather than articulated skeletons. One exception is a small juvenile *P. africanus* skeleton representing an animal that weighed 15 to 20 kilograms (33 to 44 pounds). Its postcranial anatomy lacks the specializations that characterize the posture and locomotion of the living apes. Its hindlimbs are relatively longer than its forelimbs, which is more typical of monkeys than of apes (Figure 12–14). This animal was probably an arboreal quadruped that lacked the specializations for suspensory behavior that are found in modern apes. The discovery of a last sacral vertebra shows that *Proconsul*, like all contemporary apes, had no tail.

## Continents in Collision

In general, the hominoids of the Early Miocene are found in east Africa. During the Early Miocene, the continent of Africa was isolated by water from Europe and Asia. The fossil record clearly shows that animals that were evolving in Africa were distinct from those evolving in Europe and Asia.

In the Middle Miocene, the Afro-Arabian tectonic plate came into contact with the Eurasian plate, and a land connection developed between the two continents. The fossil record reveals migrations of Asiatic species into Africa and migrations of African species, including hominoids, into Asia between 16 and 14 million B.P. (Figure 12–15).

The forces produced by the coming together of the two large tectonic plates, along with volcanic and earthquake activity, led to the development of mountainous regions. These mountain ranges had a profound effect on climatic patterns. On the side of the mountains farthest from the sea, the land lay in a rain shadow and received little precipitation. In addition, the average annual temperature gradually lowered during the Miocene.

As a result of these geological and climatic changes, glacial ice expanded in the areas known today as Antarctica and Iceland. Across the wide expanses of Africa, Europe, and Asia, the once-low-lying landscape, which had been covered by a continuous tropical forest, developed into a mosaic of discontinuous and contrasting habitats. The tropical forests diminished in size, and they were replaced in many areas by woodlands (with their lower density of trees), woodland savannas (grasslands dotted with trees), true savanna grasslands, and semiarid regions (Figure 12–16).

Many animals that were adapted to forest niches remained in the diminishing forests, but as the area occupied by tropical forests decreased, competition for forest niches became more intense. Meanwhile, other populations entered the newly developing habitats. Thus, the scene was set for an adaptive radiation of the evolving hominoids.

## Hominoids of the Middle Miocene

The Middle Miocene hominoids are known from east and south Africa. *Kenyapithecus* from east Africa differs from the African hominoids of the Early Miocene in exhibiting many features of the skull that are found in contemporary apes; but the postcranial skeleton still lacks the specializations of modern apes. A single partial mandible assigned to the genus *Otavipithecus* dates from 13 million years ago and was discovered in the Otavi Mountains of Namibia, in southwest Africa.

During the Middle Miocene, the hominoids migrated from Africa and the Arabian Peninsula across the newly formed landbridge into Europe and Asia. Although an adaptive radiation may have begun in Africa, once they arrived in Europe and Asia, the hominoids underwent a major adaptive radiation.

It is reasonable to assume that the adaptive radiation of hominoids in the Middle Miocene was due, at least in part, to ecological diversity, which is associated with differences in diet. Dietary specializations are often reflected in the structure of the dentition. *Kenyapithecus* is characterized by a thick covering of enamel on its molar teeth, which contrasts with *Otavipithecus*, which exhibits a thin layer of enamel on its molars. We see this distinction between thin- and thick-enameled dentition in other hominoid species.

**European Hominoids**   A group of hominoids belonging to the family Pliopithecidae first appeared around 16 million years ago in Europe. They lived during the Middle and Late Miocene, and they were the earliest Eurasian hominoids. The pliopithecids disappeared from the European fossil

**FIGURE 12–15 Afro-Arabian/Eurasian land bridge** (*a*) Between 25 and 18 million years ago, the Afro-Arabian Plate came together with the Eurasian Plate. The initial land bridge (II) permitted the interchange of African and Eurasian mammals. Interference with the currents of the Tethys Epicontinental Seaway brought about major climatic changes. (*b*) Between 18 and 15 million years ago, a major land corridor was established and the first hominoids appeared in Europe. During this time, woodland and woodland savanna habitats began to replace the tropical forest. (*c*) Between 15 and 12 million years ago, these open country habitats expanded, as did the number of hominoid species. These maps are based on the work of Raymond L. Bernor.

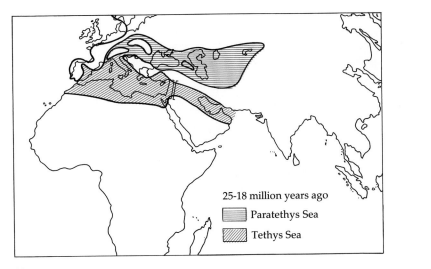

(a)

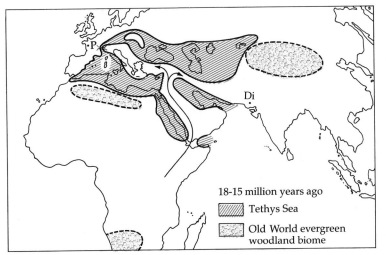

(b)

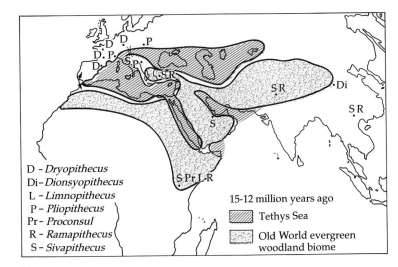

(c)

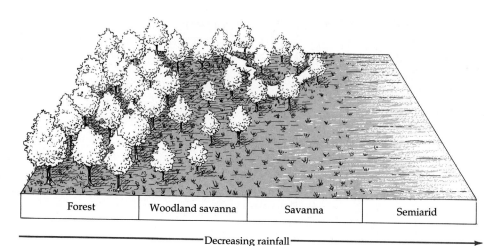

| Forest | Woodland savanna | Savanna | Semiarid |

————————————Decreasing rainfall————————————→

**FIGURE 12–16  Miocene Habitats**
During the Miocene, the once-low-lying tropical forest gave way to a mosaic of habitats including the woodland savanna, true savanna, and semiarid regions.

record about 12 million B.P., but they survived in China until 8 million B.P.

Members of genus *Pliopithecus,* which belong to the family Pliopithecidae, were small, gibbon-sized primates that weighed between 6 and 10 kilograms (13 and 22 pounds). The possession of a robust mandible and a large temporalis muscle, as indicated by the skull, suggests that *Pliopithecus* was primarily a leaf-eating primate capable of consuming tough vegetation (Figure 12–17). An analysis of the postcranial skeleton shows that *Pliopithecus* was an arboreal quadruped adapted for suspensory behavior in the manner of the New World semibrachiators such as the spider monkeys, although it lacked a prehensile tail. However, *Pliopithecus* does not show anatomical adaptations for the true-brachiation type of locomotion characteristic of modern gibbons and siamangs.

Middle Miocene European hominoids include members of the genus *Dryopithecus,* first discovered in France in 1856, and known primarily from the remains of teeth and jaws. While *Dryopithecus* has molars covered with thin enamel, other fossils from this period include specimens from eastern Europe and Turkey with thick-enameled molars like those of *Kenyapithecus.*

## Hominoids of the Late Miocene

The Miocene hominoids reached their greatest diversity in the Late Miocene. Their geographical range also appears to have expanded. Specimens have been found in sites in Spain, Italy, Greece, Hungary, Czechoslovakia, Turkey, Pakistan, India, and China. Only a few fossils are known from east Africa at this time. Important genera include *Dryopithecus, Lufengpithecus, Oreopithecus, Ouranopithecus, Rudapithecus,* and *Sivapithecus;* some paleoanthropologists recognize additional genera.

**Sivapithecus**   One of the best-known Late Miocene hominoids is *Sivapithecus* (Figure 12–18). *Sivapithecus* dentition is characterized by thick dental enamel on the molars, with the relatively low cusps of the large premolars and molars wearing flat; by relatively small canines with pronounced sexual dimorphism; and by broad central incisors. The mandible is relatively deep, the zygomatic arches are flaring, and the face is **orthognathous** (nonprojecting).

This dental pattern has been associated with the small-object-feeding complex, which is a dental adaptation to coarse materials such as grasses and seeds that are characteristic of the drier and more open habitats. Similar dental patterns have been observed in the living gelada and panda. The diet of the gelada emphasizes grasses and seeds while that of the panda consists of bamboos, which are members of the grass family. However, this view is not shared by all anthropologists. For example, some believe that this dentition was adapted for the processing of fruits with hard rinds.

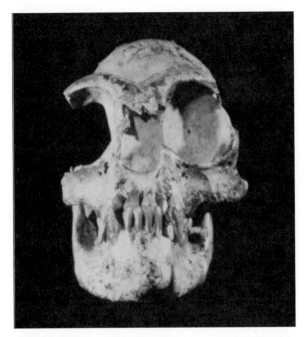

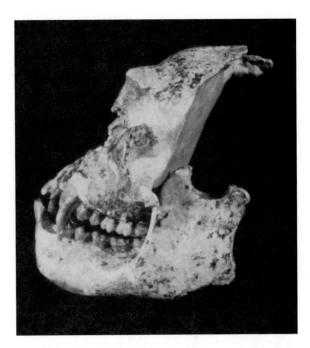

**FIGURE 12–17** *Pliopithecus*
Front and side view of *Pliopithecus* from the Miocene of Europe.

**FIGURE 12–18** *Sivapithecus*
The skull of *Sivapithecus*.

Similar problems exist in the interpretation of posture and locomotion in *Sivapithecus*. Fossilized bones of the limbs, hand, and foot lack the specializations found in the semibrachiators and knuckle walkers. The suggested pattern of locomotion has been described as arboreal quadrupedalism with a degree of climbing and suspension.

**Oreopithecus**    The first fossil to be assigned to the genus *Oreopithecus* was a juvenile mandible first described in 1872. Throughout the years, several *Oreopithecus* fossils have been found, primarily in Italy. In 1958, a badly flattened partial skeleton of a young adult male was discovered in an Italian coal mine. The material in which the skeleton was found is lignite, which is a soft form of coal that originated in a swampy forest habitat. Some fossils that may be related to the European *Oreopithecus* have been found in Africa.

*Oreopithecus* possesses large canines, a high degree of sexual dimorphism, teeth adapted to processing leafy materials, and a short, wide face (Figure 12–19). The postcranial skeleton exhibits longer

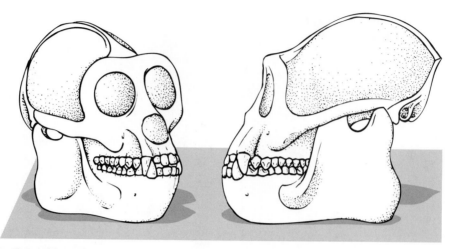

**FIGURE 12–19** *Oreopithecus*
Drawing of the reconstructed skull of the "Italian Swamp Ape."

forelimbs than hindlimbs and several features related to flexibility of the shoulder, elbow, and wrist. The ankle is very flexible, and the primate had a powerful grasping foot. Some paleoanthropologists interpret the skeleton as belonging to a primate that could climb vertical tree trunks and who moved by means of suspensory behavior. This suite of locomotor patterns would have been adapted to movement in a swampy forest region.

**Gigantopithecus**   Another important Late Miocene hominoid is *Gigantopithecus.* As its name implies, *Gigantopithecus* was a rather large primate; in fact, it was probably the largest primate that ever lived. Although there is disagreement about its actual size, *Gigantopithecus* may have been as tall as 2.75 meters (9 feet), and it may have weighed as much as 272 kilograms (600 pounds).

In traditional China, fossilized teeth known as "dragons' teeth" are used as medical ingredients. In 1935, Ralph von Koenigswald found teeth of *Gigantopithecus* in a Chinese pharmacy in Hong Kong. In the late 1950s and the 1960s, three mandibles and over a thousand teeth were discovered in caves in Kwangsi Province in southern China. These remains belonged to *G. blacki,* which inhabited China and Vietnam during the Pleistocene. *Gigantopithecus* survived to be contemporary with members of the genus *Homo.* An earlier species, *G. giganteus,* is known from the Late Miocene of India and Pakistan.

Figure 12–20 compares the mandible of *Gigantopithecus* with that of *Gorilla.* Dental features of *Gigantopithecus* include relatively small and vertically implanted incisors, reduced canines worn flat by the chewing of coarse vegetation, lack of a diastema, crowding of the molars and premolars, and so forth—all of which contrast markedly with the dentition of the gorilla. Note also the extremely heavy mandible in the region of the molars.

**The Origins of the Modern Hominoids**

It is apparent that a great number of hominoids—in addition to prosimians, tarsiers, and monkeys—were present during the Miocene. Figure 12–21 is an attempt to place many of these fossils into a diagram showing their evolutionary relationships to one another. It would be nice if we could present a diagram showing the exact relationships of the modern primates to their Miocene ancestors. When the number of fossils was few, many paleoanthropologists did just that; but as more and more specimens are recovered, we are seeing that the Miocene radiation represents a great diversification of primates. Virtually all became extinct; some left no descendants, while others left descendants that evolved through time into modern populations.

Based on some similarities in the skull, a relationship has been proposed between *Sivapithecus* and the modern orangutan. These features include a very narrow separation between the vertically elongated orbits. However, other cranial and post-

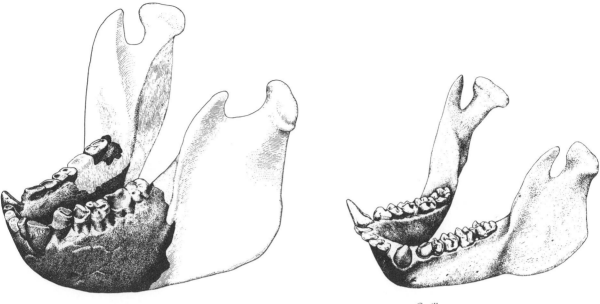

*Gigantopithecus*          *Gorilla*

**FIGURE 12–20  Mandibles of *Gigantopithecus* and *Gorilla***
(From "Gigantopithecus" by E. L. Simons and P. C. Ettel. Copyright ©1970 by Scientific American, Inc. All rights reserved.)

**BOX 12-2**

# What *Gigantopithecus* Had for Dinner

Most of what we know about fossil populations pertains to their skeletal anatomy. An important challenge in paleoanthropology is the reconstruction of other information about the life of extinct forms, including diet. Important clues about diet are provided by the structure of the teeth, the jaw, and the musculature of chewing, as well as microscopic markings on the teeth.

Another line of evidence for reconstructing diet comes from microscopic particles that are found in plants and that sometimes adhere to the surface of the teeth. Being minerals, these particles, called **phytoliths,** persist through the process of fossilization. Phytoliths are very tiny pieces of silica, and they are visible only under a scanning-electron microscope. Phytoliths form from the sil-

icon dioxide that is dissolved in the water that enters the plant. Once in the plant, the silicon dioxide solidifies into phytoliths. The phytoliths that form in different plants are often very distinctive in shape. The identification of specific phytoliths in association with archaeological and paleontological material can connect that material with a specific plant or plant group.

*Gigantopithecus* teeth were subjected to study under a scanning-electron microscope. Two kinds of phytoliths were found adhering to the surface of the tooth enamel. One is characteristic of grasses. Unfortunately, the same type of phytolith is found on different kinds of grasses, so the actual plant from which the phytoliths came could not be ascertained. The presence of these phytoliths,

however, supports the hypothesis that bamboo, a member of the grass family, formed a major part of the diet of *Gigantopithecus*. The other type of phytolith is most likely associated with durians; this is a fruit that is common throughout southeast Asia. Thus, use of modern microscopic technology in the study of microscopic structure of plants has added important information about the life of these extinct hominoids.

*Sources:* R. Ciochon et al., "Opal Phytoliths Found on the Teeth of Extinct Ape, *Gigantopithecus blacki:* Implications for Paleodietary Studies," *Proceedings of the National Academy of Sciences,* 1990; and D. R. Piperno, *Phytolith Analysis: An Archaeological and Geological Perspective* (San Diego: Academic Press, 1988).

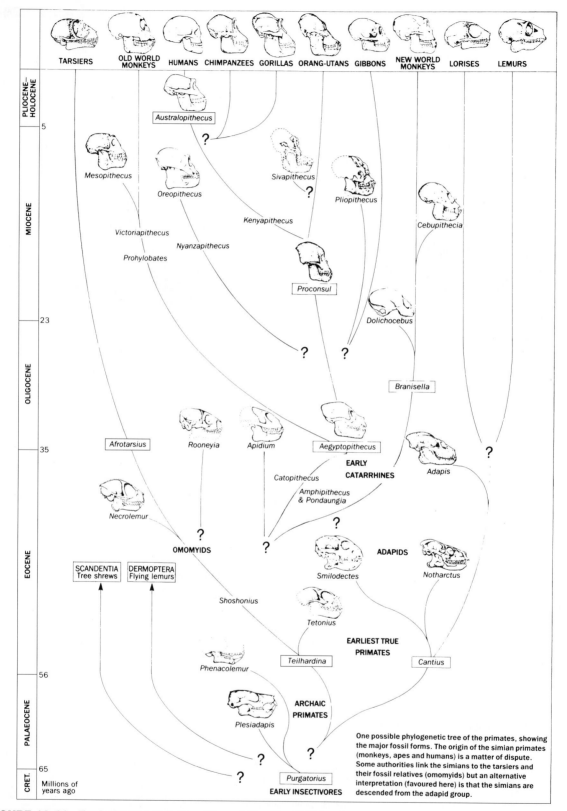

**FIGURE 12–21  Evolutionary Relationships of the Fossil Primates**

This is one of several possible schemes showing the evolutionary relationships of the fossil primates. This diagram differs in a few details from the discussion in this chapter.

cranial features are unlike that of the orangutan. The gorilla and chimpanzee probably evolved from Late Miocene primates that have yet to be discovered; the gibbon ancestor is also unknown to us.

**The Origins of the Hominidae**  Of course, from our point of view, perhaps the most significant questions are those surrounding the origins of the family Hominidae. Some paleoanthropologists hypothesize that the Late Miocene hominoid *Ouranopithecus* may be a candidate for the hominid ancestor.

*Ouranopithecus macedoniensis* is known from the Late Miocene of northern Greece, where the sites are dated from around 10 to 9 million B.P. (Figure 12–22). During the Late Miocene, the region in which *Ouranopithecus* lived was a woodland savanna; nearby mountains were covered by forests, and forests lined the large river that flowed through the area. *Ouranopithecus* is about the size of a female gorilla. The canine is smaller than the canines of other Miocene hominoids and the anterior lower premolar is not sectorial. Like many of the Miocene hominoids and the Pliocene hominids, *Ouranopithecus* possessed thick tooth enamel.

Unfortunately, there are few fossils from the time when the hominids most likely diverged from the Miocene hominoids. By the Pliocene, the earliest hominid fossils appeared; these are the subjects of the next chapter.

**FIGURE 12–22  *Ouranopithecus***
Male skull and mandible of *Ouranopithecus* reconstructed from several specimens.

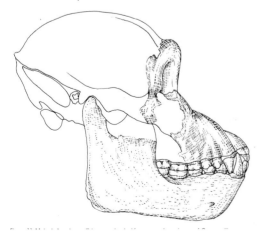

## Summary

The superfamily Hominoidea includes the living apes and humans. The earliest hominoids to appear in the fossil record are from the Early Miocene fossil beds of east Africa, dated between 22 and 18 million B.P. They are sometimes called "dental apes" because their dentition resembles the dentition of modern apes in many ways, while their postcranial skeleton is monkeylike, or perhaps simply primitive. Most of the Miocene hominoids disappeared from the fossil record by around eight million years ago during the Late Miocene. However, one genus, *Gigantopithecus,* survived into the Pleistocene of China.

Perhaps the best-known Early Miocene hominoid is *Proconsul.* The cranium shows many features that characterize the early Old World anthropoids such as a slender mandible and a robust zygomatic arch. *Proconsul* was probably an arboreal quadruped that lacked the specializations for suspensory behavior that are found in modern apes.

In the Middle Miocene, the Afro-Arabian tectonic plate came into contact with the Eurasian plate, and a land connection developed between Africa and Asia. This permitted the migration of the African hominoids into Asia between 16 and 14 million B.P. The forces produced by the coming together of the two large tectonic plates significantly altered the lay of the land, climate, and vegetation.

The Middle Miocene hominoids of Africa are represented by *Kenyapithecus* and *Otavipithecus. Kenyapithecus* differs from the African hominoids of the Early Miocene in exhibiting many features of the skull that are found in contemporary apes, but the postcranial skeleton still lacks the specializations of modern apes.

The pliopithecids were the earliest Eurasian hominoids. They first appeared around 16 million years ago in Europe and lived during the Middle and Late Miocene. Middle Miocene European hominoids include members of the genus *Dryopithecus.*

The Miocene hominoids reached their greatest diversity and geographical range in the Late Miocene. Specimens have been found in sites in Europe, Turkey, southern Asia, China, and east Africa. One of the best-known genera is *Sivapithecus.*

*Gigantopithecus* was probably the largest primate that ever lived; it may have been as tall as 2.75

meters (9 feet), and it may have weighed as much as 272 kilograms (600 pounds). Its specialized dental features appear to be an adaptation to the processing of tough fibrous material such as bamboo.

## STUDY QUESTIONS

1. What is the earliest fossil evidence of the primates? What were these animals like?
2. Two distinct morphological patterns exist in the Eocene, the adapid and omomyid. Describe the general features that distinguish one pattern from the other.
3. Describe the fossil evidence for the origins of the anthropoids.
4. While we often try to visualize fossil populations using images of living primates, now-extinct species probably do not resemble closely any living form. Using the two best-known fossil primates, *Aegyptopithecus* and *Proconsul,* write a short description of the animal as if it were living and being observed by you.
5. Contrast the relative diversity and frequency of hominoid and cercopithecoid fossils in the Early Miocene and the Late Miocene. What is the relationship between the early hominoids and the early cercopithecoids?
6. Describe the major geological event of the Miocene and describe its effect on the evolution of the primates.
7. We can divide most of the Miocene hominoids into those with thick enamel and those with thin enamel on their molars. What are some of the genera that fall

into each group? What are the possible relations between enamel thickness and diet?
8. What were some of the better-known hominoid genera of the Miocene? Which are the best candidates as ancestors of the living hominoids?

## SUGGESTED READINGS

Ciochon, R., J. Olsen, and J. James. *Other Origins: The Search for the Giant Ape in Human Prehistory.* New York: Bantam, 1990. This nontechnical book describes the search for *Gigantopithecus* fossils in Vietnam and reviews the evidence of hominoid prehistory in Asia.
Conroy, G. C. *Primate Evolution.* New York: Norton, 1990. This volume contains a very detailed and well-illustrated discussion of the fossil primates, and it includes discussions of the paleoclimates and biogeography of each period of time.
Fleagle, J. G. *Primate Adaptation and Evolution,* 2nd ed. New York: Academic, 1998. This book surveys primate evolution from 65 million years ago to the present.

## SUGGESTED WEB SITES

Fossil Hominoids from China:
   http://www.cruzio.com/~cscp/pics1.htm
Primate Evolution Links:
   http://www.oneonta.edu/~anthro/links/
   primevol.html

Additional Web sites are listed in the *Workbook* that accompanies this text.

# The Early Hominids

*No matter what kind of clothes were put on Lucy, she would not look like a human being. She was too far back, out of the human range entirely. That is what happens going back along an evolutionary line.*

*Her head, on the evidence of the bits of her skull that had been recovered, was not much larger than a softball. Lucy herself stood only three and one-half feet tall, although she was fully grown. That could be deduced from her wisdom teeth, which were fully erupted and had been exposed to several years of wear. My best guess was that she was between twenty-five and thirty years old when she died. She had already begun to show the onset of arthritis or some other bone ailment, on the evidence of deformation of her vertebrae. If she had lived much longer, it probably would have begun to bother her.[1]*

—Donald C. Johanson and Maitland A. Edey

## Chapter Outline

The 1977 television miniseries *Roots* was the most-watched series of its time. People seem to be fascinated with tracing their line of descent back through several hundred years of time. Many are drawn to physical anthropology by their curiosity about even deeper roots. The exploration of the

---

[1] D. C. Johanson and M. A. Edey, *Lucy: The Beginnings of Humankind* (New York: Simon and Schuster, 1981), pp. 20–21. Copyright ©1981 by Donald C. Johanson and Maitland A. Edey. Reprinted by permission of Simon and Schuster, Inc.

**297**

origins of humanity raises many interesting questions: With what other contemporary animals do we have a close common ancestry? Why did the hominid line go off in the direction it did? At what point should we use the word "human" to describe our ancestors? What made these ancestors human? What makes us unique?

Modern humans and a number of hominid fossils belong to the genus *Homo*. This chapter is about the three genera of early hominids that fall outside of *Homo*—*Ardipithecus*, *Australopithecus*, and *Paranthropus*. At least one species within this group, most likely a species of *Australopithecus*, is considered by paleoanthropologists to be ancestral to the genus *Homo*, and ultimately ancestral to ourselves.

## DISCOVERIES OF THE EARLY HOMINIDS

The origin of the hominids seems to lie sometime between 7.5 and 5 million years ago in Africa. No fossils found before 7.5 million years ago show enough of the hominid complex of characteristics to be considered hominid.

The early hominids of the Pliocene and early Pleistocene belong to several species of the genera *Ardipithecus*, *Australopithecus*, *Paranthropus*, and *Homo*. In this section, we will tell the story of the first three of these genera by recounting the history of their discovery and by reviewing some of the more important sites where their remains have been found. The fossil representatives of these genera are known from South Africa, from the east African countries of Tanzania, Kenya, and Ethiopia, and from Chad in north central Africa.

### The Earliest Hominids

In 1992 and 1993, paleoanthropologists Tim White, Gen Suwa, and Berhane Asfaw excavated a site in the Middle Awash area of Ethiopia known as Aramis (Figure 13–1).[2] At this site, almost 650 vertebrate fossils were collected. The collection contains 17 hominid fossils, including a fragment of a mandible, the remains of a cranial base, many teeth, and two fragmented pieces of limb bones (Figure 13–2). Early in 1995, a new find was announced that consisted of more than 90 fragments that represented about 45 percent of an adult skeleton. These include parts of the skull, arms, vertebral column, pelvis, and legs.[3]

At Aramis, carnivore tooth marks are commonly found on the bones, and the bones appear to have been fragmented before fossilization. At the time the bones were deposited, the area was a flat, wooded plain on which the carcasses of medium and large mammals were torn apart by carnivores.

The geology of this area is characterized by sedimentary beds layered between volcanic **tuffs,** layers of volcanic ash that have been solidified through the pressure of being buried in the earth. The lower Gàala Tuff Complex (*gàala* means "camel" in the Afar language), located just beneath the fossil bed, has been dated by the single-crystal laser fusion $^{40}Ar/^{39}Ar$ method to 4.4 million B.P. This date provides the maximum age of the fossils.

**The Morphology and Taxonomy of the Aramis Hominids** The teeth found at Aramis are hominidlike in many ways. For example, they exhibit a reduced incisorlike canine. Other dental features are more apelike. The canine, although incisorlike in form, is larger than the postcanine teeth. Other dental features are intermediate. The Aramis fossils possess tooth enamel of a thickness intermediate between that of the later hominids and chimpanzees.

The cranial and dental material examined so far suggests that this species is very closely related to the chimpanzee and may represent the earliest stage in the evolution of erect bipedalism. Yet because of the fragile nature of the more than 90 skeletal pieces, it will be some time before the postcranial skeleton can be studied.

The fossils from Aramis have been placed into the genus and species *Ardipithecus ramidus*. The discoverers of the new fossils propose that *A. ramidus* is not directly ancestral to the later hominids but is a sister group sharing an as-yet-

---

[2]T. D. White, G. Suwa, and B. Asfaw, "*Australopithecus ramidus,* a New Species of Early Hominid from Aramis, Ethiopia," *Nature* 371 (1994), pp. 306–312.

[3]H. Gee, "New Hominid Remains Found in Ethiopia," *Nature* 373 (1995), p. 272.

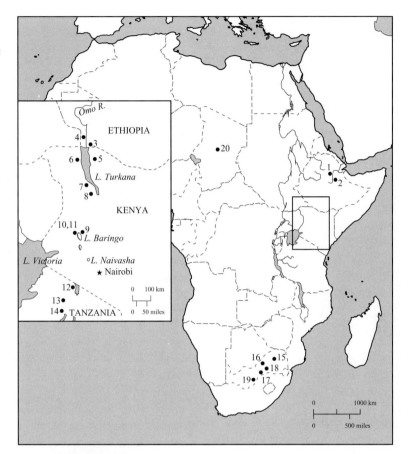

**FIGURE 13–1 Map of Early Hominid Sites**
*1* Hadar, *2* Middle Awash (Maka, Belohdelie, Aramis, Bouri), *3* Fejej, *4* Omo (Usno, Shungura),
*5* East Turkana (Koobi Fora, Allia Bay), *6* West Turkana (Lokalakei, Nariokotome), *7* Lothagam,
*8* Kanapoi, *9* Chesowanja (Chemoigut), *10* Baringo (Tabarin), *11* Baringo (Chemeron), *12* Peninj,
*13* Olduvai Gorge, *14* Laetoli, *15* Makapansgat, *16* Sterkfontein, *17* Swartkrans, *18* Kromdrai,
*19* Taung, *20* Bahr el Ghazal.

unknown common ancestor. *Ramid* is the word for "root" in the language of the Afar people who live in the region. The name suggests that this species lies near the point in hominoid evolution when the hominids split off from the line leading to the modern apes.

**The Early Hominids of South Africa**

Much of South Africa rests on a limestone plateau. Limestone is often riddled with caves, and many of the more ancient ones have become completely filled in with debris. The 1920s was a period of tremendous growth in South Africa, and the need for limestone, a constituent of cement, brought about an increase in quarrying activities. The blast-ing activities of workers in limestone quarries often expose the ancient cave fills. The material that fills these caves is **bone breccia,** which consists of masses of bone that have been cemented together with the calcium carbonate that has dissolved out of the limestone.

In 1924, fossil material from the quarry at Taung was delivered to Raymond A. Dart of the University of Witwatersrand in Johannesburg, South Africa. Embedded within the bone breccia was a small skull. Dart spent 73 days removing the limestone matrix from the skull; he spent 4 years separating the mandible from the rest of the skull. The fossil that emerged from the limestone matrix consisted of an almost complete mandible, a facial

**FIGURE 13–2** *Ardipithecus ramidus*
Jaw fragment with teeth found at Aramis, Ethiopia.

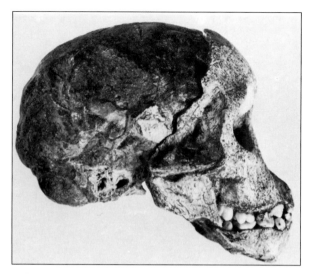

**FIGURE 13–3 Taung Baby**
The mandibular fragment, facial skeleton, and natural endocranial cast of *Australopithecus africanus* found at Taung, South Africa, in 1924.

**FIGURE 13–4** *Australopithecus africanus*
(Top) Taung mandible; (middle and bottom) mandibles from Makapansgat, South Africa (MLD 2 and MLD 18).

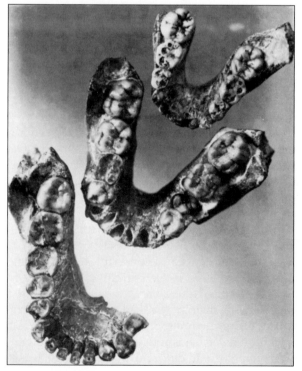

skeleton, and a natural endocranial cast (Figure 13–3). The jaws contained a set of deciduous teeth along with the first permanent molar (Figure 13–4). Dart called the find the "Taung baby"; he named it "Taung" after the quarry in which it was found, and he called it "baby" because it was a child.

Dart published his find on February 7, 1925.[4] He named the skull *Australopithecus africanus*, from *Australo*, meaning "southern," and *pithecus*, meaning "ape." Dart saw in this skull the characteristics

[4]R. A. Dart, "*Australopithecus africanus,* the Man-Ape of South Africa," *Nature* 115 (1925), p. 195; see also R. A. Dart, "Recollections of a Reluctant Anthropologist," *Journal of Human Evolution* 2 (1973), pp. 417–427.

of a primitive hominid, the most primitive of humankind's known ancestors. Dart based his opinion on the hominidlike structure of the teeth, the nature of the endocranial cast, and the forward position of the foramen magnum, which was consistent with erect bipedalism.

Other paleoanthropologists, however, were not convinced. Some noted the difficulties of making valid comparisons using an incomplete juvenile skull; some paleoanthropologists argued that the skull showed close affiliations to the apes. Others were convinced that the earliest hominids would be characterized by apelike features associated with a large brain, which was precisely what was seen in the later-discredited Piltdown skull (Chapter 11). Yet Dart persisted in his contention that the Taung baby was a bipedal hominid; the years have proved him correct.

**The Sterkfontein Valley**   In his day, Dart's interpretation of *Australopithecus africanus* was not accepted by most paleoanthropologists, and he had very little support for his ideas. One exception was Scottish physician Robert Broom. After retiring, Broom went to South Africa in the 1930s and 1940s. Broom investigated three caves in the Sterkfontein Valley, which is located between Johannesburg and Pretoria. Broom excavated the first cave, Sterkfontein, between 1936 and 1939; he almost immediately uncovered the first adult specimens of *A. africanus* (Figure 13–5). Further excavations by John T. Robinson, C. K. Brain, Phillip V. Tobias, and A. R. Hughes have brought the inventory of hominid fossils to nearly 400 (Figure 13–B in color insert).

Because of the lack of volcanic activity in the area, radiometric dating techniques cannot be used. Many attempts have been made to date the material; the most useful has been the correlation of recovered fossil mammals with similar fossils of known date from east Africa. The evidence suggests a date for the Sterkfontein fossils of around 2.5 million B.P.

Although postcranial bones are not often found, paleoanthropologists in South Africa announced in 1994 that they had recovered four bones of a left foot from a box of mammalian bones that had originally been excavated in 1980 at the site of Sterkfontein. The fossils are dated between 3.5 and 3.0 million B.P. These bones (Sts 573), nicknamed "Lit-

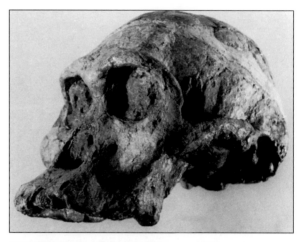

**FIGURE 13–5** *Australopithecus africanus*
Specimen Sts 5 from Sterkfontein, South Africa.

tle Foot," fit together to form an arch that extends from the heel of the foot to the beginning of the big toe. Workers then returned to the cave in an attempt to recover additional bones. In 1997, they found eight more foot and lower leg bones. Further work in 1998 uncovered even more leg and arm bones as well as a skull. The principal investigator, R. J. Clarke, believes that eventually an entire skeleton will be recovered.

In 1938, Broom excavated at the cave site of Kromdraai. Here he found a specimen that, unlike *A. africanus*, possessed a sagittal crest on the top of the cranium, a large mandible, and very large premolars and molars. He placed this fossil in the new species *Paranthropus robustus*.[5]

In 1948, the first remains of what would eventually represent over 100 individuals were recovered from the site of Swartkrans, also located in the Sterkfontein Valley. These hominids also belong to the species *Paranthropus robustus* (Figure 13–6). The Swartkrans fossils are younger than those from Sterkfontein; they date from about 1.7 to 1.1 million B.P.

C. K. Brain, who began his excavations in 1965, has reconstructed what the cave at Swartkrans was

---

[5]Originally placed in the species *Paranthropus robustus,* many anthropologists in the 1960s moved *P. robustus* into the genus *Australopithecus* as *A. robustus.* More recently, most anthropologists have returned the species to *Paranthropus. Paranthropus* means "parallel to man."

**FIGURE 13–6   *Paranthropus robustus***
Specimen SK 48 from Swartkrans, South Africa.

like when the fossils were deposited (Figure 13–7). At that time, the cave was an underground cavern connected to the surface by a vertical shaft. Because of a concentration of moisture in the relatively treeless region, trees were found in the region of the shaft. Leopards are known to drag their prey into trees, where the carcass is relatively safe from scavengers and other carnivores. For this reason, the remains of the animals of prey would have found their way down the shaft and into the cave. This accounts for the relative lack of postcranial remains, which would have been destroyed to a large extent by chewing. *A. africanus* and *P. robustus* would have been among the leopard's prey (Figure 13–8).

---

**BOX 13–1**

## Naming Fossils

Fossils are given designations that include an abbreviation for the site (and sometimes the museum housing the specimens) and an acquisition number. The latter is usually given to fossils in the order in which they are discovered. The site abbreviations used in this book are AL (Afar Locality), BOU-VP (Bouri Vertebrate Paleontology), ER (East Rudolf, the former name for East Turkana), KNM (Kenya National Museums), KP (Kanapoi), KT (Koro Toro), LH (Laetoli Hominid), MLD (Makapansgat Lime Deposit), OH (Olduvai Hominid), SK (Swartkrans), Sts (Sterkfontein), and WT (West Turkana).

---

**Other South African Sites**   In 1992, two unerupted teeth were found at Gladysvale, which is located some 13 miles east of Sterkfontein. The teeth, probably belonging to *A. africanus,* are somewhat more developed than those of the Taung child. Additional fossils from Gladysvale may contribute to our understanding of early hominid development.

Located about 200 miles north of Pretoria is the largest of the South African cave sites, Makapansgat, which has been excavated by J. W. Kitching, Dart, and Hughes. The Makapansgat hominids belong to the species *A. africanus;* they date from around 3 to 2.6 million B.P. (Figure 13–4).

### The Early Hominids of East Africa

In contrast to the tentative dating of sites in South Africa, the fossils unearthed in east Africa are associated with sound chronometric dates. Sedimentary deposits hundreds of meters thick represent former rivers, lakes, and deltas. These extensive deposits are interrupted by layers of basalt and volcanic ash. These layers, which can be dated by several chronometric techniques, act as time markers. Many volcanic eruptions produced ashfalls that were swept by the winds and fell over thousands of square miles. Since each ashfall is characterized by a unique chemical composition, it is possible to correlate layers of ash that formed in different regions from a particular eruption (Figure 13–9).

The Plio-Pleistocene sediments of east Africa are rich in fossils. Generally, the majority of fossils come from three major regions: Olduvai Gorge and the surrounding areas in Tanzania; the Turkana Basin, including Lake Turkana in Kenya, and the Omo River region in southern Ethiopia; and the Afar Basin of northern Ethiopia.

**Olduvai Gorge**   Olduvai Gorge, in east Africa, is a 25-kilometer (15½ mile)-long canyon cut into the Serengeti Plain of Tanzania (Figure 13–10). The sedimentary beds, some 100 meters (328 feet) thick, have yielded bones of ancient hominids along with the tools that they made, as well as the remains of the animals they ate.

Geologically, the sequence of sedimentary layers at Olduvai is divided into a series of beds. Bed I and the lower part of Bed II show a continuous sequence of sediments that were deposited when a

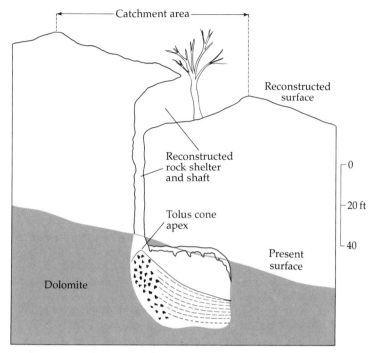

**FIGURE 13–7 Reconstruction of the Cave at Swartkrans**
Diagrammatic section through the Swartkrans hillside. The upper reconstructed part has been removed by erosion since the accumulation of the fossil deposit.

**FIGURE 13–8 Evidence of Leopard Predation**
This photograph shows part of the skull (parietal) of a juvenile hominid from Swartkrans (SK 54). The two holes in the skull match the lower canines of a leopard. The fossil leopard mandible (SK 349) comes from the same deposit.

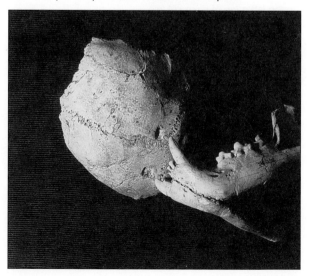

large lake existed on what is now part of the Serengeti Plain. Bed I and Lower Bed II span the time from 1.9 to 1.5 million B.P.

Hominid sites are located at what were once lake margins or stream banks. These areas provided the early hominids with a source of water as well as with a concentration of animal food. In addition, fossilization more frequently occurs in these habitats as opposed to the savanna grasslands and tropical forests. The oldest hominid site is located just above a layer of basalt with a potassium-argon date of 1.9 million B.P. Hominid material has also been recovered from Middle and Upper Bed II, dated between 1.5 and 1.1 million B.P. During this time, the freshwater lake became smaller, and much of the landscape became a dry grassland.

The story of Olduvai Gorge is the story of Louis and Mary Leakey. Louis Leakey was predisposed to think of the early South African hominids as a side branch of the hominid line that played no role in the evolution of modern humans. He saw the

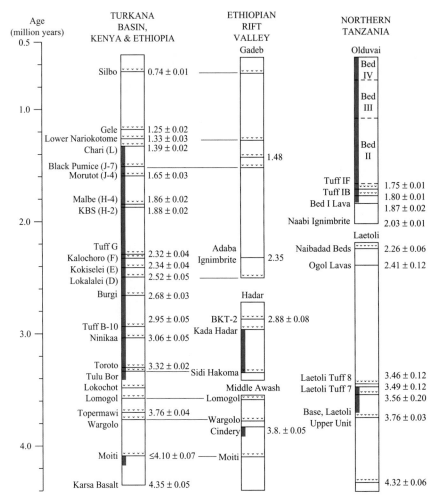

**FIGURE 13–9  Stratigraphic Beds in the Turkana Basin, the Ethiopian Rift Valley, and Northern Tanzania**

Dated units are shown in each stratigraphic column. The heavy line on the left edge of each column indicates an interval in which hominid fossils have been found. (Fossils have been lumped into 0.1-million-year intervals.)

genus *Homo* as a lineage of great antiquity whose major features were a large brain and the ability to manufacture tools. Although he and Mary later went on to make several important discoveries of early *Homo,* their earliest significant find was a hominid that did not belong to the genus *Homo.*

Louis Leakey began his work in Olduvai in 1931; Mary arrived on the scene in 1935. Although the discoveries of animal fossils and important archaeological material were made early, the first significant hominid find did not appear until 1959. In that year,

Mary Leakey found an almost-complete skull (the mandible was missing) of a hominid, designated OH 5, who lived at Olduvai Gorge around 1.75 million B.P. (Figure 13–11). This date was the first to be determined by the then-new potassium-argon dating technique. At a time when most anthropologists considered hominid evolution to be confined to the last one million years, this new information almost doubled the time span estimated for human evolution. First named *"Zinjanthropus boisei,"* this fossil is now designated as *Paranthropus boisei.*

**FIGURE 13–10   Olduvai Gorge, Tanzania**

**BOX 13-2**

# Mary Nicol Leakey (1913–1996)

History is characterized by the existence of families whose members have achieved eminence in some area of human endeavor, such as the Bach family in music, the Darwin family in science, and the Leakey family in paleoanthropology. The "matriarch" of the Leakey family died on December 9, 1996. She was 83.

Mary Leakey, along with her late husband, Louis Leakey, who died in 1972, and her son and daughter-in-law Richard and Meave Leakey, has made major contributions to our knowledge of hominid evolution in East Africa. Although her outspoken husband, Louis Leakey, re-

ceived much of the credit for their East African discoveries, most of their significant finds were made by Mary. In 1948, while on an expedition to Rusinga Island in Lake Victoria, Mary found skull fragments of *Proconsul africanus*, which at that time was thought to be a human ancestor. A decade later at Olduvai Gorge, she uncovered a 1.75-million-year-old skull of *Zinjanthropus boisei*, now called *Paranthropus boisei* (OH 5). At a time when most anthropologists considered hominid evolution to have occurred within the last million years, this find almost doubled the estimated time span for human evolution.

In 1978, Mary Leakey made what some feel was her most spectacular discovery. At the site of Laetoli in Tanzania, she found 3.6-million-year-old footprints impressed in what had been volcanic ash. These footprints showed that hominids, perhaps *Australopithecus afarensis,* were walking fully upright at a very early date. The footprints confirmed that upright walking preceded the evolution of large brains by millions of years.

---

*Sources:* F. Golden, "First Lady of Fossils—Mary Nicol Leakey: 1913–1996," *Time,* December 23, 1996, p. 69; B. Wood, "Mary Leakey 1913–1996," *Nature,* 385 (1997), p. 28.

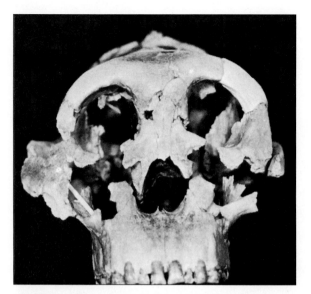

**FIGURE 13–11 Paranthropus boisei**
A hominid (OH 5) from Olduvai Gorge, originally named
"Zinjanthropus boisei."

**Omo River Basin** From 1966 to 1974, teams of American, French, and Kenyan paleoanthropologists, including F. Clark Howell, Yves Coppens, and Richard Leakey, explored the Omo River Basin of southern Ethiopia, just north of Lake Turkana. In this area are two major sedimentary formations located some 25 kilometers (15½ miles) apart. The Shungura Formation, some 760 meters (2493 feet) thick, consists of sediments representing prehistoric rivers, lakes, and deltas; the sedimentary layers are interlaced with tuffs. The Shungura Formation is divided by major tuffs into a series of members, with Member A being the lowest. Hominid fossils have been recovered from Members B through lower G; they date from 3.3 to 2.1 million B.P. The smaller Usno Formation, approximately 170 meters (558 feet) thick, overlaps the Shungura Formation in time; it dates to around 3.3 to 3.0 million years ago.

The early sediments of the Omo River basin represent fairly wet conditions. Lake Turkana was larger than it is today, and many of the fossils are associated with past marshy conditions. The earlier fossils are fragmentary and difficult to assign to a species, but they appear to belong to an early species of *Australopithecus*.

The remains of hominids similar to *P. boisei* from Olduvai Gorge appear in the middle of the Shungura sediments. The earliest appearance of *Paranthropus* is associated with major ecological changes in the Omo basin, in which the forest and marsh environments were slowly replaced by more open habitats, including grassland.

**Koobi Fora** A significant series of sites is located in the Koobi Fora region of Kenya. This area of sediments covers approximately 1000 square kilometers (386 square miles) and extends some 25 kilometers (15½ miles) inland along the eastern shore of Lake Turkana. The Koobi Fora Formation is some 560 meters (1837 feet) thick, and it is divided by tuffs into 8 members. The fossils all occur between the Tulu Bor tuff, dated at 3.3 million B.P., and the Chari tuff, dated at 1.4 million B.P. The date of the KBS tuff is of major importance in interpreting the fossils from east Lake Turkana. The fossils fall into two groups: those above and those below the KBS tuff, which is dated at 1.8 million B.P.

The Koobi Fora region has been studied since 1969 by Richard Leakey, the son of Louis and Mary, and his colleagues. More than 200 fossil hominids have been recovered so far. The early hominid material appears to include members of the species *P. boisei; Australopithecus* may be present as well (Figure 13–12).

In addition, Koobi Fora has revealed an excellent fossil record of pollen, freshwater shellfish, and many mammalian groups including prehistoric members of the pig, cattle, horse, and elephant families. This fossil record has enabled geologists to reconstruct many of the geological and climatic events in the area, and it serves to correlate the area with other regions based on similarities in the fossils recovered.

**West Lake Turkana** In 1984, excavations began west of Lake Turkana, where the Nachukui Formation extends 5 to 10 kilometers (3 to 6 miles) inland along the western shore of the lake. Investigators found a cranium, WT 17000, at the site of Lomekwi. The find was named the "Black Skull" because of its black color; the color was derived from the manganese-rich sediments in which it was found (Figure 13–13). WT 17000 appears to resemble *P. boisei*, yet this particular specimen is charac-

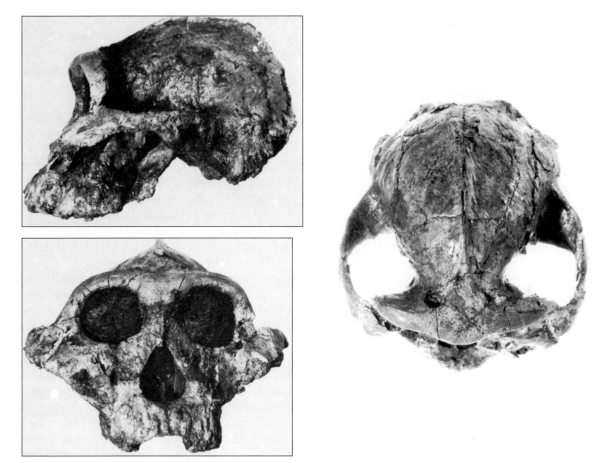

**FIGURE 13-12** *Parathropus boisei*
Side, front, and top views of KNM-ER 406 from East Lake Turkana, Kenya.

terized by a small cranium and the retention of some primitive features from the earlier *Australopithecus*. WT 17000 is dated at 2.5 million B.P., somewhat earlier than the 2.3-to-1.4-million B.P. range for *P. boisei*. Some investigators place this find into the species *Paranthropus aethiopicus*.

**Kanapoi** In 1995, Meave G. Leakey, Richard Leakey's wife, and her colleagues published the description of a new species of *Australopithecus*.[6] It

[6]M. G. Leakey, G. S. Feibel, I. McDougall, and A. Walker, "New Four-Million-Year-Old Hominid Species from Kanapoi and Allia Bay, Kenya," *Nature* 376 (1995), pp. 565–571. Additional photographs of the Kanapoi fossils and site can be seen in M. Leakey, "The Dawn of Humans: The Earliest Horizon," *National Geographic* 188 (September 1995), pp. 38–51.

was named *Australopithecus anamensis*. The name *anamensis* comes from *anam*, which means "lake" in the language of the Turkana people. The fossils were found at the site of Kanapoi, located southwest of Lake Turkana in Kenya. Additional material has also been found 48 kilometers (30 miles) away at Allia Bay on the eastern side of Lake Turkana. The sediments at both sites were once a part of an ancient lake of which Lake Turkana is a remnant. The habitat may have been one characterized by dry open woods or brush with gallery forest along the rivers.

The fossil beds at Kanapoi have been known for some time; a humerus was recovered at Kanapoi in 1965. The new material, discovered beginning in 1994, includes an incomplete mandible with all its teeth intact, a partial left temporal, additional jaw

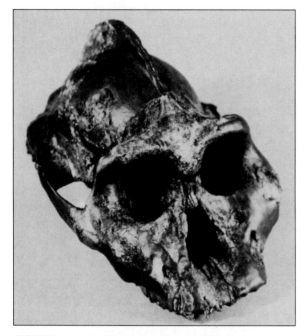

**FIGURE 13–13** *Paranthropus aethiopicus*
WT 17000, the "Black Skull," from Lomekwi, West Turkana, Kenya.

fragments and isolated teeth, a distal left humerus, and the proximal and distal sections of a right tibia (Figures 13–14 and 13–15). The Kanapoi beds also include fossil fish, aquatic reptiles, and many terrestrial mammals.

The Kanapoi fossils have been dated by $^{40}$Ar/$^{39}$Ar dating and by correlation with dated sediments at other east African sites. The fossils found in the lower horizon, dated by the $^{40}$Ar/$^{39}$Ar method, date between 4.17 and 4.07 million years ago. The upper horizon, which contains the postcranial material, is not as precisely dated, but it is thought to date from between 4.1 and 3.5 million B.P. The Allia Bay fossils, which consist mainly of teeth, were found within and below the Moiti tuff, which has been dated at 3.9 million B.P.

One of the most striking observations about this species has to do with the jaws and teeth; in many ways, they are similar to those of Miocene apes, yet they are associated with postcranial material similar in many ways to that of early *Homo*. Since at Kanapoi the dental and cranial material has

been found primarily in the lower horizon and the postcranial material in the upper horizon, the assertion that they belong to the same species will remain open to question until additional material is found.

**Hadar** In 1973, the International Afar Research Expedition, led by Yves Coppens, Maurice Taieb, and Donald Johanson, began working at Hadar, which is located in the Afar Basin in northern Ethiopia. Because of the special conditions of burial and fossilization, some fossils are very well preserved. Between 1973 and 1977, more than 240 hominid fossils were recovered. The stratigraphic beds date from between 3.6 and 2.9 million B.P.

The first hominid find, consisting of four leg bones, was made in the fall of 1973. A partial femur and tibia fit together to form a knee joint; this provided the oldest skeletal evidence of fully developed erect bipedalism. In 1975, the team discovered a collection of 197 bones representing at least thirteen individuals, both adults and immatures. Some believe that these individuals, called the "First Family," all died at the same time; they were possibly killed and buried by a sudden flood or other catastrophe. This material has been placed into the species *Australopithecus afarensis* (Figure 13–16).

Perhaps the best-known fossil is "Lucy" (AL 288-1), which was found in 1974 (Figure 13–17). This remarkable find consists of 40 percent of a skeleton. "Lucy" provided the first opportunity for anyone to study the skull and postcranial remains from the same individual of this antiquity.

After a break in time, paleoanthropologists returned to Hadar in 1990. Since then they have recovered 53 new specimens that are attributed to

---

**BOX 13-3**

## Fossil "Rock"

The 1974 find of *Australopithecus afarensis* was given the formal acquisition number AL 288-1, but to the team that found the skeleton, it is known as "Lucy," after the Beatles song "Lucy in the Sky with Diamonds."

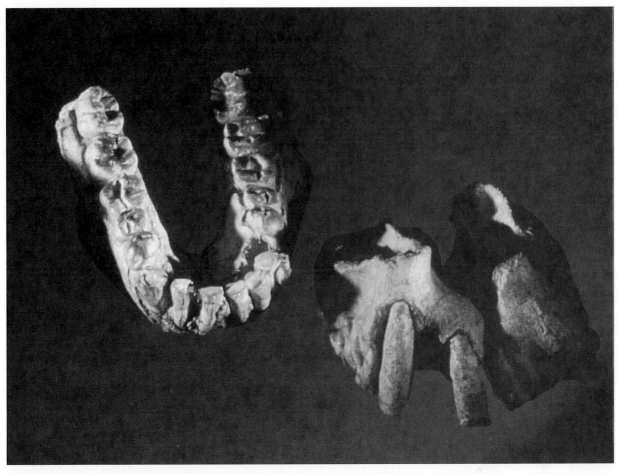

**FIGURE 13–14** *Australopithecus anamensis*
(left) A mandible (KNM-KP 29281) and (right) maxilla (KNM-KP 29283) from the site of Kanapoi, Kenya.

*A. afarensis.*[7] Among these is a cranial fragment dated at 3.9 million B.P., which makes it the oldest-known specimen of this species.

In 1994, the team announced the discovery of three-quarters of a skull that was pieced together from more than 200 fragments (Figure 13–18). This specimen (AL 444-2) is dated at approximately 3.0 million B.P., which is about 200,000 years younger than "Lucy." The skull is larger than that of "Lucy"; in fact, it is the largest known cranium outside of the genus *Homo*. Many paleoanthropologists believe that it probably represents a male. Other important finds include an ulna and a partial humerus.

**The Middle Awash** South of Hadar in the Afar Basin are several sites in a region known as the Middle Awash, named after the Awash River. A number of hominid fossils have been recovered in this region, including remains from Maka and Belohdelie.

---

[7]W. H. Kimbel, D. C. Johanson, and Y. Rak, "The First Skull and Other New Discoveries of *Australopithecus afarensis* at Hadar, Ethiopia," *Nature* 368 (1994), pp. 449–451.

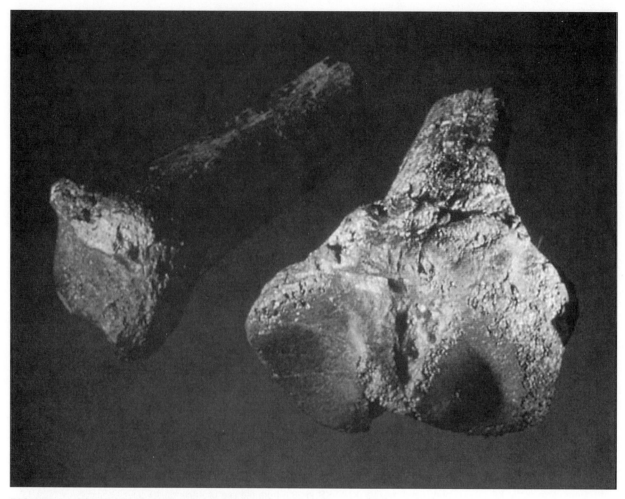

**FIGURE 13–15** *Australopithecus anamensis*
Two pieces of a right tibia from the site of Kanapoi, Kenya. The section on the right is part of the
knee, while the section on the left articulates with the foot.

In 1996 through 1998, a series of fossils were re-covered from the Hata Member of the Bouri For-mation. One of these finds was that of an incom-plete cranium (BOU-VP-12/130), which has been dated to 2.5 million B.P. (Figure 13–19). Character-ized by large anterior dentition and other distinc-tive details of dental anatomy, the cranial remains were placed in a newly created species, *Australop-ithecus garhi*.[8] (The word *garhi* means "surprise" in the language of the Afar people.) The postcranial

fossils are not associated with the cranial remains and, therefore, they cannot be placed with certainly within the new species at this time. Associated bones of other animals show clear evidence of butchering activity in association with isolated stone tools.[9]

**Konso**  In 1993, several hominid fossils were re-covered from the site of Konso, Ethiopia.[10] The

[8]B. Asfaw et al., "*Australopithecus garhi*: A New Species of Early Hominid from Ethiopia," *Science* 284 (1999), pp. 629–635.

[9]J. de Heinzelin, "Environment and Behavior of 2.5-Million-Year-Old Bouri Hominids," *Science* 284 (1999), pp. 629–635.
[10]G. Suwa et al., "The First Skull of *Australopithecus boisei*," *Nature* 389 (1997), pp. 489–492.

THE EARLY HOMINIDS **311**

**FIGURE 13–16 Reconstructed skull of**
**Australopithecus afarensis**

Konso skull, KGA 10-525, is the only specimen of
*P. boisei* known to date that includes both parts of
the cranium and mandible. The skull is that of a relatively old male with a cranial capacity of about 545
cubic centimeters. Eight other specimens have been
catalogued. The Konso skull expands the geographical range of this species, and the skull and
other material from the site show that there is a significant range of variation present among specimens
that have been placed into the species *P. boisei*.

The fossil beds at Konso were first discovered in
1991. All of the *P. boisei* material has been recovered
from the KGA 10 locality, which is thought to represent part of an alluvial fan extending into a lake.
These hominid fossils were found in deposits associated with fossils of animals that lived in grassland habitats.

The site has yielded evidence of remains of
*P. boisei, H. erectus,* and tools that date from the same
period of time. The *P. boisei* material has been recovered from tuffs dated between 1.41 and 1.43 million years B.P., as determined by $^{40}$Ar/$^{39}$Ar dating.
Since most of the other *P. boisei* specimens date between 2.2 and 1.6 million years B.P., the new skull
becomes the most recent specimen of this species.

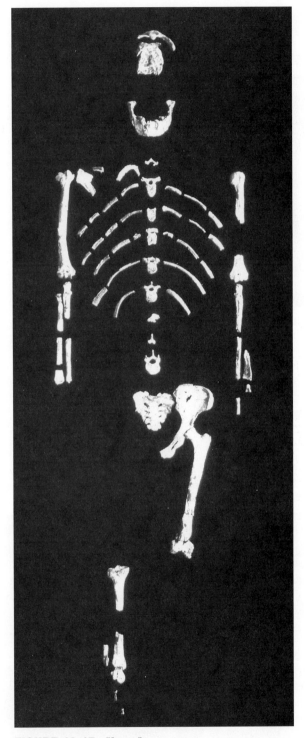

**FIGURE 13–17 "Lucy"**
A female skeleton of *Australopithecus afarensis* (AL 288-1),
from Hadar, Ethiopia.

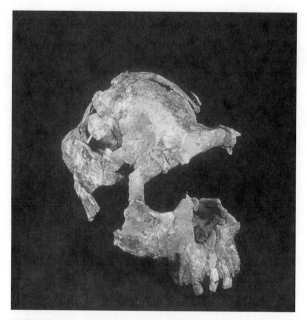

**FIGURE 13–18** *Australopithecus afarensis*
Skull of a male (AL 444-2) from Hadar.

**Laetoli**   Laetoli is located in Tanzania, near Lake Eyasi; it is approximately 50 kilometers (31 miles) south of Olduvai Gorge. Mary Leakey and Tim White excavated the remains of several hominids dated between 3.8 and 3.6 million B.P. These fossils have been placed into the species *A. afarensis* (Figure 13–20).

One day at Laetoli about 3.6 million years ago, a light fall of volcanic ash fell over the land, and a light drizzle moistened the ash; later, hominids walked across the ash field. A day or so later, another ashfall covered their tracks; the remaining impressions were discovered in 1978. The site consists of two footprint trails more than 27.5 meters (90 feet) long. Thirty-eight footprints of a small hominid make up the western trail, and 31 footprints make up the eastern trail.

The eastern trail is not as well-defined as the western trail. Some see the western trail as having been made by a female and the eastern trail having been made by a large male. The trails are so close together that Ian Tattersall sees the hominids as "walking in step and accommodating each

**FIGURE 13–19   Lateral view of *Australopithecus garhi* (BOU-VP-12/130) from the Middle Awash, Ethiopia**

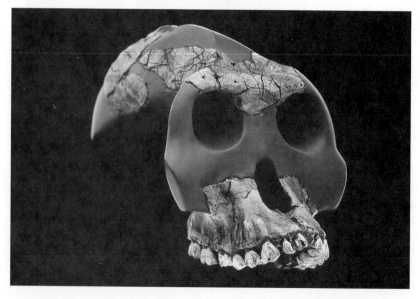

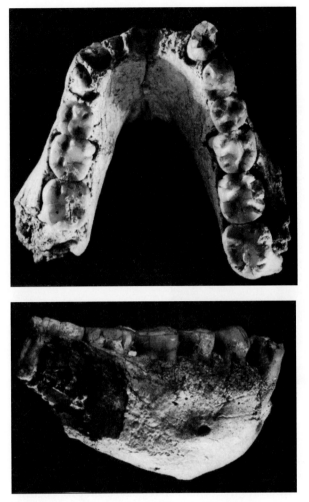

**FIGURE 13–20** *Australopithecus afarensis*
Top and side views of the mandible LH 4 from Laetoli, Tanzania.

other's stride."[11] The eastern trail is not as distinct as the western one because, as some paleoanthropologists believe, a third hominid was stepping in the large male's footprints as the three hominids walked over the sticky ash flow. The footprints exhibit specializations of the human foot, which include a well-developed arch and a nondivergent big toe (Figure 13–21).

### Early Hominids from North Central Africa

The distribution of known specimens of *Ardipithecus, Australopithecus,* and *Paranthropus* has led many paleontologists to conclude that these early hominids existed only in the eastern and southern regions of the African continent. Yet this apparent distribution of early hominid populations may simply be a reflection of the distribution of known fossil sites from this time. The announcement in 1995 that fossils had been recovered in northern Chad, some 2500 kilometers (1550 miles) west of the Rift Valley, suggests that the distribution of the early hominids may be greater than that suggested by the better-known south and east African sites.[12]

In 1993, several sites were discovered in the region of Bahr el Ghazal near Koro Toro in northern Chad. A fragment of an adult hominid mandible, which contains the crowns of several teeth, was recovered from the site known as KT 12; the fossil is known as KT12/H1 (Figure 13–22). The find is associated with other animal fossils that have been dated between 3.5 and 3.0 million years B.P.

The Chad mandible resembles *A. afarensis* in many ways yet differs from other specimens of this species in some features. In 1996, the discoverers placed the specimen into the new species *Australopithecus bahrelghazalia.*

### Drawing a Family Tree

Paleoanthropologists see a significant amount of diversity among the early hominids. The question arises: Does this variable assembly of specimens represent a few highly variable species or does it represent a larger number of different species?

Some paleoanthropologists argue that the range of variation among the early hominids may have been greater than that found among contemporary hominoids. For example, the degree of sexual dimorphism may have been considerably greater than that found among living humans and apes.

The specimens from Hadar and Laetoli provide a good example of this dilemma. Many paleoanthropologists see these fossils as representing a single species, *A. afarensis.* The smaller specimens,

[11]I. Tattersall, "The Laetoli Diorama," *Scientific American* 279 (September 1998), p. 53.

[12]M. Brunet et al., "The First Australopithecine 2,500 Kilometers West of the Rift Valley (Chad)," *Nature* 378 (1995), pp. 273–275.

**FIGURE 13–21  Hominid Footprints at Laetoli, Tanzania**

such as "Lucy," would represent females, while the larger, more robust material, represented by AL 444-2, would represent males. If there is only one species present at this time, then *A. afarensis* could be the common stock from which the later *Australopithecus, Paranthropus,* and *Homo* evolved. This viewpoint has led to an evolutionary scheme whereby *A. afarensis* is seen evolving into two branches, one leading to *A. africanus* and *Homo* and the other leading to *P. robustus* and *P. boisei.* (Other variations of this scheme have also been proposed.)

Other paleoanthropologists see the Hadar and Laetoli populations as presenting two different species. One population shows robust features that would later lead to *Paranthropus;* the other population includes "Lucy" and leads to *A. africanus* and *Homo.* (Again, other variations on these themes have been suggested.) Several "family trees" have been proposed. One is presented here in Figure 13–23.

The recent identification of the species *A. garhi* in 1999 provides a candidate for the origins of the genus *Homo.* This species is not represented in Figure 13–23 since the diagram was constructed before the discovery of *A. garhi.*

While in the 1980s the general tendency among paleoanthropologists was to see the existence of a relatively few number of variable species, today many scholars are proposing that this variation is best explained on the basis of the existence of mul-

**FIGURE 13–22  *Australopithecus bahrelghazalia***
Fragment of an adult mandible (KT12/H1) from northern Chad.

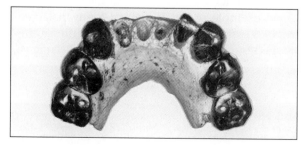

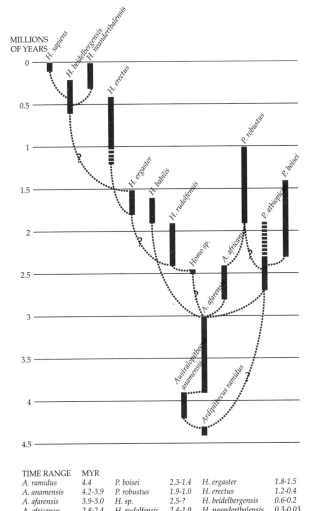

MILLIONS OF YEARS

| TIME RANGE | MYR | | | | |
|---|---|---|---|---|---|
| A. ramidus | 4.4 | P. boisei | 2.3-1.4 | H. ergaster | 1.8-1.5 |
| A. anamensis | 4.2-3.9 | P. robustus | 1.9-1.0 | H. erectus | 1.2-0.4 |
| A. afarensis | 3.9-3.0 | H. sp. | 2.5-? | H. beidelbergensis | 0.6-0.2 |
| A. africanus | 2.8-2.4 | H. rudolfensis | 2.4-1.9 | H. neandertbalensis | 0.3-0.03 |
| P. aethiopicus | 2.7-1.9 | H. babilis | 1.9-1.6 | H. sapiens | 0.1-0.0 |

**FIGURE 13–23 Phylogenetic Tree**
One of several proposed phylogenetic trees showing the relationships among fossil hominid species. This particular tree predates the discovery of *A. garhi.*

tiple species. It now appears that there may have been many more early non-*Homo* species of hominid than earlier believed, and that the early history of the Hominidae may have been marked by several evolutionary lines, perhaps the result of a modest adaptive radiation.

## Summary

The fossil evidence of hominids that fall outside of the genus *Homo* are found exclusively on the African continent: South Africa, the east African countries of Ethiopia, Kenya, and Tanzania, and the north central African country of Chad.

The first fossil of this group to be discovered was at Taung, South Africa, in 1924. Raymond Dart placed the juvenile skull into the species *Australopithecus africanus.* Today we have many fossils from several South African caves that are placed into two species: *A. africanus* and *P. robustus.*

Early hominids are well-known from several east African sites associated with extensive sedimentary deposits. Prehistoric volcanic activity associated with these beds provides material for chronometric dating. The most significant sites are those of Olduvai Gorge, the Omo River basin, Koobi Fora, west Lake Turkana, Kanapoi, Hadar, the Middle Awash, Konso, and Laetoli. The fossils have been assigned to several species. The earliest in time are *Ardipithecus ramidus, Australopithecus anamensis,* and *A. afarensis.* Later species are *Australopithecus africanus, A. bahrelghazalia, A. garhi, Paranthropus aethiopicus, P. robustus,* and *P. boisei.*

Figure 13–1 is a map of many of the African sites that have yielded the material discussed in this section. No evidence has been found to suggest that *Ardipithecus, Australopithecus,* or *Paranthropus* existed outside the African continent. It appears that Charles Darwin was correct when he stated that human ancestors originated in Africa. It was not until after the origin of the genus *Homo* that populations belonging to this genus ventured out of Africa and began the odyssey that ultimately led humans to the far corners of the planet Earth.

Table 13–1 lists most of the sites that we have discussed, including some minor sites that have not been mentioned. The table also lists for each site the hominid species found; however, there are many controversies surrounding the placement of particular fossils in particular species. The dates for many hominid sites are also tentative.

This section has introduced nine species of early hominids. These species are summarized in Table 13–2.

## EARLY HOMINIDS: INTERPRETATIONS OF THE EVIDENCE

The genera *Ardipithecus, Australopithecus,* and the later *Paranthropus* together form a group of hominids that contrast with the hominids belonging to the genus *Homo. Ardipithecus* and *Australopithecus* existed earlier in time than *Homo;* however, *Paranthropus* was contemporary with early members of

**TABLE 13-1**

**SUMMARY OF MAJOR EARLY HOMINID SITES**

| Site* | Location | Estimated age (million years B.P.) | Species present |
|---|---|---|---|
| **Taung** | South Africa | 2.6–2.4 | *A. africanus* |
| **Sterkfontein** | South Africa | 2.5 | *A. africanus* |
| **Swartkrans** | South Africa | 1.7–1.1 | *P. robustus* |
| **Kromdraai** | South Africa | ? | *P. robustus* |
| **Makapansgat** | South Africa | 3.0–2.6 | *A. africanus* |
| **Gladysvale** | South Africa | ? | *A. africanus* |
| **Olduvai Gorge** | Tanzania | 1.75 | *P. boisei* |
| Peninj | Tanzania | 1.3 | *P. boisei* |
| **Laetoli** | Tanzania | 3.7–3.5 | *A. afarensis* |
| **Koobi Fora** | Kenya | 3.3–1.4 | *P. boisei* |
| **Lomekwi** | Kenya | 2.5 | *P. aethiopicus* |
| Lothagam | Kenya | 5.5–5.0 | ? |
| **Kanapoi** | Kenya | 4.2–4.1 | *A. anamensis* |
| **Allia Bay** | Kenya | 3.9 | *A. anamensis* |
| Chesowanja | Kenya | 1.4 | *P. boisei* |
| Tabarin | Kenya | 4.2 | *A. afarensis* |
| **Omo** | Ethiopia | 3.3–2.1 | *A. afarensis* |
| | | | *P. aethiopicus* |
| | | | *P. boisei* |
| **Hadar** | Ethiopia | 3.6–2.9 | *A. afarensis* |
| Maka | Ethiopia | 3.4 | *A. afarensis* |
| **Bouri** | Ethiopia | 2.5 | *A. garhi* |
| **Aramis** | Ethiopia | 4.4 | *A. ramidus* |
| Fejej | Ethiopia | 4.2 | *A. afarensis* |
| **Könso** | Ethiopia | 1.4 | *P. boisei* |
| **KT 12** | Chad | 3.5–3.0 | *A. bahrelghazalia* |

*Sites in boldface are discussed in the text.

the genus *Homo*. Most likely a species of *Australopithecus* gave rise to *Homo*.

*Australopithecus* and *Paranthropus* are characterized by a small cranial capacity, a relatively large projecting facial skeleton, large premolars, molars with thick enamel, and postcranial features that suggest that their primary means of locomotion was erect bipedalism. Other than these general features, these genera are quite variable. The vast length of time during which these genera existed, their considerable geographical variation, and the fragmentary nature of much of the fossil material make it difficult to make broad generalizations. What follows are descriptions and interpretations of the evidence. The ideas presented here are hypotheses that will be modified as new evidence is uncovered and as new ways of interpreting the evidence are developed.

The major landmarks of hominid evolution are the evolution of habitual erect bipedalism, the development of tool use and tool manufacture, reduction in the size of the dentition, and enlargement of the brain. Generally, it is assumed that these landmarks evolved in the order listed. We will discuss the evidence in the same order.

### Early Hominids as Erect Bipeds

The anatomical evidence for erect bipedalism is found in the postcranial skeleton. Also, as Raymond Dart observed, the forward position of the foramen magnum in the base of the skull can also be used to infer upright posture. A modest number of early hominid postcranial bones are known.

The size of the early hominids can be estimated from the dimensions of the postcranial bones. They were relatively small as compared with modern hu-

THE EARLY HOMINIDS **317**

## TABLE 13-2

### SUMMARY OF EARLY HOMINID SITES

| Species | Time period (million years B.P.) | Distribution |
|---|---|---|
| *Ardipithecus ramidus* | 4.4 | East Africa |
| *Australopithecus anamensis* | 4.2–3.9 | East Africa |
| *Australopithecus afarensis* | 3.9–3.0 | East Africa |
| *Australopithecus bahrelghazalia* | 3.5–3.0 | North Central Africa |
| *Australopithecus africanus* | 3.0–2.5 | South Africa |
| *Australopithecus garhi* | 2.5 | East Africa |
| *Paranthropus aethiopicus* | 2.5 | East Africa |
| *Paranthropus robustus* | 1.9–1.0 | South Africa |
| *Paranthropus boisei* | 2.3–1.4 | East Africa |

mans and the great apes. The average reconstructed weight for the four best-known species *(A. afarensis, A. africanus, P. robustus,* and *P. boisei)* ranges from 40 to 49 kilograms (88 to 108 pounds) for males and from 29 to 34 kilograms (64 to 75 pounds) for females (Table 13-3). The average reconstructed stature ranges from 132 to 151 centimeters (52 to 59 inches) for males and from 105 to 124 centimeters (41 to 49 inches) for females. The degree of sexual dimorphism is greater than that found in the genus *Homo.*

The postcranial skeletons of *Australopithecus* and *Paranthropus* are those of erect bipeds. The pelvis, which is bowl-shaped and shortened from top to bottom, is similar in basic structure to that of *H. sapiens* (Figure 13-24); the spine shows a lumbar curve. Erect bipedalism is also deduced from analy-

sis of the footprints discovered at the site of Laetoli in Tanzania.

**Fossil Evidence for Erect Bipedalism**   The postcranial skeleton of *A. afarensis* shows several features that suggest its transitional status (Figure 13-25). On the one hand, the skeleton of *A. afarensis* exhibits a number of specializations for erect bipedalism. The blade of the ilium is short and broad, the foot possesses a humanlike arch, and the big toe is nongrasping.

Hominids maintain their center of gravity over their legs when standing and walking. This is made possible, in part, by the femur angling in toward the knee, as seen in Figure 13-26. When standing, the knees are positioned close together. In part of the walking cycle, the weight of the body is

## TABLE 13-3

### ESTIMATED SIZES OF HOMINID PALEOSPECIES

| Paleospecies | Body weight (kilograms) | | | Stature (centimeters) | | |
|---|---|---|---|---|---|---|
| | Male | Female | Female as % of male | Male | Female | Female as % of male |
| *A. afarensis* | 45 | 29 | 64 | 151 | 105 | 70 |
| *A. africanus* | 41 | 30 | 73 | 138 | 115 | 83 |
| *P. robustus* | 40 | 32 | 80 | 132 | 110 | 83 |
| *P. boisei* | 49 | 34 | 69 | 137 | 124 | 91 |
| *H. sapiens* | 65 | 54 | 83 | 175 | 161 | 92 |

*Source:* Adapted from H. M. McHenry, "How Big Were Early Hominids?" *Evolutionary Anthropology* 1 (1992), p. 18.

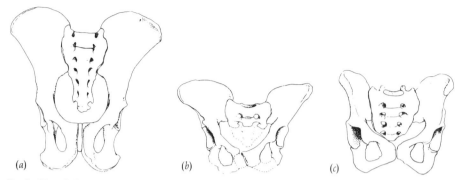

**FIGURE 13–24  Early Hominid Pelvis**
The pelvis of (b) *Australopithecus africanus* compared with the pelvis of (a) a modern chimpanzee and (c) a modern human.

**FIGURE 13–25  Reconstruction of "Lucy"**
The drawing on the right represents a reconstruction of AL 288-1 from Hadar. The original fossils are shown in gray except in the skull. The remainder of the reconstruction is based on construction of mirror images of known parts of the skeleton and reconstructions based on other fossils. Note the long arms and curved fingers. A modern human skeleton is shown for comparison.

centered over one leg while the other leg is moving. This balance on one leg is possible because the center of gravity of the body remains over the one knee while the opposite leg is raised off the ground. The short legs suggest that *A. afarensis* had a significantly shorter stride than modern humans; this means that its speed on the ground was likely to have been slower than that seen in humans today.

Other features of the postcranial skeleton suggest that *A. afarensis* engaged in some arboreal locomotion in addition to erect bipedalism. The curved, slender fingers and the curved toes are intermediate in relative length between those of apes and humans. These features suggest a degree of grasping that could have functioned as part of an arboreal locomotor pattern. The ability to sleep in trees and to use trees for protection from predators may have been an important factor in the survival of early hominid populations. In addition, these populations may have exploited arboreal food resources.

Four bones of a left foot belonging to *A. africanus* (Sts 573) fit together to form an arch that extends from the heel of the foot to the beginning of the big toe. The bones show a mixture of humanlike as well as apelike features; the apelike features are more evident in the bones closer to the toe. The investigators concluded that the foot with its grasping big toe was adapted for arboreal climbing as well as for bipedal locomotion.

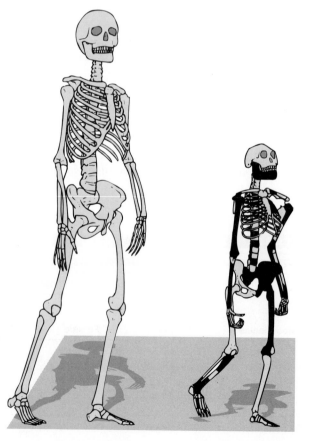

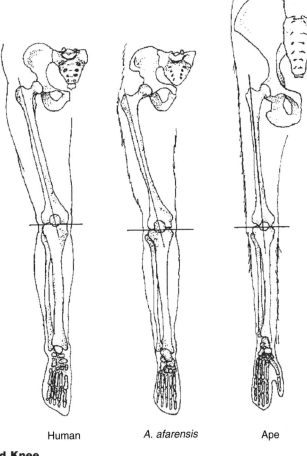

Human          A. afarensis          Ape

**FIGURE 13–26  The Hominid Knee**
In contrast with that of the ape, the human upper leg angles inward, bringing the knees directly under the body. *Australopithecus afarensis* exhibits this human pattern.

We can examine the postcranial bones of *A. ana-mensis* from Kanapoi, Kenya, which may date be-tween 4.1 and 3.5 million B.P. The region where the fibula articulates with the tibia is reduced; this sug-gests that the fibula and the associated flexors of the big toe were reduced in size (Figure 13–15). This implies a loss of mobility of the big toe. In general, the bones strongly support the conclusion that these hominids were erect bipeds.

**The Functions of Erect Bipedalism**  Many hy-potheses have been put forth to explain the ad-vantages of erect bipedalism. Upright posture po-sitions the animal's eyes high above the ground, where it can see a greater distance; this is impor-tant in spotting predators. Erect bipeds can walk a greater distance using less energy than quadrupeds can. In erect bipedalism, the hands were freed from locomotor functions and were able to evolve into organs for fine manipulation. The freeing of hands also enabled the early hominids to carry things such as food, tools, and helpless infants. Perhaps each of these hypotheses contains an element of truth, since erect bipedalism allows for a complex interaction of several functions.

Another possible function of erect bipedalism is suggested by biologist Pete Wheeler. He believes that one advantage of erect bipedalism is assisting the body to maintain a proper body temperature; this was especially important in the hot, open grasslands where many of the early hominids lived.[13] Upright posture raises the body into faster-moving air currents above the ground. It also reduces the surface area of the body that is exposed to the sun, especially when the sun is high in the sky. At noon, the sun is shining down on the entire back of a four-legged animal, but it strikes only the head and shoulders of an erect biped. While hairlessness encourages evaporative cooling through sweating, the hair remaining on top of the human head serves as a layer of insulation; this has the effect of protecting the brain from overheating.

### Early Hominid Tool Use

Raymond Dart noted the presence of many broken bones in the deposits at Makapansgat. He concluded that they were a result of the deliberate manufacture of bone tools. He termed this an **osteodontokeratic** culture, from *osteo,* meaning "bone"; *donto,* meaning "tooth"; and *keratic,* meaning "horn" (keratin is a main constituent of horn) (Figure 13–27). He saw a femur as a club, a broken long bone as a sharp cutting tool, and a piece of mandible as a tooth scraper. However, later studies by C. K. Brain of the bone material from Swartkrans demonstrated that the features of the bones that suggest deliberate toolmaking were more likely the result of carnivore activity.

In spite of the difficulties in interpreting the bone material in South Africa, paleoanthropologists still believe that tool use and tool manufacture are an important element of early hominid behavior. The report that modern chimpanzees manufacture tools suggests that such behavior could have characterized the early hominids. Although the earliest hominids may have used their hands for some degree of arboreal locomotion, the fact that they were erect bipeds means that they would have had their hands freed from primary locomotor functions. These facts lead us to expect an early expression of culture in these prehistoric populations.

The earliest hominid tools were most likely made of perishable materials such as wood, bark,

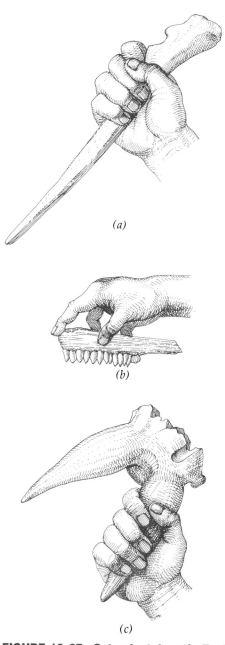

(a)

(b)

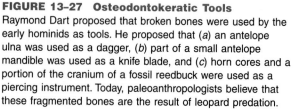

(c)

**FIGURE 13–27  Osteodontokeratic Tools**
Raymond Dart proposed that broken bones were used by the early hominids as tools. He proposed that (*a*) an antelope ulna was used as a dagger, (*b*) part of a small antelope mandible was used as a knife blade, and (*c*) horn cores and a portion of the cranium of a fossil reedbuck were used as a piercing instrument. Today, paleoanthropologists believe that these fragmented bones are the result of leopard predation.

---

[13]P. E. Wheeler, "The Thermoregulatory Advantages of Hominid Bipedalism in Open Equatorial Environments: The Contribution of Increased Convective Heat Loss and Cutaneous Evaporative Cooling,"·*Journal of Human Evolution* 21 (1991), pp. 107–115.

BOX 13-4

## What Is a Tool?

Anthropologist Joseph S. Eisenlauer notes that the term *tool* as it appears in the anthropological literature is frequently applied to such a broad range of objects that the true significance of this functionally distinct category of implements is largely obscure. He suggests a more focused definition. Specifically, he regards as "tools" only those implements that are used to make, maintain, repair and/or modify other objects or to process raw materials. The termite stick of the chimpanzee would not be a tool under this definition, whereas a hammerstone used in making a flint projectile point would be.

Another anthropologist, Wendell Oswalt, suggests the name "susistant" for implements such as the termite stick. The difference between the termite stick and the hammer is more significant than it first might appear. The termite stick is simply an implement used in helping to secure food. The hammerstone is used to manufacture something else.

Eisenlauer believes that the mental step from simply using or even making with one's hands or teeth an object to help get food to the step of using one object to manufacture another was one of the most significant steps in the evolution toward modern hominids. The use of a *hammerstone* presupposes mental processes by its user that are not necessary to the user of the termite stick. The reason one makes a hammerstone is to use it to modify something else, the finished form of which is only an idea in the maker's head. The termite stick is simply used to secure termites as food.

In the case of humans and chimpanzees, anatomy affords a limited range of technological capabilities. For instance, neither species can effectively carve wood with its teeth. Conceiving of the idea that one implement could be used to produce others is a hallmark of human evolution. This step was never taken in the evolutionary line leading to chimpanzees.

Although we continue to use the word *tool* in its general sense, Eisenlauer's point is well taken. There was an evolution in the use of implements. Perhaps the earliest stage was simply to use an unmodified object for some reason; for example, throwing a rock at another individual. Then, implements may have been modified specifically for food getting or other direct survival reasons. Next, objects would be fashioned to make other objects. In the process the human body would become a manipulator of tools rather than being a tool itself. This may have been the point where protocultural behavior at the technological level evolved into the unique technological cultural behavior of hominids.

*Sources:* J. S. Eisenlauer, Personal Communication, 1999; J. S. Eisenlauer, *Hunter-gatherer Tools: A Cross-Cultural Ethnoarchaeological Analysis of Production Technology* (Ann Arbor: UMI Dissertation Services, 1993); W. H. Oswalt, *An Anthropological Analysis of Food-Getting Technology* (New York: Wiley, 1976).

---

leaves, and fibers. However, the evidence for tool use in the archaeological record consists primarily of stone objects. Early stone tools were probably nothing more than fortuitously shaped natural objects. An example is a small, rounded stone that would fit comfortably in the hand and could be used to crack open a nut to obtain the meat or to break open a bone to obtain the marrow. Such unaltered stones were probably used as tools by early hominids for a long period of time before stones were deliberately altered to achieve a specific shape. It is very difficult to interpret stones found in a site in association with hominid fossils, since such stones may have been unaltered stones used as tools or simply stones deposited in a site through geological activity.

The first concrete evidence of the manufacture of stone tools comes from a site near the Gona River in Ethiopia; this site is dated at 2.6 million B.P. (Figure 14–21). Another early location is the Shun-gura Formation at Omo, which is dated between 2.5 and 2.4 million B.P. Stone tools are also known from many sites dated between 2.5 and 1 million B.P.

Bones of mammals found at Bouri, which are associated with the remains of *A. garhi*, exhibit evidence of cut marks made by stone tools as well as scars made by the impact of stone tools against the bone (Figure 13–28). The alterations of the bone provide evidence of several food extraction behaviors including the disarticulation of body parts, removal of flesh from the bones, and the breaking open of bones to extract the marrow. In contrast with the concentration of stone tools at Gona, relatively few, isolated artifacts were recovered at Bouri, probably because of the lack of raw materials at the site for the manufacture of stone tools. The landscape at Bouri 2½ million years ago was that of a grassy plain associated with the delta of a river as it entered a shallow lake.

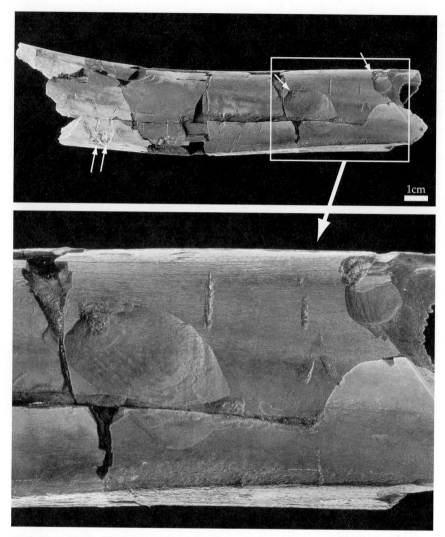

**FIGURE 13–28  Evidence of Tool Use**
This is a photograph of the midshaft of a right tibia of a large bovid (cattle-like animal) from the Middle Awash, Ethiopia. The arrows indicate the direction of the impact of a hammerstone. In the enlargement we can see large flakes produced by the impact of a hammerstone and adjacent cut marks. The goal of this activity was probably to extract the marrow from the interior cavity of the bone.

**The Early Hominid Hand**  Further evidence for early hominid toolmaking lies in the anatomy of the hand. Randall Susman has compared the hand bones of *A. afarensis, P. robustus, H. erectus,* and fossil *H. sapiens* with those of contemporary humans, chimpanzees, and bonobos.[14] He observes that ape hands are characterized by long, curved fingers, narrow fingertips, and relatively small thumbs. The ape hand is most frequently used in a power grip, where an object is held against the palm of the hand by the fingers.

Humans, on the other hand, have relatively short, straight fingers. The human thumb is relatively long; this results in a ratio of thumb to finger length that makes it possible to rotate the thumb so that the tip of the thumb can oppose the tip of

[14]R. L. Susman, "Fossil Evidence for Early Hominid Tool Use," *Science* 265 (1994), pp. 1570–1573.

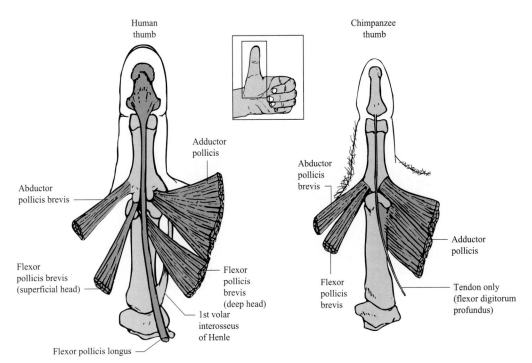

**FIGURE 13–29  Muscles of the Thumb**
In this diagram, we are looking at the bottom of the human and chimpanzee thumb. We can observe the various muscles that cross over the joint between the metacarpal and proximal phalanges (i.e., the phalanges closest to the palm). When we compare the anatomy of the two thumbs, we observe the following: (1) Humans possess a deep head of the flexor pollicis brevis muscle; chimpanzees do not. (2) Humans possess a first volar interosseous muscle of Henle; chimpanzees do not. (3) Humans have a flexor pollicis longus muscle. This muscle lies in a bony groove formed by a pair of small sesamoid bones located at the joint between the metacarpal and proximal phalanges. Chimpanzees have only a tendon that mimics this muscle. The sesamoid bones that form a bony groove are absent.

each finger in turn. The thumbs and fingers possess broad fingertips. This thumb is well adapted for a precision grip (Figure 13–29).

There are no stone tools associated with fossil remains of *A. afarensis*. The hand bones of this species show many apelike features such as a short thumb with curved phalanges in the other fingers. In contrast to the hand skeleton of *A. afarensis*, the hand of the later *P. robustus* is consistent with a precision grip. The precision grip is considered to be a requirement for complex toolmaking.

The humanlike anatomy of the *P. robustus* hand plus the presence of stone tools at the site of Swartkrans suggests that the later *Paranthropus* made tools. Yet tools may have played very different roles in *Homo* and non-*Homo* populations. The importance of tool technology to human evolution is discussed in the next chapter.

**Early Hominid Dentition**

The majority of known early hominid fossils are isolated teeth and jaw fragments with teeth. In general, the dentition of *Australopithecus* and *Paranthropus* resembles that of *Homo*. Yet the early species of *Australopithecus* show many nonhominid features, while *Paranthropus* evolved rather specialized dentition.

The dental arcade of *A. afarensis* is intermediate in shape between that of modern humans and apes (Figure 13–30*a* and 13–A in color insert). The posterior teeth lie in a fairly straight line, except for the third molar, which is positioned inward. The upper incisors are relatively large and project forward. The canines project above the tooth row, and they are conical in shape, in contrast to the spatulate shape of the modern human canine. A small diastema frequently occurs between the upper canine and premolar.

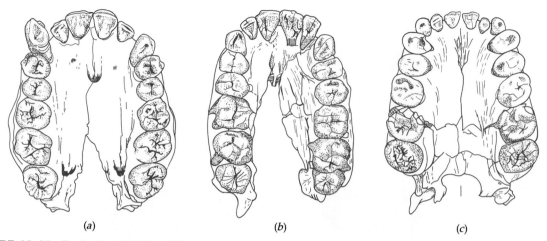

(a)  (b)  (c)

**FIGURE 13–30  Early Hominid Dentition**
Upper dentition of (a) *Australopithecus afarensis* (AL 200-1a), (b) *Australopithecus africanus* (Sts 52b), and (c) *Paranthropus boisei* (OH 5). (*Source:* From Clark Spencer Larsen, Robert M. Martter, and Daniel L. Gebo, *Human Origins: The Fossil Record,* 2nd ed., pp. 49, 59, and 66. Copyright ©1985, 1991 by Waveland Press, Inc., Prospect Heights, Ill. Reprinted with permission of the publisher.)

The anterior lower premolar is of special interest. As we saw in Chapter 8, the ape premolar is sectorial; it consists of a single cusp that hones against the upper canine. This contrasts with the modern human bicuspid premolar. The anterior lower premolar in *A. afarensis* appears to be transitional between those of apes and modern humans. It shows a slight development of the second cusp (Figure 13–31).

In many ways, the earlier dental remains of *A. anamensis* from Kanapoi show a number of similarities to the Miocene apes. For example, the jaw exhibits a shallow palate and large canines. On the other hand, the canines have long vertical roots. They are implanted vertically in the jaw, and the tooth enamel is thick, which is a characteristic of the later hominids.

The apelike character of *A. anamensis* and *A. afarensis* is no longer seen in the more recent *A. africanus* (Figure 13–30b). Although the teeth are relatively larger than those of later *Homo*, now the dentition is basically humanlike. However, the dentition of *Paranthropus* shows many specialized features (Figure 13–30c). These include thickened tooth enamel and an expansion in the size of the surface area of the premolars and molars. These

and other changes may be related to a specialized diet that consisted of tough, fibrous materials.

**Deciduous Dentition**  The early hominid fossils include dentition from infants and juveniles, including the "Taung baby." This jaw contains a complete set of deciduous teeth and first adult molars in the process of erupting. In modern humans, these features would characterize the dentition of a six-year-old child.

Because of the Taung fossil, many paleoanthropologists see evidence of a long childhood period in *Australopithecus.* One feature of modern humans is a lengthened childhood period as compared to that of apes. This prolonged maturation is related to the development of learned behavior as a major mode of hominid adaptation.

Recent analyses of the dentition of *Australopithecus,* apes, and modern humans contradict the idea that the length of the early hominid childhood was more like the human pattern than the ape pattern. In one study, the development of the dental crowns and roots of several fossil specimens were plotted against the development standards of both modern humans and apes. The dental pattern of *Australopithecus* best fits the ape pattern. For ex-

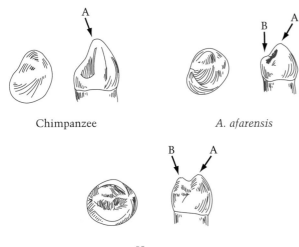

**FIGURE 13–31 The Hominid Premolar**
The anterior lower premolar from *A. afarensis* is compared with the premolars from a chimpanzee and a modern human. The human premolar is characterized by two cusps, A and B, while the chimpanzee sectorial premolar has only one cusp. Note that the premolar of *A. afarensis* is intermediate with a small development of cusp B.

ample, in the apes the canine erupts after the eruption of the first molars; this contrasts with the earlier eruption of the canine in contemporary humans. In *Australopithecus,* the eruption of the canine is delayed in the same way as it is in the apes. This fact suggests that these forms had a relatively short maturation period, which is similar to those of chimpanzees and gorillas today. On the other hand, the dental pattern of *Paranthropus* does not appear to closely resemble the dentition of either humans or apes.

New medical technology, in particular the computerized axial tomography (CAT) scan, has been used to visualize the juvenile skull from Taung. Investigators scanned the Taung skull and compared it with scans of both a human and a chimpanzee at the same stage of first-molar eruption. The scans revealed that the *Australopithecus* dentition growth and eruption pattern more closely resembled that of a three- to four-year-old chimpanzee than that of a five- to seven-year old human. Studies of bone growth in the Taung facial skeleton show a pattern similar to that of the chimpanzee. All these studies suggest that the prolongation of childhood may be a relatively late development in hominid evolution.

## The Early Hominid Brain

An important part of hominid evolution is the story of the development of the brain. Brains are not normally preserved in the fossil record. However, brain size and some very general features of brain anatomy are reflected in the size and structure of the cranium, or brain case.

The size of the brain can be estimated by measuring the volume, or cranial capacity, of the brain case. The cranial capacities of specimens of *Australopithecus* and *Paranthropus* vary from 400 to 530 cubic centimeters (Table 13–4). These cranial capacities reflect a small brain as compared to that of modern *H. sapiens*, which averages about 1350 cubic centimeters. In general, the smallest cranial capacities belong to *A. afarensis*, while the largest are found in *Paranthropus*. Not enough of the cranium of *A. ramidus* has been recovered to estimate its cranial capacity.

Some insights into the mentality of the early hominids might be revealed by an analysis of the structure of the brain. As we saw in Chapter 8, it is possible to make an endocranial cast that represents the shape and features of the inside of the brain case. Several natural endocranial casts have also survived. These casts provide some information about the pattern of convolutions and the location of grooves on the surface of the brain. Although this line of research is controversial, the early hominid brain appears to exhibit a simpler pattern of convolutions with fewer grooves than are found in the modern human brain. It is, however, very difficult to make behavioral interpretations of this evidence.

**Erect Bipedalism and the Brain** An athlete working out in a gym produces a great deal of heat, which is generated by the muscles. The evaporation of sweat from the skin is one way the human body keeps itself cool. If the rise in body temperature is too great, it can lead to dysfunction and, ultimately, death. Although it is not as obvious, the brain also produces heat. In a large-brained animal, such as a human, prevention of brain overheating is vital.

When the body temperature reaches a certain point, blood vessels just beneath the skin of the face and scalp dilate, which brings more blood to the skin, where it is cooled by sweating. (It is interesting to note that humans have the greatest sweating

**TABLE 13-4**

**CRANIAL CAPACITIES OF EARLY HOMINID PALEOSPECIES**

| Species | Specimen | Site | Cranial capacity (cubic centimeters) |
|---|---|---|---|
| A. afarensis | AL 333-45 | Hadar | 500 |
| A. afarensis | AL 162-28 | Hadar | 400 |
| A. africanus | Sts 5 | Sterkfontein | 485 |
| A. africanus | Sts 60 | Sterkfontein | 428 |
| A. africanus | MLD 37/38 | Makapansgat | 435 |
| A. garhi | BOU-VP-12/130 | Bouri | 450 |
| P. aethiopicus | WT 17000 | West Lake Turkana | 410 |
| P. robustus | SK 1585 | Swartkrans | 530 |
| P. boisei | OH 5 | Olduvai Gorge | 530 |
| P. boisei | KNM-ER 406 | Koobi Fora | 510 |
| P. boisei | KNM-ER 13750 | Koobi Fora | 475 |
| P. boisei | KNM-ER 407 | Koobi Fora | 506 |

capacity of any animal and that the density of sweat glands on the forehead is especially high.) The cooled blood flows to the head and enters the brain case by way of small veins passing through small holes, or **foramina,** in the skull. Once in the brain case, the relatively cool blood flows through the brain, helping to keep it cool.

Paleoanthropologist Dean Falk examined many modern human and ape skulls in search of these foramina.[15] She established that the skulls of modern African apes have very few, while modern humans have a large number. Falk next looked for these foramina in fossil skulls. She discovered that the skulls of *P. robustus* had very few.

Evidence suggests that *Paranthropus* may have lived in wooded areas. Being primarily vegetarians, they would have spent much of their daylight hours in shade, and therefore they did not face major problems of exposure to solar radiation.

*Australopithecus* also occupied wooded areas, yet they ventured into the savanna during the day to procure savanna resources, including the remains of animals. Like other diurnal savanna mammals, *Australopithecus* evolved mechanisms to prevent heat overload. Some foramina are present in *A. africanus;* their number increases dramatically in

*Homo* beginning about two million years ago. The increase in the number of these holes correlates with the increase in the size of the brain.

Because of the role that erect bipedalism plays in cooling the body, which was discussed earlier, and the development of a cooling mechanism for the brain, hominids are capable of being more active in the day, when many competitors are resting in the shade of trees. They are also able to survive on less water, and therefore they are able to exploit fairly dry and open habitats in contrast to the apes.

**The Early Hominid Skull**

The structure of the early hominid skull is a reflection of the relatively small cranium associated with a large dentition and powerful chewing apparatus. The skull of *A. afarensis* shows a marked **prognathism** (projecting forward) of the lower part of the facial skeleton. Air spaces, normally present within some bones of the skull, are enlarged **(pneumatized),** which reduces the weight of the skull. The temporalis muscle, an important muscle in chewing, is large. Its expansion is reflected in the development of a **temporal-nuchal crest,** which provides an expanded surface area for the attachment of the muscle to the skull (Figure 13–32).

The cranium of *A. africanus* is somewhat larger than that of *A. afarensis*. The skull of *A. africanus* is less heavily pneumatized, and the temporal and nuchal lines do not meet to form a temporal-nuchal

---

[15]D. Falk, "Brain Evolution in *Homo:* The 'Radiator' Theory," *Behavioral and Brain Sciences* 13 (1990), pp. 333–381.

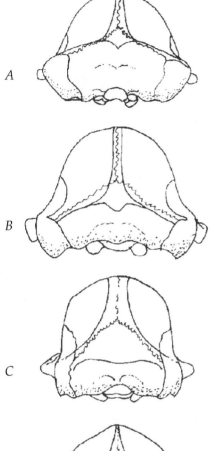

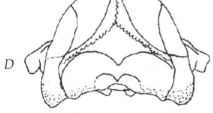

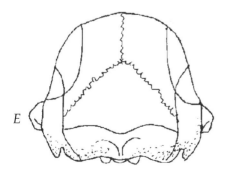

crest. The face is somewhat shorter because of a reduction in the size of the anterior dentition, and it has a very characteristic concave, or "dish-shaped," profile. The nasal bones are relatively flat. The forehead, behind the moderately large brow ridges, is low and flat. The top view shows a very marked **postorbital constriction.** When the skull is viewed from the rear, the lowest part of it is the point of greatest width.

The increase in size of the posterior dentition in *A. africanus* is related to a heavily built mandible. In these forms, chewing created powerful stresses on the bones of the skull, and bony struts evolved to withstand these stresses. For example, two bony columns, called **anterior pillars,** occur on both sides of the nasal aperture in *A. africanus* (Figure 13–33).

*Paranthropus* is characterized by a specialized chewing apparatus that includes large premolars and molars associated with a thick, deep mandible. Many features of the skull are related to the development of powerful chewing muscles that resulted in powerful forces being placed on the posterior teeth. The zygomatic arch is long and powerfully built for the attachment of the masseter muscle. It flares away from the skull to accommodate the temporalis muscle, which passes between it and the side of the skull. A small anterior sagittal crest appears on top of the skull in most specimens for attachment of the powerful temporalis muscle.

## Ecology and the Early Hominids

As is true for all animal populations, hominid evolution represents a continuous adaption to a series of ecological niches. Evolutionary modifications are

**FIGURE 13–32 Development of Crests on Early Hominid Skulls**
The relatively small size of the brain case and the relatively large size of the muscles of the jaw and neck may result in the development of crests to allow adequate surface area for the attachment of these muscles. The nuchal muscle of the neck attaches to the nuchal crest at the back of the skull. The temporalis muscle of the jaw attaches to the sagittal crest along the top of the skull. These two crests may meet and fuse to form a compound temporal-nuchal crest. Cresting can be seen in these occipital views of the skulls of (*A*) chimpanzee, (*B*) *A. afarensis* (AL 333-45), (*C*) *A. africanus* (Sts 5), (*D*) *P. boisei* (KNM-ER 406), and (*E*) *H. habilis* (KNM-ER 1813), an early member of the genus *Homo* (Chapter 14).

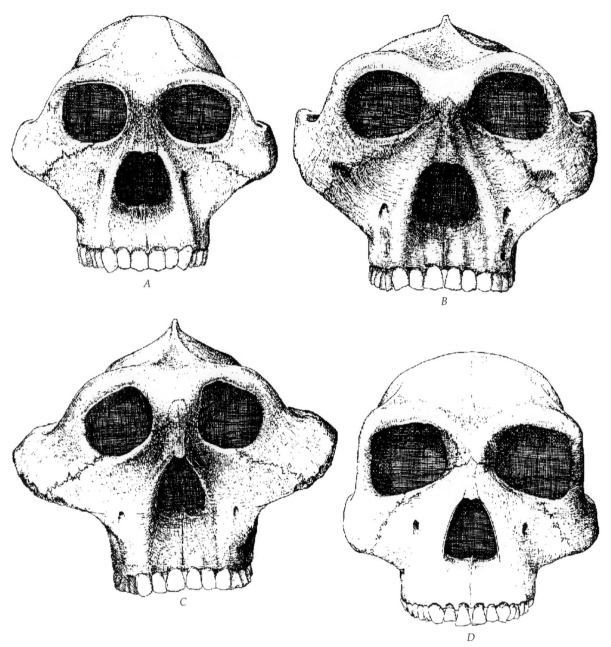

**FIGURE 13–33 Early Hominid Facial Skeletons**
Idealized composite drawings of (*A*) *A. africanus*, (*B*) *P. robustus*, (*C*) *P. boisei*, and (*D*) *Homo habilis*, an early member of the genus *Homo* (Chapter 14).

responses to changes in the environment or to competition with other populations. A challenge of paleontological studies is the great difficulty in determining the environmental factors associated with populations that are exclusively known from fossilized bones. Yet fossils do occur in a context along with the fossils of other animals and plants, archaeological material, and geological features. This allows us to develop some hypotheses regarding the lifeways of ancient populations.

**Late Pliocene Habitats** Paleoanthropologists search for environmental factors that help explain evolutionary change. Specifically, they are looking for possible explanations for the emergence of the various hominid species. It is significant that east Africa, an area associated with early hominid populations, is also an area that experienced major physical changes from Late Eocene through Late Pliocene times. Major episodes of faulting, warping, uplifting, and volcanic activity dramatically changed the east African landscape. The escarpments and gorges of the East African Rift System were formed, as were new mountains and highland areas. River systems, lakes, and deltas were created, changed, and destroyed. Associated with many of these geological changes were profound changes in climate.

Elizabeth Vrba identifies a major cooling event that took place approximately 2.5 million years ago.[16] This was a global climate change associated with the first widespread glaciation of the North Pole. This cooling event is associated with the spread of arid and open habitats in east and south Africa.

From the analyses of known dates for various fossil finds, it appears that this cooling event is associated with the appearance of the new hominid genera, *Paranthropus* and *Homo*. It is not known if the cooling event was the main factor that brought about the origins of the two lineages or whether they had already evolved before 2.5 million years ago and the cooling event was responsible for their rapid evolution into new forms.

Several reconstructions of the paleohabitats associated with early hominid remains provide us with a picture of several types of habitats. Table 13–5 lists the results of several of these studies. Nancy E. Sikes tells us that "available paleoenvironmental evidence from Plio-Pleistocene hominid fossil and archaeological localities in Africa . . . portrays a diversity of vegetation communities similar to today's topical savanna mosaic, from swamps to treeless or wooded grasslands, woodland, gallery forest, and mountain forest. Very few early hominid localities are reconstructed as open grasslands."[17]

The evidence for the extinction of *Paranthropus*, the lastest hominid not placed in the genus *Homo*, is not clear. The youngest known fossil is SK 3 from Swartkrans, South Africa. This specimen of *P. robustus* dates from about 900,000 B.P. There is some evidence for another period of cooling at about this time, but the evidence for this event is not very

---

[16]E. S. Vrba, "Late Pliocene Climatic Events and Hominid Evolution," in F. E. Grine (ed.), *Evolutionary History of the "Robust" Australopithecines* (New York: Aldine de Gruyter, 1988), pp. 405–426.

[17]N. E. Sikes, "Early Hominid Habitat Preferences in East Africa: Paleosol Carbon Isotopic Evidence," *Journal of Human Evolution* 27 (1994), p. 26.

**TABLE 13–5**

**PLIO-PLEISTOCENE HOMINID HABITAT, RESOURCE, GEOGRAPHICAL PREFERENCE***

| Habitat resource or context | P.r./P.b. | P.b. | H.h./P.b. |
| --- | --- | --- | --- |
| Montane forest[†] | x | | |
| Gallery forest/riparian woodland[‡] | | x | x |
| Closed habitat | | x | |
| Closed/mesic[§] | | x | |
| Groves of trees | | | x |
| Dambo (wet grassland) | | | x |
| Open savanna | | | x |
| Open/xeric[‖] | x | x | |
| Riverine | | x | |
| Stream channel margins | | x | x |
| Fresh water | | | x |

*P.r. refers to *Paranthropus robustus*; P.b. to *Paranthropus boisei*; H.h. to *Homo habilis.*
[†]Mountain forests.
[‡]Forests and woodlands along rivers.
[§]Associated with a moderate amount of moisture.
[‖]Associated with a small amount of moisture.
*Source:* Adapted from N. E. Sikes, "Early Hominid Habitat Preferences in East Africa: Paleosol Carbon Isotopic Evidence," *Journal of Human Evolution* 27 (1994), pp. 25–45.

clear. The fate of *P. boisei* from east Africa is uncertain since fossil evidence from between 1.2 million and 900,000 B.P. is scarce in that region.

**The Reconstruction of Diet** Associated with varying habitats are different patterns of exploitation of these habitats. For example, *Paranthropus* was adapted for a diet of tough, fibrous material. Specific anatomical adaptations for such a diet include thickened tooth enamel, expansion in size of the surface area of the premolars and molars, and an increase in the mass of the chewing muscles as seen in the robust and flaring zygomatic arch and the development of a sagittal crest. These anatomical changes parallel those of other mammals that feed on such material.

Analysis of the surfaces of the posterior teeth by the electron scanning microscope confirms this hypothesis. Richard Kay and Frederick Grine note that the wear pattern on the molars of *Paranthropus* resembles those of living primates that eat hard food items.[18]

Another approach to the reconstruction of diet is based on the ratio of two of the isotopes of carbon, $^{13}C$ to $^{12}C$, in tooth enamel. Differences in this ratio are a result of the process of photosynthesis in plants that utilize carbon dioxide in the atmosphere. Some of the carbon in carbon dioxide is the isotope $^{13}C$ and some is $^{12}C$. Different kinds of plants utilize one or the other isotope more frequently. Thus, trees, bushes, and shrubs, characteristic of more forested habitats, incorporate more $^{12}C$ than do tropical grasses and associated plants that are found in more open habitats. The former are referred as $C_3$ plants while the latter are referred to as $C_4$ plants.

When animals eat plant material, they incorporate the carbon found in the plant into their tooth enamel. Animals that consume primarily $C_3$ plants end up with a different $^{13}C$ to $^{12}C$ ratio in their tooth enamel than animals that eat primarily $C_4$ plants. Animals that eat both kinds of plants show a ratio that falls between the two; meat-eaters show a ratio similar to that of their prey.

An analysis of the tooth enamel from several fossil animals found at Makapansgat, South Africa, falls into several categories.[19] Grassland feeders had relatively high ratios of $^{13}C$ to $^{12}C$. A second group had low ratios and probably emphasized trees, bushes, and shrubs found in the forest in their diet. Two animals—scavenging hyenas and *A. africanus*—had intermediate ratios. This suggests that the hominids had a mixed diet including forest plant products as well as plant material from the more open areas. However, the microwear pattern on the *A. africanus* teeth is not that of a grasseater. This leads us to the conclusion that the $C_4$ pattern was obtained not from eating grasses, but from eating animals that subsisted on grasses. *Australopithecus* may have periodically left the forest to hunt for small animals and scavenge available carcasses.

## Summary

Four of the most significant features of the Hominidae are erect bipedalism, manufacturing of tools, reduction in the size of the dentition, and enlargement of the brain. All four hominid genera—*Ardipithecus*, *Australopithecus*, *Paranthropus*, and *Homo*—were clearly erect bipeds, as evidenced by their postcranial skeletons and the footprints preserved at Laetoli. Although the *A. afarensis* was clearly an erect biped, it was characterized by some features, such as relatively long arms and long, curved fingers and toes, suggesting that it had some proficiency in moving around in the trees.

The earliest known stone tools date from about 2.6 to 2.4 million B.P. Many researchers attribute the tools exclusively to *Homo*. However, the facts that some stone tools may predate the origin of *Homo*, and that the hands of hominids other than *Homo* were quite capable of manufacturing tools, lend credibility to the idea that *Paranthropus* made crude stone tools. Members of all three non-*Homo* genera also very likely manufactured objects of perishable materials.

---

[18]R. F. Kay and F. E. Grine, "Tooth Morphology, Wear and Diet in *Australopithecus* and *Paranthropus* from Southern Africa," in F. E. Grine (ed.), *Evolutionary History of the "Robust" Australopithecines* (New York: Aldine de Gruyter, 1988), pp. 427–447.

---

[19]M. Sponheimer and J. A. Lee-Thorp, "Isotopic Evidence for the Diet of an Early Hominid, *Australopithecus africanus*," *Science* 283 (1999), pp. 368–370.

Many dental features of *A. afarensis* are intermediate between that of modern humans and apes. For example, the canines project above the tooth row, and a small diastema frequently occurs between the upper canine and premolar. The dentition of the earlier *A. anamensis* shows even more similarities to the Miocene apes.

Although the teeth are relatively larger than those of later *Homo*, the dentition of *A. africanus* is basically humanlike. The dentition of *Paranthropus*, however, shows many specialized features. These include thickened tooth enamel and an expansion in the size of the surface area of the premolars and molars. These and other changes may be related to a specialized diet consisting of tough, fibrous materials.

The cranial capacities of *Australopithecus* and *Paranthropus* ranged from 400 to 530 cubic centimeters. This number is similar to that of the larger apes, and it is significantly smaller than the 1350-cubic-centimeter average for modern *H. sapiens*.

## STUDY QUESTIONS

1. Where have the fossils of *Ardipithecus, Australopithecus,* and *Paranthropus* been found? Are different species associated with different areas?
2. How does the skull of the genus *Australopithecus* compare with the skull of the genus *Homo?*
3. The architecture of the skull is, in part, a reflection of the dentition and the jaw. In regard to *Paranthropus,* what are some of the features of the skull of these hominids that can be associated with their large posterior dentition?
4. What evidence suggests that *Australopithecus* was an erect biped? How did the locomotor pattern of *A. afarensis* differ from that of *H. sapiens?*
5. Some paleoanthropologists consider *A. afarensis* as an intermediate between the Miocene hominoids and the hominids. What are some of the apelike characteristics of the skeleton of *A. afarensis?*
6. What are the main differences between the genera *Australopithecus* and *Paranthropus?*
7. What occurred in the Late Pliocene that may have been responsible for the appearance of the genera *Paranthropus* and *Homo?*

## SUGGESTED READINGS

Dart, R. A. *Adventures with the Missing Link.* New York: Viking, 1959. This is Raymond Dart's autobiographical account of his work with the early hominids of south Africa.

Day, M. *Guide to Fossil Man,* 4th ed. Chicago: University of Chicago Press, 1986. This guide consists of entries detailing important fossil finds.

Johanson, D., and E. Blake. *From Lucy to Language.* New York: Simon and Schuster, 1996. This is a beautifully illustrated book on human evolution with detailed descriptions of the major hominid fossils.

Johanson, D. C., and M. A. Edey. *Lucy: The Beginnings of Humankind.* New York: Simon and Schuster, 1981. This is a fascinating behind-the-scenes account of paleoanthropology. The book focuses on the fossil nicknamed "Lucy" and the change in thinking about human evolution that this find has prompted in many circles.

Johanson, D. C., and J. Shreeve. *Lucy's Child: The Discovery of a Human Ancestor.* New York: Morrow, 1989. This sequel tells the story of the discovery of new hominid fossils in Olduvai Gorge.

Morell, V. *Ancestral Passions: The Leakey Family and the Quest for Humankind's Beginnings.* New York: Touchstone, 1996. This book discusses the scientific contribution of the Leakey family with interesting bibliographic information on each of them.

Reader, J. *Missing Links: The Hunt for Earliest Man,* rev. ed. Boston: Little, Brown, 1995. This book tells the story of the hunt for and discovery of many important fossil hominids.

Willis, D. *The Hominid Gang.* New York: Viking, 1989. This easy-to-read book describes the lives and work of the paleoanthropologists responsible for our knowledge of the early hominids.

## SUGGESTED WEB SITES

Australopithecus (In Hand Museum):
   http://www.inhandmuseum.com/LA/aust.html
Institute of Human Origins:
   http://asu.edu/clas/iho/
Site of Taug:
   http://www.wits.ac.za/wits/fac/med/taung.html

Additional web sites are listed in the *Workbook* that accompanies this text.

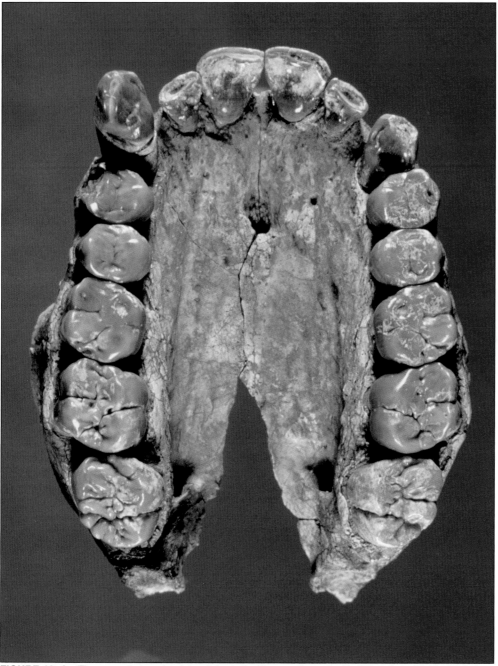

**FIGURE 13–A**  The upper jaw and palate of *Australopithecus afarensis,* AL 200-1, from Hadar, Ethiopia.

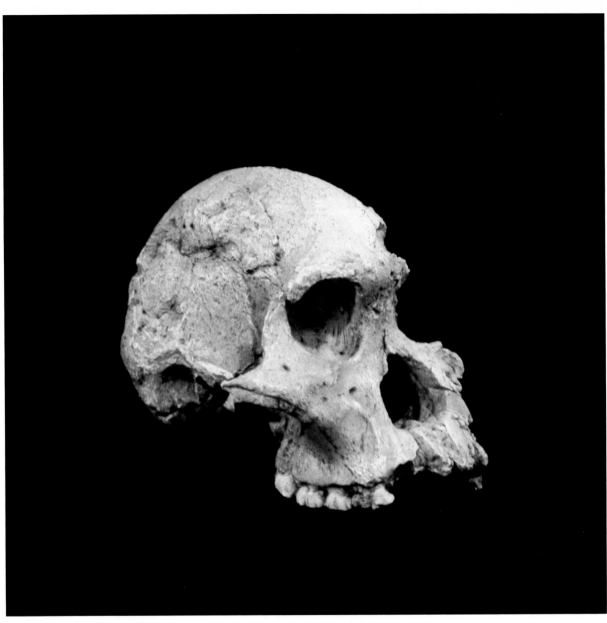

**FIGURE 13–B**   A skull of *Australopithecus africanus*, Sts 71, from Sterkfontein, South Africa.

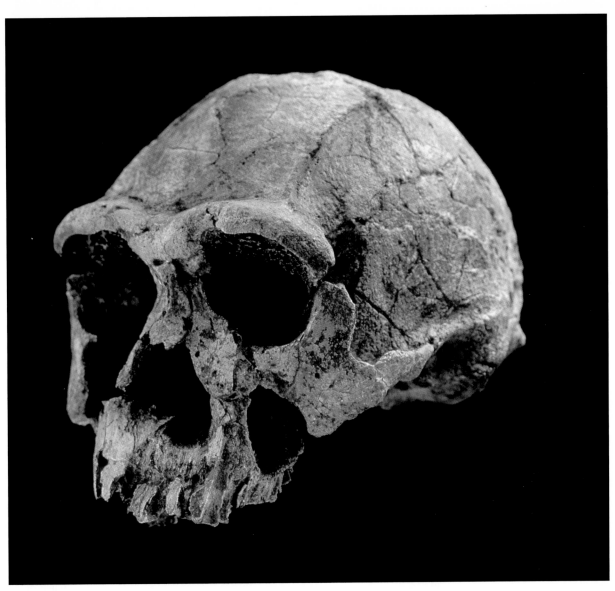

**FIGURE 13–C** A skull of *Homo erectus,* KNM-ER 3733, from Koobi Fora, East Lake Turkana, Kenya

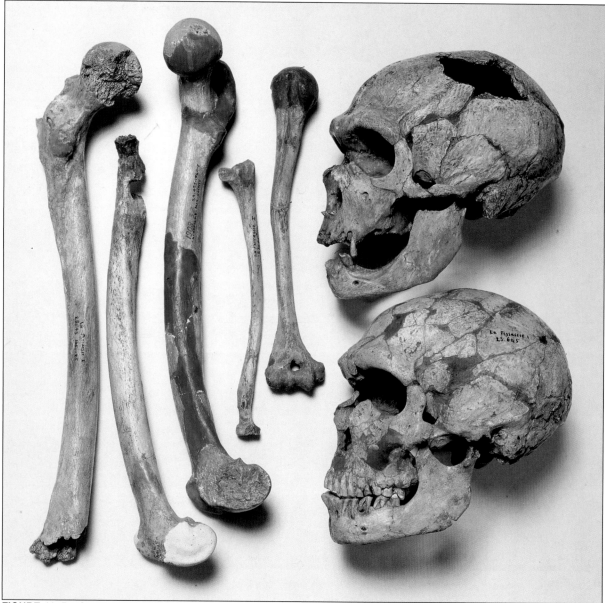

**FIGURE 13–D** Skulls of *Homo neandertalensis* from (top) La Chapelle-aux-Saints and (bottom) La Ferrassie, France, and limb bones.

# Early Species of the Genus *Homo*

*Seeing Neandertals in context, in the broad sweep of human evolution, is a valuable perspective. But we must not forget that they were neither "new and improved" versions of* Homo erectus *nor crude prototypes of modern* Homo sapiens. *They were themselves; they were Neandertals—one of the more distinctive, successful, and intriguing groups of humans that ever enriched our family history.*[1]
—Erik Trinkaus and Pat Shipman

**A**ll modern human beings belong to the genus *Homo*, *Homo* being the Latin word for "human being." While anthropologists use the term *human* in many of their discussions, *human* is not a technical term. We will leave the question of what it is to be human to the philosophers and cultural anthropologists.

The origins of our "humanity," however, lie in the origins and evolution of the genus *Homo*. What, then, are the essential characteristics that define this

---

[1]E. Trinkaus and P. Shipman, *The Neandertals: Changing the Image of Mankind* (New York: Knopf, 1992), p. 419.

genus? Since hominid adaptations are often behavioral, we must look beyond the fossil record and examine the archaeological record as well. This chapter will examine both the paleontology and the archaeology of those members of the genus *Homo* that arose before the evolution of *Homo sapiens*.

## THE EARLY *HOMO* FOSSIL RECORD

Between 2.5 and 2.3 million years ago, the fossil record reveals the emergence of several new hominid species that anthropologists place into the genera *Paranthropus* and *Homo*. Both genera most likely evolved from a late species of *Australopithecus*. Members of the genus *Homo* coexisted with *Paranthropus* until the latter became extinct some 900,000 years ago. *Paranthropus* was a subject of the last chapter; this chapter discusses the evolution of the genus *Homo*.

### The Genus *Homo*

*Homo* shares many features with *Australopithecus* and *Paranthropus* that unite the three genera in the family Hominidae. Yet *Homo* is characterized by many features that contrast with the other genera, some of which are listed in Table 14–1.

The size of the *Homo* cranium reflects an increase in cranial capacity. Cranial capacities in *Australopithecus* and *Paranthropus* generally fall between 400 and 530 cubic centimeters, while the various known representatives of *Homo* range between about 500 and 2300 cubic centimeters (Table 14–2). The lower values are found in the earlier species.

Compared with those of *Australopithecus* and *Paranthropus*, the bones of the *Homo* cranium are thinner; the cranium is more delicate and rounded; the zygomatic arch is more slender; a sagittal crest never develops on the brain case; and the cranium lacks developed muscular crests and prominent anterior pillars. In general, *Homo* is characterized by a smaller facial skeleton including smaller teeth and jaws. Some of the earlier specimens, however, exhibit front teeth that are approximately the same size as those of *Australopithecus*, but the premolars and molars show the beginning of size reduction that is characteristic of *Homo*. There is variation in

**TABLE 14–1**

**THE GENERA *AUSTRALOPITHECUS*, *PARANTHROPUS*, AND *HOMO* COMPARED**

| *Australopithecus/Paranthropus* | *Homo* |
| --- | --- |
| Cranial capacity of 400–530 cubic centimeters. | Cranial capacity of 500–2300 cubic centimeters. |
| Bones of brain case thin. | Bones of brain case very thick to thin. |
| Crests may develop on brain case. | Crests never develop on brain case. |
| Point of maximum width of brain case near bottom. | Point of maximum width of brain case bottom to top. |
| Moderate to large brow ridge. | Large to slight brow ridge. |
| Marked postorbital constriction. | Moderate to slight postorbital constriction. |
| Flaring of zygomatic arch. | Zygomatic arch not flared. |
| Facial skeleton large relative to size of brain case. | Facial skeleton small relative to size of brain case. |
| Facial skeleton often dish-shaped. | Facial skeleton never dish-shaped. |
| Suture between nasal and frontal bones upside-down V. | Suture between nasal and frontal bones horizontal. |
| Anterior pillars alongside nasal aperture. | No anterior pillars. |
| Relatively large prognathous jaw. | Jaw less massive. |
| Lack of chin. | Chin may develop. |
| Premolars and molars large to extremely large. | Smaller premolars and molars. |
| Thin postcranial bones. | Thick to thin postcranial bones. |

**TABLE 14–2**

**CRANIAL CAPACITIES OF *HOMO***

| Species | Specimen | Site | Cranial capacity (cubic centimeters) |
|---|---|---|---|
| *Homo habilis* | OH 7 | Olduvai Gorge | 674 |
| *Homo habilis* | OH 16 | Olduvai Gorge | 638 |
| *Homo habilis* | OH 24 | Olduvai Gorge | 594 |
| *Homo habilis* | KNM-ER 1813 | East Lake Turkana | 509 |
| *Homo rudolfensis* | KNM-ER 1470 | East Lake Turkana | 752 |
| *Homo ergaster* | KNM-ER 3733 | East Lake Turkana | 850 |
| *Homo ergaster* | WT 15000 | West Lake Turkana | 900 |
| *Homo erectus* | OH 9 | Olduvai Gorge | 1067 |
| *Homo erectus* | Skull III | Zhoukoudian | 918 |
| *Homo erectus* | Skull X | Zhoukoudian | 1225 |
| *Homo erectus* | Skull XI | Zhoukoudian | 1015 |
| *Homo heidelbergensis* | Kabwe | Kabwe | 1285 |
| *Homo heidelbergensis* | Steinheim | Steinheim | 1100 |
| *Homo heidelbergensis* | Swanscombe | Swanscombe | 1325 |
| *Homo neandertalensis* | Neandertal | Neander Valley | 1525 |
| *Homo neandertalensis* | La Chapelle | La Chapelle-aux-Saints | 1625 |
| *Homo sapiens* | Cro-Magnon | Cro-Magnon | 1600 |

the dimensions of the facial skeletons; some specimens retain some features found in the australopithecine face, such as facial and mandibular bone characteristics related to powerful chewing.

Erect bipedalism is a diagnostic feature of all hominids. From the known postcranial bones, individuals of the genus *Homo* are larger in body size and exhibit less sexual dimorphism than seen in the other genera.

**The Early Species of the Genus *Homo*** Many paleoanthropologists have suggested that *Homo* originated in Africa around 2.5 million years ago. Some scholars see a cooling of the earth's climate around this time that led to drier climates, more open habitats, and the development of marked seasons; others have not found convincing evidence of such changes.

A mandible from the Chiwondo Beds of Malawi and a temporal bone from the Chemeron Formation of Kenya, both in east Africa, may be the oldest known members of the genus *Homo*. However, the dating of these specimens is far from certain. A maxilla (AL 666-1) from the Hadar region of Ethiopia, found in 1994, most likely belongs to the genus *Homo*. This find, which is associated with stone tools, dates to 2.33 million B.P.

In recent years, there has been a trend toward the recognition of several species of the genus *Homo*. Only one of these ultimately gave rise to *H. sapiens*. This view is in marked contrast with the earlier idea that the hominids belonging to *Homo* were divided into only a few species. These species were seen as representing a more or less single evolutionary line.

Today there is considerable debate over the number of species within the genus *Homo* as well as the assignment of specific specimens to these species. For purposes of organization, we will describe the fossils of *Homo* in terms of the following species that have been proposed—*H. habilis*, *H. rudolfensis*, *H. ergaster*, *H. erectus*, *H. heidelbergensis*, *H. neandertalensis*, and *H. sapiens*.

### Homo habilis and Homo rudolfensis

The early fossils belonging to the genus *Homo* were originally placed into a single species, *Homo habilis* ("handy human being"). The first specimen of *H. habilis* (OH 7) was discovered by Louis and Mary Leakey in 1960 at Olduvai Gorge. The original specimen consists of a damaged mandible and parts of the brain case of a juvenile; the bones of several adult specimens were later recovered. In 1964, these specimens and others were placed into the newly defined species *H. habilis*.

In 1986, Tim White discovered another specimen of *H. habilis* (OH 62) at Olduvai Gorge (see Figure 11–H in color insert). This find is significant because it includes not only parts of the skull but also bones of the right arm and leg that belong to the same individual. For the first time, cranial and postcranial remains attributed to *H. habilis* were found in association. The association, however, is puzzling. Aspects of the skull appear to be rather *Homo*-like, yet some of the postcranial bones resemble those of *Australopithecus*.

Several hominid fossils were recovered from Koobi Fora, East Lake Turkana, between 1969 and 1976. This material shows well-defined variation. KNM-ER 1470 is an example of one of the larger specimens (Figure 14–1). It has a relatively large brain case with a cranial capacity of about 752 cubic centimeters, the face is broad and flat, the teeth and jaws are large, and it exhibits a slight brow ridge. In contrast to this fossil, KNM-ER 1813 has a smaller cranial capacity of approximately 509 cubic centimeters; the face, jaws, and teeth are small; and it displays more prominent brow ridges (Figure 13–32, 13–33, and 14–2).

**FIGURE 14–2** *Homo habilis*
Skull (KNM-ER 1813) from East Lake Turkana.

**FIGURE 14–1** *Homo rudolfensis*
Skull (KNM-ER 1470) from East Lake Turkana.

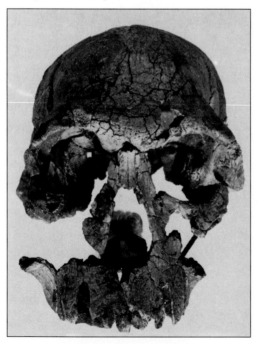

While some paleoanthropologists place all of these early fossils into the species *H. habilis*, others divide the material into two species, *H. habilis* and *H. rudolfensis*. The latter species is named after Lake Rudolf, the early name for what is now called Lake Turkana. *H. rudolfensis* includes the larger individuals, including KNM-ER 1470. *H. habilis* consists of the smaller individuals, including KNM-ER 1813 and the material from Olduvai Gorge. KNM-ER 1470, the best-known specimen of *H. rudolfensis*, dates from 1.9 to 1.8 million B.P.; the *H. habilis* fossils fall between 1.9 and 1.75 million B.P.

### *Homo erectus* and *Homo ergaster*

The best known of the early species of *Homo* is *Homo erectus*. *H. erectus* is also the earliest species of *Homo* to be found outside of the African continent. First discovered in Java in the 1890s, fossils that most paleoanthropologists place within the species *H. erectus* have been found in Java, China, the Republic of Georgia, and Africa. However, some of the early fossils from Africa differ somewhat in details of the cranium and, therefore, are placed by many paleoanthropologists into a distinct species, *Homo ergaster*.

*Homo erectus* **from Java**   One of the major arguments in the late nineteenth and early twentieth centuries centered around the location of the place where the hominids first evolved. Charles Darwin believed that hominid evolution began in Africa primarily because Africa was the homeland of our closest living primate relatives, the chimpanzee and gorilla. Other scholars, however, placed the center of hominid origins in southeast and eastern Asia.

Today the evidence clearly points to an African origin of the Hominidae with a hominid fossil record that begins some 4½ million years ago, and perhaps earlier. Yet by 1.8 million years ago, the first hominid fossils, members of the species *H. erectus*, first appear in Eurasia, on the island of Java.

Eugène Dubois, a nineteenth-century Dutch anatomist, was convinced that Asia was the place of human origin. To prove his point, he traveled to the Dutch East Indies (now Indonesia), and there, in 1890 at Kedung Brubus, he discovered a hominid jaw fragment. Dubois continued his work; in 1891, he discovered a small skullcap at Trinil, Java, and a year later he found a femur from a hominid that walked bipedally. Dubois's material is part of the Kabuh Beds of Java, which have been dated at approximately 700,000 to 500,000 B.P.

Dubois's work in Java and the discovery of a "primitive" cranium associated with a relatively modern femur excited the anthropological community. Soon paleoanthropologists traveled to Java to search for the remains of early hominids, and additional specimens of *H. erectus* were found at Sangiran, Modjokerto, Ngandong, and Sambungmachan. The latest specimen was discovered in 1993 at Sangiran.

Until recently, the oldest Asian *Homo* fossils were generally thought to be less than one million years old. Then, in 1994, Carl Swishen and Garniss Curtis, using a new dating method, redated the finds from Sangiran and Mojokerto to 1.8 and 1.6 million B.P., respectively.[2] This opens up the possibility that *Homo* populations may have migrated from Africa into Eurasia at a very early time.

Archaeological evidence suggests that early hominids, most likely *H. erectus,* spread throughout southeast Asia. Although the Indonesian islands of Java and Bali were connected to what is today the mainland of southeast Asia as falling sea levels exposed the lands lying beneath the shallow sea, islands laying to the east of these islands were not connected to Asia because they were separated by deep water. Even when the level fell to its lowest level, 19 kilometers of open water separated the eastern islands from the continental area of southeast Asia. Such a journey would have required some type of water craft. Archaeologists working on the island of Flores have fission-track dated deposits containing archaeological material to 880,000 B.P.[3]

The island of Java not only has given up the earliest evidence of *H. erectus* outside of Africa, but may also have yielded the remains of the most recent *H. erectus* specimens as well. A group of 12 hominid calvaria and partial calvaria and two tibiae were discovered between 1931 and 1933 at Ngandong, which is located on the Solo River. Additional hominid material, including two partial calvaria and pelvic fragments, were recovered between 1976 and 1980.

Some investigators have concluded that *H. erectus* survived to a late date in southeast Asia and was contemporary there with *H. sapiens.* Using a series of bovid teeth from museum collections and fresh excavations, Carl Swisher and his associates used electron spin resonance (ESR) and uranium-series dating techniques to date the tooth enamel. (The latter technique measures the decay of uranium to thorium in tooth enamel.) The results of the analysis provide a series of mean dates between 53,300 ± 4000 and 27,000 ± 2000 years ago.[4] These dates are much younger than any earlier estimates. The investigators contend that the Ngandong hominids belong taxonomically to *Homo erectus.*

***Homo erectus* from China**   In 1927, a molar tooth was discovered in a cave near the village of

[2]C. C. Swisher III et al., "Age of the Earliest Known Hominids in Java, Indonesia," *Science* 263 (1994), pp. 1118–1121.

[3]M. J. Moorwood, P. B. O'Sullivan, F. Aziz, and A. Raza, "Fission-Track Ages of Stone Tools and Fossils on the East Indonesian Island of Flores," *Nature* 392 (1998), pp. 173–176.

[4]C. Swisher III et al., "Latest *Homo erectus* of Java: Potential Contemporaneity with *Homo sapiens* in Southeast Asia," *Science* 274 (1996), pp. 1870–1874.

Zhoukoudian, near Beijing, China. The next 10 years saw the recovery of more than a dozen skulls and almost 150 teeth, but these fossils were lost at the time of the Japanese invasion of China during World War II (Box 14–1). Except for two teeth from the first excavation, all we have today of the original material are meticulous descriptions and excellent casts (Figure 14–3). Beginning in 1979, new excavations have been conducted at Zhoukoudian. Abundant stone tools and remains of nonhominid animals have been found, but *H. erectus* material has been fragmentary.

The dating of the Zhoukoudian fossils has been difficult. In 1996, the first radiometric dates were announced; these date the finds to at least 400,000 years ago. The fossils were found in an archaeological context associated with the remains of butchered animals, and many stone chopper tools.

A number of other sites have been excavated in China. In 1965, a skull was recovered in Lant'ien County, Shensi Province, China, that appears to be older than those from Zhoukoudian. Dated at approximately 800,000 to 730,000 B.P., it may be the oldest *H. erectus* find in China. The skull has a small cranial capacity, which is estimated at 780 cubic centimeters, and some of the bones of the skull are thicker than those of any other *H. erectus* yet discovered.

***Homo erectus* from Europe**   In 1991, a mandible with all 16 teeth in place was found at the site of Dmanisi in the Republic of Georgia, formerly a part of the Soviet Union. It may be older than 1.5 million years. This is the oldest *H. erectus* in eastern Europe. This specimen helps explain the existence of artifacts that have been discovered in this part of the world, without any skeletal association, that

## The Disappearance of the Zhoukoudian Fossils

The discoveries of *Homo erectus* fossils at Zhoukoudian, China, caused great excitement among anthropologists, paleontologists, and the general public. The fossils represented a wealth of information about prehistoric humans and their culture.

The invasion of China by Japan at the beginning of World War II created difficulties for the project, and the excavations were suspended in 1937. The fossils continued to be studied at the Peking Union Medical College, however, for at this time the United States was not at war with Japan and the Japanese invaders were respecting foreign interests in China. The project participants, though, expecting an eventual conflict between Japan and the United States, were concerned about the safety of the fossils.

In late November 1941, the fossils from Zhoukoudian were carefully packed into two redwood crates and placed in the college vault. From the vault, they were transported by car to the Marine headquarters in Beijing, where they were transferred to regulation footlockers. These footlockers were then transported by train to Camp Holcomb, 140 miles away, where they were stored. They were to remain in the barracks until the arrival of the USS *President Harrison,* which would transport the fossils to the United States for the duration of the war.

The Japanese attacked Pearl Harbor on December 7, 1941; in China, lying west of the international date line, it was Monday morning, December 8. The Japanese immediately took over the Peking Union Medical College and began searching for the fossils.

The fossils, however, were no longer at the college, having been moved to Camp Holcomb. The Japanese took over the camp; there were no casualties. The Americans at the camp were placed under arrest and led away from the camp; the fossils have never been seen again.

Many hypotheses have been proposed about the fate of the Zhoukoudian fossils. Some believe that they were simply destroyed by the Japanese invaders, who may not have understood their value. Others believe that they were transported to Japan, southeast Asia, or Taiwan. They may even have eventually arrived in the United States. Whatever the case may be, in spite of many attempts to discover their fate, to this day the mystery of the fossils' disappearance remains unsolved.

Exacting measurements and descriptions of the fossils were published, and fine plaster casts were made. Yet many modern analytical techniques, such as the use of x-rays and CAT scans on fossil material, did not exist in the 1930s. The rediscovery of the fossils would provide the scientific community with important new knowledge for the understanding of human evolution.

*Sources:* For detailed information on the disappearance of the Zhoukoudian fossils and the attempts to recover them, see C. G. Janus, *The Search for Peking Man* (New York: Macmillan, 1975); and H. L. Shapiro, *Peking Man* (New York: Simon and Schuster, 1974).

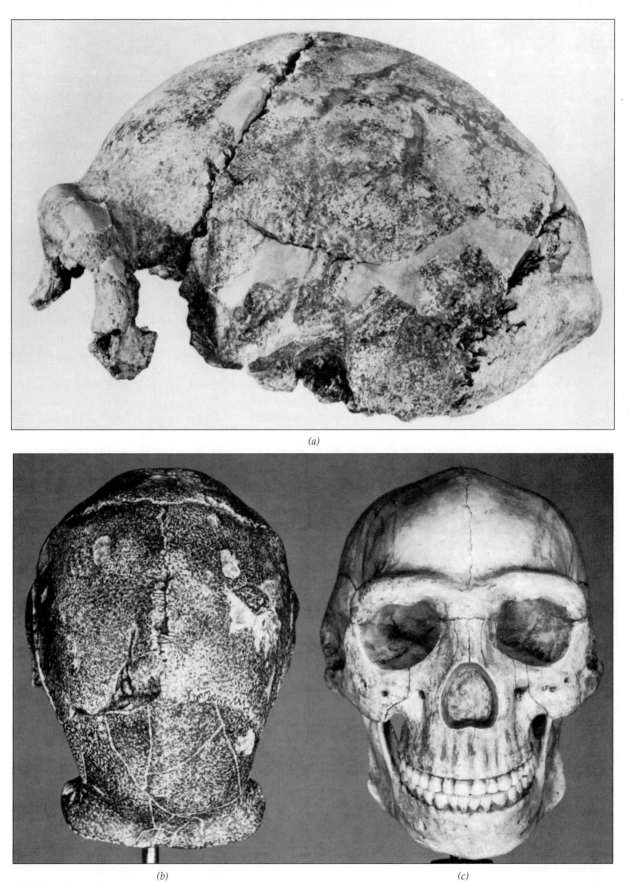

(a)

(b)                                                           (c)

**FIGURE 14–3  *Homo erectus***
Reconstructed male skull from Zhoukoudian, China. (*a*) Side view; (*b*) top view; (*c*) front view.

**FIGURE 14–4** *Homo erectus*
Skull (OH 9) from Olduvai Gorge.

show similarities to those produced by *H. erectus* in Africa.

*Homo erectus* **from Africa** Several fossils that can be attributed to *Homo erectus* are known from Olduvai Gorge. The first to be discovered (OH 9) was found by Louis Leakey in 1960 and consists of a partial cranium; it was found at the top of Bed II and is around 1.25 million years old (Figure 14–4). OH 9 is one of the largest known specimens of *H. erectus*. Other, younger fossils include a small, fragmented, and incomplete skull (OH 12), partial mandibles, and a few postcranial bones. A mandible, associated with isolated teeth and stone

tools, was discovered in 1991 at Konso-Gardula, Ethiopia, and is dated at about 1.4 million B.P.

In the early excavations at Swartkrans, South Africa, some bones were found that differed from those of *Paranthropus;* many now consider them to be *H. erectus.* Unfortunately, the remains are fragmentary. Other, less-well-known fossils are from north Africa, with the oldest from Ternifine, Algeria, dating from about 700,000 to 500,000 years ago. This material consists of three mandibles, a piece of skull, and a few teeth, all of which show many similarities to the *H. erectus* specimens from Zhoukoudian.

**The Anatomy of *Homo erectus*** The cranial capacity of *H. erectus* averages about 1000 cubic centimeters and generally ranges between about 750 and 1250 cubic centimeters (Table 14–2). The size of the brain case of most specimens falls within the lower range of variation of modern *H. sapiens,* but the distinctive shape of the *H. erectus* cranium betrays major differences in the development of various parts of the brain housed within it.

Most specimens of *H. erectus* have cranial bones that are thick when compared with the thin cranial bones of *H. sapiens.* The brow ridges are thick and continuous, and behind the brow ridges there is a pronounced postorbital constriction (Figure 14–5). The skull is low and relatively flat, or **platycephalic,** and in some specimens a bony ridge, the **sagittal keel,** is found along the midline at the top of the brain case. Unlike the sagittal crest found in *Paranthropus,* the sagittal keel is a thickening of bone along the top of the cranium. The profile of the cranium as seen from the side clearly shows the angularity of the occipital; above this angularity is

**FIGURE 14–5 A Comparison of the Skulls of (A) *Homo erectus* and (B) *Homo sapiens***

| *Homo erectus* | *Homo sapiens* |
|---|---|
| (a) Low, flat forehead | Vertical forehead |
| (b) Prominent brow ridges extending as a bar | Brow ridges slight or absent |
| (c) Occipital torus | |
| (d) Relatively large facial skeleton with large orbits and large nasal opening | Relatively small facial skeleton |
| (e) Angular occipital | Rounded occipital |
| (f) Relatively large teeth | Relatively small teeth |
| (g) Large mandible | Small mandible |
| (h) Sagittal keel | |
| (i) Horizontal nasal frontal suture | Nasal-frontal suture upside-down V |
| (j) Widest point low on brain case | Widest point high on brain case |
| (k) Pronounced postorbital constriction | Pronounced postorbital constriction |

a horizontal bar of bone, the **occipital torus.** In the rear view, the greatest width of the skull is toward the bottom. The facial skeleton of *H. erectus* is comparatively large and broad compared to that of modern *H. sapiens,* with large orbits and nasal openings. The brow ridge extends as a bar of bone across the nasal root and both orbits.

The genus *Homo* is characterized by a reduction in the size of the dentition through time. It is not surprising, therefore, that the teeth of *H. erectus* are

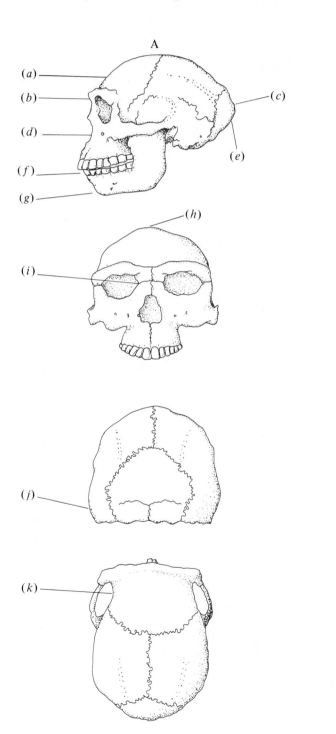
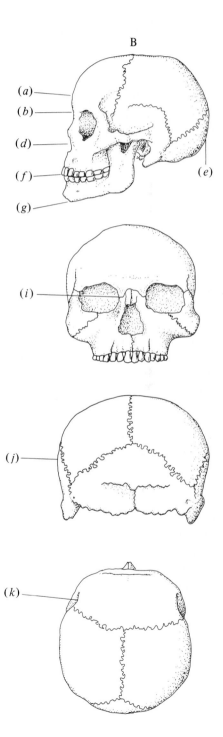

smaller than those of *Australopithecus* and larger than those of *H. sapiens*. In general, the dentition in *H. erectus* and that in *H. sapiens* appear very similar. Looking down upon the tooth row, we see that it diverges toward the back, with the greatest distance between the teeth occurring between the third molars. In *H. sapiens,* the greatest distance is between the second molars because the ends of the tooth rows turn slightly inward.

The reduction in size of the molars and premolars and the contrast in relative tooth size between *H. erectus* and *Australopithecus* and *Paranthropus* suggest that the incisors and canines of *H. erectus* were more involved in the processing of food. This may be related to major changes in diet, with an increasing emphasis on meat, and to new ways of preparing food for eating that were made possible by the development of cooking and more effective tools. The mandible lacks a chin but does have a **mandibular torus,** which is a thickening of bone on the inside of the mandible.

Although the number of postcranial bones is few, several parts of the postcranial anatomy, especially the femur, have been studied. Externally, the *H. erectus* femur resembles that of *H. sapiens*, but x-rays reveal that the outer wall of the shaft of the femur is twice as thick as that of *H. sapiens*. Although other relatively minor differences exist in the postcranial skeletons of the two species, both *H. erectus* and *H. sapiens* show an identical or very similar form of erect bipedalism. While the size of *H. habilis* remained relatively small, it appears that the evolution of large body size, characteristic of *Homo,* took place during the transition from *H. habilis* to *H. ergaster* and *H. erectus*.

*Homo Ergaster* The fossils that are attributed to *Homo ergaster* are found in the Turkana Basin of east Africa and date from about 1.9 to 1.5 million B.P. A very complete skull (KNM-ER 3733), pictured in Figure 14–6, is from an individual who lived about 1.8 million years ago. The remains of KNM-ER 3733 were found together at the same level of the same site with KNM-ER 406, a specimen of *Paranthropus boisei*.

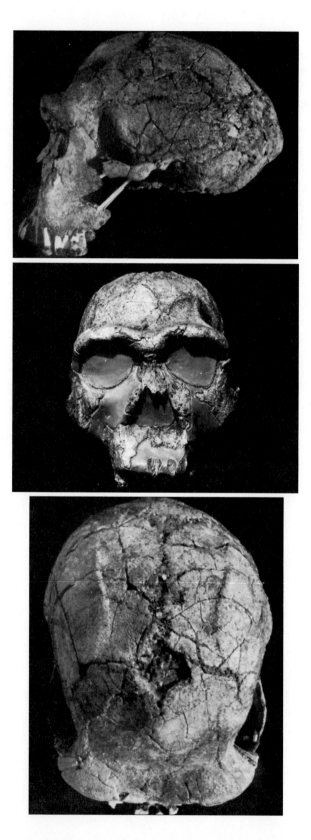

**FIGURE 14–6 *Homo ergaster***
Side, front, and top views of KNM-ER 3733 from East Lake Turkana.

A very exciting find was made in 1984 on the western side of Lake Turkana, dated at about 1.6 million B.P. This find, KNM-WT 15000, from the site of Nariokotome, consists of an almost-complete skeleton of a subadult male close to 12 years of age (Figure 14–7). It is estimated that the "Turkana Boy," if he had lived, would have reached about 183 centimeters (6 feet) in height. Until this discovery, it was generally believed that these early populations were composed of individuals who were relatively short compared with many modern *H. sapiens*. Also, the small pelvis of "Turkana Boy" suggests a small birth canal, a more helpless infant, and a longer childhood period when compared with earlier hominids.

*H. ergaster* resembles in many ways the fossils of *H. erectus*, but does vary in some ways, such as in the absence of thick cranial bones and a distinct depression behind the browridges (Figure 14–8). Some of the more important finds of *H. ergaster* and *H. erectus* are located on the map in Figure 14–9 and listed in Table 14–3. The evolutionary relationships of the species of the genus *Homo* are pictured in Figure 13–23 in the previous chapter.

### Homo heidelbergensis

The fossil record of the past million years is a very incomplete one. This is due in large part to the ebb and flow of the large continental glaciers that covered much of northern Europe and alpine areas. Conditions for fossilization were less than ideal, and the scraping action of the glaciers and the large volume of water from melting glaciers did much to destroy those fossil-bearing sedimentary beds that did exist.

Among the early hominid fossils discovered in Europe was a mandible that was found almost 24 meters below the surface in a quarry of river sand near the village of Mauer, not far from the city of Heidelberg, Germany (Figure 14–10). The year was 1907. The jaw did not clearly resemble the other hominid fossils known at that time: *H. erectus* from Java, the Neandertals of Europe, and early *H. sapiens*. More recently, the Mauer jaw has become the type specimen for a group of African, European, and Asian fossils dating between 800,000 and 250,000 years ago, which have been brought together into the species *Homo heidelbergensis*. However, there is not a complete consensus among

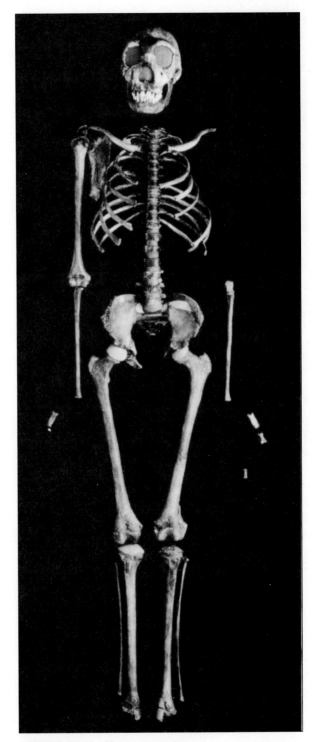

**FIGURE 14–7  *Homo ergaster***
Skeleton of WT 15000, "Lake Turkana boy," from Nariokotome, West Turkana.

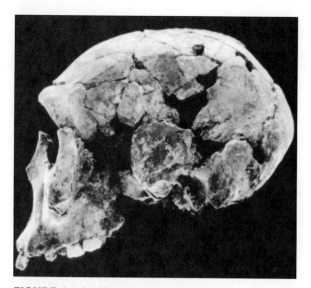

**FIGURE 14–8** *Homo ergaster*
Skull of KNM-WT 15000, "Lake Turkana boy," from Narioko-tome, West Turkana.

anthropologists about what fossils should be placed within this species.

***Homo heidelbergensis* from Africa** Several well-preserved fossils were recovered between 1921 and 1925 at Kabwe (Broken Hill), Zambia, as part of a mining operation; the cave was subsequently destroyed. The fossils include a nearly complete skull, upper jaw, pelvis, femur, tibia, and humerus; however, the postcranial material may not be contemporary with the cranium. The dating of the fossils is difficult, but they may be 300,000 years old.

The Kabwe cranium has a large cranial capacity of 1280 cubic centimeters, but it possesses massive brow ridges, probably among the thickest of any known Pleistocene hominid (Figure 14–11). It has a very long and broad facial skeleton with a sloping forehead; the teeth had dental caries (cavities), and there was an abscess (infection) in the jaw.

The skull from Bodo d'Ar, Ethiopia, is about 600,000 years ago and resembles the remains from Kabwe. Bodo has a very large, broad face with thick brow ridges. Cut marks on the skull suggest that this individual was butchered around the time of his death.

Other fossils from Africa are considered by some paleoanthropologists to belong to this group. These include a recent discovery from Buia, Eritrea, which

is discussed in Chapter 15, and the remains from Lake Ndutu in Tanzania, Omo II in Ethiopia, Saldanha in South Africa, and others.

***Homo heidelbergensis* from Europe** Among the early hominid fossils from Europe are those from the cave site of Gran Dolina in the Atapuerca Hills of northern Spain. The species designation and place in the evolutionary scheme has still to be worked out, but they date at more than 780,000 B.P. It has been suggested that these remains be placed in their own species, *Homo antecessor.*

Near the end of 1993, a human tibia and, in 1995, a tooth, were discovered at Boxgrove, England. Both ends of the very robust limb bone are missing. The fossils appear to represent hominids living during a warm interglacial that has been dated by faunal analysis to between 524,000 and 478,000 B.P., which is roughly contemporary with the Mauer mandible from Germany. Although very little can be determined about the individual from a tibia shaft, the find does place hominids in England at this early time.

In the mid-1960s, a few broken teeth and an occipital were found near the village of Vértesszöllös, not far from Budapest, Hungary. The skull is represented only by the occipital region, which is less angular and more rounded than that in *H. erectus.* It dates to between 475,000 and 250,000 B.P. The reconstructed skull has a cranial capacity of 1400 cubic centimeters.

A skull from Steinheim was found near Stuttgart, Germany, in 1933 and is dated to about 240,000 to 200,000 B.P. (Figure 14–12). Remains from Swanscombe, England, are of approximately the same age. This latter find consists of an occipital, discovered in 1935; a left parietal, discovered in 1936; and a right parietal, discovered 19 years later. All of these belong to the same individual.

The most complete of the two finds is Steinheim. The skull possesses many features that are reminiscent of *H. erectus,* including a low, sloping forehead and large brow ridges. Yet in other ways, the Steinheim skull resembles that of the later hominids, especially the Neandertals. For example, the facial skeleton is relatively small, the face and upper jaw are not prognathous, and the teeth are relatively small. The place of greatest width of the skull is higher than in the typical *H. erectus.*

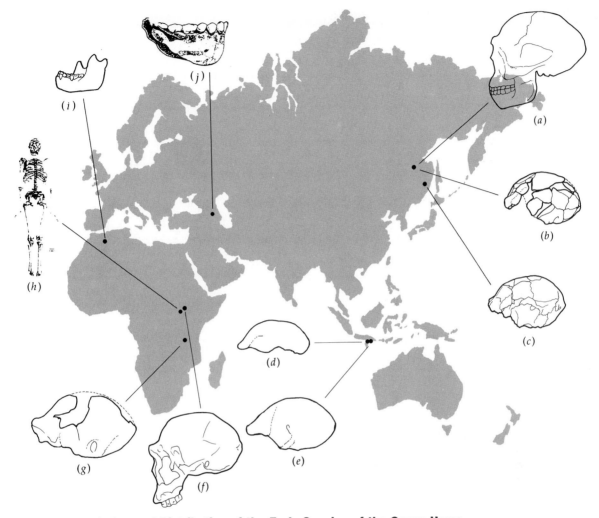

**FIGURE 14–9 Variation and Distribution of the Early Species of the Genus Homo**
(*a*) *H. erectus,* Skull XII, Zhoukoudian, People's Republic of China; (*b*) *H. erectus,* Skull XI, Zhoukoudian, People's Republic of China; (*c*) *H. heidelbergensis,* Hexian, People's Republic of China; (*d*) *H. erectus,* Trinil, Java; (*e*) *H. erectus,* Sangiran, Java; (*f*) *H. ergaster,* KNM-ER 3733, Lake Turkana, Kenya; (*g*) *H. erectus,* OH 9, Olduvai Gorge, Tanzania; (*h*) *H. ergaster,* "Turkana Boy" (KNMWT15000), west Lake Turkana; (*i*) *H. erectus,* Ternifine II, Algeria; (*j*) *H. erectus,* Dmanisi, Republic of Georgia.

Several other finds known from Europe, including a very complete skull from Petralona in northern Greece and several fossils from Arago Cave in the Pyrenees Mountains of France, are placed into *H. heidelbergensis.* Other hominid remains are known from the Second Interglacial, but knowledge of the material is limited. They include four skull fragments and a molar tooth from Bilzingsleben, Germany; a skull recovered at Salé,

Morocco; and a mandible from Montmaurin, France.

***Homo heidelbergensis* from Asia** A well-preserved cranium that was recovered in 1978 from Dali, in Shaanxi Province, China, is considered by some to belong to *H. heidelbergensis.* The skull is about 200,000 to 100,000 years old and has a cranial capacity of 1120 cubic centimeters. The skull

TABLE 14-3

**EARLY SPECIES AND REPRESENTATIVE SITES OF THE GENUS *HOMO***

| Species | Approximate dates (million years B.P.) | Some important sites |
|---|---|---|
| *Homo rudolfensis* | 2.4–1.9 | Lake Turkana, Kenya |
| *Homo habilis* | 1.9–1.6 | Olduvai Gorge, Tanzania<br>Lake Turkana, Kenya |
| *Homo ergaster* | 1.8–1.5 | Lake Turkana and Nariokotome, Kenya |
| *Homo erectus* | 1.2–0.4 | Sangiran, Modjokerto, Ngandong, Sambungmachan, Java<br>Zhoukoudian, Lant'ien, China<br>Dmanisi, Republic of Georgia<br>Olduvai Gorge, Kenya<br>Swartkrans, South Africa<br>Ternifine, Algeria |
| *Homo heidelbergensis* | 0.6–0.2 | Kabwe, Zambia<br>Bodo d'Ar, Omo, Ethiopia<br>Buia, Eritrea<br>Lake Ndutu, Tanzania<br>Saldanha, South Africa<br>Heidelberg, Steinheim, Bilzingsleben, Germany<br>Gran Dolina, Spain<br>Boxgrove, Swanscombe, England<br>Vértesszöllös, Hungary<br>Petralona, Greece<br>Arago Cave, Moutmaurin, France<br>Salé, Morocco<br>Dali, Lontangong Cave, Yunxian, China |
| *Homo neandertalensis* | 0.3–0.03 | Neander Valley, Germany<br>Spy, Belgium<br>La Chapelle-aux-Saints, Le Moustier, La Quina, La Ferrassie, France<br>Krapina, Yugoslavia<br>Tabūn, Skhūl, Israel |

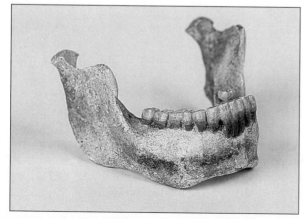

**FIGURE 14-10** *Homo heidelbergensis*
The Mauer jaw from Heidelberg, Germany.

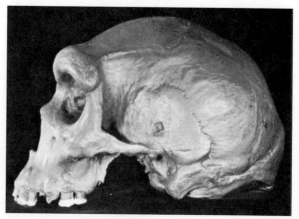

**FIGURE 14-11** *Homo heidelbergensis*
Skull from Kabwe (Broken Hill), Zambia.

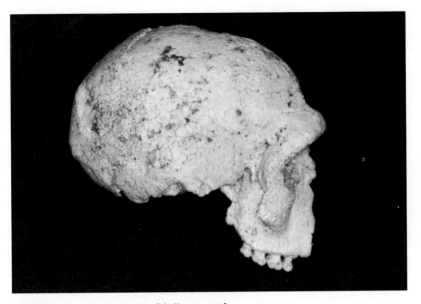

**FIGURE 14–12   *Homo heidelbergensis***
Skull from Steinheim, Germany.

and facial features resemble those of earlier hominids; these archaic characteristics include a sloping forehead and large brow ridges. The skull also has a small face that is flatter than those found in other areas of the world.

A skull found in 1980 in Lontandong Cave, Hexian County, is the first cranium to be discovered in eastern or southeastern China. It dates to between 280,000 and 240,000 B.P. Two fossil skulls, recovered in 1989 and 1990 in Yunxian, China, are considered to be 350,000 years old or younger based on the analysis of other fossil animals (Figure 14–13). The taxonomic placement of these fossils is being debated.

### *Homo neandertalensis*

The Neandertals are named after a specimen found in 1856 in the Neander Valley near Düsseldorf, Germany. Europeans of the Victorian age were totally unprepared to accept the Neander Valley fossils as the remains of one of their ancestors. The thought that this primitive-looking creature could have been related to modern people was repugnant to all but a few scholars. One Englishman considered the creature to be a "half-crazed, half-idiotic [type of man] with murderous propensities." Others considered it to be a freak, a stupid Roman legionnaire, or a victim of water on the brain.

Then, in 1886, two skeletons were removed from a cave in Belgium near the town of Spy. With the discovery of still more Neandertals, such as those at La Chapelle-aux-Saints, Le Moustier, La Quina, and La Ferrassie, all discovered in France in 1908 and 1909, the Neandertal pattern of features began to emerge (Figure 14–14). Today, the remains of

---

**BOX 14–2**

## How Do You Spell and Pronounce "Neandert_l?"

Certainly, the main controversy about the Neandertals revolves around their place in the human evolutionary tree. A much more trivial concern is how one should spell and pronounce their name. The currently preferred spelling is *Neandertal* as opposed to *Neanderthal*. The latter spelling was used in the past because the 1856 find was made in the Neander Thal of Germany; *Thal* means "valley" in German. However, the "h" in *Thal* is not pronounced in German. At the turn of this century, spelling reformers in Germany were successful in having most silent h's dropped from the German spelling system; the exception was the retention of silent h's in religious words. The accepted pronunciation of the last syllable of *Neandertal* has always been like that of the word "tall."

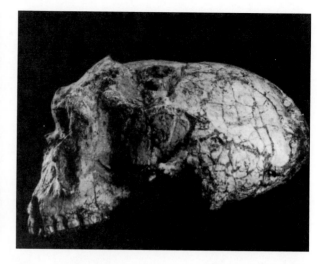

**FIGURE 14–13** *Homo heidelbergensis*
Skull from Yunxian, China.

about 400 Neandertal individuals, found in Europe and western Asia, have been collected (Figure 13–D in color insert).

**The Neandertals: Time and Place**   Clear indications of the Neandertal pattern appear approxi-

mately 130,000 years ago. However, partial skulls that display elements of this pattern have been discovered in the Atapuerca Mountains of northern Spain dated to at least 300,000 B.P.

One of the earliest sites to yield skeletons that display what might be the complete Neandertal

**FIGURE 14–14** *Homo neandertalensis*
Neandertal skull from La Ferrassie, France.

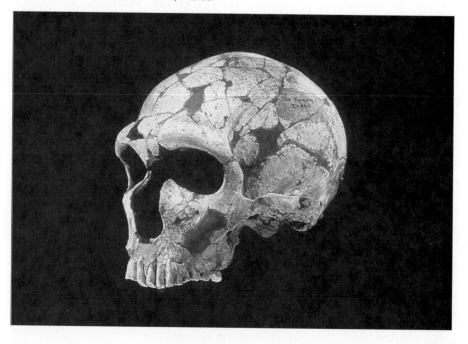

pattern is Krapina, in Yugoslavia, which contained fragmentary remains of at least 45 and perhaps more individuals. The site may be as much as 120,000 years old. Unfortunately, the site was first excavated by dynamite, so the remains of the individuals are highly fragmentary. From about 120,000 years ago to about 35,000 years ago, the Neandertal pattern, which had taken tens of thousands of years to develop, remained relatively stable.

The Neandertal pattern is also found in western Asia, including Israel, Iraq, Russia, and Uzbekistan. Fossils recovered at the sites of Tabūn and Skhūl on Mount Carmel display a surprising range of variation (Figure 14–15). Some specimens reflected the essential features of Steinheim; others showed more modern characteristics; and still others exhibited a mixture of more modern and Neandertal features. Skhūl has been dated at between 101,000 and 81,000 B.P. Some of the Neandertal fossils are located on the map in Figure 14–16.

**The Neandertal Skull**   "With slouched posture, a Neandertal man clothed in a leopard skin and carrying a crude wood club walks toward his cave. He stops, appearing dazed and confused, for he is lost. The cave he stands before is not his."

This portrait of a "caveman" that would make Forrest Gump look like a genius is a common

**FIGURE 14–15**  *Homo neandertalensis*
Skull V, Skhūl, Mount Carmel, Israel.

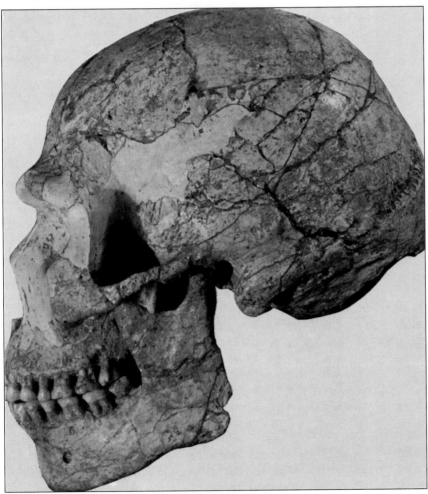

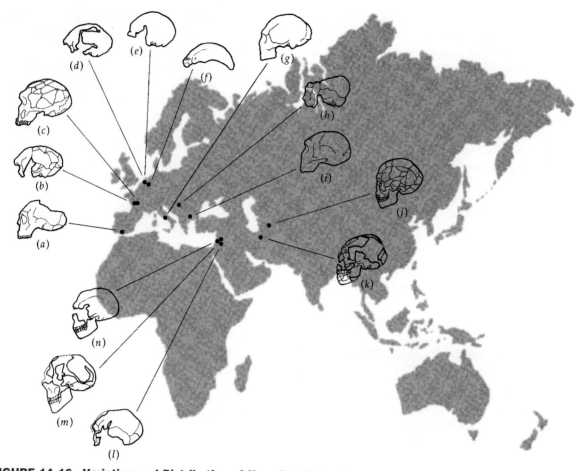

**FIGURE 14–16  Variation and Distribution of Neandertal Fossils**
(a) Gibraltar; (b) La Quina, France; (c) La Ferrassie, France; (d) Neandertal, Germany; (e) Spy I,
Belgium; (f) Spy II, Belgium, (g) Monte Circeo, Italy; (h) Krapina, Yugoslavia; (i) Petralona, Greece;
(j) Teschik Tasch child, Uzbekistan; (k) Shanidar 1, Iraq; (l) Skhūl IX, Israel; (m) Skhūl IV, Israel;
(n) Tabūn, Israel.

way of picturing Neandertals. In fact, healthy
Neandertals were not slouching or bent at the knee,
nor were they necessarily any less intelligent than
modern peoples. Anatomically, people called Neandertals displayed several unique physical characteristics; but transported to the present time and
dressed in modern clothing, Neandertals might not
elicit a second glance. Yet details of their anatomy
do contrast in several important ways with the
anatomy of modern humans.

Neandertals are "flat-headed," or platycephalic.
The distance from the top of the head to the level
of the eye sockets is less than that in modern
*H. sapiens.* However, the massive skull encases a
large brain. In fact, the average cranial capacity of
all known Neandertals is a little larger than the average capacity of contemporary *H. sapiens.* It ranges
between about 1300 and 1750 cubic centimeters,
with an average of about 1400 cubic centimeters
(Table 14–2). However, the slightly greater size of
the Neandertal brain as compared with the brain
of anatomically modern humans is not indicative
of greater mental ability. Paleoanthropologists believe that the amount of neocortex in the *H. sapiens*
brain is greater than that in the Neandertal brain.
The slightly greater average cranial capacity in the
Neandertals is more likely due to sampling error
or to the fact that the musculature of the Neander-

**BOX 14-3**

# La Chapelle-Aux-Saints

One of the great misfortunes of paleoanthropology is that one of the earliest reasonably complete skeletons of a Neandertal was that of La Chapelle-aux-Saints, found in 1908. The bones, discovered as part of a burial, were sent to Paris, where the entire skeleton was reconstructed (see figure).

Between 1911 and 1913, Marcellin Boule described La Chapelle-aux-Saints as representing a brutish, apelike population whose members walked with a shuffling, slouched gait. These descriptions colored people's perception of Neandertals for decades, as Boule and Henri V. Vallois's description of the La Chapelle-aux-Saints specimen shows:

We are impressed by its bestial appearance or rather by the general effect of its simian [apelike] characters. The brain-box, elongated in form, is much depressed; the orbital arches are enormous; the forehead is very receding; the occipital region very projecting and much depressed; the face is long and projects forward; the orbits are enormous; the nose, separated from the forehead by a deep depression, is short and broad; owing to the prolongation of the malar bones, the upper jaw forms a kind of muzzle; the lower jaw is strong and thick; the chin is rudimentary.[1]

The above description was published in 1957, several years after it was discovered that the fossil from La Chapelle-aux-Saints was that of an old man with a severe case of arthritis of the jaw, the spine, and possibly the legs. In addition, this find is not representative of the population and appears rather extreme even by Neandertal standards. It is a good example of sampling error in the fossil record. Yet this one individual has been called the "classic" Neandertal. Although Boule and Vallois's list of traits is generally correct, their interpretation of Neandertals as bestial and apelike is not.

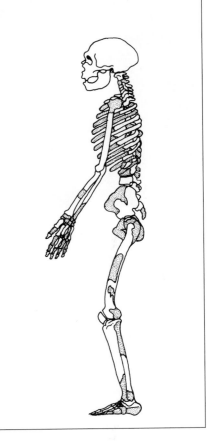

---

[1]M. Boule and H. V. Vallois, *Fossil Men* (New York: Dryden, 1957), p. 214. Printed with permission of Holt, Rinehart, and Winston, Inc.

---

tals was heavier than that of modern humans, requiring a larger surface area for the attachment of facial and cranial muscles (Figures 14–17 and 14–18).

Several interesting features of the Neandertal skull are seen from the side and back. The maximum breadth of the Neandertal skull is higher than that in *H. erectus* but lower than that in modern populations; this gives the skull a "barrel" shape when seen from behind. In the side view, the great length of the skull can be seen. The backward projection of the occipital region forms what is called a "bun."

In Neandertal children, including a 10-month-old infant, the foramen magnum, the hole in the base of the skull through which the spinal cord passes, is oval-shaped, in contrast to the round opening in modern children. The significance of this difference is unknown.

New information about Neandertals has been found in the remains of the middle ear. The semicircular canal of the inner ear functions in maintaining balance. When adjusted for body size, this structure is smaller in Neandertals than in anatomically modern humans. This may reflect a fundamental difference in posture. The shape of the Neandertal inner ear also differs from that of modern humans.

The nasal region of the Neandertal skull projects forward, is larger than that of modern *H. sapiens*, and exhibits many unique features that are not found in any other hominid or, for that matter, in any other primate. Jeffrey Schwartz and Ian

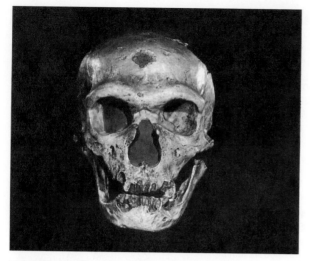
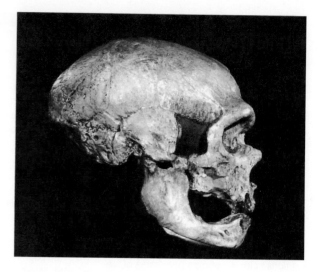

**FIGURE 14–17** *Homo neandertalensis*
Cast of La Chapelle-aux-Saints, France.

Tattersall describe several distinctive features such as

> the presence of a rim of raised bone that projects from either side of the rim of the anterior nasal aperture just within its anterior edge, forming a secondary "internal margin." This rim runs one-third to halfway up the inner nasal wall on both sides and then expands to become a wide, broad-based and bluntly pointed mass that protrudes medially into the nasal cavity.

This medial projection fades superiorly into a low ridge that continues to frame the nasal cavity within its external margin.[5]

_____

[5]J. H. Schwartz and I. Tattersall, "Significance of Some Previously Unrecognized Apomorphies in the Nasal Region of *Homo neandertalensis*," *Proceedings of the National Academy of Sciences USA* 93 (1996), pp. 10,852–10,854.

**FIGURE 14–18  The Neandertal Skull**
(*A*) Front view (Shanidar 1); (*B*) side view (reconstruction of La Chapelle-aux-Saints) with silhouette of *H. sapiens*. (*a*) Platycephalic appearance; (*b*) large, continuous brow ridge; (*c*) large orbits; (*d*) forward-projecting face; (*e*) lack of chin; (*f*) occipital "bun"; (*g*) gap between last molar and ascending branch of mandible.

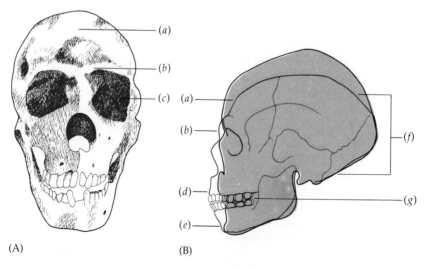

(A)                (B)

This configuration is found in all adult Neandertal skulls in which the region is preserved. On the other hand, this medial projection is not seen in any non-Neandertal skull except in a less-developed form in the Steinheim cranium, which is considered by some anthropologists to be ancestral to the Neandertals.

The Neandertal face is projecting in contrast to the flat face of modern *H. sapiens*. The forward-projecting face of the Neandertal may be due in part to the Neandertal's greatly enlarged **facial sinuses** and the positioning of the teeth. (A facial sinus is a hollow, air-filled space in the bones of the front of the skull.) The teeth project forward. From the side view, one sees a gap between the last molar and the edge of the ascending branch of the mandible (Figure 14–19). The larger sinuses are also characteristic of earlier hominids, including Steinheim, but the forward dentition pattern of the Neandertal is rare in other hominids. Neandertals, with their forward projection of the jaw, have sufficient room behind the dental arcade for an internal buttress reminiscent of the simian shelf of apes. Neandertals show varying development of a chin: in some, it is completely absent, while in others, it is slightly developed.

Many Neandertal specimens show signs of arthritis in the **temporomandibular joint,** where the mandible articulates with the rest of the skull. The presence of arthritis may be an indication of excessive strain on the joint. Could it be that the Neandertals used their teeth as tools? There is some evidence for this in the wear patterns on teeth, which suggest that Neandertals used their teeth for such tasks as softening skins.

Neandertal incisors are, on average, larger than those of modern populations, and sometimes they are as large as those of *H. erectus*. The molars and premolars are no larger than those of modern *H. sapiens,* and the third molar sometimes is very small.

**How Can We Explain the Neandertal Facial Configuration?** Until the mid-1980s, the most frequently mentioned selective agent used to explain the Neandertal face was cold. One suggestion proposed that the forward projection of the face was a means of keeping the nasal cavities away from the brain, which is sensitive to low temperatures. One function of the nasal cavities is to warm the air that moves through the head to the lungs; for people

**FIGURE 14–19   A Neandertal Mandible**
Mandible from a female Neandertal from Taʻbūn, Israel.

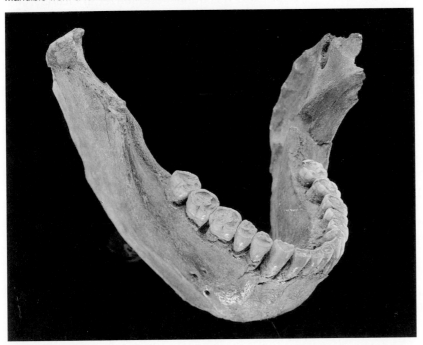

living in extremely cold climates, maximum warming means a minimum chance of damaging the brain. In addition to the projecting face, Neandertals' nasal cavities are very large, providing a greater surface area for the warming of the air.

Although the Neandertal face may have served well for cold adaptation, this hypothesis does not provide a complete explanation of the Neandertal face. For one thing, the Neandertal facial morphology is found in populations that existed before the onset of the Würm Glacial and during the glacial itself in latitudes not affected by the drops in temperature.

Yoel Rak has proposed an explanation for the Neandertal facial configuration in terms of the biomechanics of the skull.[6] The Neandertal has a robust face with large canines and incisors. The structure of the Neandertal face may have been an adaptation to withstand the considerable stresses that developed between the upper and lower teeth. The front teeth of the Neandertals often show considerable wear, indicating that, like some Inuit, they used their front teeth to chew hides and other nonfood materials.

We should not expect a single cause for a complex anatomical pattern. Rak concludes that "the unique Neandertal facial configuration is more probably the result of a combination of factors; a highly complex interaction of forces from the chewing apparatus, a response to climatic conditions and a variety of other factors as yet undetermined."[7]

**The Neandertal Postcranial Skeleton**  Compared with the modern human skeleton, the Neandertal skeleton is generally more robust and the musculature is heavier. Neandertals, who averaged a little over 152 centimeters (5 feet) tall, were generally shorter than most modern humans. Neandertals possess massive limb bones compared with the thin limb bones of modern humans. The long bones are generally curved, with larger areas for the attachment of muscles. The morphology of the finger bones indicates that Neandertals were capable of a more powerful grip than that of modern humans.

Taken together, the entire Neandertal postcranial pattern is one that allowed for great power while permitting fine control of the body.

The Neandertal scapula is characterized by a deep groove on the back surface. This suggests strong development of the teres minor muscle, which extends from the scapula to the upper end of the humerus (Figure 14–20). In modern humans, a groove is usually found on the inside (rib side) of the scapula. The Neandertal pattern indicates a powerful teres minor muscle, which functions to rotate the humerus outward while helping to keep the head of the humerus in its socket during movement. A powerful teres minor muscle working to balance other arm muscles that pull the arm down allows for powerful throwing and pounding activities while permitting fine control of movement.

Although Neandertals have often been portrayed as bowed over with their heads hung forward, capable only of an "apelike" walk, this description has no basis in fact—Neandertals were completely bipedal. However, scholars disagree whether or not Neandertal posture and locomotion were identical to those of modern humans. Like other parts of the Neandertal skeleton, and in contrast to those of modern humans, the pelvic bones are quite robust. There is an exception to this generalization, however, in the upper portion of the pubis, which is thinner and longer in Neandertals. The consequence of this feature for locomotion and posture has not been resolved.

**Neandertal DNA**  Under some circumstances, DNA remains in ancient bone, but only bone of relatively recent derivation. A 3.5 gram sample of bone was removed from the right humerus of the original Neandertal material discovered in 1856 in the Neander Valley of Germany. Using extremely careful laboratory procedures, the investigators were able to isolate a sequence of mitochondrial DNA consisting of 360 base pairs. Because this region is associated with fairly rapid mutation rates, differences in the sequence of nucleotides will show up in relatively closely related populations.

Next, the mtDNA sequence was compared with modern human and chimpanzee sequences. The average number of differences among the modern human mtDNA lineages was 8.0; between Neandertal and modern human mtDNA lineages was

---

[6]Y. Rak, "The Neandertals: A New Look at an Old Face," *Journal of Human Evolution* 15 (1986), pp. 151–164.
[7]Ibid., p. 157.

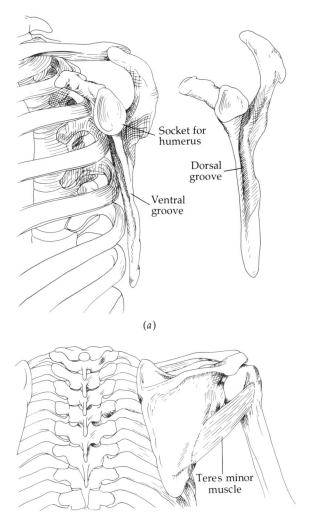

(a)

(b)

**FIGURE 14-20 The Neandertal Scapula**
(a) Side view of the left scapula of Shanidar I (right) and of
a modern *H. sapiens* (left). The ventral-groove pattern is
found in 80 percent of modern humans and is related to the
development of a shoulder muscle, the teres minor, which
connects the upper arm to the scapula by attaching to a small
portion of the dorsal surface of the scapula. In more than 60
percent of the Neandertal scapulas, we see a single, large
groove on the dorsal side of the outer border. All of the outer
edge and part of the dorsal surface provided attachment for
the teres minor muscle, indicating that it was well-developed.
(b) When the teres minor muscle contracts, it pulls the
humerus in toward the scapula, thus strengthening the shoulder joint. At the same time, it turns the upper arm, forearm,
and hand outward.

25.6; and between modern human and chimpanzee mtDNA lineages was 55.0. From these
data, we see that the average number of differences in the mtDNA sequences between modern
humans and Neandertals is three times that
among modern humans. Also, the average number of differences between modern humans and
chimpanzees is about twice that of modern humans and Neandertals.

One of the major areas of disagreement among
paleoanthropologists is whether or not the Neandertal gene pool contributed to the gene pool of
modern *H. sapiens*. If this were true, we would expect the number of substitutions between the Neandertal and European mtDNA to be significantly
greater than that between the Neandertal and other
mtDNA lineages. When the Neandertal sequence is
compared with modern human sequences from different continents, the data clearly show that this is
not the case.

One of the more controversial aspects of DNA
studies is the dating of the divergence of two DNA
lineages. Determining the timing of the molecular
clock is based on the idea that substitutions in the
DNA sequence occur on a regular basis, and that
time is directly proportional to the number of nucleotide substitutions. The problem is that the rates
of substitutions, and hence the molecular clock, differ in various segments of the genome and in different species.

Paleoanthropologists generally agree that the divergence between modern humans and chimpanzees occurred around seven to five million
years ago. Using that date in association with the
number of substitutions between modern human
and chimpanzee mtDNA, the investigators estimate that the divergence between Neandertal and
modern human mtDNA, that is the date of the most
recent common sequence, falls between 690,000
and 550,000 years ago. Using the same molecular
clock, the common ancestor of all modern human
mtDNA falls between 150,000 and 120,000 years. Of
course, we have to be very careful about these
dates, for they are only as good as the estimated divergence date of humans and chimpanzees.

The study of Neandertal mtDNA is very interesting and seems to support the contention of those
paleoanthropologists who propose that the Neandertals are a distinct species that did not contribute

**BOX 14-4**

# Shanidar I and Paleopathology

From Shanidar Cave, Iraq, come the remains of nine individuals. Besides showing the Neandertal pattern with some more modern overtones, many of the Shanidar individuals are interesting for cultural reasons. From this cave, dated about 60,000 to 46,000 B.P., comes evidence of burial with flowers and, perhaps, the first known incident of successful surgery.

**Paleopathology** is the study of diseases and injuries in fossil specimens. About 17 percent of the Neandertals from Shanidar have a joint disease called calcium pyrophosphate deposition disease.[1] Although fossilized bones

are usually all that remains of an ancient organism, soft-tissue diseases and injuries can sometimes be inferred from the evidence found in fossilized bones. One of the nine Shanidar finds, Shanidar I, is a good example of what a paleopathologist can conclude from a fossil specimen. Erik Trinkaus writes:

Shanidar I was one of the most severely traumatized Pleistocene hominids for whom we have evidence. He suffered multiple fractures involving the cranium, right humerus, and right fifth metatarsal, and the right knee, ankle, and first tarsometatarsal joint

show degenerative joint disease that was probably trauma related.[2]

In addition to the injuries listed above, Shanidar I was blind in the left eye, as inferred from a crushed orbit. Because of injuries, his right arm, clavicle, and scapula had never fully grown. The humerus had apparently been cut off slightly above the elbow, and healing of the bone indicates that the individual survived this ordeal (see figure). If this was an intentional procedure to remove a withered arm, it is the earliest known evidence of successful surgery. An unusually great amount of wear on Shanidar I's front teeth suggests that the teeth were used for grasping in place of the right arm. In addition, analysis of the skull shows that the top right side was damaged and had healed before his death.

Erik Trinkaus offers several possible explanations for Shanidar I's infirmities. What is obvious is that this individual had major debilitating injuries and lived to a relatively old age; he died a few years younger than the average life expectancy for Americans at the end of the nineteenth century. Shanidar I may not have been able to contribute directly to the food supply of his community, yet his longevity perhaps attests to other functions he was able to provide. By analogy with contemporary societies, we may surmise that his wisdom and experience were valued by the community and contributed to the survival of his society.

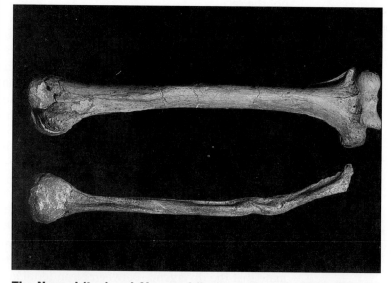

**The Normal (top) and Abnormal (bottom) Humeri of Shanidar 1**
The middle section of the normal humerus was restored in plaster and should be somewhat longer, making the abnormal humerus about 10 percent shorter than the normal one.

[1]B. M. Rothschild, "Oldest Bone Diseases," *Nature* 349 (1991), p. 288.
[2]E. Trinkaus, *The Shanidar Neandertals* (New York: Academic, 1983), p. 401.

## TABLE 14-4

### *HOMO NEANDERTALENSIS* AND *HOMO SAPIENS* COMPARED

| *Homo neandertalensis* | *Homo sapiens* |
| --- | --- |
| Flat-headed (platycephalic) brain case | Higher and rounder brain case |
| Cranial capacity of 1300–1750 cubic centimeters | Cranial capacity of 900–2300 cubic centimeters |
| Well-developed brow ridges with continuous shelf of bone | Brow ridges moderate to absent; never a continuous shelf of bone |
| Backward extension of occiput into a "bun" | Rounded occiput; no "bun" |
| Relatively flat basicrania | Bent basicrania |
| Maximum skull breadth at about midpoint (viewed from rear) | Maximum skull breadth higher on skull (viewed from rear) |
| Forward projection of face | Flatter face (nose and teeth more in line with eye sockets) |
| Variably developed chin | Well-developed chin |
| Relatively large incisors | Relatively small incisors |
| Taurodontism (molars and premolars with enlarged pulp cavities and fused roots) | No taurodontism |
| Bones thinner than in *H. erectus* | Bones thinner than in Neandertals |
| Sockets for femurs further back | Sockets for femurs further forward |
| Dorsal groove on side of outer border of scapula (in about 60% of specimens) | Ventral groove on side of outer border of scapula (in most specimens) |
| Long bones more curved with large areas for muscle attachments | Long bones straighter with smaller articular surfaces |
| More powerful muscles to flex fingers | Less powerful grip |

to the gene pool of modern *Homo sapiens*.[8] However, a fossil discovered in Portugal seems to contradict the genetic information. This 24,500-year-old individual appears to be a hybrid of Neandertal and modern human characteristics. Thus, the role of the Neandertals in human evolution remains as mysterious in the twenty-first century as it has ever been.

## Summary

One of the appeals of physical anthropology is the light paleoanthropological research sheds on the evolution of modern humans. The past century and a half of paleontological discoveries have provided a general outline of hominid evolution. Yet the specifics of the story are still illusive. Instead of a simple linear route from, let us say, *Australopithecus africanus* to *Homo habilis* to *Homo erectus* and finally to *Homo sapiens,* the route appears to be tangled and complex.

Starting around 2½ million years ago, the earliest members of our genus, *H. habilis* and *H. rudolfensis*, arose in Africa at about the same time as the early populations of *Paranthropus*. Both *Homo* and *Paranthropus* likely evolved from a late species of *Australopithecus*, perhaps *A. garhi*. At around 1.9 million years ago, we begin to see a new grade of hominids, *H. ergaster* and *H. erectus*. The latter became the first hominid to range outside of Africa. Many fossil hominids dating from about one million to 130,000 years ago show more *H. sapiens*-like characteristics than *H. erectus*-like; these are placed into the species *H. heidelbergensis*. However, populations of *Paranthropus* survived until about 900,000

---

[8]M. Krings et al., "Neandertal DNA Sequences and the Origin of Modern Humans," *Cell* 90 (1997), pp. 19–30; T. Lindahl, "Facts and Artifacts of Ancient DNA," *Cell* 90 (1997), pp. 1–3; R. Ward and C. Stringer, "A Molecular Handle on the Neanderthals," *Nature* 388 (1997), pp. 225–226; C. Stringer, "Chronological and Biogeographic Perspectives on Later Human Evolution," in K. Aoki et al. (eds.), *Neandertals and Modern Humans in West Asia* (New York: Plenum, 1998).

B.P.; some populations of *H. erectus* survived as late as 27,000 B.P.

The Neandertals existed between about 130,000 to about 30,000 years ago. They have been seen as a direct ancestor to modern Europeans by some, and a side branch of humanity that genetically contributed little or nothing to modern populations by others. Today, details of Neandertal anatomy, such as an oval-shaped foramen magnum, the distinctive structure of the middle and inner ear, and the unique shape of the nasal region, have convinced a number of paleoanthropologists that Neandertals should be placed into their own species, *Homo neandertalensis.* (The anatomy of the Neandertals is summarized in Table 14–4.) Recently, this idea has been reinforced by a study of Neandertal DNA that suggests that Neandertals are genetically distinct from modern peoples. However, a recently described fossil from Portugal suggests that modern humans and Neandertals may have interbred. A list of the hominid species discussed in this chapter is presented in Table 14–3.

## THE CULTURE OF EARLY *HOMO*

Earlier we saw that behavioral adaptability provides important ways by which humans cope with the requirements of their varied habitats. When did learned behavior begin to replace innate behavior as a major means of coping with environments? The evidence for this change is even more fragmentary than the fossil evidence of physical evolution.

Early hominids very likely made tools of perishable materials such as wood and hides long before they learned to work stone; even chimpanzees make tools out of sticks. It is not until about 2.5 million years ago that stone tools begin to appear in archaeological sites. The **Paleolithic** begins with the appearance of stone tools. *Paleo* means "old," and *lithic* means "stone"; thus the Paleolithic is the "Old Stone Age." The hominids of old stone age cultures continued to make tools out of perishable materials, but they also chipped away at stone. As time went on, they manufactured an increasing variety of durable stone tools.

The **Lower Paleolithic** begins with the manufacture of the first stone tools. The **Middle Paleolithic** refers to the stone tools of the Neandertals

and their contemporaries. Finally, the **Upper Paleolithic,** which will be discussed in the next chapter, includes the stone tools of anatomically modern peoples. Human adaptations are to a large extent behavioral. Some evidence of the behavior of early *Homo* can be seen in the archaeological record, which is the subject of this section.

### Interpreting the Archaeological Evidence

**Artifacts** are the physical remains of human activities. A carefully chipped arrow point and a highly decorated piece of pottery are in themselves works of art worthy of our admiration. In addition to their artistic merit, however, artifacts make up the evidence from which human behavior can be deduced.

An archaeological **site** is any location where manufactured objects are found. All the artifacts from a given site make up an **assemblage,** which in turn can be divided into a series of **industries.** Each industry contains all the artifacts made from one type of material, for example, a **lithic (stone) industry** or a **bone industry.** Because stone is preserved better than materials such as bone and wood, most ancient sites contain only a stone industry. Nevertheless, we must constantly keep in mind that all hominids probably utilized bone, wood, horn, and other perishable materials as well.

An artifact that appears to have been used for a specific function is a **tool;** examples of tools are choppers, scrapers, burins, and hand axes. Natural objects that are used without further modification are called **utilized material.** They include anvils, hammerstones, and utilized flakes. The word **debitage** refers to the waste and nonutilized material produced in the process of tool manufacture. Unmodified rocks brought into a site by human agency that show no signs of use are termed **manuports.**

A **core** is a nodule of rock from which pieces, or **flakes,** are removed. The individual flakes can be further altered by **retouch,** the further removal of tiny flakes, to create **flake tools.** Two examples of flake tools are the **scraper,** a flake with a scraping edge on the end or side, and the **burin,** a tool with a thick point. The remaining core can be fashioned into a **core tool,** such as a **hand ax.** A cutting edge is created by flaking on one or both ends; the little flakes are produced by hitting a **hammerstone** or a bone hammer against the core. The edge itself is often jagged, but it is quite effective in butchering animals.

Interpreting the archaeological record is often extremely difficult. Ideally, we would like to know the functions of each artifact type, but usually we must be content merely to describe its shape or to place the tool into one of a number of standardized categories such as chopper or scraper. The archaeologist must be careful not to interpret these categories as proven functions, since a scraper, for instance, may have functioned as a knife rather than as an instrument for scraping flesh off a hide.

### The Culture of Early *Homo*

Several thousand artifacts have been recovered from the site of Lokalakei in West Turkana, northwestern Kenya, dated at 2.34 million B.P. This archaeological site has yielded well-preserved artifacts and fossil bones representing 12 mammalian species, reptiles, and fish, inhabiting a grassy plain with forest along the river. The stone tools are associated with tortoise bones and fragments of ostrich shells, which suggests that these animals formed an important element in the hominid diet. Analysis of the stone tools, which included the fitting together of flakes with the cores from which they were removed, suggests that the manufacture of stone tools took place at Lokalakei. The process of tools manufacture indicates fine motor precision and coordination more advanced than previously believed.[9]

The earliest-known stone tools were discovered between 1992 and 1994 in the Gona River drainage of the Awash Basin of Ethiopia. These objects were found within the Hadar formation, which has been securely dated by radiometric dating techniques and by studies of the periodic reversal of the earth's magnetic poles to about 2.6 million B.P. Other stone tools were recovered from Bouri, also in the Awash Basin, associated with fossils of *A. garhi.*

Several sites in the Gona region have yielded more than 3000 artifacts. These artifacts include cores, flakes, and flaking debris (Figure 14–21). These well-preserved and well-made tools are sim-

**FIGURE 14–21  An Early Stone Tool**
Among the earliest known stone tools in the archaeological record is this 2.6-million-year-old Oldowan core from the Gona River basin, Ethiopia.

ilar to those first identified by Mary Leakey at Olduvai Gorge. The degree of sophistication, although primitive when compared with later artifacts, strongly suggests that the roots of stone tool manufacture extend even further back in time.

**The Archaeology of Olduvai Gorge**  The best-known early archaeological assemblages are those of Olduvai Gorge. These artifacts are assigned to the Lower Paleolithic, or Lower Old Stone Age.

Site FLK in Upper Bed I contains about 2500 artifacts and 60,000 bones, including the disarticulated remains of an extinct form of elephant (Figure 14–22). Of the 123 recovered artifacts associated with the elephant, all but five can be classified as tools; most of these are choppers.

The DK site from Bed I is older than 1.75 million B.P.; like most sites of this period, the DK site was located close to water. A large number of crocodile bones have been found, as well as bones from extinct forms of tortoise, cattle, pig, elephant, hippopotamus, horse, and giraffe; all these animals may have played some role in the early hominid diet. The DK lithic industry includes a number of tools, among them various forms of choppers (Table 14–5).

The tools known as choppers are made from round stones shaped by the tumbling effects of stream water. Once collected, a hammerstone is

---

[9]H. Roche et al., "Early Hominid Stone Tool Production and Technical Skill 2.34 Myr Ago in West Turkana, Kenya," *Nature* 399 (1999), 57–60.

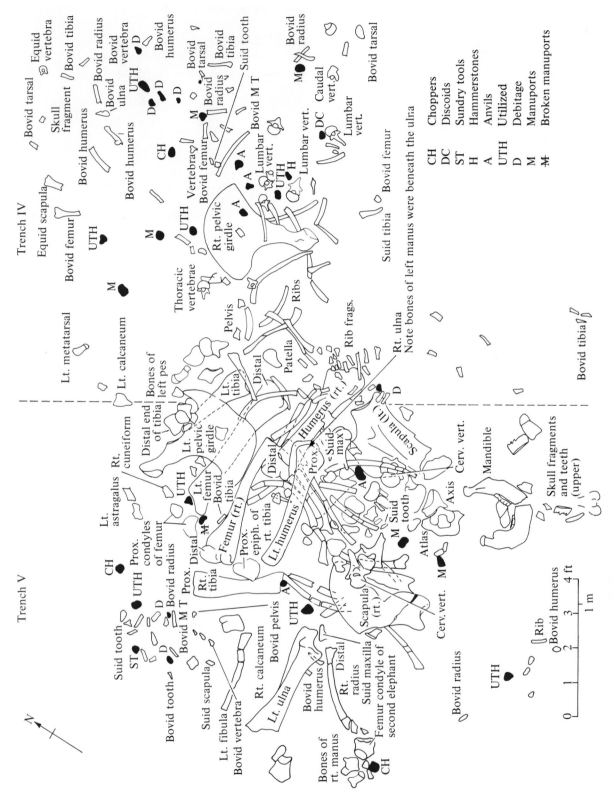

**FIGURE 14–22  Plan of Butchering Site, FLK North, Level 6, Olduvai Gorge**

## TABLE 14–5

### STONE INDUSTRY FROM DK, OLDUVAI GORGE

|  | Number | % | Number | % |
|---|---|---|---|---|
| Tools |  |  | 154 | 12.9 |
| Choppers | 47 | 3.9 |  |  |
| Scrapers | 30 | 2.5 |  |  |
| Burins | 3 | 0.3 |  |  |
| Others | 74 | 6.2 |  |  |
| Utilized material |  |  | 187 | 15.6 |
| Anvils | 3 | 0.3 |  |  |
| Hammerstones | 48 | 4.0 |  |  |
| Flakes | 37 | 3.1 |  |  |
| Others | 99 | 8.3 |  |  |
| Debitage |  |  | 857 | 71.5 |

*Source:* M. D. Leakey, *Olduvai Gorge, Vol. 3, Excavations in Beds I and II, 1963–1969* (Cambridge, England: Cambridge University Press, 1971), p. 39.

used to create a core with a sharp edge. The resulting core tool can be used for many functions, such as chopping and cutting, while the flakes knocked off the core can be used as knives and puncturing tools.

Paleoanthropologists assume that objects are tools if certain conditions are met. They look for regularity in shape among the objects and whether the objects are found in association with the things on which they may have been used, such as butchered animals. Also, tools are often found at a distance from where the material to make them is located. Many of the stones from FLK and DK display all of these features and are therefore considered to be tools.

The tools described above are characteristic of the *Oldowan culture* (Figure 14–23). This assemblage of tools is widespread during this time period throughout eastern and southern Africa. Later in time (Middle and Upper Bed II at Olduvai Gorge), we find a group of tools labeled *Developed Oldowan,* which includes new tool types such as the **awl, cleaver,** and crude hand ax.

One of the most interesting features at Olduvai Gorge is the stone circle of the DK site (Figure 14–24). This circle, about 3.7 to 4.3 meters (12 to 14 feet) in diameter, is formed of basalt blocks loosely piled up to just under 30 centimeters (1 foot) high. Associated small piles of stones may have been supports for branches, while the circle itself may have been a base to support a living structure made of brush. If this stone circle is the support of some type of hut, it would represent the earliest known human habitation structure. Other interpretations, however, have been made. The circle may simply

**FIGURE 14–23  Stone Artifacts from the Oldowan Culture of Olduvai Gorge**
(*a*) Side chopper; (*b*) discoid; (*c*) end scraper; (*d*) side scraper; (*e*) burin; (*f*) utilized flake.

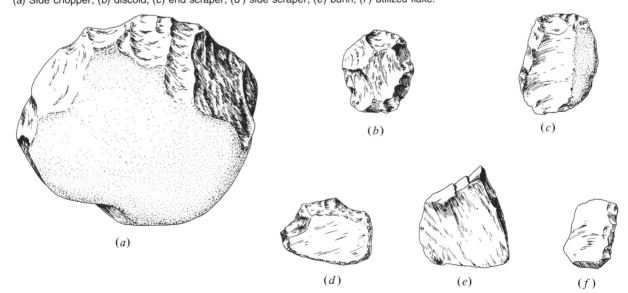

(*a*)

(*b*)

(*c*)

(*d*)

(*e*)

(*f*)

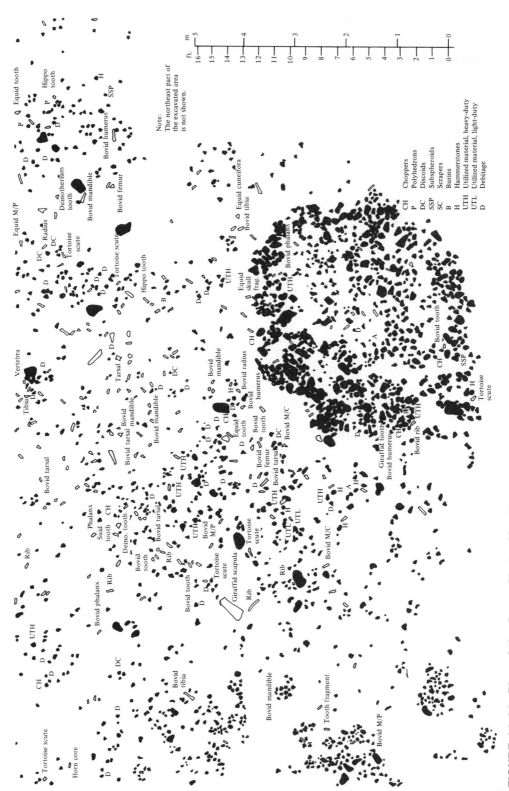

**FIGURE 14-24 Plan of the Stone Circle, Site DK, Olduvai Gorge**

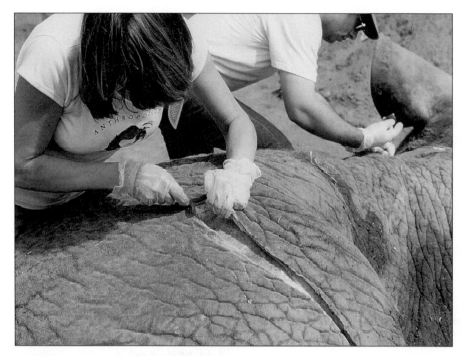

**FIGURE 14–25  The Use of Flake Tools**
Archaeologists Kathy Schick and Ray Dezzani are shown using a stone flake to cut through the thick skin of an elephant that died of natural causes.

be the result of fractured basalt having been forced up from an underlying layer of lava by the radiating roots of an ancient tree.

**The Archaeology of Lake Turkana**  Several different kinds of sites have been identified in the Koobi Fora area of east Lake Turkana. One type of site is that in which a single large animal is found associated with stone artifacts. The HAS site, which is dated at around 1.6 million B.P., consists of a hippopotamus lying in a stream channel that was part of a delta system. Paleoanthropologists believe that hominids found the animal already dead and that they used the site for their scavenging activity. Scattered among the animal bones and on the nearby bank are 119 artifacts, most of which are small, sharp flakes that could be held between the fingers and used as knives to carve up the carcass (Figure 14–25).

The KBS site at Koobi Fora presents a different behavioral picture. This site contains hundreds of stone artifacts, along with a large number of bones from many animal species: pig, gazelle, waterbuck, giraffe, and hippopotamus. The site was once the sandy bed of a stream, and perhaps a small group of hominids regularly gathered there to cut up small pieces of game. The large variety of animals represented suggests that the hominids transported game to this central location.

**The Acheulean Tradition**  The most frequent cultural manifestation of the Lower Paleolithic is the **Acheulean tradition,** which is characterized by a number of highly diagnostic tool types, including the hand ax. The hand ax may have been used for butchering animals, working wood, cracking bones, digging for roots, and many other purposes.

Throughout this period, archaeologists can trace the development of finer technological control in the manufacturing of hand axes. The earlier types were produced with hammerstones, and the flakes removed were large and thick; this resulted in a finished product that was large and had a ragged cutting edge. Later, the use of hammers of bone or other similar material produced thinner, more regular flakes; this resulted in a thinner tool with a fairly straight cutting edge.

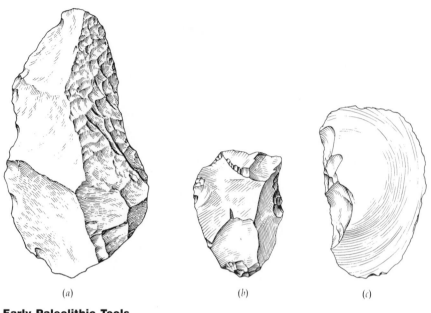

**FIGURE 14–26   Early Paleolithic Tools**
(*a*) Abbevillean hand ax from Olduvai Gorge; (*b*) chopping tools from Zhoukoudian; (*c*) cleaverlike tool from Zhoukoudian.

While hand axes are often considered diagnostic of the Lower Paleolithic, they make up only a small percentage of all the tool types from Lower Paleolithic sites; in fact, some sites lack hand axes altogether. Cores were also transformed into hammers and choppers, while the flakes were made into a variety of tools, such as scrapers, awls, and knives (Figure 14–26).

**The First Use of Fire**   Paleoanthropologists who are interested in the spread of hominids into northern latitudes recognize the importance of the controlled use of fire. Early hominids were tropical animals, and any movement northward depended to a degree on the ability to utilize fire for warmth during the winter months. Fire also played major roles in hunting and tool making.

During the original excavations at Zhoukoudian, China, in the late 1920s and 1930s, investigators found pieces of burnt bone, antler, horn cores, and pieces of wood along with burned clays. In 1996 and 1997, archaeologists reexamined Layer 10 at Zhoukoudian, the oldest of the archaeological layers at the site, and recovered 278 bone fragments, seven of which appeared burned, that they analyzed for evidence of fire. Geological material was also sampled.

A new analysis, utilizing several modern analytic techniques, found no evidence for the controlled use of fire. The few bones that were burned could have been burned naturally. There was no evidence of burned wood or hearths. Because of these results, there are no confirmed sites with evidence of controlled fires earlier than 300,000 years ago, and there is no evidence of fire associated with *H. erectus*. This could mean that the migration of *H. erectus* into northern regions was accomplished without the use of fire.

**Habitations**   The site of Terra Amata, in the city of Nice in southern France, is approximately 400,000 years old. When excavated in 1966, this site, once a part of the beach, was interpreted as containing several dwellings. If this interpretation is correct, the huts measure 6 by 12 meters (20 by 40 feet) and are characterized by oval floors. A study of what some interpret as postholes, stone supports, and hearths suggests that the hut was made of saplings or branches.

Archaeologist Paola Vila studied Terra Amata and discovered that about 40 percent of the cores and flakes could be put together to reconstruct the original stones from which these cores and flakes were manufactured.[10] Surprisingly, these pieces came from different stratigraphic levels. A specific tool was manufactured at a specific point in time, but the pieces of the tool were widely distributed at what first appear to be different time levels. This fact suggests that there has been significant disturbance at Terra Amata and that natural processes have moved artifacts made at one point in time into levels that seem to represent different points in time. Perhaps, then, the spatial arrangements of stones and postholes originally interpreted as dwellings are also the result of natural disturbances and not of human activity.

Hominids of this period probably made use of a variety of dwelling types. Some of these dwellings may have been in the open or up against a cliff, perhaps under a cliff overhang. Few habitations were constructed in caves, contrary to the popular notion of prehistoric peoples as "cavemen." Because of the good preservation of cave sites, archaeologists have tended to concentrate on their excavation.

### Hunting, Scavenging, and Gathering

The classic description of early hominid subsistence patterns was that of Lower Paleolithic hominids as big-game hunters. Today, new finds and reanalyses of previously found fossils and artifacts place some doubt on this traditional interpretation.

Not so long ago, tools found in association with bones that have cut marks on them were assumed to have been used by hominids for hunting, killing, and butchering animals. Detailed microscopic studies of bones and hominid tooth-wear patterns, however, tell a different story. Paleoanthropologist Pat Shipman has studied cut marks on bones associated with tools and has found several interesting facts (Figure 14-27).

First, many bones that were processed by hominids have carnivore tooth marks in addition to cut marks from tools. In some cases, the cut marks overlay the tooth marks, indicating that the prey animal had already been killed by a carnivore before it was butchered. Second, Shipman found that tool cut marks are often not near joints but occur

on the shafts of bones. This suggests that the hominids did not have the whole carcass to butcher and that perhaps they cut off meat that remained after carnivores had left the scene or had been chased off. Hominids could have also eaten the marrow.

It is likely that the hominids of the Lower Paleolithic were predominantly scavengers and gatherers of wild plants. They may have performed some hunting, but many anthropologists now believe that hunting of large mammals did not become a major part of any human subsistence pattern until the emergence of later hominids.

Scavenging and hunting are two quite different activities. However, all nonprimate mammalian scavengers also hunt, and this may have also been the case among early hominids. In searching for dead animals that still have some food value, animals that are primarily scavengers have to cover larger ranges than those that are primarily hunters. On the other hand, scavenging does not require as much speed as hunting, although it is aided by endurance. Shipman points out that human bipedalism is not the best locomotor pattern for speed but it is an efficient method of movement in terms of endurance. Bipedalism may have evolved, at least in part, in response to the selective pressures involved in a scavenging lifestyle.

### The Brain and Language in Prehistoric Populations

Beginning about 1.6 million B.P., brain size began to increase over and beyond that which can be explained by an increase in body size. Some researchers point to evidence that suggests that from 1.6 million to about 300,000 B.P., the brain not only dramatically increased in size but also was being neurally reorganized in a way that increased its ability to process information in an abstract (symbolic) way. This symbolism allowed complex information to be stored, relationships to be derived, and information to be efficiently retrieved and communicated to others.

In modern people, an area, usually located on the left hemisphere of the frontal lobe of the cerebral cortex, controls the muscles for speech. This area of the brain, known as **Broca's area,** may have been present as early as 1.8 million B.P. in KNM-ER 1470, a specimen of *H. rudolfensis* (Figure 14-28). The presence of Broca's area does not necessarily

---

[10]P. Vila, "Conjoinable Pieces and Site Formation," *American Antiquity* 47 (1982), pp. 276–290.

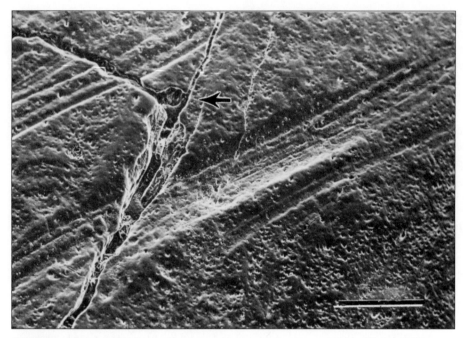

**FIGURE 14–27 Evidence of Butchering**
This photograph, taken by a scanning electron microscope, shows cut marks made with a stone tool on the surface of a fossilized bone. The cut marks are seen crossing a weathering crack (indicated by the arrow). Within the groove of each cut mark are many fine, parallel striations, features typical of such marks. The scale bar is 0.5 mm long.

mean that *H. rudolfensis* could speak, or at least not in a modern sense. The other neural features needed for fully developed language and speech, as well as the anatomical prerequisites needed for speech, may not have evolved this early. It is not possible to know exactly when the reorganization of the brain reached its modern state; many investigators believe this occurred around 300,000 years ago.

If the brain's reorganization was basically modern by about 300,000 or more years ago, and if this reorganization was a prerequisite for full language abilities, who were the first people to speak in a modern way? One type of evidence for speech comes from the examination of the shape of the **basicranium,** the floor of the brain case (Figure 14–29). A straight basicranium indicates that the larynx (voice box) is positioned high in the neck; such a vocal tract would be unable to produce many human speech sounds. In modern humans, the basicranium is flexed, or bent, indicating a larynx low in the neck; this creates an acoustic situation favorable for speech sounds. The *Australo-*

*pithecus* and *Paranthropus* basicrania are straight and are similar to those of modern apes. The basicranium of *H. erectus* is more flexed than the basicranium of *Australopithecus* but not quite as bent as that of a modern adult human skull. This may mean that the position of the larynx, and hence the shape of the vocal track, may have been approaching the modern configuration as early as 1.6 million years ago.

The other anatomical indication for speech is found in the analysis of the hyoid bone, a delicate bone in the neck that anchors muscles connected to the jaw, larynx, and tongue. This bone is so fragile that we have only one fossil specimen, that of a 60,000-year-old Neandertal found in Kebara Cave in Israel.

According to some reconstructions, the Neandertal basicranium is straighter than that of the modern human or *H. erectus,* and this has led to computer models of the Neandertal vocal apparatus that indicate that Neandertals could not pronounce certain vowel sounds such as *a, i,* and *u.* Since *H. erectus* has a quite modern basicranium,

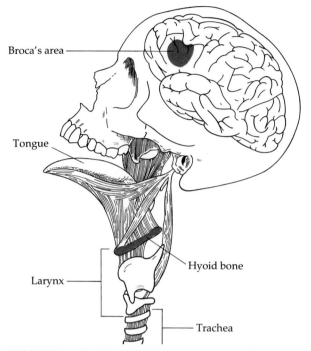

**FIGURE 14–28  Broca's Area and the Hyoid Bone**
The position and shape of the hyoid bone are important indicators of the potential for speech. The hyoid bone anchors muscles connected to the jaw, larynx, and tongue. Broca's area of the brain controls these muscles as they function to produce speech sounds.

even if Neandertals lacked articulate speech in the modern sense, it would not necessarily mean that more modern humans living at the same time as or before Neandertals could not speak as we do. For some researchers, the Kebara hyoid contradicts the basicranial data on Neandertals. It is seen by some as being almost identical in size, shape, and anatomical position to the hyoids of contemporary humans and thus indicates that the Neandertals *could* talk like modern humans.

### The Culture of the Neandertals

The cultural tradition associated most frequently with Neandertals is the **Mousterian,** named after the cave of Le Moustier in France. Some non-Neandertals are also found in association with Mousterian assemblages, and non-Mousterian cultural traditions existed during the time period of the Neandertals.

The Mousterian is a Middle Paleolithic cultural tradition. It is a continuation and refinement of the Acheulean tradition and is characterized by an increase in the number and variety of flake tools and an ultimate deemphasis of the hand ax. For example, in some early Neandertal sites, hand axes make up as much as 40 percent of the stone tools, whereas in later assemblages, they drop to less than 8 percent. In some Mousterian sites, bone tools are predominant.

The sites of the Middle Paleolithic show great variability in tool types and their frequencies (Figure 14–30). However, some paleoanthropologists see Mousterian tools as being simple variations of only about four tool types. Archaeologist Richard Klein states that Neandertals were skilled toolmakers, but they did not make tools in the standardized patterns seen later among anatomically modern *Homo sapiens.* Klein believes that Neandertals "were only interested in a point or an edge."[11] In this view, they did not conceptualize a particular type of tool.

**Were Neandertals "Cavemen"?**  Caves are among the best places in which fossils and artifacts can be found. In many areas, the cycle of wetting due to rain and drying out occurs less frequently in caves than in open sites, and hence the chance of rapid deterioration is reduced. Because of the buildup of garbage and the flaking off of material from the roof and floor, caves often provide the researcher with a well-preserved stratigraphy. Since preservation is somewhat better in caves than in open sites, caves have been extensively investigated for signs of human occupation, and most Neandertal sites have been found in this context.

Humans are not by nature cave-dwelling animals, as caves are dark, often damp, and quite uncomfortable. People did inhabit the mouths of caves, but rarely did they venture into the deep interiors. In fact, most often what are called "caves" are not caves at all but rock shelters or rock overhangs. Yet there is evidence of Neandertals using the deep interior of the cave at Bruniquel, in southern France, at around 47,600

---

[11]Quoted in C. Holden, "How Much Like Us Were the Neandertals?" *Science* 282 (1998), p. 1456.

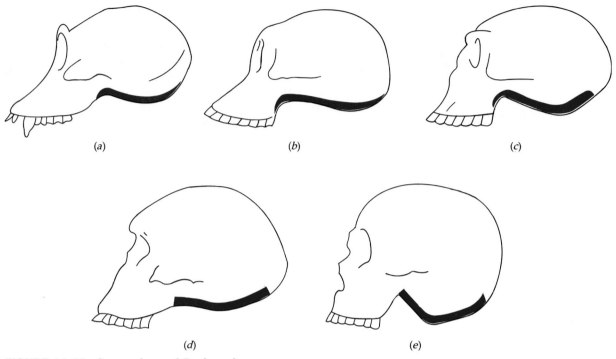

(a)    (b)    (c)

(d)    (e)

**FIGURE 14–29  Comparison of Basicrania**
The shape of the base of the cranium in living forms is correlated with the position of the larynx.
The flatter the basicranium, the higher the larynx in the neck. In turn, the position of the larynx in
the throat influences the type of vocalizations that can be produced. The figure shows a series of
composite representations of (a) the chimpanzee, (b) *Australopithecus africanus*, (c) *Homo erectus*,
(d) *Homo neandertalensis*, and (e) *Homo sapiens*. (Skulls are not drawn to scale.)

B.P. Hundreds of meters from the cave entrance, archaeologists found a complex quadrilateral structure of unknown function. Since only Neandertals inhabited Europe at this time, we can postulate the existence of portable light sources and complex patterns of communication and social organization.

Neandertals also may have spent a great deal of their time in open-air sites, but these have not been preserved with as great a frequency as have cave sites. This is an example of how differential preservation influences the data.

However, some open-air sites are known; among the most famous is Molodova I, in the western part of Ukraine. At this site, mammoth bones served as the support for animal hides that created a house with an inside area 5.4 meters (18 feet) in diameter. Fifteen hearths have been found in the floor of this ancient home.

## How Neandertals Behaved

As stated previously, behavior does not fossilize. Therefore, drawing conclusions about the behavior of ancient hominids is more speculative than making conclusions about their anatomy. Nowhere is this more evident than in the reconstruction of Neandertal behavior.

Neandertals, at one time or another, have been characterized as either dimwitted or superintelligent. They have also been characterized as the first hominids to systematically, and perhaps ritually, bury their dead (Figure 14–31). Some paleoanthropologists interpret artifacts associated with Neandertal skeletal remains as grave goods. Taking this one step further, grave goods can be seen as indicating a belief in the afterworld. The objects would aid the dead in a supposed next world.

However, an alternative view has been gaining support over the last several years. Anthropologist

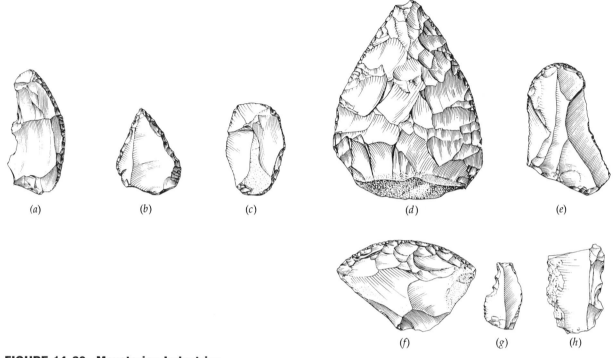

**FIGURE 14–30  Mousterian Industries**
(*a*) Typical Mousterian, convex side scraper; (*b*) typical Mousterian, Mousterian point; (*c*) Mousterian of Acheulean, backed knife; (*d*) Mousterian of Acheulean, hand ax; (*e*) Mousterian of Acheulean, end scraper; (*f*) Quina-type Mousterian, traverse scraper; (*g*) and (*h*) denticulate Mousterian, denticulate tools.

Harold Dibble expresses that view. He believes that supposed grave goods were "incidental intrusions" and that Neandertals may not have purposefully buried their dead.[12] Dibble also sees the lack of art and other forms of symbolizing, as well as the lack of variation in tool types, as indications that Neandertals were significantly different from anatomically modern people in the way the Neandertals adapted to and perceived their environment.

Lewis Binford also believes that Neandertals may have differed in many ways from *H. sapiens*. Based on evidence from a site in southwestern France, Binford sees a pattern in which Neandertal men and women lived basically separate lives and may not have had the ability to plan for future

events. Even Binford, however, admits that this is speculation.

**Summary**

The oldest known archaeological material dates from around 2.6 million B.P. from the Gona River basin. Other important east African archaeological sites include the Omo River basin, Hadar, Olduvai Gorge, and east Lake Turkana. While both *Australopithecus* and *Homo* were for the most part contemporary at these sites, it is assumed that the development of technology was largely an adjustment of *Homo* and that the artifacts recovered represent the behavior of this genus.

The earliest stone tools are predominantly choppers and flakes. Later Paleolithic tools, attributed to *H. erectus*, are associated with hand-ax traditions such as the Acheulean. The degree to which

---

[12]Ibid.

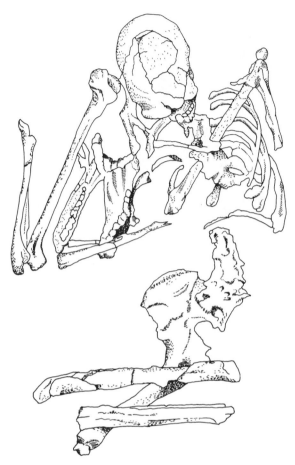

**FIGURE 14–31   Neandertal Burial**
An adult male burial from Mount Carmel. The body was buried with the jawbones of a great wild boar.

*H. erectus* depended on hunting for subsistence is debated. Today, many researchers believe that gathering wild vegetation and scavenging for meat and marrow were important methods of obtaining food.

Neandertals used tools made of stone, bone, wood, and shell. Their cultural tradition, called the Mousterian, continued the use of hand axes, but the number and variety of flake tools increased throughout the Neandertal period. Neandertals lived in both rock shelters and open-air sites, and although some groups were probably more settled than others, most groups were probably nomadic.

To some, Neandertals seem to show a consciousness that we can recognize as "human." They may have buried their dead and placed artifacts and flowers in the graves, although this view has been challenged. Some anthropologists believe that the Neandertals may have differed from modern people in many ways. Some investigators believe that the Neandertals evolved into *H. sapiens* in Europe while others think they are a side branch of human evolution that did not contribute to the gene pool of contemporary peoples. Neandertal behavior and their relationships to modern humans remain a mystery of paleoanthropology.

## STUDY QUESTIONS

1. Compare the anatomical characteristics of the genera *Homo* and *Australopithecus*.
2. What was the distribution of *H. erectus* and *H. ergaster*? Briefly describe the finds made in each major geographical area.
3. List the members of the species *H. heidelbergensis* mentioned in this chapter. Tell where they were discovered, and explain how this group of fossils differs from both earlier and later species of the genus *Homo*.
4. What are some of the major anatomical differences between Neandertals and modern humans?
5. What evidence exists to justify the idea that *H. erectus* was primarily a gatherer of wild plant material and a scavenger of already killed animals as opposed to an efficient big-game hunter?
6. Summarize what is known about the origins of the Neandertals.
7. What type of evidence is used to construct models on the potential for language and speech abilities in fossil populations?
8. Discuss assumptions that have been made about the Neandertals' world view.

## SUGGESTED READINGS

The following handbooks list individual fossils along with pertinent information:

Day, M. *Guide to Fossil Man: A Handbook of Human Paleontology,* 4th ed. Chicago: University of Chicago Press, 1986.
Larsen, C. P., R. M. Matter, and D. L. Gebo. *Human Origins: The Fossil Record,* 3rd ed. Prospect Heights, Ill.: Waveland, 1998.

Also recommended are the following:

Fagan, B. *The Journey from Eden: Peopling the Prehistoric World.* New York: Thames and Hudson, 1990. This book is a general survey of prehistory.

Klein, R. G. *The Human Career: Human Biological and Cultural Origins,* 2nd ed. Chicago: University of Chicago Press, 1999. This is a comprehensive, readable book detailing current research in paleontology and archaeology.

Lanpo, J., and H. Weiwen. *The Story of Peking Man.* Beijing: Foreign Languages Press, 1990. This translation of a book written by two Chinese paleoanthropologists describes the history, discoveries, and current research at Zhoukoudian.

Mellars, P. *The Neanderthal Legacy: An Archaeological Perspective.* Princeton, N.J.: Princeton University Press, 1995. This book is an overview of western European Neandertal material culture, subsistence patterns, and society.

Reader, J. *Missing Links: The Hunt for Earliest Man,* rev. ed. Boston: Little, Brown, 1995. This book tells the story of the hunt for and discovery of many important fossil hominids.

Shreeve, J. *The Neandertal Enigma: Solving the Mystery of Modern Human Origins.* New York: William Morrow, 1995. This is a beautifully written and informative book on the Neandertals and the possible relationships they had to modern peoples.

Solecki, R. S. *Shanidar: The First Flower People.* New York: Knopf, 1971. This is the story of Solecki's excavation of the Neandertals in Iraq.

Trinkaus, E. *The Shanidar Neandertals.* New York: Academic, 1983. This is a book detailing the finds of nine early eastern Neandertals. The final chapter gives an overview of the evolution of the Neandertals.

Trinkaus, E., and P. Shipman. *The Neandertals: Changing the Image of Mankind.* New York: Knopf, 1992. This is a survey of perceptions and attitudes about the Neandertals from the time of their discovery until today.

## SUGGESTED WEB SITES

The Human Lineage:
http://www.wf.carleton.ca/Museum/man/evnman.html
Flintknapping through the Ages:
http://www.ucs.mun.ca/~t64tr/history.html
The Fossil Evidence for Human Evolution in China:
http://www.cruzio.com/~cscp/index.htm

Additional web sites are listed in the *Workbook* that accompanies this text.

# The Evolution of *Homo Sapiens*

*Few topics in anthropology have generated more interest and debate over the past few years than the biological and behavioural origins of fully "modern" human populations. The debates have arisen partly from new discoveries and the application of new dating methods, and partly from the use of more sophisticated approaches to the modelling of human evolutionary processes, both in terms of biological evolution, and the associated (and inevitably interrelated) patterns of cultural change. A central factor in much of this rethinking has of course been the recent developments in molecular genetics, which are now opening up an entirely new perspective on the evolutionary origins of modern human populations.*[1]
—Paul Mellars and Chris Stringer

## Chapter Outline

---

[1]P. Mellars and C. Stringer (eds.), *The Human Revolution* (Princeton, N.J.: Princeton University Press, 1989), p. ix.

**373**

Anthropocentrism is the belief that humans are the most important elements in the universe and that everything else exists for human use and fancy. This belief runs counter to modern scientific thought. Yet since the nineteenth century, scientists have debated what it is to be human. These discussions often seem to be anthropocentric or, if we may coin a new term, *sapiencentric.*

As an example, some scholars see the origins of creative thought and behavior, such as that seen in pictorial art, as occurring only after the origins of modern humans. Although the Neandertals and their contemporaries do not appear to have expressed themselves through pictorial art, they may have developed other creative outlets, such as story-telling. We just don't know!

As we will see shortly, anatomically modern peoples may have originated at the same time as or even before the time of the Neandertals, yet *H. sapiens* may not have developed pictorial art until about 30,000 years ago. Why? Perhaps art and other new behaviors originated because of changes in the environment or as the result of cultural exchanges, and not because of any physical or mental changes. This chapter will focus on what it means to be modern, and it will examine the debate over modern human origins and evolution.

### HOMO SAPIENS

Today, modern *H. sapiens* populations are distributed widely over the globe. This section will survey the earliest appearances of modern *H. sapiens* in various areas of the world (Figure 15–1).

### The Distribution of Fossil *Homo sapiens* in the Old World

**Asia** Two early modern hominids from Israel, one from Jebel Qafzeh and the other from Tabūn, place anatomically modern humans well back into the Neandertal time range. The Jebel Qafzeh fossil has been dated by electron spin resonance dating to between 115,000 and 96,000 B.P. (Figure 15–2). The dating of Tabūn is less certain, but it is probably older than 100,000 B.P.

Although many paleoanthropologists conclude that Jebel Qafzeh and Tabūn are about 100,000 years old, the earliest reliable dates for *H. sapiens* in Asia are much more recent. One of these early reliable dates is associated with an anatomically modern human from Niah Cave in north Borneo; the fossil has been dated by radiocarbon dating at about 41,500 B.P. The adult female found in the cave is delicately built; the skull lacks brow ridges, the forehead is high, and the back of the head is rounded. The Niah Cave individual resembles modern populations of New Guinea.

Many finds have been made in China, but perhaps the best known is a series of skulls from the Upper Cave of Zhoukoudian. They are relatively recent, dating to between 18,000 and 10,000 years ago. The skulls are all modern, but they are interesting in that each one differs in some respects from the others; they provide a good example of intra-population variability. One skull shows a forward-jutting zygomatic arch and **shovel-shaped incisors** similar to those of present Asian populations. Shovel-shaped incisors are incisors that have a scooped-out shape on the tongue side of the tooth. These skulls also closely resemble many Native American skulls.

**Europe** Early modern humans are often seen in terms of a population called Cro-Magnon, which lived about 28,000 years ago or later (Figure 15–3). In 1868, several partial skeletons were discovered in a rock shelter in southwestern France. They became the prototype of *H. sapiens.* Early scholars envisioned Cro-Magnon people as light-skinned, beardless, upright-walking individuals who invaded Europe and destroyed the bestial Neandertals. In general, Cro-Magnon people are characterized by broad, small faces with high foreheads and prominent chins and cranial capacities as high as 1590 cubic centimeters. Their height has been estimated at 163 to 183 centimeters (5 feet 4 inches to 6 feet), but their skin color and amount of body hair can only be surmised.

In other parts of Europe, even older fossil populations of modern people existed. At the 38,000-year-old site of Mladeč in Czech Republic, paleontologists found a cranium that was quite robust yet basically modern in appearance. It and other finds in eastern, central, and southern Europe show modern features; yet these specimens also exhibit characteristics, such as brow ridges, that are intermediate in size between those of the Neandertals and modern humans.

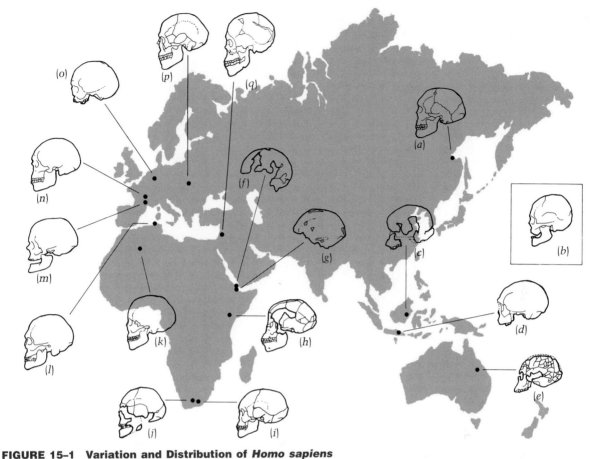

**FIGURE 15–1  Variation and Distribution of *Homo sapiens***
(a) Upper Cave 101, Zhoukoudian, People's Republic of China; (b) Tepexpan, Mexico; (c) Niah
Cave, Borneo; (d) Wadjak, Java; (e) Talgai, Australia; (f) and (g) Omo, Ethiopia; (h) Lothagam Hill,
Kenya; (i) Fish Hoek, South Africa; (j) Cape Flats, Cape Peninsula, South Africa; (k) Asselar, Mali;
(l) Afalou, Algeria; (m) Cro-Magnon, France; (n) Combe Capelle, France; (o) Oberkassel, Germany;
(p) Predmost, Czechoslovakia, (q) Jebel Qafzeh IX, Israel.

**Africa**  A recent discovery of a skull at a site near
the village of Buia, Eritrea, east Africa, shows a mixture of *H. erectus* and *H. sapiens* features at around
one million years ago. Between 1995 and 1997, the
site yielded a nearly complete cranium, two pelvic
fragments, and two adult lower incisors.[2]

The cranium exhibits a mosaic of features, some
of which, such as the high position of the greatest
width of the parietals, are typical of *H. sapiens*. Yet

the low cranial capacity (750–800 cubic centimeters)
and long oval-shaped brain case associated with
large browridges bear a resemblance with other
African fossils most often classified as *H. erectus*
and *H. ergaster*.

The oldest sub-Saharan fossils that show a
greater number of modern characteristics than the
Eritrian fossils are fragmentary finds from the
Klasies River mouth in South Africa. This material
is about 120,000 years old as dated by electron spin
resonance dating. Also in South Africa, finds from
Border Cave that have many modern features have
been dated to between 115,000 and 100,000 B.P.
However, the dating from both sites has been

[2]E. Abbate et al., "A One-Million-Year-Old *Homo* Cranium from
Danakil (Afar) Depression of Eritrea," *Nature* 393 (1998), pp.
458–460.

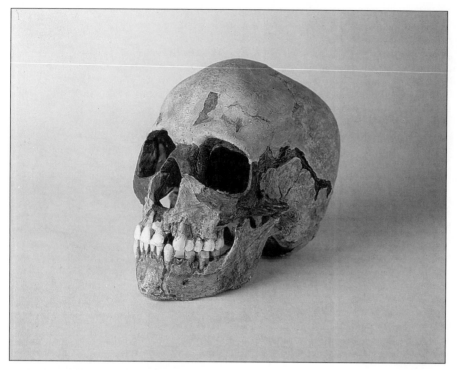

**FIGURE 15–2** *Homo sapiens*
Jebel Qafzeh skull, Israel.

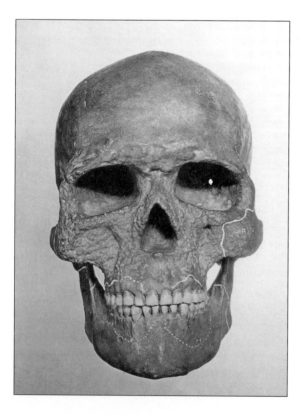

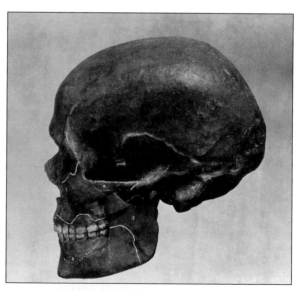

**FIGURE 15–3** *Homo sapiens*
Cast of the skull from Cro-Magnon, France.

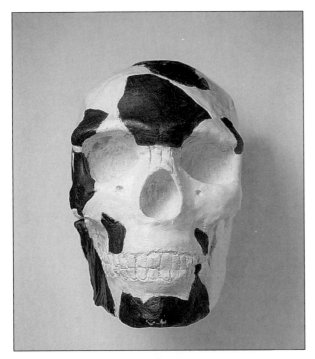

**FIGURE 15–4** *Homo sapiens*
Omo I skull, Ethiopia.

questioned, as has the degree to which they exhibit modern features. Other African fossils, such as Omo I from Ethiopia, dated at 130,000 B.P., are quite modern in appearance (Figure 15–4). Still other early African hominids show a mixture of archaic and modern features.

## The Anatomy of *Homo sapiens*

Modern humans have a distinctly round head that contains a large brain that averages 1350 cubic centimeters. From front to back, the cranial arch, or vault, is short but high. The occipital bone is delicate; it lacks the large bony crests that in other anthropoids function as surface areas for the attachment of large neck and jaw muscles.

Compared with earlier hominids, the modern human face and eye sockets are smaller; the front of the upper jaw and the mandible are also small. The modern human has a strong **chin,** which is the bony projection of the lower part of the mandible. Compared with the earlier hominid skeletons, the modern human skeleton is generally less robust and the musculature is lighter.

## Ideas on the Origins of *Homo sapiens*

During the past two decades, paleoanthropologists have uncovered new evidence and have developed new hypotheses to explain the origins of *Homo sapiens*. Although there are several competing models, most are variations of two basic models, labeled the replacement model and the regional continuity model (Figure 15–5).

In the **replacement model,** which anthropologist William Howells calls the "Noah's Ark" model, *H. sapiens* are seen as having evolved in Africa some 200,000 years ago. They then radiated out of this area and spread throughout Asia and Europe. These *H. sapiens* ultimately replaced earlier hominid populations, including the Neandertals.

This replacement occurred because *H. sapiens* either killed off archaic forms or exploited the resources of the environment into which they moved more effectively than other hominids. The inability of the indigenous hominids to compete with *H. sapiens* for such resources as food may have led to their decline. Or both processes may have operated. At any rate, the proponents of the replacement model, in its original form, believe that the earlier forms did not interbreed with *H. sapiens* populations, and therefore they did not contribute genes to contemporary *H. sapiens*. Gene flow did not occur between existing hominid populations, and there are no transitional forms outside of Africa. Physical variation in modern populations would have evolved only after the origin of modern humans.

The **regional continuity model** assumes multiple origins of *H. sapiens* from existing local populations. For example, Neandertals gave rise to modern European populations. This is not to say that each regional *H. sapiens* population evolved in total isolation. On the contrary, enough gene flow and migration between these populations would have occurred to maintain a single species, *H. sapiens*. This gene flow and similar selective forces in the different regions are seen as reasons for parallel evolution in the direction of modern humanity.

According to this latter model, modern-population differences in physical characteristics are deeply rooted. They point to possible physical features, especially in Asia, that characterize specific regions that are seen in both modern and fossil forms. Such similarities suggest the existence of

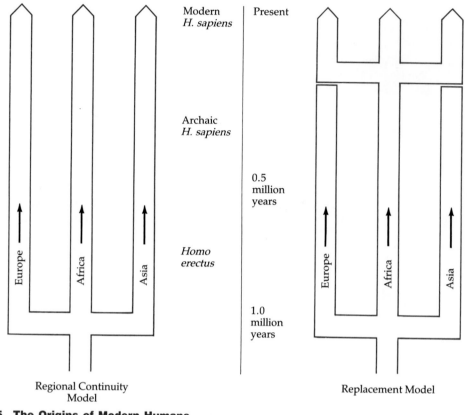

**FIGURE 15–5  The Origins of Modern Humans**

These two diagrams represent two views of the origins of modern *H. sapiens*. The regional continuity model assumes that modern human populations are direct descendants of local *H. erectus* populations. The replacement model assumes that local *H. erectus* populations were replaced by migrations of *H. sapiens* that originated in Africa.

transitional forms. Proponents of the regional continuity model believe that modern *H. sapiens's* last common ancestor existed 1 million to perhaps 1.8 million years ago.

**The Story of "Mitochondrial Eve"**  The "mitochondrial" in "Mitochondrial Eve's" name refers to mitochondrial DNA (mtDNA). Mitochondrial DNA is found in the cytoplasm of the cell, and it is inherited exclusively from the mother's sex cell. Since there is no recombination of the two parents' mtDNA, the only difference in a child's mtDNA and that of its mother, grandmother, great-grandmother, or any other direct female relative is due to mutation. Alan Wilson, Rebecca Cann, and Mark Stoneking proposed that the mtDNA of all modern populations can be traced back to a population of African women who became known collectively as "Mitochondrial Eve."[3] By assuming a mutation rate of 2 percent per million years, they believe that the current variation in mtDNA suggests a common ancestral population to all current people that lived about 200,000 years ago.

Led by Milford Wolpoff, paleoanthropologists have pointed out that in order for the geneticists' model to work, the only thing affecting the differences in the structure of mitochondrial DNA would be random mutation. However, any genes entering the gene pool of "Eve's" descendants from other populations would create a different degree of

---

[3]R.L. Cann, M. Stoneking, and A. C. Wilson, "Mitochondrial DNA and Human Evolution," *Nature* 325 (1987), pp. 31–36.

variation than would be expected if random muta-tion was the only cause for such variation. There *were* people before "Eve"; so if all modern people are the descendants of "Eve's" gene pool only, all of the people not of her line would have died off without breeding with any of "Eve's" descendants.

Some anthropologists also see flaws in the ge-neticists' techniques for calculating mutation rates and in some basic assumptions they make about evolution. They point out that the same data used in the original studies that established an African origin can also be used to generate phylogenetic trees that show non-African origins.

Like other scientific controversies, the debate be-tween proponents and opponents of the "Mito-chondrial Eve" hypothesis illustrates the self-correcting nature of science. As the research used to compile the data for a hypothesis is constantly repeated and reanalyzed, the new research either validates the old hypothesis or invalidates it. The construction of specific phylogenetic trees showing an African origin for *H. sapiens* is questioned by some, but the research did illustrate that there is greater mtDNA variation in African populations. This reinforces the idea inferred from the fossil record that hominids have existed in Africa longer than on any other continent.

**Other Lines of Evidence**  The argument over the two models for the origins of *H. sapiens* revolves around several lines of evidence. The first is ge-netic, especially the mtDNA evidence that was re-viewed in the previous section.

A study published in 1995 reported on the analy-sis of a section of the Y chromosome of humans, chimpanzees, gorillas, and orangutans. The re-searchers calculated a mutation rate, based on the supposed time that pairs of each of the above species had a common ancestor, and the differences in the area of the Y chromosome under study. On the basis of this mutation rate, they propose that *H. sapiens* originated 275,000 years ago. However, even the investigators consider their findings to be tentative.[4]

[4]R. L. Dorit, H. Akashi, and W. Gilbert, "Absence of Polymor-phism at the ZFY Locus on the Human Y Chromosome," *Sci-ence* 268 (1995), pp. 1183–1185.

The second area of investigation involves phys-ical similarities and differences between fossil and contemporary populations. The regional continuity model is strengthened by similarities in cranial and dental features between fossil and modern popu-lations in Asia. Yet the proponents of the replace-ment model note the relatively abrupt change in Europe between the earlier *H. neandertalensis* and later *H. sapiens* populations.

The final area of study involves new methods of dating, which have suggested some very early dates for *H. sapiens* in Africa that are much older than those in Europe and Asia. These data suggest the presence of what appears to be anatomically modern humans 120,000 years ago at the Klasies River mouth in South Africa, 130,000 years ago at Omo, and between 115,000 and 92,000 years ago at Jebel Qafzeh in Israel. Yet the dating techniques themselves are open to question.

There are also several intermediate models of the evolution of modern *H. sapiens* that combine the ideas of the replacement and regional continuity models. These intermediate models assume differ-ent degrees of inbreeding between earlier hom-inids and *H. sapiens* populations. For instance, in 1999 it was reported that a 24,500-year-old skele-ton found in Portugal had physical characteristics of both the Neandertals and *H. sapiens*. The promi-nent chin looks very modern, yet its stocky trunk and short arms and legs are reminiscent of the Ne-andertals. Some paleoanthropologists see this skeleton of a 4-year-old child as the product of in-terbreeding between Neandertals and anatomically modern humans. If this is indeed the case, Nean-dertals might best be classified as a subspecies of *H. sapiens*, *H. sapiens neandertalensis*, instead of a separate species, *Homo neandertalensis*.

### The Migrations of *Homo sapiens* to Australia and the New World

There is evidence of modern-looking populations in Africa as early as 130,000 years ago, in Asia some-what after that, and in Europe at 38,000 B.P. and per-haps earlier. Except for the mysterious Kow Swamp fossils, to be discussed shortly, all hominids in Aus-tralia and the New World are modern in appear-ance. No representatives of *Australopithecus*, *Paran-thropus*, or *Homo* other than *H. sapiens* have been found.

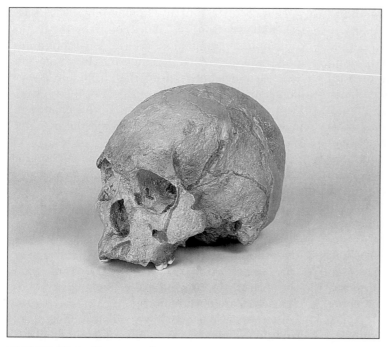

**FIGURE 15–6** *Homo sapiens*
Skull from Wadjak, Java.

**Australia** People reached New Guinea and nearby islands from the mainland of southeast Asia by crossing over land connections formed by the lowering of ocean levels associated with glacial periods. Australia was never connected by land to the mainland of Asia, yet humans may have reached Australia more than 60,000 years ago, or even earlier. Although Australia was separated from Asia, the periodic lowering of the sea level may have made migration by watercraft from Asia to Australia possible at an early date.

Many of the skeletal finds from southeast Asia resemble the modern Australian aborigine. The Wadjak skulls from Java, discovered in 1890, show large brow ridges, a receding forehead, a deep nasal root, and large teeth (Figure 15–6). A find from Lake Mungo in New South Wales, Australia, dated at 25,500 B.P., represents the oldest skeletal remains in Australia. It is also the earliest evidence of cremation burial anywhere in the world. Large fragments of bone remain after cremation. The remains of the Lake Mungo individual, whose bones had been broken and placed in a depression, are those of a person of fully modern appearance.

One of the mysteries of prehistory concerns a second population from Australia. This population, from Kow Swamp in the state of Victoria, displays a low, retreating forehead; large brow ridges; and other features reminiscent of earlier forms. The surprising thing is that the Kow Swamp finds are dated between 14,000 and 9500 B.P. This is thousands of years after earlier patterns ceased to be recognizable elsewhere in the world. Since 40 burials have been excavated, we cannot attribute this to sampling error.

**The New World** Most anthropologists believe that the Americas were populated by Asian big-game hunters who followed their prey across the Bering Strait to North America. American aborigines show similarities to Asian populations in body build, head shape, eye and skin color, hair type, dentition, presence of the Diego blood antigen, and many other physical characteristics. They also share many features of their languages.

When did the first migrants arrive in the New World? Today, on a clear day, the shore of Siberia is visible from Cape Prince of Wales, Alaska. At times in the past, Siberia and Alaska were connected by a landmass, as much as 2000 kilometers (1250 miles) from north to south, called **Beringia.** Beringia was exposed during the Pleistocene when large amounts of water were trapped in glacial ice, causing a drop in sea level.

Current geological and biological evidence suggest that Beringia existed at 80,000 B.P. or before. Before that time, North America and Asia had not been connected for about 15 million years. A warm period from 35,000 to 27,000 years ago flooded Beringia. During that time, people may have crossed the open water during the winter when the channel froze, or they may have even used simple watercraft. From approximately 27,000 to 11,000 years ago, Beringia again provided a wide grassy plain to those moving between Asia and North America. This plain was exposed as dry land for the last time about 11,000 years ago.

The firmest dates for the first presence of people in the New World are about 11,500 B.P., but dates of up to 27,900 years ago have been suggested. Most of the evidence for the early presence of humans in the New World is archaeological rather than paleontological; we will discuss this archaeological evidence in a later section of this chapter.

There is little skeletal evidence of early hominids in the New World. An electron spin resonance date of 15,400 B.P. has been determined for human bones found in Kansas and a date of around 13,000 B.P. has been suggested for a woman found on one of the Channel Islands of southern California. If these

---

**BOX 15-1**

## Genes and Language

Anthropologists agree that the first Americans came from Asia, although they debate precisely from where they came. They also agree that these early migrants walked to North America during a period of time when sea levels were low and the land that had been under water between what is modern Russia and Alaska was exposed. Two questions are more problematic: When was the first time that people entered the New World? Was there more than one early migration?

A study carried out by an anthropological linguist, an archaeologist, and a geneticist concluded that the data from all of their disciplines indicated that there were three separate early migrations from Asia to the New World. Called the Greenberg hypothesis after linguist Joseph Greenberg, they hypothesized that three waves of migrants established three different genetic patterns, which corresponded to three different language families.[1]

The first of the three migrant groups was the Eskimo-Aleut. This population included people who settled in Alaska, northern Canada, and Greenland. The second group was called the Na-Dene, which included populations living today in parts of Alaska, northwest and north-central Canada, the American Southwest, and northern Mexico. The last group included the ancestors of populations living today in the rest of the New World. This idea has received widespread popularity within anthropology, although most linguists have not been convinced. Now, a new generation of geneticists are placing doubt on the Greenberg hypothesis.

The Greenberg hypothesis is based, in part, on the presence of three distinct genetic populations in the New World. New and more precise genetic tests, however, lead to the conclusion that New World populations are not as diverse as previously thought, and that differences that exist between contemporary populations could have evolved after an initial migration or perhaps two migrations. The authors of a recent study examined 574 mitochondrial DNA control region sequences from aboriginal Siberians and Native Americans.[2] They conclude that a major wave of northeastern Siberians entered the Americas between 25,000 and 20,000 years ago. This date corresponds to new archaeological data that predate the traditional 12,000- and 11,000-year-old materials.

The original migrant population arose near the Bering Land Bridge. About 11,300 years ago, another wave of people moved from that area deeper into the Americas. This second wave were the ancestors of the present Eskimo and Na-Dene populations.

Although this idea corresponds well to archaeological data, the new genetic analysis is by no means considered firm. As with mitochondrial DNA studies of the origin of all modern humans (the "Mitochondrial Eve" hypothesis), the use of genetic data to establish migrations and the time of those migrations remains controversial. Even among geneticists, there is no consensus on the number of migrations to the New World. For instance, a Japanese geneticist recently suggested that there were four migrations. In the meantime, Joseph Greenberg is in a holding pattern. He says that if a hypothesis is refuted, it should be given up. However, he is not willing to see his hypothesis become history yet.

---

[1] A. Gibbon, "The Peopling of the Americas," *Science* 274 (1996), pp. 31–33.
[2] P. Foster et al., "Origin and Evolution of Native-American mtDNA Variations: A Reappraisal," *American Journal of Human Genetics* 59 (1996), pp. 935–945.

dates are correct, the remains would be the oldest yet found in the Americas. Fossils with dates of about 11,000 to 10,000 years have been recovered in North, Central, and South America. All fossil hom-inids found in the Americas possess Asian characteristics, and they also appear similar to modern Native American populations.

A recent study based on a series of cores from the floor of the Bering and Chukchi Seas indicates that Beringia was a tundra similar to that of Arctic Alaska today.[5] Instead of a rich grassland supporting a high density of herd animals, this tundra was relatively unproductive and required the development of a specialized technology for survival, not unlike that seen among the Inuits of the Arctic in this century. Since Beringia existed for thousands of years at a time, the migration from Asia to North America could have been a very slow one.

**Kennewick Man**   In 1996, a 9300-year-old skeleton called Kennewick Man was found along the banks of the Columbia River in Washington State. With about 90 to 95 percent of the skeleton found, Kennewick Man is the most complete and the oldest skeleton found in the Pacific Northwest (Figure 15–7).

Scientists are just beginning to have an opportunity to study the skeleton. Because of the 1990 Native American Graves Protection and Repatriation Act (NAGPRA), the Army Corps of Engineers, which has jurisdiction over the land where the skeleton was found, locked it away. NAGPRA specifies that Native American remains are to be given to the Native American group that can best show an ancestral link to the remains. The problem with the Kennewick Man skeleton is that its affiliation is unclear. Anthropologists who initially were able to study the remains note that it exhibits many "Caucasoid" features and that it could not be shown to be connected to any existing Native American group.[6]

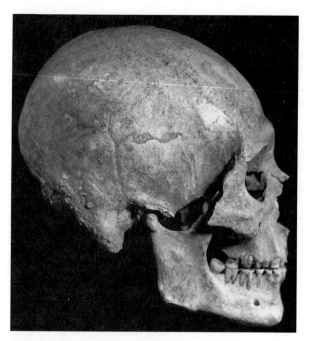

**FIGURE 15–7   *Homo sapiens***
"Kennewick Man" from the State of Washington.

In early 1999, the Interior Department, which took over control of the fossils from the Army Corps of Engineers, announced that it would allow scientists to study the more than 300 bone fragments that make up the Kennewick material. It is hoped that this research will determine the genetic affiliations of Kennewick Man.

### Summary

We cannot say exactly when fossils classified as *H. sapiens* first appeared; the precise point in time is a relative and arbitrary matter. However, the earliest *H. sapiens* may be from Africa at about 130,000 years ago. The "Mitochondrial Eve" hypothesis proposes an even earlier date for an African origin of modern humans. Modern *H. sapiens* may have been present in Asia as early as 115,000 years ago, and they were in Australia and Europe about 60,000 and 38,000 years ago, respectively. The only hominid populations found in Australia and the New World are classified as *H. sapiens*. Although considerably older dates have been proposed, firm dates for people in the New World go back to only about 11,500 years ago.

[5]S. A. Elias, "Life and Times of the Bering Land Bridge," *Nature* 382 (1996), pp. 60–63.
[6]C. Holden, "Kennewick Man Realized," *Science* 279 (1998), pp. 1137; R. Jantz, "Polemicizing Kennewick Man," *Anthropology Newsletter* 39 (March 1998), p. 56; and E. Miller, "Whose Ancestor Is He? The Case of Kennewick Man and the Science of Repatriation," *Southwestern Anthropological Association* 38 (January, 1998), pp. 1, 5, 8, 10, 13–14.

Two models have been proposed to account for the appearance and spread of *H. sapiens*. According to the replacement model, modern *H. sapiens* evolved in a limited area, such as Africa, and then moved into other areas of the world; they completely replaced the Neandertals and other non–*H. sapiens* populations. On the other hand, proponents of the regional continuity model believe that the Neandertals contributed to the origin of modern Europeans while other populations evolved into *H. sapiens* in other geographical areas. Intermediate models see different degrees of interbreeding between archaic hominids and *H. sapiens* populations. By about 30,000 years ago, *H. sapiens* was the only type of hominid existing on earth.

## THE CULTURE OF *HOMO SAPIENS*

During the Upper Paleolithic, human cultural development achieved a level of complexity that had never before existed. The cultural traditions associated with the Upper Paleolithic are found throughout Europe, northern Asia, the Middle East, and northern Africa.

### Humans' Relationship to the Environment

The development of the Upper Paleolithic must be seen in relation to the nature of the environment during that time. The period comprises the latter part of the last glaciation. Northern and western Europe was essentially a **tundra,** a land that was frozen solid throughout most of the year but thawed during the summer. A proliferation of plant life in the summer was capable of supporting large herds of animal life. The tundra of Canada today teems with animal life, such as the moose and caribou, but the Pleistocene European tundra was a low-latitude tundra that received more solar radiation than that received by the Canadian tundra today; thus, it was able to support a huge mass of herd animals.

Upper Paleolithic peoples hunted the large herd animals, often specializing in one or two types. This was in contrast to the scavenging or perhaps more individualistic hunting techniques of the Neandertals. This shift in orientation toward cooperative hunting of herd animals with improved projectile technology may have been responsible for the development of the Upper Paleolithic complex.

Among the more important animals hunted were reindeer, horse, and bison; fish, such as salmon, were also important.

Unfortunately, humans' growing mastery in the utilization of these natural resources may have been matched by the disruption of ecological balances. During the Late Pleistocene, more than 50 genera of large mammals became extinct. Yet the extinction of large animals was not accompanied by the extinction of large numbers of smaller animals or plants, and analysis of the record has shown no evidence of droughts in most areas. One factor does correspond with these extinctions: *H. sapiens*. Most extinctions can be correlated with the movements of people into an area. It seems very possible that human technology and social efficiency had developed to a point at which the environment could have been endangered.

One thing that humans may have done when they entered an area was to alter the vegetation by burning it. New information on the use of fire by Australia's earliest inhabitants indicates that their use of fire contributed to the extinction of at least 60 species, including all animals larger than people. The use of fire may have led to mass extinctions elsewhere in the world.[7]

The Upper Paleolithic of Europe was characterized by alternating periods of very cold and mild climate; people had to develop the technology to survive in such an environment. The archaeological record contains evidence of tailored clothing. Humans in a cold environment also need housing. In southwestern France, they used rock shelters, but many open settlements have also been found. Villages in this area were built in the river valleys, where they were somewhat protected from the cold of the plateau.

### Upper Paleolithic Technology

The Upper Paleolithic is often defined in terms of the stone **blade.** Blades are not unique to this period, but the high frequency of their use is.

Blades are stone flakes with roughly parallel sides and extremely sharp edges that are generally

---

[7]G. H. Miller et al., "Pleistocene Extinction of *Genyornis newtoni*: Human Impact on Australian Megafauna," *Science* 283 (1999), pp. 204–208.

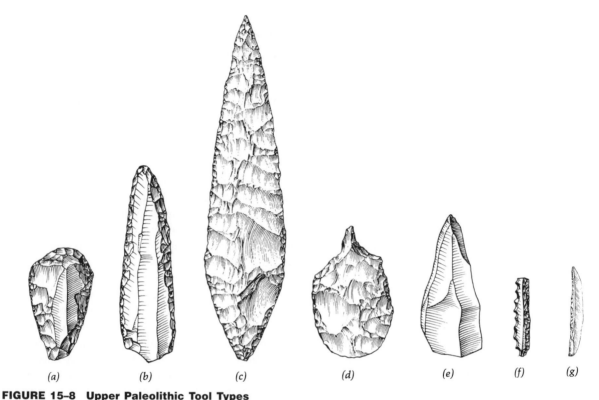

**FIGURE 15–8  Upper Paleolithic Tool Types**
(a) Aurignacian, scraper on retouched blade; (b) Aurignacian, Aurignacian blade; (c) Solutrean, laurel-leaf point; (d) Solutrean, borer end scraper; (e) Perigordian, burin; (f) Perigordian, denticulated backed bladelet; (g) Magdalenian, backed bladelet.

about twice as long as they are wide. They are manufactured from carefully prepared cores, and they can be made quickly and in great numbers. The manufacture of blades represents an efficient use of a natural resource—in this case, flint. François Bordes points out that from a pound of flint, the Upper Paleolithic blade technique could produce 305 to 1219 centimeters (10 to 40 feet) of cutting edge, whereas the early Mousterian flake technique could produce only 102 centimeters (40 inches).[8]

From the basic blade, a wide variety of highly specialized tools can be manufactured. Unlike humans of the Lower Paleolithic, who used the general-purpose hand ax, humans of the Upper Paleolithic used tools designed for specific purposes. The primary function of a number of these tools

was the making of other tools. Figure 15–8 illustrates some of the Upper Paleolithic tool types.

Bone, along with antler, horn, and ivory, became a very common raw material. Bone has many advantages over stone; for example, it does not break as easily. The widespread use of bone resulted from the development of the burin, which had a thick point that did not break under pressure when used to work bone. Some of the later Upper Paleolithic cultures became very dependent on bone implements, and stone points practically disappeared.

One of the major reasons for the success of Upper Paleolithic populations was the development of new projectile weapons. These are **compound tools,** that is, tools composed of several parts. Hafting appears in the archaeological record; the ax is no longer a hand ax but an ax with a handle. Although some compound tools may have been produced as part of the Late Middle Paleolithic, they became more common in Upper Paleolithic cultures.

[8]F. Bordes, *The Old Stone Age* (New York: McGraw-Hill, 1968).

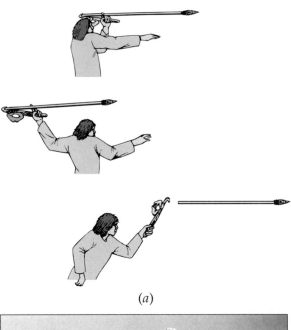

(a)

(b)

**FIGURE 15–9  The Spear Thrower**
(a) The hook of the spear thrower is inserted into the base of the spear and, using the spear thrower, the spear is thrown. (b) A spear thrower from the Magdalenian site of Enlène, France, showing two headless ibexes embracing. The handle is missing.

A spear was made by hafting a bone point to a shaft, and to add to the force of penetration, it was often used with a spear thrower (Figure 15–9). A harpoon consisted of a barbed bone point that detached from the shaft after entering the animal yet remained tied to the shaft by a cord; the dragging of the shaft behind the animal would impede its flight. The shaft could be retrieved and used again. In glacial climates, long pieces of wood were rare and the shafts were valuable; the points were eas-

ily made from antler or bone. Later in the period, the bow and arrow appeared. Several types of fishing gear, such as barbed fishhooks and fish spears, are also known.

Another innovation of the Upper Paleolithic is the eyed needle, which first appeared about 25,000 years ago (Figure 15–10). It was usually made of bone or ivory. Many presume that the needle was used to make waterproof tailored clothing similar to that commonly worn by contemporary people living in high northern latitudes. Evidence of European Upper Paleolithic clothing also comes from images of clothed humans found in some cave paintings and in sculptures, beads that were probably sewn onto shirts and pants, and the presence of stone tools that appear to have been used for working hides. The impression of woven material made in wet clay reveals the existence of weaving 27,000 to 25,000 years ago. Woven materials may have been used for clothing or flexible baskets.

**Art of the Upper Paleolithic**

The Upper Paleolithic is characterized by a variety of artistic methods and styles. Paintings and engravings can be seen developing from early beginnings to the colorful and skillful renderings of the Magdalenian peoples. Realistic, stylized, and geometric modes were used.

**FIGURE 15–10  Upper Paleolithic Eyed Needles**
Eyed needles were first manufactured about 25,000 years ago. They were usually made of bone or ivory.

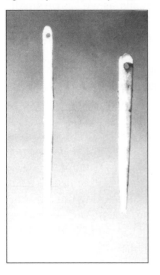

**FIGURE 15–11 Venus Figurine**
The Venus of Willendorf, from Austria, 11.1 centimeters
(4.3 inches) high.

Paleolithic art also found its expression in the rare modeling of clay; sculpturing in rock, bone, ivory, and antler; and painting and engraving on large surfaces such as cave walls, as well as on small objects. Utensils were decorated, but perhaps the most interesting works are the statues and cave paintings.

Some of the most famous statuaries are the statues called **Venus figurines,** which were carved in the round from a variety of materials. Although they are only a few centimeters high, some figures have extremely exaggerated breasts and buttocks and very stylized heads, hands, and feet (Figure 15–11). Perhaps they represent pregnant women, motherhood, or fertility. Upper Paleolithic artists also made models of animals, including the famous set of clay figures of a bison, a bull, a cow, and a calf that were found deep in a cave in France. The earliest Upper Paleolithic sculptures date to about

32,000 B.P. Painting was developing at about the same time.

Upper Paleolithic cave art is found in France, Spain, Italy, the south Urals, Australia, and other parts of the world. Dates of older than 32,000 years have been proposed for some cave art.

For the most part, the subject matter of cave art is animals, although humans are also depicted. These were hunting peoples, and we might suppose that the art expressed their relationship to the fauna that supported them (Figure 15–12) . Several hypotheses have been suggested to explain the meaning of cave art.

Some researchers believe that most representations of nature served magical purposes. This conclusion is based on several facts. First, some cave paintings are found in almost inaccessible areas of caves. Perhaps rituals, not open to the majority of the people, were performed using the paintings and engravings. For example, some modern societies believe that if a person harms an image of an animal or a person, the act will have a similar effect on the real animal or person. This is called **imitative magic.** An Upper Paleolithic shaman may have performed similar rituals so that the animal depicted would be weakened and would therefore be easier to capture and kill.

Other investigators see no evidence of imitative magic. They suggest that the cave may have acted as a meeting place where people shared information on hunting. A recently discovered cave, Grotte Chauvet, contains hundreds of animal images, many of which are not of food animals. So at least for the people who created these images, some of the art seems to have had no relation to hunting, magical or otherwise. Still other caves contain ancient footprints of men, women, and children. This suggests that entire groups, not just specific individuals such as shamans, visited the galleries. Perhaps the artworks served primarily aesthetic purposes.

The decoding of the meaning of ancient pictures and other symbols may prove to be illusive. If archaeologists 20,000 years from now were to find evidence of late twentieth century objects, would they be able to determine what these objects mean to us today? A logo representing a company performing tune-ups on automobiles might be interpreted as an important religious symbol. One thing does

**FIGURE 15–12 Cave Art**
Painted reindeer from the Dordogne, France.

seem likely. The people who made the paintings were attempting to develop symbolic and descriptive ways of transmitting and storing information. This would later be manifested in the development of writing systems.

## Upper Paleolithic Cultural Traditions

The Upper Paleolithic tool technologies of Europe are often divided into five traditions, which are, from earliest to most recent, Châteperronian, Aurignacian, Gravettian, Solutrean, and Magdalenian. Much of the archaeological evidence of these traditions comes from France. We will briefly survey how these traditions manifested themselves in France.

The Châteperronian (also called the Lower Perigordian) is in many ways a transitional combination of industries. Beginning about 32,000 years

ago, it contains many tools that are characteristic of the Mousterian tradition of the Neandertals. Yet mixed with these older tool types are tools that are found in the next tradition, the Aurignacian. The Aurignacian is associated only with modern peoples such as the Cro-Magnon. Beginning about 28,000 years ago, these people began making tools of bone and antler.

Bone became a very important material for the manufacture of tools. This is seen in the Gravettian tradition (also called the Upper Perigordian), beginning about 25,000 years ago. They made bone awls, punches, and points. The Solutrean, beginning about 20,000 years ago, took flint working to a high level of sophistication. The Solutreans were replaced about 17,000 to 16,000 years ago by the Magdalenians, who at first made very poorly crafted stone-tools. Although the Magdalenians

BOX 15-2

# Upper Paleolithic Cave Art

Until 1995, the most spectacular of the approximately 300 caves known to contain Upper Paleolithic paintings was Lascaux Cave in France. In 1942, the Lascaux cave paintings were accidentally discovered by four boys searching for hidden treasure. One of the boys, Jacques Marsal, was so impressed by the cave's 80 multicolored paintings and 1500 engravings that as an adult he became the curator of the cave, one of France's major tourist attractions. Marsal held this position until his death in 1989. Because of the deterioration of the paintings due to problems created by tourism, however, the cave is now closed to the public. In its place, a full-scale replica of the main hall, dubbed Lascaux II, has been built by the French government.

In January 1995, the French government announced that Jean-Marie Chauvet and other explorers had found an underground limestone cavern that contained about 300 Upper Paleolithic paintings and engravings. The cavern, known as Grotte Chauvet, which is located near the town of Vallon-Pont-d'Arc, is about five times larger than the cave at Lascaux, with four larger chambers yet to be explored.

The cave at Vallon-Pont-d'Arc appears to be undisturbed, and it is interesting in several ways. It contains murals of about 50 extinct woolly haired mammalian species, which is more than twice as many as in all other Paleolithic caves combined. Many large animal groupings are portrayed. In other caves, animals are usually depicted individually. Hyenas, bears, lions, owls, and a panther are depicted here; they are less common in other Paleolithic caves. In other caves, the animals pictured are usually not carnivores but herbivores, which are generally harmless to people. Grotte Chauvet also contains about 40 rhinoceros paintings. Both carnivores and rhinoceroses were not food animals. Archaeologists are attempting to explain why they, and not food animals such as reindeer, are depicted on the cave walls.

The cave's explorers also found ancient human footprints, tracings of human hands, brushes, pigments, pieces of flint, evidence of the use of controlled fire, and the skeletal remains of bears. Geometric shapes such as dots and bars are found associated with the paintings.

In addition to human-made images, the cave contained a bear skull that appears to have been carefully placed on a stone slab. Was the slab an altar of some type? Some investigators have characterized the cave as a sacred place. Yet perhaps what looks sacred to a modern Westerner was something entirely different to the people who used and decorated the cave. The cave was occupied an estimated 30,000 years ago, but accurate dating has yet to be completed.

Sources: J.-M. Chauvet et al., *Dawn of Art: The Chauvet Cave* (London: Thames and Hudson, 1996); J. Pfeiffer, "The Emergence of Modern Humans," *Mosaic* 21 (1990), p. 20; A. Marshack, "Images of the Ice Age," *Archaeology* 48 (July/August 1995), pp. 28–39.

**Cave Paintings at Grotte Chauvet, France**
Pictured are horses, bison, a rhinoceros, an elephant, and wild cattle.

were not the best stone tool makers, they excelled in the use of bone and antler. They also developed Upper Paleolithic art to its peak.

**Non-European Upper Paleolithic Cultures** European-type assemblages are found in the Middle East, India, east Africa, the Crimea, and Siberia. On the other hand, some African traditions differed from those in Europe, and the hand ax remains the most commonly found tool. The retention of the hand ax in some parts of Africa was not an indication of backwardness; rather, it was an adjustment to forest conditions. The hand ax has a long history of development in some parts of Africa.

Recently it has been suggested that some people who lived in Africa as long as 90,000 years ago developed certain tool types, such as bone harpoon points, that are not seen in Europe until 14,000 B.P. At Katanda in Zaire, archaeologists found barbed and unbarbed bone points. These points may have been hafted to a wood shaft and used to spear fish. The Katanda people also used materials such as ocher pigment and stones that were brought in from distant localities. They may have developed a semisettled lifestyle based on fishing tens of thousands of years before people did in other parts of the world.[9]

In east and southeast Asia, simple chopping tools were used until the end of the Paleolithic. According to one suggestion, this was the result of reliance on materials other than stone, such as bamboo, for tool manufacture.

Similarly, chopping tools and crude flake tools made up most of the stone artifacts of the natives of Australia. When the first inhabitants reached the continent about 60,000 to 40,000 years ago, they found an environment whose largest animal was the kangaroo. Australia also lacked the types of raw materials needed for producing good blade tools. Although they did have resources of bone and wood and they made a variety of tools out of these materials, their overall technology was restricted by the lack of resources and by their isolation from ideas that were developing elsewhere.

## Archaeology of the New World

Early inhabitants of the New World entered Alaska from Asia. Once in Alaska, where did the earliest inhabitants of the New World go? Southern Alaska, much of Canada, and the northwestern United States were covered with glacial ice, but ice-free routes were open during most of the Pleistocene through central Alaska, along the eastern foothills of the Rocky Mountains, and along the West Coast. Like Beringia, these routes provided large game for migrating hunters.

Most likely, the migrants entered the New World in very small groups. Since there was no competition for food from other human groups, the first

populations in the New World increased rapidly in size and range. According to some estimates, the founding population in America could theoretically have been as small as 25 people. Such calculations are interesting, but they are not direct evidence of what actually occurred. Some evidence does exist that people moved across Beringia more than once. Each migration may have been very small, but every time a new group entered the New World, its members would have brought with them a new influx of genes and gene combinations.

Most New World sites contain cultural remains only; skeletal material dated before 11,500 B.P. is extremely rare. One of the many candidates for a pre-11,500-year-old date is Meadowcroft Rockshelter in Pennsylvania. This site contains flakes, a projectile point, and other tools from a level that has been dated by radiocarbon dating to 16,000 to 11,000 B.P. A possible basket fragment comes from an even lower level; it is dated at $19,000 \pm 2400$ years. The dates have been questioned because of possible contamination of the site by naturally occurring coal. The coal is derived from ancient trees, and it has lost all of its radioactive carbon. The nonradioactive carbon from these trees, dissolved in water, may have mixed with the carbon in the basket and other organic material in the level. If this occurred, the older carbon would make the artifacts appear older than they really are.

Another possible early site is Orogrande Cave in southern New Mexico, which is dated at 27,000 B.P. The evidence includes what archaeologist Richard MacNeish believes is a human palm print on a piece of fire-baked clay. Other archaeologists are not yet convinced of the antiquity of the print or even that it was made by a human. Recently, dates of 18,000 to 12,260 B.P. have been suggested for sites in the Mojave Desert and the Petrified Forest in Arizona. While finds from Kansas, Pennsylvania, New Mexico, California, Arizona, and other areas of the New World suggest the possibility of pre–11,500 B.P. dates for humans in the New World, archaeological finds from Clovis, New Mexico, provide the oldest agreed-upon dates for people in the New World. The finds from Clovis and surrounding sites date from 11,500 to 11,000 B.P.

Early sites are also known from South America. In general, the great tropical forests of South America are seen as having been uninhabitable until the advent of horticulture, yet recently archaeologists

---

[9]J. E. Yellen et al., "A Middle Stone Age Worked Bone Industry from Katanda, Upper Semliki Valley, Zaire," *Science* 268 (1995), pp. 553–556.

located stratified Paleoindian deposits in association with a painted sandstone cave at Caverna da Pedra Pintada in the state of Monte Alegre, Brazil. They recovered 24 tools and more than 30,000 flakes, which included triangular, stemmed bifacial points. Both conventional and the accelerator mass spectrometry method of radiocarbon dating were used to date many plant samples, from which the investigators estimate that the site was first occupied from about 11,200 to 10,500 B.P. Thousands of carbonized fruits and wood fragments were also found. These provide evidence as to the food resources of the occupants of the site. One familiar food resource is the Brazil nut. Remains of bone and shell testify to a diverse diet obtained from animal sources.

**Folsom and Clovis Points**  Just as fossils are not found in the chronological order in which they were deposited, neither are artifacts. In 1926, a cowboy discovered "arrowheads" near the town of Folsom, New Mexico; these and similar artifacts are now called Folsom points. These artifacts are associated with a type of bison that had been extinct for about 10,000 years (Figure 15–13). In the light of current speculation on relatively early dates for the first Americans, 10,000 years ago might not seem startling. Yet in the 1920s, the belief was that humans had not been in North America anywhere near this long.

In 1932, another important "arrowhead" find was made in New Mexico when blade tools were discovered near the town of Clovis; these Clovis points are larger than the later Folsom points. The term "arrowhead" is placed in quotation marks because neither the Folsom nor the Clovis points were really arrowheads, nor were they spearheads; they were used to tip lances. A lance is a weapon that is

**FIGURE 15–13  Folsom Point**
A Folsom point in association with ribs of extinct bison, Folsom, New Mexico.

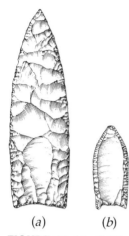

**FIGURE 15–14  Artifacts from the New World**
(*a*) Clovis point; (*b*) Folsom point.

held and repeatedly thrust into the prey. On the other hand, a spear is made to be thrown, not held, and it often has barbs to keep it from falling out of the prey animal.

Both the Folsom and Clovis points are **fluted;** that is, each type has a rounded groove in the shaft of the point (Figure 15–14). This furrow made hafting of the wood lance shaft to its point easier. With the possible exception of a point recently found in Siberia, fluted points are not found in other parts of the world, and they are assumed to be an American invention. Clovis and Folsom assemblages are the most common tool types found from about 11,500 to 9000 B.P. Clovis and similar kinds of points have been found in all U.S. states except Hawaii, and their distribution extends from the Arctic to South America.

The Clovis and Folsom people were basically hunters of large game. The Clovis people, whose remains first appeared in the western United States, hunted mammoths. They appear to have followed the herds eastward, ultimately reaching the northeast coast. However, the mammoth declined to the point of extinction, perhaps due to overhunting, and in the Great Plains and the Rocky Mountains valleys, the Folsom tradition replaced that of the Clovis people. Bison was the mainstay of the Folsom hunters.

### Summary

The Upper Paleolithic traditions generally represent an increase in the percentage of blade tools over time; sometimes these blades were hafted to ax or spear handles. In addition to stone tools, tools of bone, antler, horn, and ivory became more varied and complex than those of earlier times. *H. sapiens* may have been the first big-game hunters.

In the Upper Paleolithic, artistic development showed mastery of both painting and sculpting, as well as the use of complex symbols. Large cave paintings were expertly executed in western Europe and east to the Urals; small objects were also decorated, and numerous small statues were produced. Although some art may have been created for its own sake, most of this early art may have had symbolic significance. Some "decorations" may actually be calendrical, mathematical, or even writing systems.

The earliest established New World lithic industries are the Folsom and Clovis, which have been dated to about 11,500 and 9000 B.P. These unique fluted points are not found in other parts of the world. The Clovis people were hunters of mammoth, while the later Folsom hunters relied on bison.

### POST-PLEISTOCENE *HOMO SAPIENS*

The Pleistocene ended about 10,000 years ago. A few thousand years before, human populations in some parts of the world entered a period of rapid sociocultural change. Paleolithic cultures were replaced by other types of cultures and, ultimately, modern agricultural and industrial societies.

### The Mesolithic: Transition from Hunting-Gathering to Farming

The changes from a hunting-gathering existence to a farming economy did not occur overnight. The dependence on group living, along with the biological and technological developments, created a potential for new systems of subsistence. This potential began to be expressed at an increased pace in the period between the retreat of the last glaciers and the advent of agricultural communities, a period known as the **Mesolithic.**

During the Mesolithic, societies began to utilize the land around them more intensively. The last part of the Upper Paleolithic was characterized by enormous herds of large mammals in the grasslands of Eurasia, but about 12,000 years ago, climatic changes began to occur that ultimately converted these grasslands into forests. With the advance of the forests came the disappearance of the herds; they were replaced by less abundant and more elusive animals such as elk, red deer, and wild pigs.

**Aquatic and Vegetable Resources** Along with changes in hunting patterns came an intense exploitation of aquatic resources, and Mesolithic sites are often found near seas, lakes, and rivers. A characteristic type of site is the **shell midden,** a large mound composed of shells, which provides evidence of the emphasis on shellfish as a food resource. Fishing was an important activity, and remains of boats and nets from this period have been recovered. Waterfowl also made up an important part of the diet in many areas.

In addition, people began to intensively exploit the plant resources of their habitats. Much of this exploitation was made possible by the development of a technology for processing vegetable foods that cannot be eaten in their natural state; for example, the milling stone and the mortar and pestle were used to break up seeds and nuts. Storage and container vessels found in Mesolithic sites allowed for easy handling of small and pulverized foods (Figure 15–15). Out of this utilization of plant resources, farming developed.

### The Origins of Farming

**Domestication** involves the control of the reproductive cycle of plants and animals. Through the use of farming techniques, people were able to plant and harvest large quantities of food in specific areas; in time, they selected the best food-producing plants to breed. Domestication thus led to selection initiated by humans, which over the centuries has created new varieties of plants. Many theories have been proposed regarding the origins of plant domestication, but the important point to note is that farming was probably not a deliberate invention. It most likely arose from an intensive utilization of and dependence upon plant material, a pattern that developed out of Mesolithic economies.

Current evidence suggests that hunter-gatherers first domesticated rye in the Near East as long as 13,000 years ago. However, people living in the

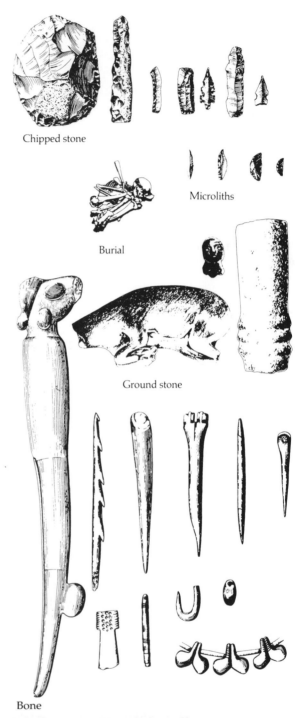

Chipped stone

Microliths

Burial

Ground stone

Bone

**FIGURE 15–15 Mesolithic Artifacts**
Various artifacts from the Mesolithic of Palestine (Natufian), ca. 10,000 B.P.

Near East did not become dependent on farming until about 10,000 years ago.[10] In addition to its development in this Near East location, plant and animal domestication developed in other areas of the Old World and in Mexico and Peru. Domestication occurred independently in the Near East and the New World, and perhaps in southeast Asia and west Africa as well.

Although the development of farming has been seen as the great revolution leading to modern civilization, we must emphasize that farming was a revolution in potential only. Many hunting-gathering peoples rejected farming because it would have brought about a decline in their standard of living. For example, even in a semiarid region during a drought, the food supply of the San of South Africa is reliable and plentiful. The farming and pastoral communities are the ones that suffer the most in such times.

**Origins of Domestication in the New World**  The origins of domestication have always been thought to have been much earlier in the Old World than in the New World. Old World plant domestication has been placed at about 13,000 years ago; plant domestication in the New World has been thought to have begun between 5000 and 3500 years ago.

New studies using an improved radiocarbon dating technique, called *accelerator mass spectrometry*, have provided a date for squash seeds and stems as early as 10,000 B.P. These squash parts, from a cave at Oaxaca, Mexico, show signs of domestication, such as thicker stems than are found in wild squash.

If the antiquity of this sample is correct, then domestication in the New World started thousands of years before the date currently accepted. Yet there is little evidence that any plants other than squash were domesticated at this time; beans and maize were domesticated much later. Perhaps the transition between hunting and gathering to farming in the New World was somewhat longer than in the Old World. In the latter areas, farming was in full swing by about 2700 years after initial domestication. Of course, a perceived gap in time between

---

[10]H. Pringle, "The Slow Birth of Agriculture," *Science* 282 (1998), p. 1446.

**BOX 15–3**

## "Man's Best Friend"

In the United States today there are about 50 million domesticated dogs. Some of these dogs fulfill utilitarian functions: guide dogs, guard dogs, police dogs, and hunting dogs. Most dogs, however, are pets and companions. Dogs are so much a part of our culture that there is now a Dog Genome Project similar to the Human Genome Project discussed in Chapter 3. A goal of this project is to learn how the different breeds of dog evolved.

Domestic dogs derived from gray wolves, which can still breed with domesticated dogs. In fact, most experts classify dogs in the same species, *Canis lupus*, as wolves; dogs are placed in the subspecies *Canis lupus familiaris*.

Why were dogs domesticated? There are many ideas on this. One scenario is that in areas where forestation had occurred, hunters had to play hide-and-seek with well-hidden animals. The domestication of the dog may have been the result of the increased pressures of hunting in dense, dark forests. As we discussed in the chapters on primates and the fossil record, the development of a refined visual sense in primates was accompanied by a decrease in the sense of smell. The wolf's nose seems to have been employed by people to sniff out nonvisible prey. By 14,000 to 10,000 years ago, the wolf had already been domesticated in such widespread places as southwestern Asia, Japan, Iran, England, Illinois, and Idaho.

*Source:* R. Mestel, "Ascent of the Dog," *Discover*, October 1994, pp. 90–98.

initial domestication and full-scale farming in either the Old World or New World may be simply due to a lack of evidence rather than an actual delay.

### The Neolithic

Ultimately, in some areas over a period of thousands of years, and sometimes quickly, food production came to dominate hunting and gathering in many parts of the world. With farming came an increase in the frequency of village life. This stage of human history is called the **Neolithic.**

The Neolithic was a time of great change in both technology and social organization. Although some people who were predominantly hunters and gatherers cultivated some crops or altered the terrain to encourage the growth of wild plants, it was the shift

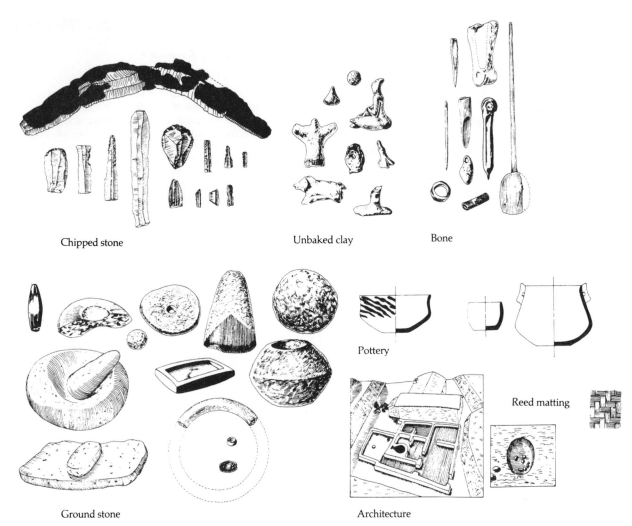

Chipped stone    Unbaked clay    Bone

Pottery

Reed matting

Ground stone    Architecture

**FIGURE 15–16  Neolithic Artifacts**
Various artifacts from the Neolithic of Jarmo, Iraq, ca. 8750 B.P.

to full-scale farming that ushered in great changes. By producing food in one place rather than searching for it, societies developed a more settled pattern of existence. Farming meant that more food could be acquired in less space, and as a result, population densities increased. This led to the interaction of greater numbers of people, and thus it brought about a greater exchange of ideas and an increase in innovation, which is dependent on such exchanges.

The Neolithic was characterized by the elaboration of tools for food preparation: querns, milling stones, mortars, and pestles. Pottery, used only rarely by nonfarming peoples, became refined and varied, and the techniques of weaving and spinning cloth were developed (Figure 15–16).

Most Neolithic villages were small, self-sufficient farming communities. During the Neolithic, many technological and social systems were being developed that would later be important in the first civilizations. This can be seen at the settlement of Çatalhüyük in Turkey, which dates from 8500 to 7700 B.P.

At Çatalhüyük, timber, obsidian, marble, stalactite, and shell were all imported, and skillfully made artifacts attest to the development of occupational specialization. Wooden bowls and boxes, jewelry, bone awls, daggers, spearheads, lance heads, arrowheads, ladles, spoons, spatulas, hooks and pins, and obsidian mirrors, as well as other beautifully made objects, contributed to a rich material inventory. The residents at Çatalhüyük lived in plastered mud-brick houses that were contiguous to one another; they entered them from the roof. Murals painted on the walls depicted animals, hunters, and dancers, and statues portrayed gods and goddesses, as well as cattle.

Because Çatalhüyük may have had a population as high as 10,000 people, early research saw it as a highly organized community with centralized authority. New archaeological investigations, which began in the 1990s, question the nature of the social organization at Çatalhüyük. The data suggest that Çatalhüyük was made up of groups of extended families that were relatively autonomous.[11] This view would place this settlement in a transitional phase between the more or less autonomous social pattern of hunters and gatherers and the more centralized farming societies. Excavations on this site continue and perhaps will provide a clear picture of the life at this Neolithic village.

### The Rise of Civilization

For the vast majority of prehistory, that time before the first true writing, hominids lived in small bands. Their population densities were generally under one person per square mile. Leaders led by example and reputation. The bands' subsistence depended on combinations of hunting, fishing, gathering, and scavenging.

Then, about 13,000 years ago, evidence of the first domestication of plants appears. Beginning in the Middle East, plant and animal domestication gradually came to dominate earlier subsistence patterns, and the first civilizations arose. A **civilization** is a society in which the population density is higher than in earlier systems. The right to lead is often hereditary and absolute. There are considerable differences in access to power, wealth, and prestige. Technology is far advanced from that of band societies.

There are many thoughts on the origins of civilization, but one of the major factors involved was the increase in population (Table 15–1). Techniques such as irrigation and flood control made farming possible in special areas such as the floodplain of the Tigris and Euphrates rivers, and this supported large populations. Once populations reached a certain number, which was dependent on environmental and social variables, the older patterns of social organization broke down and new ones developed. In the older systems, each individual participated in food production, and all members maintained a similar standard of living. Kinship served as the cornerstone of social organization. These patterns were replaced by the occupational division of labor, class systems, political and religious hierarchies, public works such as road and public building construction, codes of law, markets, new forms of warfare, and urban centers. Allied with these important sociological traits were material traits such as monumental architecture, the development of science, and, in many cases, metallurgy and writing systems.

The earliest civilization, Sumer, developed in the Middle East. During this period, known as the **Bronze Age** of the Old World, people first developed the art of metallurgy. Civilizations also arose in other parts of the Old World: first in Egypt, China, and India and later in Europe and sub-Saharan Africa. In addition, civilization also developed independently in the New World—in Mexico, Peru, and adjacent areas.

Because of increased food supplies and the increased number of children a family could take care of, populations increased rapidly with the development of the Neolithic and Bronze Age cultures. A couple living in a mobile society can usually deal with only one infant at a time. This is because the mother has to carry the infant everywhere and the child normally nurses until five years of age or later. Until the infant walks and is weaned, a second child would be a great burden. In contrast, a farming couple can usually support a large family with babies born only a year apart. Even today, it is not unusual for an Amish farming family in the United States to have 10 or more children; these children become valued farmworkers.

In the Old World, the Bronze Age was followed by the **Iron Age.** This period saw the rise and fall

---

[11]M. Balter, "Why Settle Down? The Mystery of Communities," *Science* 282 (1998), pp. 1442–1445.

**TABLE 15-1**

**HUMAN POPULATION GROWTH**

| Years ago (from 2000) | Years elapsed* | World population (thousands) | Comment |
|---|---|---|---|
| 1,000,000 | | 125 | |
| 300,000 | 700,000 | 1,000 | |
| 10,000 | 290,000 | 5,320 | Domestication begins |
| 6,000 | 4,000 | 86,500 | |
| 2,000 | 4,000 | 133,000 | |
| 250 | 1,750 | 728,000 | Industrialization |
| 100 | 150 | 1,610,000 | Medical "revolution" |
| 50 | 50 | 2,400,000 | |
| 40 | 10 | 3,000,000 | |
| 0 (the present) | 40 | 6,300,000 | Information Age |
| Year 2100 | 100 | 10,400,000 | |

*Note that (1) it took 700,000 years to reach the first million from a population of 125,000; (2) it took only 50 years (1950 to 2000) for an increase of about 3.3 billion to occur; (3) it is estimated that between 2000 and 2100 about 4.1 billion people will be added to the world population.
*Source:* Adapted from Edward S. Deevey, Jr., "The Human Population," *Scientific American,* September 1960. Copyright © 1960 by Scientific American Inc. All rights reserved. Data for projection for the years 2000 and 2100 are reported in G. Tyler Miller, Jr., *Living in the Environment,* 6th ed. (Belmont, Calif.: Wadsworth, 1990), p. 2.

of great empires, as well as the shift of power from the Middle East to Greece and Rome, and then to western Europe. The 1700s marked the beginning of the **Industrial Age,** which led directly to the modern civilizations of today.

### Summary

Humans were exclusively foragers and scavengers for the vast majority of prehistory. About 13,000 years ago, domestication of plants and animals became a subsistence option for the people in the Near East. Plant and animal domestication spread widely throughout the Old World; it was independently developed in the New World. In most parts of the world, the foraging way of life was gradually replaced by farming. A few foraging societies, however, still exist.

In the places where farming and raising animals occurred, settlement patterns changed, sometimes gradually, from nomadic to settled, and population size increased dramatically. Ultimately, the kinship-based organization of society was supplemented by government control. Cities arose to produce goods, to distribute these goods and farm products, and to ship excesses to other societies. Cities also served as religious and political centers. Writing, mathe-

matics, science, and metallurgy became features of most developing civilizations. In addition, animals were "drafted" to do farmwork such as pulling plows. Eventually, beginning in the eighteenth century, human and animal power was joined by machine power, and the Industrial Age was born.

### STUDY QUESTIONS

1. What are some of your ideas on where and when *H. sapiens* appears in the fossil record?
2. How do the replacement model and the regional continuity model of the origin of *H. sapiens* differ from each other? What is the evolutionary role of the Neandertals in each of these models?
3. Who is Kennewick Man? What does the debate over the fossils involve?
4. Discuss the cultural innovations of the Upper Paleolithic.
5. To what do the terms *Mesolithic* and *Neolithic* refer? What characterizes each of these cultural stages?
6. In what area of the world did plant domestication first originate? Where else did it independently develop?
7. What data suggest that domestication in the New World might have occurred at an earlier date than is traditionally thought?
8. How did the first civilizations differ from the Neolithic farming societies?

## SUGGESTED READINGS

The following handbooks list individual fossils along with pertinent information:

Day, M. *Guide to Fossil Man: A Handbook of Human Paleontology,* 4th ed. Chicago: University of Chicago Press, 1986.

Larsen, C. S., R. M. Matter, and D. L. Gebo. *Human Origins: The Fossil Record,* 3rd ed. Prospect Heights, Ill.: Waveland, 1998.

Also recommended are the following:

Brace, C. L. *The Stages of Human Evolution,* 5th ed. New York: Prentice-Hall, 1995. This edition of a book first published in 1967 is a detailed inventory of hominid fossils with chapters on evolutionary theory.

Conroy, G. C. *Reconstructing Human Origins: A Modern Synthesis.* New York: Norton, 1997. This text presents an overview and synthesis of our current knowledge of the human fossil record.

Fagan, B. *The Journey from Eden: Peopling the Prehistoric World.* New York: Thames and Hudson, 1990. This book is a general survey of prehistory.

Mellars, P., and C. Stringer (eds.). *The Human Revolution: Behavioural and Biological Perspectives on the Origins of Modern Humans.* Princeton, N.J.: Princeton University Press, 1990. This is an encyclopedic volume on the emergence of modern humans from primarily the replacement model point of view.

Reader, J. *Missing Links: The Hunt for Earliest Man,* rev. ed. Boston: Little, Brown, 1995. This book tells the story of the hunt for and discovery of many important fossil hominids.

Trinkaus, E. (ed.). *The Emergence of Modern Humans: Biocultural Adaptations in the Late Pleistocene.* Cambridge, England: Cambridge University Press, 1989. This book contains nine essays on the appearance of modern humans throughout the world as well as the relationship of modern humans to other forms such as Neandertals. This book basically takes the regional continuity approach.

Williams, S. *Fantastic Archaeology: The Wild Side of North American Prehistory.* Philadelphia: University of Pennsylvania Press, 1991. This book explores the misinterpretations of North American archaeological data as well as outright hoaxes, followed by an up-to-date summary of the prehistory of the Americas.

## SUGGESTED WEB SITES

Institute for Ice Age Studies (Paleolithic Art):
http://www.insticeagestudies.com/library.html
Archaeological Excavations at Boxgrove:
http://www.ucl.ac.uk/boxgrove
Neanderthal Museum:
http://www.neanderthal.de

Additional web sites are listed in the *Workbook* that accompanies this text.

# The Biology of Modern *Homo Sapiens*

*The genetic basis of man's capacity to acquire, develop or modify, and transmit culture emerged because of the adaptive advantages which this capacity conferred on its possessors.[1]*
—Theodosius Dobzhansky (1900–1975)

**A** common dream, which has served as the plot of more than one novel, involves viewing or meeting an exact duplicate of oneself who lives in another place or time. This "second self" can be no more than illusory. Except for identical twins and the possibility of clones, genetic variables alone reduce the probability that two people can be exactly the same to all but zero. Even identical twins show variation due to differences in their environments.

---

[1]T. Dobzhansky, *Mankind Evolution* (New Haven, Conn.: Yale University Press, 1962), p. 20.

There are three principal mechanisms that bring about variation among individuals and populations. The first is nongenetic adaptations called adjustments: behavioral adjustments are cultural responses to environmental stress, and acclimatory adjustments are reversible physiological responses to such stress. The second mechanism that brings about variation is microevolutionary change or adaptation. Finally, there are the processes of growth and development. These mechanisms are the subjects of this chapter.

## HUMAN ADAPTABILITY: ADJUSTMENTS

Physiologically, humans are animals who evolved under conditions of the tropicals. Yet today human populations occupy a wide range of habitats, from the equatorial deserts of north Africa to the icy wastelands of the Arctic.

One reason that the human species survives in a wide diversity of habitats is because of nongenetic changes termed **adjustments.** However, the genetic potentials that allow for nongenetic adjustments are themselves the products of the evolutionary process. A major problem facing researchers in this area is the determination of the relative importance of genetic and nongenetic forms of adaptability, which we have termed here adaptation and adjustment, respectively. In fact, in most situations, both processes are working together.

### Behavioral Adjustments

**Behavioral adjustments** are cultural responses to environmental stresses. Because these adjustments are nongenetic, they may be continuously altered to meet new environmental situations.

An example of how culture allows people to survive in stressful habitats is housing. The type of housing that is used in an area is influenced by such factors as temperature, humidity, wind, rain, and light. A classic example of the use of housing in a stressful habitat is the igloo of the Inuit (Figure 16–1). The igloo consists of a dome-shaped structure connected to the outside by a tunnel. The construction material is snow, which is an excellent insulator because air is trapped within the snow itself. Heat within the structure is produced by a small seal-oil lamp. The heat of this lamp causes the snow to melt slightly during the day and re-

freeze at night, forming an icy reflective layer on the inside. This reflective layer plus the dome shape serve to reflect the heat throughout the igloo. Relatively little heat is lost to the outside, since the dome shape minimizes the surface area from which heat can radiate. A long entryway gradually helps warm the air as one enters the structure, and it also serves to block the entry of wind into the habitation area.

Habitation structures are only one aspect of a people's technology. It is through all aspects of technology that people can survive under difficult environmental conditions. In fact, through behavioral adjustments, humans have been able to spend limited periods of time deep under the ocean and in outer space.

### Acclimatory Adjustments

**Acclimatory adjustments** are reversible physiological changes to environmental stress. Examples of acclimatization may be seen in three particularly stressful environments: the Arctic, the desert, and high altitudes.

**Arctic Habitats**   Perhaps one of the more stressful habitats occupied by humans is the Arctic. Not surprisingly, people occupied the Arctic regions late in human prehistory, and humans can become acclimatized to the climate only to a very limited degree.

The primary environmental stress in the Arctic is very low temperatures. Cold stress can lead to frostbite, an actual freezing of the tissues, which usually occurs in exposed, high-surface-area parts of the body such as fingers, toes, and earlobes. Another result of cold stress is **hypothermia,** or lowered body temperature. Normal body temperature, as measured in the mouth, averages 37°C (98.6°F). When the body temperature falls below 34.4°C (94°F), the ability of the hypothalamus of the brain to control body temperature is impaired. Temperature-regulating ability is lost at 29.4°C (85°F), and death may result.

Unlike other animals that occupy the Arctic, humans are not well-adapted to cold stress; this fact is probably a reflection of people's tropical origins. Humans do not possess thick layers of subcutaneous fat or thick fur; in fact, the human body has remarkably little in the way of insulation. The most important factor for survival in the hostile Arctic

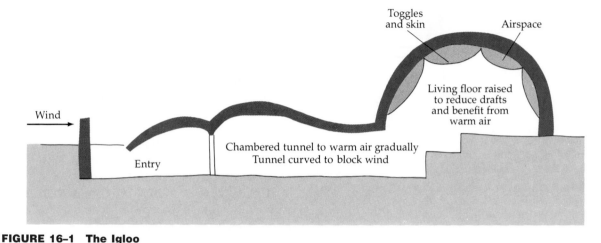

**FIGURE 16–1  The Igloo**
The Inuit igloo is designed to permit people to survive in the extremely hostile Arctic environment.

climate is responding with behavioral adjustments, such as specialized housing, clothing, and other technologies.

While clothing and shelter provide insulation for humans in the Arctic, it is interesting to see what happens when a human is exposed to cold without the necessary behavioral adjustments. The nude human body at rest must begin to combat a lowering of body temperature when the air temperature stands at approximately 31°C (87.8°F). This temperature is known as the **critical temperature.**

The subject of this experiment must both increase the heat produced by the body and reduce the loss of heat to the air. Two short-term methods of producing additional body heat are exercise and shivering. As any jogger knows, a high degree of muscle activity yields heat, but such exercise can be maintained only for limited periods of time. More important is shivering. Low body temperature causes the hypothalamus of the brain to stimulate increased muscle tone, which, when it reaches a certain level, results in shivering. At the height of shivering, the increase in muscle metabolism can raise body heat production to five times normal; but, as with exercise, shivering cannot continue indefinitely. A major mechanism for conserving heat is peripheral **vasoconstriction.** Constriction of the capillaries in the skin prevents much of the warm blood from reaching the surface of the skin, where much of the body's heat would be lost to the air.

People living under Arctic conditions for long periods of time are less affected by the cold as time passes. Perhaps the most important acclimatory adjustment is in the **basal metabolic rate.** The basal metabolic rate, which represents the total energy used by the body in maintaining those body processes necessary for life, is a measure of the minimum level of heat produced by the body at rest. Under cold stress, individuals are able to acclimatize by increasing their basal metabolic rate; this increase can be as much as 25 percent in adults and 170 percent in infants. The increased basal metabolic rate results in the production of additional body heat, but the production of this heat requires that individuals consume a great quantity of high-energy food sources. The native diet in Arctic regions, which consists largely of protein and fat, provides the necessary types of food.

**Desert Habitats**   In some ways, humans are better able to survive in the hot and arid climates of the world than in the Arctic regions. This ability is due to the general lack of body hair, which, if present, would act as insulating material.

In desert habitats, the human body must get rid of excess heat that is being absorbed by the body. In general, a nude human body loses heat in any one of four ways (Figure 16–2). The first is **conduction,** which occurs when heat appears to move from a warmer object to a cooler object by direct

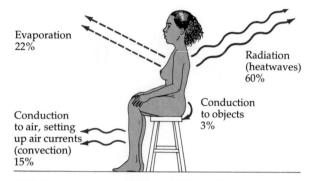

Evaporation
22%

Radiation
(heatwaves)
60%

Conduction
to objects
3%

Conduction
to air, setting
up air currents
(convection)
15%

**FIGURE 16–2  Heat Loss in a Nude Human Figure**
This figure illustrates the various mechanisms by which heat
is lost from a nude human body at rest. The percentages refer
to the contribution of each mechanism to the total heat loss.

contact. Thus, if you touch an object cooler than yourself, heat will move from your body to the cooler object. The second is **convection,** in which the warm object is surrounded by a cooler fluid, either liquid or air. A person who is hot from absorbing solar radiation will lose heat as the heat from the body is transferred to the cooler air. As the air next to the body warms up, it expands, and expanding air rises. As the warm air rises from the skin, cooler air flows down to replace it. Thus, currents set up in the air carry away heat.

The third way in which an object can rid itself of heat is by **radiation.** Radiation represents electromagnetic energy that is given off by an object as electromagnetic waves of a characteristic wavelength. Other forms of electromagnetic waves include visible light, ultraviolet radiation, and radio waves.

The fourth way in which an object can lose heat is through **evaporation.** When water is turned from a liquid to a gas, in this case water vapor, a certain amount of energy, in the form of heat, is required. Therefore, when you get out of the swimming pool on a warm day, you feel cool because some of your body heat is being used in the process of transforming the pool water left on your skin into water vapor.

While conduction, convection, radiation, and evaporation are used by the human body to rid itself of excess heat in warm climates, in air temperatures above 35°C (95°F), body heat is lost primarily through evaporation. Therefore, **sweating** is the

most important method of controlling body temperature in warm climates. Humans have a greater capacity to sweat than any other mammal.

Humans have a high density of sweat glands over their bodies, although the number of sweat glands per square centimeter does differ in different parts of the body. Interestingly, people who go to live in desert environments do not develop additional sweat glands; the number of sweat glands does not differ significantly between desert- and nondesert-dwelling populations.

Acclimatizing to desert life is not well understood, but within a few weeks, people living in hot, arid climates seem to reach some type of acclimatory adjustment. In time, the sweat glands become more sensitive and produce more sweat. Of course, sweat is not all water; it also contains salts, and much sodium is lost through sweating. With time, the concentration of salt in sweat is reduced, and the relatively high salt concentrations found in desert water usually compensate for salt loss. Urine volume is also reduced, thus helping the body conserve the water so badly needed for sweating. This same acclimatization ability has been found in peoples from all parts of the world. It appears to represent a basic ability of the human species instead of an adaptation of certain populations.

In addition, there are other short-term responses to increased heat loads. A physiological response is **vasodilation** of the capillaries of the skin. In vasodilation, the bloodstream brings more heat to the body surface as the capillaries of the skin dilate; then the heat is removed by sweating. People can also make a number of behavioral adjustments to hot climates. In desert regions people reduce physical activity during the heat of the day, thereby reducing heat production by the body. Also, desert-dwelling people adopt a relaxed body posture that increases the surface area of the body from which sweat may evaporate.

Adjustment to hot climates is aided by cultural factors such as clothing and shelter. Desert dwellers cover their bodies to protect the skin from sunlight and to reduce the amount of heat from the sun that directly heats the body. Their clothing is designed to permit the free flow of air between the clothing and the body. This airflow is necessary to carry off the water vapor formed by the evaporation of sweat.

It is interesting to note that the color of clothing does not seem to make much difference in hot climates. An experiment involving black and white Bedouin robes showed that the black robes gained about 2½ times as much heat as the white robes. Yet the temperature of the skin under black robes is the same as that under white robes. Most likely, the greater convection currents between the black robe and the skin are responsible for this phenomenon.

**High-Altitude Habitats** Many people experience **high-altitude,** or **mountain, sickness** when they travel into the mountains. The symptoms of high-altitude sickness may include "shortness of breath, respiratory distress, physical and mental fatigue, rapid pulse rate, interrupted sleep, and headaches intensified by activity. There may also occur some slight digestive disorders and in some cases a marked loss of weight. In other cases the individual may feel dyspnea, nausea, and vomiting."[2] Although most people eventually become acclimatized to high altitude, many do not. They will continue to suffer from chronic mountain sickness as long as they remain at high altitude.

Less than 1 percent of the world's population lives at high altitude, yet these people are of great interest to anthropologists. High-altitude environments pose many stresses on human populations, including low oxygen levels, high levels of solar radiation, cold, high winds, and, often, lack of moisture, rough terrain, and limited plant and animal life.

Our previous discussions of Arctic and desert environments stressed the great importance of culture as a means of adjustment to stressful environments. Culture plays a major role at high altitudes as well, and it helps people adjust to many of the environmental problems that they face. However, a major situation in which culture plays virtually no role is **high-altitude hypoxia.**

Hypoxia refers to low oxygen pressure, which occurs when low levels of oxygen are supplied to the tissues of the body. High-altitude hypoxia is one of the few environmental stresses that cannot be ad-

justed to by some cultural means. Although the use of oxygen tanks provides limited adjustment, this solution is available only in high-technology cultures and is practical only for short periods of time.

The earth's atmosphere exerts an average of 1.04 kilograms of pressure on every square centimeter (14.7 pounds per square inch) of surface area at sea level. At sea level, this pressure raises a column of mercury in a closed tube to an average height of 760 millimeters (29.92 inches). Therefore, we say that the average air pressure at sea level is 760 millimeters (29.92 inches) of mercury.

The atmosphere is composed of many gases. Approximately 21 percent of air is oxygen; that portion of the total atmospheric pressure that is due to the pressure of oxygen is the **partial pressure** of oxygen. At sea level, the partial pressure of oxygen is 159 millimeters (6.26 inches) of mercury. As one gains altitude, the total air pressure and the partial pressure of oxygen decrease (Figure 16–3). At 4500 meters (14,765 feet), the partial pressure of oxygen decreases by as much as 40 percent, thus substantially reducing the amount of oxygen that can reach the tissues of the body.

The actual entry of oxygen into the bloodstream takes place in the approximately 300 million **alveoli** of the lungs. The alveoli are small air sacs that are richly endowed with blood capillaries. Although the partial pressure of oxygen at sea level is 159 millimeters (6.26 inches) of mercury, the partial pressure of oxygen in the alveoli at sea level is 104 millimeters (4.16 inches) of mercury. This is because not all the air in the lungs is replaced with each breath. The partial pressure of oxygen in the arteries and capillaries of the circulatory system is 95 millimeters (3.80 inches) of mercury, while the partial pressure of oxygen in the tissues is 40 millimeters (1.60 inches) of mercury.

Oxygen diffuses from the higher to the lower partial pressure; therefore, oxygen moves from the blood into the tissues. At high altitudes, however, where the partial pressure of oxygen in the atmosphere is low, the partial pressure of oxygen in the blood would be too low to allow diffusion of oxygen from the blood to the tissues unless special physiological adjustments take place. These are the adjustments that make possible human habitation of high-altitude environments.

---

[2]A. R. Frisancho, "Functional Adaptation to High Altitude Hypoxia," *Science* 187 (1975), p. 313. The term **dyspnea** refers to difficult or painful breathing.

BOX 16-1

## How High Can People Live Without Bottled Oxygen?

The highest human settlement in the world is Aconquija, located at an elevation of 5000 meters (16,400 feet) in the Andes. It is possible for some individuals to perform at higher altitudes for short periods of time. "While the well-adapted climber can survive and function adequately for months at 19,000 feet, at 26,000 feet this is possible only for days, if no artificial oxygen is used."[1]

The highest place on earth is the summit of Mount Everest, which lies 8848 meters (29,028 feet) above sea level. The first humans known to stand atop Mount Everest were Edmund Hillary and Tenzing Norgay on May 29, 1953. Since then, several expeditions have reached the summit with the aid of bottled oxygen. In fact, it was believed that it was impossible for humans to climb that high without the use of bottled oxygen.

On May 9, 1978, two members of an Austrian expedition, Peter Habeler and Reinhold Messner, were the first humans to reach the top of Mount Everest without the use of bottled oxygen.[2] In 1981, the American Medical Research Expedi-

tion moved into the Himalayas to conduct research on human physiology at extreme altitudes. Research stations were established at several altitudes and two members of the team reached the summit of Mount Everest without bottled oxygen and were able to take a limited number of physiological measurements.[3]

The symptoms of high-altitude sickness become exaggerated at extremely high altitude, even in those who have become acclimatized to some degree. Reinhold Messner describes his feelings on route to Mount Everest:

My rucksack weighed between 12 and 16 kilos [26 and 35 pounds], and to carry it was such an effort for me that it took all my strength and all the oxygen in my muscles, simply to thrust out my chest to take in air, and then to let it out again. . . I could only manage 30 or 40 steps without oxygen, and they cost me so much strength, that the possibility of my climbing Everest without oxygen didn't even enter into the question.[4]

At high altitude, mental functions begin to become impaired, as described by Peter Habeler:

Our altitude was now 28,500 feet, and we had obviously reached a point at which normal brain functions had broken down, or at least were severely limited. Our attentiveness and concentration declined; our instinct no longer reacted as reliably as before; the capacity for clear logical thinking had also apparently been lost.[5]

---

[1]O. Ölz, "Everest without Oxygen: The Medical Fundamentals," in P. Habeler, *The Lonely Victory* (New York: Simon & Schuster, 1979), p. 220.
[2]Habeler, *The Lonely Victory*; R. Messner, *Everest: Expedition to the Ultimate* (New York: Oxford Univ. Press, 1979).
[3]J. B. West, "Human Physiology at Extreme Altitudes on Mount Everest," *Science* 223 (1984), pp. 784–788.
[4]Messner, *Everest*, p. 156.
[5]Habeler, *The Lonely Victory*, p. 183.

---

**Moving into High Altitudes**   When a person who normally lives near sea level first travels into high mountains, he or she will probably notice an increase in the breathing rate, which may reach twice that at sea level. The increased breathing rate brings more oxygen into the alveoli, and it helps increase the partial pressure of oxygen in the blood. This **hyperventilation,** or increased breathing rate, eventually is reduced, and it levels off as the person becomes acclimatized to the high altitude.

About 97 percent of the oxygen in the blood is carried in chemical combinations with hemoglobin in the red blood cells; the other 3 percent is dissolved in the plasma and may be ignored. The chemical association of oxygen and hemoglobin is loose and reversible. When the partial pressure of oxygen is high, as in the alveoli of the lungs, oxy-

gen will combine with hemoglobin. When the hemoglobin reaches the capillaries, where the partial pressure of oxygen is low, the oxygen is released from the hemoglobin molecule and is free to diffuse into the cells.

When the blood leaves the lungs, the hemoglobin is about 97 percent saturated; that is, oxygen has combined with about 97 percent of the hemoglobin molecules. Some of the oxygen is then given up in the capillaries of the tissues. As a result, the hemoglobin in the veins returning to the heart and lungs is only about 70 percent saturated. At high altitudes, several factors operate to alter these percentages, thereby permitting the hemoglobin molecules to carry more oxygen to the tissues. For example, because of hyperventilation, the concentration of carbon dioxide in the blood decreases,

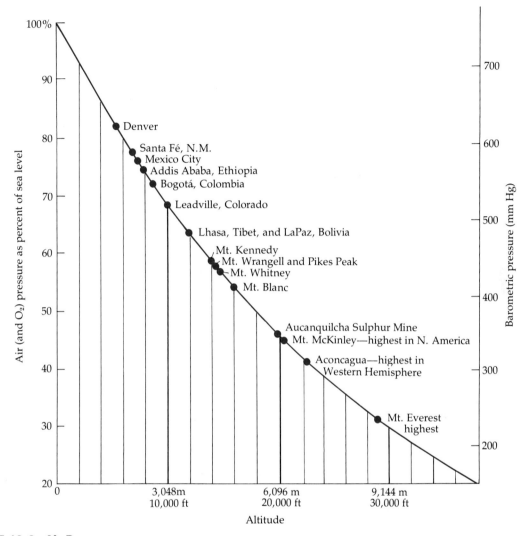

**FIGURE 16–3  Air Pressure**
This graph shows the decrease in air pressure with increase in altitude.

thus altering the blood chemistry in such a way as to increase the amount of oxygen carried in the blood.

Many other acclimatory adjustments take place. In time, the number of capillaries in the body increases, thereby shortening the distance that the oxygen must be carried by the blood to the tissues. In addition, the number of red blood cells increases, and hence the amount of hemoglobin being carried by the blood also increases. Therefore, although the partial pressure of oxygen as it enters the lungs differs at sea level and at high altitude, the partial

pressure of oxygen in the blood is not very different by the time it reaches the capillaries (Figure 16–4). Many changes also occur at the cellular level that enable cells to carry out their metabolic functions at lower oxygen levels.

While the factors discussed above permit people to live at high altitudes, people cannot overcome all the negative biological effects from high-altitude living. For example, high altitude affects reproduction; birth weights are lower, and infant mortality is greater. In addition, as we will discuss later, the growth and development of children are slower.

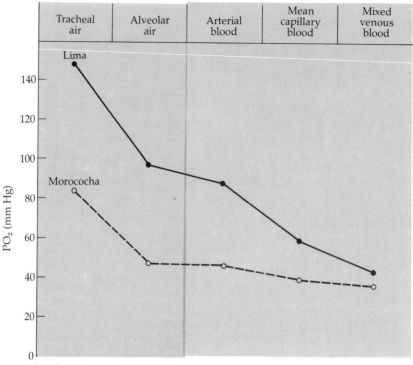

**Figure 16–4    Average Partial Pressure of Oxygen**
This chart shows the partial pressure of oxygen in the lungs and in various parts of the circulatory system, comparing individuals living at sea level (Lima, Peru) and at high altitude [Morococha, Peru, at 4540 meters (14,891 feet)].

## Summary

Although *Homo sapiens* is physiologically a tropical species, human populations today occupy a great variety of habitats and are able to survive under stressful environmental conditions. Adjustments are nongenetic mechanisms by which animals can survive in specific habitats.

Behavioral adjustments are cultural responses to environmental stress. The utilization of technology, such as specialized clothing, housing, and tools, and the development of particular forms of social behavior are cultural ways in which humans are able to adjust to hostile conditions.

Humans can also adjust in physical ways by means of reversible physiological responses to environmental stress; these are termed acclimatory adjustments. For example, under conditions of extreme Arctic cold, the basal metabolic rate of the body increases, resulting in an increased production of body heat. Under desert conditions, the sweat glands become more sensitive and produce more sweat; urine volume is reduced. Changes in blood chemistry permit humans to survive the dangers of hypoxia at high altitudes. Through such mechanisms, human populations have been able to spread over the earth and have come to terms with some of the earth's most difficult habitats.

## HUMAN ADAPTATION

Microevolutionary change, or **adaptation,** is an important factor bringing about variation within and among populations. Here we will discuss two examples of adaptation in human populations, skin color and body build.

### The Nature of Skin Color

People are commonly referred to as red, white, black, yellow, or brown. Yet in spite of this apparent rainbow of humanity, only one major pigment,

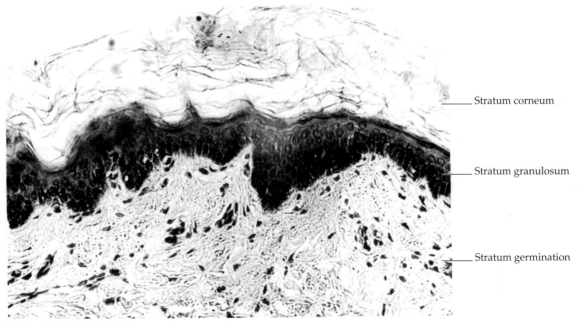

Stratum corneum

Stratum granulosum

Stratum germination

**FIGURE 16–5  Human Skin**
A photograph of the outermost layer of the skin (epidermis) as seen through the microscope. In this cross section of dark skin, the concentration of melanin can be seen in the stratum granulosum.

**melanin,** is responsible for human coloring. Skin color is also affected by hemoglobin: the small blood vessels underlying the skin give lighter-skinned persons a pinkish cast. The larger the number of blood vessels, the greater the influence of hemoglobin on skin color.

Melanin is produced in the outermost layers of the skin, the **epidermis** (Figure 16–5). The pigment is produced in specialized cells called **melanocytes.** People with dark skin and people with light skin have, on the average, the same number of melanocytes in the same area of the body. Skin color is determined by the amount of melanin produced, the size of the melanin particles, the rate of melanin production, and the location of the melanin in the skin.

**Skin Color as an Adaptation**  People with dark skin are often found in more equatorial regions while persons with light skin are found farther from the equator. Why would darker skin color be adaptive in equatorial regions?

One hypothesis holds that dark skin provides protection against the harmful effects of ultraviolet radiation from the sun. This radiation can cause sunburn and sunstroke and can stimulate the development of skin cancers. Since melanin absorbs ultraviolet radiation, dark skin cuts down the amount of this radiation that passes through the outer layers of the skin.

In many parts of the world, the amount of ultraviolet radiation reaching the surface of the earth varies with the seasons. Since ultraviolet radiation stimulates melanin production, the increased amount of radiation during the summer in the middle latitudes causes people to tan. All people are capable of some degree of tanning.

Another hypothesis links skin color with production of vitamin D, which is vital for calcium absorption in the intestines. Calcium is necessary for normal bone development, and the lack of this mineral leads to bone diseases, such as **rickets.** Excessive calcium leads to **hypercalcemia,** a condition characterized by malfunctions of the nervous system. Although some vitamin D comes from digested foods, most is manufactured within the skin. This biochemical reaction requires ultraviolet radiation. The amount of ultraviolet radiation that reaches those layers of the skin where vitamin D synthesis takes place is influenced by the concentration of melanin in the skin.

The geographical areas of most intense ultraviolet radiation are the grasslands of the equatorial regions. People in these areas often have extremely dark skin that always remains dark, as we can see in the Nilotic peoples of the grasslands of east Africa and the aboriginal populations of the Australian desert. Even with very dark skin, the intense ultraviolet radiation characteristic of equatorial regions guarantees that more than enough vitamin D will be produced.

Extremely dark skin is not characteristic of indigenous tropical-forest dwellers, since the heavy vegetation filters out much of the solar radiation. The pygmies of the Congo Basin of Africa, for example, are lighter than the people who entered the forest some 2000 years ago from the Cameroons, which lies northwest of the Congo. On the other hand, peoples living in the Arctic are darker than one might expect. Snow reflects ultraviolet radiation, thereby increasing the amount of such radiation that ultimately reaches their skin.

Another hypothesis about the distribution of human skin color revolves around the chances that one might be injured by cold temperatures. It has been noticed for decades that soldiers with dark skin suffer from frostbite more frequently than do light-skinned troops. For instance, there were up to six times as many frostbite-related deaths among African-American troops during the Korean War than among white soldiers. Thus, cold would have selected against people with heavily pigmented skin in early European populations who were living under glacial conditions, thus establishing light skin in the area.

All of the hypotheses about the variation and distribution of human skin color have their strengths and weaknesses. It is likely that several selective pressures are involved. One thing that seems to be certain is that the distribution of skin color prior to the mass migrations of the past 500 years is associated with sunlight.

**Determination of Skin Color**    As we have just seen, ultraviolet radiation can act as a selective agent on a population's gene pool, bringing about differences in skin color in different parts of the world. We know that the inheritance of skin color is polygenic. A small number of genes are involved, but the exact genetic mechanisms are not known.

Cultural factors may also affect skin color. For instance, light-skinned people who wear little clothing or make a practice of sunbathing will appear darker in the summer than genetically similar people who protect themselves from tanning. Suntan lotions also alter the color of the skin. Of course, darkened skin produced by exposure to ultraviolet radiation or tanning lotions will not be passed on to the next generation. However, if there is an advantage or disadvantage in the ability to tan, natural selection will increase or decrease the frequency of this trait.

## Adaptation and Body Build

Natural selection plays a major role in determining the size and shape of the human body. The effects of natural selection are greatest under the most stressful conditions. Thus, if people live in a generally mild climate that is frigid for three months of the year, they must be adapted to the harsh conditions as well as to the mild ones. Each time the stressful conditions arise, the genes of those individuals who do not survive will be eliminated. Their nonadaptive genes will not be transmitted to the next generation. Over time, the population will become increasingly adapted to its local circumstance.

**Radiation of Heat and Body Build**    We have already discussed some aspects of the problem of heat loss in desert habitats. Radiation is the most significant mechanism for heat loss in the nude human body at rest, accounting for 67 percent of the heat loss at an air temperature of 24°C (75.2°F). The efficiency of radiation as a heat-reducing process depends largely on body build.

The amount of heat that can be lost from an object by radiation depends on the ratio of surface area to body mass. Suppose two brass objects of identical weight, a sphere and a cube, are heated to the same temperature and then left to cool. Which object cools faster? The cube cools faster. Although both objects have the same weight, the cube has more surface area from which the heat can radiate. On the other hand, the sphere has the smallest surface per unit weight of any three-dimensional shape.

## TABLE 16-1

### RATIO OF BODY WEIGHT TO BODY SURFACE AREA IN MALES*

| Population | Median latitude | Ratio (kilograms per) square meter) |
|---|---|---|
| China | | |
| North | | 36.02 |
| Central | | 34.30 |
| South | | 30.90 |
| North Europe to north Africa† | | |
| Finland | 65°N | 38.23 |
| Ireland | 53°N | 38.00 |
| France | 47°N | 37.78 |
| Italy | 42½°N | 37.15 |
| Egypt (Siwah) | 26°N | 36.11 |
| Arabs (Yemen) | 15°N | 36.10 |

*Women show ratios different from men's. This may be due to differences in the mechanisms of heat regulation between men and women. For example, the ratio for France (women) is 38.4, compared with 37.78 for men, as seen above.
†There is some discontinuous variation in the north Europe to north Africa range. For example, the ratio for Germany is 39.14, even though it is south of Finland.
*Source:* Eugene Schreider, "Variations morphologiques et différences climatiques," *Biométrie Humaine* 6 (1971), pp. 46–49. Used with permission of Dr. Schreider.

While weight increases by the cube, surface area increases only by the square. This is generally true of human beings as well. As seen in Table 16–1, the ratio of body weight to surface area of skin is higher in cooler northern regions and decreases toward the equator. Just as a sphere has the smallest surface area per unit weight, a short, stocky human body also has a low surface area per unit weight. Thus, we would expect that people in Arctic regions, in order to reduce heat loss, would be short and stocky, with short limbs. When the Inuit's body is examined, this expectation is confirmed. In contrast, the Nilotes live in the hot equatorial regions of east Africa and have long, linear trunks with long arms and legs. Such linearity provides a large surface area for the radiation of heat (Figure 16–6).

Variability extends to other parts of the anatomy. Anthropologists have studied variation of many features, including the nose, hair texture, and hair color, but the reasons for variability in these features are poorly known. Variation also occurs in various physiological traits, in molecular traits such as blood types, and in the frequencies of genetic disease.

### Summary

Adaptation refers to microevolutionary changes. This section has examined two examples of adaptation in human populations: skin color and body build.

Human skin color is due primarily to the pigment melanin. In general, people living in equatorial regions tend to have darker skin than those living at higher latitudes. In this case, melanin may be acting to protect the body from the harmful ultraviolet rays of the sun and also to regulate the production of vitamin D. People living in equatorial regions also tend to be tall and linear, a body build that maximizes the amount of surface area per unit of body weight. This body shape maximizes the efficiency by which excess heat can be removed from the body.

### THE NATURE OF HUMAN GROWTH AND DEVELOPMENT

The patterns of growth and development differ among human groups. These patterns also differ among individuals within groups due to variations in heredity, nutrition, disease, and health care.

**Growth** can be defined as an increase in the size or mass of an organism. For example, we may observe growth by measuring the increase in a child's height and weight over time. On the other hand, **development** is change over time from an immature to a mature or specialized state. The appearance of the specialized tissues that make up the various organs of the body from the undifferentiated cells of the early embryo, and the changes in the sex organs and other features that occur as an individual passes through puberty, are both examples of development.

Each of the estimated 100 trillion cells of the adult human is ultimately derived from a single fertilized ovum. The process of growth from this single cell occurs in three ways: increase in the number of cells, which is accomplished by the process of mitosis **(hyperplasia);** increase in cell size **(hypertrophy);** and increase in the amount of intercellular material **(accretion).**

The different rates at which various types of cells divide is largely responsible for the differences in body proportions and in body composition that develop with age. As we see in Figure 16–7, the

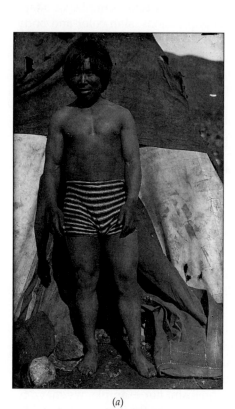

(a)

(b)

**FIGURE 16–6  Body Build**
The body builds of an (a) Inuit of the Arctic and a (b) Nilote of the African savanna conform
to Bergmann's and Allen's rules.

tonsils, the thymus gland, and the lymph nodes are composed of lymphoid tissue that grows very rapidly in early childhood. Lymphoid tissue traps foreign particles in the body and plays a major role in the development of immunity to diseases. By the end of five or six years, the nervous system has reached 90 percent of its adult size; after this, the growth rate is extremely slow. In contrast, the elements of the reproductive system grow very slowly until puberty, when their growth accelerates. Growth rates of fatty tissues will be discussed when we examine puberty.

### Growth and Development of the Human Body

Anthropologists study the process of human growth most extensively in the skeleton. Interest in **osteology**, the study of bones, stems from archaeological and paleontological fieldwork that in-

volves careful study of skeletal remains. Information about populations, including sex ratios, age at death, and diseases, provides insights into the biology of prehistoric populations. Methods of burial and artificial deformation of the skeleton tell us much about the cultural practices surrounding life and death.

**The Growth of Bones**   Initially, a fetal limb bone is formed of cartilage. The actual bone first appears at the center of this cartilage, an area that is called the **primary center of ossification;** in many bones, this center appears before birth. The process of **ossification** soon turns most of the cartilage into bone.

The formation of other centers of ossification occurs most frequently near the ends of long bones such as the humerus. Although considerable variation exists, primary and secondary centers of ossification generally appear in a characteristic order

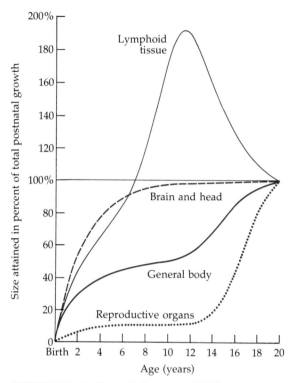

**FIGURE 16–7 Growth Curves of Different Parts and Tissues of the Body**
This graph illustrates the differences in growth of different tissues and parts of the body, expressed in terms of percent of total growth attained after birth.

at particular ages. Figure 16–8 shows examples of ages at which centers of ossification appear, from birth to 5 years, in females. As ossification continues, bone replaces the remaining cartilage and ultimately the centers of ossification unite to form a single bone.

Growth of mammalian long bones does not occur at the ends, but in very narrow areas between the centers of ossification. As the individual increases in size, these areas, called **growth plates,** become increasingly thinner and eventually disappear as the centers of ossification fuse. Once fusion occurs, growth stops. As is true with the appearance of centers of ossification, fusions of growth plates generally occur in a characteristic order and at certain average ages, although individuals vary. Figure 16–9 shows the average ages of fusion for selected growth plates in males.

The appearance of a center of ossification or the fusion of a growth plate may be used to define a standard **bone age.** These standards vary among populations and between males and females. The standard bone age represents the average chronological age at which these events take place. In contrast, **chronological age** is the time since birth. For example, Figure 16–10 shows the x-rays of the wrists of two boys, each with a chronological age of 15 years. The x-ray on the left shows more unfused growth plates than does the x-ray on the right. The boy on the left has a bone age of 12½ years; the boy on the right has a bone age of 15½ years.

**The Development of Dentition** Like other mammals, humans develop two sets of teeth. The first is a set of **deciduous,** or baby, teeth; the second is a set of **permanent teeth.** Humans have 20 deciduous teeth and 32 permanent teeth.

In humans, teeth begin to develop in the five-month-old fetus, and the first deciduous tooth erupts (appears through the gum) about six months after birth. By the average age of three years, all 20 deciduous teeth have fully erupted and the permanent teeth are developing in the jaws. At six or seven years of age, the deciduous teeth begin falling out, to be replaced by the permanent teeth.

Although variation does occur, most of the deciduous and permanent teeth erupt in a fairly consistent order at particular ages. For example, the second permanent molar erupts at an average age of 12 years. (In England the eruption of the second molar was formerly used to decide when a child was old enough to go to work.) Other teeth are not so regular: third molars, the "wisdom teeth," may erupt between the ages of 18 and 80 years and in some individuals may never erupt at all.

Figure 16–11, developed by the American Dental Association, shows the status of the different teeth at various ages. This chart depicts the "typical" sequence and average age of tooth eruption; there is considerable variation in both.

**Puberty**

Of all the events in an individual's life cycle, one of the most significant both biologically and socially is **puberty.** In most human societies, the onset of puberty occasions a ritual that marks a major transition in the social life of the individual.

One of the major physical changes that occurs in puberty is a rapid increase in stature. If we plot the height of a child on a series of dates (on the child's

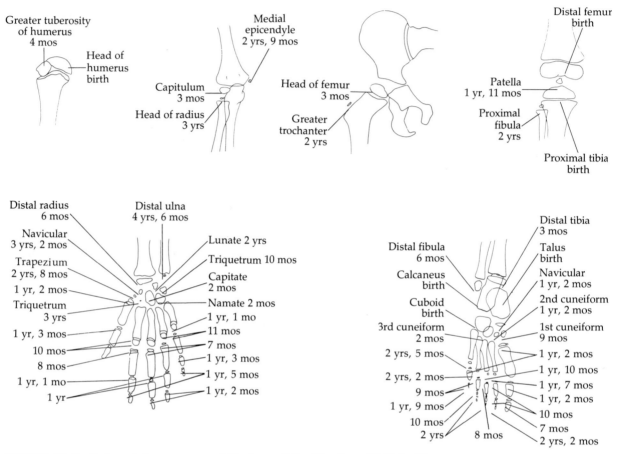

**FIGURE 16–8   Dates of Appearance of Centers of Ossification, Birth to Five Years of Age, in "White" Females.**

birthday, for example), we obtain what is called a **distance curve.** An example of a distance curve for a male is shown in Figure 16–12. At about 14½ years of age, there is a major increase in the growth rate known as the **adolescent growth spurt.** This is most clearly seen in a **velocity curve,** which plots the height gained for each year (Figure 16–13). Females experience a similar growth spurt, but it occurs earlier than in males. Also, the increase in stature and the speed of growth are less in girls than in boys.

The later onset of puberty in males may account for their greater stature as adults. The hormones involved in the sexual changes at puberty also bring about the end of bone growth in the long bones. Thus, the later onset of puberty gives males a longer time to grow.

The earliest signs of puberty in males are the enlargement of the testes and changes in the texture and color of the scrotum; these are soon followed by the enlargement of the penis and the growth of pubic hair. Individuals vary in the age at which these events occur. Growth of the penis begins at 12½ years on the average, but it may begin as early as 10½ or as late as 14½. A problem of social adjustment at this time is that some boys may be just beginning puberty after their peers have completed it.

The earliest sign of puberty in the female is the development of the **breast bud,** which is an elevation of the breast as a small mound. Also, there is a slight enlargement of the **areolar area,** the dark area surrounding the nipple. In the female, there is a sudden and visible event known as **menarche**

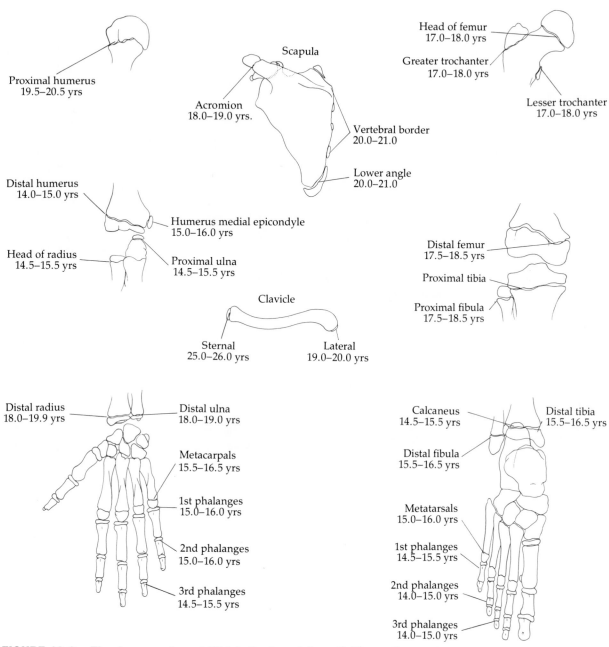

**FIGURE 16–9 The Average Age at Which Fusion of Growth Plates Occurs in "White" Males**

(rhymes with "monarchy"), the first menstrual flow. Menarche actually appears late in puberty; it represents a mature stage of development of the uterus. It does not, however, mark the development of full reproductive functions. These occur a year or so later.

Within a given population, the age at menarche is quite variable. In addition, when *averages* from different populations are compared, great variation is apparent as well. In some populations, the average age at menarche may be under 13, whereas in other populations, the average age may exceed 18 (Table 16–2).

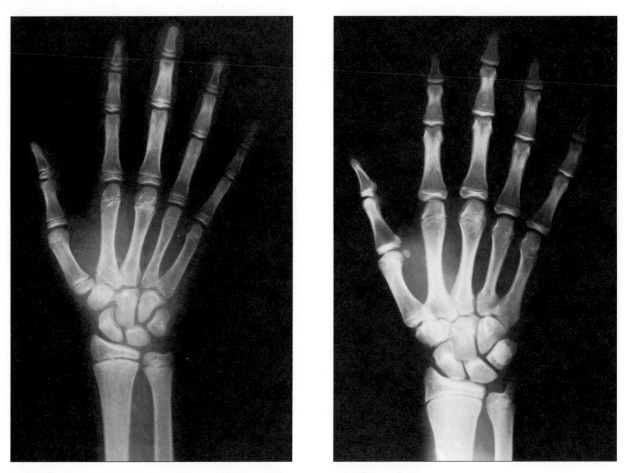

**FIGURE 16–10  X-rays of Hands and Wrists of Two Boys 15 Years of Age**
Boy on left has a skeletal age of 12½ years; boy on right has a skeletal age of 15½ years.

In addition to changes in the reproductive organs, other changes that differentiate males and females occur at puberty. These are the **secondary sexual characteristics.** An example found in males is the development of facial hair and of a deeper voice. The voice change is due to lengthening of the vocal cords, which, in turn, results from the growth of the larynx. Voice change also occurs in the female. Perhaps more important for both sexes, however, are changes in body proportions and body composition.

**Dimensions of the Body**   One of the oldest studies within physical anthropology is **anthropometry,** the "systematized art of measuring and taking observations on man, his skeleton, his brain, or other organs, by the most reliable means and methods for scientific purposes."[3]

Anthropometric measurements can be plotted as growth curves. Different parts of the body grow at different rates, and many differences that characterize the sexes after puberty simply represent differences in relative growth rates. For example, Figure 16–14 plots two anthropometric measurements against age in the form of velocity curves. The first plots **biacromial width,** a measurement of the width of the shoulders. At puberty, males develop relatively broad shoulders. The second graph plots

[3]A. Hrdlička, *Practical Anthropology* (Philadelphia: Wistar Institute of Anatomy and Biology, 1939), p. 3.

**Prenatal**     **Infancy**     **Early Childhood**     **Late Childhood**

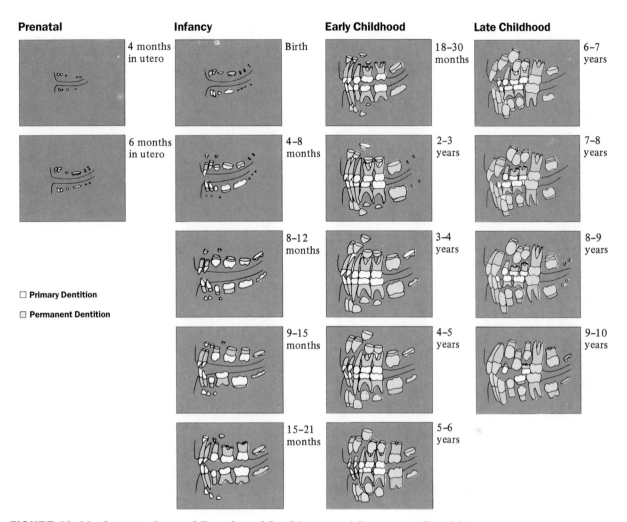

**FIGURE 16–11  Average Ages of Eruption of Deciduous and Permanent Dentition**
The deciduous teeth are shown in solid color. (Copyright by the American Dental Association.
Reprinted by permission.)

**bitrochanteric width,** a measurement of hip width. Here the greatest growth at puberty is in the female.

Some variations in the pattern of growth and development provide a means of adjustment to environmental stress. Such adjustments are called **developmental adjustments.** A good example of developmental adjustment can be seen in differences in growth rates involving chest circumference.

It has been known for some time that individuals growing up at high altitudes develop greater chest circumferences than do those growing up at lower elevations (Figure 16–15). This is related to greater lung volume, primarily in what is termed the **residual volume,** the amount of air still remaining in the lungs after the most forceful expiration. Greater residual volume in children growing up at high altitude appears to develop as a result of a rapid and accelerated development of the lungs in childhood.

**Changes in Body Composition**  Along with the adolescent growth spurt is a change in the composition of the body. The amount of muscle tissue

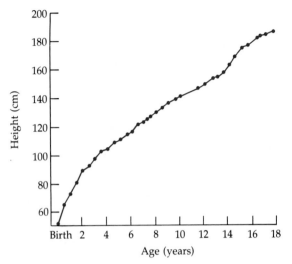

FIGURE 16–12 **Growth in Height of de Montbeillard's Son from Birth to 18 years, 1759–1777**
This example of a distance curve shows total height on each of several dates.

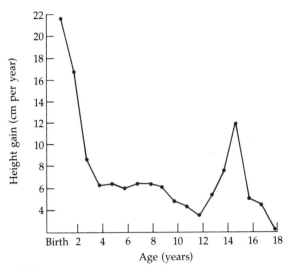

FIGURE 16–13 **Growth in Height of de Montbeillard's Son from Birth to 18 Years, 1759–1777**
This example of a velocity curve shows increments of height gained from year to year.

increases, especially in males. Apart from the large muscles, males develop larger lungs, larger hearts, and a greater capacity for carrying oxygen in the blood in comparison with females. These differ-

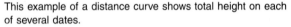

**MEDIAN AGE AT MENARCHE (FIRST MENSTRUATION) IN SEVERAL POPULATIONS**

| Population or location | Median age (years) |
|---|---|
| Wealthy Chinese (Hong Kong) | 12.5* |
| Wroclaw (Poland) | 12.6* |
| California (United States) | 12.8* |
| Moscow (U.S.S.R.) | 13.0* |
| Tel Aviv (Israel) | 13.0† |
| Burma (urban) | 13.2* |
| Oslo (Norway) | 13.5* |
| Wealthy Ibo (Nigeria) | 14.1* |
| Transkei Bantu (South Africa) | 15.0* |
| Tutsi (Rwanda) | 16.5* |
| Hutu (Rwanda) | 17.1‡ |
| Bundi (New Guinea) | 18.8* |

*J.M. Tanner, "The Secular Trend towards Earlier Physical Maturation," *Trans. Soc. Geneesk.* 44 (1966), pp. 524–538.
†A. Ber and C. Brociner, "Age of Puberty in Israeli Girls," *Fertility and Sterility* 15 (1964), pp. 640–647.
‡J. Hiernaux, *La Croissance de écoliers Rwandais* (Brussels: Outre-Mer, Royal Academy of Science, 1965).

ences are associated with greater speed, strength, and physical endurance (Figure 16–16).

Changes also occur in the amount of **subcutaneous fat,** the fat deposited under the skin. These changes are especially observed in the limbs. With the onset of the growth spurt, the relative proportion of subcutaneous fat decreases. Because this decrease is greatest in males, females enter adulthood with relatively more subcutaneous fat, especially over the pelvis and on the breasts, the upper back, and the upper arms.

### Control of Growth and Development

The nature and rates of growth and development are controlled by the complex interaction of many factors. Among these are the endocrine glands, nutrition, and heredity.

The **endocrine glands** produce a special group of chemicals called **hormones,** which are secreted directly into the bloodstream and are carried throughout the body. A number of hormones have an effect on growth and development. For example, **growth hormone,** produced by the pituitary gland, is essential for normal growth, particularly the growth of bone. Children deficient in this hormone reach an average adult height of only 130

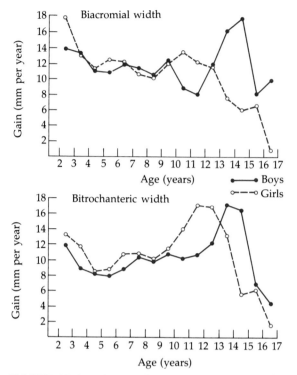

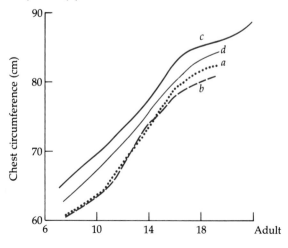

**FIGURE 16–14   Annual Change in Shoulder (Biacromial) Width and Hip (Bitrochanteric) Width in Boys and Girls**

**FIGURE 16–15   Chest Circumferences**
This graph compares the growth of chest circumference of three Peruvian populations found at (*a*) sea level, (*b*) moderate altitude of 2300 meters (7544 feet), and (*c*) high altitudes between 4000 and 5000 meters (13,120 and 18,040 feet). A growth curve from the United States is included for comparison (*d*).

centimeters (51 inches) although they have normal body proportions.

Sex hormones play major roles in growth and development, especially at puberty. **Testosterone** is manufactured by cells of the testes. At puberty, testosterone stimulates the growth of the testes and the male sex organs, such as the penis and the prostate, and also stimulates the development of secondary sexual characteristics such as facial hair. In the female, **estrogens** are produced by the ovaries. Estrogens stimulate the growth of the female sex organs, such as the vagina and the uterus, and cause secondary changes such as breast development. Other hormones, produced by other glands, also influence the pattern of growth and development in the individual.

**The Effects of Nutrition and Disease on Growth and Development**   The processes of growth utilize the raw materials taken into the body as food. Nutrients help sustain growth and development, repair damage, and maintain vital processes, and they provide energy for bodily activities. The lack of proper nutrition can seriously retard normal growth and development.

**Protein-caloric malnutrition** is a broad term covering many nutritional problems. Malnutrition is especially prevalent among developing nations, primarily those undergoing the transition to urbanized societies. Severe malnutrition is also frequent during war.

One form of protein-caloric malnutrition is **kwashiorkor,** a Ghanaian word meaning "second-child disease" (Figure 16–17*a*). Kwashiorkor is usually associated with the period immediately following weaning, which often takes place when a second child is born. In many parts of the world, especially in the tropics, the child moves from its mother's milk to a diet of carbohydrates and little protein. The main food is usually a starchy gruel made from yams, taro, corn, rice, or millet; animal protein is scarce and, when available, expensive. Thus, the child may receive enough food to satisfy hunger but does not receive the proteins vital to normal health, growth, and development.

Several symptoms characterize kwashiorkor. **Edema,** or water retention, occurs in the feet and lower legs and may occur in other parts of the body. Growth is retarded. Muscle wasting occurs, as seen

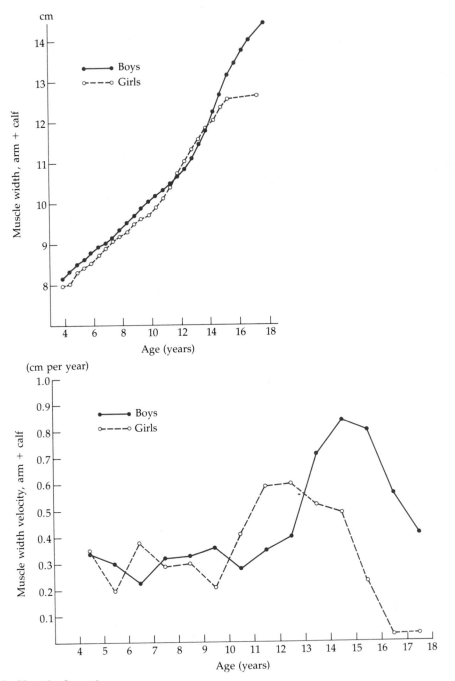

**FIGURE 16–16 Muscle Growth**
Distance and velocity curves showing the sum of widths of upper arm and calf muscles as seen in x-rays.

(a)

(b)

**FIGURE 16–17  Kwashiorkor and Marasmus**
(a) Child with kwashiorkor in Agra, India. (b) Child with marasmus, from Diamond Harbor, near Calcutta, India.

in the thinness of the upper arms and by the child's difficulty in holding up its head when pulled from a lying to a sitting position. Because the diet is high in carbohydrates, a relatively thick layer of subcutaneous fat and a distended belly are often seen. Many psychomotor changes occur, including retarded motor development. The child is apathetic, miserable, withdrawn, and indifferent to its environment.

**Marasmus** results from a diet low in both protein and calories (Figure 16–17b). It occurs in all ages, but usually in children soon after weaning. Symptoms of marasmus include extreme growth retardation, wasting of muscles and subcutaneous fat, diarrhea, and severe anemia. Since vital nutrients are absent during a critical time for brain growth, mental retardation often occurs. Early death is the rule.

Kwashiorkor and marasmus represent extreme examples of malnutrition and growth retardation. In addition to these, less severe forms of malnutrition and the lack of specific nutrients, or an excessive amount of many nutrients, in the diet can also lead to problems.

Growth and development are affected by many diseases. Many genetic abnormalities, such as PKU, and chromosomal abnormalities, such as Down syndrome (Chapter 3), clearly affect growth. Likewise, nongenetic diseases, such as those caused by bacteria, viruses, fungi, and parasites, can also influence growth.

Many childhood diseases may retard normal growth and development. Although measles and chicken pox may have no lasting effect on well-nourished children, severe and prolonged nongenetic

## TABLE 16-3

### AVERAGE DIFFERENCES BETWEEN MONOZYGOTIC AND DIZYGOTIC TWINS AND PAIRS OF SIBLINGS

| Difference in | Monozygotic twins | Monozygotic twins reared apart | Dizygotic twins | Same-sex siblings (not twins) |
|---|---|---|---|---|
| Stature (centimeters) | 1.7 | 1.8 | 4.4 | 4.5 |
| Weight (kilograms) | 1.9 | 4.5 | 4.5 | 4.7 |

*Source:* H. H. Newman et al., *Twins: A Study of Heredity and Environment* (Chicago: University of Chicago Press, 1937), p. 72.

diseases inevitably impair growth, especially in malnourished populations.

**Heredity and Growth and Development**  Growth is a complex process involving the interaction of cultural, environmental, and genetic factors. The exact role of heredity is not precisely known, but it is certainly polygenic (Chapter 3). Tall parents tend to have, on the average, tall children, but genetic factors are complex and difficult to analyze.

One method of estimating the relative influence of heredity and environment is through twin studies, which were discussed in Chapter 2. Tables 16–3 and 16–4 present data on growth from such twin studies. The similarities between monozygotic twins in stature, weight, and age at menarche, together with the differences between dizygotic twins and pairs of nontwin siblings, suggest a strong genetic influence on these traits. Yet the differences between monozygotic twins, especially when twins are reared apart, show that environmental influences are also present.

Twin studies suggest that genes strongly influence growth, primarily by establishing optimal lim-

its for growth. Thus, an individual may have the genetic potential for a particular stature, yet that stature may not be reached because of malnutrition or childhood disease. The nature of the genetic mechanism, however, is unknown.

### The Secular Trend in Growth and Development

Occasionally we read a newspaper or magazine article that reports that people are getting larger each generation. Scientists have long been aware of this phenomenon, which is called the **secular trend.** The secular trend is the tendency over the last hundred or so years for each succeeding generation to mature earlier and grow larger (Figure 16–18). This

**FIGURE 16–18  Secular Trend**
This graph shows the mean height of "white" Australian males and females measured in 1901–1907 and in 1970.

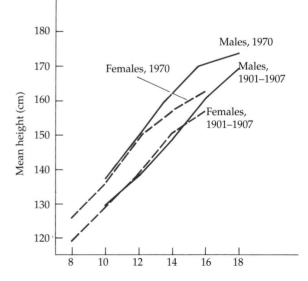

## TABLE 16-4

### AVERAGE DIFFERENCE IN MENARCHE

| Relationship | Difference (months) |
|---|---|
| Monozygotic twins | 2.8 |
| Dizygotic twins | 12.0 |
| Pairs of sisters | 12.9 |
| Pairs of unrelated women | 18.6 |

*Source:* E. Petr, "Untersuchungen zur Erbbedingtheit der Menarche," *Zeitschrift für Morphologie und Anthropologie* 33 (1935), pp. 43–48.

**BOX 16-2**

# Aging

Someday, genetic-engineering techniques may be used to arrest the aging process, although today the idea is a fantasy of science fiction. All people age. **Aging** is the uninterrupted process of normal development that leads to a progressive decline in physiological function and ultimately to death.

It has been suggested for decades that certain groups of people age at a much slower rate and live considerably longer lives than other groups. Russians from the Caucasus Mountains, Hunzas from the Karakoram Mountains in Pakistan, and Ecuadorans have been represented in the popular literature as including within their populations a very high percentage of people who are well over 100 years old. However, when these cases are carefully examined, these people usually turn out to be in their 70s and 80s.[1] In fact, these populations do not show average life expectancies any greater than the general U.S. population.

So, then, why do people exaggerate age? One reason may be that the society is attempting to show that its culture is better than others, or even to display a biological superiority. In some groups, a man of draftable age customarily takes the identity of his father in order to avoid military service. In many societies, great age brings with it increased prestige or fame.

The rates of aging and the time of death are influenced by both genetic and cultural factors. **Life expectancy** is how long a person can, on the average, expect to live. Although average life expectancies differ considerably from population to population, the oldest ages that people attain in different cultures are very similar. For humans, as for each other animal species, there seems to be a theoretical maximum age determined by genetic predestiny. This is called the **life span**. The life span for humans is about 120 years. A French woman, Jeanne Calmut, lived longer than any other person for whom we have a record. At the time of her death in 1997, she was 122 years and 164 days old.[2]

Many investigators of the aging process believe that the maximum life span of a species is due to a developmental "clock." The timing of this clock is controlled, in part, by regulatory genes. These genes determine the appearance and disappearance of biochemical products that control the aging process. Recent studies indicate that another aspect of the genetic developmental clock might involve mitochondrial DNA. As mutations accumulate in mtDNA, the body might age. These models of aging, as well as others that have been proposed, are hypothetical. As of yet, aging is inadequately understood.

Many developmental events contribute to old age. The following will or may occur as one gets older: loss of bone density, gain of fat but loss of muscle tissue, loss of teeth, dry skin, menopause, decline in sperm count, decline in near and far vision, diminished senses of hearing and taste, rise in cholesterol levels, and increase in susceptibility to many diseases, including heart disease, cancer, cerebrovascular disease, chronic pulmonary disease, diabetes, and chronic liver disease. The occurrence and degree of these events are highly variable among individuals within a population as well as variable among populations.

[1] A. Leaf, "Long-Lived Populations: Extreme Old Age," *Journal of American Geriatrics* 30 (1982), pp. 485–487.
[2] J-M. Robine and M. Alland, "The Oldest Human," *Science* 279 (1998), pp. 1834–1835. *See also:* T. Overfield, *Biologic Variation in Health and Illness: Race, Age, and Sex Differences* (Menlo Park, Calif.: Addison-Wesley, 1985), and J. S. Olshansky, B. A. Carnes, and C. Cassel, "In Search of Methuselah: Estimating the Upper Limits to Human Longevity," *Science* 250 (1990), pp. 634–640.

---

trend has occurred worldwide. In the twentieth century, the change in mean body height per decade has been about 0.6 centimeter (0.25 inch) in early childhood, about 1.3 centimeters (0.5 inch) in late childhood (8 years old for girls and 10 years old for boys), and about 1.9 centimeters (0.74 inch) at mid-adolescence (age 12 for girls and age 14 for boys).[4]

What causes secular trends? No one knows for sure. Some researchers believe that a general improvement in nutrition, better sanitation, better health services, and less tedious lifestyles are responsible. These factors have permitted individuals to more closely approach their genetically determined potential weight and stature. Today, a leveling off of the secular trend appears to be occurring among the higher socioeconomic, urban population.

### The Adult Skeleton

By the early 20s, most of the growth plates have closed and all the teeth, with perhaps the exception of the highly variable third molars, are fully

[4] H. V. Meredith, "Findings from Asia, Australia, Europe, and North America on Secular Change in Mean Height of Children, Youths, and Young Adults," *American Journal of Physical Anthropology* 44 (1976), pp. 321–322.

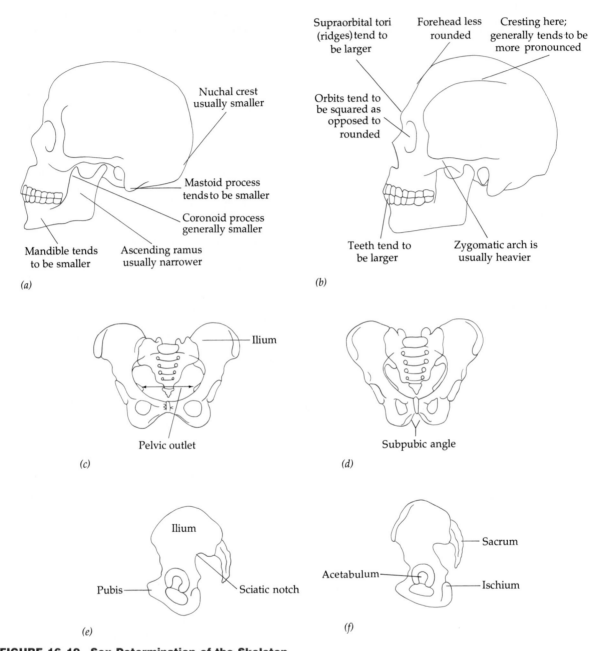

Supraorbital tori (ridges) tend to be larger

Forehead less rounded

Cresting here; generally tends to be more pronounced

Orbits tend to be squared as opposed to rounded

Nuchal crest usually smaller

Mastoid process tends to be smaller

Coronoid process generally smaller

Mandible tends to be smaller

Ascending ramus usually narrower

Teeth tend to be larger

Zygomatic arch is usually heavier

(a)

(b)

Ilium

Pelvic outlet

Subpubic angle

(c)

(d)

Ilium

Pubis

Sciatic notch

Sacrum

Acetabulum

Ischium

(e)

(f)

**FIGURE 16–19 Sex Determination of the Skeleton**
Comparison of the stereotypic (a) female skull and (b) male skull, and (c) female pelvis and (d) male pelvis; side view of (e) female pelvis and (f) male pelvis.

erupted. Age-related changes in the adult skeleton are generally degenerative changes such as the closure and obliteration of sutures in the skull, loss of teeth, and degeneration of bone in the skull and other parts of the anatomy.

An example of age-related changes in the post-cranial skeleton may be seen in the analysis of the **pubic symphysis,** which is the part of the pelvis where the two innominates join. (The pelvis consists of two halves, the innominates, that in turn are divided into sections. The front section is the pubis.) Age can be estimated by separating the two innominates and carefully examining the **symphyseal face,** or the surface where one pubis joins the other. Using analysis of the skull and the postcranial bones in the adult, a reasonable estimate of age at death can be made.

**The Male and Female Skeletons** The adults of many mammalian and primate species show marked differences in size and structure between males and females, a feature referred to as **sexual dimorphism.** Sexual dimorphism is relatively slight in humans, yet various parts of the male and female skeleton do show noticeable differences.

In Figure 16–19, which compares the male pelvis with the female pelvis, adaptations for childbearing can be seen in the female pelvis. Note, for example, that the female pelvis is characterized by a U-shaped and broader subpubic angle; a smaller acetabulum; a larger, wider, and shallower sciatic notch; a circular or elliptical pelvic inlet; and many other features.

Many sexual differences in the human skeleton reflect the male's greater size and heavier musculature. Areas where muscles attach to bone are seen as roughened areas and projections, and the size of these areas and projections is a reflection of the size of the attached muscle.

### Summary

Growth is an increase in the size of an organism; development is a change from an undifferentiated to a highly organized, specialized state. There are three ways in which growth occurs: hyperplasia is an increase in the number of cells; hypertrophy is a general increase in cell size; and accretion is an increase in the amount of intercellular material.

Bone growth begins with the appearance of primary and secondary areas of ossification, areas where bone is replacing cartilage. In long bones, growth takes place in growth plates that close when growth ceases in a fairly regular order at characteristic ages. Bone age is the average chronological age at which these events occur. The pattern of tooth formation and eruption serves a similar purpose.

Growth can be charted in distance and velocity curves that plot the increase in stature, or some other variable, over time. When examining a growth curve, we notice a period known as the adolescent growth spurt. This is an aspect of puberty, which also includes changes in the reproductive organs and the secondary sexual characteristics. Specific anthropometric measurements can also be plotted against age and illustrate aspects of sexual dimorphism. Differences in patterns of growth and development may be seen in children growing up in stressful environments; these are known as developmental adjustments.

The nature and rates of growth and development are controlled by the complex interaction of internal and external factors. These factors include the hormones, which are particularly involved in the control of puberty; environmental factors, including the availability and usage patterns of food; diseases, both those that are genetic and those caused by disease organisms; and heredity, which plays a major role by setting the potential limits to growth measurements such as stature. Improvement in nutrition, better sanitation, and better health services may be responsible for an increase in average stature and weight over the years, a tendency referred to as the secular trend.

### STUDY QUESTIONS

1. How does *adaptation* differ from *adjustment?*
2. Why would one expect peoples living in hot equatorial grasslands to be very tall and linear and to have dark skin?
3. How are skin color and general body build related to one another?
4. A human wearing little clothing sets out into the Arctic winter. Another, similarly dressed, sets out into the Sahara Desert. Describe the physiological events that will take place in each situation.
5. Very high altitude presents what is perhaps the most difficult habitat for human habitation. Describe the various stresses found at high altitude and the human responses to these stresses.
6. What is the major difference between *growth* and *development?*
7. What factors are responsible for differences in the patterns of growth and development among individuals or groups of individuals?
8. What is the secular trend?
9. An archaeologist excavates a prehistoric burial. Using the information from osteology, what can we find out about the skeletons?

## SUGGESTED READINGS

Bogin, B. *Cambridge Studies in Biological Anthropology, No. 23: Patterns of Human Growth.* Cambridge, England: Cambridge University Press, 1999. This book provides a basic introduction to the topic of human growth and development from an anthropological pespective.

Frisancho, A. R. *Human Adaptation: A Functional Interpretation,* rev. ed. Ann Arbor: University of Michigan Press, 1993. This book discusses human adaptations to stressful environments, including heat and cold stress, high-altitude hypoxia, and malnutrition.

Harrison, G. A., J. M. Tanner, D. R. Pilbeam, and P. T. Baker. *Human Biology,* 3rd ed. Oxford: Oxford University Press, 1988. The section on human growth, written by J. M. Tanner, provides a concise introduction to the study of growth and related topics.

Joyce, C., and E. Stover. *Witness from the Grave: The Stories Bones Tell.* Boston: Little, Brown, 1991. This book discusses the methods used to decipher the information from skeletal material. The book highlights the work of Clyde Snow, a leading forensic anthropologist.

Sinclair, D., and P. Dangerfield. *Human Growth after Birth,* 6th ed. Oxford: Oxford University Press, 1999. This book is a basic text on human growth and development.

Tanner, J. M. *Foetus into Man: Physical Growth from Conception to Maturity,* 2nd ed. Cambridge, Mass.: Harvard University Press, 1990. This is a general introduction to the study of human growth and development.

## SUGGESTED WEB SITES

Princeton University Outdoor Action Guide to High Altitude:
http://www.princeton.edu/~oa/safety/altutide.html

Ultraviolet Radiation (New Zealand National Institute of Water & Atmospheric Research):
http://katipo.niwa.cri.nz/lauder/uvinfo.htm

Zeno's Forensic Page (extensive list of links in the area of Forensic Anthropology):
http://users.bart.nl/~geradts/forensic.html

Additional web sites are listed in the *Workbook* that accompanies this text.

# The Analysis of Human Variation

*The whole human species, of course, is tremendously variable. Even within one nation, no matter how isolated, even within one family, we find innumerable differences between individuals. In ways that we do not fully understand, these differences have become partially sorted out according to geographic area (or, as we must say in the modern world, area of ancestry). . . . Some of the differences correlated with area of ancestry probably arose many thousand years ago, when small bands, perhaps a few families, left a group and went out to found new tribes. Their individual and family characteristics became the heritage of what later became large populations. Thus population and racial differences are, in a sense, the lengthened shadow of individual differences.[1]*

—Alice Brues

## Chapter Outline

In the previous chapter, we examined the nature of three sources of human variation. The first is adjustments, nongenetic responses to environmental stress. These are behavioral, acclimatory, and development adjustments. The second source of

---

[1]A. Brues, "Foreword," in T. Overfield, *Biologic Variation in Health and Illness: Race, Age, and Sex Differences* (Menlo Park, Calif. Addison-Wesley, 1985), p. x. Reproduced by permission of Theresa Overfield and Alice Brues.

variation is the differences that result from the pattern of growth and development.

The third source of variation is microevolutionary changes called adaptations. This chapter will examine the distribution of human variation and the classification of this variation.

## THE DISTRIBUTION OF VARIABILITY

Adjustments and adaptations are responses to particular environmental conditions. Many of these environmental conditions are associated with particular habitats. For example, dark skin color and linear body build are associated with hot, open, tropical climates. Since such climates are found near the equator, it follows that there will be a characteristic distribution of these traits when they are plotted on a map. This section will examine the distribution of variable features of human populations.

### Some Generalizations about Mammalian Variation

Scientists have made several generalizations based on the data on the physical nature of the bodies of various "warm-blooded" animals. One such generalization is **Gloger's rule.** This rule states that within the same species, there is a tendency for more heavily pigmented populations to be located toward the equator and for lighter populations to be farther from it.

**Bergmann's rule** refers to the relationship between surface area and mass or volume of the body. It states that within the same species, the average weight of the members of a population increases and the surface area of the body decreases as the average environmental temperature decreases. **Allen's rule** states that within the same species, the relative size of protruding parts of the body, such as the nose and ears, and the relative length of the arms and legs increase as the average environmental temperature increases.

From our discussion of skin color and body build in the previous chapter, we see that these generalizations hold true for humans in many situations. However, there are also many exceptions. For example, body size is affected by diet, and dietary differences in different parts of the world may account for some of the observed variation in weight.

Other facts include the migration of many human groups into new areas to which they bring a body characteristic adapted to their region of origin.

### Clinal Distributions

The frequencies of a particular trait may vary systematically from place to place, which can be seen when frequencies are plotted on a map. This is seen in Figure 17–1, which plots the frequencies of blood-type B in Europe. Note that the frequencies of blood-type B decrease along a line from the upper right-hand corner of the map to the French-Spanish border.

A distribution of frequencies that shows a systematic gradation over space is known as a **clinal distribution.** Clinal distributions develop in at least two ways. A cline might be determined by a gradual change in some selective pressure. For instance, an increase in the prevalence of the malaria-carrying mosquito as one moves from temperate into more tropical areas may be related to an increase in the frequency of the allele for sickle-cell anemia. As the selective pressure changes, so might the distribution of the trait.

A cline may also develop when a particular trait originates in a specific area and spreads outward by means of gene flow. The farther away one is from the center of origin, the lower the frequency will tend to be. The distribution of blood-type B may be the result of this process: blood-type B has its highest frequencies in central Asia and may have originated there.

**Discontinuous variation** occurs when a particular trait appears in high or low frequencies in various areas with little or no gradation between those areas. An example is the frequency of red hair in the United Kingdom (Figure 17–2).

Skin color and body build are generally clinal in nature. Since human populations are mobile, discontinuous variation in skin color and body build occurs as peoples with different skin colors and body builds migrate into new areas. Also, the interbreeding of these migratory peoples has produced multiple skin-color variants and a variety of body builds. In the following sections, we will examine the distribution of other factors.

**Distribution of Blood Types**   In Figure 17–1, we see the clinal distribution of blood-type B in Eu-

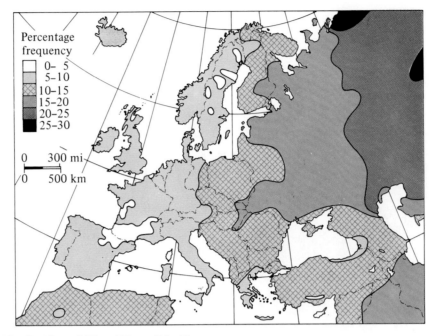

**FIGURE 17–1  Distribution of Blood-Type B in Europe**
This is an example of a clinal distribution.

**FIGURE 17–2  Distribution of Red Hair in the United Kingdom**
This is an example of discontinuous variation.

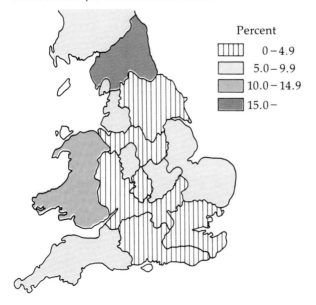

rope. The clinal distribution of many blood-type antigens, coupled with the nonclinal distribution of still other antigens, suggests that considerable variation occurs in the frequencies of particular blood types from population to population.

Some populations are characterized by particular blood-type frequencies. For example, high frequencies of blood-type A are found in Scandinavia and among the Inuit; high frequencies of blood-type B are found in central Asia, north India, and west Africa (Figure 17–3); and high frequencies of blood-type O are found throughout most of North and South America and in Australia. The distribution of blood types and their use in the classification of human variation will be discussed more thoroughly in the next section.

As discussed in Chapter 5, selective pressures are operating on the ABO blood-type system. For example, researchers have hypothesized that smallpox is more severe and mortality rates are higher among peoples of blood-types A and AB than

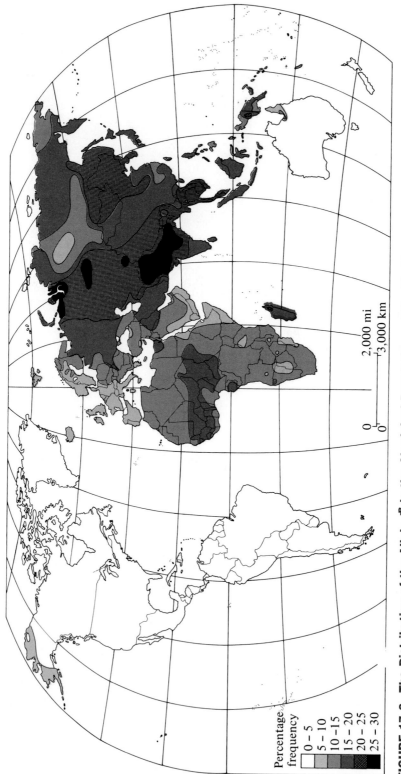

**FIGURE 17-3  The Distribution of the Allele $I^B$ in the Aboriginal Populations of the World**

Percentage
frequency

0 – 5
5 – 10
10 – 15
15 – 20
20 – 25
25 – 30

## TABLE 17-1

### FREQUENCIES (PERCENT) OF DIEGO-POSITIVE PHENOTYPE IN VARIOUS POPULATIONS

| Population | Frequency of Diego-positive |
|---|---|
| Caingangs (Brazil) | 45.8 |
| Carajas (Brazil) | 36.1 |
| Caribs (Venezuela) | 35.5 |
| Maya Indians (Mexico) | 17.6 |
| Guahibos (Venezuela) | 14.5 |
| Japanese | 12.3 |
| Chippewas (Canada) | 10.8 |
| Koreans | 6.1 |
| Guajiros (Venezuela) | 5.3 |
| Apaches (United States) | 4.1 |
| Eskimos (Alaska) | 0.8 |
| Lapps (Norway) | 0.0 |
| Polynesians | 0.0 |
| Aborigines (Australia) | 0.0 |
| Whites (United States) | 0.0 |
| Asiatic Indians | 0.0 |
| Africans (Liberia, Ivory Coast) | 0.0 |
| Bushmen (South Africa) | 0.0 |

*Source:* G. A. Harrison et al., *Human Biology* (New York: Oxford University Press, 1964), p. 275.

among peoples of types O and B. If this hypothesis is correct, smallpox, in areas where it is common, would act as a selective agent tending to eliminate A and AB individuals. O and B individuals would be left to reproduce most of the next generation. Maybe this is why in countries such as India, where smallpox was once common, B is the most common blood type today.

An interesting distributional study focuses on the Diego blood antigen. Table 17–1 shows that this antigen is found only in eastern Asian populations and in the aboriginal populations of the New World who are derived from the peoples of eastern Asia. According to one hypothesis, the Diego antigen is of fairly recent origin. Presumably, the antigen was carried to the New World when the ancestors of the Native Americans migrated across the Bering Strait (Chapter 15).

### Variability in Frequency of Genetic Disease

Specific genetic diseases, or high frequencies of genetic diseases, characterize all populations. For example, cystic fibrosis is a recessive genetic abnormality. While the abnormal allele is relatively frequent in European populations, it is rare in Asiatic and African populations. Another example is the allele associated with Tay-Sachs disease among Ashkenazi Jews. Table 17–2 lists some genetic abnormalities associated with particular groups of people.

Why are certain genetic diseases associated with particular populations? Major factors in establishing high frequencies of particular alleles in specific populations include inbreeding in small populations, the preference for consanguineous matings in many societies, and the founder principle operating in small migrant populations.

Balanced polymorphism, or heterozygous advantage (Chapter 5), has been identified as the mechanism responsible for the relatively high frequency of sickle-cell anemia in many populations of Africa and elsewhere. This mechanism may also be involved with the elevated frequencies of cystic fibrosis, phenylketonuria, schizophrenia, Tay-Sachs disease, and other conditions. Modern technology has alleviated the selective advantage of many balanced polymorphisms, so it may be impossible to discover the nature of the former advantage that a heterozygous genotype bestows on individuals of a population.

### Cultural Variation

Different populations have different technologies, marriage patterns, religions, and economies. They possess different ideas of nature, justice, and law. Even body movements and thought patterns are culturally tempered. Within a group, all these factors are integrated into a functional system, with each element related in some way to the others. The cultural system, in turn, is intimately related to the noncultural environment and to human biology.

Different peoples have different ideas of beauty, based on their cultural traditions. To achieve effects that they consider to be aesthetically pleasing, many groups permanently alter the shape and the structure of the body by artificial means. This alteration often serves to distinguish individuals of high status in cultures in which little clothing is worn. Various societies provide medical and religious justifications for body alterations. Examples of body alterations include circumcision, clitoridectomy (surgical removal of the external portion of the clitoris), scarification, body piercing, and tattooing.

**TABLE 17–2**

**THE ETHNIC DISTRIBUTION OF GENETIC DISEASE***

| Population | Disease | Inheritance pattern[†] |
|---|---|---|
| Europeans in general | Alkapoturnia | AR |
| | Anencephaly | PG |
| | Cystic fibrosis | AR |
| | Oculocutaneous albinism | AR |
| | Porphyria variegata | AD |
| | Spina bifida | PG |
| Ashkenazi Jews | Gaucher's disease | AR |
| | Hyperuricemia (gout) | AD |
| | Tay-Sachs disease | AR |
| Greeks, Italians, and Armenians | G-6-PD deficiency | XLR |
| | Thalassemia major (Cooley's anemia) | AR |
| Northern Europeans | Lactase deficiency | AD |
| | Pernicious anemia | PG |
| Irish | Phenylketonuria (PKU) | AR |
| Amish and Icelanders | Ellis–van Creveld syndrome | AR |
| Africans | G-6-PD deficiency | XLR |
| | Hemoglobinopathies (hemoglobin S, hemoglobin C) | CD |
| | Polydactyly | PG |
| Chinese | Alpha thalassemia | AR |
| | G-6-PD deficiency, Chinese type | XLR |
| Japanese | Acatalasia | AR |
| | Cleft palate | PG |
| | Wilson's disease | AR |

*This table indicates some of the genetic diseases found in high frequencies in particular populations.
[†]AR, Autosomal recessive; AD, autosomal dominant; PG, polygenic; XLR, X-linked recessive; CD, codominant.
*Source:* V. McKusick, *Mendelian Inheritance in Man: Catalogs of Autosomal Dominant, Autosomal Recessive, and X-Linked Phenotypes,* 5th ed. (Baltimore: Johns Hopkins, 1978).

The face and the head are frequently subject to modification. The Kwakiutl Indians of British Columbia place a board on the soft foreheads of their infants to flatten the front of the skull (Figure 17–4*a*). Punan women of Borneo slit their earlobes and insert brass rings, eventually drawing each lobe down to the shoulder.

Societies throughout the world alter the body to enhance their beauty, attain status, or become initiated. Several groups pierce the nasal septum, others slit the lips, and, in the United States, many pierce the ear (Figure 17–4*b*). Each method allows ornaments to be attached. Foot-binding, plastic surgery, hair and skin transplants, and many other methods of surgically or cosmetically altering the body are practiced in various parts of the world.

**Summary**

Several generalizations have been proposed to describe the distribution of features in "warm-blooded" animals. Gloger's rule states that within the same species, there is a tendency for more heavily pigmented populations to be located toward the equator and for lighter populations to be farther from it. Bergmann's rule states that within the same species, the average body weight of the individuals of a population increases and the surface area of the body decreases as the average environmen-

(a)

(b)

**FIGURE 17–→  Deformation of the Head**

(a) An example of head flattening: woman from the Koskimo (Kwakiutl) tribe, Vancouver Island; (b) American showing body piercing.

tal temperature decreases. Allen's rule states that within the same species, the relative size of protruding parts of the body, such as the nose and ears, and the relative length of the arms and legs increase as the average environmental temperature in-

creases. However, especially among human populations, there is considerable deviation from these generalizations.

Human variation is often clinal in nature, that is, expressed as gradations. Yet some traits appear

**BOX 17-1**

# Skeletal Evidence of Cultural Practices

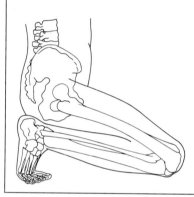

While many alterations of the human body are deliberate, many other changes in anatomy are nondeliberate side effects of cultural practices. For example, humans in all cultures habitually assume particular resting postures. In adulthood, the postures learned in child-hood have become normal and comfortable. Postures encountered in other cultures may prove difficult and often painful to assume and may permanently affect the anatomy.

D. H. Ubelaker excavated a large number of skeletons at Hacienda Ayalan on the southern coast of Ecuador. On analysis, he found that many of the bones of the foot, specifically the metatarsals and the phalanges (see the appendix), showed several unusual features such as small bony extensions.

Analysis of the Ecuadoran skeletons suggests that the unique features in the foot skeleton developed from the stresses produced from frequent and extreme hyperdorsiflexion of the metatarsophalangeal joints. The figure illustrates this extreme backward movement of the joints between the metatarsal bones of the ankle and the phalanges of the toes.

This movement would result from the individual's assuming a kneeling position with the weight of the body pressing down on the joints within the foot. Since these features are found most frequently in female skeletons, Ubelaker suggests that this body position was assumed by women as they ground maize on stone metates. Thus, whether describing skeletal material or a living human body, anthropologists must know whether they are dealing with genetic traits, environmentally produced features, or cultural modifications of some genetically determined trait.

*Source:* D. H. Ubelaker, "Skeletal Evidence for Kneeling in Prehistoric Ecuador," *American Journal of Physical Anthropology* 51 (1979), pp. 679–686.

almost exclusively within one or a few populations. These traits are said to show a distribution that is discontinuous.

Humans differ in their anatomy, physiology, ontogeny, and culture. Except for culture, which is by definition learned, all these factors can have a genetic component. In many instances, the environment also plays a powerful role in creating variation. In fact, it would be more accurate to say that human morphology (form) and behavior are products of the dynamic interaction between cultural, biological, and environmental variables. Because the relationship between these variables is dynamic, the differences between human groups are in a constant state of flux. For any particular trait, two groups may become more or less similar to each other at different times, depending on the particular situations.

## THE CLASSIFICATION OF HUMAN VARIATION

People are natural classifiers. They see nature as being composed of types of things rather than individual entities. If every rock, tree, or animal had a unique label attached to it, effective communication would be impossible. So people speak in categories; they talk of igneous rocks, pine trees, and mammals.

Each group of people classifies the world around it. Any human group has an answer to the question "What kinds of rocks, trees, or animals are there?" but the categories expressed by people do not necessarily describe the world as seen by objective science. These categories reflect specific cultural traditions and differ from society to society. Anthropologists refer to such classifications as **folk taxonomies.**

Categorization or classification is necessary in everyday communication as well as in science. Without the ability to generalize, conversation would be difficult and laws and theories could not exist. Nevertheless, folk taxonomies do not always correspond to reality. When the inaccuracies apply to categorizations of people, they often mirror hatred and mistrust.

## Folk Taxonomies of Race

In coping with the world, people visualize human variation in terms of categories. The simplest type of classification is one in which a particular people will classify themselves as "human" and everyone else as "less than human." For instance, the Navahos call themselves *diné*, which, roughly translated, means "the people." This label implies "a strong sense of difference and isolation from the rest of humanity."[2] This frequently encountered type of conceptualization also existed among the ancient Greeks, who divided humankind into two categories, Greeks and barbarians. Some Greeks believed that the barbarians just made noises or babbled. Today we play a reversal on the Greeks with the saying, "It's all Greek to me."

In urban centers, and to a lesser degree elsewhere, a person encounters daily a variety of people of different statures, skin colors, and facial features. If people at an American suburban shopping center were asked to list the different types of people in the world, the most frequent answers would probably be Caucasoid, Mongoloid, and Negroid; or Black, Brown, Yellow, Red, and White; or African American, Indian or Native American, Hispanic, and Asian; or some other combination of terms (Figure 17–5).

Such classifications are examples of folk taxonomies that reflect how many Americans perceive human differences. Do they also reflect reality? The answer is both yes and no. Folk taxonomies do have a social reality in that many forms of behavior are determined by them. In a situation requiring interaction with another person, an American may behave differently if the other individual is perceived as "Hispanic" or "African American." On the other hand, physical anthropologists deal with biological reality, and here folk taxonomies just do not reflect what we know about human variation.

Few Americans have seen aboriginal peoples from remote regions of the world, such as the Ainu, the Australian aborigine, the San, or the Lapp. Most Americans have contact primarily with peoples whose origins are in Europe, the Middle East, West Africa, Latin America, and parts of Asia, particularly Japan, China, and southeast Asia. A person who looks somewhat different from the people normally encountered is forced into an existing category. Thus, American soldiers during World War II often classified the Melanesians of the western Pacific as "Negro" even though there was no direct genetic link with the peoples of the African continent.

## Anthropological Classifications of Human Variation

"Races do not exist; classifications of mankind do."[3] Scientific classifications of people, like folk taxonomies of people, are attempts to divide human beings into specific groups, but this is where the similarity ends.

A scientific classification is a means of discovering the processes that create the phenomenon being classified, in this case, human variation. A scientific classification of human variation would be a model serving a function similar to that of other scientific models, such as the Hardy-Weinberg formula. This formula is a way of discovering whether forces of evolution are working on a population. Similarly, a classification of human variation should be a way of discovering the processes involved in creating human genotypic and phenotypic variation.

Folk taxonomies are usually based on ethnocentric ideas about the inherent differences in physical appearance and behavior between groups. Although some of these beliefs may be partially based on observation, most are based on folklore or

---

[2]C. Kluckhohn and D. Leighton, *The Navaho*, rev. ed. (New York: Doubleday, 1962), p. 23.

[3]G. A. Dorsey, "Race and Civilization," in C. A. Beard (ed.), *Whither Mankind: A Panorama of Modern Civilization* (New York: Longmans, Green, 1928), p. 254.

(a)

(b)

(c)

**FIGURE 17–5  Four American Racial Stereotypes**
(a) Jay Silverheels as Tonto in *The Lone Ranger*, (b) Warner Oland as "Charlie Chan," and (c) Hattie McDaniel and Vivian Leigh in *Gone with the Wind*.

stereotypes. In contrast, the criteria used in scientific classification must be derived from empirical studies. In other words, the attributing of different characteristics to different populations must be validated through procedures of the scientific method.

**Attempts at Scientific Classification**

Carolus Linnaeus (1707–1778) was perhaps the first person to apply systematic criteria in a uniform way in classifying humans. His contribution, the first scientific taxonomy of the living world, included people. Linnaeus labeled all humans *Homo sapiens*, from *Homo*, meaning "man," and *sapiens*, meaning "wise." He then divided the human species into four groups based on the criteria of skin color, geographical location, and personality traits.

These four categories are *H. sapiens Africanus negreus* (black), *H. sapiens Americanus rubescens* (red), *H. sapiens Asiaticus fucus* (darkish), and *H. sapiens Europeus albescens* (white).

Among scientists, this classification did not stand the test of time. For one thing, it excluded many peoples. Where were the peoples of Oceania, India, and other areas to be placed? Could it legitimately be said that all peoples of Africa had the same skin color? North Africans are light-skinned; the San of south Africa are brownish-yellow; and the Bantu are dark. While Linnaeus's general system of classification of plants and animals was readily adopted by the scientific community, his classification of people was not. Nevertheless, his notion of four races is still used by many Europeans and Americans.

**Nineteenth-Century Classification** Johann Friedrich Blumenbach (1752–1840) was a German physician and student of comparative human anatomy. He divided the human species into five "races": *Caucasian, Mongolian, Ethiopian, Malayan,* and *American.* The term *Ethiopian* was later changed to *Negro.*

Anders Retzius (1796–1860) noted many variations within the five types proposed by Blumenbach. Deciding that the shape of the head was an important criterion for classifying people, Retzius developed the cephalic index as a means of comparing populations. The **cephalic index** is the breadth of the head relative to the length, as given by the formula

$$\frac{\text{Head breadth}}{\text{Head length}} \times 100$$

These early attempts set up two criteria for the classification of human variation: outward physical characteristics and geographical origin. The measurements made and the indices calculated led to classifications that were wholly descriptive in nature. They did not explain the process that created the observed variations. Often the classifications arrived at did not appear to fit the real world, as when members of the same family were placed into different "races" on the basis of the criteria used.

**Use of Blood Types in Classification** With the development of genetic theory, anthropologists began to question the use of the traditional criteria of classification. Skin color, they argued, was a poor standard, since its mechanism of inheritance is unknown and it is affected by environment and culture. Therefore, some anthropologists turned to the blood-type systems as a basis for classification. Blood type is easy to determine; in most cases, blood-typing can be done in the field. A given blood type is either present or absent, and it is not affected by environmental factors. Finally, the mechanisms of inheritance of blood types are, for the most part, known.

William Boyd published in 1950 the following classification based on an analysis of the frequencies of specific blood types: (1) *Early European* (hypothetical category, represented today only by the Basques of Spain), (2) *European* (Caucasoid), (3) *African* (Negroid), (4) *Asiatic* (Mongoloid), (5) *American Indian,* and (6) *Australoid.*[4]

Boyd defined these categories on the basis of blood-type frequencies. For example, he defined the European group in terms of a high frequency of Rh-negative and $A_2$, one of the two major varieties of blood-type A. The Asiatic group, however, was characterized by a low frequency of Rh-negative and $A_2$ but a high frequency of $A_1$ and a variety of Rh-positive, $Rh_2$.[5]

The basic problem with this method is that clearly defined categories do not always emerge. Although it is possible to generalize for a large geographical area, specific groups often deviate from this generalization. For instance, most Native Americans show a high frequency of blood-type O; the Cherokee are 96 percent O, and the Chippewa are 88 percent. However, the Blackfeet show an O frequency of only about 25 percent.[6]

On the other hand, specific populations from different parts of the world can show similar blood-type frequencies. For example, the frequencies of blood-types O, A, B, and AB for the Atayal of Taiwan are 45.2, 32.6, 17.1, and 5.1 percent, respectively. The same frequencies for a population from Macedonia, Greece, are 45.2, 32.3, 19.3, and 3.2 percent.[7] Although their blood-type frequencies are very similar, these two populations clearly belong to different categories on the basis of geography and physical appearance. Are we therefore to say that the Blackfeet are not Native Americans because the frequencies of their blood types deviate from those of most other Native Americans? Are we to place the Atayal and Macedonians in the same group purely on the basis of similarity of blood types?

A major problem with the use of blood-type frequencies as the sole criterion for categorizing of human populations is that most of these frequencies

---

[4]W. C. Boyd, *Genetics and the Races of Man* (Boston: Little, Brown, 1956).
[5]Ibid., p. 268.
[6]A. E. Mourant, A. C. Kopeč, and K. Domaniewska-Sobczak, *The Distribution of the Human Blood Groups and Other Polymorphisms,* 2nd ed. (London: Oxford University Press, 1976). Figures for Native Americans are for groups with no known, or minimal, gene flow from Europeans.
[7]Ibid.

show a clinal distribution. Although major differences may exist in two populations from either end of the cline, this distinctiveness is blurred by subtle differences in frequencies in intermediate populations.

**Classification and the Fossil Record**   To some people, there are a fixed number of categories of people that correspond to basic divisions from the remote past. A classification based on the fossil record is that of Carlton S. Coon, who, in his 1962 book *The Origin of Races,* divided the human species into five categories: *Australoids, Mongoloids, Caucasoids, Congoids* (dark-skinned Africans), and *Capoids* (the San and Hottentots of southern Africa).[8]

Coon postulated that humankind separated into his five divisions before the evolution of our species, *Homo sapiens.* To him, human fossils represented early stages in this pre-*sapiens* development. An early fossil found in Java would be an early Australoid, while a fossil from China would be an early Mongoloid, and so on. Coon also proposed that hominids in each of the five evolutionary lines evolved into *Homo sapiens* at different times and, hence, different living races have developed on a *Homo sapiens*–level for differing amounts of time, which accounts for differences in cultural development. This clearly racist conclusion is not consistent with the evidence.

In Chapter 15, we discussed the regional continuity model of human evolution that links certain finds with contemporary populations. The problem with such links, however, is that human variation does not follow clear-cut evolutionary lines. Gene flow between adjacent groups and migrations serve to confuse such lines. While distinct populations may have existed among human ancestors, it is extremely unlikely that such groups maintained themselves as distinct entities over long periods of evolution.

**Geographical Races**   Another approach to the classification of human variation is the 1961 scheme of Stanley Garn.[9] He observed that people living in the same large geographical area tend to resemble one another more closely than they do people in different geographical areas. Of course, this is a generalization with many exceptions. Garn divided the human species into nine large **geographical races.** Geography alone is the major criterion for classification, not some arbitrarily chosen trait such as skin color, blood type, or cephalic index. Since gene flow does take place more frequently within a major geographical zone than between adjacent zones, populations in the same major geographical areas will generally show some similar gene frequencies.

Garn's nine geographical human races are (1) *Amerindian* (the aboriginal inhabitants of North and South America), (2) *Asiatic,* (3) *Australian,* (4) *Melanesian* (peoples of New Guinea and neighboring islands), (5) *Micronesian* (peoples of the islands of the northwest Pacific), (6) *Polynesian,* (7) *Indian* (peoples of the subcontinent of India), (8) *African,* and (9) *European.*

Garn divided these large geographical races into a series of **local races,** which are of two basic types. The first type consists of distinctive, partially isolated groups, usually remnants of once-larger units. Examples used by Garn include the Ainu of Japan and the San of southern Africa. Much larger local races make up the second basic type. Large local races are not as isolated as small ones, and a greater degree of gene flow occurs between them. An example of a large local race is the northwestern European.

Considerable variation exists within larger local races. If allele frequencies within the northwestern European local race are mapped, for example, constant changes in frequencies often are found as we travel in a particular direction—a clinal distribution exists. Garn divided the large local races into several small units called **microraces.** Microraces are arbitrary divisions of large local races. Precise boundaries cannot be drawn, and specific individuals within one microrace may look more like members of another microrace than like each other. Still, one fact remains: people living in the same community tend to mate more frequently with one another than with individuals of other communities.

**The Changing Nature of Human Variation**   Human variation is dynamic, and the shape of clines

---

[8]C. S. Coon, *The Origin of Races* (New York: Knopf, 1962).
[9]S. M. Garn, *Human Races* (Springfield, Ill.: Charles C. Thomas, 1961).

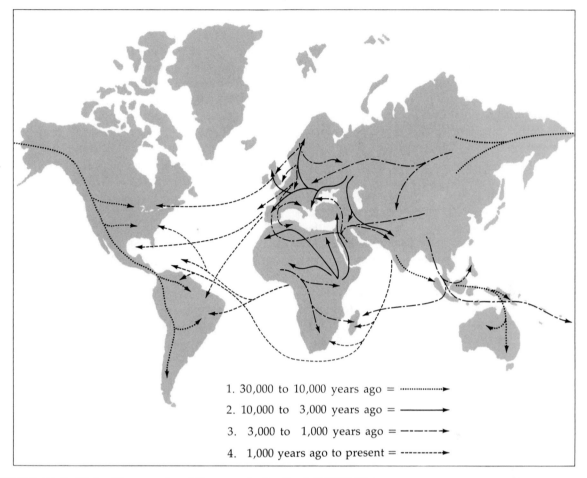

1. 30,000 to 10,000 years ago = ···············▶
2. 10,000 to 3,000 years ago = ───────▶
3. 3,000 to 1,000 years ago = ─ ─ ─ ─▶
4. 1,000 years ago to present = ‐‐‐‐‐‐‐‐▶

**FIGURE 17–6   Major Movements of Humans in the Last 30,000 Years**

is constantly changing. Old populations are broken down, and new ones are established. Between 1845 and 1854, 3 million people migrated to the United States. Between 1881 and 1920, 23½ million people entered the United States from such countries as Great Britain, Italy, Germany, Spain, Russia, Portugal, and Sweden. Some of these people formed partial isolates, such as Germans in Pennsylvania, Welsh in upper New York, and Scandinavians in Wisconsin and Minnesota.

The U.S. Immigration and Naturalization Service reported that in 1996, about 915,900 persons legally immigrated to the United States. In that one year, 163,572 immigrated from Mexico, 55,876 from the Philippines, 44,859 from India, 42,067 from Viet-

nam, and 41,728 from China. The balance represented virtually every geographic area of the world. With each migration, the gene pool is reconstituted, and hence a description of the people in a geographical area at one specific time may not hold at another time (Figure 17–6).

## The Genetic Relationship between Human Populations

We discussed earlier the work of William Boyd, who used blood-type frequencies in developing a classification of human races. His was an early attempt to employ the study of human variation on the molecular level. Since the 1950s, great progress has been made in the analysis of molecular variation. Now, both nuclear and mitochondrial DNA can be studied directly. The methodologies that have been developed for such studies have provided scientists with a wealth of data for studying the genetic relationships among populations.

Two important conclusions can be drawn from the molecular data. First, the average genetic differences between geographically separated human populations are fewer than the genetic differences within a single population. Second, because of the relatively small number of genetic differences among geographically separated populations, these populations should not be assigned to separate subspecies. The differences in human populations are fewer than those that zoologists consider significant enough to separate nonhuman species into subspecies.

In 1988, Luigi Luca Cavalli-Sforza and his colleagues collected published data on gene frequencies from 42 aboriginal populations of Africa, North and South America, Oceania, Europe, and Asia.[10] They then constructed a genetic tree that diagramed these genetic relationships. A tree showing the relationships among 38 populations is shown in Figure 17–7.

According to this study, the 42 human populations may be separated into two large divisions. The first contains the Africans; the second may be broken down into two major groupings: the north Eurasians and the southeast Asians.

The north Eurasian "supercluster" includes the Caucasoids, a group comprising the peoples of Europe, north Africa, southwest Asia, and India. A major subdivision includes two further groupings. The first includes the peoples of northeast Asia, such as the Mongols, Tibetans, Japanese, Arctic peoples of Asia, and the Inuit of the North American Arctic. The second grouping includes the aboriginal peoples of North and South America.

The second major "supercluster" is that of the southeast Asians. This group includes the peoples of mainland and insular southeast Asia, such as those of Thailand, Indonesia, Malaya, and the

Philippines; the peoples of the Pacific islands, including those of Polynesia, Micronesia, and Melanesia; and the peoples of Australia.

This study does not attempt to develop a classification of human populations per se; rather, it attempts to determine the genetic relationships among these populations. Linguistic models on the distance between groups generally correspond to the genetic data. Two linguistic superfamilies show very close correspondence with the two major divisions based on genetic data markers.

## The Nature of Human Variation and Its Classification

In traditional systems of classification, arbitrary traits are often used to divide humankind into a finite number of groups. When 1, 2, or 20 traits are used in such classifications, the underlying assumption is that groups so classified will be different from each other in traits not used in the classification. This is not necessarily true. If another set of traits is used, the classification might be different. The species *H. sapiens* is a collection of thousands of characteristics. Isolating the variation between groups for a few of these characteristics does not explain all similarities and differences or even a small portion of them. Also, when a trait shows continuous gradation, the point at which the cline is broken into two groups becomes arbitrary.

Many populations that resemble each other in one way differ in other respects. This is illustrated in Table 17–3. Here we see the frequencies of phenylthiocarbamide (PTC) nontasting, blood-type B, lactase deficiency (an enzyme required to break down lactose, or milk sugar), and sickle-cell trait and anemia. With respect to PTC nontasting and lactase deficiency, west Africans are closest to South American Indians; yet, in relation to sickle-cell anemia, west Africans are closest to Greeks.

**Do Human Races Exist?** The answer to this question depends on what is meant by "race" and by "exist." People certainly act toward other people in specific ways that depend on perceptions of how those other people fit into stereotyped groups called "races." However, this only means that "races" exist in a social sense.

Do races exist in a biological sense? The answer to this question is unequivocably no. No one de-

---

[10]L. L. Cavalli-Sforza et al., "Reconstruction of Human Evolution: Bringing Together Genetic, Archaeological, and Linguistic Data," *Proceedings of the National Academy of Sciences* 85 (1988), pp. 6002–6006.

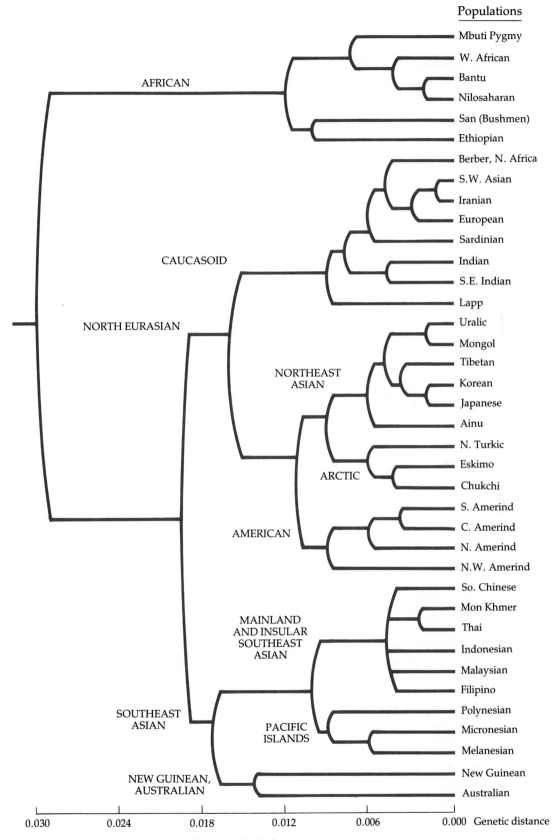

**Populations**

Mbuti Pygmy
W. African
Bantu
Nilosaharan
San (Bushmen)
Ethiopian
Berber, N. Africa
S.W. Asian
Iranian
European
Sardinian
Indian
S.E. Indian
Lapp
Uralic
Mongol
Tibetan
Korean
Japanese
Ainu
N. Turkic
Eskimo
Chukchi
S. Amerind
C. Amerind
N. Amerind
N.W. Amerind
So. Chinese
Mon Khmer
Thai
Indonesian
Malaysian
Filipino
Polynesian
Micronesian
Melanesian
New Guinean
Australian

AFRICAN

CAUCASOID

NORTH EURASIAN

NORTHEAST
ASIAN

ARCTIC

AMERICAN

MAINLAND
AND INSULAR
SOUTHEAST
ASIAN

SOUTHEAST
ASIAN

PACIFIC
ISLANDS

NEW GUINEAN,
AUSTRALIAN

0.030        0.024        0.018        0.012        0.006        0.000   Genetic distance

**FIGURE 17-7  Genetic Tree Showing Human Variation**

## TABLE 17-3

### COMPARISON OF TRAITS IN FIVE POPULATIONS*

| Trait | Population | | | | |
| --- | --- | --- | --- | --- | --- |
| | South American Native | West African | English | Japanese | Greek |
| PTC nontasting[†] | 1.2 | 2.7 | 31.5 | 7.1 | |
| Blood-type B[‡] | 0–5 | 15–20 | 5–10 | 20–25 | 10–15 |
| Lactase deficiency[§] | Up to 100 | Up to 100 | 32 | 90 | 88 |
| Sickle-cell trait and anemia[¶] | Up to 16 | Up to 34 | 0 | 0 | Up to 32 |

*Data are expressed in average percentages.
[†]G. A. Harrison et al., *Human Biology* (New York: Oxford University Press, 1964), p. 274.
[‡]A. E. Mourant, A. C. Kopeč, and K. Domaniewska-Sobczak, *The Distribution of the Human Blood Groups and Other Polymorphisms,* 2nd ed. (London: Oxford University Press, 1976).
[§]See Robert D. McCracken, "Lactase Deficiency: An Example of Dietary Evolution," *Current Anthropology* 12 (1971), pp. 479–517; and Norman Kretchner, "Lactose and Lactase," *Scientific American* 277 (October 1972), p. 76.
[¶]Frank B. Livingstone, *Abnormal Hemoglobins in Human Populations* (Chicago: Aldine, 1967), pp. 162–470.

bates the existence of human variation—that certainly does exist. Yet analysis of the evidence leads us to the inescapable conclusion that we cannot divide the human species into a finite number of groups, each having a label attached to it and representing a bounded gene pool. The best we can do is to describe human variation in terms of distribution and the adaptive significance of specific traits.

Because human variation is so complex and dynamic, it is not subject to categorization. Just as not all phenomena are amenable to empirical study, perhaps not all things can be organized into neat categories that have explanatory potentials. An approach that looks at each trait individually is more logical and explanatory in light of what we do know about human variation. It would facilitate the description of the distribution, clinal or discontinuous, of each trait and the generation of hypotheses regarding the reasons for the distribution that is observed. Are natural selective forces at work? To what degree is sampling error responsible for the distribution? What contributions do nonrandom mating patterns make to the establishment of the distribution in question?

### The Politics of "Race"

The exploration of differences between human groups is a valid scientific pursuit. However, history is filled with examples of genocide, slavery, and discrimination based, in part, on false notions of bi-

ological differences between peoples. Any examination of the relationship of human biological variation and differences in behavior is sure to cause controversy. A proposed 1992 conference on "Genetic Factors in Crime" was cancelled because of fears that certain populations might be labeled as biologically more prone toward crime than others. At the annual meeting of the American Association of Physical Anthropologists in 1995, a session on human variation turned emotional as participants argued over whether or not the Human Genome Diversity Project would reinforce the false idea that some populations are "purer" than others. These and other concerns make it difficult to make any conclusions about human variation without being accused of having some political motive.

As controversial as delving into the nature of human biological diversity is, there is general consensus that the idea of a fixed number of groups has not been fruitful, and it is the wrong way to approach the subject. Not only has this approach failed to explain most human variation, but it has allowed people to conclude, erroneously, that a group different for a few traits must be different for a large number of traits. Such conclusions have been stated in several popular books, including *The Bell Curve,* published in 1994.[11] These conclusions,

---

[11]R. Herrnstein and C. Murray, *The Bell Curve: Intelligence and Class Structure in American Life* (New York: Free Press, 1994).

in turn, have led to judgments concerning the superiority or inferiority of particular populations. These judgments are not based on empirical data, as scientific conclusions must be. The following sections deal with this error and with the idea mentioned at the beginning of this discussion—the social "reality" of race.

**Race and Intelligence**    There have been great debates over the relationship between race or ethnic affiliation and intelligence. In the early part of this century, the focus of this question was on the relative intelligence of members of ethnic groups, such as the Poles, Greeks, Italians, and Jews, who were entering the United States in great numbers. Immigrant populations were extensively tested during World War I, and they were consistently found to average about 20 points lower than the national average on IQ tests. By the 1970s, the descendants of these immigrants were scoring at the national level or higher. It has become obvious to researchers that the early low scores were due primarily to environmental and cultural factors, such as malnutrition, language difficulties, and lack of experience with tests and the types of questions being asked.

**Race and Intelligence Testing**    Psychological testing in the United States is big business. Yet intelligence or IQ testing has been under attack for a variety of reasons. During most of the twentieth century, intelligence has been equated with IQ score, and the results of IQ tests show that different ethnic groups have different average scores. For instance, people socially classified as "African Americans" score about 15 points lower on the average than do "whites." Is this difference due to environmental causes or differences in innate potentials?

IQ tests use symbols that are common within the particular culture that develops the test. The test is said to be **culture-bound.** This means that if the test has relevance at all, it would have relevance only for members of the culture that uses the language and general concepts employed in the test.

As an example, most Americans may think that the question illustrated in Figure 17–8 is a perfectly logical one to ask. Yet making the correct choice in the time given depends on previous experience. If

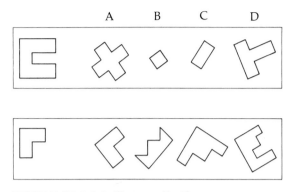

**FIGURE 17–8 Intelligence Testing**
This is an example of a test for the measurement of spatial ability. The subject is asked to mark the drawing that will make a complete square with the first figure. Speed is important. This type of test would be extremely difficult for members of a society in which geometric shapes are not utilized to the same degree as in U.S. society.

this question were given to Australian aborigine trackers, for example, who had little or no contact with the concepts of two-dimensional geometry, they would probably answer it incorrectly because of their lack of experience with the things pictured. On the other hand, if a city-dwelling American were asked to identify if a set of footprints were made by a man or a woman, an adult or a child, he or she would probably fail where the Australian tracker would succeed.

Verbal exams are equally biased. In one of these, a battery of questions is asked, such as the name of the person who wrote *Faust*. The answer to this, Goethe (Gounod wrote the opera), might be familiar to children who emigrated from Germany or who have German parents. Or it might be known by a college student who enrolled in world literature as opposed to one who enrolled in English literature. Going one step further, the upper-middle-class teenager who does not have to work after school to help support his or her family may spend leisure time reading. A person from a poor family who must work may have no time or motivation to read books. Also, a poor family may simply maintain a household without books.

On the same test, by the way, is the question: What is ethnology? Ethnology is a branch of anthropology, but the answer given as correct for this question conforms to none of the modern anthropological definitions of this term.[12] In other words, an incorrect response might be marked "correct"! The point is that these tests are biased toward "white" middle-class experiences; in some cases, the answers expected by the testers are grounded in the middle-class experience.

In the light of the preceding observations, one can easily see why various ethnic groups in the United States tend to score, on the average, lower than "whites" on standard IQ tests. These tests embody questions that are considered important to the "white" middle-class population. In fact, such commonly used tests as the Stanford-Binet were standardized by using "white" subjects only, "with no explanation about this on the part of the authors."[13]

IQ tests emphasize mathematical manipulation, a subject to which middle-class children usually are exposed early in life. Their parents may have been to college, and many of these children have had early preschool experience as well. In lower socioeconomic communities, the parents often had to go to work early in life; few have gone to college. Thus, mathematical logic is both less important and less attainable to them. Such parents often do not value the existing educational systems because they do not see the schools as helpful in preparing their children for jobs or in providing social mobility. As a result, children from lower socioeconomic groups often do not attend preschool. In addition, vocabulary and other dialect differences exist between social classes, ethnic groups, and regions of the country. Lower IQ scores often reflect a lack of understanding of the question because of the way in which it is worded.

Another important point is that even when comparisons are made between ethnic groups in the United States with differing lifestyles and experiences, the differences in IQ scores within each group greatly exceed the differences between groups. Whereas the scores of people from the same ethnic group might differ by 50 points or more, the averages of two different groups might vary by

only about a dozen or so points. This means that many members of one population will individually score either higher or lower than the average score of another population.

Little evidence exists to suggest that the average differences in IQ scores that are observed between groups are due to innate differences. Richard Herrnstein and Charles Murray in *The Bell Curve* state that such innate differences do exist. They point out that "African Americans" who have attained middle-class or higher economic status on the average score higher than lower socioeconomic class "African Americans" and "whites." Yet these middle-class "African Americans" still on the average score lower than middle-class "whites."

People matched for economic status, however, are not necessarily matched for other social dimensions. "African Americans" as a social group have had very different social experiences in the United States than have "whites" who have not suffered prejudice and discrimination. The behaviors and values most inducive to creating children with high IQ scores might be less frequently found in "African American" and other minority groups, even if they have attained middle or higher economic status. Cross-culturally, it can be shown that economic status is correlated with IQ scores.

**The Many Dimensions of Intelligence**  IQ scores tell us little or nothing about a person's creative, social, musical, or artistic talents. Intelligence as tested by an IQ test leaves us with an imprecise and culture-bound definition of intelligence. Howard Gardner believes that there are several relatively separate types of intelligence, including linguistic, musical, logical-mathematical, spatial (the perception and recreation of the visual world), bodily-kinesthetic (skill in handling objects), and personal (skill, for instance, that gives "access of one's own feelings").[14]

Robert Sternberg believes that intelligence is exercised in three areas. Contextual intelligence guides a person in selecting the appropriate envi-

[12]M. L. Moerman, "Ethnology, the Dictionary, and IQ," *Anthropology Newsletter* 16 (May 1975), p. 24.
[13]J. Ryan, "IQ, the Illusion of Objectivity," in K. Richardson and D. Spears (eds.), *Race and Intelligence* (Baltimore: Pelican, 1972), p. 53.

[14]H. Gardner, *Frames of Mind: The Theory of Multiple Intelligence* (New York: Basic Books, 1983); and W. Winn, "New Views of Human Intelligence," *New York Times Magazine,* special section, April 29, 1990, p. 16.

BOX 17-2

# Are the Japanese, on the Average, Smarter than American?

In October of 1986, Yasuhiro Nakasone, prime minister of Japan, offered an explanation of why Japan competes so well against the United States: the Japanese people score higher on IQ tests than Americans. Indeed, the mean national IQ score in Japan is about 111 as compared to 100 in the United States. Nakasone's remark seems to suggest a belief in a connection between race and intelligence. Nakasone seems to be blaming the differences in scores on innate factors. In examining Japanese culture, no innate factors need be postulated to explain the 11-point IQ-score advantage that the Japanese appear to display.

Here are some reasons that could explain the differences in average scores between Japanese and Americans.

1. Japanese children attend school for an average of 240 days a year; American children attend school for less than 180 days a year.
2. The quality of education is uniformly high in Japan. Most Japanese are of the same social class, and about 99 percent are of the same ethnic group.
3. Discipline and expectations of students in Japan are much greater than in the United States.
4. Japanese students are assigned heavier course loads and more homework than their American counterparts.
5. Economic success in Japan is absolutely dependent on academic achievement. Although academic achievement increases the chances of economic success in the United States, it is not absolutely essential.
6. Almost all Japanese value education. The consequences of dropping out of school are extremely negative. Only 2 percent of Japanese high school seniors drop out of school as compared to 27 percent of the high school seniors in the United States.

It is therefore no wonder that mean IQ scores are higher in Japan than in the United States. The Japanese place a greater value on education. As a result, Japanese children take educational goals more seriously and spend more time in school and on homework than American children. The differences in average IQ scores between groups labeled as different races or ethnic groups in the United States are most likely also due to a mix of sociocultural factors rather than innate differences.

Even though the American mean IQ is not as high as that of the Japanese, Americans are responsible for innovating more of this century's new technologies than any other nationality and they have won more Nobel Prizes than the members of any other culture. IQ scores do not test such things as creativity. American society emphasizes creativity.

*Sources:* E. Brown, "Nakasone's World-Class Blunder," *Time,* October 6, 1986, pp. 66–67; "A Racial Slur Stirs Up a Storm," *Newsweek,* October 6, 1986, p. 35; T. Watanabe, "Cookie-Cutter Education," *Los Angeles Times,* June 24, 1990, pp. D10–D11.

ronments in which to be and in adapting to environments. Experiential intelligence is the ability to confront new situations on the basis of previous experiences. And internal intelligence is the ability to plan, monitor, and change an approach to solving a problem.[15] Both Gardner and Sternberg agree that intelligence is more than a single score on a single type of test.

**Race and Cultural Capabilities** It's believed by some that the non-European peoples are incapable of developing civilizations. The term *civilization* is like the term *culture:* everyone has a different idea of what it is. It is beyond the scope of this text to discuss the various schools of thought on the subject. Instead, let us define it in terms of the common elements in most definitions. Civilization usually implies technological complexities, such as a large number and variety of artifacts, often including monumental architecture, metallurgy, and a body of "scientific" knowledge. Most important, it implies complex social arrangements, such as occupational specialization, centralized governments, religious and political hierarchies, social classes, and codes of law and conduct. In civilizations, the individual becomes subject to regulations of a state, whereas in noncivilizations, the family (including extensions of the family, such as clans) is the single most important regulating agent.

[15]R. Sternberg, *Beyond IQ: A Triachic Theory of Human Intelligence* (New York: Cambridge University Press, 1985).

Civilization arose in areas characterized by a maximum of trade and movement of people, which provided for the diffusion of artifacts and ideas. Because innovation is basically a recombination of things existing in a society into new forms, as the number of elements increases in a society, the rate of innovation increases. The cart could not have been invented if the wheel did not already exist.

Civilizations did not arise in central Africa because the terrain was not suitable for quick movement of people or goods. The rivers of this area are not navigable because of great fault systems that create rapids along their courses. Restricted travel; a hot, humid climate; dense vegetation; and endemic disease, not innate inferiority, hampered the early development of civilization in the Congo Basin. Yet in areas of Africa where these conditions did not exist, early civilizations did arise and spread into the forest areas. The empires of Ghana, Kanem-Bornu, Mali, and Songhai rose to greatness when their goods were traded throughout the world. The people involved were not members of the "white race."

**Are There "Pure Races"?**  The assertion that some races are "purer" than others, which Hitler used to justify the killing of millions of people, is not validated by any factual data. People are spread over an extremely large area, and physical variation exists in all directions without extensive discontinuities. Through gene flow and migration or invasion, all areas of the world are constantly interchanging genes. This may be an extremely slow process, as in the case of the Australian aborigine, or a very dynamic process, as in Europe.

The picture of human variation is a constantly changing one. Since no two people are alike through time and space, the same is true of human populations. If we were to move back in time 10,000 years, the people inhabiting the earth would not fall into the groupings or clinal patterns of today. Even today, certain groups, such as the Ainu and the San, are changing, primarily through intermarriage with other groups. New groups are emerging.

Those Americans labeled as "African American" are in many ways dissimilar to the African populations from which some of their ancestors came. Estimates indicate that today's African American gene pool contains between 20 and 30 percent European and Native American alleles. This is seen in the statistics for such traits as lactase deficiency. The Africans who were brought to America came from such groups as the Yoruba and the Ibo of west Africa, groups that display close to 100 percent lactase deficiency. African Americans, on the other hand, are only 70 percent lactase-deficient. This is partially due to the flow of northern European genes into this population's gene pool. In addition, a limited number of Native American genes have entered gene pools that are derived predominantly from Africa and Europe. On the other side of the coin, the groups in the United States generally classified as "white" have a certain frequency of genes within their gene pools that are derived from African, Native American, Asiatic, and other non-European sources. As we have emphasized throughout this chapter, human gene pools are always being reconstituted; there are no stable divisions of *Homo sapiens*.

## Summary

People are socially classified into "races" that do not correspond to biological facts. Folk taxonomies of race are frequently linked to ideas of superiority and inferiority, and they serve as justification for the socioeconomic stratification that benefits the ruling group. It is easier to subject a group to harsh and unjust treatment if the people in it are relegated to a completely different ancestry and if they are portrayed as being inferior.

While anthropologists have become more realistic about the nature of human variability, people in general still use the simplistic division of humankind into a small number of stereotyped "races." This section has discussed the problems that concern race as a social category. Race has often been correlated with differences in intelligence and cultural capabilities. Upon examination, these differences either are not supported by factual data or, where they do exist, are not traceable to genetic components.

In the case of intelligence, an additional problem exists. There is no consensus on just what intelligence is—so how can it be measured? In the 1980s, new ideas about the nature of intelligence were proposed by investigators who were generally critical of IQ-type intelligence tests. We conclude that behavioral differences between peoples are almost always the result of cultural influences. Nevertheless, a genetic component may be involved in such things as the linearity of the Nilotes, which facilitates spear throwing. Researching the heritability of human traits is a legitimate activity of scientists, but as in any research, the variables must be carefully defined and controlled.

## STUDY QUESTIONS

1. What factors are responsible for the clinal nature of the distribution of some traits? Why are the distributions of many traits discontinuous?
2. What are some characteristics of mammals that are generally found to be distributed in a clinal manner?
3. In what ways are folk taxonomies different from scientific classifications?
4. Briefly describe the ideas on racial classification of Carolus Linnaeus, Johann Friedrich Blumenbach, William Boyd, and Carlton S. Coon.
5. Many people classify "races" on the basis of a single criterion, such as skin color. What are the inherent dangers of using only one or a few criteria to classify human populations?
6. What do your textbook authors conclude about the nature of human variation?
7. A legitimate scientific pursuit is the exploration of possible intellectual differences between groups. Explain why IQ and other standardized tests are not good measures of the comparative intelligence of different populations.
8. Many writers have correlated the origin of civilization with the "white race." Why is this a false correlation?

## SUGGESTED READINGS

Two general texts in the field of human biological variation are

Brues, A. *People and Races,* 2nd ed. Prospect Heights, Ill.: Waveland, 1990.
Molnar, S. *Human Variation: Race, Type, and Ethnic Groups,* 4th ed. Englewood Cliffs, N.J.: Prentice Hall, 1998.
The *American Anthropologist,* volume 100 (September 1998), contains a series of articles on the concept of race.

The following books deal with intelligence and intelligence testing:

Gould, S. J. *The Mismeasure of Man,* rev. ed. New York: Norton, 1996.
Sternberg, R., and W. M. Williams (eds.) *Intelligence, Instruction, and Assessment: Theory into Practice.* Hillsdale, N.J.: Lawrence Erlbaum Associates, 1999.

Additional books that deal with human variation are

Cavalli-Sforza, L. L., P. Menozzi, and A. Piazza. *The History and Geography of Human Genes.* Princeton, N.J.: Princeton University Press, 1994. Using genetic, geographic, archaeological, ecological, anthropological, and linguistic data, the authors attempt to reconstruct the origin and evolution of human populations. This 1,032-page book is a detailed analysis of human variation—and it is not without its critics.
Harding, S. (ed.) *The "Racial" Economy of Science: Toward a Democratic Future.* Bloomington, Ind.: Indiana University, 1993. This book is a group of essays that deal with a number of issues on race, including how Western science has contributed to racist ideas.
Jenkins, J. B. *Human Genetics,* 2nd ed. New York: Harper & Row, 1990. Chapter 14 of this book offers an excellent discussion of the relative contribution of genetic and sociocultural factors to intelligence (as measured by IQ tests).
Mascie-Taylor, C. G. N., and G. W. Lasker (eds.). *Biological Aspects of Human Migration.* Cambridge: Cambridge University Press, 1988. The editors have included eight essays on the evolutionary significance of migration.

## SUGGESTED WEB SITES

Modern Human Variation:
  http://daphne.palomar.edu/vary/default.htm
Population Estimates by Age, Sex and Race (National Center for Health Statistics):
  http://govinfo.kerr.orst.edu/document/pestimates/peconv.html

Additional web sites are listed in the *Workbook* that accompanies this text.

# THE FACES OF HUMAN VARIATION

**Figure 17–A** San, Kalahari Desert, Botswana

*Homo sapiens* is a highly variable species. People live in local populations, and populations and groups of populations take on particular physical characteristics. Many of these characteristics are those that evolve through natural selection as an adaptive response to environmental circumstances. For example, an adaptive relationship exists between ultraviolet radiation, melanin production in the skin, and vitamin D production.

These pictures show a very few faces of human variation. As you examine them, keep the following facts in mind. First, there are no typical individuals; every population is greatly varied. Second, physical differences are relatively minor, and in the final analysis, the major differences among people are learned cultural ones.

**Figure 17–B** Efe, Ituri Forest, Zaire

**Figure 17–C** Somba, Dahomey

Figure 17–D   Ainu, Hokkaido, Japan

Figure 17–E   Bagish, China

Figure 17–F   Bangalore, India

Figure 17–G   Hmong, Laos

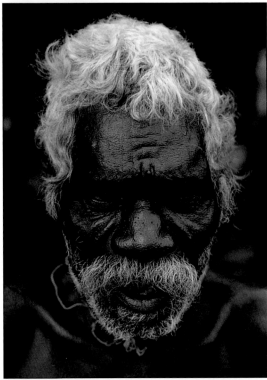

**Figure 17–H** Aborigine, Arnhem Land, Australia

**Figure 17–J** Tonga, Polynesia

**Figure 17–I** Mendi, South Highlands, New Guinea

Figure 17–K  Hamadan, Iran

Figure 17–M  Tbilisi, Goergia

NEW WORLD

Figure 17–N  Yanomama, Brazil

Figure 17–L  Kauto Keino Lapp, Norway

Figure 17–O  Taos Pueblo, New Mexico

# Epilogue

*We travel together, passengers on a litle*
*spaceship, dependent on its vulnerable*
*resources of air, water, and soil. . . preserved*
*from annihilation only by the care, the work,*
*and the love we give our fragile craft.*
—Adlai E. Stevenson (1900–1965)

**A**re humans still evolving? All of the factors that influence evolution—mutation, sampling error, migration, nonrandom mating, and natural selection—are still operating on human populations. So it is safe to say that the human gene pool continues to evolve.

Domestication of plants and animals created new conditions that affected the human gene pool. More recently, urbanization and industrialization have produced conditions such as the use of medical x-rays that, among other effects, increase mutation rates. A whole array of other factors such as

**447**

the information revolution, genetic engineering, weapons of modern warfare, the depletion of the ozone layer, acid rain, and the reduction of biological diversity could affect future human evolution.

## THE AGE OF INFORMATION AND THE AGE OF BIOTECHNOLOGY

In Chapter 15, we traced the evolution of humans through several stages: Paleolithic, Mesolithic, Neolithic, Bronze Age, Iron Age, and the Industrial Age. We can ask a sample of people today: what should we label the "age" that characterizes today's industrial nations? The response might be "The Age of Information." Looking further into the future, we might predict that the age that follows will be "The Age of Biotechnology."

### The Age of Information

Prior to the nineteenth century, most information could travel from one place to another only as fast as people or horses could walk or run or as fast as ships could sail. In some cases, smoke signals, signal flags, and signal lamps allowed for messages to be sent more rapidly over some distance or even relayed from one area to another.

The modern era of telecommunications (from *tele*, meaning "operating at a distance") began in 1837, the year in which Samuel F. B. Morse patented the telegraph. The telegraph was the first electric instrument that instantaneously transmitted information over a significant distance. The first telegraph message was sent in 1844 in Morse code from Baltimore to Washington, D.C., a distance of 24 kilometers (15 miles). The distance a message could be sent increased dramatically. By 1861, the east and west coasts of the United States were linked, and by 1866, a message could be sent across the Atlantic Ocean.

New methods of rapid communication were rapidly introduced. In 1876, the first telephone message was heard when Alexander Graham Bell spoke to his assistant in the next room. Radio entered the scene in 1895, and television made its debut in 1929. Personal computers were introduced in 1975 and their popular use began two years later with the introduction of the Apple II computer. Today, information can be instantaneously sent and received by telephone, television, radio, fax, and computers. Stored information is available in an instant on the Information Superhighway or Internet. From an evolutionary perspective, one of the most significant things that the information revolution has done is made the sharing of information easier and faster. This allows people from a variety of places to quickly pool their knowledge and ideas to solve problems. The down side of the Information Age is that the thirst for the technology that allows for the rapid dispersal of information has added to our ecological problems. The manufacturing of televisions, computers, cellular phones, and so on creates and releases chemicals that pollute the water, soil, and air. The Information Age has also made dangerous information, such as instructions on how to make bombs, easily available to anyone. On the Internet, errors in information can be transmitted world wide in an instant. Personal information that an individual may want to keep private is often retrievable through a computer.

### The Age of Biotechnology

Just as schools and colleges gear up for the information age by building computer labs and expanding computer science curricula, schools and corporations are now preparing for the Age of Biotechnology. Of course, this "Age" has already begun. All cultural stages are dependent on one another, and many overlap. In Chapters 3 and 4, we discussed some of the elements of the Age of Biotechnology, such as gene therapy.

In 1998, the entire genome of an animal, a flat worm, was deciphered for the first time. In the near future, we will know the entire genetic code of a human. This feat might allow us to cure genetic diseases and make normal conditions better. For instance, aging might be slowed down or even halted. Also in 1998, embryonic stem cells were isolated and kept alive for the first time. Stem cells can grow into any type of cell in the body. In the future, stem cells might be used to replace and develop into any type of damaged tissue, such as muscle, nerve, heart, and kidney tissue. Perhaps some day people will be as highly engineered as a Porsche.

Is this all good? Many people are disturbed by many of the possibilities of the Age of Biotechnology. The ethics of the biotechnical revolution is an important issue. For instance, if a person is genetically screened and is found to have a strong disposition for cancer or heart disease, does an insurance company or employer have the right to know and to deny insurance or a job?

The most general concern about changing biology is whether people should interfere with the very basic elements of life. Some of this concern is of a religious nature, the fear of people playing God. But there are also many biological concerns. Will we reduce biological variation through genetic engineering and thereby reduce our ability to adapt to unknown and unpredictable environmental factors? The twenty-first century will be a time of exploring the possibilities and consequences of biological engineering.

## MODERN ISSUES IN ECOLOGY

Each era is associated with its own set of environmental changes. Today's challenges include eliminating the environmental hazards of modern warfare, stopping the destruction of the ozone layer, ceasing to spew chemicals into the atmosphere that come back to land and water as acid rain, managing our resources better, stopping the rapid extinction of animals and plants, controlling population growth, and preventing industrial and other environmental disasters. To accomplish this requires a change in philosophy from one that sees resources as infinite and the earth as indestructible to one that sees resources as finite and the earth as fragile. This change is starting to spread worldwide. Conferences on world problems have drawn representatives from most of the countries of the world. Agreements have been reached to eliminate or reduce many of the threats to human survival. Yet these agreements represent only the very beginnings of the solutions to the world's ecological problems.

### The Depletion of the Ozone Layer

**Ozone,** a molecule composed of three oxygen atoms ($O_3$), forms in the **stratosphere,** the area of the atmosphere 20 to 50 kilometers (12 to 31 miles) above the earth's surface. The ozone layer encircles the earth, and it absorbs 99 percent of the ultraviolet radiation from the sun. High amounts of ultraviolet radiation interrupt normal cell activity, so without this protection, most life on earth would cease.

It was in 1974 that we were first warned of the causal relationship between the thinning of the ozone layer and industrial activities. These activities included the use of products that produced chlorofluorocarbons (CFCs), a class of chemicals used as refrigerants, in plastic foams, and in some spray cans. Natural factors such as volcanic eruptions and the 11-year solar cycle also increase or decrease the amount of ozone. Currently, the depletion of ozone is increasing the frequency of skin cancer in humans. Each 1 percent deletion of ozone may increase skin cancer by about 6 percent. In the northern midlatitudes (roughly between Seattle and New Orleans), ozone losses are between 5 and 10 percent per decade depending on the season.[1]

In addition, ozone depletion could eventually decrease certain food crops, affect food chains, and cause changes in world climatic patterns. If the depletion were to go unchecked, it could ultimately threaten all life on earth. In the meantime, an international agreement, the Montreal Protocol, was reached to end the production of ozone-destroying chemicals. This is one environmental agreement that seems to have been taken seriously. Most countries are rapidly phasing out the destructive chemicals, and the ozone layer may be "healthy" again by the middle of the twenty-first century.[2]

### Acid Rain

Some industrial plants, such as those that burn fossil fuel, release sulfur dioxide into the atmosphere; automobile exhaust also contains nitrogen oxides that enter the atmosphere. Sulfur dioxide and nitrogen oxides are carried back to the earth in rain; they oxidize to form sulfuric acid and nitric acid, respectively. **Acid rain,** as this precipitate is called, has acidified lakes to the point where life cannot be maintained (Figure E–1). In Canada alone, aquatic life has been depleted or threatened in at least 48,000 lakes; this is mainly due to U.S. industry. Acid rain has changed environments, sometimes drastically, and therefore it has created new

---

[1]U.S. Environmental Protection Agency, "Ozone Science," http://www.epa.gov/docs/ozone/science_facts.html, December 24, 1997.
[2]M. Prather et al., "The Ozone Layer: The Road Not Taken," *Nature* 381 (1996), pp. 551–554.

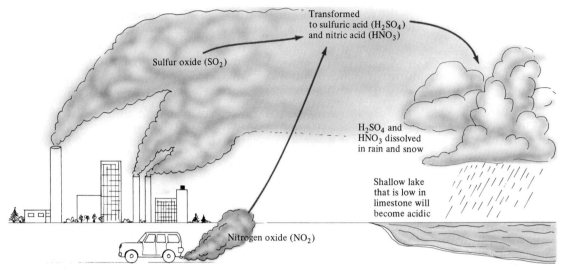

**FIGURE E–1   Acid Rain**

selective pressures on humans by destroying food, water, and other resources.

Even though sulfur emissions from factories and other sources have been reduced by about 50 percent by the year 2000 as compared to 1980, ecosystems are not recovering as fast as predicted. The problem appears to be that the acid rain has been destroying large quantities of basic ions, such as calcium ions, that neutralize acid in the soil. These basic ions are essential for plant growth. The ions are not being replaced from the weathering of rocks and minerals fast enough to quickly return soils to their preindustrial health. In fact, even if we continue to cut the emissions that cause acid rain, it could be decades or even centuries until that preindustrial state is reestablished.[3]

### The Reduction of Biological Diversity

The rain forests contain about half of the earth's species, yet by 1990, human activities had led to a 55 percent reduction in the rain forests. By the year 2035, the remaining rain forests will be gone or greatly disturbed. What does this mean to humans? A partial list of the effects of the loss of the world's

rain forests includes reduction in atmospheric oxygen, which is created by green plants; loss of the plants used in making medicines; loss of fuel plants; loss of as many as 20,000 species food plants; possible transformation of tropics into deserts; major changes in world climates; and crop failures due to the extinction of insects that formerly pollinated the crops.

### Nuclear, Chemical, and Biological Warfare

In December 1987, the United States and the Soviet Union agreed to destroy 2611 nuclear warheads carrying missiles; this would eliminate all intermediate-range missiles. In 1991, it was announced that there would be a reduction in short-range nuclear weapons and other military cutbacks. In 1994, the Ukrainian president agreed to destroy all nuclear warheads that Ukraine inherited as the result of the breakup of the Soviet Union. Yet the world is still left with thousands of megatons of nuclear power. As of 1994, 44 countries had or were developing nuclear weapons. New and even more devastating weapons are being developed by the United States and other countries. On April 6, 1998, Britain and France became the first nuclear powers to ratify the Comprehensive Test Ban Treaty, which bans all nuclear weapon test explosions. However, later in that year, India and Pakistan each conducted numerous nuclear test explosions.

---

[3]J. Kaiser, "Acid Rain's Dirty Business: Stealing Minerals from the Soil," *Science* 272 (1996), p. 198.

Concern also exists over chemical weapons, such as nerve gas. The United States and more than 24 other countries are actually working on or developing chemical weapons, or they have already stockpiled them.

A third tool of war is biological weapons. Current research is attempting to use genetic engineering and other methods to create deadly viruses, bacteria, parasites, and venoms. Although a 1972 treaty ratified by 103 nations bans the use and production of biological weapons, research goes on. In 1998, the United States and Great Britain conducted missile attacks on Iran, in part to damage Iran's ability to produce nuclear, biological, and chemical weapons.

The use of nuclear, chemical, and biological weapons could threaten the survival of the human species. Any of these destructive agents could cause environmental damage that would render the earth uninhabitable.

## Environmental Disasters

In December 1984, a catastrophe occurred that dwarfed, in terms of deaths, any previous industrial accident. Methyl isocyanate leaked from a Union Carbide pesticide factory in Bhopal, India, killing more than 8000 people.[4]

In April 1986, human error was responsible when a nuclear power plant at Chernobyl in Ukraine dumped nearly 100 million curies of radioactivity into the environment.[5] About 135,000 people living within 30 kilometers (19 miles) of the plant were evacuated, and although there is disagreement on the exact number, as many as 100,000 people may die over the next decade from cancer as a direct result of the explosion at Chernobyl.[6]

The 1991 war in the Persian Gulf resulted in several ecological disasters. They include the purposeful dumping of oil into the gulf and the destruction or setting ablaze of more than 1000 oil wells.

## Are There Too Many People?

At its present rate of growth, the human species could eventually crowd everything else off the earth (Figure E–2). Of course, before that could hap-

**FIGURE E–2  People Crowd Broadway in New York City after the Bicentennial Parade**

[4]D. Kurzman, *A Killing Wind* (New York: McGraw-Hill, 1987).
[5]C. Norman and D. Dickson, "The Aftermath of Chernobyl," *Science* 233 (1986), pp. 1141–1143.
[6]Ibid.

pen, widespread disease, mass starvation, and other catastrophic events would come into play. In the late 1980s and early 1990s, up to 40 million people per year died from a lack of food or from normally nonfatal infections that were worsened by deficiencies in food resources.

Many of the world's governments have at least begun to tackle the problem of population growth. Some countries mandate sterilization for males who have fathered a specified number of children; others impose economic or other social punishments on people who have what is defined by the country in question as too many children. Between 1978 and 1983, family-planning programs led to about 130 million fewer people being born than would have been born without such plans.

Population reduction policies have not had the predicted effect. Although the peak population growth rate was about 2 percent annually, which was registered in the mid-1960s, it is now down to about 1.8 percent; however, the world population has still climbed to more than 6.3 billion in 2000. Two factors account for the increase: people are living longer and nearly 34 percent of the world's population is below the age of 15. At an annual growth rate of 1.8 percent, the world population will double in 39 years.

### Learning from Our Mistakes

Publicity about the above incidents and other environmental problems has focused at least some concern on environmental programs. Yet concern is not enough. Culture—learned, patterned, transmittable behavior—is humankind's major tool for survival. The next years will test just how good a tool it is. For what is needed, if humans are not to go the way of the dinosaurs, is a willingness to change basic beliefs and behaviors that have proven to be nonadaptive. Ideas that place humans above nature must be replaced with ideas that see people as a *part* of nature. Rather than subdue the world around us, we should intelligently interact with the environment. Rather than reproduce ourselves into situations of increasing starvation, disease, and general degradation, we should use reproductive restraint.

We must also avoid the trap of thinking that technology will always save us; the misuse of modern technology is one cause of the ecological crisis. We must learn to be more selective in the types of technology we use and develop. Why not put our money and effort into technologies such as solid-waste recycling, nonpolluting machinery, and efficient and nondisruptive energy sources instead of innovations that lead to the darkening of our lungs; the poisoning of our food, air, and water; and the possible dehumanizing of the human species?

In your daily life, you can also help restore the quality of the environment by doing such things as choosing a simpler lifestyle. In this light, G. Tyler Miller, Jr., offers the following suggestions: "Refuse, Reduce, Reuse, Recycle."[7] Refuse to buy things that you do not really need or want. Reduce your consumption of energy and resources by buying energy-efficient cars and appliances, for instance. Reuse things that you have got in the habit of throwing out. And recycle those things that can be efficiently reprocessed into new material.

Above all, we must not fall into a gloom-and-doom trap. In many respects, the next 50 or so years may be the most exciting in human history. Each of us can be a "hero" by virtue of our own involvement in the social and technological revolution that has already begun. Apathy will be the worst enemy of the struggle to prove that we, as well as termites, can efficiently interact with nature.

## WHAT CAN WE SAY ABOUT THE FUTURE?

Some have said that people of the future will lose all their hair or that people's legs will degenerate from lack of use. This pattern of thought is similar to the nineteenth-century Lamarckian theory of evolution. The assumption is that when something becomes unnecessary, it will disappear, and when something becomes necessary, it will materialize. Thus, one might reason that body hair will totally disappear because clothes can take its place. This type of thinking becomes dangerous when it is applied to something like smog: some maintain that smog is not dangerous to humanity because eventually people will evolve lungs that can cope with it.

Evolution does not proceed by way of necessity or lack of necessity. A trait will appear only if there is genetic potential for it and only if that potential is expressed. The chance that any particular new

---

[7]G. T. Miller, Jr., *Living in the Environment,* 10th ed. (Belmont, Calif.: Wadsworth, 1998), pp. 756–757.

trait will appear, and appear at the right time and in the right place, is infinitesimally small.

Likewise, a trait will disappear only if it is selected against or if it diminishes because of random genetic drift. If it is selectively neutral, there will be no reason for it to vanish. Hair will not become more scarce unless the *lack* of hair has selective advantage over the retention of hair. Lungs will not adapt to smog unless mutations occur that would allow this to happen. *But there is no reason to believe that this will happen;* taking into account the ingredients of smog at high concentrations, extinction is a greater possibility.

The anthropologist cannot describe what the human form will be like in the future, nor can anyone predict random changes or the effects that unknown environmental conditions of the future will have on the genetic material. Nevertheless, there are some absolutes—for instance, existence or nonexistence.

For the human species to continue, certain conditions are necessary for survival. First, certain resources are nonreplenishable—for example, fossil fuels (such as coal and oil) and natural gases (such as helium). Humans depend on these energy sources, and they have no guarantee of a substitute if they run out.

Second, the earth is, in effect, a container with the ground acting as the bottom and the atmosphere acting as the sides and lid. Pollution is pumped into the ground, water, and air, where it often becomes trapped. Humans reside in that container, and they require that healthful conditions exist within it.

Third, the earth has a finite amount of space. Humans cannot occupy all that space, since the things on which they depend for food and environmental stability must also have room to exist.

## THE APPLICATION OF ANTHROPOLOGICAL KNOWLEDGE

The knowledge gained through anthropological investigation is not purely academic. The study of genetics has aided in building theories of inheritance that have been important in recognizing, treating, and, through counseling, preventing genetic disease. In this light, research into genetics and general evolutionary theory has awakened people to the dangers of actually increasing the frequency of genetic disease by arresting a disease without curing it. We have also developed hypotheses on the long-range evolutionary effects of artificially increased mutation rates, which are a result of human-caused environmental contamination by radiation and chemicals.

Studies of human variation have put differences among people into an empirical perspective instead of one based on social and biological myths; these studies have very definitely affected policy making as well as the ideas held by the educated public. In fact, the works of an early anthropologist, Franz Boas, were extensively cited in the historic 1954 U.S. Supreme Court decision that legally ended racial segregation in the United States. Anthropological studies have shown that the tendency of some groups within our society to score lower on IQ tests is due to social deprivation and environmental deterioration, as well as to cultural bias in the tests themselves, rather than to supposed innate differences. This has been realized by some educators and administrators, and we hope that the implementation of policies aimed at correcting these situations will increase the standard of living for everyone.

Anthropology is an ecological discipline, and one of its main contributions has been the investigation of relationships between humans and their environment. From these studies, it has become clear that people, like all animals, must maintain a proper balance with nature. People's great potential for cultural behavior provides adaptive flexibility, but it is limited; if this potential is used carelessly, it could create a sterile environment.

Studies of humans' closest relatives, the primates, and of evolutionary history have provided a multidimensional picture of human nature. Through these anthropological studies, many current biological and social problems, such as those that arise in urban situations, are put into an understandable perspective in which solutions can be sought.

### Anthropology and You—A Personal Note to the Student

Most of you are probably taking an anthropology course because it is a general education requirement or because you chose it as an elective. For you, we hope that this course has provided perspectives and information that have been enriching. Some of you, however, may have become interested in pursuing anthropology further, and you may even be interested in anthropology as a career.

Traditionally, anthropologists with M.A.s and Ph.D.s have worked almost exclusively as teachers, researchers, curators, and writers attached to colleges, universities, and museums. In addition, we believe that a B.A. in anthropology is a valuable liberal arts degree. H. Russell Bernard and Willis E. Sibley found that a B.A. degree in anthropology "if it is combined with appropriate personal training [provides] . . . an excellent competitive position for careers in many fields."[8] These fields include various health professions, public administration, government work, counseling, advertising, market research, journalism, and many others. The sources in the Suggested Readings provide information on both academic and nonacademic careers for anthropology majors.

## SUGGESTED READINGS

The following sources provide information on anthropology as a career or on the uses of anthropology in nonanthropological fields. One of the main sources for such information is the American Anthropological Association. You can consult their web page at http://www.aaanet.org, or you can write or call them at the American Anthropological Association, 4350 North Fairfax Drive, Suite 640, Arlington, VA 22203, (703) 528-1902. Additional sources are:

Baba, M. "The Fifth Subdiscipline: Anthropological Practice and the Future of Anthropology." *Human Organization* 53 (1994), pp. 174–186.

Bodo, D., and E. Briody. "Anthropologists at Work: Careers Making a Difference." 36-minute VHS color video. American Anthropological Association and EXPOSE: Communication Network, 1994.

Hyland, S. *Guide to Training Programs in the Application of Anthropology,* 4th ed. Oklahoma City: Society for Applied Anthropology, 1994.

## SUGGESTED WEB SITES

This site is called the WWW Virtual Library—Anthropology. It has links to numerous anthropological sites, including ones that discuss jobs and career opportunities.
http://anthrotech.com/cgibin/search/ressearch.cgi.

This web page uses graphs to discuss what anthropology majors do after graduation.
http://weber.ucsd.edu/~jmoore/bioanthro/brochure2.html

This site provides numerous links to sites that give information on careers in anthropology.
http://wings.buffalo.edu/anthropology/Grad/career.html

---

[8]H. R. Bernard and W. E. Sibley, *Anthropology and Jobs* (Washington, D.C.: American Anthropological Association, 1975), pp. 1–2.

# An Introduction to Skeletal Anatomy and the Anatomy of the Brain

Important evidence for evolution is found in anatomy. Because of the interest of anthropologists in the skeletons of living primates, the fossil record, and human burials, physical anthropologists have become specialists in the skeleton. Skeletal evidence is also used in studies of growth and development and in forensic anthropology.

Various aspects of the skeleton are discussed in several chapters of this text. Because different readers may study these chapters in different orders, a general introduction to skeletal anatomy is presented in this appendix so that it can be used with any chapter.

In order to understand the primate skeleton, it is important to constantly refer to the drawings and to locate on them the bones and features that are being discussed. Important bones and features that can be seen in the drawings in this appendix appear in bold type. This is a general discussion designed to provide the reader with tools necessary for understanding the text. More detailed discussions of skeletal anatomy may be found in the Suggested Readings and Suggested Web sites at the end of this appendix and in the *Workbook* and CD ROM that accompanies this text.

## SKELETAL ANATOMY OF PRIMATES

### The Postcranial Skeleton

The postcranial skeleton is that part of the skeleton behind the skull or below the skull in bipedal animals such as humans; it is all the skeleton except the skull (Figures A–1 and A–2). The axis of the skeleton is the spine, or **vertebral column,** which consists of a series of

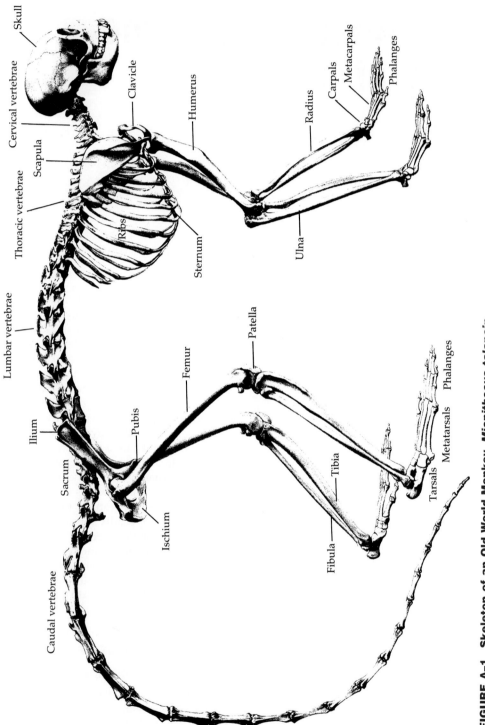

**FIGURE A–1** **Skeleton of an Old World Monkey,** *Miopithecus talapoin*

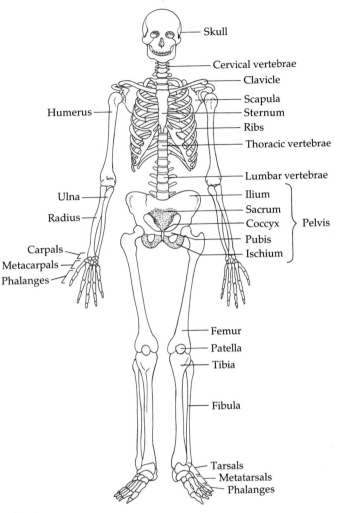

Skull

Cervical vertebrae

Clavicle

Scapula

Sternum

Ribs

Thoracic vertebrae

Humerus

Lumbar vertebrae

Ilium

Sacrum

Ulna

Coccyx
Pelvis
Radius

Pubis

Ischium

Carpals

Metacarpals

Phalanges

Femur

Patella

Tibia

Fibula

Tarsals

Metatarsals

Phalanges

**FIGURE A–2  The Human Skeleton**

interlocking vertebrae. The vertebrae differ in morphology in various regions of the spine. The vertebrae in these regions may be identified as **cervical, thoracic, lumbar, sacral,** and **coccygeal.** The term *articulation* refers to the coming together of two bones at a joint. All ribs articulate with the vertebrae, and most of the ribs articulate in front with the **sternum.**

The forelimbs and hindlimbs are connected to the spine at the **shoulder girdle** and the **pelvis,** respectively. The shoulder girdle consists of two bones, the **clavicle** (collarbone), which articulates with the sternum, and the **scapula** (shoulder blade). The scapula articulates with the clavicle and the **humerus,** the bone of the upper arm. The articulations of the clavicle with the scapula and the scapula with the humerus are close together, providing

for movement and flexibility in the shoulder. The humerus articulates with the scapula as a ball in a socket.

The lower arm consists of a pair of bones, the **radius** and the **ulna.** The radius articulates with the humerus in such a way that it can rotate around an axis; in so doing, the wrist and hand rotates. The wrist consists of eight bones, the **carpals;** the palm region of the hand contains the five **metacarpals.** The bones of the fingers are the **phalanges,** two in the thumb and three in each finger. (However, there has been a reduction in the number of bones in the fingers in some primates, such as the potto, spider monkeys, and colobus monkeys.)

The hindlimbs articulate with the spine by means of the pelvis. The pelvis itself is composed of three units: a pair of **innominate** bones and the **sacrum.** The latter is made up of fused sacral vertebrae. Each innominate in the adult is divided into three regions corresponding to what are three separate bones in the fetus. These regions are the **ilium,** the **ischium,** and the **pubis.**

The bone of the upper leg is the **femur.** The lower leg, like the lower arm, consists of two bones, the **tibia** and the **fibula;** unlike the lower arm, the lower leg does not rotate. The small **patella** is commonly called the kneecap. The ankle consists of the seven **tarsals;** the arch of the foot, five **metatarsals;** and the toes of the **phalanges,** two in the big toe and three in each of the others.

## The Skull

The skull consists of 28 separate bones plus the teeth. The skull has two major parts: the **mandible,** or lower jaw, and the **cranium.** The skull may also be partitioned into a **facial skeleton** and the **cranium,** or **brain case.** The facial skeleton includes the mandible and the skeleton of the upper jaw, along with the regions of the nose and eyes (Figures A–3, A–4, and A–5).

**The Brain Case** The brain is housed in the brain case, or cranium. The brain case is made up of several separate bones. As we can see from the top or side, the bones of the cranium come together at immovable joints called sutures. The part of the skull surrounding the sides and top of the brain is the **calvarium,** which is composed of the **frontal, parietals, temporals,** and **occipital.**

The cranial base is the floor of the brain case. It consists of the ethmoid and sphenoid, plus parts of the occipital, temporals, and frontal bones. A large hole, the **foramen magnum,** is found in the occipital bone. The spinal cord passes through this opening and enters and merges with the brain. On either side of the foramen magnum are two rounded surfaces, the **occipital condyles,** which fit into a pair of depressions on the top of the uppermost vertebra. This is how the skull articulates with the spine. Finally, the auditory bulla, a balloonlike structure, houses the middle ear.

**The Facial Skeleton and Mandible** The skeletal supports for the senses of smell, sight, hearing, and taste, and the skeletal apparatus for chewing, are all parts of the facial skeleton. The facial skeleton is composed of a number of small bones. It can be divided into several regions, including the nasal cavity, upper jaw, and mandible.

The upper jaw is made up of two pairs of bones, the **premaxillae** and **maxillae.** The top of the nose is formed by the nasal bones. Within the nose itself, the inner surface of the nasal cavity is covered with membranes containing the receptors for the sense of smell. These mem-

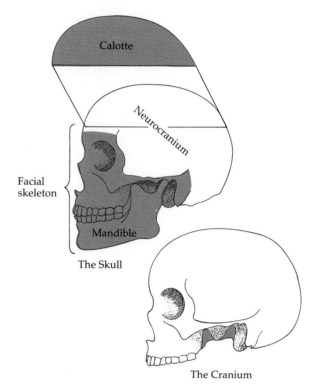

**FIGURE A–3  Divisions of the Skull**

branes sit on a series of thin, convoluted bony plates, the turbinals and nasal conchae, which may be extensive in animals with a keen sense of smell.

The mandible, or lower jaw, is composed of two halves fused in the middle in many primates (Figure A–6). The **horizontal ramus** contains the teeth. Behind the molars, the **vertical ramus** rises at an angle and ends in a rounded surface, the **mandibular condyle,** which articulates with the rest of the skull. To the front of the vertical ramus is a projection, the **coronoid process.** There are four types of teeth embedded in the mandible: the incisors, canines, premolars, and molars. In addition, the facial skeleton includes the lacrimals, **palatine,** vomer, and **zygomatics,** as well as part of the frontal.

## THE ANATOMY OF THE HUMAN BRAIN

We may identify several structures that are parts of the brain. The major parts of the human brain that appear below in bold type are identified in the figures (Figure A–7).

The **brainstem** is involved with certain body functions that are essential to life, such as the regulation of

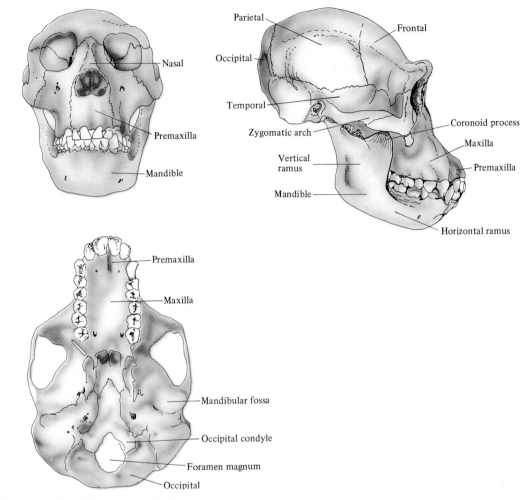

**FIGURE A–4  The Chimpanzee Skull**

breathing and heartbeat. Attached to the brainstem is a major structure of the hindbrain, the **cerebellum.** The cerebellum has a number of functions, including those that are basic to movement of the body: balance, body position, and position in space.

In the center of the brain, immediately above the brainstem, is a group of cells that make up the limbic system. Like the brainstem and cerebellum, the limbic system is involved with basic functions of the body. These functions include regulating body temperature, blood pressure, blood sugar levels, and more. Sexual desire and self-protection through fight or flight, emotional reactions critical to the survival of the individual, lie within the limbic system.

A critical part of the limbic system is a structure known as the **hypothalamus.** The hypothalamus regulates hunger, thirst, sleeping, waking, body temperature, chemical balances, heart rate, sexual activity, and emotions. It also plays a major role in the regulation of hormones through control of the **pituitary gland.** The pituitary gland regulates the estrous cycle and reproductive behavior.

### The Cerebrum

The most prominent structure of the human brain is the **cerebrum,** which is so large that it covers and obscures many structures of the brain. The cerebrum is divided into two halves, or hemispheres; the right

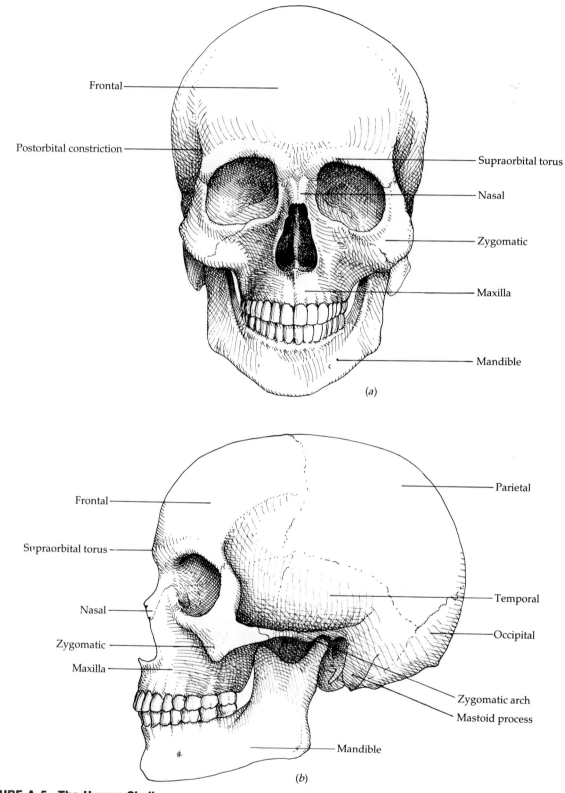

Frontal

Postorbital constriction

Supraorbital torus

Nasal

Zygomatic

Maxilla

Mandible

(a)

Parietal

Frontal

Supraorbital torus

Nasal

Zygomatic

Maxilla

Temporal

Occipital

Zygomatic arch

Mastoid process

Mandible

(b)

**FIGURE A–5  The Human Skull**

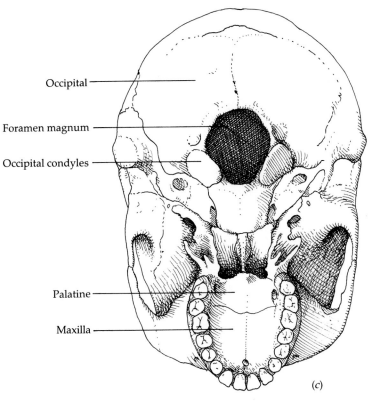

Occipital

Foramen magnum

Occipital condyles

Palatine

Maxilla

(c)

**FIGURE A-5  Continued**

hemisphere controls the left side of the body, and the left controls the right side of the body. The two halves are connected by nerve fibers that make up the **corpus callosum.**

The human cerebrum is covered by the **cerebral cortex,** a layer about 3 millimeters (0.125 inch) thick. The human cortex is intricately folded into a series of rounded ridges, or convolutions, separated from one an-

**FIGURE A-6  The Human Mandible**

*The human mandible.*

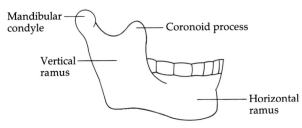

Mandibular condyle

Coronoid process

Vertical ramus

Horizontal ramus

other by fissures. The convolutions increase the surface area of the cerebral hemispheres since a convoluted surface has a greater surface area than a smooth surface.

Each hemisphere is divided into four lobes by deep grooves, and each lobe is named after the bone of the skull that overlays the lobe. The functions of the cortex in the various lobes have been determined by studies of electrical stimulation of the area, observations of persons with specific brain damage, and animal experimentation. The **temporal lobes** deal with perception and memory, and a section of the temporal lobe, the **auditory cortex,** is responsible for hearing. The **occipital lobes** handle the sense of sight; the cortex in this area is often called the visual cortex. The **parietal lobes** receive sensory information from the body. The largest parts of the cerebrum are the **frontal lobes,** which deal with purposeful behavior.

While the two cerebral hemispheres look alike, there are many subtle differences. In general, the left side deals more with language than the right side does; the right is involved more with spatial abilities.

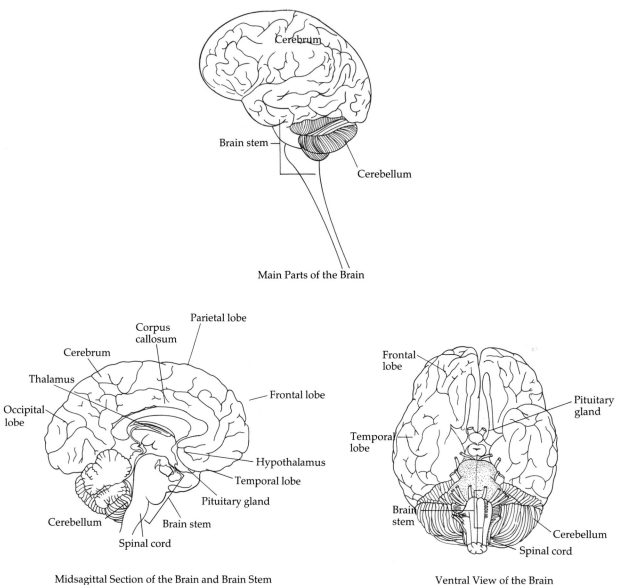

Main Parts of the Brain

Midsagittal Section of the Brain and Brain Stem

Ventral View of the Brain

**FIGURE A–7  The Human Brain**

## SUGGESTED READINGS

Aiello, L., and C. Dean. *An Introduction to Human Evolutionary Anatomy.* London: Academic, 1990. This is a very detailed description of human anatomy from an evolutionary perspective.

Steele, D. G., and C. A. Bramblett. *The Anatomy and Biology of the Human Skeleton.* College Station, Tex.: Texas A&M University Press, 1988. This book features a large number of excellent photographs of human bones carefully labeled.

Swindler, D., and C. D. Wood. *An Atlas of Primate Gross*

*Anatomy.* Melbourne, Fla.: Krieger, 1982. This book contains a series of detailed line drawings illustrating the comparative anatomy of the baboon, chimpanzee, and human.

White, T. D., and P. A. Folkens. *Human Osteology.* San Diego, Calif.: Academic, 1991. This book is a detailed discussion of the human skeleton for the paleoanthropologist.

## SUGGESTED WEB SITES

The Human Bones & Muscles (Leeds University): http://pc65.frontier.osrhe.edu/hs/science/bbones.htm

The Human Brain: http://wwwl.vh.org/Providers/Textbooks/BrainAnatomy/BrainAnatomy.html

# Glossary

**abductor**   A muscle that moves a part of the body away from the midline of the body.

**ABO blood-type system**   A blood-type system that consists of two basic antigens, A and B. Blood-type O is the absence of both antigens.

**acclimatory adjustment**   Reversible physiological adjustments to stressful environments.

**accretion**   Growth by virtue of an increase in intercellular materials.

**Acheulean tradition**   The most frequent cultural manifestation of the Lower Paleolithic, characterized by several highly diagnostic tool types, including the hand ax.

**achondroplastic dwarfism**   Form of dwarfism in which the individual's head and trunk are of normal size, but the limbs are quite short; inherited as a dominant.

**acid rain**   Rain that carries acids that pollute water systems and soils.

**acrocentric chromosome**   Chromosome in which the centromere is near one end, resulting in arms of very unequal length.

**adaptation**   Changes in gene frequencies resulting from selective pressures being placed on a population by environmental factors; results in a greater fitness of the population to its ecological niche.

**adaptive radiation**   The evolution of a single population into a number of different species.

**adenine**   One of the bases found in DNA and RNA.

**adenosine triphosphate (ATP)**   The main fuel of cells. ATP is manufactured by the mitochondria.

**adjustment**   The ability of humans to survive in stressful environments by nongenetic means.

**adolescent growth spurt** A rapid increase in stature and other dimensions of the body that occurs during puberty.

**adult** The period in an individual's life cycle after the eruption of the last permanent teeth.

**agglutination** A clumping together of red blood cells in the presence of an antibody.

**aging** The uninterrupted process of normal development that leads to a progressive decline in physiological function and ultimately to death.

**agonistic behavior** Behavior that involves fighting, threats, and fleeing.

**albinism** A recessive abnormality that leads to little or no production of the skin pigment melanin.

**allantois** Sack within the amniote egg in which waste products produced by the embryo are deposited.

**allele** An alternate form of a gene.

**Allen's rule** Among endotherms, populations of the same species living near the equator tend to have body parts that protrude more and to have longer limbs than do populations farther away from the equator.

**allogrooming** Grooming another animal.

**allometric growth** Pattern of growth whereby different parts of the body grow at different rates with respect to each other.

**allopatric species** Species occupying mutually exclusive geographical areas.

**alpha chain** One of the two polypeptide chains that make up the globin unit of the hemoglobin molecule.

**alpha-feto protein (AFP)** A compound, produced by the fetus, that enters the mother's blood through the placenta. Excessive amounts of AFP may indicate neural tube defects or other fetal abnormalities.

**altruism** Behaviors characterized by self-sacrifice that benefit others.

**alveoli** Small air sacs, located in the lungs, that are richly endowed with blood capillaries. Oxygen is absorbed by the blood in the alveoli.

**amino acid** A type of molecule that forms the basic building block of proteins.

**amino acid racemization** Chronometric dating method based on change in the three-dimensional structure of amino acids from one form to its mirror image over time.

**amniocentesis** A medical technique in which amniotic fluid is removed for study of the fetus.

**amnion** A fluid-filled sac, formed from embryonic tissue, that contains the embryo in the amniote egg.

**amniote egg** An egg with a shell and several internal membranes, which made reproduction on land possible.

**amniotic fluid** The fluid surrounding the fetus.

**analogies** Structures that are superficially similar and serve similar functions, but have no common evolutionary relationship.

**anterior pillars** Bony columns located on both sides of the nasal aperture of some fossil hominids that help withstand the stresses of chewing.

**anthropocentricity** The belief that humans are the most important elements in the universe.

**anthropoid** A member of the suborder Anthropoidea; includes the New World monkeys, Old World monkeys, apes, and humans.

**anthropological linguistics** The study of language in cross-cultural perspective; the origin and evolution of language.

**anthropology** The broad-scope scientific study of people from all periods of time and in all areas of the world. Anthropology focuses on both biological and cultural characteristics and variation as well as biological and cultural evolution.

**anthropometry** The study of measurements of the human body.

**antibody** A protein manufactured by the body to neutralize or destroy an antigen.

**antigen** A substance that stimulates the production or mobilization of antibodies. An antigen can be a foreign protein, toxin, bacteria, or other substance.

**ape** A common term that includes the lesser apes (the gibbons and siamang) and the great apes (the orangutan, chimpanzee, bonobo, and gorilla).

**applied anthropology** A branch of anthropology devoted to applying anthropological theory to practical problems.

**arbitrary** A characteristic of language. A word, or other unit of sound, has no real connection to the thing to which it refers; the meanings of the arbitrary elements of a language must be learned.

**arboreal** Living in trees.

**archaeology** The scientific study of the past and current cultures through the analysis of artifacts and the context in which they are found.

**archetype** The divine plan or blueprint for a species or higher taxonomic category.

**areolar area** The dark area surrounding the nipple of the breast.

**argon 40/argon 39 dating** A method of chronometric dating based on making measurements of the relative amounts of argon 40 and argon 39 in a sample.

**artifact** Any physical remains of human activity.

**artificial gene** A gene that is made in a laboratory and used in place of a defective or undesirable gene.

**artificial selection** See **selective breeding.**

**assemblage** All the artifacts from a given site.

**assortative mating** Preference for or avoidance of certain people as mates for physical or social reasons.

**aster** In cell division, the fibers that radiate from the centrosome.

**asymmetry of function** The phenomenon in which the

two hemispheres of the brain specialize in regard to different functions.

**atom**  A building block of matter.

**auditory bulla**  A flat or inflated structure that forms in the floor of the skull that houses the middle ear.

**autapomorphic feature**  A feature that is unique to a particular species.

**autogrooming**  Self-grooming.

**autosome**  A chromosome other than a sex chromosome.

**awl**  A type of tool that is used to puncture a hole in a soft material such as wood or skin.

**back cross**  The process of crossing a hybrid with its homozygous recessive parent.

**balanced polymorphism**  Maintenance of two or more alleles in a gene pool as the result of heterozygous advantage.

**band**  Among geladas, a social group consisting of a number of harems and all-male units.

**band**  Among humans, the basic social unit of hunting and gathering peoples, which typically consists of about 35 to 50 members.

**basal metabolic rate**  The measure of the total energy utilized by the body to maintain those body processes necessary for life; the minimum level of heat produced by the body at rest.

**base**  A subunit of a nucleotide that makes up the DNA and RNA molecules: adenine, cytosine, guanine, thymine, uracil.

**basicranium**  The floor of the brain case.

**behavioral adjustment**  Survival in stressful environment made possible by cultural means, primarily technology.

**behavioral thermoregulation**  Using behavior, such as avoiding or seeking sources of heat, to regulate body temperature.

**Bergmann's rule**  Within the same species of endotherms, populations with less bulk are found near the equator while those with greater bulk are found farther from the equator.

**Beringia**  The landmass, some 2000 kilometers (1250 miles) from north to south, that connected Siberia and Alaska during the glacials.

**beta chain**  One of the two polypeptide chains that make up the globin unit of the hemoglobin molecule.

**biacromial width**  A measurement of the width of the shoulders.

**bilaterally symmetrical**  A situation where, when cut down the middle, the two halves formed are generally mirror images of each other.

**bilophodont**  Refers to a form of molar found in Old World monkeys consisting of four cusps with a small constriction separating them into two pairs.

**binocular field**  The visual field produced by the overlapping of the separate visual fields from each eye when the eyes are located on the front of the face.

**binomen**  A two-part name given to a species; the first name is also the name of the genus. An example of a binomen is *Homo sapiens*.

**binomial nomenclature**  A system of naming species that uses a double name such as *Homo sapiens*. The first name alone names the genus; both names used together name the species.

**biological environment**  The living elements surrounding the organism.

**biological evolution**  Change in the frequencies of alleles within a gene pool of a population over time.

**bipedalism**  See **erect bipedalism.**

**bitrochanteric width**  A measurement of hip width.

**blade**  Flakes with roughly parallel sides and extremely sharp edges; blades are frequently found in Upper Paleolithic sites.

**blending theory**  An early and incorrect idea that the inherited characteristics of offspring are intermediate between maternal and paternal genetic characteristics.

**bone age**  A standard age based on the appearance of centers of ossification and fusion of growth plates.

**bone breccia**  Cave fill consisting of masses of bone cemented together with calcium carbonate that has dissolved out of limestone.

**bone industry**  All of the bone artifacts from a particular site.

**brachiation**  Hand-over-hand locomotion along a branch with the body suspended underneath the branch by the arms.

**branch running and walking**  A form of quadrupedalism in which the animal is walking along a branch grasping with both hands and feet.

**breast bud**  An elevation of the breast as a small mound; the earliest sign of puberty in the female.

**Broca's area**  A small area in the human brain that controls the production of speech.

**Bronze Age**  The stage of cultural history that includes the earliest civilizations and the development of metallurgy.

**brow ridge**  Ridge of bone above the eye sockets.

**burin**  A stone tool with a chisel-like point used for engraving or manufacturing bone tools.

**calendrical system**  A system of measuring time based on natural recurring units of time, such as the revolutions of the earth around the sun; it notes the number of such units that have preceded or elapsed with reference to a specific point in time.

**call system**  A system of vocalized sounds that grades one into another.

**carbohydrates** Organic compounds composed of carbon, oxygen, and hydrogen; includes the sugars and starches.

**carnivore** An animal that eats primarily meat.

**carrier** A person who possesses a recessive allele in the heterozygous condition.

**cast** A representation of an organism created when a substance fills in a mold.

**cataract** Opacity of the eye lens, often inherited as a dominant. The type may vary according to the action of a modifying gene.

**catarrhine nose** Nose in which nostrils open downward and are separated by a narrow nasal septum; found in Old World monkeys, apes, and humans.

**catastrophism** Idea that the earth has experienced a series of catastrophic destructions and creations and that fossil forms found in each layer of the earth are bounded by a creation and destruction event.

**cell** The smallest unit able to perform all those activities collectively called life. All living organisms are either one cell or composed of several cells.

**centiMorgans (cM)** A measurement of distance between genes on a chromosome. One centiMorgan represents a crossing-over rate of 1 percent.

**centriole** A pair of small bodies found near the nucleus of the cell from which the spindle is formed.

**centromere** A structure in the chromosome holding the two chromatids together; during cell division, it is the site of attachment for the spindle fibers.

**centrosome** A body that lies near the nucleus of the cell that contains two centrioles.

**cephalic index** The breadth of the head relative to its length.

**cerebral cortex** The "gray matter" of the brain; the center of conscious evaluation, planning, skill, speech, and other higher mental activities.

**cheek pouch** Pocket in the cheek that opens into the mouth; some Old World monkeys store food in the cheek pouch.

**cheek teeth** The premolars and molars.

**chin** A bony projection of the lower border of the outside of the mandible.

**chordate** A member of the phylum Chordata; chordates are characterized by the presence of a notochord, dorsal hollow single nerve cord, and gill slits at some point in the life cycle.

**chorion** A membrane derived from the amnion that lies just beneath the shell in the amniote egg and acts as a surface for oxygen absorption.

**chorionic villus biopsy** A method of analyzing the embryo by sampling the tissue of the placenta surrounding the developing embryo.

**chromatid** One of the two strands of a replicated chromosome. Two chromatids are joined together by a centromere.

**chromosomal aberration** Abnormal chromosome number or chromosome structure.

**chromosomal sex** The number of X and Y chromosomes a person has. The chromosomal sex of a person with two X chromosomes is a female. The chromosomal sex of a person with one X and one Y chromosome is a male.

**chromosome** A body found in the nucleus of the cell containing the hereditary material.

**chron** A large division of a geomagnetic time scale that shows primarily a single polarity.

**chronological age** Period of time since birth.

**chronometric dates** Dates that refer to a specific point or range of time. Chronometric dates are not necessarily exact dates, and they are often expressed as a probability.

**chronospecies** Arbitrarily defined divisions of an evolutionary line.

**civilization** A type of society with relatively high population density; based on the deemphasis of kinship as a method of social control and the rise of central authority in the form of a government and powerful priesthood. Civilizations often also include monumental architecture, writing, mathematics, public works, and full-time armies.

**clade** A group of species with a common evolutionary ancestry.

**cladistics** A theory of classification that differentiates between shared ancestral and shared derived features.

**cladogram** A graphic representation of the species, or other taxa, being studied, based on cladistic analysis.

**class** Major division of an phylum, consisting of closely related orders.

**classification** A system of organizing data.

**cleaver** A large core tool with a straight, sharp edge at one end.

**clinal distribution** A distribution of frequencies that show a systematic gradation over space; also called continuous variation.

**cloning** The process of asexual reproduction in an otherwise multicellular animal.

**codominance** The situation in which, in the heterozygous condition, both alleles are expressed in the phenotype.

**codon** A sequence of three bases on the DNA molecule that codes a specific amino acid or other genetic function.

**communication** Occurs when some stimulus or message is transmitted and received; in relation to animal life, when one animal transmits information to another animal.

**community** Among chimpanzees, a large group of chimpanzees that, through fission and fusion, is composed of a series of constantly changing smaller units including the all-male party, family, unit, nursery unit, consortship, and gathering.

**comparative cytogenetics** The comparative study of the heredity mechanisms within the cell.

**competition** The situation in which two populations occupy the same or parts of the same niche.

**complementary pair** A set of two nucleotides, each on a different polynucleotide chain, that are attracted to each other by a chemical bond. In DNA, adenine and thymine, and cytosine and guanine, form complementary pairs.

**compound tool** A tool that is composed of several parts, for example, a harpoon.

**computerized tomography** A technology used in medicine that permits visualization of the interior of an organism's body.

**conduction** The movement of heat from one object to another by direct contact.

**cones** Cells of the retina of the eye; each of the three types of cones is sensitive to a specific wave length of light, thereby producing color vision.

**consanguineous mating** Mating between biological relatives.

**consort pair** A temporary alliance between a male and an estrus female.

**constitutive heterochromatin** Chromosomal material that is not thought to contain any actual genes.

**control** In the scientific method, a situation in which a comparison can be made between a specific situation and a second situation that differs, ideally, in only one aspect from the first.

**convection** Movement of heat from an object to the surrounding fluid, either gas or liquid; heat causes the fluid to move away from the object.

**convergence** Nonhomologous similarities in different evolutionary lines; the result of similarities in selective pressures.

**coprolite** Fossilized fecal material.

**core** A nodule of rock from which flakes are removed.

**core area** Sections within the home range of a primate population that may contain a concentration of food, a source of water, and a good resting place or sleeping trees, and in which most of the troop's time will be spent.

**core tool** A tool that is manufactured by the removal of flakes from a core.

**cranial capacity** The volume of the brain case of the skull.

**creation-science** The idea that scientific evidence can be and has been gathered for creation as depicted in the Bible. Mainstream scientists and the Supreme Court discount any scientific value of "creation-science" statements.

**critical temperature** The temperature at which the body must begin to resist a lowering of body temperature; occurs in the nude human body at approximately 31°C (87.8°F).

**cross-cousin preference marriage** Marriage between a person and his or her cross-cousin (father's sister's child or mother's brother's child).

**crossing-over** The phenomenon whereby sections of homologous chromosomes are interchanged during meiosis.

**cultural anthropology** The study of the learned patterns of behavior and knowledge characteristic of a society and of how they vary.

**cultural environment** The products of human endeavor including technology and social institutions.

**culture** Learned, nonrandom, systematic behavior and knowledge that can be transmitted from generation to generation.

**culture-bound** The state or quality of having relevance only to the members of a specific cultural group.

**cusp** A point on a tooth.

**cytogenetics** The study of the heredity mechanisms within the cell.

**cytology** The study of the biology of the cell.

**cytoplasm** Material within the cell between the plasma membrane and the nuclear membrane.

**cytosine** One of the bases found in the DNA and RNA molecule.

**Darwinian psychology** The study of the influence of biology and natural selection on human behavior.

**debitage** Waste and nonutilized material produced in the process of tool manufacture.

**deciduous teeth** The first set of teeth that develop in mammals; also known as the baby or milk teeth.

**deletion** A chromosomal aberration in which a chromosome breaks and a segment is not included in the second-generation cell. The genetic material on the deleted section is lost.

**deme** The local breeding population; the smallest reproductive population.

**dendrochronology** Tree-ring dating.

**dental arcade** The tooth row as seen from above.

**dental comb** A structure formed by the front teeth of the lower jaw projecting forward almost horizontally; found in prosimians.

**dental formula** Formal designation of the types and numbers of teeth. The dental formula 2.1.2.3/2.1.2.3 indicates that in one-half of the upper jaw and lower jaw there are two incisors, one canine, two premolars, and three molars.

**deoxyribonucleic acid (DNA)** A nucleic acid that

controls the structure of proteins and hence determines inherited characteristics; genes are portions of the DNA molecule that fulfill specific functions.

**deoxyribose** A five-carbon sugar found in the DNA molecule.

**development** The process whereby cells differentiate into different and specialized units; change over time from an immature to a mature or specialized state.

**developmental adjustments** Alterations in the pattern of growth and development resulting from environmental influence.

**diabetes** Failure of the body to produce insulin, which controls sugar metabolism; has a complex genetic basis influenced by environmental factors.

**diaphragm** A muscle that lies beneath the lungs. When the diaphragm contracts, the volume of the lungs increases, causing a lowering of pressure within the lungs and movement of air from the outside into the lungs. When the diaphragm relaxes, air is expelled from the lungs.

**diastema** A space between teeth.

**diphyodonty** Having two sets of teeth, the deciduous and the permanent teeth.

**directional selection** A type of natural selection characterized by a generation-after-generation shift in a population in a specific direction, such as toward larger body size. In this example, individuals with smaller body size are being selected against.

**discontinuous variation** Distribution of alleles, allele combinations, or any traits characterized by little or no gradation in frequencies between adjacent regions.

**discrete** A characteristic of language. Signals, such as words, represent discrete entities or experiences; a discrete signal does not blend with other signals.

**displacement (behavior)** The situation in which one animal can cause another to move away from food, a sitting place, and so on.

**displacement (language)** A characteristic of language. The ability to communicate about events at times and places other than when they occur; enables a person to talk and think about things not directly in front of him or her.

**disruptive selection** A type of natural selection characterized by a generation-after-generation shift in the population away from the average individual, such as toward both larger and smaller body size. In this example, individuals with average (mean) body size are being selected against.

**distance curve** A graph that shows the total height (or other measurement) of an individual on a series of dates.

**diurnal** Active during daylight hours.

**dizygotic twins** Fraternal twins; twins derived from separate zygotes.

**domestication** The control of the reproductive cycle of plants and animals.

**dominance (behavior)** Behavior in which one animal displaces another and take preference in terms of sitting place, food, and estrus females.

**dominance (genetic)** When in the heterozygous genotype only one allele is expressed in the phenotype, that allele is said to be dominant.

**dominance hierarchy** A system of social ranking based on the relative dominance of the animals within a social group.

**dorsal** Toward the top or back of an animal.

**Down syndrome** Condition characterized by a peculiarity of eyefolds, malformation of the heart and other organs, stubby hands and feet, short stature, and mental retardation; result of extra chromosome 21.

**duplication** Chromosomal aberration in which a section of a chromosome is repeated.

**dyspnea** Difficult or painful breathing.

**ecological isolation** Form of reproductive isolation in which two closely related species are separated by what is often a slight difference in the niches they occupy.

**ecological niche** The specific microhabitat in which a particular population lives and the way that population exploits that microhabitat.

**ecology** The study of the relationship of organisms or groups of organisms to their environment.

**ectotherm** An animal that derives most of its body heat from external heat sources.

**ectotympanic** A bony element within the middle ear that supports the tympanic membrane or ear drum.

**edema** Retention of water in the tissues of the body.

**electron spin resonance (ESR) dating** A chronometric dating technique based on the behavior of electrons in crystals exposed to naturally occurring radioactivity; used to date limestone, coral, shell, teeth, and other materials.

**electrophoresis** A method for separating proteins in an electric field.

**Ellis–van Creveld syndrome** A rare recessive abnormality characterized by dwarfism, extra fingers, and malformations of the heart; high incidence among the Amish.

**embryology** The branch of biology that studies the formation and development of the embryo.

**empirical** Received through the senses (sight, touch, smell, hearing, taste), either directly or through extensions of the senses (such as a microscope).

**encephalization quotient (EQ)** A number reflecting the increase in brain size over and beyond that explainable by an increase in body size.

**endocranial cast** A cast of the inside of the brain case.

**endocrine glands**   Organs that produce hormones.

**endotherm**   An animal whose body heat is regulated by internal physiological mechanisms.

**environment**   Everything external to the organism.

**epidermal ridges**   Fine ridges in the skin on the hand and foot that are richly endowed with nerve endings and are responsible for the highly developed sense of touch; responsible for fingerprint pattern.

**epidermis**   The outermost layer of the skin.

**epoch**   A unit of geological time; a division of a period.

**era**   A major division of geological time defined by major geological events and delineated by the kinds of animals and plant life it contains. Humans evolved in the Cenozoic era.

**erect bipedalism**   A form of locomotion found in humans in which the body is maintained in an upright posture on two legs while moving by means of a heel-toe stride.

**erythroblastosis fetalis**   A hemolytic disease affecting unborn or newborn infants caused by the destruction of the infant's Rh+ blood by the mother's anti-Rh antibodies.

**erythrocyte**   Red blood cell. Cell found in blood that lacks a nucleus and contains the red pigment hemoglobin.

**estrogen**   Hormone produced in the ovary.

**estrus**   Time period during which the female is sexually receptive.

**eugenics**   The study of the methods that can improve the inherited qualities of a species.

**eutherian mammal**   A placental mammal, member of the infraclass Eutheria.

**evaporation**   Liquid is transformed into a gas utilizing energy.

**evolution**   See **biological evolution.**

**extensor**   A muscle that straightens out the bones about a joint.

**extinction**   The disappearance of a population.

**facial sinus**   A hollow, air-filled space in the bones of the front of the skull.

**familial hypercholesterolemia**   A rare dominant abnormality controlled by a multiple allele series of at least four alleles. The disease is caused by a defective protein that can result in extremely high levels of cholesterol in the blood.

**family**   Major division of an order, consisting of closely related genera.

**female-bonded kin group**   Primate social groups that are based on associations of females.

**fetal hemoglobin (Hb F)**   A normal variant of hemoglobin, consisting of two alpha and two gamma polypeptide chains, found in the fetus and early infant; it is gradually replaced by hemoglobin A.

**field study**   A study conducted in the natural habitat of an animal with minimal interference in the animal's life.

**fission-fusion society**   Constantly changing form of social organization whereby large groups undergo fission into smaller units and small units fuse into larger units in response to the activity of the group and the season of the year.

**fission-track dating**   The determination of a chronometric date by counting the proportion of atoms of a radioactive isotope such as uranium 238 that have decayed, leaving visible tracks in a mineral relative to the total number of atoms of the isotope.

**fitness**   Measure of how well an individual or population is adapted to a specific ecological niche.

**flake**   A small piece of stone that is removed from a core when the core is struck by a hammerstone or bone hammer.

**flake tool**   A tool manufactured from a flake.

**fluted**   Referring to fluted points where a rounded groove has been made in the shaft of the point, most likely to facilitate hafting.

**folivore**   An animal that eats primarily leaves.

**folk taxonomy**   Classification of some class of phenomena based on cultural tradition.

**foramen magnum**   A large opening in the occipital bone at the base of the skull through which the spinal cord passes.

**foramina**   Small holes found in bone that permit the passage of nerves and blood vessels.

**forebrain**   The anterior of three swellings in the hollow nerve cord of the primitive vertebrate brain formed by a thickening of the wall of the nerve cord.

**forensic anthropology**   Application of the techniques of osteology and skeletal identification to legal problems.

**fossil**   Remains or trace of any ancient organism.

**founder principle**   Situation in which a founding population does not represent a random sample of the original population; a form of sampling error.

**four-chambered heart**   A heart that is divided into two sets of pumping chambers, effectively separating oxygenated blood from the tissues from deoxygenated blood from the body.

**fovea**   A depression within the macula of the retina of the eye that contains a single layer of cones with no overlapping blood vessels; region of greatest visual acuity.

**frugivore**   An animal that eats primarily fruits.

**gamete**   A sex cell produced by meiosis that contains one copy of a chromosome set (23 chromosomes in humans). In a bisexual animal, the sex cell is either a sperm or an ovum.

**gametic mortality** Form of reproductive isolation in which sperm are immobilized and destroyed before fertilization can take place.

**gene** A section of DNA that has a specific function.

**gene flow** The process in which alleles from one population are introduced into another population.

**gene pool** The sum of all alleles carried by the members of a population.

**gene therapy** A genetic-engineering method in which a gene is altered and then inserted into a cell to correct an inherited abnormality.

**generalized species** Species that can survive in a variety of ecological niches.

**generalized trait** A trait used for many functions.

**genetic counselor** A medical professional who advises prospective parents or a person affected by a genetic disease of the probability of having a child with a genetic problem.

**genetic drift** The situation in a small population in which the allelic frequencies of the $F_1$ generation will differ from those of the parental generation due to sampling error.

**genetic engineering** The artificial manipulation of the genetic material to create specific characteristics in individuals.

**genetic equilibrium** A hypothetical state in which a population is not evolving because the allele frequencies remain constant over time.

**genetic load** The totality of deleterious alleles in a population.

**genetic sex** In humans, male sex is determined by the presence of the *Sry* gene, which is located on the Y chromosome. Persons who lack the Y chromosome, and hence the *Sry* gene, or who possess an abnormal allele of the *Sry* gene, are genetically female.

**genetics** The study of the mechanisms of heredity and biological variation.

**genome** All of the genes carried by a single gamete.

**genotype** The genetic constitution of an individual.

**genus** A group of closely related species.

**geographical isolation** Form of reproductive isolation in which members of a population become separated from another population through geographical barriers that prevent the interchange of genes between the separated populations.

**geographical race** A major division of humankind into large geographical areas wherein people resemble one another more closely than they resemble people in different geographical areas.

**geomagnetic reversal time scale (GRTS)** A chart showing the sequence of normal and reversed polarity of the earth's magnetic field.

**gestation** The period of time from conception to birth.

**gill bar** Skeletal element supporting the gill slit in nonvertebrate chordates and some vertebrates.

**gill pouches** Structures that form in the early human embryo that are thought to be homologous to the gill slits of other chordates.

**gill slits** Structures that filter out food particles in nonvertebrate chordates and are used for breathing in some vertebrates.

**glacial** Period of expansion of glacial ice.

**globin** A constituent of the hemoglobin molecule; the globin consists of two alpha and two beta polypeptide chains.

**Gloger's rule** Within the same species of warm-blooded animals, there is a tendency to find more heavily pigmented forms near the equator and lighter forms away from the equator.

**glucose-6-phosphate dehydrogenase (G6PD) deficiency** Lack of an enzyme of the red blood cell inherited as an X-linked recessive. Afflicted individuals develop severe anemia when in contact with the fava bean or certain antimalarial drugs.

**gluteus maximus** In humans, the largest muscle of the human body, acts as an extensor; acts to extend the leg in running and climbing.

**gluteus medius** Muscle of the pelvis that in monkeys and apes acts as an extensor, but in humans acts as an abductor.

**gluteus minimus** Muscle of the pelvis that in monkeys and apes acts as an extensor, but in humans acts as an abductor.

**gonad** General term used for an organ that produces sex cells; the ovary and testis.

**gout** Abnormal uric acid metabolism inherited as a dominant with variation expression.

**grammar** A set of rules used to make up words and then to combine the words into larger utterances such as phrases and sentences.

**great apes** The orangutan from Asia and the chimpanzee, bonobo, and gorilla from Africa.

**grooming** In primates, the activity of going through the fur with hand or teeth to remove insects, dirt, twigs, dead skin, and so on; also acts as a display of affection.

**grooming claw** A claw found on the second toe of prosimians that functions in grooming.

**grooming cluster** A small group of closely related females that engage in a high degree of grooming.

**ground running and walking** A form of quadrupedalism that takes place on the ground as opposed to in the trees.

**growth** Increase in the size or mass of an organism.

**growth hormone** A hormone produced by the pituitary gland, essential for normal growth.

**growth plate**   Narrow zone within which bone growth occurs.

**guanine**   One of the bases found in the DNA and RNA molecules.

**habitat**   The place in which a particular organism lives.

**half-life**   The time in which one-half of the atoms of a radioactive isotope have decayed.

**hammerstone**   A stone that is used to remove flakes from a core by striking the hammerstone against the core.

**hand ax**   Large core tool with a sharp cutting edge, blunted at one end so it can be held in the hand.

**hard palate**   The bony roof of the mouth that separates the mouth from the nasal cavity, permitting the animal to breath and chew at the same time.

**Hardy-Weinberg equilibrium**   A mathematical model of genetic equilibrium: $p^2 + 2pq + q^2 = 1$.

**harem**   A subunit of a larger social group consisting of a male associated with two or more females.

**heel-toe stride**   Method of progression characteristic of humans where the heel strikes the ground first; the person pushes off on the big toe.

**heliocentric**   A sun-centered model of the universe.

**heme**   A constituent of the hemoglobin molecule; each heme unit contains an atom of iron.

**hemochorial placenta**   Type of placenta found in most anthropoids in which materials pass between the maternal and fetal bloodstreams through a single vessel wall.

**hemoglobin**   Red pigment in red blood cells that carries oxygen to and carbon dioxide from body tissues.

**hemoglobin A (HbA)**   Normal adult hemoglobin whose globin unit consists of two alpha and two beta chains.

**hemoglobin A2**   A normal variant of hemoglobin A consisting of two alpha and two delta polypeptide chains that is found in small quantities in normal human blood.

**hemoglobin C**   An abnormal variant of hemoglobin A that differs from the latter in having a single amino acid substitution on the beta chain at the same position as the substitution producing hemoglobin S.

**hemoglobin F**   A normal variant of hemoglobin, also known as *fetal hemoglobin*, that consists of two alpha and two gamma polypeptide chains found in the fetus and early infant; it is gradually replaced by hemoglobin A.

**hemoglobin S (HbS)**   An abnormal variant of hemoglobin A that differs from the latter in having a single amino acid substitution on the beta chain; known as sickle hemoglobin.

**hemolytic disease**   Disease involving the destruction of blood cells.

**hemophilia**   A recessive X-linked trait characterized by excessive bleeding due to a faulty clotting mechanism.

**herd**   Among geladas, a large social unit consisting of several bands that come together under very good grazing conditions.

**heterodont dentition**   Dentition characterized by regional differentiation of teeth by function.

**heterozygous**   Having two different alleles of a particular gene.

**high-altitude hypoxia**   Low oxygen pressure due to being at high altitude.

**high-altitude (mountain) sickness**   Includes shortness of breath, physical and mental fatigue, rapid pulse rate, headaches; occurs in persons not acclimatized to high altitudes.

**higher taxa**   Taxa above the species level, such as family, order, class, phylum, and kingdom.

**hindbrain**   The posterior of three swellings in the hollow nerve cord of the primitive vertebrate brain formed by a thickening of the wall of the nerve cord.

**home range**   The area occupied by an animal or animal group.

**homeothermic**   The ability to control body temperature and maintain a high body temperature through physiological means.

**hominid**   A member of the family Hominidae, which includes modern humans and species of the genera *Ardipithecus, Australopithecus, Paranthropus,* and *Homo.*

**hominoid**   A member of the superfamily Hominoidea, which includes the apes and humans.

**homodont dentition**   Situation in which all teeth are basically the same in structure, although they may differ in size, as is found in reptiles.

**homologous chromosomes**   Chromosomes of the same pair containing the same genes but not necessarily the same alleles.

**homology**   A similarity due to the inheritance from a common ancestor.

**homoplasy**   A similarity that is not homologous. Homoplasy can arise from parallelism, convergence, analogy, and chance.

**homozygous**   Having two like alleles of a particular gene; homozygous dominant when the allele is dominant and homozygous recessive when the allele is recessive.

**homozygous dominant**   Having two dominant alleles of the same gene.

**homozygous recessive**   Having two recessive alleles of the same gene.

**hormones**   Complex molecules produced by the endocrine glands that regulate many bodily functions and processes.

**hybrid**   The result of a cross or mating between two different kinds of parents.

**hybrid inviability**   Form of reproductive isolation in which a mating between two species gives rise to a hybrid that is fertile but nevertheless does not leave any offspring.

**hybrid sterility**   Form of reproductive isolation in which a hybrid of two species is sterile.

**hydraulic behavior**   The transport and dispersal of bones in water.

**hypercalcemia**   High levels of calcium in blood caused by excessive amounts of vitamin D; sluggish nerve reflexes and calcification of soft tissues.

**hyperplasia**   Growth by virtue of increase in the total number of cells resulting from mitosis.

**hypertrophy**   Growth by virtue of increase in the size of cells.

**hyperventilation**   Increased breathing rate producing a high level of oxygen in the lungs.

**hypothermia**   Lowered body temperature induced by cold stress.

**hypothesis**   An informed supposition about the relationship of one variable to another.

**imitative magic**   A type of magic that is based on the belief that one can affect an actual entity such as a person or animal by manipulating the image of that entity.

**immunological comparison**   Method of molecular biology that compares molecules by use of antigen–antibody reactions.

**immunological distance (ID)**   A measure of the strength of an antigen–antibody reaction that is indicative of the evolutionary distance separating the populations being studied.

**immutable**   Unchanging.

**inclusive fitness**   An individual's own fitness plus his or her effect on the fitness of any relative.

**incomplete penetrance**   The situation in which an allele that is expected to be expressed is not always expressed.

**independent assortment**   A Mendelian principle that states that differing traits are inherited independently of each other. It applies only to genes on different chromosomes.

**index fossil**   A paleospecies that had a very wide geographical distribution but existed for a relatively short period of time, either becoming extinct or evolving into something else.

**induced mutation**   Mutation caused by human-made conditions.

**Industrial Age**   A cultural stage characterized by the first use of complex machinery, factories, urbanization, and other economic and general social changes from strictly agricultural societies.

**industry**   All artifacts in a site made from the same material, such as bone industry.

**infantile**   That period in an individual's life cycle from birth to the eruption of the first permanent teeth.

**insectivore**   An animal that eats primarily insects; also a member of the mammalian order Insectivora.

**interglacial**   Period of warming between two glacials.

**intermediate expression**   The situation whereby a heterozygous genotype is associated with a phenotype that is more or less intermediate between the phenotypes controlled by the two homozygous genotypes.

**intermembral index**   The length of the humerus and radius relative to the length of the femur and tibia.

**intersexual selection**   A form of sexual selection; selection for traits that make males more attractive to females.

**intrasexual selection**   A form of sexual selection. Selection for characteristics that make males better able to compete with one another for sexual access to females.

**inversion**   Form of chromosome aberration in which parts of a chromosome break and reunite in a reversed order. No genetic material is lost or gained, but the positions of the involved alleles are altered.

**Iron Age**   A cultural stage characterized by the use of iron as the main metal.

**ischial callosities**   A thickening of the skin overlying a posterior section of the pelvis (ischial tuberosity), found in Old World monkeys and some apes.

**isotopes**   Atoms of the same element but of different atomic weight.

**juvenile**   That period in an individual's life cycle that lasts from the eruption of the first to the eruption of the last permanent teeth.

**karyotype**   The standardized classification and arrangement of photographed chromosomes.

**kin selection**   A process whereby an individual's genes are selected for by virtue of that individual's increasing the chances that his or her kin's genes are propagated into the next generation.

**kinetochore**   Protein structures that form on each side of each centromere in cell division that function in chromosome orientation within the cell.

**kingdom**   A major division of living organisms. All organisms are placed into one of five kingdoms: Monera, Protista, Fungi, Planti, and Animalia.

**Klinefelter syndrome**   A sex-chromosome count of XXY; phenotypically male, tall stature, sterile.

**knuckle walking**   Semierect quadrupedalism, found in chimpanzees and gorillas, with upper parts of the body supported by knuckles as opposed to palms.

**kwashiorkor**   A form of protein-caloric malnutrition

brought about by a protein-deficient diet that contains a reasonable supply of low-quality carbohydrates.

**lactation**   Act of female mammal producing milk.

**lateralization**   See **asymmetry of function.**

**lesser apes**   The gibbons and siamang of Asia.

**lethals**   Defects that cause premature death.

**leukocyte**   A white blood cell; cell in blood that functions to destroy foreign substances.

**lexicon**   In linguistics, the total number of meaningful units (such as words and affixes) of a language.

**lexigram**   A symbol that represents a word.

**life expectancy**   How long a person can, on the average, expect to live.

**life span**   The theoretical genetically determined maximum age.

**linguistics**   The scientific study of language.

**linkage**   Association of genes on the same chromosome.

**linkage groups**   Sets of genes that are found on the same chromosome.

**lipids**   Class of compounds that includes fats, oils, and waxes.

**lithic (stone) industry**   All artifacts in a site that are made of stone.

**lithosphere**   The hard outer layer of the earth.

**local race**   Distinctive, partially isolated groups, usually remnants of once-larger units and large local races with a greater degree of gene flow occurring between them.

**Lower Paleolithic**   A cultural stage that begins with the manufacture of the first stone tools.

**lumbar curve**   A curve that forms in the lumbar region of the spine in humans.

**macroevolution**   "Large-scale" evolution; the evolution of new species and higher taxa.

**macula**   The central area of the retina consisting of cones only.

**mammals**   Members of the class Mammalia, a class of the subphylum Vertebrata, that are characterized by a constant level of activity independent of external temperature and by mammary glands, hair or fur, heterodonty, and other features.

**mammary glands**   Glands found in mammalian females that produce milk.

**mandible**   The bone of the lower jaw; contains the lower dentition.

**mandibular symphysis**   The area where the two halves of the mandible join together.

**mandibular torus**   A thickening of bone on the inside of the mandible.

**manuport**   An unmodified, natural rock, brought into a site by human agency, that shows no sign of alteration.

**marasmus**   A form of protein-caloric malnutrition caused by a diet deficient in both protein and carbohydrates.

**marsupial**   A member of the infraclass Metatheria of the class Mammalia; young are born at a relatively less-developed stage than in placental mammals. After birth, young attaches to a mammary gland in the pouch, where it continues to grow and develop.

**masseter**   A muscle of chewing that arises on the mandible and inserts on the zygomatic arch of the skull.

**maximum parsimony principle**   The principle that the most accurate phylogenetic tree is one that is based on the fewest changes in the genetic code.

**mechanical isolation**   Form of reproductive isolation that occurs because of an incompatibility in structure of the male and female sex organs.

**meiosis**   Form of cell division occurring in specialized tissues in the testes and ovary that leads to the production of gametes or sex cells.

**melanin**   Brown-black pigment found in the skin, eyes, and hair.

**melanocyte**   Specialized skin cell that produces the pigment melanin.

**menarche**   First menstruation.

**Mesolithic**   A cultural stage characterized by generalized hunting and gathering.

**messenger RNA (mRNA)**   Form of RNA that copies the DNA code in the nucleus and transports it to the ribosome.

**metacentric chromosome**   Chromosome in which the centromere appears roughly in the center and the two arms are roughly the same length.

**metaphase plate**   During cell division, the central plane of the cell.

**microenvironment**   A specific set of physical, biological, and cultural factors immediately surrounding the organism.

**microevolution**   "Small-scale" evolution; genetic changes within a population over time.

**microhabitat**   A very specific habitat in which a population is found.

**microrace**   Arbitrary division of large local races.

**midbrain**   The middle of the three swellings in the hollow nerve cord of the primitive vertebrate brain formed by a thickening of the wall of the nerve cord.

**Middle Paleolithic**   Refers to the stone tools of the Neandertals and their contemporaries.

**mitochondria**   Bodies found in the cytoplasm that convert the energy in the chemical bonds of organic molecules into ATP.

**mitochondrial DNA (mtDNA)**   A double-stranded loop of DNA found within the mitochondria; there can be as few as one or as many as a hundred mitochondria per cell, and each mitochondrion possesses between 4 and 10 mtDNA loops.

**mitosis**   Form of cell division whereby one-celled organisms divide and whereby body cells divide in growth and replacement.

**model** A representation of a phenomenon on which tests can be conducted and from which predictions can be made.

**modifying gene** A gene that alters the expression of another gene.

**mold** A cavity left in firm sediments by the decayed body of an organism.

**molecular biology** The comparative study of molecules.

**molecule** Two or more atoms linked by a chemical bond.

**monkey** Any member of the superfamilies Ceboidea (New World monkeys) and Cercopithecoidea (Old World monkeys).

**monocausal explanation** Attributing one cause to the explanation of a phenomenon.

**monogamous pair** A social group, found among lesser apes and other primates, consisting of a single mated pair and their young offspring.

**monotreme** A member of the subclass Prototheria of the class Mammalia; the egg-laying mammals.

**monozygotic twins** Identical twins; derived from a single zygote.

**morphology** The study of structure.

**mounting** A behavioral pattern whereby one animal jumps on the posterior area of a second animal as a part of the act of copulation or as a part of dominance behavior.

**Mousterian tradition** A Middle Paleolithic cultural tradition associated with the Neandertals, characterized by an increase in the number and variety of flake tools and an ultimate deemphasis of the hand ax.

**multicausal explanation** Attributing more than one cause to the existence of a phenomenon.

**multimale group** A social unit consisting of many adult males and adult females.

**multiple-allele series** A situation in which a gene has more than two alleles.

**mutation** An alteration of the genetic material.

**natural selection** Differential fertility and mortality of genotypes within a population.

**negative eugenics** Method of eliminating deleterious alleles from the gene pool by encouraging persons with such alleles not to reproduce.

**neocortex** Gray covering on the cerebrum of some vertebrates; site of higher mental processes.

**Neolithic** A cultural stage marked by established farming.

**New World semibrachiation** Locomotor pattern involving extensive use of hands and prehensile tail to suspend and propel the body in species otherwise quadrupedal.

**niche** See **ecological niche.**

**nocturnal** Active at night.

**nondisjunction** An error of meiosis in which the members of a pair of chromosomes move to the same pole rather than moving to opposite poles.

**notochord** A cartilaginous rod that runs along the back (dorsal) of all chordates at some point in their life cycle.

**nuchal crest** Flange of bone in the occipital region of the skull that serves as the attachment of the nuchal musculature of the back of the neck.

**nuchal muscle** The muscle in the back of the neck that functions to hold the head up. In primates with heavy facial skeletons, the large nuchal muscle attaches to a nuchal crest.

**nuclear DNA (nDNA)** DNA found within the nucleus of the cell.

**nuclear membrane** A structure that binds the nucleus within the cell.

**nucleic acid** The largest of the molecules found in living organisms; it is composed of chains of nucleotides.

**nucleotide** The basic building block of nucleic acids; a nucleotide is composed of a five-carbon sugar (either ribose or deoxyribose), a phosphate, and a base.

**nucleus** A structure found in the cell that contains the chromosomes.

**occipital condyles** Two rounded projections on either side of the foramen magnum that fit into a pair of sockets on the top of the spine, thus articulating the skull with the spine.

**occipital torus** A horizontal bar of bone seen above the angularity in the occipital.

**Old World semibrachiation** Locomotor pattern involving extensive use of hands in leaping in a basically quadrupedal animal.

**olfactory** Referring to the sense of smell.

**omnivorous** Eating both meat and vegetable food.

**one-male group** A social unit consisting of a single male associated with several females.

**ontogeny** The processes of growth and development of the individual from conception to death.

**ontology** The study of ontogeny.

**oogenesis** The production of ova.

**openness** A characteristic of language that refers to the expansionary nature of language, which enables people to coin new labels for new concepts and objects.

**opposable thumb** Anatomical arrangement in which the fleshy tip of the thumb can touch the fleshy tip of all the fingers.

**order** Major division of a class, consisting of closely related families.

**orthognathous** Describes a face that is relatively vertical as opposed to being prognathous.

**orthograde** Vertical posture.

**ossification** Process of bone formation.

**osteodontokeratic culture** An archaeological culture based on tools made of bone, teeth, and horn.

**osteology** The study of bones.

**outgroup** Species used in a cladistic analysis that are closely related to the species being studied and are used to differentiate between shared derived and ancestral derived features.

**ovulation** The point during the female reproductive cycle, usually the midpoint, when the ovum has matured and breaks through the wall of the ovary.

**ovum** A female gamete or sex cell.

**ozone** A molecule composed of three oxygen atoms ($O_3$). Atmospheric ozone shields organisms from excessive ultraviolet radiation.

**paleoanthropology** Scientific study of fossils and artifacts and the context in which they are found.

**paleoecology** The study of the relationship of extinct organisms or groups of organisms to their environments.

**Paleolithic** A type of culture called the "Old Stone Age."

**paleontology** The study of fossils.

**paleopathology** The study of injuries and disease in prehistoric populations.

**paleospecies** A group of similar fossils whose range of morphological variation does not exceed the range of variation of a closely related living species.

**palynology** The study of fossil pollen.

**pangenesis** An early and inaccurate idea that acquired characteristics of the parents are transmitted to their offspring.

**parallelism** Homoplastic similarities found in related species that did not exist in the common ancestor; however, the common ancestor provided initial commonalities that gave direction to the evolution of the similarities.

**partial pressure** The pressure exerted by a particular gas in the atmosphere.

**pedigree** A reconstruction of past mating in a family, expressed as a diagram.

**penetrance** The degree to which an allele is expressed in the phenotype.

**pentadactylism** Possessing five digits on the hand and/or foot.

**peptide bond** A link between amino acids in a protein.

**pericentric inversion** A type of inversion whereby two breaks occur in a chromosome, one on either side of the centromere, and the centerpiece becomes turned around and rejoined with the two outside pieces.

**period** A unit of geological time; a division of an era.

**peripheralization** Process whereby an adolescent animal encounters aggressive behavior from adults and gradually moves away from the group over time.

**permanent teeth** The second set of teeth that erupts in mammals; humans have 32 permanent teeth.

**phenotype** The observable and measurable characteristics of an organism.

**phenotypic sex** The sex that a person is judged to be, based on his or her physical appearance. Phenotypic sex may not correspond to chromosomal sex.

**phenylketonuria (PKU)** A genetic disease, inherited as a recessive, brought about by the absence of the enzyme responsible for the conversion of the amino acid phenylalanine to tyrosine; phenylalanine accumulates in the blood and then breaks down into by-products that cause severe mental retardation in addition to other symptoms.

**phenylthiocarbamide (PTC)** An artificially created substance whose main use is in detecting the ability to taste it; ability to taste PTC is inherited as a dominant.

**phosphate unit** A unit of the nucleic acid molecule consisting of a phosphate and four oxygen atoms.

**phyletic gradualism model** The idea that evolution is a slow process with gradual transformation of one population into another.

**phylogenetic tree** A graphic representation of evolutionary relationships among species.

**phylogeny** The evolutionary history of a population or taxon.

**phylum** Major division of a kingdom, consisting of closely related classes; represents a basic body plan.

**physical anthropology** A branch of anthropology concerned with human biology and evolution.

**physical environment** The inanimate elements that surround an organism.

**phytoliths** Microscopic pieces of silica that form within plants; the distinctive shapes of phytoliths found in different plants permit their identification when observed imbedded in fossil teeth.

**placenta** An organ that develops from fetal membranes that functions to pass oxygen, nutrients, and other substances to and waste material from the fetus.

**placental mammal** A member of the infraclass Eutheria of the class Mammalia; mammals that form a placenta.

**plasma** Liquid portion of the blood containing salts, sugars, fats, amino acids, hormones, plasma proteins, and so on.

**plasma membrane** A structure that binds the cell but allows for the entry and exit of certain substances.

**plate tectonics** The theory that the surface of the earth is divided into a number of plates that move in relationship to each other. Some of these plates carry the continents.

**platelets**   Cell fragments in the blood that function in blood clotting.

**platycephalic**   Having a low, relatively flat forehead.

**platyrrhine nose**   Nose in which nostrils open sideways and are usually separated by a broad nasal septum; characteristic of the New World monkeys.

**play**   Energetic and repetitive activity engaged in primarily by infants and juveniles.

**play group**   A group of juveniles within a larger social unit that engage in play behavior.

**pleiotropy**   Situation in which a single allele may affect an entire series of traits.

**pneumatized**   The presence of air spaces within some bones of the skull.

**point mutation**   An error at a particular point on the DNA molecule.

**polar body**   A cell that develops in oogenesis that contains little cytoplasm and does not develop into a mature ovum.

**polyandrous group**   A form of social organization found in primates in which a female has multiple mates.

**polygenic**   The result of the interaction of several genes.

**polymorphism**   The presence of several distinct forms of a gene or phenotypic trait within a population with frequencies greater than 1 percent.

**polypeptide**   Chain of amino acids.

**polyphyodonty**   The continuous replacement of teeth such as found in reptiles.

**population bottlenecking**   A form of sampling error in which a population is reduced in size, which in turn reduces variability in the population. The population that descends from the reduced population is therefore less variable than the original population.

**populationist**   The viewpoint that only individuals have reality and that the type is illusory; since no two individuals are exactly alike, variation underlies all existence.

**positive eugenics**   Method of increasing the frequency of desirable traits by encouraging reproduction by individuals with these traits.

**postmating mechanism**   Any form of reproductive isolation that occurs after mating.

**postorbital bar**   A feature of the skull formed by an upward extension of the zygomatic arch and a downward extension of the frontal bone that supports the eye.

**postorbital constriction**   As seen from a top view, a marked constriction in the skull immediately behind the orbits and brow ridge.

**postorbital septum**   A bony partition behind the eye that isolates the eye from the muscles of the jaw and forms a bony eye socket or orbit in which the eye lies.

**potassium-argon dating**   Chronometric dating technique based on the rate of decay of potassium 40 to argon 40.

**power grip**   A grip in which an object is held between the fingers and the palm with the thumb reinforcing the fingers.

**preadaptation**   The situation in which a new structure or behavior that evolved in one niche is by chance also suited, in some cases better suited, to a new niche.

**precision grip**   A grip in which an object is held between one or more fingers with the thumb fully opposed to the fingertips.

**predation model**   This is one of several models that give an explanation of why primates form groups. It is based on the hypothesis that a group of individuals can protect itself better from or even ward off attacks from predators better than an individual animal could do.

**prehensile tail**   A tail found in some New World monkeys that has the ability to grasp.

**premating mechanism**   A form of reproductive isolation that prevents mating from occurring.

**prenatal**   That period of an individual's life cycle from conception to birth.

**presenting**   A behavior involving a subordinate primate showing his or her anal region to a dominant animal.

**preservation potential**   The probability of a bone's being preserved after death.

**primary center of ossification**   Area of first appearance of bone within the cartilage model of a long bone.

**primatology**   The study of primates.

**prognathism**   A jutting forward of the facial skeleton and jaws.

**pronograde**   Posture with the body held parallel to the ground.

**prosimians**   Members of the suborder Prosimii; includes the living Madagascar lemuriformes and the lorises, potto, angwantibo, and galagos.

**protein**   Long chains of amino acids joined together by peptide bonds (a polypeptide chain).

**protein-caloric malnutrition**   A class of malnutrition that includes kwashiorkor and marasmus.

**protoculture**   The simplest or beginning aspects of culture as seen in some nonhuman primates.

**prototherian mammal**   A mammal belonging to the subclass Prototheria; a monotreme or egg-laying mammal.

**provisioned colony**   Groups of free-ranging primates that have become accustomed to humans because of the establishment of feeding stations.

**puberty**   An event in the life cycle that includes rapid increase in stature, development of sex organs, and the development of secondary sexual characteristics.

**pubic symphysis**   The area of the pelvis at which the two innominates join.

**punctuated equilibrium**  A model of evolution characterized by an uneven tempo of change.

**purine**  Base found in nucleic acids that consists of two connected rings of carbon and nitrogen; in DNA and RNA, adenine and guanine.

**pyrimidine**  Base found in nucleic acids that consists of a single ring of carbon and nitrogen; in DNA, thymine and cytosine; in RNA, uracil and cytosine.

**quadrumanous**  Locomotor pattern found among orangutans who often suspend themselves under branches and move slowly using both forelimbs and hindlimbs.

**quadrupedalism**  Locomotion using four limbs, with hands and feet moving on a surface such as the ground or top of a branch of a tree.

**race**  A division of a species; a subspecies.

**radiation**  Electromagnetic energy that is given off by an object.

**radioactivity**  The phenomenon whereby an atom that is unstable will radioactively decay into another type of atom and in the process emit energy and/or particles.

**radiocarbon dating**  A method of chronometric dating based on the decay of carbon 14.

**radiometric dating techniques**  Chronometric dating methods based on the decay of radioactive materials; examples are radiocarbon and potassium-argon dating.

**range**  See **home range.**

**recessive**  An allele that is expressed only in the homozygous recessive condition.

**recombination**  A mechanism of meiosis responsible for each gamete's uniqueness. As the chromosomes line up in metaphase, they can combine into several configurations.

**red blood cell**  See **erythrocyte.**

**regional continuity model**  The hypothesis stating that modern *H. sapiens* had multiple origins from existing local populations; each local population of archaic humans gave rise to a population of modern *H. sapiens.*

**regulatory gene**  A segment of DNA that functions to initiate or block the function of another gene.

**relative fitness (RF)**  The fitness of a genotype compared to the fitness of another genotype in the same gene system. Relative fitness is measured on a scale of 0 to 1.

**reliable**  Predictable.

**replacement model**  The hypothesis that states that modern *H. sapiens* evolved in Africa and radiated out of this area, replacing archaic hominid populations.

**reproductive isolating mechanism**  A mechanism that prevents reproduction from occurring between two populations.

**reproductive population**  A group of organisms capable of successful reproduction.

**reptiles**  Members of the class Reptilia; terrestrial vertebrates that include the lizards, snakes, and turtles.

**residual volume**  The amount of air still remaining in the lungs after the most forceful expiration.

**resource-defense model**  This is one of several models that give an explanation of why primates form groups. It is based on the hypothesis that a group of individuals can defend access to resources such as food and keep other animals and other groups away from these resources better than an individual can.

**restriction enzyme**  Enzyme used to "cut" the DNA molecule at specific sites; used in recombinant DNA technology.

**retina**  The layer of cells in the back of the eye that contains the cells, rods and cones, that are sensitive to light.

**retinoblastoma**  A cancer of the retina of the eye in children, inherited as a dominant.

**retouch**  Further refinement in the manufacture of stone tools by the removal of additional small flakes.

**Rh blood-type system**  A blood type system consisting of two major alleles. A mating between a Rh− mother and Rh+ father may produce in the infant the hemolytic disease erythroblastosis fetalis.

**rhinarium**  The moist naked area surrounding the nostrils in most mammals; absent in most primates.

**ribonucleic acid (RNA)**  A type of nucleic acid based on the sugar ribose; exists in cells as messenger RNA and transfer RNA.

**ribose**  A five-carbon sugar found in RNA.

**ribosome**  Small spherical body within the cytoplasm of the cell in which protein synthesis takes place.

**rickets**  A bone disease that is usually caused by a lack of calcium, phosphate, or vitamin D.

**rods**  Cells of the retina of the eye that are sensitive to the presence or absence of light; function in black-and-white vision.

**sagittal crest**  Ridge of bone along the midline of the top of the skull that serves for the attachment of the temporalis muscle.

**sagittal keel**  A bony ridge formed by a thickening of bone along the top of the skull; characteristic of *H. erectus.*

**sampling error**  In population genetics, the transmission of a nonrepresentative sample of the gene pool over space or time due to chance.

*Scala naturae*  A rank-order sequence of contemporary animals that falsely suggests an evolutionary sequence.

**scent marking** Marking territory by urinating or defecating, or by rubbing scent glands against trees or other objects.

**science** A way of learning about the world by applying the principles of scientific thinking, which includes making empirical observations, proposing hypotheses to explain those observations, and testing those hypotheses in valid and reliable ways; also refers to the organized body of knowledge that results from scientific study.

**scraper** A tool manufactured from a flake with a scraping edge on the end or side.

**seasonal isolation** Form of reproductive isolation in which the breeding season of two closely related populations do not exactly correspond.

**secondary center of ossification** Area of bone development, usually near the end of a long bone.

**secondary sexual characteristic** Physical feature other than the genitalia that distinguishes males from females after puberty.

**sectorial premolar** Unicuspid first lower premolar with a shearing edge.

**secular trend** The tendency over the last hundred or so years for each succeeding generation to mature earlier and become, on the average, larger.

**sediment** Material that is suspended in water; in still water, it will settle at the bottom.

**sedimentary beds** Beds or layers of sediments called strata.

**sedimentation** The accumulation of geological or organic material deposited by air, water, or ice.

**segregation** In the formation of sex cells, the process in which paired hereditary factors separate, forming sex cells that contain either one or the other factor.

**selective agent** Any factor that brings about differences in fertility and mortality.

**selective breeding** The deliberate breeding of domesticated animals or plants.

**selective coefficient** A numerical expression of the strength of a selective force operating on a specific genotype.

**selective pressure** Pressure placed by a selective agent on certain individuals within the population that results in the change of allele frequencies in the next generation.

**sex chromosomes** The X and Y chromosomes. Males usually have one X and one Y chromosome; females usually have two X chromosomes.

**sex-controlled trait** Non-sex-linked trait that is expressed differently in males and females.

**sex-limited trait** Non-sex-linked trait that is expressed in only one of the sexes.

**sexual dimorphism** Differences in structure between males and females of the same species.

**sexual isolation** Form of reproductive isolation in which one or both sexes of a species initiate mating behavior that does not act as a stimulus to the opposite sex of a closely related species.

**sexual selection** Selection that favors characteristics that increase reproductive success, usually due to male competition or female mate choice.

**sexual skin** Found in the female of some primate species; skin in anal region that turns bright pink or red and may swell when animal is in estrus.

**shared ancestral (symplesiomorphic) feature** Compared with shared derived features, a homology that did not appear as recently and is therefore shared by a larger group of species.

**shared derived (synapomorphic) feature** A recently appearing homology that is shared by a relatively small group of closely related taxa.

**sharing cluster** Among chimpanzees, a temporary group that forms after hunting to eat the meat.

**shell midden** A large mound composed of shells, which provides evidence of the emphasis on shellfish as a food resource.

**shovel-shaped incisors** Incisors that have a scooped-out shape on the tongue side of the tooth.

**sickle-cell anemia** Disorder in individuals homozygous for hemoglobin S in which red blood cells will develop into a sickle shape, which, in turn, will clog capillaries, resulting in anemia, heart failure, and so on.

**sickle-cell trait** The condition of being heterozygous for hemoglobin A and S, yet the individual usually shows no abnormal symptoms.

**simian shelf** A bony buttress on the inner surface of the foremost part of the ape mandible, functioning to reinforce the mandible.

**single-crystal fusion** A form of potassium-argon dating that uses a laser to melt individual crystals to release the argon.

**site** A location where artifacts are found.

**social Darwinism** The application of the principles of biological evolutionary theory to an analysis of social phenomena.

**social intelligence** The knowledge and images that originate in an individual's brain that are transferred by speech (and in the last 5000 years, writing) to the brains of others.

**sonogram** The image produced by ultrasound equipment.

**specialized species** A species closely fitted to a specific niche and able to tolerate little change in that niche.

**specialized trait** Structure used primarily for one function.

**speciation** An evolutionary process that is said to occur when two previous subspecies (of the same species) are no longer capable of successful interbreeding; they are then two different species.

**species**   The largest natural population whose members are able to reproduce successfully among themselves but not with members of other species.

**sperm**   Male gamete or sex cell.

**spermatid**   Cells produced by meiosis in the male that are transformed into mature sperm.

**spermatogenesis**   Sperm production.

**spindle**   Structure that appears in the cell undergoing cell division that is responsible for the movement of the chromosomes.

**spontaneous generation**   An old and incorrect idea that complex life forms could be spontaneously created from nonliving material.

**spontaneous mutation**   Mutation that occurs spontaneously, that is, in response to the usual conditions within the body or environment.

**stabilizing selection**   A type of natural selection characterized by a generation-after-generation shift in a population in the direction of the average (mean) individual, such as, for example, towards average body size. In this example, individuals with small and large body size are being selected against.

**standard deviation**   A statistical measurement of the amount of variation in a series of determinations; the probability of the real number falling within plus or minus one standard deviation is 67 percent.

**stereoscopic vision**   Visual perception of depth due to overlapping visual fields and various neurological features.

**strata**   Layers of sedimentary rocks.

**stratigraphy**   The investigation of the composition of the layers of the earth, used in relative dating; based on the principle of superposition.

**stratosphere**   That part of the atmosphere 20 to 50 kilometers (12 to 31 miles) above the earth's surface where ozone forms.

**structural gene**   A segment of DNA that codes for a polypeptide that has a phenotypic expression.

**subchron**   A small subdivision within a chron.

**subcutaneous fat**   The fat deposited under the skin.

**subera**   A division of an era. The Cenozoic is divided into two suberas, the Tertiary and Quaternary.

**submetacentric chromosome**   Chromosome in which the centromere lies to one side of the center, producing arms of unequal length.

**submission**   In a primate dominance hierarchy, submission is the act of giving way to a more dominant individual

**subspecies**   Interfertile groups within a species that display significant differentiation among themselves.

**superposition**   Principle that under stable conditions, strata on the bottom of a deposit were laid down first and hence are older than layers on top.

**suspensory behavior**   Form of locomotion and posture whereby animals suspend themselves underneath a branch.

**sweating**   The production of a fluid, sweat, by the sweat glands of the skin; the evaporation of the sweat from the skin leads to a cooling of the body.

**symbol**   Something that can represent something distant from it in time and space.

**sympatric species**   Different species living in the same area but prevented from successfully reproducing by a reproductive isolating mechanism.

**symphyseal face**   The surface of the pubis where one pubis joins the other at the pubic symphysis.

**symplesiomorphic feature**   See **shared ancestral feature.**

**synapomorphic feature**   See **shared derived feature.**

**syndrome**   A complex of symptoms related to a single cause.

**synthetic theory of evolution**   The theory of evolution that fuses Darwin's concept of natural selection with information from the fields of genetics, mathematics, embryology, paleontology, animal behavior, and other disciplines.

**system**   A collection of parts that are interrelated so that a change in any one part brings about specifiable changes in the others.

**tactile pads**   The tips of the fingers and toes of primates; areas richly endowed by tactile nerve endings sensitive to touch.

**taphonomy**   The study of the processes of burial and fossilization.

**taxon**   A group of organisms at any level of the taxonomic hierarchy. The major taxa are the species and genus and the higher taxa: family, order, class, phylum, and kingdom.

**taxonomy**   The theory of classification.

**Tay-Sachs disease**   Enzyme deficiency of lipid metabolism inherited as a recessive; causes death in early childhood.

**tectonic plate**   A segment of the lithosphere.

**telocentric chromosome**   Chromosome in which the centromere is located at the very end of the chromosome.

**temporalis**   A muscle of chewing that arises on the jaw and inserts on the side of the skull.

**temporal-nuchal crest**   A crest on the back of the skull, forming on the occipital and temporal bones.

**temporomandibular joint**   The joint formed at the point of articulation of the mandible and the base of the skull.

**termite stick**   Tool made and used by chimpanzees for collecting termites for food.

**territory**   The area that a group defends against other members of its own species.

**testosterone**   A male sex hormone.

**thalassemia**   Absence or reduction of alpha- or beta-chain synthesis in hemoglobin; in the homozygous condition (thalassemia major), a high frequency of hemoglobin F and fatal anemia occurs; in the heterozygous condition (thalassemia minor), it is highly variable but usually occurs with mild symptoms.

**theory**   A step in the scientific method in which a statement is generated on the basis of highly confirmed hypotheses and used to generalize about conditions not yet tested.

**theory of acquired characteristics**   Concept, popularized by Lamarck, that traits gained during a lifetime can then be passed on to the next generation by genetic means; considered invalid today.

**therian mammal**   A mammal belonging to the subclass Theria; the "live-bearing" mammals including the marsupials and placental mammals.

**thermoluminescence dating**   A chronometric dating method based on the fact that when some materials are heated, they give off a flash of light. The intensity of the light is proportional to the amount of radiation to which the sample has been exposed and the length of time since the sample was heated.

**threat gesture**   A physical activity that serves to threaten another animal. Some threat gestures are staring, shaking a branch, and lunging toward another animal.

**thymine**   One of the bases found in DNA.

**tool**   An object that appears to have been used for a specific purpose.

**trait**   One aspect of the phenotype.

**transfer RNA (tRNA)**   Within the ribosome, a form of RNA that transports amino acids into the positions coded in the mRNA.

**translocation**   Form of chromosomal mutation in which segments of chromosomes become detached and reunite to other nonhomologous chromosomes.

**tree-ring dating**   Chronometric dating method that determines the age of a wood sample by counting the number of annual growth rings.

**trisomy**   The state of having three of the same chromosome, rather than the normal pair. For example, trisomy 21 or Down Syndrome is a tripling of chromosome number 21.

**troop**   A multimale group found among baboons and other primates.

**true brachiation**   Hand-over-hand locomotion along a branch with the body suspended underneath the branch by the arms.

**true-breeding**   Showing the same traits without exception over many generations.

**tuff**   Geological formation composed of compressed volcanic ash.

**tundra**   A type of landscape where the ground is frozen solid throughout most of the year but thaws slightly during the summer.

**Turner syndrome**   Genetic disease characterized by 45 chromosomes with a sex chromosome count of X–; phenotypically female, but sterile.

**twin studies**   Comparisons of monozygotic twins to dizygotic twins for the purpose of estimating the degree of environmental versus genetic influence operating on a specific trait.

**tympanic membrane**   The ear drum.

**typological**   The viewpoint that basic variation of a type is illusory and that only fixed ideal types are real; two fossils that differ from each other in certain respects represent two types and, hence, are two different species.

**ultrasound**   A method of taking a picture of the fetus using sound waves.

**unconformity**   The surface of a stratum that represents a break in the stratigraphic sequence.

**uniformitarianism**   Principle that states that physical forces working today to alter the earth were also in force and working in the same way in former times.

**uniquely derived feature**   See **autapomorphic feature.**

**Upper Paleolithic**   Refers to the stone tools of anatomically modern peoples.

**uracil**   One of the bases found in RNA.

**utilized material**   Pieces of stone that have been used without modification.

**variable**   Any property that may be displayed in different values.

**vasoconstriction**   Constriction of the capillaries in the skin in response to cold temperatures that prevents much of the warm blood from reaching the surface of the body where heat could be lost.

**vasodilation**   Opening up of the capillaries of the skin in response to warm temperatures, increasing the flow of blood to the surface of the body and thereby increasing the loss of body heat.

**velocity curve**   A curve that illustrates the velocity or rate of growth over time by plotting the degree of growth per unit of time.

**ventral**   The front or bottom side of an animal.

**Venus figurines**   Small Upper Paleolithic statues characterized by exaggerated breasts and buttocks and very stylized heads, hands, and feet.

**vertebrate**   A member of the subphylum Vertebrata; possesses a bony spine or vertebral column.

**vertical clinging and leaping** A method of locomotion in which the animal clings vertically to a branch and moves between branches by leaping vertically from one to another. The animal moves on the ground by hopping or moves bipedally.

**white blood cell** See **leukocyte.**

**X chromosome** The larger of the two sex chromosomes. Females usually possess two X chromosomes; males usually possess one X and one Y chromosome.

**X-linked** Refers to genes on the X chromosome.

**Y chromosome** The smaller of the two sex chromosomes. Females usually possess no Y chromosome; males usually possess one X and one Y chromosome.

**Y-5 pattern** Pattern found on molars with five cusps separated by grooves, reminiscent of the letter Y.

**Y-linked** Refers to genes on the Y chromosome.

**yolk sac** A sack formed from embryonic tissue in the amniote egg that contains yolk.

**zygomatic arch** The "cheek" bone; an arch of bone on the side of the skull.

**zygote** A fertilized ovum.

**zygotic mortality** Form of reproductive isolation in which fertilization occurs but development stops soon after.

# Glossary of Primate Higher Taxa

Extinct taxa are indicated by a †.

**Adapidae†** Family of Eocene prosimians found in North America, Asia, Europe, and possibly Africa; may be related to lemurs and lorises.

**Adapinae†** Subfamily of the Adapidae found in Europe and Asia.

**Alouattinae** Subfamily of the Cebidae; includes the howler monkeys.

**Anthropoidea** Suborder of the order Primates; includes the New World monkeys, Old World monkeys, apes, and humans.

**Aotinae** Subfamily of the Cebidae; includes the owl monkeys.

**Callitrichidae** A family of New World monkeys consisting of the marmosets and tamarins.

**Catarrhini** Infraorder of the order Primates that includes the superorders Cercopithecoidea and Hominoidea.

**Cebidae** A family of New World monkeys that includes the squirrel, spider, howler, and capuchin monkeys, among others.

**Cebinae** Subfamily of the Cebidae; includes the capuchin and squirrel monkeys.

**Ceboidea** A superfamily of the suborder Anthropoidea; includes all the New World monkeys, consisting of the families Callitrichidae and Cebidae.

**Cercopithecidae** Family of the superfamily Cercopithecoidea; includes the Old World monkeys.

**Cercopithecinae** Subfamily of the family Cercopithecidae; includes the Old World monkeys that are omnivorous and possess cheek pouches such as the macaques, baboons, guenons, and mangabeys.

**Cercopithecoidea** Superfamily of the suborder Anthropoidea; consists of the Old World monkeys.

**Colobinae** A subfamily of family Cercopithecidae; the Old World monkeys that are specialized leaf-eaters, possessing a complex stomach and lacking cheek pouches, such as the langurs and colobus monkeys.

**Daubentoniidae** Family of Madagascar prosimians consisting of the aye-aye.

**Hominidae** Family of the superfamily Hominoidea; includes humans.

**Hominoidea** Superfamily of the suborder Anthropoidea; includes the apes and humans.

**Hylobatidae** Family of the superfamily Hominoidea; the lesser apes consisting of the gibbons and siamang.

**Indriidae** Family of Madagascar prosimians that includes the indri, sifaka, and avahi.

**Lemuridae** A Madagascar prosimian family that includes the lemurs.

**Lorisidae** Prosimian family that includes the loris, potto, angwantibo, and galago.

**Omomyidae†** Family of Eocene and Oligocene primates, showing some resemblance to the tarsiers, found in North America, Europe, Asia, and Africa.

**Panidae** Family within the superfamily Hominoidea that consists of the chimpanzee, bonobo, and gorilla.

**Parapithecidae†** Family of the order Primates consisting of Early Oligocene primates from the Fayum, Egypt.

**Parapithecoidea†** Suborder of the order Primates that contains the family Parapithecidae.

**Pithecinae** Subfamily of the Cebidae; includes the titis, sakis, and uakaris.

**Platyrrhini** Infraorder of the order Primates that includes the New World monkeys and various New World fossil taxa.

**Plesiopithecidae†** Family within the superfamily Plesiopithecoidea; contains the genus *Plesiopithecus,* from the Oligocene of the Fayum, Egypt.

**Plesiopithecoidea†** Superfamily within the suborder Prosimii; contains the genus *Plesiopithecus,* from the Oligocene of the Fayum, Egypt.

**Pongidae** Family within the superfamily Hominoidea that consists of the orangutan.

**Primates** Order of the class Mammalia that includes the living prosimians, tarsiers, New World monkeys, Old World monkeys, lesser apes, great apes, and humans.

**Proconsulidae†** Family of miocene hominoids from Africa.

**Propliopithecidae†** Family of the infraorder Catarrhini from the Middle Oligocene to Late Miocene of Africa and Europe; they may have given rise to the Old World monkeys and the hominoids.

**Prosimii** Suborder of the order Primates that includes the lemurs, indris, and aye-aye of Madagascar, and the lorises, potto, angwantibo, and galagos.

**Tarsiidae** Family of the suborder Tarsioidea that consists of the tarsiers.

**Tarsioidea** Suborder of the primates consisting of the tarsiers.

**Victoriapithecidae†** Family of Early and Middle Miocene Old World monkeys from north and east Africa.

# Photo Credits

**Chapter 1**

Figure 1–1     Peter Weit/SYGMA
Figure 1–3     Culver Pictures
Figure 1–5     National Portrait Gallery, London
Figure 1–6     David Muench/Tony Stone Images
Figure 1–7     Photograph by Dodie Stoneburner
Figure 1–8     National Portrait Gallery, London
Figure 1–10    Brown Brothers
Figure 1–11    *(a)* Fred Bavendam/Peter Arnold, Inc. *(b)* David Cavagnaro/Peter Arnold, Inc.
Figure B1–2    Culver Pictures

**Chapter 2**

Figure 2–6     *(a) (b)* Leonard Lessin/Peter Arnold, Inc.

**Chapter 2 Color Insert**

Figure 2–A     Ray Simmons/Photo Researchers
Figure 2–B     Michael Abbey/Photo Researchers
Figure 2–C     Leonard Lessin/Peter Arnold, Inc.
Figure 2–D     Tony Stone Imaging/Tony Stone Images

**Chapter 3**

Figure 3–4     *(b)* Gernsheim Collection, Harry Ransom Humanities Research Center, The University of Texas at Austin
Figure 3–5     *(a)* Science VU/© Valerie Lindgren/Visuals Unlimited *(b)* Courtesy of the National Foundation, March of Dimes

Figure 3–6     *(a) (b)* Courtesy of Patricia Farnsworth, Ph.D., UMD–NJ Medical School
Figure 3–7     Photograph by Philip L. Stein

**Chapter 4**

Figure B4–1    Courtesy Victor A. McKusick, Johns Hopkins University

**Chapter 5**

Figure 5–8     Werner H. Muller/Peter Arnold, Inc.
Figure 5–9     San Diego Zoo

**Chapter 6**

Figure 6–1     Culver Pictures
Figure 6–12    Zoological Society of San Diego
Figure 6–13    Ron Garrison/Zoological Society of San Diego

**Chapter 7**

Figure 7–3     *(a) (b) (c)* Photograph by Dodie Stoneburner
Figure 7–6     Courtesy of Jeffery H. Schwartz, University of Pittsburgh
Figure 7–8     Courtesy of Prof. Bernhard Meier, Ruhr–Universität Bochum
Figure 7–9     Courtesy of Prof. Bernhard Meier, Ruhr–Universität Bochum

## Chapter 10 Color Insert

**Figure 10–A**  Robert C. Bailey
**Figure 10–B**  Robert C. Bailey
**Figure 10–C**  Robert C. Bailey

## Chapter 11

**Figure 11–1**  Sygma
**Figure 11–2**  (a) Neg. #315485, Courtesy Department of Library Services, American Museum of Natural History (b) Neg. #325097, Courtesy Department of Library Services, American Museum of Natural History (c) Neg. #125158, Courtesy Department of Library services, American Museum of Natural History
**Figure 11–4**  Photograph by Rick Freed
**Figure 11–6**  (a) (b) (c) (d) (e) (f) From John Buettner–Janusch, *Origins of Man*, 1966. Used with permission of John Wiley & Sons, Inc.
**Figure B11–2**  E.M. Fulda/American Museum of Natural History
**Figure B11–3**  Breck P. Kent/Earth Scenes

## Chapter 11 Color Insert:

**Figure 11–A**  Institute of Human Origins
**Figure 11–B**  Institute of Human Origins
**Figure 11–C**  Institute of Human Origins
**Figure 11–D**  Institute of Human Origins
**Figure 11–E**  Institute of Human Origins
**Figure 11–F**  Institute of Human Origins
**Figure 11–G**  Institute of Human Origins
**Figure 11–H**  Institute of Human Origins

## Chapter 12

**Figure 12–5**  (b) Courtesy of Russell Ciochon, University of Iowa
**Figure 12–7**  Courtesy of Elwyn L. Simons and the Peabody Museum of Natural History, Yale University, New Haven, CT
**Figure 12–8**  Courtesy of Elwyn L. Simons and the Peabody Museum of Natural History, Yale University, New Haven, CT
**Figure 12–10**  Courtesy of T. Setoguchi and A.L. Rosenberger
**Figure 12–11**  National Geographic Society
**Figure 12–12**  The Natural History Museum, London
**Figure 12–13**  The Natural History Museum, London
**Figure 12–17**  (a) Courtesy of and Copyright © Eric Delson
**Figure 12–17**  (b) Courtesy of and Copyright © Eric Delson

**Figure 12–18**  W. Sacco/Anthro–Photo

## Chapter 13

**Figure 13–2**  Copyright © 1994 Tim D. White/Brill Atlanta
**Figure 13–3**  Alun R. Hughes by permission of Professor Philip V. Tobias
**Figure 13–4**  Alun R. Hughes, Paleoanthropology Research Unit, University of Witwatersrand
**Figure 13–5**  Photograph by J.F. Thackery, Courtesy of the Transvaal Museum, Pretoria
**Figure 13–6**  Photograph by J.F. Thackery, Courtesy of the Transvaal Museum, Pretoria
**Figure 13–8**  Photograph by J.F. Thackery, Courtesy of the Transvaal Museum. Pretoria
**Figure 13–10**  National Geographic Society, courtesy of Hugo Van Lawick
**Figure 13–11**  National Geographic Society
**Figure 13–12**  (a) (b) (c) Courtesy of R.E.F. Leakey, National Museums of Kenya
**Figure 13–13**  Photo by Alan Walker/National Museums of Kenya
**Figure 13–14**  Kenneth Garrett/National Geographic Image Collection
**Figure 13–15**  Kenneth Garrett/National Geographic Image Collection
**Figure 13–16**  Institute of Human Origins
**Figure 13–17**  © David L. Brill 1985
**Figure 13–18**  Don Johanson/Institute of Human Origins
**Figure 13–19**  © David L. Brill 1999/Atlanta
**Figure 13–20**  Tim White
**Figure 13–21**  Andrew Hill/Anthro–Photo
**Figure 13–22**  Michel Brunet
**Figure 13–28**  (A) (B) © David L. Brill 1999/Atlanta

## Chapter 13 Color Insert:

**Figure 13–A**  Donald C. Johanson/Institute of Human Origins
**Figure 13–B**  Jay Kelley/Anthro–Photo
**Figure 13–C**  David L. Brill/National Geographic Society and the National Museums of Kenya
**Figure 13–D**  John Reader/Science Photo Library, Science Source/Photo Researchers

## Chapter 14

**Figure 14–1**  Courtesy of R.E.F. Leakey, National Museums of Kenya
**Figure 14–2**  Natural History Museum, London
**Figure 14–3**  (a) Neg. #336185, Courtesy Department

of Library Services, American Museum of Natural History *(b) (c)* Neg. #336412 Courtesy Department of Library Services, American Museum of Natural History

**Figure 14–4**   Natural History Museum, London

**Figure 14–6**   *(a) (b) (c)* Courtesy of R.E.F. Leakey, National Museums of Kenya

**Figure 14–7**   David L. Brill/National Geographic Society and the National Museums of Kenya

**Figure 14–8**   David L. Brill/National Museums of Kenya

**Figure 14–10**   Natural History Museum, London

**Figure 14–11**   Neg. #410816, Courtesy Department of Library Services, American Museum of Natural History

**Figure 14–12**   Milford H. Wolpoff

**Figure 14–13**   *(a) (b)* Li Tianyuan

**Figure 14–14**   David L. Brill photo of Musee de l'Homme, Paris Artifact/Brill Atlanta

**Figure 14–15**   From the collection of the Peabody Museum, Harvard. Courtesy of Erik Trinkaus

**Figure 14–17**   *(a)* Neg. #327423, Courtesy Department of Library Services, American Museum of Natural History *(b)* Neg. #327424, Courtesy Department of Library Services, American Museum of Natural History

**Figure 14–19**   David L. Brill/Brill Atlanta

**Figure B14–4**   Copyright © Erik Trinkaus. Used with permission of Erik Trinkaus

**Figure 14–21**   Photograph courtesy of Sileshi Semaw, Department of Anthropology, Douglas College, Rutgers university, New Brunswick, NJ

**Figure 14–25**   Courtesy of Kathy D. Schick and Nicholas Toth, CRAFT Research Center, Indiana University. From Schick and Toth, *Making Silent Stones Speak*, 1993, p. 167.

**Figure 14–27**   Courtesy of Pat Shipman

## Chapter 15

**Figure 15–2**   Natural History Museum, London

**Figure 15–3**   *(a)* Neg. # 109229, Courtesy Department of Library Services, American Museum of Natural History *(b)* Neg. # 310705, Courtesy Department of Library Services, American Museum of Natural History

**Figure 15–4**   Natural History Museum, London

**Figure 15–6**   Natural History Museum, London

**Figure 15–7**   Courtesy James C. Chatters © 1996

**Figure 15–9**   *(b)* Collection Phototheque de Musee de l'Homme, Paris

**Figure 15–10**   Professor Randall White, New York University

**Figure 15–11**   Neg. # 326474 Courtesy Department of Library Services, American Museum of Natural History

**Figure 15–12**   Neg. # 15038 Courtesy Department of Library Services, American Museum of Natural History

**Figure B15–2**   Jean Clottes/Ministere de al Culture/Sygma

**Figure 15–13**   Denver Museum of Natural History

## Chapter 16

**Figure 16–5**   Philip L. Stein

**Figure 16–6**   *(a)* Neg. # 231604/R. MacMillan. Department of Library Services, American Museum of Natural History *(b)* Mark M. Lawrence/The Stock Market

**Figure 16–10**   *(a) (b)* Courtesy of J.M. Tanner, Institute of Child Health, University of London

**Figure 16–17**   *(a)* Steve Mains/Stock Boston *(b)* Sygma

## Chapter 17

**Figure 17–4**   *(a)* Anthropological Archives, Smithsonian Institution Photo 3084 *(b)* Gaye Hilsenrath/The Picture Cube

**Figure 17–5**   *(a)* Culver Pictures *(b)* The Bettmann Archive/Bettmann Newsphotos *(c)* Culver Pictures

## Chapter 17 Color Insert

**Figure 17–A**   Irven DeVore/Anthro–Photo

**Figure 17–B**   Tronick/Anthro–Photo

**Figure 17–C**   Victor Englebert/Photo Researchers, Inc.

**Figure 17–D**   George Holton/Photo Researchers, Inc.

**Figure 17–E**   Anthro–Photo

**Figure 17–F**   Mike Yamashita/Woodfin Camp & Associates

**Figure 17–G**   Halpern/Anthro–Photo

**Figure 17–H**   George Holton/Photo Researchers, Inc.

**Figure 17–I**   Michael McCoy/Photo Researchers, Inc.

**Figure 17–J**   Jack Fields/Photo Researchers, Inc.

**Figure 17–K**   Paolo Koch/Photo Researchers, Inc.

**Figure 17–L**   Ch. et J. Lenars/Explorer, Science Source/Photo Researchers

**Figure 17–M**   Daniel Zirinoky/Photo Researchers, Inc.

**Figure 17–N**   Rapho Division/Photo Researchers, Inc.

**Figure 17–O**   Emil Muench, ASPA/Photo Researchers, Inc.

## Epilogue

**Figure E–2**   Ray Ellis/Photo Researchers

# Illustration Credits

**Figure 2–11** Postlethwait, John H., and J. L. Hopson, *The Nature of Life.* Copyright © 1989 by McGraw-Hill, Inc. Reprinted by permission of McGraw-Hill, Inc.

**Figure 2–12** Postlethwait, John H., J. L. Hopson, and R. C. Veres, *Biology.* Copyright © 1991 by McGraw-Hill, Inc. Reprinted by permission of McGraw-Hill, Inc.

**Figure 2–13** Postlethwait, John H., J. L. Hopson, and R. C. Veres, *Biology.* Copyright © 1991 by McGraw-Hill, Inc. Reprinted by permission of McGraw-Hill, Inc.

**Figure 2–E** Mader, S. S., *Biology,* 6th edition, 1998, Figure 9.5 on pp. 152–153. Copyright 1998. Reprinted by permission of The McGraw-Hill Companies.

**Figure 2–F** Mader, S.S., *Biology,* 6th edition, 1998, Figures 10.4 & 10.5 on pp. 164–165. Copyright 1998. Reprinted by permission of The McGraw-Hill Companies.

**Figure 3–9** Mader, S. S., *Biology,* 6th edition, 1998, Figure 17.10 on p. 279. Copyright 1998. Reprinted by permission of The McGraw-Hill Companies.

**Figure 4–3** Cavalli-Sforza, L. L., "Genetic Drift in an Italian Population," *Scientific American,* August, 1969, p. 32. Copyright © 1969 by Scientific American, Inc. All rights reserved. Reprinted by permission of Scientific American and Academic Press.

**Table 4–7** Stern, Curt, *Principles of Human Genetics,* 3rd edition, 1973. Copyright © 1973 W. H. Freeman and Company. Reprinted by permission.

**Figure 5–6** Buettner-Janusch, John, *Origins of Man.* Copyright © 1966 by John Wiley & Sons, Inc. Reprinted by permission of John Wiley & Sons, Inc.

**Figure 5–14** Postlethwait, John H., and J. L. Hopson, *The Nature of Life.* Copyright © 1989 by McGraw-Hill, Inc. Reprinted by permission of McGraw-Hill, Inc.

**Figure 5–15** Lack, David, *Darwin's Finches,* 1947. Reprinted with the permission of Cambridge University Press.

**Box 6–1** Wilson, E. O., *The Diversity of Life.* Cambridge, Mass.: The Belknap Press of Harvard University Press, Copyright © 1992 by E. O. Wilson. Reprinted by permission of the publisher.

**Figure 6–2** Beck, William S., and George G. Simpson, *Life: An Introduction to Biology,* 2nd edition. Copyright © 1965 by Harcourt, Inc. and renewed 1993 by William S. Beck, Elizabeth Simpson Wurr, Helen S. Vishniac and Joan S. Burns. Reproduced by permission of the publisher.

**Box 6–2** Thewissen, J. G. M., S. T. Hussain, and M. Arif, "Fossil Evidence for the Origin of Aquatic Locomotion in Archaeocete Whales," *Science,* **263** (1994), 210–212. Copyright © 1994 American Association for the Advancement of Science. Reprinted by permission.

**Figure 6–9** Beck, William S., and George G. Simpson, *Life: An Introduction to Biology,* 2nd edition. Copyright © 1965 by Harcourt, Inc. and renewed 1993 by William S. Beck, Elizabeth Simpson Wurr, Helen S. Vishniac and Joan S. Burns. Reproduced by permission of the publisher.

**Figure 6–10** Romer, A. S., *The Vertebrate Body.* Copyright © 1959 by A. S. Romer. Reprinted with permission of the University of Chicago Press and A. S. Romer.

**Box 6–3** Ostrom, J. H., "Osteology of *Deinonychus antirrhopus,* an Unusual Theropod from the Lower

Cretaceous of Montana," *Bulletin of the Peabody Museum of Natural History,* **30** (1969). Reprinted by permission of the Peabody Museum of Natural History and John H. Ostrom.

**Figure 6–11** Clark, W. E. LeGros, *The Antecedents of Man.* Edinburgh University Press, 1959. Reprinted by permission.

**Figure 6–14** Novacek, M. J., "Mammalian Phylogeny: Shaking the Tree," *Nature,* **356** (12 March 1992), 121–125. Copyright © 1992 American Association for the Advancement of Science. Reprinted by permission from M. J. Novacek.

**Figure 7–1** Clark, W. E. LeGros, *The Antecedents of Man.* Edinburgh University Press, 1959. Reprinted by permission.

**Figure 7–4** Schultz, A. H., *The Life of Primates.* © 1969 by Adolph H. Schultz. Reprinted by permission of Universe Books / Weidenfeld / Orion Publishing Group and A. H. Schultz.

**Figure 7–5** Amoroso, E. C., "Placentation," in *Marshall's Physiology of Reproduction,* 3rd edition, vol. 2, 1952. Reprinted with permission of Longmans, Green & Co. and E. C. Amoroso.

**Table 7–1** Hendrick, A. G., and M. L. Houstion, "Gestation," in E. S. E. Hafez (ed.), *Comparative Reproduction of Nonhuman Primates,* 1971. By permission of Charles C. Thomas, Publisher, Ltd., Springfield, IL.

**Table 7–2** Napier, J. R., and P. H. Napier, P. H., *The Natural History of the Primates,* 1985, p. 14. Reprinted by pemission of the M.I.T. Press, Cambridge, MA.

**Figure 7–7** Hockett, C. F., *Man's Place in Nature.* Copyright © 1973 by McGraw-Hill, Inc. Reprinted by permission of McGraw-Hill, Inc., and C. F. Hockett.

**Figure 7–13** Hockett, C. F., *Man's Place in Nature.* Copyright © 1973 by McGraw-Hill, Inc. Reprinted by permission of McGraw-Hill, Inc., and C. F. Hockett.

**Figure 7–24** Hockett, C. F., *Man's Place in Nature.* Copyright © 1973 by McGraw-Hill, Inc. Reprinted by permission of McGraw-Hill, Inc., and C. F. Hockett.

**Figure 8–6** Schultz, A. H., *The Life of Primates.* © 1969 by Adolph H. Schultz. Reprinted by permission of Universe Books / Weidenfeld / Orion Publishing Group and A. H. Schultz.

**Figure 8–7** Schultz, A. H., *The Life of Primates.* © 1969 by Adolph H. Schultz. Reprinted by permission of Universe Books / Weidenfeld / Orion Publishing Group and A. H. Schultz.

**Figure 8–8** Buettner-Janusch, John, *Origins of Man.* Copyright © 1966 by John Wiley & Sons, Inc. Reprinted by permission of John Wiley & Sons, Inc.

**Figure 8–9** Schultz, A. H., "The Skeleton of the Trunk and Limbs of Higher Primates," *Human Biology,* **2**

(1930). Copyright © 1930 by Warwick and York, Inc. Reprinted by permission of Wayne State University Press.

**Figure 8–10** Neg. # 320654, Courtesy Department of Library Services, American Museum of Natural History.

**Figure 8–14** Simpson, George G., and William S. Beck, *Life: An Introduction to Biology,* 2nd edition. Copyright © 1957, 1965, by Harcourt & Company, and reprinted by their permission.

**Figure 8–15** Simpson, George G., and William S. Beck, *Life: An Introduction to Biology,* 2nd edition. Copyright © 1957, 1965, by Harcourt & Company, and reprinted by their permission.

**Table 8–3** Jerison, H. J., *Evolution of the Brain and Intelligence* (London: Academic Press Ltd., 1973). Used by permission.

**Figure 8–16** Penfield, W., and T. Rasmussen, *The Cerebral Cortex of Man.* Copyright © 1950 by Macmillan Publishing Co., Inc. Reprinted with permission.

**Figure 8–17** Tague, R. G., and C. O. Lovejoy, "The obstetric pelvis of A. L. 288-1 (Lucy)," *Journal of Human Evolution,* **15** (1986), 237–255. Adapted by permission of Academic Press Ltd.

**Table 8–4** Tobias, P. V., "The Distribution of Cranial Capacity Values Among Living Hominoids," *Proceedings of the Third International Congress of Primatology, Zurich, 1970,* Vol. 1 (1971), 18–35. Reproduced with permission of S. Karger AG, Basel.

**Figure 8–19** Illustration by Jo Cameron in Aiello, L., and C. Dean, *An Introduction to Human Evolutionary Anatomy,* 1990. Reprinted by permission of Leslie Aiello and Academic Press Ltd.

**Figure 8–20** Drawings from Fleagle, J. G., *Primate Adaptations and Evolution,* 1988, p. 240. Reprinted by permission of Academic Press.

**Figure 8–21** Swindler, D. R., *Dentition of Living Primates,* 1976. Reprinted by permission of Daris R. Swindler and Academic Press Ltd.

**Figure 8–23** Swindler, D. R., *Dentition of Living Primates,* 1976. Reprinted by permission of Daris R. Swindler and Academic Press Ltd.

**Figure 8–24** Illustration by Jo Cameron in Aiello, L., and C. Dean, *An Introduction to Human Evolutionary Anatomy,* 1990. Reprinted by permission of Leslie Aiello and Academic Press Ltd.

**Figure 8–25** Illustration by Jo Cameron in Aiello, L., and C. Dean, *An Introduction to Human Evolutionary Anatomy,* 1990. Reprinted by permission of Leslie Aiello and Academic Press Ltd.

**Table 8–6** Hsu, T. C., and Benirschke, K. *Atlas of Mammalian Chromosomes,* Vol. 10, 1977, pt. 4. Reprinted by permission of Springer-Verlag.

**Figure 8–27** Yunis, J. J., J. R. Sawyer, and K. Dunham, "The Striking Resemblance of High-Resolution

G-Banded Chromosomes of Man and Chimpanzees," *Science,* **208** (1980), 1145–1149. Copyright © 1980 by the American Association for the Advancement of Science. Used by permission.

**Table 8–7**  Adapted from Sarich, Vincent, "A Molecular Approach to the Question of Human Origins," in P. Dolhinow and Vincent Sarich (eds.), *Background for Man,* 1971, 66. Reprinted by permission of Scott, Foresman & Company, Glenview, IL.

**Table 8–8**  Adapted from Beard, J. M., and Goodman, M., "The Hemoglobins of Tarsius bancanus," in M. Goodman, R. E. Tashian, and J. H. Tashian (eds.), *Molecular Anthropology,* 1976, 243. Reprinted by permission of Plenum Publishing Corp.

**Figure 8–29**  Goodman, M., Alejo E. Romero-Herrera, Howard Dene, John Czelusniak, and Richard E. Tashian, "Amino Acid Sequence Evidence on the Phylogeny of Primates and Other Eutherians," in Morris Goodman (ed.), *Macromolecular Sequences in Systematic and Evolutionary Biology,* 1982. Reprinted by permission of Plenum Publishing Corp.

**Table 8–9**  Adapted from Goodman, M., "Protein Sequence and Immunological Specificity," in W. P. Luckett and F. S. Szalay (eds.), *Phylogeny of the Primates,* 1975, 224. Reprinted by permission of Plenum Publishing Corp.

**Table 8–10**  Reprinted from King, M. C., and Wilson, A. C., "Evolution at Two Levels in Humans and Chimpanzees," *Science,* **188,** 1975, 108. Copyright 1975 by the American Association for the Advancement of Science. Reprinted by permission.

**P. 201**  Quotation from Hinde, Robert A., "Can Nonhuman Primates Help Us Understand Human Behavior?" in B. B. Smuts et al. (eds.), *Primate Societies,* 1987, 413. Copyright 1987. Reprinted by permission of University of Chicago Press.

**Figure 9–6**  DeVore, I., ***Primate Behavior: Field Studies of Monkeys and Apes.*** Copyright © 1965 by Holt, Rinehart and Winston, Inc. Reprinted by permission of the publisher and Irven DeVore.

**Pp. 241–242**  Quotation from Essock-Vitale, Susan, & Robert M. Seyfarth, "Intelligence and Social Cognition," in B. B. Smuts et al. (eds.), *Primate Societies,* 1987, 452. Copyright 1987. Reprinted by permission of the University of Chicago Press.

**Figure 10–11**  Cheney, D. L. and R. M. Seyfarth, *How Monkeys See the World.* Copyright © 1990 by the University of Chicago Press. Reprinted by permission of the publisher.

**Table 11–1**  Adapted from Shipman, P., *Life History of a Fossil: An Introduction to Taphonomy and Paleoecology,* 1981. Cambridge, Mass: Harvard University Press, Copyright © 1981 by the President and Fellows of Harvard College. Reprinted by permission of the publisher.

**Figure 11–3**  Drawing by Dave Bichell from Shipman, P., *Life History of a Fossil: An Introduction to Taphonomy and Paleoecology,* 1981. Cambridge, Mass: Harvard University Press, Copyright © 1981 by the President and Fellows of Harvard College. Reprinted by permission of the publisher.

**Figure 11–5**  Isaac, Glen L., "Early Hominids in Action: A Commentary on the Contribution of Archaeology to Understanding the Fossil Record in East Africa," *Yearbook of Physical Anthropology,* **19** (1975). Reprinted by permission of John Wiley & Sons, Inc.

**Figure 11–8**  Leakey, M. D., *Olduvai Gorge, vol. 3, Excavations in Beds I and II, 1960–1963* (Cambridge: Cambridge University Press, 1971). Reprinted by permission of Cambridge University Press.

**Table 11–2**  Paul, C., *The Natural History of Fossils,* 1980, 184. Reprinted by permission of Holmes & Meier Publishers, Inc.

**Figure 11–13**  Harland, W. B., et al., *A Geologic Time Scale 1989,* 1990. Adapted by permission of Cambridge University Press and W. Brian Harland.

**Figure 11–14**  Postlethwait, John H., and J. L. Hopson, *The Nature of Life.* Copyright © 1989 by McGraw-Hill, Inc. Adapted by permission of McGraw-Hill, Inc.

**Figure 11–15**  Hamblin, W. Kenneth, *The Earth's Dynamic System,* 2nd edition, 1978. Burgess Publishing Co.

**Figure 11–16**  Chard, Chester S., *Man in Prehistory,* 2nd edition. Copyright © 1975 by McGraw-Hill, Inc. Reprinted by permission of McGraw-Hill, Inc.

**Figure in Box 12–1**  Drawing by Rudolph Freund in Simons, E. L., "The Early Relatives of Man," *Scientific American,* July, 1964, pp. 56–57, bottom. Copyright © 1964. Reprinted by permission of the Estate of Rudolph Freund.

**Figure 12–1**  Drawing by Rudolph Freund in Simons, E. L., "The Early Relatives of Man," *Scientific American,* July, 1964, pp. 56–57, bottom. Copyright © 1964. Reprinted by permission of the Estate of Rudolph Freund.

**Figure 12–2**  Simons, E., and D. Russell, "Notes on the Cranial Anatomy of *Necrolemur,*" *Breviora,* 127 (1960). Museum of Comparative Zoology, Harvard University. Copyright © President and Fellows of Harvard College. Used by permission.

**Figure 12–3**  Simons, E. L., *Primate Evolution.* Copyright © 1972 by Elwyn Simons. Reprinted by permission of Macmillan Publishing Co., Inc.

**Figure 16–12** Tanner, J. M., *Growth at Adolescence,* 2nd edition, 1962. Reprinted by permission of Blackwell Scientific Publications.

**Figure 16–13** Tanner, J. M., *Growth at Adolescence,* 2nd edition, 1962. Reprinted by permission of Blackwell Scientific Publications.

**Figure 16–14** Tanner, J. M., *Growth at Adolescence,* 2nd edition, 1962. Reprinted by permission of Blackwell Scientific Publications.

**Figure 16–15** Friancho, A. R., and P. T. Baker, "Altitude and Growth: a Study of the Patterns of Physical Growth of a High Altitude Peruvian Quechua Population," *American Journal of Physical Anthropology,* **32** (1970), 290. Used by permission of The Wistar Institute Press.

**Figure 16–16** Courtesy of Open Books and Harvard University Press.

**Table 16–3** Newman, H. H., et al., *Twins: A Study of Heredity and Environment,* 1937, 72. Copyright 1937. Used by permission of The University of Chicago Press.

**Figure 17–1** Mourant, A. E., A. C. Kopéc, and K. Domaniewski-Sobczak, *The Distribution of the Human Blood Groups and Other Polymorphisms,* 2nd edition, 1976. Reprinted by permission of Oxford University Press.

**Figure 17–2** Sunderland, E., "Hair-Colour Variation in the United Kingdom," *Annals of Human Genetics,* **21** (1955–56). Reprinted by permission of Cambridge University Press.

**Figure 17–3** Mourant, A. E., A. C. Kopéc, and K. Domaniewski-Sobczak, *The Distribution of the Human Blood Groups and Other Polymorphisms,* 2nd edition, 1976. Reprinted by permission of Oxford University Press.

**Table 17–1** Harrison, G. A., et al., *Human Biology,* 1964, 275. Used by permission of Oxford University Press.

**Table 17–2** McKusick, V., *Mendelian Inheritance in Man: Catalogs of Autosomal Dominant, Autosomal Recessive, and X-linked Phenotypes,* 5th edition, 1978. Used by permission of Johns Hopkins University Press.

**Box 17–1** Ubelaker, D. H., "Skeletal Evidence for Kneeling in Prehistoric Ecuador," *American Journal of Physical Anthropology,* **51** (1979), 683. Reprinted by permission of The Wistar Institute Press.

**Figure 17–6** Klass, M., and H. Hellman, *The Kinds of Mankind* (Philadelphia: J. B. Lippincott). Copyright © 1971 by Morton Klass and Hal Hellman. Used by permission of the publisher.

**Figure 17–7** Cavalli-Sforza, L. L., et al., "Reconstruction of Human Evolution: Bringing Together Genetic, Archaeological, and Linguistic Data," *Proceedings of the National Academy of Sciences,* **85** (1988), 6002–6006. Adapted by permission of L. L. Cavalli-Sforza.

**Figure 17–8** Bischof, L. J., *Intelligence: Statistical Concepts of Its Nature.* Copyright © 1954 by Doubleday & Company, Inc. Reprinted by permission of Random House, Inc.

**Figure A–1** Neg. # 37408, Courtesy Department of Library Services, American Museum of Natural History.

**Figure A–2** Reprinted from Brothwell, D. R., *Digging Up Bones,* 3rd edition, Revised and Updated. Copyright © 1981 by D. R. Brothwell. Used by permission of the publisher, Cornell University Press.

# Index